Cities in the International Marketplace

Cities in the International Marketplace

THE POLITICAL ECONOMY OF URBAN DEVELOPMENT IN NORTH AMERICA AND WESTERN EUROPE

H. V. Savitch and Paul Kantor

PRINCETON UNIVERSITY PRESS

PRINCETON AND OXFORD

307676

JUN 1 6 2005

Second printing, and first paperback printing, 2004
Paperback ISBN 0-691-12014-5

The Library of Congress has cataloged the cloth edition of this book as follows

Savitch, H. V.
Cities in the international marketplace : the political economy of urban development
in North America and Western Europe / H. V. Savitch and Paul Kantor.
p. cm.
Includes bibliographical references and index.
ISBN 0-691-09159-5 (alk. paper)
1. Urban economics. 2. Urban policy. 3. Cities and towns — North America.
4. Cities and towns — Europe, Western. I. Kantor, Paul, 1942– II. Title.

HT321 .S29 2002
307.76 — dc21   2002019844

British Library Cataloging-in-Publication Data is available

This book has been composed in Sabon

Printed on acid-free paper. ∞

pup.princeton.edu

Printed in the United States of America

3   5   7   9   10   8   6   4   2

*The authors wish to acknowledge the assistance of
Serena Vicari Haddock, University of Pavia, Italy*

For Luke Benjamin Savitch, may he grow up in a world filled with the splendor of urban life — HVS

For my wonderful wife, Anna, and to the memory of Pauline Kantor — PK

CONTENTS

PHOTOGRAPHS

FIGURES

Notes and source information for figures and tables appear in the appendix.

TABLES

PREFACE

Books frequently derive their inspiration from a larger culture and supporting environment. *Cities in the International Marketplace* reflects that rule. In recent years the fields of urban affairs, city politics, and political economy have been filled with new approaches, clashing perspectives, and fresh data of enormous value. Despite this, much of the debate on urban development became encapsulated into separate worlds. During recent decades urban theory focused on uncovering political dimensions of economic development in an attempt to avoid the economic determinism of past approaches. Though insightful, this change in direction often seemed to be excessively absorbed in looking at the processes of local political agency to the neglect of powerful constraining forces in the economy and cultures extending beyond city borders. Urban regimes, decision makers, and policies became the object of many case studies. Yet the advance of global capitalism, demographic shifts, and historical change sweeping the world seemed neglected. Of particular importance, a new international marketplace has been forming, pulling cities into its orbit. We concluded that theories of local politics and urban development should not ignore these new realities. So many interesting and urgent questions begged to be answered, but needed to be captured within a comparative and systematic conceptual net. The challenge of finding answers to problems posed by these larger forces and local politics became tantalizing.

In pursuing this challenge we found that available cross-national research was quite limited. Most studies beyond the Anglo-American experience consisted of case studies or of cities within one or perhaps two nations. Language barriers, lack of comparable data sources, differences in political systems, and governmental practices as well as cultural variations confounded rigorous comparative analysis. Yet anything short of a truly comparative analysis would not allow us to answer bigger questions.

This book represents our attempt to answer those questions. It also represents many compromises we needed to make in order to pursue our inquiry. Heeding James Burnham's admonition to "do things boldly," we cast about for ways of surveying the experiences of multiple cities without sacrificing accuracy and context. At the outset we decided it would be necessary to do the actual site investigations ourselves, rather than farming out the task to local academic experts. In the end our venture brought forth an infusion of ideas from European colleagues who introduced us to new ways of examining old problems. Our American colleagues also challenged us to reconcile European comparisons with American realities.

Trying to examine a wide swathe of the Western experience without losing critical depth was an uncertain challenge. How many cities might fulfill our criteria? Initially we thought that at least seven and as many as seventeen cities were appropriate. We thought it necessary that our selection of cities mirror a reasonable degree of variation in the West. Otherwise we would be unable to test our propositions about the comparative dynamics of urban development.

Over a period of time we collected data, tested our propositions and initially settled on sixteen cities. This led to our first paper on the subject, "Can Politicians Bargain With Business?" which was published in *Urban Affairs Quarterly*. Gradually we whittled down the final number of cities to the present ten. In aggregate, they reflect a wide range of variation. Our cities include three in the United States — New York, Detroit, Houston — and one in Canada — Toronto. The remaining cities are located in Western Europe. They include two in the United Kingdom — Glasgow and Liverpool — two cities in France — Paris and Marseilles — and two cities in Italy — Milan and Naples.

We also decided to focus on a time frame between 1970 and 2000. This period encompasses years in which most Western cities faced similar challenges. As our work advanced, we became especially interested in how cities responded to pressures of the international marketplace. Hence, we increasingly focused on the interaction among cities, governmental systems, and the manner in which governments bargained with private capital. What eventually stood out was how government and policy mattered in providing alternative economic choices. Ironically, by looking at the big picture, we found a smaller one also emerging. We especially appreciated how local government and its decisions mattered.

These themes constitute the organizing principles of this volume. Chapter 1 begins by introducing the reader to the new international marketplace that has been sweeping through the Western industrial world. This "great transformation" has simultaneously dispersed populations and jobs, recast the economic functions of cities, and unleashed a process of globalization that precipitates intense and widespread competition among cities. This chapter draws on a larger universe of cities to illustrate global trends and shows how those urban centers experienced varying impacts. We then show how our ten cities mirror much of that variation.

Chapter 2 is devoted to theory building. Our framework explains how urban development works and how it is influenced by political, economic, and sociocultural factors that interact in important ways.

This helps to explain why cities vary in their development policies and how cities tap different kinds of resources in order to obtain bargaining leverage. We go on to elucidate why different urban policies emerge in different cities and offer a bargaining model that helps account for different development patterns.

The next several chapters are devoted to testing this model, illustrating how bargaining works, identifying the different types of development politics, surveying the strategic behavior of cities, and examining the interplay between structure and agency. In chapter 3, we introduce our ten case cities, offering thumbnail sketches of their political economies. In doing so, we describe how the great transformation has changed these cities and assess their bargaining position. This chapter presents data in a comparative format, so that all ten cities can be assessed along common criteria.

Chapter 4 systematically charts the policy responses of all of the case cities, gauging patterns of change and the relative weight accorded to different social and economic values in making development policy. We assess two types of development policy, contrasted as "social-centered" versus "market-centered" strategies. We show that cities governments often "mix and match" or adopt even inconsistent directions in development policy, a finding that challenges some commonly held assumptions about development strategies.

Chapter 5 tests our development model in all ten cities. Our approach consists of what Karl Hempel might call a "deductive-nomological" explanation. In offering this explanation we examine how ten cities match up to our variables and we deduce some key observations. Most important, we find that the resources a city brings to the international bargaining table influence development strategies. It explains how "driving" resources powerfully structure bargaining opportunities while "steering" resources play a different role. This enables us to identify different kinds of bargaining environments within which cities navigate the international marketplace, what we term *dirigiste, entrepreneurial,* and *public* and *private dependent* contexts. It concludes by highlighting how political forces at all governmental levels interact in dynamic ways with economic circumstances to empower or limit local politicians.

Chapters 6 and 7 probe the dynamics of political, economic, and cultural forces in our ten cities. Particular governing regimes exhibit important variations in the kinds of interests that get represented, policy agendas that rise to the fore, and decisions that are taken. In these pages we observe how various types of local governing regimes are linked to external pressures and how these go into the making of political choice. In our ten cities we identify four kinds of bargaining contexts. At the same time, we are able to show how political struggles to change the regimes occur, allowing citizens opportunities to pursue changes of direction in bargaining strategy and public policy. In the end, this survey shows that political agency and structural circumstances are in constant interaction, producing patterns of stability and change.

Chapters 8 and 9 look at the big picture of urban change. Both try to glean lessons from three decades of development. Chapter 8 investigates whether the forces of internationalization are precipitating a new convergence in urban economic development politics. Are cities becoming similar in development strategy, urban policy, and local governance, or is diversity alive and well? By probing emerging practices we find that the cities may be converging in some respects, but in many others they remain quite different from one another. Rather than homogenizing, we find that cities continue to respond to globalization by bringing national cultures and indigenous institutions to bear. While the "American model" may influence some cities, it is far from having become a universal guide. Differences in bargaining resources and development strategy are pretty much intact, enabling cities to chart their own courses.

Chapter 9 surveys policies that do or do not work as well as those that provide a measure of choice in city building. By comparing urban experiences over thirty years, we are able to assess institutional innovations. Specifically, we evaluate four different approaches that were utilized in some or all of the cities: pro-growth strategies, community development politics, regional strategies, and national urban policy. We find that each of these has some value in coping with global development pressures but that they are best seen working in concert with one another. We also describe ways in which community, regional, and national governments can supply overlapping policy nets to enhance urban choice.

We conclude this volume by reviewing evidence and highlighting our most important observation: namely, that cities are not mere leaves in the wind, passively responding to international change. Instead, we can use global change as an opportunity to enhance urban life. Our investigation describes how cities as well as governments at all levels have powerful roles to play in maximizing public choices.

ACKNOWLEDGMENTS

We are indebted to the community of urban scholars for the knowledge and inspiration it has provided over the years. Forerunners in the field comprise the Urban Politics Section of the American Political Science Association, the Urban Affairs Association, the European Urban Research Association and Research Committees 03 and 21 of the International Sociological Association, and the Urban Affairs Division at the Organization for Economic Cooperation and Development. Not the least our students were a source of immense intellectual stimulation and fulfillment. On an individual level, both of us are grateful to an international cast of scholars. These include, Dennis Judd, Peter Eisinger, Terry Clark, Susan Clarke, Paolo Calzabini, Bob Whelan, Hal Wollman, Robin Hambleton, Murray Stewart, Robin Boyle, Mauro Calise, Jens Dangschat, Jan Van Weesop, Frank Moulaert, and many others. Over the years their comments and conversation enriched this work. Both authors extend their warm appreciation to friends who, sadly, have passed away. Edward T. Rogowsky and Robert Bailey will be missed and we mourn that loss. Finally, our editors at Princeton University Press have been exceptional. The staff at Princeton made life infinitely easier for us. Special gratitude goes to editors Chuck Myers and Debbie Tegarden and copy editor Linda Truilo for their expertise, their patience, and their ability in putting a complicated manuscript through production. Back in Louisville Diane O'Regan did a wonderful job on the index.

Many individuals on the other side of the Atlantic helped us offset the difficulties of doing cross-national research. In Glasgow, Ivan Turok, Ronan Paddison, Gerry Stoker, and Michael Keating all shared their knowledge of planning and politics. David Webster at the Glasgow City Council and Steward Gulliver and Gordon Kennedy at the Glasgow Development Agency provided first-rate perspectives. In Liverpool, the European Institute for Urban Affairs was a marvelous resource. As usual, Michael Parkinson graciously gave his time, insight, and energy. At the European Institute, Richard Evans and Hillary Russell were generous with their time and knowledge. Elsewhere in Liverpool help came from different sides of the political spectrum. City councilors Richard Kemp and Gideon Ben Tovim gave unstintingly of their knowledge and perspective.

In Paris, Nathan Starkman's and Elizabeth Duflos's understanding of planning and design provided superb insights. Christian Lefevre's knowledge of the city and its region proved invaluable. Others lending help were Patrick Le Galès, Sophie Gendrot, and François Ascher. Much of the research on Marseilles was made possible by the Agence d'Urbanisme de l'Agglomération Marseillaise, or AGAM. At AGAM thanks go to Jean François Brillet and Etienne Tulasne for their time, help, and knowledge. AGAM's archives managed by P. Antalovsky and her staff made research infinitely easier. The eminent scholarship and kindness of Marcel Roncayolo provided a foundation for whatever was done on Marseilles. The work and time given by André Donzel also provided an indispensable core of knowledge about the city.

Special recognition goes to Serena Vicari Haddock, who played a unique role. Serena became an active collaborator in the Italian research and in helping to adapt the theoretical constructs to Western European situations, in refining parts of the manuscript dealing with Italy, as well as in critiquing or editing other draft chapters. Serena also helped coauthor an article, "The Political Economy of Regime Politics: A Comparative Perspective" in the *Urban Affairs Review*, which in part informs this book.

Each of us also offers separate thanks. Paul Kantor thanks *Urban Studies* for providing a fellowship at the Department of Social and Economic Research at Glasgow University. This stimulating experience with Bill Lever and his colleagues afforded a grand opportunity to learn about the Scottish experience. Thanks to Enrico Pugliese for all his help and to his colleagues at the Department of Sociology at the University of Naples. They provided invaluable support and advice in guiding this author through the political and social mysteries of one of Italy's most intriguing and magnificent cities. Similarly, Enzo Mingione's warm fellowship and his generosity in providing clerical and research assistance at the *Fondazione Bignaschi* and the University of Milan were indispensable to the project. Guido Martinotti gave sage advice and as well as access to the offices of the *Istituto Superiore di Sociologia* in Milan. All of these fine people played a critical role, especially in orienting this author to Italian urban politics. Not least, the most incredibly patient Italian language training was provided by Ms. Nilde Rosati of Florence, Italy, work that was also guided by a wonderful colleague at Fordham University, Wayne Storey.

In Naples, Enrica Morlicchio and her husband, Sandro Staiano, mayor of Pompei, helped in critical interviews, finding people, and, in Enrica's case, sharing her research. Enrico Rebeggiani at the University of Salerno and Simonetta Capecchi provided immeasurable assistance in every way—from extended conversations about Neapolitan politics, to finding published and unpublished materials, to giving fast rides to interviews on the back of a motor scooter through death-defying traffic in the city. In Milan, many people gave valuable help in understanding the planning, politics, and sociology of the city despite their pressing schedules. Special thanks goes to Alesandro Balducci, Stefano Draghi, and Paolo Fareri.

Hank Savitch is especially grateful to The Woodrow Wilson International Center for Scholars and The Hebrew University of Jerusalem for affording him precious research time to work on issues of globalization. At the Wilson Center, Blair Ruble and Joseph Tulchin were excellent hosts and lively commentators. At The Hebrew University, Gabbie Sheffer, Ira Sharkansky, Arie Shachar, Danny Felsenstein, and Eran Razin were terrific colleagues. At the Organization for Economic Cooperation and Development, much appreciation goes to Josef Konvitz and Lindsay MacFarlane. Good friends were always available to help. Ron Vogel read portions of the manuscript and offered valuable suggestions. Martin Schain was always on hand to guide Hank through the labyrinth of French politics. In Canada, Richard Stren was an immense help. He provided access to the Centre for Urban and Community Studies and was a good friend. Richard also read the manuscript and was generous with his time. Frances Frisken's good counsel and access to officials gave Hank a bird's eye view of Toronto.

Hank Savitch is equally grateful for the time he was able to spend in France, and to those who made that possible. Vincent Hoffman-Martinot sponsored an appointment for him at the Institut d'Etudes Politiques in Bordeaux. Jean-Claude Boyer made a stay possible at the Institut Français d'Urbanisme at Champs-sur-Marne. Marcel Roncayalo arranged a research opportunity for him at the Institut d'Urbanisme de Paris at Val-de-Marne. Jacques Brun was always a good friend and a wonderful guide through the academic terrain of Paris. One could hardly expect better places to live, work, or play than Paris or Marseilles.

Closer to home, Hank Savitch would like to express his appreciation to the University of Louisville for the short-term project completion grants and longer-term assistance given to him. The University of Louisville has been a real friend to urban affairs, and those of us in the field are deeply appreciative. The university's College of Business and Public Administration contains a mix of colleagues whose presence enhanced this work. The School of Urban and Public Affairs and the Urban Studies Institute provided an exemplary professional home. Hank is particularly grateful to Paul Coomes, Lyle Sussman, Steve Bourassa, and former graduate assistants Kevin DuPont and Greg Ardashev. In New York, long-time friend Jesse Vazquez has always been a source of inspiration. Finally, Hank is fortunate to be blessed with a wonderful family. Susan Savitch was always encouraging and patient. Adam, Jonathan, and Jennifer Savitch frequently wondered why it took so long to get a book written, but were lovingly supportive. Without their chiding this book might have taken even longer.

On Paul Kantor's home front, he thanks Bob Stein for his kind invitation to take part in the Houston Metropolitan Study, which enabled him to learn about the city in a unique way. Particularly critical insights came from stimulating conversations about Houston politics with Bob, Richard Murray, and Robert Thomas at the University of Houston as well as from developer David Hawes. Not least, Paul Kantor is deeply appreciative of Fordham University for furnishing two faculty fellowships and to the Research Council of the university for providing grant assistance for completing some of the site visits abroad. The continuous support of Fordham University, its Graduate School of Arts and Sciences, and Dean Robert Himmelberg really made this project possible. Finally, Paul's greatest debt is to his wife, Anna, and his daughter, Elizabeth. Their love and unselfish tolerance of the work and separations occasioned by the research made all the difference in the end.

Of course, none of these individuals shares responsibility for the words that follow. We alone bear that responsibility.

Cities in the International Marketplace

Chapter One

THE GREAT TRANSFORMATION
AND LOCAL CHOICES

The city lives by remembering.
—Ralph Waldo Emerson

THE CONTOURS OF TRANSFORMATION

An enormous transformation engulfs the industrial world. The rapidity and consequences are unparalleled. The change is breathtaking. The ancient world lasted for three thousand years, the medieval age for less than a millennium, and the industrial era for about a century. Our post-industrial society has been brought about in roughly three decades, and its pace is quickening. This new revolution has already remade the economic fabric of society, radically altered the behavior of capital, broken down national boundaries, and is remodeling government.

This transformation is particularly profound within liberal democratic states in North America and Western Europe. Since 1970, these states have shed their older industrial capacity and have become societies dominated by the tertiary sector—business, professions, services, high technology, and government. Within these societies capital has changed its configuration. It is more nimble and more multinational.[1] "Flexible production" and "just-in-time inventory" are not only techniques for quick action but they have also changed the operations of capitalism. Corporate ownership is not confined solely to a single nation but can span the globe, putting management in the hands of unlikely collaborators. Archrivals continue their rivalries but also find themselves in partnership with one other; fiercely competing one day and collaborating the next. The giant plane-manufacturer Airbus is a case in point. Its operations are a product of a European high-tech face-off with America. At the same time, it buys products from its American nemesis, Boeing, and 40 percent of Airbus components are made in the United States.

Migration is another part of the story. Counting refugees alone, one finds that within the last decade 4.3 million have flocked into Germany, France, Italy, and the United Kingdom. Over one million have turned to the United States and Canada.[2] Recent immigrants now make up roughly 10 percent of these last two societies. While North America is regarded as the traditional immigrant haven, the numbers in Western Europe have exploded. During the past decade European officials expected that more than 25 million legal or illegal immigrants would settle on that continent.[3] Meanwhile birth rates of nationals within most Western countries have flattened or declined. The birth rate crisis is most acute in France and Italy, where the newborn cannot keep pace with the rate of mortality. As those birthrates continue to plummet, Europeans will have to rely on even more immigrants to support high living standards and generous pensions.

On the political front transnational pacts have nurtured the transformation by facilitating the movement of goods, people, and common policies across boundaries. The most prominent of these pacts are in the West and include the European Union (EU), which comprises fifteen nations, and the North American Free Trade Association (NAFTA), composed of the United States, Canada, and Mexico.[i] The EU already has a supranational government and bureaucracy that imposes policy on member nations. NAFTA is not that far advanced, but it has begun to affect political life in North America by forcing choices over freer trade, currency supports, and labor policy.

Technology plays a central role in this transformation. Just as previous periods may have been driven by steam locomotion (1780–1840), rail transportation (1840–90), electric power (1890–1930), or petroleum energy (1930–70), so the current era is propelled by the transmission of information. The last quarter of the twentieth century was appropriately called "the information age," and it portended revolutionary technological achievements into this millennium.

By now it may be a commonplace observation that warrants repeating. Ordinary people are communicating faster, they are more directly in touch with events, and they often exchange information person to person. The new world of cyberspace is just one technology that allows this. At the dawn of the postindustrial age, during the mid-1970s, just 50,000 computers existed in the world. That number has now rocketed to 556 million, giving common individuals access to each other across the globe. More than half of Americans and more than a quarter of Western Europeans own computers. In North America and Western Europe, big and small cities are hard-wired for instant communication. Carriers, like BBC or CNN, have established global news networks, allowing the world to witness the same events at the same time. Impressions are created instantly, and reactions occur swiftly. The decreasing cost of telephone service and the spread of fiber optic cables (simultaneously transmitting 1.5 million conversations within the diameter of a human hair) catapulted personal information to new levels. By the year 2000 international telephone calls reached an all-time high of 100 billion minutes.[4] None of these developments can create democracy, but collectively they assure wider dissemination of information, they facilitate freer exchange among people, and they hold potential for greater accountability between rulers and the ruled. Under these conditions, it becomes increasingly difficult to monopolize information, control public opinion, or ignore citizen demands.

The combination of economic, demographic, technological, and political change is cumulative, and will continue to impact the social order. No society encapsulates this transformation more than urban society. Cities are the crucibles through which radical experiments become convention. They are concentrated environments in which people adapt and their resilience is tested. They are the world's incubators of innovation — made possible by critical mass, diversity, and rich interaction. And cities have steadily grown over the centuries to fulfill that role. In the tenth century one of the world's largest cities, Cordoba, held just 300,000 people. Later Constantinople became the leading metropolis and held half a million people. By the eighteenth century London had surpassed every other Western city with one million inhabitants. In the twentieth century New York rose to ascendancy with several million people. Now in the twenty-first century Tokyo, São Paulo, and Mexico City have climbed above ten million inhabitants.

What is more, cities have complemented their role as global innovators with geophysical centrality. Despite enormous changes in technology, cities remain at the juncture of world transportation, as transit points for business, science, and travel of every stripe. This puts cities at the very pivot of transformation. Few statistics demonstrate this better than air traffic. Table 1.1 presents information for passenger and cargo traffic in fifteen major cities between 1991 and 2000.

In just nine short years average passenger traffic jumped by 51 percent while cargo increased by 131 percent. Already a global transit point, Paris more than doubled both its air passengers and cargo. Seoul showed a similar doubling in passengers and cargo, while Amsterdam and London also showed impressive gains. All told, every one of these cities registered gains, and we note that these advances have been made on very substantial bases. Cities are continuing to grow in this global transformation, and indeed are at its very heart. Despite the dip in passenger air traffic after September 11, that transformation is likely to continue and cities will resume their station at the junctures of air travel.

This tells us something not only about the future, but also about the recent past. Cities have been the terrain on which technological, social, and global transformation has taken place. Cities hold the machinery that furnishes each era with a distinct product; they are the progenitors of national culture; and, they are the great mixing cauldrons that supply

TABLE 1.1
Air Passengers and Cargo in Fifteen Cities, 1991–2000

City	Passengers			Cargo		
	1991	2000	Change	1991	2000	Change
Chicago	60010234	66981786	11.6%	986674	1342057	36.0%
Tokyo	40188083	51862564	29.0%	484901	1767773	264.6%
Frankfurt	29373436	45926771	56.4%	1240484	1561450	25.9%
Paris	21975289	44713463	103.5%	615699	1266951	105.8%
Amsterdam	16470983	36864802	123.8%	630153	1150572	82.6%
Seoul	16821121	33558857	99.5%	703654	1708009	142.7%
Detroit	21783980	32949283	51.3%	191717	NA	NA
Houston	17518791	32294534	84.3%	223013	NA	NA
London	18820902	29989760	59.3%	212908	1286507	504.3%
Bangkok	15917666	26928356	69.2%	405855	791463	95.0%
Los Angeles	45668204	62971893	37.9%	1141196	1883936	65.1%
Miami	26591415	30685658	15.4%	877479	1485869	69.3%
New York	29794350	30268324	1.6%	1322434	1675973	26.7%
Hong Kong	19747543	30008737	52.0%	849786	2070573	143.7%
Toronto	20304271	26776648	31.9%	322929	NA	NA
Average Increase			51.1%			130.1%

a unique human hybrid. In providing all of these functions, cities continually remake themselves, reconstruct their productive base, and adapt their physical environment to the necessities of the time.

We examine this transformation in greater detail along with the tremendous impact it has had upon cities. In this chapter we trace this transformation along three distinct trajectories: 1) the deindustrialization of urban economies, 2) the deconcentration of older cities, and 3) the globalization process. As we shall see, cities are not necessarily the passive recipients of this change, but have the capacity to guide it and shape its impact. That capacity may be constrained and mediated by underlying structures, and it may differ from city to city, but it is nonetheless present. Choice, then, is an essential part of urban development, and this book focuses on the underlying components of that discretion. Exactly what are those choices, how are they initiated, why are they made, and can they be maximized? Before turning to that, we take up the elements of the great transformation.

DEINDUSTRIALIZATION: FOR WHAT?

Just thirty years ago, cities in North America and Europe were bustling with factories, workshops, warehouses, and open air markets. While the great primate cities of New York, London, and Paris had always held financial houses and corporate headquarters, they also were balanced by textile manufacture, light industry, chemical production, and warehousing.[ii]

At the same time, secondary cities took on the heavy lifting. Cleveland, Pittsburgh, Birmingham, Newcastle, Essen, Lille, and Turin were centers for tool and dye making, automobile manufacture, and steel production. These industrial towns were complemented by cities of passage. New Orleans, Liverpool, Marseilles, Hamburg, and Naples were glorious ports, which boasted the world's finest bistros and bawdiest night life.

Secondary cities were the workshops of the industrial world. They also housed large numbers of blue-collar families in a rich social milieu. From London's East End to New Orleans's Garden District, neighborhoods anchored the social life of the city. To be sure, the housing was often substandard and the neighborhoods overcrowded, but they spawned a host of vibrant institutions. Labor unions, shops, schools, churches, and social clubs bound communities together, allowed citizens to connect to public institutions, and gave the city meaning.

The bulk of those factories are now gone and many of the ports are closed. Some workers hold on to remnants of the old economy, some have joined the ranks of the unemployed, and others have found jobs elsewhere. While some working-class neighborhoods are intact, others have been gentrified and enriched with boutiques and expensive specialty shops. Still other inner-city neighborhoods now accommodate immigrants who bring with them a new culture, different foodstuffs, and an altogether distinct way of life (from tea salons to mosques). A substantial number of old neighborhoods, mostly in America and Great Britain, have not been recycled for the gentry or for immigrants. Instead they have fallen into disuse: the houses are abandoned, stores are boarded up, sidewalks are littered, and streets are dangerous. Many social institutions are gone—either they have disappeared or taken new form in the suburbs.

Figure 1.1 provides a glimpse of the economic magnitude of this transformation. The figure shows employment patterns for major cities in North America and Europe. It focuses on jobs within secondary (blue-collar) and tertiary (white-collar) sectors between the approximate period of 1970–90, and these economic sectors are grouped for each city by their respective periods.

Deindustrialization is generating uneven development and social imbalance. We see this in the relatively steep declines and rises in the bars. Some cities remain in decay while others have succeeded in remaking themselves. Chicago, Cleveland, Madrid, and Rotterdam saw the col-

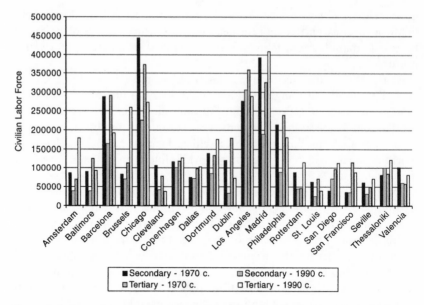

Figure 1.1. Secondary and Tertiary Employment in North American and European Cities, ca. 1970–ca. 1990.

lapse of blue-collar employment. Some of these same cities (Madrid and Rotterdam) made up their losses in manufacture through white-collar employment. Other cities like Cleveland, Philadelphia, and St. Louis have not yet recovered from this trauma. The crises of transformation is more widespread in Anglo-American cities than on the European continent. American cities were particularly hard hit, and account for the bulk of those that have yet to recover. In part, this is due to the nineteenth- and early-twentieth-century genesis of American central cities as locations for heavy industry. This is also true for some British cities (Newcastle, Liverpool, Glasgow). Continental cities mostly developed in the trading eras of the seventeenth and eighteenth centuries, and wealth was largely vested in the urban core. Thus, the ecological structure of European cities permitted them to shift more easily to tertiary economies.[iii]

By and large, primate cities did well. London emerged as the banking center where capital could be concentrated, New York as a producer of financial instruments where loans and mergers could be consummated, and Paris as a seat for corporate headquarters and professional services where deals could be struck. Each of these cities carved out niches for themselves as command posts in a larger world economy.[5] In large measure London, New York, and Paris became the forerunners of postindustrialism and established the pace for others.[6] To be sure, these cities already had thriving nests of banks and corporate headquarters, and they were able to build upon economies of agglomeration. Yet primate cities are complex, and during the 1950s high finance made up just a fraction of their economies. Manufacture, ports, and warehousing held the bulk of employment, and losses in these sectors were enormous. After deindustrialization struck, London, New York, and Paris had to refill huge holes in their economies just to stay even.

Secondary cities show greater variation in outcome. Cleveland experienced fiscal collapse in 1978, and nearly 40 percent of its residents are now below the poverty line.[7] Detroit and countless other rustbelt cities in America suffered a similar fate.[8] By contrast, Pittsburgh guided its shrinkage, revived its economy through research and technology, and kept its downtown healthy. In France, grimy, industrial Lille was rebuilt as the crossroads for Northern Europe. Industrial Glasgow has acquired a new downtown, but the rest of the city remains mired in decline.

Port cities have also turned out differently from one another. New Orleans and Liverpool fell into deep decline and have yet to recover. For a while, Hamburg reeled under successive economic blows, but recovered by modernizing its port and diversifying its industry. Today it is one of Europe's success stories and exults in the fact that it has more millionaires per capita than any other city on the continent.[9] Rotterdam, too, managed a partially successful transition by retaining its role as Europe's leading port and by building commercial linkages with Amsterdam and Utrecht.

Deindustrialization has also paved the way for new types of cities. So-called new-age boomtowns or sunbelt cities owe their urban form to late-twentieth-century technology.[10] Their economies usually are based on computers, software, electronics, space technology, or other emerging economic sectors. Their social structure is founded on middle-class outlooks, small families, and private housing. Especially in North America, new-age boomtowns enjoy an abundance of space, and their development spreads out along the corridors of modern freeways.

The United States has a concentration of these cities in its southwest and counts among them Phoenix, Houston, Albuquerque, and San Diego. Canada's boomtowns are found in its westerly open spaces and include Calgary and Vancouver. Boomtowns are not as common in Europe, which is already highly urbanized and lacks much vacant land. Nevertheless, European versions of these cities can be found in Southeast London (Croydon) and Oxford, in Grenoble and Montpellier, in Bavaria (Munich), and in the smaller towns of Italy's Northeast.

In America these boomtowns grew rapidly during the late 1960s and through the 1970s. Upheavals in petroleum and real estate sometimes threw cities like Houston into shock. But Houston recovered and continues to grow. In Canada, Vancouver is fueled by investments from Hong Kong, and it continues to lead that nation. The picture in Europe is hazy, though cities like Oxford and Grenoble have embraced high technology and believe that they are Europe's answer to the Silicon Valley.

In a nutshell, cities in North America and Europe changed substantially during the previous three decades. While the most successful became postindustrial, that status represented a dominant layer of activity, superimposed upon a diminished base of manufacture, shipping, and skilled trades. Less successful cities underwent shrinkage, though many of these managed to secure some postindustrial activity (small downtowns, tourism, stadiums, and exhibition centers). New-age boomtowns thrived on a combination of office employment, services, electronics, and light industry — set in the midst of universities, research centers, and low density development.

This reshuffling of the urban hierarchy has brought old and new cities into a competitive scramble to secure their economic well-being. As old industries decline and new investment patterns emerge, citizens and politicians are drawn into finding a niche for their communities in the new economic order. In the process, cities may be gripped by a certain angst — internal conflicts over means and ends, a belief that if a community does not grow it will surely die, and a rush to move faster.

DECONCENTRATION: THE SPREADING URBAN LANDSCAPE

The great transformation has also influenced human settlement and mobility. Overall, central cities have lost population. This deconcentration of population encompasses a range of different demographic processes, some healthy for cities, others not. Deconcentration entails movement away from places. This includes a movement out of healthy central cities, which allows remaining residents more space and gives departing residents more economical accommodations. We call this *dedensification*. Of course, dedensification also involves movement toward other places. This includes a burgeoning of low-density, metropolitan peripheries, brought about by rising living standards and a desire for single-family housing in the suburbs. It can also mean an entry into newer boomtowns and a search for fresh opportunities and economic betterment (new migration). This kind of movement can facilitate prosperity. On the other hand, deconcentration can also entail an exodus from urban cores because of decaying conditions, leaving these cities as segregated reservations for the poor. We refer to this as *decline*. In this case, population loss usually leaves cities in deeper distress.

Just as population loss does not necessarily mean decline, population growth does not always mean prosperity. Impoverished growth can occur when people move off rural land in search of opportunities elsewhere and fail to find them. We label this *impaction*. Migration into or around cities can also be accompanied by poorer living conditions and unemployment. The upshot has been massive growth without commensurate development. While this experience is uncommon among more mobile North Americans, it does occur in Africa and Latin America. A few European cities have grown while living conditions deteriorated. Whether accompanied by affluence or poverty, new migration and impaction create sprawling urban regions or megalopoli.[11]

In the United States, deconcentration often meant urban decline. As cities lost employment and neighborhoods decayed, some people escaped to the suburbs, while others remained behind in segregated ghettos. Even major cities that managed to remake themselves incurred the ravages of decline because whole neighborhoods fell apart. New York and Chicago did manage population gains during the past decade, but white residents continued to flee and the gains were due to immigration from Latin America or Asia. Population decline was rampant in secondary cities, where immigration was marginal and could not offset losses. Detroit, Cleveland, and St. Louis, once cities with close to or above a million residents, shrunk to less than half that size. Even after devastating losses of the 1970s and 1980s, the past decade was scarcely better, with those cities losing between 5 and 10 percent of their population.[12]

At the same time, urban deconcentration brought enormous prosperity to sunbelt boomtowns and swelled their suburbs. Boomtowns are the paragons of what we think of as urban *growth*. These areas experienced dramatic increases in residential populations, which gave rise to new shopping malls, office complexes, and single-family houses. The transformative years saw a virtual upheaval of inner-city populations, a massive shift of the white middle class into new settlements, and the trek of blacks and Hispanics into what remained of the urban cores.[13]

Some cities in Europe also suffered urban decline and now resemble their American counterparts. For the most part, however, European deconcentration was more genteel, taking the form of urban dedensification. Having begun in the Middle Ages and matured in the industrial era, Europe's cities were already overcrowded. Families often lived in small apartments within congested communities where shopping, recreation, schools, and factories were tightly clustered. Some urban theorists hailed this as the realization of community, but the realities were less quaint.[14] Space was scarce, private bathrooms often absent, and sanitary conditions dubious. By the 1970s, if people could afford to live in the city, they bought extra space and renovated. If not, they moved out.

A push-pull operated in European cities to shift populations around. The rich, the upwardly mobile, and the single people stayed. Modest income families left because of financial pressures, but were also attracted by the ease of living outside the central city. In contrast to the United States, suburbs were built for those who could not afford to live closer to the center. The best of these were in outlying villages, in "new towns," or further away in new-age boomtowns; and they accommodated middle-class citizens. They were clean, spacious, and featured supermarkets, playgrounds, and schools woven into the residential fabric. The worst, were low-income projects built in segregated edges or as extensions to impacted cities. They were massive, dingy concrete blocks that accommodated immigrants.

In sum the great transformation produced massive population shifts with different kinds of consequences. A profile of these consequences can be seen in tables 1.2 and 1.3. Table 1.2 presents a fourfold typology by using population change and patterns of deconcentration. Table 1.3 shows how this is worked out for thirty-five cities in North America and Western Europe. We rely on published indices for European and American cities to determine whether a particular city falls into the category of "distressed" or "prosperous."[iv] The last columns in table 1.3 show growth, decline, dedensification or impaction for each major city.

Despite differences in geography, size, and population, major cities across the industrial West have undergone economic restructuring, brought on by similar forces. On both continents, populations spread throughout metropolitan areas. Suburbs and boomtowns radically expanded and urbanization proceeded apace. Rural areas shrank and fewer people earned their living through agriculture. Distant towns and rural villages

TABLE 1.2
Patterns of Deconcentration

| | Patterns of Deconcentration | |
	Prosperity	*Distress*
Population Change		
Gain	Growth (new-age boomtowns, high tech corridors, edge cities)	Impaction (squatter villages, "favelas")
Loss	Dedensification (renewed central business districts, luxury high-rises, gentrified and/or stable neighborhoods)	Decline (hollowed-out central business districts, derelict, high-crime neighborhoods)

City	ca. 1970	ca. 1990	ca. 2000	Net Change (ca. 1970–ca. 2000)	Prosperity & Distress Indices		Type of Deconcentration
					Chesire et al. Index	Nathan & Adams Index	
Amsterdam	820000	701000	715148	−12.79%	Prosperous		Dedensification
Baltimore	906000	736000	645593	−28.74%		Distressed	Decline
Barcelona	1745000	1694000	1505581	−13.72%	Distressed		Decline
Birmingham	1098000	970000	1008381	−8.16%	Distressed		Decline
Berlin[1]	3273074	3347512	3425759	4.66%	Prosperous		Growth
Brussels	1075000	976000	950597	−11.57%	Prosperous		Dedensification
Chicago	3367000	2784000	2802079	−16.78%		Distressed	Decline
Cleveland	751000	574000	485817	−35.31%		Distressed	Decline
Copenhagen	725000	556000	487969	−32.69%	Prosperous		Dedensification
Dallas	844000	1008000	1075894	27.48%		Prosperous	Growth
Detroit	1511000	1028000	970196	−35.79%		Distressed	Decline
Dortmund	542396	584600	594274	9.56%	Distressed		Impaction
Dublin	568000	485000	481854	−15.17%	Distressed		Decline
Frankfurt	657776	623700	643469	−2.18%	Prosperous		Dedensification
Glasgow	940000	734000	680000	−27.66%	Distressed		Decline
Hamburg	1781621	1603070	1704731	−4.32%	Prosperous		Dedensification
Houston	1233000	1631000	1786691	44.91%		Prosperous	Growth
Liverpool	610000	479000	474001	−22.29%	Distressed		Decline

TABLE 1.3 (cont.)

City	ca. 1970	ca. 1990	ca. 2000	Net Change (ca. 1970–ca. 2000)	Prosperity & Distress Indices		Type of Deconcentration
					Chesire et al. Index	Nathan & Adams Index	
London[2]	7800000	6638109	6962319	-10.74%	Prosperous		Dedensification
Los Angeles	2814000	3486000	3597556	27.84%	Prosperous	Prosperous	Growth
Lyons	520000	413000	445257	-14.37%	Prosperous		Dedensification
Madrid	3146000	3124000	2881506	-8.41%	Prosperous		Dedensification
Marseilles	881000	840000	797486	-9.48%	Distressed		Decline
Milan	1725000	1200000	1302808	-24.47%	Prosperous		Dedensification
Naples	1234000	1025000	1035835	-16.06%	Distressed		Decline
New York, N.Y.	1514642	1487536	1536220	1.42%	Prosperous	Prosperous	Growth
Paris	2591000	2176000	2123261	-18.05%	Prosperous		Dedensification
Philadelphia	1949000	1586000	1436287	-26.31%		Distressed	Decline
Rotterdam	687000	574000	589987	-14.12%	Distressed		Decline
St. Louis	622000	397000	339316	-45.45%		Distressed	Decline
San Diego	697000	1111000	1220666	75.13%		Prosperous	Growth
San Francisco	716000	724000	745774	4.16%		Prosperous	Growth
Seville	548000	668000	701927	28.09%	Distressed		Impaction
Toronto[3]	2089729	2275771	2400000	14.85%		Prosperous	Growth
Valencia	654000	739000	739412	13.06%	Distressed		Impaction

lost population and, in some instances, fell into near vacancy. All told, we see substantial variation among these cities. The ramifications are deeply political. Citizens face a new set of urban challenges, driven by deindustrialization, migration, and a need to adapt.

GLOBAL SWEEP, LOCAL BROOMS

Globalism is an encompassing concept; it covers a broad range of activities, and it has brought both positive and negative results. Foremost among its characteristics is free trade. Open markets rest on a theory of competitive advantage, whereby each locale finds it beneficial to produce goods or services it can most efficiently turn out and to use international markets to acquire products that are best made elsewhere. This has sharpened and refined the division of labor among nation-states. The upshot is an explosive process, in which productivity, consumption, and participation rise at exponential rates. As we have seen and will continue to explore, urban growth has been nothing short of colossal, but it has also been accompanied by deep inequalities and paradoxes.[15]

Fundamentally, globalism and its attendant free trade are derived from a technological revolution that has shrunk time and distance. We have already mentioned the revolutionary effects of instant communication, and here we amplify how that technology allows nations to achieve deeper levels of economic integration within competitive markets. By now, advanced technology moves $1.5 trillion around the world each day. In the United States international flows of bonds and equities are fifty-four times higher today than in 1970. The comparable figures for Germany and Japan are sixty and fifty times higher. Other research has shown that international trade sustains the global patterning and has brought about changes in economic relationships, social structure, and the significance of geographical place.[16]

A corollary characteristic is standardization. Once goods and information are alike, they become recognizable and interchangeable. Common standards of measurement, universal criteria, interchangeable parts, and identical symbols are essential for globalization. Just as the grid system of streets helped land-development, so too does standardization facilitate globalization. This includes a common currency, established procedures for registering and enforcing patents, and compatible mechanical or electronic equipment. Licenses and professional certification have also become standardized in order to allow human resources to flow across boundaries. Even sports has become standardized. The Olympic Games and Olympic committees legitimate certain sports and sanction rules through which athletic contests are held. Traditionally, American baseball has been capped by the misnomer of a "World Series." Up until recently this was entirely an American affair, but increasingly players and even some teams have been drawn from other nations. The progressive universality of sports today is incontrovertible.

Another wave of global change is heavily political. Globalization has magnified the intercourse between states, localities, and social movements across the world.[17] Signs of this are visible in the rise of multilateral organizations, regional pacts, and talk of a borderless world. States, localities, nongovernmental organizations, and labor increasingly ignore old boundaries and are driven more than before by the seemingly contradictory stimuli of cooperation and competition. For some this has opened new worlds of opportunity, where masses of people can be mobilized for democratic ends. This interaction, both on site and across cyberspace, makes government more accountable and also more replaceable. For others, globalism signifies a concentration of wealth and power, and a threat of lower living standards. This has led to a perilous instability and a thunderous reaction from both left- and right-wing protestors.[v]

An additional wave of globalization is sociocultural. This involves diffusion of a more open, multipolar, and multicultural society in which migration is a major by-product.[18] What distinguishes current migration from preceding movements is its truncated and temporary patterns of settlement. Commonly, single men live abroad for lengthy periods, while sending remittances to the homeland. When whole families do migrate, they often are treated as long-term aliens, rarely assimilating, and even children born in the host country may not acquire citizenship. Indeed, the telecommunications revolution has given permanency to this temporary status. Cheap, efficient technology compresses space and time, enabling groups to retain homeland ties and preserve indigenous culture. Overseas, ethnic cultures are now said to thrive in "transnational space" in which language, habit, and tradition continue regardless of geography.[19]

These aspects of globalization also foster a greater sense of mutual vulnerability. Free trade and competitive advantage have made societies more efficient, but they have also made societies more fragile and susceptible to crisis. In a matter of minutes, turmoil in a single great bank can upset finance at the other end of the world. Currency fluctuations can overturn decades of progress, hitting those at the bottom of the economic scale hardest. As economies become more integrated, localities share more closely both the good and bad times of globalization. Through the 1990s Taipei, Tel Aviv, and Santiago experienced an unprecedented boom. After 2000 the global economy was hit by recession and those cities went bust. The more integrated and the more synchronized the locality with globalization, the greater the upturn and the steeper the downturn.

Vulnerability has many dimensions. Disease travels as swiftly as airline flights and has acquired an international character. The recent exuberance and then depression of stock markets as well as the AIDS epidemic are unfortunate examples of this exposure. Still another dark side of globalism is the spread of terrorism.[20] The ease of travel, instantaneous communication, and quick transfer of money make it possible for terrorists to do their work and attack fragile international linkages.[vi] International terror most vividly illustrates the underside of global interdependence. The multinational character of its actors and the slippery content of its operations are especially well suited for porous boundaries. As we explain in chapter 10, it was at the seams of globalization where international cities and international terror were tragically joined on September 11.

How do cities fit into this overall picture? One might suppose that globalization makes cities less important, as they are swept into a common world of economic competition and social interchange. Presumably, people could be located anywhere, and conduct business via the internet from a mountaintop retreat.[21] In fact, the opposite is true — at least for some cities. A knowledge-based economy has accelerated face-to-face and informal contact. It has increased an appetite for conferences, seminars, and annual meetings. Additionally, business searches for that extra edge that comes from personal contact.

Globalization also has generated a need for central direction in which financial, legal, and professional services are concentrated within a common locale. Cities have made free trade much easier to accomplish, they have facilitated a new international division of labor, and they have absorbed waves of migration.[22] While not all cities have been blessed with these advantages, many are still efficient and enormously productive work stations for the postindustrial era. Whether one selects a handful of global cities, a larger number of primate cities, or a sampling of regional ones, urban centers lead national productivity, and their total output in goods and services has quickened during the last few decades.[23]

Rising urbanization has occurred concomitantly with globalization and is associated with rising GDP. Metropolitan areas of Europe and North America grew rich during the transformation, though clearly as the process matures the rate of urbanization flattens. Figure 1.2 portrays rates of urbanization and GDP in North America and Europe. Note the proportion of people living in all types of urban settlement is remarkably high.

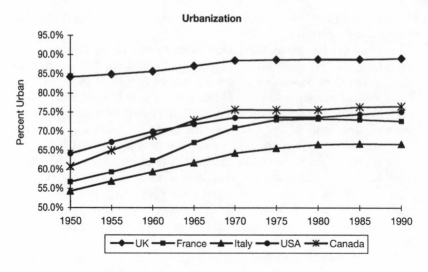

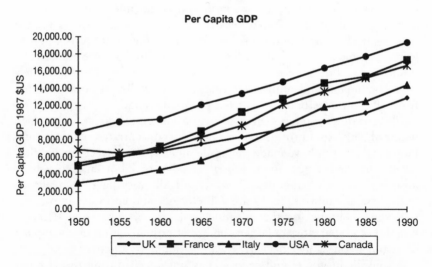

Figure 1.2. Urbanization and Gross Domestic Product in Europe and North America, 1950–90.

Globalization has not made all urban places alike. Where you live and work matters more than ever in accessing jobs, income, public amenities, schools, and green space. These things are contingent upon "place." Location does make a huge difference. Neat suburban residential enclaves, edge cities, busy commercial downtowns, urban ghettos, vacated industrial areas, and campus-like office parks are all part of a complex urban fabric that differentiates opportunities. Some cities have taken advantage of those opportunities and the enormous wealth that springs from global trade. By the end of the millennium, Foreign Direct Investment (FDI) had reached an all-time high of $865 billion. While it is not possible to trace that investment to every locality, an overwhelming proportion of it went to advanced industrial nations, mostly located in the West. Banks held that money and facilitated investments, and almost all of these institutions were located in major cities. Moreover, along with investment flows, banking assets have gushed over the last few decades. Table 1.4 shows the growth of these assets (adjusted for inflation) in thirty-five cities across the globe.

Even during this short period, most banks substantially increased their holdings. In some cases the aggregation of capital crested by over 300 percent. Place often shapes perspective, and location cannot help influencing decisions. More than ever, cities serve as the command and control centers of those decisions. They have benefited not just from saturated white-collar employment and offshoot industries, but also from their strategic placement in international capital markets. Not all of this has produced salutary results. There are always paradoxes and contradictions connected to change, and the impact of globalization on cities is no exception.

One paradox is that while most metropolitan areas have become wealthier, they also contain rising numbers of the poor. In Western Europe 10 percent of city residents are classified as poor, while the percentage rises in suburbs to roughly 20 percent. The United States reverses these proportions, so that central cities and suburbs respectively hold 21 percent and 9 percent of residents who fall below the poverty line.[24] Quite expectedly, migrants searching for opportunities in cities account for a substantial portion of the poor. More than 50 percent of the populations in New York and Toronto are classified as either ethnic minorities or foreign born. In Paris, the percentage is above 15 percent.

Another paradox is that urban transformation has both expanded the sphere of central cities and shrunk it. In some ways deconcentration has extended central cities by making suburbanites dependent upon them for income, investment, jobs, and culture. One can see this in the huge numbers of commuters pouring into urban cores each day as well as in the many monetary transactions (mortgages, business loans, venture capital) that occur between city financial institutions and the hinterlands. In other ways, deconcentration has also meant an escape from the central city and has created an altogether new urban form. Green cities have sprung up in the more distant countryside and eliminated distinctions between urban and rural life. A newer urban life is built

TABLE 1.4
Major Banks and Bank Holdings, 1994–98

Rank	City	Country	# Banks (top 100)	Assets, 1998 (billions US$)	Assets, 1994 (adjusted, in billions 1998 US$)	Percent Change, 1994–98
1	Tokyo	Japan	13	3,494.45	5,014.66	69.7
2	Paris	France	6	1,964.99	1,627.36	120.7
3	Frankfurt	Germany	5	1,932.81	887.57	217.8
4	London	United Kingdom	6	1,811.88	773.61	234.2
5	New York	United States	4	1,428.69	448.44	318.6
6	Zurich	Switzerland	2	1,162.39	320.89	362.2
7	Osaka	Japan	4	1,096.65	1,480.67	74.1
8	Amsterdam	Netherlands	2	970.81	387.23	250.7
9	Brussels	Belgium	4	853.43	390.02	218.8
10	Munich	Germany	2	826.09	441.70	187.0
11	Milan	Italy	3	484.24	280.34	172.7
12	Toronto	Canada	3	453.24	255.41	177.5
13	Düsseldorf	Germany	1	415.95	176.87	235.2
14	Montreal	Canada	2	323.24	205.76	157.1
15	Utrecht	Netherlands	1	293.14	136.64	214.5
16	Nagoya	Japan	1	264.45	292.00	90.6
17	Chicago	United States	1	261.49	NA	NA
18	Melbourne	Australia	2	241.32	135.14	178.6
19	Edinburgh	United Kingdom	2	233.09	65.59	355.4
20	Rome	Italy	2	224.18	232.83	96.3
21	San Francisco	United States	1	202.48	141.45	143.1
22	Stockholm	Sweden	2	199.89	147.45	135.6
23	Turin	Italy	1	185.40	172.27	107.6
24	Santander	Spain	1	182.01	65.70	277.0
25	Hanover	Germany	1	178.34	99.19	179.8
26	Sydney	Australia	2	164.17	137.28	119.6
27	Bilbao	Spain	1	157.28	93.95	167.4
28	Weisbaden	Germany	1	141.67	60.56	233.9
29	Vienna	Austria	1	140.16	NA	NA
30	Brasilia	Brazil	1	107.21	73.94	145.0
31	Madrid	Spain	1	96.69	143.27	67.5
32	Yokohama	Japan	1	92.45	112.56	82.1
33	Hamburg	Germany	1	83.87	NA	NA
34	Shizuoka	Japan	1	63.83	70.41	90.7
35	Chiba	Japan	1	63.71	78.97	80.7

around asphalt, glass, trees, and grass, and it functions apart from traditional central cities.

Still another oddity is that while transformation has made cities into hard-working centers of productivity, it has also made them into sites of gluttonous leisurely consumption. Scholars often write about the di-

chotomy between investment and consumption whereby different locales tend toward one or the other.[25] Postindustrial cities have united
these dichotomies. Complementing an enormous white-collar apparatus
of producer services is a burgeoning industry in leisure and consumption. The rise of the office-complex city has been accompanied by the
rise of the tourist city. Cities are today in the midst of what Judd and
Fainstein describe as a "tourist bubble," whose growth is among the
fastest in the world.[26]

Put in historical perspective, these paradoxes are not unusual. Cities
have always grown or shrunk alongside technological advance. The introduction of elevators and steel framing allowed for skyscrapers but
broke up traditional neighborhoods. Metro lines were a boon for central business districts, but a bust for out-of-the-way small towns. Invention is often a conveyance for what Schumpeter called "creative destruction"[27] and brought about very different results. Creative destruction
caused cities to rise and fall, and nothing demonstrates this so completely as our profile of ten cities, their choices over development strategy and their role in the international marketplace.

"Glocal" Choices

Deindustrialization, deconcentration, and globalization have put cities
on trajectories of change. It is this unusual blend of global challenge
and local response that confronts us, and this combination is sometimes
denoted by the inelegant terms "glocal" or "glocalization".[28] Like the
industrial revolution before it, this revolution can be decisively influenced by government as well as other social institutions.[29] Governments
have responded to these challenges in diverse ways. First, leaders and
citizens have made strategic decisions about *what kind of community*
they want. Some political leaders look to the marketplace for strategic
direction, placing a high priority on gaining a competitive advantage for
their communities. They ask, how can we find our niche in the regional,
national, or world market? What can we do best? Where can we garner
capital investment? How can we grow by helping business operate more
efficiently? For cities that choose competition, answers to these questions have produced a variety of strategic responses. We see cities remaking waterfronts into tourist attractions, refurbishing downtowns
with office towers and convention halls, and trying to attract big bang
events such as the World Cup, Expo, or Olympic games, as well as
revenue sources such as sports teams, theme parks, or gaming casinos.

Cities then do not just react to the movement of capital but act upon
these forces. Although local governments have only limited control over
the marketplace, they use public power to engage it. They do so when-

ever land is recycled, development rights are granted, housing is built, taxes are collected, or capital is borrowed. Moreover cities can profoundly affect factors of production. They can lower overhead costs by building bridges, ports, and airfields. They can tighten up or loosen controls over air pollution. Cities can even affect labor costs by making it easier or more difficult for individuals to access welfare benefits.[30] In making decisions over these issues, cities struggle to resolve an array of problems and influence their own restructuring.

Some leaders try to induce capital investment by reducing risks for business. They may put up bonds that guarantee the building of stadiums or convention halls, they may underwrite loans to potential investors, and they may find themselves forming public private-partnerships in order to assure private investors of unified backing.[31] Cities also aggressively solicit business by lobbying for private capital, bidding for company headquarters, or establishing international offices to stimulate trade.

Cities seeking competitive advantages may also tolerate increased migration, allow informal economies to flourish, and facilitate the supply of cheap goods and services. They may countenance permissive building codes, lax licensing, and an abundance of substandard housing. These newfound resources explain the partial resurgence of textile manufacture in some cities, where old-fashioned sweatshops arise and where illegal immigrants are exploited as low-cost labor. The upscale life-style of postindustrial cities generates a demand for low-paying service jobs. A virtual night shift of unskilled workers commutes into downtowns to clean the office towers, staff the restaurants, and drive the taxicabs. The "reverse commute" of marginal workers into affluent suburbs also helps to maintain an attractive low cost of living.

Alternatively, cities sometimes defy the swells of the marketplace. Local leaders can remain politically sensitive and rely on a logic of populist, anti-growth policies.[32] This logic may well clash with the rationality of the marketplace. Cities may resist the lure of growth and opt for preservationist or caretaker strategies.[33] They may want to protect historic neighborhoods, guard surrounding farmland, or prohibit large discount outlets and suburban malls. Some fear higher taxes and increased congestion. They may want to remain as quiet residential communities.

Large and small cities have resisted economic growth by invoking moratoria on the construction of office towers, using zoning exactions to force concessions from developers, adopting strict architectural codes, requiring underground facilities for automobile parking, and setting aside large tracts for open space.[34] In Western Europe the upsurge of "green parties" has affected urban policies. Green legislators have placed controls on housing costs, limited the price of apartment rentals, and closed off streets to automobiles. Reciprocally, they have used public funds to renovate housing, protected rights of squatters, and reserved sections of the streetscape for bicycles. Populist movements have sometimes arisen to challenge the power of corporate decision makers in places such as Cleveland, Ohio, the Mon Valley in Pennsylvania, and Liverpool, England.

There is variation in the response to globalization. In important ways, world competition has sparked a quest for capital investment and growth. In other ways, the free exchange of ideas and possibilities for collaboration has enabled groups to mobilize. Some scholars have found evidence of a new urban politics based on social issues, increased diversity, and a concern for the environment.[35] They also envision globalized cities as hothouses for the spread of postmaterialist values with its emphasis on citizen activism.[36] The concerns of migrant workers coupled to environmental and populist sentiment could generate counterpressures. Whatever the outcomes, globalization is not a leveling process, and it has created new alternatives.

Who makes decisions over *what* is another question of choice. This ultimately depends upon the existence of assets and the distribution of power within a city. Some scholars argue that urban decision-making is shaped by economics, and they stress growth and competition as the predominant force. From this perspective, cities must give priority to economic growth because they are disciplined by a market that punishes them with loss of jobs and tax revenue.[37] Other scholars argue that political preferences matter more than economic pressures. They see powerful leaders, coalitions, regimes, and growth machines operating to shape economic preferences.[38] There is something to both interpretations. Cities are certainly limited by the assets at their disposal, and they cannot deal with global change unless they have the wherewithal to do so. By the same token, dealing with change requires initiative, and coalitions must be built by political entrepreneurs who mobilize groups and classes.

The important questions deal not only with differences of alternatives taken, but also with the reasons why some cities might be able to chose particular alternatives. Are there structural characteristics that are common to cities choosing similar strategic alternatives? If so, can they be identified and how do they interact? Likewise, do cities that share similar strategic responses to globalism also share similar cultural or political characteristics. If so, what are these and how do they operate? Can we make sense of these varying influences on choice and put them into some logical schema? Finally, what are the lessons learned from this inquiry? Does the international marketplace have a tendency to homogenize cities so that they become alike, or are cities becoming more dis-

TABLE 1.5
Transformation and Urban Choice

Trajectory of Change		Alternatives: Developmental and Political
From (ca. 1970)	To (ca. 2000)	
Deindustrialization	Postindustrialization	Developmental: Attempt to retain old industry through public support, worker ownership, and cooperatives versus aggressively convert to a post-industrial economy by recruiting new investors and retraining workers. Political: Establish alliances with blue-collar classes and racial or ethnic groups versus forge coalitions with business leaders, banks, or chambers of commerce.
Deconcentration	Growth of suburbs and boomtowns	Developmental: Attempt to stop or slow population change through growth controls versus attempt to stimulate population growth, increase jobs, and expand investments through supply-side incentives and low taxes. Political: Build voting blocs in neighborhoods through social investment, public housing, and collective goods versus enlist business support through reinvigorated downtowns and new industrial areas.
Preglobal (national-regional-indigenous business)	Globalization (international-extramural-absentee-owned business)	Developmental: Invoke building moratoria and height restrictions, adopt exactive zoning, and preserve historic districts versus aggressively attract international business through trade centers, new airports, and containerized ports. Political: Cultivate anti-growth coalitions and award allies with collective benefits versus court business with free land and infrastructure for corporate headquarters, free trading zones, and side payments.

similar? Given the tension between the global and the local, can one decide which side, if any, prevails?

This study compares urban strategic choices during a period of transformation. Table 1.5 provides a schematic representation of the juxtaposition between trajectories of change and strategic choices. The first two columns list trajectories of change between 1970 and 2000. The last column lists strategic alternatives (developmental and political). The strategic choices are not mutually exclusive and cities may adopt any in combination. Nevertheless, cities are constrained by the availability of resources and conflicting constituency objectives.

The classic development conflict occurs between "anti-growth" and "pro-growth" coalitions, and includes such debates as whether to adopt building moratoria and preserve historic districts or aggressively recruit private investors and turn downtowns into rows of towering office complexes. This conflict often encompasses a political component where the sides are poised for battle—neighborhood groups, preservationists, and environmentalists on one side versus developers, chambers of commerce, and media boosters on the other. Pro-growth impulses are often driven by a desire to standardize development (trade centers, office towers, tourist attractions) and expand the contributions of multinational firms in the local economy. Anti-growth impulses frequently stem from a desire for citizen participation and local autonomy.[39] These tensions reflect the degree to which local development agendas are influenced by the international market.

Looking at the situation more broadly, we can appreciate that issues of international import are fought on local battlegrounds, and that ultimately these conflicts change the character of cities. Many local challenges and responses have global proportions; decisions flow to and from an international marketplace. This marketplace can either saturate cities with massive investment and political pressure or marginalize them. Either way, cities must respond by accommodating, managing, or resisting these forces.

Ten Cities

We examine choice of development strategy through the medium of ten cities, as they dealt with trajectories of change between 1970 and 2000. These cities are not necessarily representative of all cities in North America and Western Europe. It is doubtful that any ten cities—or twice that number—could provide such a representative profile. Rather, our cities have been chosen because they illustrate a broad range of variation on variables that we believe are critical to urban development politics (for reasons discussed in chapter 2). Specifically, these cities display wide diversity in their market conditions, their intergovernmental arrangements, and the political behavior (participation and culture) of their citizens. As such, they illustrate the vicissitudes of fortune as well as common currents.

The cities include three in the United States — New York, Detroit, and Houston — and one in Canada — Toronto. The remaining cities are located in Western Europe. They include two in the United Kingdom — Glasgow and Liverpool — two cities in France — Paris and Marseilles — and two cities in Italy — Milan and Naples. For the most part, and unless stated otherwise, cities are defined as central cities contained within boundaries.

On both continents we selected cities that enjoyed favorable market conditions (Paris, Milan, Houston, Toronto, and New York) and several that have experienced adverse conditions (Naples, Marseilles, Liverpool, Glasgow, and Detroit). This permits us to assess the role of investment attractions and a city's wealth in the making of developmental choices. These cities also vary in their intergovernmental arrangements. Some are in federal systems that devolve considerable control to local governments, while others are in unitary-systems of governments.

Toronto, Detroit, Houston, and New York exemplify North America's federal pattern. Revenues, budgets, land use, and discretion are largely in the hands of local government. This is true for both Americans and Canadians. American cities are exemplars of local autonomy and are subject to some federal or state intervention. Federated Canada also grants a good deal of autonomy to its cities, but the provinces are more apt to intervene in local affairs.

At the other end of the spectrum are the European cities. In different degrees Paris, Marseilles, Naples, Milan, Liverpool, and Glasgow function within unitary national systems. National governments in Great Britain, France, and Italy often intervene in local affairs — from setting land-use standards to remaking local boundaries. Revenues, budgets, and institutions are heavily influenced by national elites and are subject to a host of national or regional regulations. Governmental differences enable us to probe how national governments influence strategic choice.[40] Will cities within the same nation tend to resemble each other's pattern of development or do transnational forces have a greater influence on decision making?

These cities also reflect differences in their political behavior and culture. Some are characterized by activism and widespread support for what has come to be called "postmaterialist" values (Paris, Toronto), while others are politically more passive and hold traditional values (Naples, Detroit). The diversity is considerable and reflects the realities of urban life in the Western world. At the same time, our selection of subjects has retained a certain constancy. All ten cities are major industrial centers, all ten are part of a Western, liberal, democratic polity, and all ten have gone through the crucible of postindustrial restructuring.

The choice of these ten cities also allows us to examine how the great transformation has shaped these communities. Cities within different nation-states have experienced differentiated patterns of development. In most cases, each nation-state has held one prosperous city that has either dedensified or grown into a boomtown and another distressed city that has experienced severe decline. In the United States, Detroit (distressed and in decline) and Houston (prosperous and growing) represent these polar cases. In France, Paris (prosperous and dedensified) and Marseilles (distressed and in decline) demonstrate this contrast. In Italy, Milan (prosperous and dedensified) and Naples (distressed and in decline) also illustrate this distinction. The cities selected in the United Kingdom are less illustrative of such polarity. Liverpool (distressed and in decline) does conform to the pattern, but Glasgow is also quite poor and dedensified, although it has experienced some recovery.[vii]

Table 1.6 below provides a profile of each of our ten cities. The table shows variation in ten cities according to economic, demographic, and political characteristics. This variation is consistent with previous patterns of variation found in a larger number of cities (see table 1.3).

A systematic analysis of these cities allows us better to generalize about the theoretical implications of urban development. One issue, already mentioned, is strategic choice. That is the extent to which cities can exercise discretion and the degree to which it is embedded in the marketplace and in other structural factors. Another theoretical issue is the degree to which our ten cities are converging or diverging. That is, how might these ten cities be adopting similar or dissimilar characteristics? Here again, our selection of ten cities helps us test this proposition under conditions of significant variation. Too often case studies rely on a few similar cities, or even one municipality, for conceptual insight. While the few or single-city approaches can provide valuable depth, they are often confined by special circumstance and limit our ability to generalize. For example, to conclude that "growth coalitions" do or do not rule leaves the reader in the dark about the multiple circumstances under which growth coalitions could exercise varying degrees of power. Although our approach sacrifices some depth, its broadly constructed comparative perspective can reap rich generalizations.

The central argument of this book is that urban development policies are formulated at the juncture of local politics and the international marketplace. While city governments may be constrained, they are also active managers of development strategies. They play a critical role by mobilizing resources, exercising policy choices, and bargaining over

TABLE 1.6
Variation in Ten Cities of North America and Europe

Country	City	Economic Assessment	Type of Deconcentration	National/ Intergovernmental Arrangements	Political Behavior
United States	New York, N.Y.	Prosperous	Growth	Federal	Active/Mixed
	Detroit	Distressed	Decline	Federal	Passive/Materialist
	Houston	Prosperous	Growth	Federal	Passive/Materialist
Canada	Toronto	Prosperous	Growth	Federal/Regional	Active/Postmaterialist
United Kingdom	Glasgow	Distressed	Decline	Unitary/Regional	Mixed/Materialist
	Liverpool	Distressed	Decline	Unitary	Mixed/Materialist
France	Paris	Prosperous	Dedensification	Unitary/Regional	Active/Postmaterialist
	Marseilles	Distressed	Decline	Unitary/Regional	Mixed/Mixed
Italy	Milan	Prosperous	Dedensification	Unitary	Active/Postmaterialist
	Naples	Distressed	Decline	Unitary	Mixed/Materialist

capital investment. At the heart of development choice lies bargaining ability, which explains important policy differences because cities draw upon a variety of political, economic, and social assets in order to conduct that bargaining. Further, cities are bounded by differences in resources. Some will be able to exercise greater discretion than others: some possess the wherewithal, the political relationships, and the energy to strike favorable bargains, while others must accept much less. We find that the poltical discretion of cities increases when they are economically secure and anchored in strong intergovernmental arrangements, with an active citizenry and supportive local cultures. We conclude that while cities are constrained by the global economies, they are not necessarily its prisoners. After all is said and done, postindustrial change is a product of human decisions—of public policies made in international organizations, the seats of national government, and city halls. We focus on the local nexus and conclude that ultimately the welfare of cities is a matter of balanced development strategies, coordinated public action, and intelligent citizenship.

Before turning to our ten cities, we offer a theoretical framework for assessing urban development. Here we examine why cities might choose different development strategies, what factors should be taken into account in explaining differential development patterns, and whether cities are more likely to pursue economic or social objectives.

Notes

i. Other parts of the world have also formed transnational associations, including the Association of South East Asian Nations (Brunei, Indonesia, Malaysia, Philippines, Singapore, Thailand, and Vietnam) and Mancusor (Argentina, Brazil, Paraguay, and Uruguay).

ii. Primate cities are giant entities, at least twice as large as the next largest city in the nation, and not infrequently they hold 20 percent or more of a nation's population. While primate cities are not always at the nexus of the global economy, they are central to a national economy and generate a substantial portion of its GDP.

iii. There are also cultural, social, and geographical reasons for this. Anglo-American traditions favor country and low-density living, while Continental traditions are more disposed to high-density or clustered environments. In America, the availability of greater space and racial enmity contributed to middle-class white flight.

iv. Combining two somewhat different indices for Western Europe and America is problematic, but can still provide a reasonable picture of prosperity and distress. The index for European cities can be found in Cheshire, Carbonaro, and Hay, "Problems of Urban Decline." This index uses per capita income, unemployment, immigration, and travel demand to determine varying degrees of prosperity or distress. The index for American cities can be found in Nathan and Adams's "Understanding Central City Hardship" and "Four Perspectives on Hardship." This index uses poverty, unemployment, dependency, education, and crowded housing to determine varying degrees of prosperity or distress. We also have used this index to construct a score for Manhattan and classify it accordingly.

v. Instances of both democratic and antidemocratic movements can be traced in some ways to globalization. In 1999 the overthrow of the Indonesian government was made possible by internet communication in that nation's archipelago. Within the next year, populist, protest movements held large-scale demonstrations in Seattle and Washington, D.C. Populist demonstrations against Iran's repressive theocracy have also been held and gained resonance through telecommunications. On the other side, in the United States neo-Nazi and racist groups have been able to mobilize followers through the Internet. Also, marginal political parties in both America and Europe have capitalized on a reaction against global trade (in the U.S., Patrick Buchanan's Reform Party; in France, Jean-Marie Le Pen's National Front; in Italy Gianfranco Fini's neofascists).

vi. Every action has its reaction, and globalism is no different. Vulnerability also has a more fortunate side that can be found in cross-national cooperation and synergy. This kind of complementary interdependence has brought about cooperation in regulating currencies, controlling AIDS, and combating terrorism.

vii. New York and Toronto also afford a look at the behavior of cities that are metropolitan in their scope of government and their geographic composition and that differ in some respects from traditional municipalities. New York is a giant city that spans five boroughs and is run by a single government. Differences between New York's five boroughs are considerable, and we sometimes treat its most important one (Manhattan) separately. Toronto is Canada's leading city and during the transformation period was run through a federation of six municipalities. Since 1998 Toronto has been turned into a single "mega city." Also, Metropolitan Toronto has continued to thrive without becoming a new-age boomtown or losing its historic character.

Chapter Two

TOWARD A THEORY OF URBAN DEVELOPMENT

> In a storm there must surely be a great advantage in
> having the aid of a pilot's compass.
> — Plato

ECONOMIC VERSUS POLITICAL LOGIC

As chapter 1 points out, cities have responded to deindustrialization, decentralization, and globalization in various ways. Before elaborating on these responses and explaining how and why they differ, we offer our own theory of comparative urban development. Few scholars have systematically probed how cities develop within different national contexts or why they choose different pathways. In the absence of a comprehensive theory that applies to diverse contexts, analysts have only been able to report case studies of cities or survey general trends.[1]

As much as we can glean from the literature on urban development, we find two major strands of thought. One strand claims that cities compete in a competitive marketplace and must strive to promote economic growth. This perspective is oriented toward an "economic logic" and stresses the notion of rational actors who maximize advantages and pursue individual interests. It draws upon the assumptions of public choice theory.[2] According to one leading study by Paul Peterson, cities are constrained by local and regional economic competition and must give priority to policies that promote economic growth.[3] Policies that conflict with these forces are bound to fail because the marketplace will punish rebellious cities with loss of private investment, jobs, and tax revenue. Ultimately, the public will vote against politicians if they fail to promote the city's economic position. A central point of this economic logic is that cities must conceive of themselves as business corporations — as efficiency-maximizing organizations, which hold a unitary interest in enhancing economic productivity.[4]

Another strand of thought stresses that internal political forces shape urban development choices. What counts, according to these theorists, is the "space" or "slack" in a political system. This space allows political pressures to mount and determine development priorities.[5] This perspective relies upon a "political logic" to explain the behavior of cities. It suggests that cities are not business corporations but political entities whose leaders must build coalitions and win political support. According to this political logic, cities disperse the benefits of development, seek to reward a majority of constituents, and provide collective benefits.[6]

For all the light these theories shed on urban development, they leave many shadows. The research offers few propositions about why cities might differ from one another and how their particular political or economic contexts might matter. Why do some cities follow free-market strategies and inducements for private investors to accomplish their objectives, while others use a political process to promote collective benefits? Contrasting approaches to development in New York and Paris may better elucidate the point. During the 1990s officials in New York wanted to develop a decaying area in the city. They agreed to relax density controls and building height regulations in Times Square in order to build office towers. They later gave millions of dollars in tax concessions to a giant multinational corporation so that it would move several hundred jobs to this location. At about the same time in Paris, officials and planners decided to develop a large unused swath of land on the eastern side of the city. Public funds estimated at more than $3.5 billion were employed to anchor the development with four towers housing the national library. The library was to be accompanied by promenades, recreational facilities, publicly assisted housing, and commercial space. The project was capped off by the construction of modern high-tech transit lines to service the area. No subventions were given to developers and they were not called upon to shape the project.

Here we have contrasting cases where, in the first instance, environmental regulations are suspended and public money is used to pay a private corporation to develop prime real estate. In the second instance, public money is applied through a comprehensive plan designed to service multitudes of citizens with public facilities. Clearly, there are different institutions, practices, and attitudes at work here. New Yorkers were prompted to chase after private investors, and the public paid a handsome sum for their cooperation. Though potential profits were a part of Parisian considerations, officials paid considerably less attention to the private sector and anchored their project in collective benefits. Contemporary theory has little to say about these contrasts. And while scholars have debated whether economic or political logics are most important, few have trod into the area of why or when one logic might prevail rather than another.

Looking at development in terms of different logics and their underlying contexts also raises a fundamental issue about the interplay between structure and agency.[7] The idea of structure entails long-term, underlying, relatively fixed forces that configure decision making and make it quite difficult for human actions to overcome. Economic benefits that spring from geographic location is an example of a structural factor that cities can do little about. By contrast, the idea of agency conveys human volition, personal discretion, and freedom of action. The ability of elected leaders to adopt development strategies that solely satisfy popular preferences represents an instance of agency. Scholars who favor an economic logic are more apt to focus on structural factors and claim that cities have no choice but to follow the strictures of a competitive marketplace.[8] Scholars who stress political logic are inclined to focus on the latitude given to leaders and citizens.[9]

The actual facts of urban development may well reveal an interaction between structure and agency, but unless we specify how different political, social, and economic contexts shape choices, any theory will have limited utility. An economic logic will put research into an impersonal, deterministic box, which lacks reference to realities. By comparison, a political logic will be superficial and fail to explain how actors actually respond to underlying constraints when making policy.

Without an explanatory theory, it is impossible to say how and when structure or agency matters. Ironically, this difficulty hinders us in achieving the very thing that theorists set out to do, which is to demonstrate the constraints upon leaders or the scope of freedom they can exercise. We pursue this task by attempting to incorporate the interaction of both structure (underlying constraints) and agency (manifest personal discretion). Although the impersonal forces of structure and the personal volition of agency are not always easy to distinguish, our theory helps weigh or assess their interaction. Cities may differ in their underlying structure — in the cards they hold. But political leaders can use that structure — play those cards — in any number of ways. The challenge is to understand what specific economic and political contexts underpin choices regarding development options and how they explain variations between cities.

LINKING MARKETS AND POLITICS

How cities go about the process of overseeing urban development springs from the resources at their disposal. These resources define their bargaining position with business, their urban development strategies, and their disposition to balance economic and sociopolitical considerations. Variation among cities is strongly tied to the ways in which the larger political economy shapes local discretion and accords cities differential bargaining advantages. As we later elaborate, poor cities do worse in this bargaining, because they have the scarcest resources. No matter how well or poorly off cities may be, bargaining is an integral component of development. Local officials operate within different bargaining parameters and within a broader milieu of tension-ridden cooperation between public and private sectors.

Following Lindblom,[10] it is useful to look at local governments in

Western Europe and North America as sharing a liberal-democratic system in which there is a division of labor between business and government.[11] The private sector is responsible for the production of wealth in a market system in which choices over production and exchange are organized by price mechanisms. For its part, the public sector is organized along democratic or "polyarchal" lines in which public decisions are subject to popular control. Public officials are responsible for the management of political support for governmental projects, while business leaders manage investments and market-driven enterprises.

This perspective suggests that even though public and private sectors are theoretically separate, in reality they are highly interdependent. So far as government is concerned, the private sector produces wealth and economic growth that are necessary for public well-being — including jobs, a higher tax base, and revenues for public programs. Private prosperity also exerts a positive spinoff for politicians, who profit from popular satisfaction with economic conditions. Most politicians know that a prosperous economy brings them votes. For business, the public sector is important because government intervention in the marketplace is necessary for economic affluence and healthy enterprise. These interventions include inducements to business that permit risky investments (tax abatements, zoning variances, favorable financing), the resolution of conflict (assuaging irate neighborhoods, settling labor disputes), the creation of an infrastructure (highways, ports, airports, metro lines), making the local environment safe for business (police and fire protection), and work force training.

Most of these actions are not left solely to cities but are undertaken within a complex set of economic and political interactions. A theory of development cannot be limited to the internal behavior of city hall; it must have a sufficient scope to include external influences. The twists and turns of an international, national, or regional economy are also important. Of considerable significance, too, are measures taken by other governments (regional, provincial, state, national, or supranational). Any attempt at theory building must encompass a range of market and political variables that are bound to influence urban development. These include market conditions, the exercise of popular control, the intergovernmental mesh of policy interventions, and the dispositions of business leaders.

Markets and Political Choice

The greatest bargaining resource held by business is its control over the generation of investment and wealth. It is this attribute that provides so much plausibility for the economic logic described above. The rationale for this logic is based on a powerful set of facts. Cities are fragmented corporate bodies, they lack autonomy, and they are devoid of political sovereignty. Cities also compete with each other for investment in a world where business is increasingly mobile. If cities are to survive, they must show a friendly attitude toward business and promote economic growth. Economic theorists make a credible case showing that local governments are highly motivated to limit their social expenditures, spend more on infrastructure to encourage business, and to adapt their policies to market conditions.[12] Failure to meet these conditions will lead to disinvestment and bring about an "automatic punishing recoil" of the marketplace.[13]

The implications for political choice are far reaching. It means that cities are almost always forced to give highest priority to economic development in pursuit of a more attractive tax base. Most urban scholars interpret this as a struggle between business and the citizenry. Case studies claim that pro-business decisions work to the detriment of ordinary citizens.[14] Conflicts are often cast as taking place between "pro-growth" and "anti-growth" coalitions or between "downtown" and "neighborhood interests."[15]

While these perspectives are sometimes useful in explaining certain instances of urban development, they do not capture many others, and they fail to account for other sides in the development game. Most particularly, this perspective highlights those advantages that accrue to business and neglects the advantages that remain with public-sector actors. We suggest the advantages attributed to business may be overstated. The marketplace works in two directions, not one. Cities possess not only resources but also opportunities to leverage business with those resources. The following sections take up some commonly held propositions that cities are helpless, and puts them into perspective. We begin our discussion with four commonly held arguments: 1) the assumption that "cities lose, if business gains," 2) the belief in unqualified "capital mobility," 3) the proposition that "cities cannot choose," and 4) the notion that almost invariably "cities will maximize growth."

The "cities lose if business wins" argument.   Many researchers assume that public and private actors represent competing institutions whose goals are mutually exclusive. In the analogy of a zero-sum game, if one side wins, the other must automatically lose.[16] While this may sometimes be true, the zero-sum analogy may not always hold. We should distinguish between interests and goals. Governments often have different interests than does business, but can share the same goals. Thus, local government may have an interest in raising public revenue by increasing retail sales, while investors have an interest in maximizing profits. Though the interests of each are different, both may share the common goal of bringing about higher sales through expanded development. When this happens, bargaining between government and business shifts from rivalry over competing interests to sorting out common goals.

This kind of scenario enhances the value of bargaining resources that are mostly owned by the public sector. Development politics focuses on such things as the ability to amass land, grant legal privileges and rights, control zoning, provide appropriate infrastructure, and enlist public support. Public officials, motivated by different stakes, frequently choose to pursue economic goals that are also favored by business.[17] Although many academics are suspicious of pro-growth policies, these options are often supported by local electorates who are interested in jobs and higher property values.

To take a different tack on Charles Wilson's aphorism, scholars may be too anxious to suggest that if it's good for General Motors, it must be bad for Detroit. Yet popularly supported government and elite-dominated business are often in genuine agreement. Under these conditions, the ability of political authorities to create political support for specific projects can become an important bargaining resource. At the very least, the extent to which agreement between business and local government is a by-product of political choice rather than of economic constraint should be a premise for empirical investigation, rather than an a priori conclusion.[i]

The capital mobility argument. This argument assumes that bargaining advantages accrue to business as it becomes more mobile. As discussed in chapter 1, decentralization and technological innovation continue to have a profound impact on cities. Changes in the organization of capital have increased business mobility and made urban locations more interchangeable. Automation, robotics, and the postindustrial revolution have also added to business mobility and eliminated old-fashioned Fordist processes in favor of flexible production.[18]

It would seem logical that increasing capital mobility must favor business interests, yet this conclusion does not always follow. To begin, capital is not always portable. Although cities are frequently viewed as interchangeable by some corporations, many cities retain inherent advantages of location (Brussels), of agglomeration (New York), of technological prowess (Grenoble), and of political access (Washington, D.C.). In an era where human resources and skill are enormously important, capital may find it difficult to move away from a well-educated work force. Indeed, cities that establish comparative advantages for particular functions are also able to dominate certain business markets and make themselves into nearly indispensable locations.[19]

A corollary to the previous point is that decentralization may in fact have increased the importance of location and place. Cities are required for the concentration of resources, talent, and producer networks. They also accumulate specific resources and enable business to reach into regional hinterlands. New trends and technology may actually enhance the importance of place and the vitality of cities because the communities in which they are lodged are difficult to duplicate. All this actually discourages business mobility. So-called "flexible production" relies on a local milieu of knowledge, labor, and interfirm networks that combine economies of scale, scope, and versatility.[20] Local jurisdictions offer enormous benefits to businesses that depend upon complex information systems, concentration of human resources, proximity to research centers, just-in-time production, and small-batch manufacture. Examples of such places include Silicon Valley in California, the "Third Italy" industrial district in Emilia-Romagna, and Baden-Wurttemberg in Germany.

Next, the dispersion of capital has triggered a need to centralize communication and the coordination and support of far-flung corporate units, again limiting capital mobility. In fact, the growth and importance of great cities has risen concomitantly with technology, not in contradiction to it. Large, global cities have become command posts and nerve centers for global trade — most of which are located in huge office towers.[21] The enormity of these sunk costs ties not only corporations to cities but also to banks, mortgage companies, and thousands of other investors. New York's downtown and midtown, London's financial district and Canary Wharf, Paris's "golden triangle" and La Défense, and Tokyo's Shinjuku are some outstanding examples of postindustrialism that have generated billions in fixed investments. Movement by individual enterprises away from such established corporate business centers is more easily said than done.

A study of London's mortgage-backed securities industry found that financial services appear to be highly concentrated in order to take advantage of information networks, to facilitate face-to-face communication, to exploit social investments, and to improve access to support services.[22] Clustering of this sort called for a myriad of public services, supportive planning and policy intervention, which business could not easily give up. This is also the case in other industries.[23]

At least some cities have taken political advantage of their ascendant market positions. As property values and development pressures have risen, local politicians have imposed new planning requirements and demanded financial contributions in exchange for development rights.

In San Francisco, a moratorium on high-rise construction regulates the amount and pace of investment.[24] In Boston and several other large cities, linkage policies have exacted fees on office development in order to support moderate income housing.[25] In Paris, differential taxes have been placed on high-rise development and the proceeds used to support city services.[26]

We should also recognize that market relationships between business and government are not immutable. Several scholars have found that as business changes, so too does its grip on local government.[27] This is particularly true as urbanization proceeds and business grows. Over time, business may extend elsewhere and become less involved in local politics. In the same vein, local governments may be subject to the blandishments of business at an early stage of development, when there is great eagerness for development and capital has wide investment choices. Once business puts stakes in the ground, it sometimes finds that they are not easily moved. In this case, bargaining relationships can change, emboldening local officials to impose new demands on business enterprise.

This kind of change occurred in Orlando, Florida, where Disney World exacted early concessions from the local governments only to be faced with new sets of public demands afterward.[28] Prior to building a vast entertainment complex, Disney planners capitalized on their impending investment and won huge concessions from state, county, and local governments. Soon after Disney World opened, the corporation was awarded tax advantages and planning autonomy. However, as Disney transformed the region into a sprawling tourist center, local and county governments began making demands on the corporation to give up some autonomy and contribute toward infrastructure improvements. Disney eventually conceded to political pressures. With huge sunk investments in place, its executives had little choice but to agree to public demands.

So while some industries have grown more mobile, others have not. The issue turns on the relative costs incurred by business and by government when facilities, jobs, and people are moved. How these relative costs are assessed and the likelihood that businesses will absorb them affect the relative bargaining strengths of business and government.

The cities cannot choose argument. A commonly held view is that mobile business makes investment choices among stationary cities. Because cities cannot move, the advantages lies with business. While this is sometimes the case, it is also true that cities have investment choices. Economic change works both ways, and local governments have been able sell themselves as tourist cities, as research or technical centers, or as retirement communities. Further, economic diversification enhances a locality's ability to withstand economic pressure from any particular segment of the business community. This has occurred in cities as far-ranging as Seattle, Singapore, and Rome, enabling them to maintain substantial market positions for decades despite profound changes in the world and national economies.

Experience sometimes teaches cities to sense their vulnerabilities and develop defenses against dominance by a single industry. Through diversification these cities can gain a good deal of strength, not only in weathering economic fluctuations but also in dealing with prospective investors. Houston's experience after the crash of oil prices moved city leaders to develop high-tech and service industries. Hamburg not only recovered from the effects of automation on its port trade, but converted itself into a nexus between Eastern and Western Europe. Lille used its experience with deindustrialization to become a leading transportation center and the crossroads of the European Union.

The lesson for urban politicians is clear. Instead of vainly hanging onto old industry, it may be possible to go for new, preferably clean, business. Diversity also begets still more economic variation and helps build public bargaining advantages.

The cities maximize growth argument.   Although economic logic is built upon the assumption that it is in the interest of cities to promote economic growth, not all localities seek to compete in capital markets. Santa Barbara, Vancouver, and Stockholm are cities that despite pressures have resisted growth and instituted extensive land-use controls. These cities are in enviable positions as they deal with business and developers.

Aside from major cities, there are smaller communities that do not seek to compete for capital investment, such as suburban areas and middle-size cities that, after years of expansion, now face environmental degradation. Even if these localities have a stake in maintaining competitive advantages as bedroom or mixed-use communities, they need not be subordinate to business. University towns, which value their traditions and have a self-sustaining and alert population, have managed to resist the intrusions of unwanted industry. Coastal cities, which seek to preserve open space, have successfully acquired land or used zoning to curtail development.

In sum, the argument that market imperatives and business invariably dominate cities is too simplistic. Market forces are powerful and exert strong pushes and pulls, but they work in multiple ways. Localities can use market forces to enhance their own bargaining with business and fulfill their own strategic purposes. How this is achieved and what kinds of conditions are necessary for this to occur are questions taken up in the next two sections.

Shaping Urban Development through Integrated Multiple Governments

Despite globalization and the perforation of sovereignty, national government still reigns supreme. Only national governments have the authority to enact laws, impose tariffs, issue passports, create money, employ fiscal or monetary policy, and regulate the movement of capital. State and provincial governments can also play a useful role in shaping development. These governments have a longer territorial reach over a tax base and can channel development. Depending on the political system, governments at the national, state, and provincial levels have established urban development corporations, urban enterprise zones, and urban service districts that reach across central cities and suburbs.

Such activity creates a vertical integration between multiple governments that acts to unify the public sector vis-à-vis private capital. Political systems that allow for vertical integration among cities, regions, provinces, and national government will enhance opportunities for achieving policy objectives. Vertical integration is not only a mechanism for creating public allies, but a way for cities to garner assets from other governments and shed liabilities. Assets can be created by accessing a broader tax base, by securing direct financial aid, by having other governments pay for infrastructure, and by carrying out strategic regional planning. Liabilities are shed by having national, provincial, or state governments regulate the movement of capital or restrict urban development.

This is why tight networks between the center (nation) and the periphery (localities) can be important. Formal and informal collaboration between national ministries and city halls can provide cities with tangible resources and with political leverage in bargaining with business. Nations do accomplish this in different ways.[29] In the Netherlands, center-periphery networks are formed through elaborate plans. In Great Britain, special inspectors from Whitehall play an active role in local decision making. In Italy, political parties serve as integrative networks, while France allows local mayors to hold seats in the central ministries and sometimes in the national legislature. On this score the United States and Canada are weaker, but they do use informal access to knit center and periphery.

Also, a unified territorial administration can provide favorable bargaining advantages to local public officials. Systems that are organized on a national basis provide a number of advantages to local public sectors. Consolidated territorial control of metropolitan regions can limit the economic consequences of capital mobility — especially if regions co-ordinate common policies. By contrast, fragmented political jurisdictions allow business interests to play one local government against the other. Fragmentation reinforces the bargaining advantages of business by discouraging local political cooperation and encourages competition over jobs and money.[30]

Three distinct methods stand out as ways in which a unified territorial administration can curb footloose capital or strengthen public bargaining. First, integrated systems ensure that threats of capital mobility among local and regional political jurisdictions will be subject to national planning. Although national governments may choose not to restrict capital mobility, they do possess regulatory authority and on occasion have used it to channel business expansion.[31] Great Britain's containment of growth in major cities during the 1970s was achieved by a combination of national and local land-use controls and subsidies.[32]

Second, unified territorial administration can provide bargaining advantages for local government by ensuring that policies are consistently applied across jurisdictions.[33] Public officials are less able to escape responsibility for local results when localities belong to a national system of urban planning and regulation. As Michael Keating suggests, "relations with the central state may serve to reinforce a narrow conception of development or to broaden it out and constrain or increase the supply of scarce resources."[34]

Integrated systems are more common in Western Europe than in North America. In the United States and (to a lesser degree) Canada, local accountability over economic development is often unclear in that it is shared or contained within one or few political jurisdictions.[35] This limits the ability of citizens to organize region-wide coalitions on matters of community development. In the United States, the development of suburbia as racially segregated, upper-income communities was directly tied to state policies that allowed for the easy incorporation of small separate jurisdictions. This increased the fragmentation of metropolitan areas and encouraged exclusionary land-use practices, hampering the ability of local government to ensure equitable land-use policies.[36]

Third, cities in nations with unified territorial administration are better able to draw upon extensive regulatory authority. Localities can rely on national planning systems that bring together local, regional, and national administrators within a single professional tradition.[37] Authority over development varies widely among the nations of Western Europe. In the Netherlands' Randstad, the Dutch property system enables municipalities to own almost all the undeveloped land within their jurisdications. Provincial land-use planning works in conjunction with local regulation, and extensive central government subsidies favor equalization of land costs for different categories of household. Dutch development is overwhelmingly dominated by government agencies, whose policies have minimized the importance of land prices in favor of equal usage and have given local governments considerable leeway to enforce this value.[38]

Systems also differ in the degree to which national governments provide fiscal support and services to local authorities. The most integrated systems utilize national fiscal support to pay for all or most of local operating costs. National or provincial governments also absorb the costs of borrowing for infrastructure and other construction. Less integrated systems devolve fiscal responsibilities for raising, borrowing, and spending money onto local authorities, who in turn rely almost entirely upon private capital markets. This impacts upon their development practices, making them parochial and short term.

Differences between American and Western European institutions illustrate the bargaining relationships that underlie development as well as differences in priorities. In America, capital investment is highly decentralized and unconnected to national planning. Local and state governments obtain revenues for long-term capital investment from the private sector, whose priorities are to maximize dividends and satisfy investor confidence. In order to market long-term debt, public corporations must contend with investor fears that borrowed funds might be diverted to nonprofitable operations. This is why profit-making bridges, airports, and highways are built rather than mass transit. American public benefit corporations are well known for courting private investors and treating them as constituents, rather than as bargaining rivals.[39] Moreover, the reliance on private capital markets disciplines American cities and prevents them from moving toward collective benefits. Should a city reach beyond its financial capability in launching social programs, its bond ratings would soon drop on Standard and Poor's or Moody's. Lower ratings automatically bring higher interest payments, and the threat of default for any American city is enough to chasten political leaders.

The European experience is quite different. There, most capital expenditures are supported by the central government, which draws upon funds from public or semipublic treasuries. In France upward of 40 percent of local budgets are financed by central government, while in the Netherlands the subvention exceeds 90 percent. This relieves the pressure on local authorities to compete with one another for capital investment in order to finance basic services.[40] While local governments are not entirely free of constraint, they are better able to deal with business from a position of greater strength. Because of publicly supported fiscal arrangements, tensions are more likely to occur between national and local governments than between local governments and capital markets. Beyond this, national government is not as dependent upon private capital as local government, and can turn to vast financial and regulatory powers in order to reinforce public bargaining with business.

The literature on governance has a good deal to say about this. R.A.W. Rhodes[41] and others point out that European governments are bound together not just by institutions, but also by an embracing process that links local and central authorities. Horizontal connections among bureaucracies are overlain with vertical relationships between governments. This web of public power is compounded by differentiated partnerships with the private sector, in which public authorities often set the agenda. Hence, intergovernmental relations are not so much hierarchical as they are a honeycomb of relationships knit together by a system of "cross regulation."[42] While intergovernmental relations may be characterized by tensions, it also integrates the social order into a larger process of "governance" in ways that are not conceivable in the United States or even Canada.[ii]

Regional or metropolitan governments are also a source of strength for cities. Unlike the vertical integration between localities and national governments, metropolitan linkages are more akin to lateral integration. This type of integration allows for a division of labor, whereby localities work on the narrow terrain of service delivery and metropolitan authorities deal with a wider scope of functions such as transportation and strategic planning. Lateral integration allows localities to pool resources and coordinate the placement of industry, housing, and recreation. In effect, lateral integration is a series of partnerships, which enable localities to allocate development and engage the process of capital investment more actively and decisively.

Shaping Urban Development through Popular Control and Local Culture

Popular control not only provides a means of making elites accountable, but also forces them to legitimize their actions. Development projects get stopped when they lack a compelling public rationale and generate significant community opposition. Is popular participation a "loose cannon" that can only have a negative influence and lead to veto groups?[43] Not entirely, and from our perspective popular opinion can also be a resource for local leaders.

If popular control is to be effective, a number of conditions must be satisfied. To begin with, public approval must be connected to the capital investment process. This is not easy to accomplish because investment decisions often fall outside local government. The use of public benefit corporations, whose boards are appointed and whose revenue sources are independent, insulates development from public account-ability.[44] Nevertheless, even public benefit corporations must hold hear-ings, entertain popular motions, and justify their actions. Quite often issues spill over their ordinary boundaries and into public arenas. When this occurs, elected political authorities gain bargaining advantages by putting together coalitions that can play a vital role in the urban devel-opment game.

Next, public authorities must have the managerial and organizational capability to muster political support for business. Credible bargaining requires a stable and active constituency, whose collaboration can be offered to business in a quid pro quo process. In the United States and Canada, nonprofit organizations have filled a gap between public and private sectors and have served as a vehicle for low- and moderate-income housing. Great Britain, Austria, France, and Nordic countries rely on forms of corporatism to bring about negotiated settlements, and "mixed corporations" carry out certain kinds of development.[45]

Last, popular participation must be bolstered by sufficient "social capital." As scholars have recognized, democratic institutions require an attitude of cooperation and trust among the citizenry. For democracy to work, citizens must share similar values and pursue common objectives.[46] This depends upon the social culture of an area. The culture of a city expresses values and norms that underlie development priorities. Some distressed cities are characterized by persistent racial or class polariza-tion, and this deeply affects the development agenda. Here, the popular call is for jobs and housing. Other, more affluent, cities may embrace a postmaterialist or "new political" culture.[47] Here, an activist citizenry puts a great deal of attention on environmental issues and collective benefits.

The institutional expression given to urban culture will differ. Cities vary in their capacity to organize public approval. Some cities work though neighborhood councils that exercise discretion over land use. Other cities give expression to popular opinion through programmatic political parties. Still others, offer few outlets for popular participation and actually design institutions so that local democracy is discouraged.

Some Western European cities combine neighborhood government with cohesive party systems. This combination stimulates popular ex-pression, furnishes bargaining leverage, and influences development. In Paris, political control over major development rests on a system of neighborhood city halls and an organized party system that stretches into central government. The upshot is a city filled with public ameni-ties, collective benefits, and massive housing subsidies. Amsterdam tells much the same story. A system of neighborhood councils and disciplined political parties assures a strong popular voice. As a result, the city enforces stringent rent controls and has established historic preservation districts.

In London, a system of borough governance is tied to disciplined, highly competitive political parties (and more recently to an at-large mayor-regional council system).[iii] Given the political significance of development issues for British parties, it is difficult for nonparty interests to offer inducements that split politicians away from their partisan agendas.[48] During the 1980s radical Labour-dominated councils succeeded in organizing economic development initiatives in opposition to the Tory government.[49] Similarly, programmatic political parties are capable of providing a powerful bargaining resource to elected governmental authorities. In Italy, the relatively stable ideological character of party loyalties up to the 1990s assured elected politicians of constituency support. This stable base of political power afforded significant bargaining advantages in dealing with business interests and shaped development priorities.[50]

BARGAINING AND URBAN DEVELOPMENT

Having set the premises of our argument, we now boil it down to essentials. Our approach is based on the idea of city bargaining. We define this as the ability of a city to garner resources in order to maximize its choices and ultimately realize its objectives in the capital investment process. Further, bargaining over urban development is shaped by specific kinds of resources that have a cumulative impact on city choices. These are 1) market conditions, 2) intergovernmental support, 3) popular control systems, and 4) local culture.

Market conditions consist of circumstances or forces that make cities more or less appealing to private capital. This may be due to geographic characteristics (Singapore as a gateway to Asia), or because of political reasons (Brussels as the seat of the European Union), or as a by-product of business circumstance (New York as a financial capital) or because of a vital strategic role (Berlin as a transit point between Eastern and Western Europe), or for religious cultural reasons (Jerusalem as a sacrosanct city). Whatever the reasons, market conditions make a city highly valued and constitute an inherent advantage for attracting investment and continuing attention.

Naturally, favorable market conditions put a city in a stronger bargaining position and give it greater control over capital investment and development. Cities that are diversified and have a varied employment base are usually in a better position to control capital investment. By contrast, single-industry towns have difficulty turning down any kind of capital investment. This weak position is particularly acute in cities whose resources have been used up or whose geographic advantages have been circumvented. The flight of investment from cities like Detroit, Liverpool, and Essen have left them desolate, and they are desperate to give away property.

Market conditions are a composite of many different circumstances. They reflect larger economic fluctuations that put urban investment at a premium (the office building boom of the 1980s) or put urban investment at risk (the savings and loan bust of the 1990s). The indicators of market conditions are dependent upon the state of a national or regional economy as well as how a city fares in the global revolution. Most cities can measure their market condition by the creation of a modern employment base, the increase or decrease in available jobs, the value of office space, and a willingness to invest in property within a jurisdiction. As mentioned in chapter 1, population growth or decline may or may not be associated with a city's market condition.

Intergovernmental support refers to practices used in conjunction with city, regional, provincial, or national authorities to intervene in the marketplace. Support mechanisms are brought to bear in order to strengthen public control over development. They include planning, land-use controls, fiscal support, differential tax policies, and infrastructure or housing construction. These supports are often carried out on a metropolitan or regional basis and usually involve the integration of functions or fiscal capacity between governments.

As previously mentioned, intergovernmental integration may be vertical and take place between higher and lower levels of authority such as city to province to national government. Integration can also be lateral and include cooperation among equal levels of government over a wider region. In either vertical or lateral integration, localities can "borrow" bargaining resources or transfer negotiations with business into more favorable arenas. Integration can also include more encompassing and irregular processes of governance that unite officials at all levels and incorporate public private partnerships. We suggest that intergovernmental systems that are well integrated are better able to channel economic development and shape the marketplace. Poorly integrated or diffuse systems have less capacity, though such systems may hold other advantages and be better at economic stimulation.

A combination of qualitative assessments and quantitative indicators can be used to analyze intergovernmental support. These include descriptions of intergovernmental institutions and their impact, accounts of intergovernmental cooperation on planning and development, explanations of housing policies, assessment of housing subsidies, and analyses of intergovernmental aid.

Popular control systems refer to the means by which citizens express their preferences and make elites accountable. Popular control also encompasses a larger process through which urban development decisions are legitimized. This process may vary along several dimensions, including the scope of public participation, the extent to which participation is organized, and the effectiveness of electoral mechanisms in ensuring accountability in the process of legitimization. Cities may organize popular control around formal neighborhood governments or civic groups, they may work through mass-member or programmatic political parties, they may use voting to encourage widespread awareness and involvements, or they may organize legislative councils around small wards. Generally, electoral districts based on representation by neighborhood wards are more sensitive to popular expression than at-large representation.

Cities with strong popular control systems exercise greater influence over capital investment and influence the course of economic development decisions. Popular control may either work to enhance development and provide projects with legitimacy, or popular control may serve as a focal point of opposition. Popularly elected councils have been known to welcome new business and endorse the construction of office towers. They have also opposed highways and airport construction.

It is not easy to measure popular control, because of cross cultural differences. Voting and political party participation may mean one thing in Naples and quite another in Houston. Nevertheless, we can gauge popular control by investigating local institutions, by examining citizen access to decision making, and by looking at the prevalence of citizen groups. We also assess competition for elected positions and the role played by political parties in transmitting citizen demands.

We apply the concept of *local culture* in a particular way. Briefly, it refers to the norms and values that create a disposition toward the development agenda. Cities bear a history, an experience with conflict and cooperation as well as a social structure that go into the making of local culture. That culture ultimately helps determine what kind of development popular opinion most values. Is it jobs and construction? Or is it historic preservation and green space?

There is a connection between what leaders negotiate for their constituents and the values of those constituents. Cities with a high "materialist" culture will generally opt for jobs, income, and tangible benefits that are easily divisible. Cities with a strong degree of "postmaterialist" culture are more concerned with preservation of the built or natural environment, and those benefits are generally indivisible.[51] These preferences often mean that cities with materialist cultures are more likely to agree with business objectives than cities with postmaterialist cultures. Bargaining and urban development will then take different courses.

We can draw upon measures of local culture by examining data on social composition. This data can tell us whether a particular city is predominantly blue collar or white collar. We can also rely on household size to determine whether cities are disposed toward a "materialist" or "postmaterialist" culture. Finally, we can look at attitudes toward development and assess popular priorities.

AN URBAN DEVELOPMENT MODEL

Our perspective suggests that local governments compete for private capital in the international marketplace and that they adopt policy strategies to influence the terms of their participation. City governments draw upon a variety of bargaining advantages or resources in support of these strategies. The more bargaining advantages held by a city, the greater its ability to shape urban development. Variation in outcomes is a product of four variables — market conditions, intergovernmental support, popular control, and local culture.

When these variables work cumulatively toward a strong public position, public actors are able to shift the risks and costs of development onto the private sector. An advantageous bargaining position means that cities will pursue a development policy that we call "social centered." A social-centered development policy puts priority on strong public direction, activist planning, and preservationist policies. It also emphasizes collective benefits or public amenities. Social-centered development means that cities will make demands upon business and pursue "linkage policies" (defined as compensation to support a collective benefit in exchange for the right to develop). These include charging environmental impact fees, requiring contributions for moderate-income housing or mass transit, exacting public amenities, and imposing stringent architectural standards. In many European cities, social-centered development is part of a comprehensive planning process that establishes the location, placement, and design of construction.

On the other hand, when these variables work cumulatively toward a weaker public position, the public sector tends to absorb risks and costs. Often a disadvantaged bargaining position means that cities rely more heavily on an economic logic and pursue development that we label as "market centered." This kind of development policy emphasizes free development, minimalist planning, and strong economic growth. It accomplishes this by offering inducements to business such as tax abatements, providing public aid for capital projects, making land contributions, relaxing architectural standards, and doing away with zoning regulations. Some American cities follow this pattern and adhere to a "build as one may" principle.

To this we add an important distinction or clarification. The difference between a social-centered and a market-centered orientation concerns the manner in which a city conceives of its development strategy, controls its resources, and conducts its strategy. This should not be confused with a lack of competitiveness or unwillingness to compete. Some cities legitimately see social-centered development in their long-term interests and as enhancing their competitive edge. Cities may see careful planning and an abundance of public amenities as a genuine attraction for investors, particularly for company headquarters or high-tech industry. To be social centered has more to do with how a city conceives and manages its development than with whether it competes in the international marketplace. Indeed, as we show in chapters 8 and 9 social-centered cities have become more competitive, but they also have retained their taste for collective benefits. Naturally, market-centered cities are more consistently competitive — both internally and externally. Their own development strategies are based on competition and are undertaken because they are seen as the best way to perform in the international marketplace.

Figures 2.1 and 2.2 portray these propositions and list major attributes of each variable. To clarify the alternatives, we present the figures as "ideal types."[52] The figures link each of these four variables to a bargaining and development process.

Note that two variables — market conditions and intergovernmental support — are designated as "driving variables" while the other two — popular control systems and local culture — are designated as "steering variables." Driving and steering variables are derived from the metaphor of an automobile, whereby the drive train furnishes power to propel the vehicle, while manipulation of the steering mechanism puts the vehicle on its actual route. In this sense, driving variables confer economic power to cities and grant public leaders leverage as they bargain with business. By comparison, steering variables have more to do with choices about the strategic direction of development. Because steering variables focus on local preferences, they can be used by public leaders to garner indigenous support for a given policy preference. Each set of variables plays distinct, though complementary, roles in the development process.

As a driving variable, market conditions provide cities with resources, investment initiative, and jobs. Without some positive market condition that makes capital available to enhance a city's economic base, development is simply not likely to occur. Our next driving variable, intergovernmental support, provides the finance and infrastructure that are also essential for development. By comparison, steering variables pinpoint the strategic destination of a given development policy. Popular control will focus public attention on whether development should be

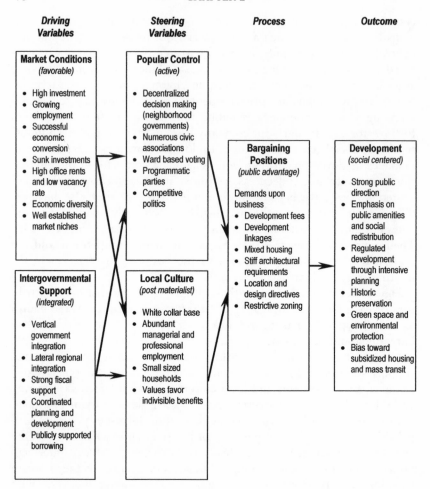

Figure 2.1. Social-centered Development.

used to produce jobs or green space. Local culture will underlie the values that shape the cohesion and consistency of those choices over time. It is not too much to say that driving variables, like market conditions and intergovernmental support, determine *if things can be built*. By the same token, a steering variable like popular control will give expression to *how, where, and whether things are built*, while local culture will reveal dominant priorities about *what is likely to be built*. These particular steering variables mobilize and funnel bargaining resources in strategic directions.

Still another way to sharpen the distinction between driving and

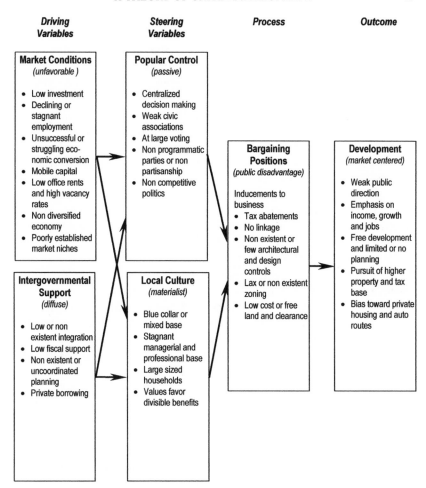

Figure 2.2. Market-centered Development.

steering variables is to see them as usually originating from two different sources — one is predominantly exogenous and mostly beyond local
political control, while another is mostly endogenous and more amenable to local control. Market conditions and intergovernmental support
are mostly exogenous because they constitute "hard" resources that are
either subject to larger forces of capital investment or derived from
other governments. They change slowly in response to forces such as
technology, geographical advantages, and constitutional developments.
By contrast, popular participation and local culture are usually more
endogenous because they are strongly linked to the behavior of local

citizens and their way of life.[iv] Although these resources do not usually change rapidly, they are more likely to reflect local habits and institutional developments. For instance, steering resources can change in response to electoral reforms, immigration of new social groups into the community, voter registration drives, or even the rise of civic leaders with new ideas about politics.

The distinction between steering and driving forces is significant because it allows us to examine the play of structure versus agency in city building. One of our central questions has to do with the actual choices (agency discretion) that citizens have in coping with global restructuring. Do local political efforts and resources matter? Or are cities driven to accommodate forces of global magnitude? The driving concept helps us to identify variables closely connected to structural circumstances; the steering notion points to things over which there is more agency. By examining their interplay we are able to highlight what, if anything, cities can do to alter their trajectories of development. This also enables us to compare the constraints on policy choices in different cities and to explain why particular cities take different policy roads.

Further, we have labeled the variables in each figure within their respective development patterns. Market conditions are categorized as favorable or unfavorable, and the attributes follow. Intergovernmental support can be analyzed as integrated or diffuse and the attributes are listed. Popular control can be classified as active or passive. Local political culture is shown as materialist or postmaterialist. Each attribute of either type of culture is listed. The process is explained in terms of two bargaining positions — public advantage or public disadvantage. The outcome is explained as social-centered or market-centered development.

We stress that these are heuristic models and starting methods for conducting our investigation of ten cities. Although they enable us to explain policy directions and alternatives, we cannot claim them to form a powerful causal theory of development. The world is more complicated than these models suggest and we do not attempt to find the motivating forces behind all the variables we examine. Yet they do enable us to start with simple cases and go on to complex ones. A more complex model would mix elements of social- and market-centered development. Not all characteristics would be reinforcing. For example, a city could very well have a mixture of driving variables in which favorable market conditions would combine with diffuse intergovernmental support. Add to this a mixture of steering forces in which an active popular control would combine with a materialist culture. Once we arrive at determining a city's bargaining position and its development strategy, we could yield an amalgam of social and market traits.

Figure 2.3 displays this possibility as a hybrid pattern. The charac-

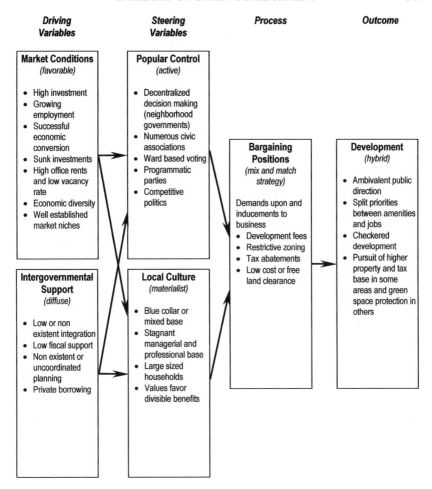

| Driving Variables | Steering Variables | Process | Outcome |

Market Conditions *(favorable)*
- High investment
- Growing employment
- Successful economic conversion
- Sunk investments
- High office rents and low vacancy rate
- Economic diversity
- Well established market niches

Popular Control *(active)*
- Decentralized decision making (neighborhood governments)
- Numerous civic associations
- Ward based voting
- Programmatic parties
- Competitive politics

Bargaining Positions *(mix and match strategy)*

Demands upon and inducements to business
- Development fees
- Restrictive zoning
- Tax abatements
- Low cost or free land clearance

Development *(hybrid)*
- Ambivalent public direction
- Split priorities between amenities and jobs
- Checkered development
- Pursuit of higher property and tax base in some areas and green space protection in others

Intergovernmental Support *(diffuse)*
- Low or non existent integration
- Low fiscal support
- Non existent or uncoordinated planning
- Private borrowing

Local Culture *(materialist)*
- Blue collar or mixed base
- Stagnant managerial and professional base
- Large sized households
- Values favor divisible benefits

Figure 2.3. Hybrid Development.

teristics of each variable and outcome are derived from an amalgam of previous ideal types. As in the previous figures, arrows show tendencies and pressures toward a development outcome.

Of course any variation of market- or social-centered development is possible, even likely. Later chapters will show that development is not bipolar, that cities may mix and match development options, and that the variables operate in different and uneven ways. For the time being, we can keep these models in mind, using them to decipher the actions of cities and trace common strands.

This suggests that urban development has more to do with nuance than with a simple set of choices about whether or not to develop.

Many studies on the politics of development are phrased as "yes" or "no" alternatives, such as whether "pro-growth" or "anti-growth" coalitions are able to prevail or whether "growth machines" or "anti-growth machines" hold sway.[53] These perspectives may oversimplify the issue because the norm for most cities, most of the time, is to undertake some kind of development. That development may be market centered and produce jobs or it may be social centered and create museums. Both kinds of development are different, but both are also meaningful, and to relegate public amenities to the category of "non-growth" excludes vital information about the nature of choice.

In a parallel manner, some scholars make distinctions between policies that promote "development" versus those that promote "consumption." Presumably, building infrastructure for an industrial park is "development" while constructing a museum is "consumption." In reality those distinctions are difficult to make because the line between development and consumption is quite porous. Access roads for industrial development can also be used by private motorists on a consumer vacation. Museums visited by consuming local residents can also attract tourists and stimulate a recreational industry. Whether a policy is developmental or consumptive can be subject to rapid and incessant shifts in usage.

Indeed, we show that public amenities (a type of social-centered development) are used to enhance job development in some cities. Our own bargaining perspective takes account of multiple but complementary objectives and cuts the issues more finely. While we begin with a simple dichotomy of market- versus social-centered development, we are able to show hybrid variations and permutations of choice. This perspective allows us to frame urban choices within a larger number of contexts and show how they relate to driving and steering variables.

Bargaining Contexts and Regimes

We now arrive at some final theoretical considerations, namely what circumstances structure development, who determines its course of action, and how do these factors interact with one another. Here we return to the earlier discussion of structure versus agency. To begin with, structure, our bargaining model looks at the strength and type of resources a city brings to the negotiating table. We posit that cities that possess strong driving resources (favorable market conditions and integrated intergovernmental support) will have more advantages and greater choice in bargaining with private investors. We refer to this combination of advantage and choice as a *bargaining context*. Cities operate in different contexts, each of which structures local bargaining. In chapter

5, we describe a hierarchy of contexts and show how they liberate or limit urban choices. Most leaders are aware of their latitude and are careful not to move beyond contextual bounds. Occasionally, city leaders decide to break free of those contexts. More often than not, a radical departure from context has met with "punishing recoils" from other sources of power, and radicals either have retreated from their initiatives or have been cast out of office.[v]

At the same time, city leaders do frequently maneuver within contextual bounds. To examine this issue, we rely on the concept of a regime, and we use it in a very limited manner — namely to focus on governing coalitions that engage in bargaining over development. Our work is comparative and designed to capture a variety of societies. Accordingly, governing coalitions may or may not include the private sector, because in some societies private developers do not have sufficient clout or cohesion to make a difference. Conceivably, regimes could be composed of coalitions of different public actors. We are interested in how regimes use driving and steering variables to bargain over development as well as the principles, rules, norms, and decision-making procedures around which they converge.[54] Simply put, a regime is a regularized pattern of political cooperation for mobilizing city resources in support of a common, identifiable agenda.

We employ the regime concept within a bargaining context. Using the concept in this way, we are able to highlight the interplay between structure and agency. That is, we are better able to focus on how politics may be constrained by economics and how change comes about in the face of those constraints. While regimes work within contextual restraints, they can also change those contexts. Agency can work upon structure, enabling a city to move into another context and change its development strategy. Neither market condition nor intergovernmental support is immutable, and cities have been successful in remaking their economic base as well as tightening their intergovernmental support.

Such agency accounts for how cities might evolve over time, and we illustrate how this has worked and continues to operate in some cities.[vi] If cities are anything, they are entities that continually change, mutate, or adapt. Those changes can be for better or worse, and cities can also remain in transitional or indeterminate states. Depending upon how a city manipulates its essential variables or resources, it can move up or down the hierarchy of contexts.

The next chapter introduces each of our ten cities in terms of these variables. We show how these cities have weathered postindustrial transformation, we provide a picture of their economic, political, and social conditions, and we situate the cities on a continuum of social-centered and market-centered development.

Notes

i. The universe of cases is likely to be mixed. Obviously, there are instances where citizens and business are in accord over development and instances where they are not. Whether constraint and conflict are norms is a highly suspect proposition, and it may be that cases chosen for study are highly selective.

ii. For further discussion on governance see chapter 9.

iii. London's new mayor, Ken Livingston, was a maverick in the Labour Party who ran as an independent. While Livingston successfully bucked Labour, the party system is still alive and well.

iv. We recognize that the fit is not perfect. Market conditions can have a strong local component while political participation can be tied to national parties. As we say, the exogenous-endogenous distinction is not invariable but is a usual and reasonable one to make.

v. See, for example, the case of Liverpool in chapter 7.

vi. See, for example, the case of Toronto in chapter 6 and the case of Marseilles in chapter 7.

Chapter Three

TEN CITIES, THIRTY YEARS

Nobody goes there any more. It's too crowded.
— Yogi Berra

THE VARIABLES OF URBAN TRANSFORMATION

At the outset of the 1970s our ten cities entered the international marketplace with very different bargaining advantages. Differences in market conditions, intergovernmental support, popular control, and local culture illustrate the driving and steering variables present in Western cities. In this chapter, we describe our cities as they simultaneously confronted the winds of global economic and social change over a thirty-year period. Some emerged from this transformation stronger, viable, and affluent. Others went through deep devastation and continue to feel the sting of economic and social depression. Some radically changed their social makeup, while others retained their continuity. Transformation also brought selective political change and periodic turmoil. Rioting, militant confrontation, earthquakes, and near bankruptcy hit a few cities, while others had a relatively easy time.

MARKET CONDITIONS: A DRIVING VARIABLE

The quest for economic development is not always even, and economists explain that there are a number of reasons why some cities are more resilient than others. A city's economic strength is derived from its capacity to provide a complex and diverse system of exchange.[1] Cities that have shallow complexities and that are dependent upon a single industry may find it difficult to survive, while those with deep complexities and a diverse industrial base are more resilient. Overall we find that cities with an insufficient mass of existing wealth, talent, and resources are more liable to encounter difficulties, while those fortunate enough to take advantage of "forces of agglomeration" will find it easier. Loosely put, forces of agglomeration operate through a kind of circular causation. Investors, capital, and people choose particular areas because sources of commercial opportunity are already situated there. Opportunity then attracts further opportunity, and this process snowballs into a rich dynamic city.

Formally explained, forces of agglomeration consist of a concentrated mixture of economic activities that create synergies and stimulate further growth. This quality provides a city with economic depth and a capacity to survive the trauma of change while adapting to new conditions. Sir Peter Hall specifies how this works for global cities and cites four critical functions.[2] These are defined as concentrations of 1) command and control services, including government agencies, international organization, or corporate headquarters, 2) financial and business services like advertising, banking, accountancy, and law, 3) tourist and cultural features, encompassing museums and the performing or creative arts, and 4) a media network, including newspapers, publishers, and television or film studios. "Place luck" can make all the difference. Cities that possess forces of agglomeration often resurrect themselves into even more powerful entities during periods of change, while cities that are dependent on a single industry find it difficult to recover.

Forces of agglomeration are just one component of market condition. As mentioned in the previous chapter, market conditions refer to a series of factors that make cities attractive to private investment, enhance their economic base, and enable them to export goods and services.[3] We begin with the most distressed cities, move to cities with mixed tendencies, and then turn to the more prosperous ones.

Disfavored Cities: Detroit, Glasgow, Liverpool, Marseilles, and Naples

For most of the twentieth century Detroit, Glasgow, Liverpool, Marseilles, and Naples were either single-industry towns or heavily dependent on a single industry. Automobile production dominated Detroit while ports and warehousing defined Liverpool, Marseilles, and Naples. Glasgow was less of a single-industry town, but relied heavily on ship construction as a major employer. These cities lost their competitive advantage to surrounding, often younger, localities.

By the 1960s massive changes occurred within heavy manufacture and shipping. Detroit's ill fortune was tied directly to overseas competition for the automobile market. In 1960 that city held nearly half the world market. Thirty years later Detroit's share of automobile trade had shrunk to 19 percent and was still falling.[4] Detroit is also surrounded by a good deal of open land and competitive suburbs quite capable of building a new central business district. Suburban areas like Southfield have successfully reaped Detroit's harvest, and corporations are known to settle just across the city boundary lines in order to take advantage of lower taxes. Indeed, new firms often cite their suburban locations as being in "Near Detroit."

Glasgow can be described as a "dual city" with an attractive business core surrounded by poverty and decay. Glasgow's downtown sparkles with upscale retail stores, restored Victorian buildings, and cultural attractions. Yet this vibrant square mile has not succeeded in halting Glasgow's decline, and all the indicators point downward. The city continues to struggle against industrial obsolescence, a dwindling job base, and chronic unemployment. Much of the middle class has left the city, leaving pockets of distress where nearly half the work force remains idle. While commuters may still use the central city for jobs and shopping, the rest of Glasgow is caught in a vicious cycle. All this is in sharp contrast to Scotland's princely capital of Edinburgh, which is solidly upscale and stands as Glasgow's indomitable competitor.

Liverpool lost much of its competitive advantage when trade and immigration shifted away from North America and toward Western Europe. Automation also took its toll on Liverpool and decimated employment on the docks. In 1950, 27 percent of Liverpool's employment was to be found in its port. By the mid-1970s that proportion had dropped to just 12 percent and fell below 4 percent in the 1990s.[5] Today barely 500 people work the docks, and Liverpool continues to lose jobs.[6] Whatever manufacturing opportunity exists, it is likely to drift to Manchester, which is barely fifty miles away. Compounding these losses is the absence of a versatile capitalist class, and the middle class continues to leave. At the turn of the twenty-first century the city has begun to show improvement. Its downtown shows significant signs of regeneration and its docklands are going through a renaissance, with new housing and tourist attractions. While there is no mistaking this most recent trend, we should not overstate its extent. Liverpool is still a depressed city. Eight percent of its land is either vacant or derelict, its neighborhoods are worn and gripped by unemployment.[7]

In general, French cities are attractive places and urban depression on the continent is not quite the same as it is in the Unites States or Great Britain. Marseilles is no exception to that tradition. It has an exceptional waterfront, a bustling central core, and decent neighborhoods. Recent efforts at revitalization have built upon these assets, especially along the city's outstanding coastline. But the past thirty years have also been filled with economic woes, and this has hit the city's most desperate neighborhoods. As in other older port cities, shipping no longer holds its former preeminence. Port activity moved fifty kilometers away to modern facilities at Fos-sur-Mer.[8] By the 1990s Marseilles was left with just 6 percent of the region's economic activity. Nearby cities like Aix-en-Provence and Nice have absorbed the bulk of new growth in tourism, services, and high technology. Other smaller cities like Aubagne and Vitrolles have attracted heavier industry and are strong competitors for scarce capital.

Naples reached its peak during Europe's Renaissance and continued to prosper up through the seventeenth century. Its power rested on the twin pillars of royal privilege and a strategic port. But as industry spread, Naples was mired in one of the poorest regions of Europe, known as "Mezzogiorno." Unlike cities in northern Italy, Naples was unable to exploit potential wealth in the countryside and catalyze development. Instead it relied on state-subsidized industry, particularly on assistance for a faltering steel mill. With such a weak industrial base, the city has been vulnerable to larger currents of change. Closure or downsizing of state-subsidized heavy industries have left an economy dominated by small, family-owned construction businesses.

A Mixed Tendency City: Houston

Houston is a young city that did not go through the trauma of deindustrialization. By virtue of its oil and gas industries, it took off in the mid-1960s. The city has since leveraged that base with a burgeoning aerospace industry and rising medical business. Also, it has held onto a substantial manufacturing presence and is still a growing city. Yet with all these attributes, Houston did fall on difficult times and remains vulnerable to economic downturns. The most severe recession occurred in the 1980s when oil prices plummeted. During that period, new office space stood vacant and business fell on hard times. In addition to this, Houston was hit years later by exuberant mortgage lenders and its housing market fell apart. The federal government stepped in to insure payments and most banks were taken over. These crises left an indelible mark on the city and revealed its dependence on a narrow industrial base. Since that time the city has worked hard to diversify and to some extent has succeeded. Computer manufacture, port trade, and healthcare have become major industries. Partial diversification is Houston's Achilles' heel, and the city's slab ugliness still hampers outside interest.

Favored Cities: New York, Paris, Milan, and Toronto

Very different market conditions operated in New York, Paris, Milan, and Toronto. For one, these cities are either national capitals (Paris) or they dominate the urban landscape (New York and Milan) or they hold unusual strategic or spatial advantage (Toronto).[i] When deindustrialization struck, most of these cities also incurred massive declines in manufacture, yet decades later they are thriving.

Perception of business climate also affects market conditions. Some cities may be regarded as too dangerous or outmoded to accommodate business. Others can be seen as "hot spots" or as furnishing a particularly sound environment for economic growth. A survey of *Fortune* magazine's "best cities for business" confirms our own assessments.

Ratings between 1994–97 show the following frequencies of mention: New York (3 mentions), Paris (two), Milan (one), Houston (one). Detroit, Marseilles, Glasgow, Liverpool, and Naples received no mentions.[9]

Despite its reputation as the nation's garment center, New York kept a vibrant financial sector, a world-class stock market, and numerous professional services in law, advertising, and media. Its ready supply of banks and real estate developers created a flow of capital into office and apartment towers, hotels, and cultural attractions (museums, theater, etc.). Manhattan stood as the city's economic generator and built upon its reputation as the world's banking and cultural capital. A vast commercial infrastructure replaced abandoned factories, and the re-creation of artistic talent fueled a different kind of production. Much of this was propelled during the 1980s by market-oriented development. By the end of that decade and through the 1990s, the stock market revived causing land values to soar and creating whole new layers of wealth and spending.

On the other side of the Atlantic, Paris exploited a different set of diversities. It too had lost enormous amounts of manufacturing in apparel, machinery, and chemicals. But the city could play to its strengths as a political and cultural capital. Also, the built environment and architecture of Paris were treasures that demanded protection and replenishment. Enormous amounts of public funds were used to plan and leverage private expenditures. Paris has no rival in all of France, and while it has lost population, the middle class remains. Indeed, whole neighborhoods have been gentrified, and over the last three decades property values have soared.

Milan won a formidable market position during Italy's postwar "economic miracle" and is today a major player in the Western European economy. It is strategically located among Italy's most productive Northern provinces, and has exploited opportunities to become the nation's foremost commercial city . Unlike other cities in Italy's "industrial triangle" (Turin and Genoa), Milan has managed to avoid decline by balancing its economic structure with multiple industries. These include professional services, advanced technology, producer services, fashion, and other leading-edge industries.

Toronto has differed from its industrial counterparts in the United States. Unlike Detroit, it has always maintained a balance between automobile manufacture, finance, and professional services. Toronto also retained a strong corporate headquarters and a research and a university base that put it in good stead once postindustrialism took hold. This diversity enabled it to build on a number of resources and make a successful transition. Toronto also played to its competitive advantage as Canada's major Anglophone city. At one time Montreal and Toronto held an equal number of corporate headquarters, but as the national debate over language and culture heated up, Toronto profited from corporations seeking a stable Anglophone environment.[10] By the mid-1990s Toronto was the third largest city in North America in terms of the number of its corporate headquarters. Only New York and Chicago now surpass it in corporate headquarters. And finally, Toronto has been able to capitalize on its location in the center of Canada, between Montreal to the east and Vancouver to the west. Toronto's per capita income growth has exceeded its two urban rivals.[11]

Comparing Cities

Whatever the variation in outcome, certain constants affect most cities in advanced societies. During the past thirty years all ten central cities experienced spatial decentralization of industry and population. Urban sprawl had become an endemic feature of the modern metropolis. Population continued to move out of the urban cores (old or new) and settled into surrounding suburbs and countryside. The rate and extent of decentralization may vary and the content of nonurban settlement may differ, but advanced nations are facing similar dynamics. Increased automobile usage, technological change, and, cultural shifts have had a profound effect on human settlement. Regardless of workers' proximity to cities—and no matter what country—more commuters now rely on automobiles, which make hinterlands more accessible for shopping and living. Technology now makes it more possible for people to carry out their work at greater distances from urban cores. Contemporary attitudes now favor open spaces as better places to raise children, enjoy freedom, and avoid pollution.

Figure 3.1 displays population change for ten cities and their outlying areas. The figure shows central cities relative to their metropolitan area or agglomeration.

The most dramatic central-city declines occurred in Detroit (down 37 percent), Glasgow (down 38 percent), Liverpool (down 38 percent), and Milan (down 25 percent). Less severe losses could be found in Paris (down 8 percent), Marseilles (down 13 percent), and Naples (down 15 percent). Registering gains were Houston (up 59 percent) and Toronto (up 14 percent), while New York remained stable (up 1 percent).

More significantly, outside the central cities most of the suburban areas gained population. Detroit experienced one of the more radical transformations. Its urban core changed from predominantly white and middle class to mostly black and heavily impoverished. Meanwhile, Detroit's white population fled to outer-ring suburbs—so-called "golden corridors"—and built an alternative business district elsewhere.[12]

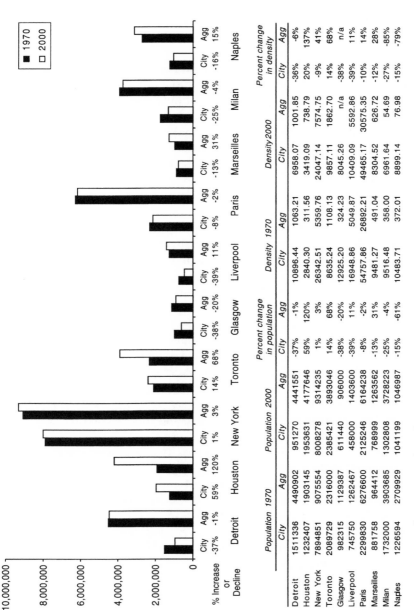

	Population 1970		Population 2000		Percent change in population		Density 1970		Density 2000		Percent change in density	
	City	Agg	City	Agg	City	Agg	City	Agg	City	Agg	City	Agg
Detroit	1511336	4490902	951270	4441551	-37%	-1%	10896.44	1063.21	6958.07	1001.85	-36%	-6%
Houston	1232407	1903145	1953631	4177646	59%	120%	2840.30	311.56	3419.09	738.79	20%	137%
New York	7894851	9075554	8008278	9314235	1%	3%	26342.51	5359.76	24047.14	7574.75	-9%	41%
Toronto	2089729	2316000	2385421	3893046	14%	68%	8635.24	1108.13	9857.11	1862.70	14%	68%
Glasgow	982315	1129387	611440	906000	-38%	-20%	12925.20	324.23	8045.26	n/a	-38%	n/a
Liverpool	745750	1262467	458000	1403600	-39%	11%	16948.86	5049.87	10409.09	5592.86	-39%	11%
Paris	2299830	6276600	2125246	6164238	-8%	-2%	54757.86	26892.21	49465.17	30575.35	-10%	14%
Marseilles	881758	964412	768999	1263562	-13%	31%	9481.27	491.04	8304.52	626.72	-12%	28%
Milan	1732000	3903685	1302808	3728223	-25%	-4%	9516.48	358.00	6961.64	54.69	-27%	-85%
Naples	1226594	2709929	1041199	1046987	-15%	-61%	10483.71	372.01	8899.14	76.98	-15%	-79%

Figure 3.1. Population Growth and Loss in Ten Cities, 1970–2000.

Spreading populations gripped both North America and Western Europe. People were moving into nearby agglomerations, and in some cases the growth was spectacular. The American exodus usually settled in sprawled suburbs, while Europeans were more apt to be clustered in new towns or more compact suburbs.

The greatest spread into suburbs occurred in the prosperous and growing cities of Houston and Toronto. Outlying areas in these cities ballooned by more than two-thirds. Not only were these cities growing, but they appeared to be generating growth well beyond their bounds. Jacobs's observation that "cities are unique in their abilities to shape and reshape economies" beyond their borders holds true.[13] Urban prosperity was contagious and interaction between some central cities and their suburbs profoundly marked the course of development. Cities, in fact, have become city-regions, bringing together numerous common economies and interdependent futures.[14]

How did some of these ten cities prosper? Older dedensified cities filled manufacturing vacuums with massive replacements of jobs in services as well as finance, insurance, and real estate (FIRE). Newer growth cities expanded in multiple directions — retaining some manufacturing but mixing it with warehousing, transportation, services, high technology, or a burgeoning public sector.

Figure 3.2 portrays changes in manufacture, transportation, and utilities for ten central cities and their agglomerations (near suburbs). Complementary data can be found in figure 3.3, which shows these changes for services and FIRE in those same cities and their agglomerations. Numbers and percentages are presented for employment by place of work. For purposes of comparison we have collapsed employment into secondary (manufacture, transportation, and utilities) and tertiary (services, FIRE) sectors.

With the exception of Houston, every city and its agglomeration lost manufacturing. Once again, Detroit, Liverpool, and Glasgow were hard hit, losing between 64 percent (Detroit) and 73 percent (Liverpool) of their manufacturing base. Two other distressed cities joined the pack — Marseilles and Naples respectively lost 56 percent and 45 percent of their blue-collar employment. On this criterion, however, the most distressed cities were joined by the prosperous ones. New York lost a third of its manufacturing (Manhattan plummeted by 47 percent), while sister cities like Paris and Milan fell by more than half. Even Toronto dropped slightly, by almost five percent. Houston was the sole city enjoying a healthy gain of 12 percent. Note, too, that suburbs were not spared. In many cases these suburbs were blue-collar industrial communities surrounding large urban cores.

When urban recovery did occur, it could be seen in booming tertiary

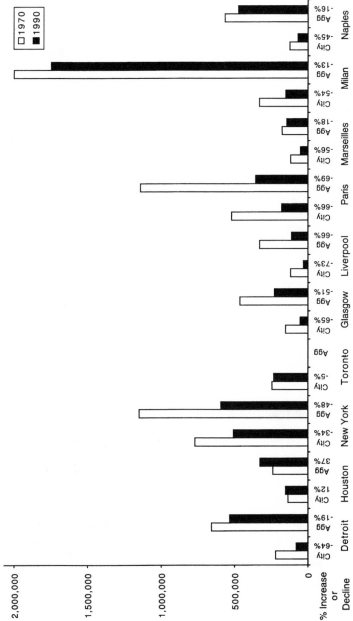

Figure 3.2. Secondary Sector Change in Ten Cities, 1970–1990.

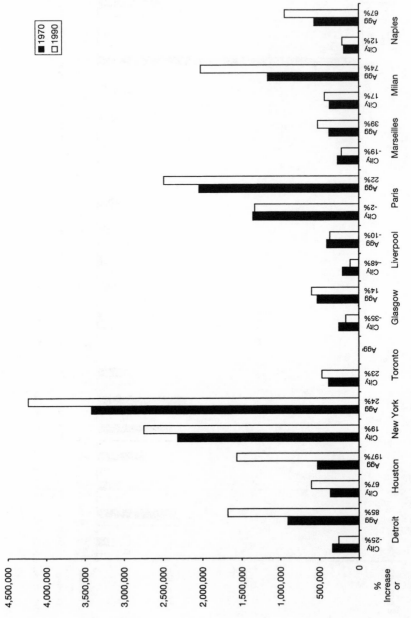

Figure 3.3. Tertiary Sector Change in Ten Cities, 1970–1990.

sectors. What marked distressed cities was a failure to build in this sector. At least during this period Detroit, Liverpool, and Marseilles continued to lose sizeable percentages of tertiary employment, ranging from a fifth to nearly half of their existing base. Even the suburbs of Liverpool failed to come to life. Glasgow also lost a hefty proportion of service and white-collar employment—more of these jobs vanished or moved out of town than were created. While it is still too early to determine its success, there are signs of a partial rebound in the downtown and surrounding neighborhoods.[15]

By contrast, prosperous cities made successful transitions into services, professional, and office employment. New York's and Milan's tertiary employment moved upward by substantial proportions, while Paris and Naples were basically stable. Toronto enjoyed a surge of white-collar employment, amounting to 23 percent, while Houston exploded with a gain of 67 percent (mostly aerospace and high-tech industry). We can also see tertiary employment enjoyed a healthy life in the rest of the agglomerations.

Thus far we have divided our cities into those disfavored or favored by market conditions. We now draw closer comparisons between these cities by ranking them along some basic market indicators—the cost and vacancy rate of their office space and their labor force. The office data provides us with a glimpse of a city's appeal for white-collar employment, while labor force data give us an idea of a city's productive capacity within each national economy.

Table 3.1 displays each city office vacancy alongside the cost per square foot. Each factor is then combined to produce a rank order of

TABLE 3.1
Office Markets in Ten Cities, 1995–96

City	Occupancy Rate (%)	Cost / Sq. Foot (USD)	Index: Office Demand	Rank
Paris	91.70	52.00	97.76	1
New York	86.90	35.13	67.29	2
Toronto	84.90	36.00	64.98	3
Marseilles	93.00	18.30	55.66	4
Milan	83.56	27.50	51.49	5
Detroit	85.20	14.00	36.55	6
Liverpool	80.00	19.07	34.26	7
Naples	70.00	17.29	31.92	8
Houston	81.00	14.20	29.57	9
Glasgow	64.00	28.33	18.86	10

market demand. The figures are derived for each central city based on information from the mid-1990s.

Observe that despite some shifting, the results are fairly consonant with the previous descriptions. Paris leads the other cities followed by New York, Toronto, Marseilles, and Milan. Marseilles's high standing is a surprise, and this is because of recent efforts to restore its business district and the proximity of its port to the downtown area. At the lower end of the order are Detroit, Liverpool, Naples, and Glasgow. Despite the shift to tertiary services in these lower-end cities, most did not experience robust office growth. Most of this growth has been confined to the public sector (education, health services), and did not carry into the office market. Moreover, cities like Liverpool may have added white-collar workers, but these were often poorly paid clerks who could be put to work in small and modest offices.[16] As for Houston, its low office demand is due to excess supply rather than a shortage of demand. The city's sprawling urban fabric, its absence of a strong central business district, and its lack of zoning hold down both occupancy rate and rents.

Next we turn to a ranking of civilian labor forces. Table 3.2 shows the proportion of the civilian work force in each city relative to its national total. The table covers the years 1970 and 1990, ranks each city for that year, and shows change over two decades.

Again, taking into account some shifting, the cities bear out previous descriptions. Paris takes the lead followed by New York, Toronto, and Milan. This time, however, Marseilles turns up in the middle followed by cities in the lower half — Naples, Glasgow, Liverpool, Houston, and

TABLE 3.2
Civilian Labor Force in Ten Cities, 1970–90

City	City Labor Force (% of nation)			
	1970	Rank 1970	1990	Rank 1990
Paris	5.79	1	4.67	1
New York	4.04	3	2.82	2
Toronto	4.28	2	2.74	3
Milan	3.56	4	2.43	4
Marseilles	1.61	6	1.39	5
Naples	1.60	7	1.18	6
Glasgow	1.86	5	1.08	7
Liverpool	1.37	8	0.72	8
Houston	0.64	10	0.68	9
Detroit	0.73	9	0.33	10

Detroit. We should also note that nine of our ten cities lost ground over the past two decades. This is largely a result of the decentralization of employment into suburbs and metropolitan peripheries. Only Houston gained employment relative to the national total. That city has freely annexed land where investment and jobs have thrived.

A final piece of the market puzzle is educational achievement. Education is often equated with human resources and sometimes considered a form of social capital. Educated workers are also better able to experiment, collaborate, think systematically, and convert existing resources into the generation of new wealth.[17] The transition to a new information-based economy requires high levels of literacy, skill, and cognition. Levels of education are not so much an indicator of past market success as they are a measure of current strategy and future accomplishments. A properly educated work force is a key to economic transition and vital for continued success.

Figure 3.4 shows different levels of educational achievement in each of our ten cities. The figure shows the proportion of the total population possessing two or more years of college or its equivalent.

While there are some exceptions, we generally observe a certain concordance between educational level and prosperity. Better educated populations usually reside in cities whose market conditions are favorable. This is the case for Paris, Milan, New York, Houston, and Toronto. At least 17 percent of residents in each of these cities have two or more years of higher education, and in some cases the number rises to roughly a third of the population. At the opposite pole we find lower levels of educational attainment in Detroit, Glasgow, and Liverpool. The proportion of residents with two or more years of higher education falls to roughly 10 percent in these disfavored cities. Local trends often reflect national policies. Less prosperous cities like Marseilles and Naples have high attainment levels because advanced education in France and Italy is very inexpensive, readily available, and paid for by the state. This is less true for the United Kingdom and especially less true for the United States.

Last, we put these bits of information together and offer an overview of economic transition in our ten cities. We do this by constructing a continuum of how our cities are distributed by market condition. Figure 3.5 shows market conditions varying from disfavored to favored. In order to better place our cities on the continuum, we turn again to select indicators that include economic factors, industrial composition, and office demand.[ii] These indicators are converted into a composite score, shown for each city. The score ranges from a low of 1.0 to a high of 3.0. Scores and indicators for each city are shown and explained in table 3.ii in the notes at the end of this chapter.

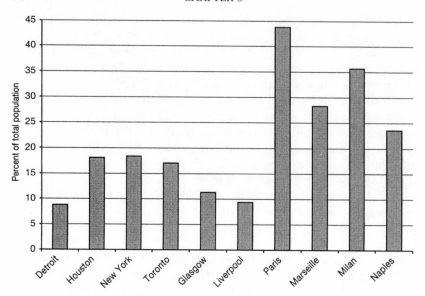

Figure 3.4. Educational Attainment in Ten Cities, ca. 1990.

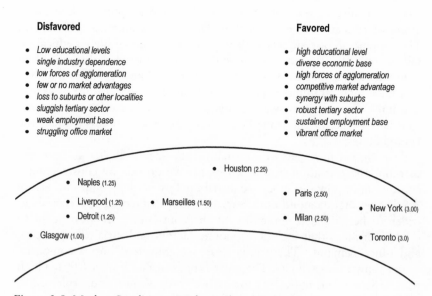

Figure 3.5. Market Conditions: Disfavored and Favored.

Intergovernmental Support: A Driving Variable

One reason why some cities are more successful than others has to do with interventions permitted by intergovernmental arrangements. As mentioned earlier, intergovernmental support encompasses practices carried out among multiple governments to intervene in the marketplace. Markets do not function autonomously but are part of a political environment. They are often targets of national and subnational governments that seek to improve economic performance or redistribute resources. While policy targeting may not be decisive, it affects public-private bargaining and accounts for variation between cities. Cities are nested within various intergovernmental arrangements, the capacities and coordination of which differ. In considering these arrangements, we look beyond formalities and focus on the actualities of intergovernmental support. We are interested not so much in the letter of the law, but in how intergovernmental mechanisms succeed or fail to sustain cities.[iii]

Diffuse Cities: Houston, Detroit, and New York

Houston's rise as the "shining buckle" of the Sunbelt has not been entirely a matter of chance. It is located in a region where individual initiative is honored and local autonomy is sacred.[18] Barring defense and aerospace contracts, national aid is sparse, and both federal and state governments are loathe to intervene in local matters. In recent years just 4 percent of Houston's revenues were derived from Washington, and state support amounts to less than 2 percent.[19]

Any kind of horizontal integration is also limited by fragmentation around the city. Surrounding Houston are 790 governments and special districts, whose jurisdictions frequently overlap, and they are eager to compete for capital investment.[20] Houston has been able to blunt some of this competition by taking advantage of the state's easy annexation laws and gobbling up unincorporated areas. Today Houston covers an immense, sparsely settled terrain of over 600 square miles. Land expansion enables the city to attract capital, and the city has an easy-going laissez-faire policy toward development. Houston lacks a zoning ordinance. People can build almost anywhere, although deed restrictions rein in some wildcat development.

For Detroit, intergovernmental relations are at best avoided or at worst hostile. Vertical integration is weak. Except for grants in aid, Washington has learned to keep its distance from local affairs. In fact, federal aid declined during the last decade, shrinking to less than 6 percent of the city's revenues.[21] State aid has compensated for some of Detroit's shortfalls, but Michigan is at a loss to do anything about the internecine struggles for jobs and investment. Racial tensions have created long-term divisions and have made it difficult to work with surrounding suburbs. Attempts at creating tax-base sharing or undertaking regional planning have failed.[22] Suburban growth has created nearly 400 fragmented jurisdictions.[23] Proposals for some kind of regional coordination have been soundly defeated, with the press describing white attitudes toward cooperation as "feared and despised."[24] Racial animosities work both ways, and even Detroit's former mayor looked askance at efforts to create regional authorities for water and mass transit.[25]

Like its sister American cities, New York operates within a federal system, and this makes for loose relations with the center. The stand-aside propensities of federalism are moderated by a relatively cohesive congressional delegation that sometimes succeeds in prying dollars from Washington. But city-federal relationships are erratic and subject to personal connections. The best-known accounts of the New York region see it as hugely fragmented and lament the fierce competition between the city and its suburbs.[26] The city contends with over 200 other jurisdictions in its proximate metropolitan area. Other governments regularly raid it for business investment, sports teams, and consumer spending. New York has returned this dubious favor by trying to outbid its competitors. "Nonaggression" pacts between neighboring states have failed to stop raids for private capital.[27]

While this description has merit, the portrayal of New York as intensely fragmented may be overstated. Recall that New York is a consolidated metropolitan government spanning five counties (boroughs). This gives the city marginal geographical leverage over development along its less dense periphery. Next, New York's Public Benefit Corporations, or PBCs, have played an impressive role in working across localities. PBCs operate freely throughout the state and region in creating infrastructure, building housing, and investing in all sorts of projects. They are powerful vehicles for uniting public and private capital and financing projects across the metropolitan area. PBC investments are tied to the interests of its financial sources, and they must ultimately satisfy bankers, bond holders, and consumers.

Mixed-Tendency Cities: Toronto and Liverpool

Canada's federal system also makes for moderate vertical integration. Canada's federal government expects the provinces to fill much of the center-periphery vacuum, though it has funded urban infrastructure and home mortgages and has donated valuable land to the localities.[28] For their part, the provinces have acted with great gusto. They have been instrumental in furnishing urban aid, creating mass transit, and overseeing the environment. Decades ago conservative legislators from Ontario successfully organized the Toronto area into a metropolitan government. What Toronto lacked in vertical integration was made up laterally by "Metro Toronto."

Metro began to take shape in the 1950s, and by 1967 a new two-tier government took root among six localities. Metro was essentially a federation of cities that included Toronto plus East York, Etobicoke, North York, Scarborough, and York. While the localities retained a narrow role as lower-tier units, Metro Toronto acted as an upper-tier government with broad responsibilities. Constituent localities funded Metro government through property assessments. During its heyday Metro covered 20 percent of welfare costs for the area and administered payments.[29] With its powers Metro Toronto built a modern, accessible rail system and it put affordable housing in all parts of the area. Metro guided development through a combination of local (municipal) and structure (strategic) plans.[30] However Metro has not been able to protect Toronto from localities outside its purview. Some of these like Vaughan and Missisauga have used media advertising and site relocation experts to lure business out of Toronto. Raiding for business has been particularly aggressive in recent years, and as the exurbs have grown, such raiding has loosened Metro's integrating force.

What the province has given Toronto, it also has shown it could take away. The most startling demonstration of Ontario's power occurred in 1998, when it abruptly terminated Metro Toronto (despite acknowledged achievements and massive support in referenda). In place of Metro, Ontario consolidated six former localities into a single "mega city." Toronto is now governed by a single mayor and city council. While the city has begun to function as a composite entity, it is still too early to know the extent to which amalgamation has changed Toronto's development politics. We do know however, that Ontario has reversed crucial social policies by "downloading" responsibilities to the city. This has had significant fiscal impact on the new mega city and could impact its approach to development (see chapters 4, 6, and 8).

While Great Britain's unitary system gives central authorities enormous powers of intervention, local government is an entirely different matter. National politics generally operates on a loftier plain and relegates urban issues to "low politics." National leaders climb different career ladders than their local colleagues, and their connections with city halls are stunted. Moreover, prevailing attitudes in Whitehall treat local governments as agents of a national hierarchy.[31] Other practices contribute to the sclerosis of the intergovernmental system. Central-local relations are characterized by rule making in Whitehall and rule application by local governments. Unlike that in France, the British system lacks flexibility and too often is inclined toward the arbitrary exercise of central power.[32]

Despite these limitations central government has sometimes been helpful to Liverpool and other cities. It has acted to restrain wildcat development and preserved green belts around the central city. Notwithstanding the tensions between central and local authorities, Liverpool has been the beneficiary of a host of renewal programs. One writer points out that "Liverpool has been the recipient of nearly every urban experiment devised."[33] The city has been the object of "enterprise zones," "challenge grants," and "urban regeneration strategies." Thus far too little has come of these efforts, but they have created an embryo of growth that holds some promise.

Integrated Cities: Paris, Marseilles, Milan, Naples, and Glasgow

In France, intergovernmental relations are a vital component of national politics. While a host of laws govern these relations, the system is characterized by open, overlapping networks of power, and it is extraordinarily flexible.[34] As a rule, the country is parceled into regional councils that unify resources for infrastructure investment and other spending. Also, the French state pays for more than 40 percent of local budgets, thereby mitigating intense "place wars" so common in the United States. One of the ways in which French cities have established center-periphery networks is through an accumulation of public offices, known as *cumul des mandats*. Traditionally, the *cumul des mandats* has enabled elected officials to hold more than one office at the same time. It is common for a mayor to also hold office in the National Assembly or to serve as a cabinet minister or to sit as prime minister. Since 1985 the *cumul des mandats* has been curtailed, but mayors in Paris and Marseilles have made and continue to make considerable use of this mechanism.[iv] Also, the national government intervenes directly in local affairs and it has poured billions of francs into mass transit and the creation of a new business district just astride Paris. A state agency, called DATAR, also spearheads development. Along with national, city, and regional authorities, DATAR has channeled development through differential taxes, special zoning, and elaborate partnerships with private investors.

In 1964 DeGaulle's government reorganized the region into a number of jurisdictions encompassing the Ile-de-France. Today, the Ile-de-France consists of eight departments (equivalent to counties) and 124 municipalities stretched over more than 6,000 square miles. These eight departments include Paris, Haute-de-Seine, Val-de-Marne, Seine-St-Denis, Yvelines, Essone, Seine-et-Marne, and Val-d'Oise. Presided over by an elected council that selects its chief executive, the Ile-de-France is able to fund infrastructure, undertake strategic planning, and coordinate common policies.

In the past Marseilles had difficulty developing horizontal integration within its region, though today it is part of a larger *Communauté Urbaine* consisting of surrounding smaller municipalities. The Communauté Urbaine is a metropolitan organization covering eighteen communes. Encouraged by the hope of building a Greater Marseilles, these localities have adopted tax-sharing agreements and cooperate on matters of industrial development and environmental protection. Initially the effort to create a larger urban community was resisted. Major competitors, like Aix-en-Provence, refused to join and still remains outside the Communauté Urbaine, but some progress has been made. The national government also boosted vertical integration by incorporating Marseilles within a system of *"contrat de ville,"* or cities that have contracted for additional aid from the state.[35] These are new experiments at further integration, and it is still too early to tell how far they will evolve.

Italy lacks a formal urban policy, yet Milan and Naples are positioned within one of the most integrated urban systems in Western Europe. Although there is no Italian equivalent to the *cumul des mandats*, the Italian party system affords enormous access to national policy makers and resources. Milan and Naples are dominated by a highly organized party system that combines partisanship, ideology, and patronage to constitute a strong base for local politicians. The reach of major parties is felt in most areas of Italian society. Parties maintain a strong presence in the economy, where they routinely appoint managers in large public companies and financial institutions. Voting for dominant parties (Socialist or Christian Democratic until 1992) and partisan loyalty provide access to patronage, finances, and power. Even after the decline of major parties in 1990s, new factions emerged to take on old partisan roles.

Italy draws much of its constitutional inspiration and intergovernmental system from France. Even more so than their French counterparts, Italian cities receive fiscal support from higher-level governments. City governments hold extensive control over land-use decisions, and they can turn to regional governments for cooperation and assistance. Milan has also benefited from extensive national intervention. It has taken advantage of national initiatives in transportation, infrastructure, and subsidized sports arenas.

In Naples, intergovernmental aid is often used to rescue the city from distress rather than enhance existing development. Again, political parties are an integrative feature in the national system, though in recent years they have been discredited because of corruption and scandal. National government is highly interventionist, and few matters are not influenced by Rome. Along with substantial income transfers, Rome provides huge assistance for industrial development, infrastructure, and housing. This was carried out by special agencies, such as the Cassa per il Mezzogiorno. During the 1980s a major earthquake in the region precipitated a massive emergency program for reconstruction of Naples. So massive in scope was this program, that it drove the city's policy agendas through the early 1990s.

Great Britain's intergovernmental system puts a good deal of discretion in the hands of Scottish authorities and this limits Glasgow's connection to the center.[36] Instead Glasgow has developed strong horizontal relationships within its region, and this has muted tensions with Whitehall. The Scottish office has enabled the region to enjoy a degree of autonomy, including a different legal and educational system as well as some separate urban programs. During the 1970s massive economic problems led to the creation of a network of regional development institutions. The dominant player in Glasgow was the Scottish Development Authority, or SDA. That agency was empowered to plan and modernize the city in cooperation with the city government and new regional councils. Through the decades, the SDA acquired broad powers to confiscate and clear land, establish development areas, and provide new investment. The agency survived the Thatcher years to continue to assert power over the region during the 1990s. Indeed, in recent years the spark of Scottish nationalism has increasingly encapsulated Glasgow's politics in the warp of regional governance.[37]

Comparing Diffuse, Mixed, and Integrated Cities

As previously mentioned, the budgets of European cities are heavily supported by national government. Currently, this support ranges upward of 50 percent in Great Britain to more than 90 percent in Italy. By comparison, national aid to American cities amounts to between 2 and 7 percent of their budgets. State aid varies enormously, but a recent study of major American cities shows that state assistance amounted to approximately 21 percent of city budgets.[38] In recent years, state budgets have expanded to assist some U.S. cities, but this has not made up for the shortfalls in city revenues.[39] Canadian cities do somewhat better, but rely more heavily on the provinces than the national government.

Even these gaps in intergovernmental support do not show the full contrast between Europe and the United States. In European cities, the national government takes full responsibility for many more services, such as welfare, mass transportation, and education, and is sometimes a major provider for housekeeping services. Because local responsibilities are so different, it is difficult to compare city budgets. With some caution and adjustments we can, however, present varying levels of intergovernmental aid.

TABLE 3.3
Intergovernmental Aid to Ten Cities, ca. 1970–1990

	Total (unadjusted)	Rank by Highest (unadjusted)	Total (adjusted)	Rank by Highest (adjusted)
Naples	80.0	1	96.5	1
Milan	80.0	2	96.5	2
Glasgow	64.0	3	80.5	3
Liverpool	54.5	4	71.0	4
Paris	40.0	5	56.5	5
Marseilles	40.0	6	56.5	6
Toronto	33.0	7	33.0	7
New York	32.5	8	32.5	8
Detroit	30.9	9	30.9	9
Houston	5.6	10	5.6	10

Table 3.3 shows total amounts of intergovernmental aid as a proportion of city revenues. The table includes total aid from national, state or provincial governments. Because of sharp differences in the kinds of responsibilities cities must fund, the table also contains a column for adjusted aid.[v] Cities are ranked for both unadjusted and adjusted aid.

We can observe that while the adjusted figures give us a better idea of the proportion of intergovernmental aid in each city, the rankings do not change. Naples and Milan receive especially generous amounts while Glasgow and Liverpool follow. Paris and Marseilles receive relatively less aid as a proportion of revenue, though they are significantly above the U.S. and Canadian cities.[vi] Interestingly, Toronto's proportion is similar to that received by Detroit and New York.

We now put both qualitative and revenue information together, and offer a continuum of where each city stands on intergovernmental support. Figure 3.6 lists these cities as diffuse moving toward integrated. To better place our cities on the continuum, we turn again to indicators that include ties with national, regional, state, or provincial governments, as well as intergovernmental aid.[vii] These indicators are converted into a composite score, shown for each city. The score ranges from a low of 1.0 to a high of 3.0. Scores for each city are also shown and explained in the table 3.vii in the notes at the end of this chapter.

POPULAR CONTROL: A STEERING VARIABLE

Popular control refers to the availability of institutions and practices through which citizens can participate. Normally, cities with an abundance of participatory institutions and viable voting practices will have

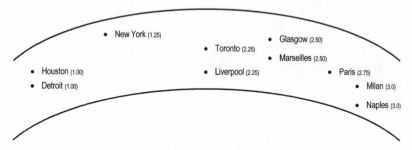

Figure 3.6. Intergovernmental Support: Diffuse and Integrated.

a greater capacity to steer economic development and strengthen public bargaining.

Cities will differ in the kinds of popular control they employ. Cities with active popular control contain competitive and programmatic parties, they have high voter turnout, they facilitate political access through neighborhood institutions, and they are replete with voluntary associations. In contrast, passive cities lack most of these characteristics. They are characterized by entrenched political monopolies (political machines or one-party systems), they have low voter turnout, their neighborhoods lack political access, and they experience a paucity of civic life.

Rarely will cities possess all or none of these features. While cites have variable strengths and weaknesses, they exhibit predominant patterns, ranging from passive participation, to mixed tendencies, to active participation.

Cities with Passive Participation: Detroit and Houston

In form and substance, Detroit's popular control has been ineffectual. A nine-member city council is elected at large and in nonpartisan balloting. These aspects of the system lessen the importance of neighborhoods, they diminish citizen representation, and they tend to deflect responsibilities onto personalities. Nor has Detroit stood for competitive politics. Its former mayor Coleman Young held power for twenty years. Young's popularity and decisive victories at the ballot booth enabled him to monopolize power and dominate a weak city council. Young's successor, Dennis Archer, was also elected without much opposition. In 1997, only 28 percent of the electorate went to the polls, and they gave him 73 percent of the vote. What remains of the city's civic organization is weak.[40] The system affords scant opportunity for neighborhood expression, and the city's singular racial composition has been coupled to a politics of black symbolism that has impeded pluralist opposition. More than in most other cities, real power is tied to economic resources. Big corporations grew up in the city and some retain enormous influence. One scholar has described Detroit as ruled by a tight-knit elite, while two other researchers believed that the city's power has been exercised at the peaks of major sectors within the city.[41]

Houston's politics is marked by weak civic traditions and a low level of neighborhood activism. This is partly due to spread settlement and physical obstacles to social cohesion. It is also due to a weak civic involvement by unions, civic groups, and other nonbusiness voluntary organizations. In Houston, business leadership towers over almost everyone else.[42] Most important, Houston's nonpartisan system shrouds popular participation in a politics of personality. Except for pervasive support for growth, politics is nonprogrammatic. Rather than parties, private interest groups (chamber of commerce, newspapers, and realtors) field political candidates. The absence of political parties diminishes competitive politics, emphasizes personality over program, and dampens voter turnout.[43] During recent decades voter turnout averaged only 22 percent of the electorate. In 1995 it fell to 15 percent of the electorate, as Mayor Robert Lanier ran unopposed.[44]

There also are other limits on popular participation in Houston. Mayors are elected for limited terms, hampering efforts to build stable constituencies, and legal requirements make it difficult for labor unions to become a strong force. Recently, there are signs of change. Houston's minorities have grown and adopted a politics of ethnic identity, infusing a mild pluralism into the system. In 1997, a black candidate ran for and won the mayoralty; voter turnout jumped to an unprecedented 35 percent. The rising use of voter referenda may also portend increased opportunities for citizens.

Cities with Mixed Tendencies: Glasgow, Liverpool, and Naples

In some ways Glasgow can be said to have passive attributes. Its voter turnout is low, and the city lacks formal neighborhood political institutions. The Labour Party has dominated local politics, except for a brief interlude of Scottish nationalism during the late 1970s. The Scottish National Party and the Conservative Party have a modest presence. Despite the lack of a strong partisan opposition, it would be wrong to conclude that citizens are deprived of political access. Glasgow's vivid blue-collar union traditions are a focal point for political organization. Popular participation is organized around trade unions with strong links to the local labour party.

Party agendas are guided by trade unions, national party programs, and a pragmatic socialist philosophy that is peculiar to Glasgow. Policy issues usually get thrashed out in public, rather than in party closets. Glasgow's pragmatism encourages politicians to mobilize residents and grass roots organizations. Also, Glasgow's city council sees itself as the single organization in touch with popular opinion. It considers itself the voice of the people in dealing with distant bureaucracies like the Scottish Office and Whitehall.

Liverpool shows some of the same tendencies found in Glasgow, but with an added flavor of political polarization. Its lack of formal neighborhood government has not prevented citizens from using party institutions for populist causes. Like Glasgow, programmatic partisanship lies at the core of this political tradition. Party membership is open and institutions are organized around neighborhoods, housing estates, and trade unions.

Strong and explicit ideologies resonate through Liverpool's different neighborhoods. This hardens an already endemic social polarization, which is split along ethnic, religious, and even racial lines. Catholics vote for Labour, while Protestants follow the Liberal or Social Democratic Party. Blacks, mostly of West Indian origin, live at the margins of the society. Through the transformation years of the 1980s, Liverpool was either blocked by "hung councils" or it was in outright rebellion. While Liverpool often supports Labour, its politics is ridden by factions. On the Left have been several Labour breakaway groups (Militant Labour, Socialist Labour, Ward Labour). At the center are various amalgams of Liberals and Social Democrats (now called Liberal Democrats), and they command a stable proportion of the vote. The Right is quite small and draws well under 10 percent of the vote. While turnout has been remarkably low and continues to decline, Liverpool's politics is robust. During the elections of 1998 the Liberal Democrats won a plurality of the vote, and held a majority of seats on the city council.

Naples also exhibits a strong ambivalence between party dominance and popular activism. Naples is characterized by well-organized parties and high rates of electoral participation. For decades, the city has been contested by local branches of the major national parties, resulting in coalition governments. Christian Democrats and right-wing coalitions were dominant until the mid-1970s. Since then, left-wing coalitions also have run the city. Until 1993 mayors were dependent upon shifting coalitions, but recent electoral reforms have helped stabilize leadership. As in other Italian cities, vigorous registration systems and national partisanship encourage voter turnout. Elections bring out more than 60 percent of the electorate, who split their vote among half a dozen parties.

What diminishes real popular control is the dominance of party bosses coupled to a submissive popular base. The postwar years brought on a corrupt party system in which bosses could buy electoral support. Although elections produce a sense of deep party rivalry, political chieftains often ignore adopted policy in order to collaborate over the spoils of power. These aspects of Neapolitan party politics have dampened real political competition. Italian local governments have been empowered to organize elected neighborhood councils, but Naples has not taken this seriously. City hall leaders have been unable or unwilling to pass enabling ordinances for neighborhood empowerment. One researcher suggests that most of the city's trade unions and civic groups subordinate themselves to political bosses.[45] While the institutions of popular control may be present, the absence a large middle class and the paucity of independent voluntary organizations leave a great void.

Having said this, we find are hints of change in Naples' politics. During the 1990s, Neapolitan corruption was brought to the attention of the nation. This led to national campaigns for reform, including legal prosecutions and electoral changes. Leading politicians were put in prison. In 1993 the national government permitted the direct election of mayors, bringing Antonio Bassolino into power. Bassolino is a former Communist with a strong reformist bent. His new agenda took shape in the 1990s, and has begun to make the city work. While the media cheer these reforms, only time will tell whether the changes will endure.

Cities with Active Participation: New York, Paris, Marseilles, Toronto, and Milan

New York has a highly competitive, pluralistic, and accessible system of popular control. Although residents often vote Democratic, party organization has been disintegrating for decades. Factional struggles within Democratic primaries ensure lengthy lists of challengers for major offices and hard fought elections. Opposition movements have managed to win mayoralty elections through "fusion parties" or by creating coalitions around popular Republicans. Fiorello La Guardia, John Lindsay, and Rudolf Giuliani are the most outstanding examples of Republicans who brought opposition coalitions to power. Indeed, opposition parties have captured the mayoralty during roughly half the city's one-hundred-year history. Voting turnout is generally high by American standards, although it is erratic — running as high as 61 percent in 1989, but down to 35 percent in 1997.

Besides this, contests for public office are supported by a plethora of active neighborhood associations, civic groups, and voluntary organizations — buttressed by fifty-nine community boards. These community boards can comment on land use, and their advice is forwarded to city-wide institutions.[46] That advice carries not only community sentiment but also political weight, and one study claimed that community board advice is followed in 98 percent of the cases.[47] But even here, community boards can be circumvented by New York's PBCs, which have the power to override local ordinances. Another flaw in the electoral process allows big money from developers to influence political candidacies. On balance, however, few issues get past the city's interest groups, neighborhoods, political opponents, and its vigilant voters.

Both Paris and Marseilles reflect the vigor of French politics. Overlapping centers of power among the national governments, the parties, and the regions place enormous resources in the hands of big-city mayors. Differences between Right and Left are sharp and elections are strongly contested. While Paris has remained in Gaullist hands until recently, its arrondissements were gradually drifting toward the Socialists. Socialists were also gaining power in the muncipal council, and this portended the Socialist victory in 2001. On the other side of the nation, Marseilles took a different turn. For decades it was in the hands of the Socialists. But a right-center coalition successfully challenged the Socialists in the 1990s, and by 2001 they had retained control.

Paris and Marseilles supplement their city-wide institutions with a system of neighborhood city halls, consisting of mayors and municipal legislators. In Paris each of the twenty arrondissements (neighborhoods) elect neighborhood officials and offer outreach services. In Marseilles, sixteen arrondissements cover the city and are divided into eight sectors that choose officials for neighborhood city halls.[viii] Neighborhood mayors have substantial resources at their disposal and can influence the distribution of subsidized housing to constituents. In most instances politicians serve in more than one capacity, and a neighborhood mayor will also serve on the municipal council. Their overlapping offices work to enhance democratic representation, so that elected officials can ply their influence in several venues. Moreover, the ability of parties to establish a foothold within a particular neighborhood enables minority parties to challenge dominant coalitions and ultimately win city hall.

Added to this blend of citizen participation is the extraordinary vibrancy of civic and neighborhood groups. Paris and Marseilles allocate portions of their budgets to citizen groups, and this encourages both the quantity and adherence of citizen activists. Paris has seen a virtual explosion of voluntary associations. One journalistic report says that the number of citizen committees has more than doubled since the mid-

1970s, and it puts the current number at 125,000.[48] Roughly 8,000 of these associations receive funding from the city, contributing to what the French call "*la vie associative.*" Another report estimates that over sixty of these associations are dedicated to challenging urban development projects.[49] Marseilles has a particularly dense network of neighborhood associations that are equally engaged in politics. Hundreds of neighborhood associations containing over 75,000 members are said to function in that city.[50] These associations aggressively deal with a variety of issues that range from the allocation of public housing to plans for building mega projects and the preservation of green space.[51]

For thirty years Toronto's federated government enabled voters to exercise influence within their respective city councils. Metro's six constituent cities were small, ranging from 629,000 in the City of Toronto down to 104,000 in East York.[ix] The respective city councils have numerous wards and a low ratio of citizens to representatives. Toronto's neighborhoods have a powerful (albeit informal) voice in the conduct of local affairs.[52] While Toronto is officially nonpartisan, many politicians identify with one party or another. Politicians are often perceived as belonging to "lefty" or "righty" groups and voters readily respond to informal partisan cues. Provincial politics often carries into the city, and discussions are organized around the contrasting platforms of Progressive Conservatives, Liberals, and the New Democratic Party. Real voter turnout reaches 70 percent, and in 1997 the incumbent won 53 percent of the vote.

In Milan political parties are the centerpiece of civic life. During the postwar decades, coalitions of right-wing parties led by Christian Democrats held power, although they increasingly alternated with Socialists. Political competition surged during the 1990s. A new right-wing party, the Lombardy League, advocates a federalist Italy and won control. The league would grant autonomy to the affluent North and guarantee a deeper separation from the poorer South. By 1997 the league fell to a left-center party coalition.

While Milanese politicians use patronage networks to cement party loyalties, this is offset by strong interparty rivalry and aggressive civic groups. The city's robust private sector and highly developed civic traditions support a dense network of professional groups, trade unions, business associations, and other voluntary groups that make themselves heard. Milan also experimented with a system of elected neighborhood councils several years before the national legislation requested cities to do so. During the 1970s city leaders quickly delegated extensive powers to a network of twenty neighborhood councils over a wide range of policy areas. Although the power of these councils should not be exaggerated, they provided a forum that permitted public participation in

TABLE 3.4
Electoral Participation and Party Competition in Ten Cities, 1989–97

City	Average % of Registered Voters Voting	Average % Minority Party(ies) Votes	Index: Voter Party Activism	Rank
Milan	69.30	71.17	99.23	1
Naples	63.70	67.47	89.07	2
Toronto	70.00	52.80	79.98	3
Marseilles	62.88	52.59	71.96	4
Paris	55.44	49.02	59.93	5
New York	51.97	46.40	53.27	6
Glasgow	43.85	50.90	49.29	7
Liverpool	24.95	52.46	30.29	8
Detroit	37.00	34.67	24.10	9
Houston	24.33	25.28	0.00	10

economic development decisions. Neighborhood councils and groups became more active as partisan political upheaval and fragmentation continued through the 1990s and populist-style council leaders emerged.

Comparing Passively and Actively Participatory Cities

Table 3.4 offers a view of electoral behavior in each of our ten cities. The table lists "turnout" for registered voters in two previous mayoral elections prior to the year 2000, as well as "party competition" calculated as percentage of the vote gained by minority parties in the last two elections.[x] The composite rank for a city's "voter/party activity" is compiled through an index of the two scores.

Generally, Europeans and Canadians vote in greater proportions and have firmer party loyalties than do Americans. This is due to the differing structure and traditions of political parties as well as to differences in how voters view these organizations.[53] Both voter turnout and party competition are higher in French, Italian, and Canadian cities than in their American and British counterparts. Toronto, Milan, Naples, Marseilles, and Paris have the highest voter/party activity.[xi] At the low end of the spectrum are the American and British cases. As expected, Houston and Detroit have the lowest voter/party activity. New York is an exception and is closer to its European counterparts. Liverpool's and Glasgow's are relatively low.

If we consider voter/party activism in light of our qualitative descriptions, we can get a better comparative picture. Figure 3.7 depicts our ten cities on a continuum ranging from passive to active. To better place

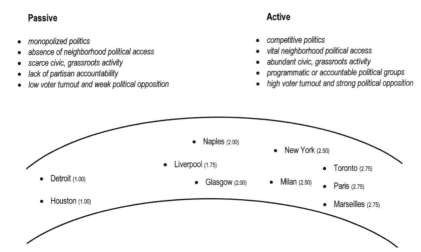

Passive

- *monopolized politics*
- *absence of neighborhood political access*
- *scarce civic, grassroots activity*
- *lack of partisan accountability*
- *low voter turnout and weak political opposition*

Active

- *competitive politics*
- *vital neighborhood political access*
- *abundant civic, grassroots activity*
- *programmatic or accountable political groups*
- *high voter turnout and strong political opposition*

- Naples (2.00)
- New York (2.50)
- Liverpool (1.75)
- Toronto (2.75)
- Detroit (1.00)
- Glasgow (2.00)
- Milan (2.50)
- Paris (2.75)
- Houston (1.00)
- Marseilles (2.75)

Figure 3.7. Popular Control: Passive and Active.

our cities on the continuum, we turn again to indicators that include neighborhood political access, civic participation, the nature of political parties, and voter/party behavior.[xii] These indicators are converted into a composite score, shown for each city. The score ranges from a low of 1.0 to a high of 3.0. Scores for each city are also shown and explained in the table 3.xii in the notes at the end of this chapter.

LOCAL CULTURE: A STEERING VARIABLE

When we speak of local culture we refer to the attitudes that a city brings toward development and the values that it holds toward the built environment. Prevailing norms on these issues are manifest in a city's history, its experience with issues of class, race, or social policy, its attitude toward business, and its social makeup. Briefly, we point up a city's traditions in order to illustrate how it creates cultural pathways and establishes values toward the built environment.

In applying the concept of local culture, we borrow from scholars who distinguish "materialist" from "postmaterialist" values as well as "divisible" from "indivisible" benefits.[xiii] Materialist cultures emphasize personal needs and see development as bringing divisible benefits to individuals. These benefits are often delivered through piecemeal initiatives so that they can be more easily granted or withheld. Conceived in this manner, materialist cultures use public power to produce jobs, income, contracts, or favors. There are cases where materialist cities sacrifice environmental quality or build freeways to achieve jobs and income.[54] Understandably, materialist cultures often (though not always) spring from a blue-collar, working-class base and from distressed social conditions. Economic necessity holds little choice for hard-pressed cities, and their populations will seek to satisfy immediate, tangible concerns.

By contrast, postmaterialist cultures stress the "interests of the whole," and see development as leading to indivisible benefits designed for the larger commonweal. These are generally considered to be collective benefits or public amenities that are provided through long-term planning and investment. Logically, postmaterialist cultures employ public power to provide collective goods like the protection of open space, growth management, and environmental safeguards. Postmaterialist cultures also favor interventionist planning that entail architectural controls, historic preservation districts, and mass transit. There have been instances where postmaterialist cities invoked building moratoria or stopped massive highway projects.[55] Logically, postmaterialist cities have substantial proportions of professionals, artists, and upper-level managerial occupations. Put bluntly, social privilege brings choices and evokes broader concerns because populations can afford it.

Naturally, most cities will contain elements of both materialist and postmaterialist cultures, and we draw distinctions by locating predominant tendencies. When these tendencies cannot be discerned, we place cities in a hybrid category. We begin our discussion with an examination of dominant traditions, and then consider how population characteristics contribute to the makeup of local culture.

Materialist Cities: Detroit, Liverpool, Naples, and Houston

In Detroit cultural outlooks are driven by a tradition of trade unions, racial issues, and desperation for private capital. Throughout the past fifty years, Detroit was a union, mostly single-industry town — often torn by conflicts between labor and management. This contributed to a culture of endemic distrust, later compounded by issues of race. The fault line on race broke open during the summer of 1967, when rioting tore that city apart. Detroit's violence was among the worst in the nation's history and required intervention by armed soldiers.[56] Coupled with rising crime, the events of 1967 accelerated the white exodus to the suburbs. Detroit has continued to suffer through chronic episodes of violence. It has one of the highest homicide rates in the nation, and the once renowned "motor city" is now dubbed America's "murder city." In the past, Halloween eve (popularly called "Devil's Night") offered an especially grim scene of self-destruction as whole blocks were often set ablaze.

In the wake of rioting and racial tumult, citizens took a dim view of public authority and professional expertise. They began to see planners as "villains" and "perpetrators of wrongs against central city residents."[57]

Placed against the backdrop of abusive urban renewal practices, planning lost its legitimacy and disintegrated.[58] Such fear and district influenced perceptions, attitudes, and ultimately investment. Ironically, both the fear of planning and flight of capital have made the city desperate enough to agree to almost any investment. Detroit has built freeways that slice it in half and has agreed to razing whole neighborhoods to obtain capital investment from a major automobile manufacturer.[59] While the public approved of these job initiatives, redistribution policies were also favored. Public surveys rated "aid to the needy" as the city's highest priority, winning endorsement by 88 percent of the population.[60] These attitudes were embellished by public toleration of political clientelism built up by former mayor Coleman Young. Young built a personal machine, fed by development contracts and federal grants.[61] While the mayor was investigated by the FBI for alleged kickbacks, no indictments were returned.

Liverpool also took root as a working-class city beset by social tensions. It experienced its own share of sporadic violence and confrontation. Unlike Detroit, which relied on private industry, Liverpool aggressively used the public arm to sustain jobs and selective benefits. The city's Irish Catholic, working-class population had been identified with the more militant wing of the Labour Party. In recent years, things have changed, but old perceptions linger. Liverpool itself has a weak middle class, deep income disparities, and high public-sector employment. More than half the population now draws public benefits of one type or another.[62] A concentrated black underclass makes the social composition all the more volatile. In 1981 the Toxteth riots broke out with open warfare between police and youth (see chapter 7). Liverpool still bears the reputation of "riot city" because of confrontations a decade ago, and it is still at a loss for investment.

These troubles have been accentuated by political turmoil. Once unemployment set in, so did political militancy. During the mid-1980s radical Trotskyites went into open battle with the Conservative central government. The Trotskyites were eventually sacked, but not until they created a national spectacle by trying to spend the city into bankruptcy. Even today, residents rely on the public sector as the economy's mainstay. A third of all jobs are in the public sector. While the new leadership has altered older practices and reduced patronage, much of it still exists. Liverpool employs 30 percent more public servants per capita than the average English city.[63] Traditions are hard to erase, and Liverpool is still a city where the public sector is regarded as the major source for jobs and development. One particularly cynical investor is quoted as saying, "Liverpudlians had this attitude that the world owes them a living, and it was this attitude that concerned us. All they wanted were handouts."

Naples comes into the world of globalization with a strong material-ist tradition. The city's huge number of unemployed and its poor have been unable to challenge landed interests that continue to dominate the society. Even with democratization, the old order has perpetuated its power through a system of patron-client relationships. Clientelism over-rides broader values and touches everything, from business contracts to personal relationships. Whether Christian Democrat or Socialist, the culture is geared toward exchanging jobs and favors for social support or political votes.[64]

This tradition also colors public planning. While urban master plans are required by law, it has taken decades to bring them about. Even when plans are published, policymakers ignore them.[65] Despite the city's tremendous overcrowding, for example, little has been done to claim open space for parks. Today, Naples is one of the least green cities in Italy. Traffic congestion plagues the city and suffocates it with pollution. Neapolitans seem unwilling to do away with clientelism, and this is made worse by the existence of organized crime. Rather than clean up the city, local politicians have operated as middlemen between marginal enterprise and several crime syndicates.[66] Clientelism is reinforced by a social base heavily laden with small-family firms that count on public contracts for sustenance. Remaking the built environment is then viewed as an opportunity for jobs, favors, profit, and bribery.

Houston's materialism is quite different from more collectivist and densely settled European cities. Its new-age materialism is rooted in a geography of open land and cowboy individualism. Rather than kinship or political parties, personal initiative is most valued and encouraged. Often called the "free enterprise city," Houston has been quick to pro-mote the idea that rapid growth — no matter where — is good for every-body.[67] It has a well-established tradition of limited government, low taxes, and respect for private property. Opposition to zoning, planning, trade unions, and public amenities are articles of faith. Developers are given a free hand to shape the city's built environment around massive bands of highways and sprawling suburbs. During the 1960s Houston's leaders rejected federal urban renewal monies. Civic gospel says that city government should be managed like a business corporation by lim-iting public expenditures and maximizing personal revenues.

Cities of Mixed Tendency: New York, Marseilles, and Glasgow

By virtue of its size and complexity, New York is a polyglot city. Its tradition of immigration and trade unions collide with its legacy of phi-lanthropy and Wall Street aristocracy. The conservative, blue-collar bungalows of Queens clash with Manhattan's artistic, loft-living com-munities. During the first half of the century, New York spawned notorious political machines like Tammany Hall. At the same time, it also laid claim to impressive movements for "good government" and magnificent public amenities (museums, cultural centers, parks).

The result is a culture that encompasses competing materialist and postmaterialist traditions. Issues regarding the built environment generate mixed reactions. On one hand, the city earned a reputation as an innovator in land-use planning (the first zoning law) and public enterprise.[xiv] Its high taxes and activist government created an enormous reservoir of indivisible, public goods. On the other hand, the city's social characteristics and fragmentation encouraged NIMBYism, patronage, and deal making.[xv] A city with so many elements can rise in opposition to massive highway construction and the pollution it would cause, while tolerating skyscrapers that shut out sunlight and create massive wind tunnels.

Judging from its blue-collar complexion, Marseilles might seem like it would have a solidly materialist culture. But history and tradition give the city a more complex cast. For one, Marseilles has been France's entrance to the Mediterranean and to Africa. At one time its port made it wealthy, gave it imperial importance, and enhanced its bourgeois flavor. Second, French institutions and manners are seductive integrators and provide a powerful identity for politicians, businessmen, and citizens. Marseilles's elites are part of a a civic establishment and play an important role in conserving the city's heritage. Last, the city has its own architectural and planning traditions.[68] Neighborhoods may be old but they are reasonably well kept and intact. Citizens are passionate about protecting the local fabric and have forced decision makers to build auto routes below grade level. For the average resident, preserving Marseilles as France's "port city" is quintessential, and they do so with fierce pride.[69]

At the same time, Marseilles is a Mediterranean city where kinship and connections are important. The city is composed of neighborhoods with distinct social characters and ethnic attributes. Blue-collar residents and Maghrebians (Algerians, Moroccans, and Tunisians) occupy neighborhoods in the northern and central areas. Italians and Armenians cling to neighborhoods on the eastern side, while the native bourgeoisie holds the southern arrondissements. "Marseilles," writes Marcel Roncayolo, "is a civil society which happens to have a system of government."[70] The clustering of this civil society into different social enclaves and clans produces a mentality amenable to the trading of divisible benefits. *Who* you know may count for more than *what* you know. Divisible benefits and patronage are also part of the city's politics. Marseilles's reputation was also built on illegal port traffic and underworld ties. This combination of neighborhood, kinship, and port gives local politics a clientelist character.

Glasgow's major waves of immigration have come from Ireland and contributed a Catholic outlook to its politics and society. Like other industrial cities at the beginning of the century, life was hard and grimy. Rent strikes and labor disputes gave the city a reputation as a "Red Clydeside." Over the years this radicalism has been incorporated into a pragmatic, if not eclectic, socialist philosophy. Studies of Labour councillors during the 1950s and 1960s showed that most constituted a relatively apolitical group, the interests of which were local.[71] Other writers suggest Glasgow followed values of "municipal labourism," which puts an emphasis on both individual and collective benefits acquired through public expenditure.[72]

While Glasgow's working-class orientation has meant support for social redistribution, it has also supported indivisible benefits. Britain's once renowned "second city of the empire" can still muster pride of public achievement, and a British sense of fair play dispels any temptation for clientelism.[xvi] Public support is high for green belts, environmental protection, and amenities. Glasgow's collectivism has a nonmaterial side that values public goods. Its sooty river has been cleaned up and its downtown restored without resort to massive bulldozing. Its center is now a network of attractive Victorian buildings and thriving commerce. The restoration has impressed the preservationists enough to be designated as "Britain's City of Architecture and Design."[73] It is this curious blend of divisible benefits coupled with a concern for the larger commonweal that sets Glasgow apart.

Postmaterialist Cities: Paris, Toronto, and Milan

Paris is France's great city, and its penchant for fine architecture and meticulous planning runs deep. During the nineteenth century Baron Von Haussmann shaped the modern city with grand boulevards and luxurious residential buildings. A century later that tradition was followed in the planning maps by Paul Delouvrier, who laid out the region as a postindustrial mecca. Green spaces, new towns, and a network of railways laid out the region in a grand radio centric pattern. Those pathways have left indelible marks on the Parisian mindset. Everything is debated and decided via plans, maps, and special development zones. Citizens have stopped proposed plans for a highway along the Left Bank, and neighborhoods have prevailed against massive construction projects.[74] In recent years Parisians have clamored about deteriorating air quality and traffic congestion. Nearly 80 percent of the public supports banning automobiles from city streets in favor of mass transit.[75] Bicycles and special riding paths are now popular.[76]

The often quoted description of Toronto as "New York run by the Swiss" captures its cultural diversity and orderliness. Its master plan goes back to the 1940s, and it has a tradition of seeking to balance development among neighborhoods, downtown, and the rest of the region. Well-kept Victorian neighborhoods are woven into the downtown core, which in turn is surrounded by "streetcar suburbs" — all served by extensive tramways. The city's British inheritance and continued respect for civil order contribute to its sense of fair play and reputation for clean dealing. Debates animate the many middle-class neighborhoods that fill the city. Former mayor John Sewell symbolized Toronto's "postmaterialist" and populist streak. With avid public support, Sewell pressed hard for neighborhood preservation, he was an energetic environmentalist, and decried the pervasiveness of automobiles by commuting to city hall on his bicycle. The city's gentrified residents (so-called "white painters") launched campaigns against expressways.[77] Popular norms place value on a vibrant center, a healthy downtown, and mass transit.[78] This also includes support for historic preservation, density controls, strict zoning enforcement, and mandatory underground parking facilities.

Milan never shared Naples's long history of feudalism and repressive landowners. Instead it arose as a trading center and developed a powerful middle class. Milan's robust private sector and civic traditions have supported a dense network of professional groups, business associations, educational institutions, and trade unions. The city defines itself as the moral capital of the country because of its Calvinistic work environment. This contrasts with the dolce vita and baroque attitudes prevalent in Rome and the South.[79] Bureaucratic traditions were transmitted to Milan via the Austro-Hungarian Empire, and serve as an efficient instrument of public policy.

We should also recognize that Milan is a city of contradictions. Despite the collective pride, clientelist practices touch every rung of the social order. Policies are made with the best of intentions and with the broadest concerns in mind. But once decided, the clientelist features of the culture can also be seen. Divisible rewards seep into the implementation of decisions and are distributed to those who are well connected. Neighborhood preservation, environmental quality, and mass transit are surely on the agenda, but they compete for attention with materialist concerns over jobs, contracts, and public spoils. All this should be seen in light of the fact that Milan's judicial system has little hesitation imposing itself on a sometimes unruly public. This occurred during the 1990s when prosecutors waged a campaign against bribery.

Comparing Materialist and Postmaterialist Cities

As mentioned earlier, materialist cities are usually associated with a stronger blue-collar base, while postmaterialist cities are more inclined

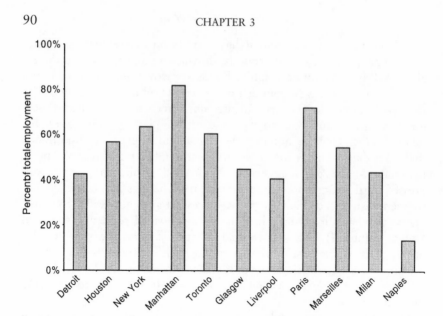

Figure 3.8. Professionals and Managers in Ten Cities, 1990s.

to contain white-collar workers. Scholars also find that materialist (or "progressive") cultures emphasize nontraditional norms, new kinds of household arrangements, and higher disposable incomes.[80] Finally, "slimmer families" with two adult working partners typify the post-materialist streak, while larger families and traditional norms are more frequent in materialist cultures.[81]

We rely partially on demographic data to assess materialism and postmaterialism in our cities. Taking our cues from earlier research on the subject, we assess these differences by turning to social composition in our ten cities.[xvii] Figure 3.8 provides a glimpse of how professionals and managers are arrayed in our ten cities as of 1990. Tables 3.5 and 3.6 show respectively percent of persons in poverty and household size between 1970 and 1990.

As we see, Manhattan and Paris hold the highest proportion of professionals and managers. Toronto, Marseilles, and Milan follow. At the other end, Detroit, Glasgow, Liverpool, and Naples have fewer professionals and managers. Taking a glimpse at poverty, we see that Milan, Paris, Marseilles, and Toronto have relatively low rates of impoverishment. Somewhere in between are New York and Houston. Manhattan is a bipolar case, with a poverty rate of 20 percent juxtaposed against extraordinarily high per capita income. Comparing this to household size puts our picture into sharper relief. As of 2000, cities with the

TABLE 3.5
Persons in Poverty in Ten Cities, 1970 and 1990

Central City	1970	1990	Rank Lowest Poverty, 1990
Milan	NA	4.0%	1
Paris	13.0%	14.0%	2
Marseilles	NA	14.9%	3
Toronto	14.5%	16.0%	4
New York (5 boroughs)	14.9%	18.9%	5
New York (Manhattan)	18.9%	20.0%	6
Houston	14.1%	20.4%	7
Naples	NA	22.0%	8
Glasgow	NA	30.0%	9
Detroit	14.9%	32.0%	10
Liverpool	NA	40.0%	11

lowest household size were (New York's) Manhattan and Milan. Those with the highest household size were Detroit and Naples.[xvi]

Despite some exceptions, our cities show consistent traditions and social attributes. We combine this data with our earlier accounts of attitudes toward planning and environmental concerns to construct a profile for each city. Putting these patterns together, we offer a continuum that shows where our cities stand on a particular aspect of local culture.

Figure 3.9 is based on a number of indicators (attitude toward planning, divisible benefits, poverty, household size) and lists the cities along a continuum ranging from materialist to postmaterialist cultures.[xix] These indicators are converted into a composite score, shown for each

TABLE 3.6
Average Number of Persons per Household in Ten Cities, 1970–ca. 2000

Central City	1970	ca. 2000	Rank by Lowest: ca. 2000
Paris	2.19	1.87	1
New York (Manhattan)	2.36	2.00	2
Milan	2.80	2.08	3
Glasgow	3.09	2.25	4
Toronto	3.32	2.26	5
Liverpool	3.84	2.28	6
Marseilles	3.10	2.30	7
New York (5 Boroughs)	2.74	2.59	8
Houston	3.09	2.67	9
Detroit	2.99	2.77	10
Naples	3.94	2.80	11

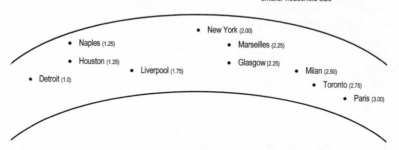

Materialist

- divisible, personal benefits, interests of the individual
- jobs, income, contracts
- development as a vehicle for expected side payments, corruption as a commonly accepted practice
- blue collar social base, higher poverty rates, larger household size

Post Materialist

- indivisible, widespread benefits, interests of the whole
- planning, growth management, historic and environmental preservation
- robust debate over development choices, more surreptitious (or scarcer) side payments and corruption
- white collar social base, low poverty rates, smaller household size

Figure 3.9. Local Culture: Materialist and Postmaterialist.

city. The score ranges from a low of 1.0 to a high of 3.0. Scores for each city are also shown and explained in table 3.xix in the notes at the end of the chapter.

CONCLUSIONS

All told, our ten cities show remarkable variation. They experienced industrial transformation with different market conditions, different kinds of intergovernmental support, different types of popular control, and different local cultures. In previous sections, our ten cities were evaluated by each of these variables and placed on a continuum. Table 3.7 presents a different version of this continuum by highlighting characteristics for each city.

As noted in chapter 2, our hypothesis states that when these characteristics are cumulative or reinforce each other, they are likely to have the clearest impact upon bargaining and development. Also notice that only a few cities hold these cumulative features. They come close to being "pure types," either where *disadvantaged bargaining* is associated with *market-centered* development or where *advantaged bargaining* is associated with *social-centered* development.

Detroit, with disfavored market conditions, diffuse intergovernmental support, passive popular control, and a materialist culture theoretically lies at the "market-centered" end of the spectrum. Except for its very different market condition, Houston would join Detroit. By contrast,

TABLE 3.7
Summary Characteristics: Ten Cities

City	Market Conditions	Intergovernmental Support	Popular Control	Local Culture
New York	Favored	Diffuse	Active	Mixed
Detroit	Disfavored	Diffuse	Passive	Materialist
Houston	Mixed	Diffuse	Passive	Materialist
Toronto	Favored	Mixed	Active	Postmaterialist
Glasgow	Disfavored	Integrated	Mixed	Mixed
Liverpool	Disfavored	Mixed	Mixed	Materialist
Paris	Favored	Integrated	Active	Postmaterialist
Marseilles	Disfavored	Integrated	Active	Mixed
Milan	Favored	Integrated	Active	Postmaterialist
Naples	Disfavored	Integrated	Mixed	Materialist

Toronto, Paris, and Milan—with favored market conditions, integrated intergovernmental support, active popular control, and a postmaterialist culture—theoretically lie at the "social-centered" end of the spectrum. The rest of our cities theoretically fall between these polar types. Subsequent chapters will deal with the impact of these four variables in greater detail and enable us to match theory with fact.

NOTES

i. New York and Paris are giant entities whose agglomerations are roughly twice as large as the next biggest city in their respective nations, and not infrequently they hold 20 percent or more of their nation's population. While the New York and Paris agglomerations can be called primate cities, Milan and Toronto miss the mark. Milan's agglomeration of over 4 million is Italy's largest, but it falls short of having twice the number of Rome's 2.9 million inhabitants or Naples 3 million. Toronto is Canada's largest agglomeration with 4.4 million, but it too is closely followed by Montreal's 3.3 million and more distantly by Vancouver's 1.8 million.

ii. Table 3.ii combines ordinal and interval data. While the ordinal data are interpretive, we find this to be the best way to realistically capture a complex reality and provide the most complete and accurate picture for each city. In table 3.ii we rank cities according to four criteria. Rankings are generally consistent with the contextual descriptions and market condition scores. Criteria rated as "low" are assigned one point, those rated as "moderate" are given two points, while those rated as "high" are given three points. A market condition score is assigned to each city, and the outcome designated in the last column.

iii. Thus Liverpool is formally part of a tight set of intergovernmental arrangements. In reality however, these arrangements have been ridden with ten-

TABLE 3.ii
Market Conditions: Summary Characteristics

City	Forces of Agglomeration	Economic Diversity	Tertiary Growth: >18% = High 17–5% = Moderate <5% = Low	Office Market Index: >55 = High 55–34 = Moderate <34 = Low	Market Condition Score: 1.00–1.66 = Disfavored 1.67–2.33 = Mixed 2.34–3.00 = Favored	Outcome: Disfavored Mixed Favored
New York	High	High	High	High	3.00	Favored
Detroit	Low	Low	Low	Moderate	1.25	Disfavored
Houston	High	Moderate	High	Low	2.25	Mixed
Toronto	High	High	High	High	3.00	Favored
Glasgow	Low	Low	Low	Low	1.00	Disfavored
Liverpool	Low	Low	Low	Moderate	1.25	Disfavored
Paris	High	High	Low	High	2.50	Favored
Marseilles	Low	Low	Low	High	1.50	Disfavored
Milan	High	High	Moderate	Moderate	2.50	Favored
Naples	Low	Low	Moderate	Low	1.25	Disfavored

sion through a substantial part of Liverpool's recent history. For this reason we classify it as a city of mixed tendency (see note table 3.vii).

iv. Since 1985 the *cumul des mandats* has been reduced to just two offices, and further restrictions were placed on the ability of big-city mayors also to hold seats in the National Assembly or Senate.

v. Intergovernmental aid can vary quite a bit from country to country and cross-national calculations are likely to be inexact. In the United Kingdom, cities carry out many functions, but central government gives localities substantial grants; in France, some functions like education are split between the national government and localities; while in Italy the national government absorbs the cost of most local services. Given these complications we have been cautious about the amount to be adjusted. Four major functions often undertaken by American cities are police, fire, education, and, to some extent, welfare. We take just two functions that are often carried out by European national governments: police and fire. Actual percentages for these functions were calculated for 1970 and 1990 and they amount to an average of 16.5 percent. Since these functions are not carried out by American national government, we add these revenue percentages to British, French, and Italian cities. Because Metro Toronto carried out these functions during the period examined, we made no adjustments for that city.

vi. Rémy Prud'homme claims that France is more fiscally decentralized than other European cities. Prud'homme's analysis is based on taxation and other fiscal measures. While Prud'homme does make a strong case, he does not account for substantive policy interventions, the force of the national bureaucracy, and the degree to which political elites at all levels are integrated within a national framework. See Prud'homme, "La France."

vii. Table 3.vii combines ordinal and interval data. While the ordinal data are interpretive, we find this to be the best way to realistically capture a complex reality, and provide the most complete and accurate picture for each city. In the table we rank cities according to four criteria. Rankings are generally consistent with the contextual descriptions and intergovernmental aid rankings. Criteria rated as "low" are assigned one point, those rated as "moderate" are given two points, while those rated as "high" are given three points. An intergovernmental support score is assigned to each city, and the outcome designated in the last column. Note also that the table shows how cities can be integrated in different ways. Naples is integrated through a centralized government, massive aid programs, and the power of political parties. By contrast, central government in Canada plays a limited role, and Toronto's integration was brought about by Metro government. Despite the fact that both Glasgow and Liverpool share a common national government, Glasgow is more strongly integrated within its subnational region.

viii. In fact, national legislation affords some uniformity to neighborhood governance. Legislation passed in the 1980s for Paris, Marseilles, and Lyon mandated that these three cities establish neighborhood governance led by local mayors.

ix. In 1994 the respective populations for each of Metro's cities were as follows: Scarborough, 548,000; Toronto, 629,000; East York, 104,000; North York, 575,000; York, 143,000; Etobicoke, 316,000.

TABLE 3.vii
Intergovernmental Support: Summary Characteristics

City	Unified Territorial Administration	Center-Periphery Networks	Regional or Metro Government	Intergovernmental Aid (adjusted): >60% = High 60–33% = Moderate <33% = Low	Intergovernmental Support Score: 1.00–1.66 = Diffuse 1.67–2.33 = Mixed 2.34–3.00 = Integrated	Outcome: Integrated Mixed Diffuse
New York	Low	Low	Moderate	Low	1.25	Diffuse
Detroit	Low	Low	Low	Low	1.00	Diffuse
Houston	Low	Low	Low	Low	1.00	Diffuse
Toronto	Moderate	Moderate	High	Moderate	2.25	Mixed
Glasgow	Moderate	Moderate	High	High	2.50	Integrated
Liverpool	High	Moderate	Low	High	2.25	Mixed
Paris	High	High	High	Moderate	2.75	Integrated
Marseilles	High	High	Moderate	Moderate	2.50	Integrated
Milan	High	High	High	High	3.00	Integrated
Naples	High	High	High	High	3.00	Integrated

x. Where possible, mayoral elections are used to gauge turnout. In cases where there were no direct elections for a mayor, council elections are used.

xi. In official statistics Toronto registers 46.9 percent turnout. This relatively low figure is due to the practice of counting all eligible voters and not just registered voters. We should also note that we were informed that provincial authorities overestimate eligible populations, which makes turnout appear to be even lower. Interviews with local officials in Toronto indicate that actual turnout is closer to 70 percent, and we have used that estimate.

xii. The table below combines ordinal and interval data. While the ordinal data are interpretive, we find this to be the best way to realistically capture a complex reality and provide the most complete and accurate picture for each city. In the table below we rank cities according to four criteria. With the exceptions mentioned in the text, rankings are generally consistent with the contextual descriptions and voter party activism scores. Criteria rated as "low" (or "passive") are assigned one point, those rated as "moderate" (or "mixed") are given two points, while those rated as "high" (or "active") are given three points. A popular control score is assigned to each city, and the outcome designated in the last column.

xiii. Wilson and Banfield, "Political Ethos Revisited"; Clark, Urban Innovation. Divisible benefits are distinguished by the fact that they can be offered to one person and withheld from another. This gives it great utility when dealing with materialist cultures that use clientelist practices to assure individual compliance. Redistribution, however, is a more a slippery concept. This is because it can entail both divisible and indivisible benefits, making it appropriate for materialist as well as postmaterialist cultures. Thus, subsidized mass transit will bring benefits to all who use it, albeit disproportionately for the poor who are less able to afford automobiles. Given their greater operational utility, we emphasize divisible and indivisible benefits as the best distinction between materialist and postmaterialist cultures. Redistribution is treated more cautiously.

xiv. Caro, Power Broker. Interestingly, June Manning Thomas contrasts New York's willingness to establish the first zoning law in 1916 with Detroit's opposition to such an initiative, which the latter city regarded as "Prussian and socialistic" (see Thomas, Redevelopment and Race).

xv. "NIMBY" is the acronym for the expression "Not in my backyard."

xvi. Both Marseilles's and Glasgow's cultures are influenced by a history of second-city colonial glory.

xvii. Thus noted authors on the subject say that cities tend to have new political culture or postmaterialist patterns when they are larger and have citizens who are more affluent, more educated, and who more often work in services, especially in professional and high-tech occupations. (See Clark and Hoffman-Martinot, The New Political Culture).

xviii. There are outlying cases here, and for good reason. Relatively low household size in Glasgow and Liverpool is as much due to outmigration of younger residents as anything else. Larger households in Houston may well be a function of the city's sprawling character and extensive land mass.

xix. Table 3.xix combines ordinal and interval data. While the ordinal data are interpretive, we find this to be the best way to realistically capture a com-

TABLE 3.xii
Popular Control: Summary Characteristics

City	Neighborhood Political Institutions (access)	Participatory Practices (civic life)	Programmatic Political Parties	Index of Voter/Party Activism: >70 = High 40–69 = Mixed <40 = Low	Popular Control Score: 1.00–1.66 = Passive 1.67–2.33 = Mixed 2.34–3.00 = Active	Outcome: Passive Mixed Active
New York	High	High	Moderate	Mixed	2.50	Active
Detroit	Low	Low	Low	Low	1.00	Passive
Houston	Low	Low	Low	Low	1.00	Passive
Toronto	Moderate	High	High	High	2.75	Active
Glasgow	Low	Moderate	High	Mixed	2.00	Mixed
Liverpool	Low	Moderate	High	Low	1.75	Mixed
Paris	High	High	High	Mixed	2.75	Active
Marseilles	High	Moderate	High	High	2.75	Active
Milan	Moderate	Moderate	High	High	2.50	Active
Naples	Low	Low	High	High	2.00	Mixed

TABLE 3.xix
Local Culture: Summary Characteristics

	City Traditions		Social Composition			
City	Preference for Long-Term Planning & Preservation: Positive, Mixed, Negative	Preference for Indivisible over Divisible Benefits: Positive, Mixed, Negative	Population Not in Poverty: >83% = High 83–71% = Mixed <70% = Low	Smaller Household Size: <2.27 = Small 2.28–2.59 = Mixed >2.6 = Large	Postmaterialist Score: 1.00–1.66 = Materialist 1.67–2.33 = Mixed 2.34–3.00 = Postmaterialist	Outcome: Materialist Mixed Postmaterialist
New York (5 boroughs)	Mixed	Mixed	Mixed	Mixed	2.00	Mixed
New York (Manhattan)	Positive	Positive	Mixed	Small	2.75	Postmaterialist
Detroit	Negative	Negative	Low	Large	1.00	Materialist
Houston	Negative	Negative	Mixed	Large	1.25	Materialist
Toronto	Positive	Positive	High	Small	3.00	Postmaterialist
Glasgow	Positive	Mixed	Low	Small	2.25	Mixed
Liverpool	Mixed	Negative	Low	Mixed	1.50	Materialist
Paris	Positive	Positive	High	Small	3.00	Postmaterialist
Marseilles	Mixed	Mixed	High	Mixed	2.25	Mixed
Milan	Mixed	Mixed	High	Small	2.50	Postmaterialist
Naples	Negative	Negative	Mixed	Large	1.25	Materialist

plex reality and provide the most complete and accurate picture for each city. With the exceptions mentioned in the text, rankings are generally consistent with the contextual descriptions and data. In the table we rank cities according to four criteria. The most materialist features (negative, low, large) are assigned one point, mixed features are given two points, while cities with postmaterialist features (positive, high, small) are given three points. A postmaterialist score is assigned to each city, and the outcome designated in the last column.

Chapter Four

SOCIAL- AND MARKET-CENTERED STRATEGIES

Science begins with comparison.
— Emile Durkheim

During the past three decades our cities responded to economic restructuring by choosing a variety of policy responses. Over time these discrete decisions culminated in strategies. In this chapter we describe these pathways of development and explore their character. We focus on two different kinds of urban development — social and market centered. Do cities pursue different strategic directions or do local policy responses suggest a common trend? What are the dominant patterns of variation? Do cities behave strategically over a sustained period? How can we understand their policies in a comparative context?

COMPARING LOCAL POLICY

Comparing development policies has its pitfalls. Within different nation-states, city governments vary enormously in their legal authority, their political scope, and their social disposition. This enables some local governments to undertake more ambitious forms of intervention than others. Local authorities in Britain, France, and Italy are unable on their own to provide many of the business incentive subsidies that are sometimes used by American city governments in order to promote job growth. These subsidies are often prohibited by national governments and have been restricted by the European Union.

Further, specific programs for encouraging urban development are far from universal. Various types of urban enterprise zones can be found in Great Britain, the United States, and France, but they are not duplicated in Italy or Canada. Besides, the content of these zones is quite different — some are simply tax-free havens while others engage citizens in an array of self-help programs. To add to problems of comparability, many — perhaps most — local governments are accustomed to working in cooperation with national or regional agencies. Recently, the European Union has entered the development game by funneling aid to distressed urban areas. Multiple actors make it difficult to distinguish exactly who is doing what or if a policy is more a creature of state, provincial, regional, or national authority, rather than a direct choice of local governments.

Despite these problems, it is possible to conduct a qualitative comparison of local policy responses. This can be done by focusing on the priorities of local government, by examining their willingness to seek opportunities from higher levels of government, and by understanding their specific political contexts.

Local political authorities exercise choices among competing values whenever they actively support, oppose, or ignore policy opportunities. This is true whether these opportunities arise as matters of purely local governance or are provided by higher-level governments or private-sector investors. This observation echoes Easton's dictum that politics is about the authoritative allocation of values for society.[1] Accordingly, our analysis focuses on the priorities that are found in the policies and activities of local governments.

SOCIAL- AND MARKET-CENTERED DEVELOPMENT

As mentioned in chapter 2, social-centered development puts a priority on public enhancement. Proponents of social-centered policies seek to distribute the benefits directly, and widely. Tangible evidence of these policies can be seen in green belts, low- and moderate-income housing, and historic preservation districts, as well as by material exactions from the private sector. This does not mean that cities with social-centered policies do not compete, but that they compete by offering collective benefits and portraying their environments as desirable.

By contrast, market-centered governments act much like Peterson's efficiency-maximizing organization and weigh their gains by the criterion of economic growth. This strategy places the highest priority on attracting jobs, increasing population, adding buildings, and revenue. Market-centered strategies target benefits to business or stress benefits that will accrue to individuals through market behavior. This distinction between the two approaches is often drawn in the scholarly literature, though there have been few systematic attempts to define it rigorously.[2]

Social- and market-centered strategies view economic and social enhancement differently and utilize different means for bringing it about. Table 4.1 summarizes these differences.

Social-centered strategies make demands upon private investors, often requiring them to furnish amenities or build for nonmarket purposes. These include tying development to public purposes (through linkage policies), higher taxes on business, and sharply curtailed funding for private projects. It may be that social-centered strategists seek votes and are motivated more by popular pressures to distribute benefits or demonstrate the collective uses to which capital can be put.

TABLE 4.1
Social- and Market-centered Policies

Social-centered Policies	Market-centered Policies
Economic Enhancement	
• high taxation on business and commerce	• low taxation on business and commerce
• restrictive zoning	• free land use
• few or no business subsidies	• extensive business subsidies
• integrated, planned land use	• discrete, market-driven land use
• public-sector-led development	• private sector-led development
• social criteria in business promotion	• commercial criteria in business promotion
• rail, metro, and other forms of mass transit	• expressways and freeways for private automobiles
• planned job development and re-training	• open job development by consumer demand
Social Enhancement	
• land-use exactions, linkage to public amenities	• free, "no strings attached" development
• public funding for land preservation	• private rights for land development
• strict architectural controls	• loose architectural controls
• neighborhood emphasis	• downtown emphasis
• publicly subsidized housing	• privately financed housing

In contrast, market strategists rely on supply-side methods to create capital. Their objectives are to stimulate the market place by removing restrictions on capital flow or infusing that flow with public/private funding. Ideally, this should entail limited public intervention, such as deregulating land use or lowering taxes. In reality, these objectives actually require government intercession. Methods for doing this include tax abatements, direct subsidies (grants, loans), or "packaging" deals for land acquisition and clearance (through development corporations). Growth through a market-centered strategy depends on the willingness of elites to furnish capital, and accordingly benefits are targeted toward those who assume risk.

When it comes to social enhancement, social approaches place a high priority on linking private investment to "place value," including neighborhood preservation and green spaces.[3] These approaches also emphasize redistributive policies and seek job access for the poor as well as "set-asides" for minorities or women. By comparison, market-centered strategists believe that individual freedom and greater choice enable the market to register broader community concerns. For market-centered strategists, development projects are more likely to be treated piece-meal. Discrete development is the norm, with no or few strings attached to employers or developers. Developers have few obligations imposed upon them, and they are not required to share benefits with the public or adhere to social criteria. In fact, market-centered strategists view the use of social criteria as hindering competitive enterprise. This distinction in urban policy affords a way of comparing and evaluating directions in local development policy. Are there important differences in policy agendas among the cities? Are social- and market-centered strategies mutually exclusive and do cities experience a conflict in managing what we have called a dual struggle? Or do cities employ a mix of both strategies, which can complement each other?

Social- and Market-centered Policy in the Cities

In order to capture strategic direction, we evaluate each of our city's most important policies. This is done over a thirty-year time span (1970–2000). We gauge the dominant direction and relative mix of policy strategy by reviewing each city. This allows us to offer ordinal rankings for each development model, ranging from high to moderate to low. Note also that the rankings for social- and market-centered models are not orthogonal. That is, it is possible for a city to hold the same ordinal ranking for both social- and market-centered models. As we shall see, Naples fits this category and ranks low on both scales. We begin with cities that are the most social centered and move to those that are moderate and lower.

Highly Social-centered, Least Market-centered Cities:
Paris and Toronto

PARIS: DEVELOPMENT THROUGH RIGHT-WING SOCIALISM

Paris is France's great city. It plays an usually prominent role in defining the rest of the nation, and for this it has always been a special case. In discussing Paris, we must keep in mind two fundamentals. The first is that one can hardly talk about major urban development without including national government. State initiatives are present everywhere — in the monuments, buildings, commercial complexes, cultural and sporting establishments, and ubiquitous public transit systems. This may be more or less true for other French cities, but it is especially valid for Paris. Second, one can hardly speak of the city's transition without paying close attention to Jacques Chirac. He became its first modern mayor in 1977, held that position while he was also prime minister, and resigned only after he was elected president in 1995. For eighteen years

Chirac and his Gaullists shaped modern Paris, overseeing the city during some of its most formative phases.[4]

While there is no doubting national presence in Paris or Chirac's personal imprint, Parisian development also transcends any single person. This is because the tools of development are both abundant and potent. The city's built environment is governed by elaborate plans, zoning regulations, and other controls. Limitations on building heights and architectural controls are strictly enforced. Whole neighborhoods are designated as historic districts in order to guard against overzealous developers. Some types of retail outlets also have size limitations, designed to ward off an American-style invasion of jumbo malls and supermarkets. While Paris has no shortage of mega projects, it also has kept its small shops and conserved its character as a city of small villages.

On a more general scale, large pieces of the city's terrain have been set aside as coordinated development zones (ZACs), special development zones (ZADs), or priority development zones (ZUPs). Density controls, or what is called the POS, are also used aggressively. Between the ZACs, ZADs, ZUPs, and energetic use of the POS, development is largely a public affair.[i] These tools enable a cadre of policymakers and technocrats to pour public money and infrastructure into the city's most strategic sites. ZACs enable the public arm to assemble land, ZADs permit it to guard against speculation by freezing land prices, ZUPs allow it to allocate exceptional funding, and the POS authorizes localities to control the utilization of space.

Enhancing these formidable public controls are Public Development Corporations (EPADs) and mixed corporations. Statutes governing EPADs and mixed corporations permit the public sector to establish administrative bodies to carry out development. While EPADs are almost entirely in the hands of public officials, the mixed corporation combines majority shares of public capital with private contributions (up to 49 percent). Supplementing these tools is an arm of the national government called DATAR.[ii] This agency is able to regulate development across local boundaries and sets the pace for the nation. DATAR's carrots and sticks have included the capacity to offer monetary inducements, withhold construction permits, or impose differential taxes in order to channel development.[5]

The activities of ZACs, ZADs, ZUPs, EPADs, mixed corporations, and DATAR have paid off handsomely. Major projects (shopping centers, cultural and sports facilities, museums) were located in special zones, while "mixed corporations" or EPADs carried out the work. An underground retail complex and park were built at Les Halles, at the very epicenter of Paris. Retail shops reach five stories below the earth and are joined by a terminal for modern rail and metro lines that ribbon city. Crowning Les Halles are a children's playground, a garden, and pastoral pathways for strollers. All building within Les Halles is governed by stringent density controls or the POS.

Not far from Les Halles, land was "ZADed" in order to build a massive cultural center. Chirac made sure that Paris's largest cultural center was named after his Gaullist mentor — Georges Pompidou. The mayor established social priorities by using development to create lavish gardens and promote exuberant street festivals. The virtual reconstruction of the center had a profound impact on adjoining neighborhoods. Elsewhere, old railway stations have been converted into museums and vacant areas filled with libraries, art galleries and housing. These areas have become hot spots for tourism and nightlife.

Further from the center, neighborhoods have withstood the test of time and in many instances have been revitalized. Typically, residents are relocated to subsidized housing estates built by mixed corporations. Social housing, or HLMs, are not just for the working class but are also a valuable commodity sought by the middle class.[iii] They are often located in good neighborhoods, and affluent families clamor to get onto HLM waiting lists. Poorer neighborhoods in the north of Paris have also been sites for social housing, and during the 1970s this sometimes uprooted the neighborhood fabric. More recently, the city has pursued a "softer touch." It has designated some of the most distressed northern neighborhoods as ZUPs and invested additional money into their revitalization. Special programs also enable residents to rehabilitate and modernize existing dwellings rather than resorting to the bulldozer. One well-known neighborhood, Belleville, succeeded in halting the construction of large apartment buildings and instead substituted smaller-scaled housing to preserve the neighborhood's mixed character.[6]

In the west of the city is the so-called "golden triangle," based in the eighth arrondissement and extending at opposite angles toward the sixteenth and seventeenth arrondissements. These three neighborhoods house the city's largest and most chic establishments. Banks, insurance companies, and corporate offices saturate the area. The eighth arrondissement alone contains 32 percent of the corporations listed on the Parisian stock exchange.[7] In the absence of massive demolition, development appears to be very limited in any of these arrondissements. There is virtually no space left in the eighth arrondissment, and the city recently cancelled plans to establish a ZAC in the sixteenth and seventeenth arrondissments (at Port Maillot).

The French have gone to great pains to preserve older sections of the city from the intrusion of mega complexes. To do this, office towers have sprung up just outside the Parisian boundary. Thirty years ago an

EPAD began the construction of an alternative central business district on a near-empty western plain, known as La Defense. Today La Defense sits on a massive 1,875-acre site with huge office towers that hold some of the world's largest corporations. This vast complex is connected to the rest of the region by sleek, fast-moving modern metro trains. All kinds of development tools were used to ensure La Defense's success. This included special zoning, differential taxes, prodigious financing, French ingenuity for a superb mass transit system, and the authority of DATAR to restrict competition.

Paris's last urban frontier is now being developed as an eastern counterweight to La Défense. Open land on the southeastern rim of the city is now the site of a large ZAC. The new area, now called "Paris Rive Gauche," covers 337 acres and stretches along one-and-a-half miles of the Seine River. The new ZAC already holds the National Library, built as huge slates of cement and glass cast in the shape of four open books. Over the next two decades Paris Rive Gauche anticipates building 10 million square feet of modern office space, residential housing for 15,000 people, parks, a sports complex, and a university. Esplanades, boulevards, and new metro stations already grace Paris's newest neighborhood. A subterranean highway was also planned for the area, but has been cancelled.[iv] The projected cost to finish Paris Rive Gauche is over $3.5 billion.

Chirac had demonstrated how a rightist political movement can bring about a municipal welfare state. He ably provided extensive public services, ranging from day-care to free outdoor theater and seven-day-a-week sanitation pickup. Music and art festivals are held periodically in neighborhoods, all at city expense. Streets are washed down daily. During his tenure nearly half the budget was dedicated to social expenses.[8] Of all the major French cities, Paris spends the most per inhabitant — 3,500 francs ($473) per capita as compared to a national average of 2,500 francs ($338).[9]

The mayor also boasted that his city could pay the bill. Unlike its poorer brethren, Paris has been able to mix business and pleasure. It has the highest per capita income in the nation, the highest land values in the region, and the biggest employment base. The city is ranked second, behind London, as Europe's most desired business location.[10] Because of its massive corporate wealth, Paris has one of the lowest tax rates and lowest level of indebtedness in the nation.[11]

Municipal welfare made Chirac enormously popular as mayor. At one point, the French magazine *L'Express* ran its front cover with a muscular Chirac flying above the city dressed in Superman attire. The caricature showed that Chirac the "Supermayor" was master of his domain. To the consternation of his Socialist foes, Chirac knew how to please business and the voters. During his race for the presidency he campaigned on the slogan "I will do for the rest of France what I've done for Paris."[12] Chirac is now gone from city hall, succeeded by his protégé Jean Tiberi, who was recently replaced by Socialist Betrand Delanoe. Notwithstanding allegations about fiscal improprieties during his tenure, Chirac's legacy endures.

TORONTO: DARLING OF RATIONAL, COMPREHENSIVE URBAN POLICY

To many Americans, Canada stands as the exemplar of urban policies that work. Those policies have a populist content and a penchant for rational, comprehensive planning.[13] Canadians also believe that markets should be subordinated to collective interests and that development can be controlled and evaluated as a long-term comprehensive, orderly process. There is some legitimacy to this view—at least there was up through the 1980s.[14]

While Americans were building freeways through their cities, Canadians paid attention to mass transit and rail lines. As America's downtowns fell into decline, Canadians were busily concentrating their efforts in city centers. And as suburban sprawl became the hallmark of American metropolitan development, Canadians were carefully laying out relationships between high- and low-density uses. Metro Toronto has been a remarkable illustration of these contrasts. Its policies have carefully nurtured a downtown core, extensive land preservation through high-density and diverse land use, and a network of cheap, accessible transportation (metro, rail, tram, bus).

The framework for these initiatives stemmed from an aggressive transportation policy that began in the 1950s. At that time the Toronto Transportation Commission (TTC) enlarged its jurisdiction from 35 to 240 square miles, enabling it to coordinate policies between the city and its suburbs. While TTC's recommendations for downtown metro lines were welcomed, its plan for expressways ran into headlong opposition—mostly from neighborhood and environmental groups. Popular opposition took aim at the Spadina Expressway, and as cities like Toronto and York joined the fray, the highway was severely curtailed. "The city does not belong to the automobile," declared Ontario's premier.[15]

By the 1980s rail and mass transit covered the downtown, and lines ran into the suburbs. From a mere 46 million miles of total service in 1955, TTC had increased its carrying capacity to over 120 million miles of service by 1987.[16] Toronto's mass transit not only served all parts of the metropolitan area but also held its own in the face of the automobile. More than 70 percent of peak-hour commuters through downtown Toronto still use mass transit — and this proportion has not changed for fifty years.[17] Toronto continued to build new metro lines up through the turn of the century.

Housing is also carefully managed. Rent controls legislated by the provincial government are popular and, for some groups, have kept the price of housing down. Metropolitan Toronto also had its own non-profit corporation that built low and moderate income housing. In principle, all six localities are supposed to take a "fair share" of publicly assisted housing units. In fact the suburbs have resisted and left Toronto with the bulk of that responsibility. All told, 16 percent of the metropolitan area's housing units are subsidized.[18]

Most subsidized units are well constructed and contain little of the social stigma attached to public housing. The most notable achievement occurred in the 1970s with the construction of the St. Lawrence neighborhood. The new project created a neighborhood where none had existed. Located in the downtown area, in the midst of historic landmarks, St. Lawrence occupies forty-four acres of highly valued terrain. Its 3500 housing units are built as a high-density, low-rise series of buildings, built in a grid-like pattern. It features a "city square" running through the center of the neighborhood, which provides its residents with an eight-acre, six-block-long park (18 percent of the site).[19] St. Lawrence is hailed as a project built in defiance of land values and as an example of how inner-city neighborhoods should be built.

Downtown development followed along. Throughout the 1970s and 1980s newly elected city councils led the charge for consistent, though restrained, economic growth. These efforts coincided with the election of two populist mayors, David Crombie and John Sewell. The prevailing idea was to pay more attention to the city's burgeoning neighborhoods and channel already robust downtown development into the suburban municipalities. Toward these ends some downtown projects were stopped, and the city encouraged new office development in suburban nodes around rapid transit stations. The city also adopted codes for maximum building heights, put a freeze on the construction of some office towers, and established tighter density controls on others. Historic areas enjoyed extensive protection. Even the city's aging though beloved trams were favored over less costly diesel engine buses.

There were, of course, differences in the city council over development, and a willingness to bargain over those differences. Mayor John Sewell and other left-wing allies defended the construction of high-rise towers, so long as developers provided a number of affordable units.[20] Other linkages were created between public and private sectors by granting bonuses to investors who met specific conditions. This practice

of "bonusing" meant that the city would allow greater densities in exchange for developer contributions in open land, landscaping, or recreational facilities.

All this is not to say that Toronto was without its grand projects.
Indeed, the list is impressive — Harbourfront, the Skydome, Euston Centre, and the theater district are some examples of how affluent residential areas, sports stadia, and office and entertainment complexes can
bolster the center city. But in so far as Toronto is one of the world's
great cities, these mega projects are relatively modest. More importantly, they are integrated with the rest of the metropolitan area.

For most of its thirty-year transition, Toronto emphasized the diversity and complementary features of its many parts. Balanced development was promoted by pooling municipal resources in order to minimize interlocal competition. During its metro period, Toronto's six
localities shared funding in order to equalize municipal services and educational expenditures. This kind of tax pooling allowed the poorest of
metro's municipalities, the City of York, to maintain a modicum of social and infrastructure services (public health, parks, street maintenance). Mass transit helped promote balanced development because
planners were able to painstakingly route bus, rail, and metro lines to
outlying residential areas. Despite outcries from the municipalities, both
the provincial and metro authorities managed to build low-cost residence throughout the area. This mitigated social disparities between the
six constituent cities, allowed them to build at higher densities, and
made the entire metro area more alike. Indeed, coordination among the
municipalities allowed developers to build office space downtown in
exchange for residences built elsewhere.[21]

Add to this interlocal coordination a strong governmental impulse to
intervene in capital markets. During the mid-1980s the Toronto Economic Development Corporation (TEDCO) bought mass amounts of
vacant industrial sites along the waterfront. TEDCO then proceeded to
attract small firms with loans, business incubators, and special taxing
districts that could provide amenities. While the strategy did not succeed, it did serve as a progenitor for new Harbourfront projects. Moreover, a provincial injunction against subsidies to business also reduced
interlocal competition. Recounting his years in dealing with the market,
one high-level official referred to supply side incentives "as a fool's
game" that he never really needed to play. "Why it's absolutely mad,"
he continued, "because the last deal you cut becomes public knowledge,
and you just ratchet down the costs to business while ratcheting up the
price for us."

Beginning in the late 1990s, the course of Toronto's development has
possibly been shifting. At $2,500 per capita, Toronto already lays claim

to having the highest social expenditures in Canada, and its appeal is wearing thin.[22] Top quality office space is taxed at an average of $10 per square foot, and this has contributed to a slump in downtown business. More office buildings lie vacant and for a time property revenues dipped. Complaints about high taxes, persistent unemployment, and an unfriendly business environment are frequently seen on the editorial pages of local newspapers. And most seriously, the election of the Progressive Conservative Government in the Province of Ontario has set a different standard. The conservatives now promote "A Common Sense Revolution," stressing markets and global competition. These ideas are coupled with a single mega-city intended to put Toronto at the forefront of world commerce.

Moderately Social-centered, Least Market-centered Cities: Marseilles and Liverpool

MARSEILLES: SOCIALISM GONE STALE?

Postwar Marseilles was largely in the hands of the Socialists, and this political fact defined its development strategy through the 1990s. Under the leadership of Mayor Gaston Deferre, the Socialists navigated between a centrist or moderate right and a Communist left. At first Deferre collaborated with the Right in an anticommunist block, but when the Communists showed strength among the voters, he moved decidedly to the Left. These maneuvers not only provided a considerable margin of autonomy, but kept Deferre in power for more than three decades. Socialist policies have left a strong imprint on the city.

In carving their own path, the Socialists adopted a third way strategy, which followed neither capitalism nor communism. As it was defined, the "third way" coupled high social benefits to a guided local economy. Commentators often referred to this as "municipal socialism" because of its blue-collar trade union constituency. Rather than economic development and grand projects, urban policy favored full employment and collective benefits.[23] Immense amounts of money were put into public housing and parks. Metro lines were also constructed and designed to carry the city's large working class to jobs and leisure. Added to the amenities were hospitals, schools, and day-care centers. On the economic side, Deferre was ready to collaborate with the chamber of commerce, but frequently under the veto of his working-class constituency. Office centers were planned in conjunction with massive public works, but most never came to fruition.

These initiatives were guided by a series of master plans and zoning regulations, beginning in the late 1960s. The master plans envisioned a city that would 1) function as the commercial heart of the Mediterranean basin, 2) represent balanced development within the larger region, 3) improve urban life for all social classes, and 4) accommodate a growing work force and demographic base, estimated to increase by nearly 40 percent. These plans were supported by investments in infrastructure and transportation. Strict zoning controlled population densities and separate areas were designated for industrial use, white-collar commerce, residential neighborhoods, and recreational spaces.[24]

"Third way" policies also had their political cachet. The poorest neighborhoods in the north of the city received social housing, working classes in the east got hospitals and day-care centers, while the bourgeoisie in the southern reaches of the city was promised a splendid downtown. At least some of the results were impressive. Between 1978 and 1993 over 40,000 subsidized housing units were built to accommodate 100,000 people.[25] Today, Marseilles has one of the highest proportions of social housing in France, amounting to 46 percent of the total stock.[26] A good many residents feel a deep attachment to their neighborhood, and even the poorest northern neighborhoods are able to claim strong popular loyalty. A survey of ten major French cities shows that Marseilles's residents have the strongest neighborhood attachment, and part of this must be attributed to social policies geared to its sixteen distinct arrondissements.[27]

All this was well and good, so long as the economy kept pace and population grew. But such was not the case. Instead, Marseilles's economy plummeted and its population fell. During roughly the same period of social expansion, Marseilles lost 17,000 jobs and 74,000 inhabitants. Unemployment rose from just 3.5 percent during the 1960s, to 14 percent during the 1980s, to more than 18 percent by the mid-1990s. As the economy went through a crisis, so too did the city's fiscal solvency. City services held up, but at a cost of mounting municipal debt. Social expenditures generated economic strain. Marseilles's debt has doubled in the past twenty years, and its repayment accounts for 25 percent of the city's budget.[28] The city now has the seventh highest per capita debt in the country.[29]

By the mid-1980s, Deferre's policies had run their course. While his successors were obliged to maintain municipal services and social programs, they also had to reach beyond Socialist nostrums. The Right blamed Deferre for having failed to stop the city's economic hemorrhage and business flight. The Left was fed up not only with its own patriarchal elite but also with social policies that reinforced the city's class segregation.[30] For a time the Socialists tried to hold onto old industry and resuscitate the center. During the 1960s and 1970s they came up with ideas for building office towers and locating a center for Mediterranean and international trade within one of the office complexes. None of these ideas could attract enough private investment, and they even engendered resentment by those on the Left who felt that these projects would exacerbate economic segregation.[31]

By the end of the decade, Deferre veterans were replaced, and other incarnations of the Left came into power. These new regimes tried to resuscitate older industrial wastelands and sought openings to the private sector. New leaders worked with the national government to create "enterprise villages" where small business could thrive. Despite the nomenclature, "enterprise villages" were publicly led. One of the largest areas, Château Gombert, was designated as a special development zone. The idea was to boost the city's sagging economy with high technology, but this failed to resonate. As the nation has moved to the Right, neighborhoods in the northern (most depressed) reaches of the city have been designated as "zones franches," or "free zones." These zones are versions of the Anglo-American enterprise zone. In France, zones franches are tracts of land that are free of taxes and other fees. Industry, labor, and residents also receive funding to stimulate employment, enhance training, and strengthen security. Zones franches are still quite limited and still in embryonic form.

A more distinct change occurred in the 1990s when the voters of Marseilles turned in a more conservative direction. A center right party under Mayor Jean-Claude Gaudin led the development charge. Business, labor unions, and neighborhoods joined the struggle. But even here the difficulties were daunting. Private developers were underfunded and weak, labor clung to wage/lesiure issues, and the neighborhoods held to a narrow vision of future policies. In response, Gaudin and his party pinned their hopes on an outside strategy—a grand scheme called "EuroMéditerranéen." The idea initially incubated in the chamber of Commerce and a local think tank. Their strategy was to link the city's most valued assets—its port and business center—into a single urban renewal project. EuroMéd would combine modern office towers, a new university center, housing, and recreation. It turned out to be an essentially massive venture, whose parts are interconnected by tunnels, highways, and local mass transit. In total EuroMéd covers a huge triangle of 750 contiguous acres running from the city center down to the port. The project encompasses Marseilles's railroad station and is boosted by the prospect that the national railway system's "fast train" will bring fourteen million travelers per year into the heart of Marseilles.

EuroMéd is cast in a public mold and has been suffused with 1.7 billion francs ($230 million) to launch it (50 percent paid by the national government, 25 percent by the city, and 25 percent by regional bodies). Over the course of fifteen years and jutting into 2010, the project is supposed to attain an investment of 20 billion francs ($2.7 billion). The expectation is that EuroMéd will "reconquer Marseilles's center" and restore the city's rightful place as Europe's great Mediterranean city. It has, in fact, been designated as a "national priority."[32] EuroMéd's design, architecture, and construction are carried forward by a public corporation led by technocrats. Despite its technocratic élan, the project is unusually sensitive to popular opinion. Housing comprises a substantial part of the project, supplying 4,000 new units to the city. These are to be equally divided among luxury, middle-class, and low-income units. More to the point, the bulk of existing housing will remain and will be rehabilitated at public expense. Very few households, perhaps a hundred inhabitants or so, will be moved. EuroMéd is determined to accomplish the impossible — at once not upsetting the existing urban fabric while also creating a "big bang" for the city.[33]

Part of that "big bang" means that other development in the city center should complement EuroMéd. Nearby neighborhoods are now targets for a series of mega projects (commercial and retail establishments, a grand theater, a municipal library, and new housing). The strategy is to create a critical mass around an attractive port, inject the adjacent areas with economic life, and lure other investors. This strategy is also assisted by the national government, which has promoted a spate of legislation designed to help cities. One piece of this legislation is known as the "*contrat de ville*," or city contract, and it is essentially a mutual agreement between individual cities and the state. These contracts integrate metropolitan areas at different geographical scales, so that Marseilles is linked not only to its department but also to the larger region. Collective action by all these localities is then used to spur development and combat social problems. Other pieces of national legislation enacted during the late 1990s and the early 2000s reinforce Marseilles's collective action with additional funding and more discretion over land use (see chapters 8 and 9).[v] The total impact of these policies is yet to be assessed, but whatever one might say, the French have put a powerful process into place.

LIVERPOOL: SPLINTERED POLICIES

Urban policies in Liverpool have deep fault lines. From the 1970s into the mid-1990s, the city made good on its left-wing reputation. Despite chronic economic decline, social spending continued to mount. Much of the spending was directed toward the city's working class. A bloated public payroll absorbed the dockers and assemblers whose private-sector jobs had disappeared. Public housing gave blue-collar workers bargain rental rates. Social services for the poor and elderly kept family life afloat, and youth programs kept potential delinquents off the streets.

Despite the obvious benefits, all this took place gradually and lacked direction. Led by the city council, the National Health Service, the university, and nationalized industries, the public sector soaked up part of the labor pool and provided needy citizens with services. Liverpool's splintered politics sustained the policy inertia. For much of 1970s and through the beginning of the 1980s, the city was governed by "hung councils" in which no party could achieve a majority. Liberals, Tories, and Socialists were either unwilling or unable to stand up to the unions and blue-collar majorities.[34]

For a while the city was held together by these nebulous coalitions, but 1983 proved decisive. In that year Labour took control of the council. This was no mainstream Labour movement in that it was heavily influenced by a Trotskyite faction called the "Militant Tendency."[35] While still a minority within Labour, Militant Tendency used its organizational coherence to run the party and, ultimately, the council.

The new leadership argued that private investment was not responding to inducements and would continue to abandon the city. In its view, only the public sector could restore the local economy, and public employment had to be the engine of growth. Militant Tendency also felt that the city had been too solicitous of business and immediately closed the council's promotional agency. It also embarked upon an "Urban Regeneration Strategy" (URS), which put resources into rebuilding housing for its blue-collar constituency. Working-class neighborhoods were designated in seventeen "priority areas," and public money flowed into neighborhood improvement. To make ends meet, the council resorted to creative accounting and foreign borrowing.

Although Labour's strategy alienated most of the private sector, it proved successful as a means of building support within party circles, the city's unions, council employees, and the unemployed.[36] Within a short period of time, 4,000 housing units were built and 8,000 units were refurbished. Leisure centers, sports facilities, and parks were also built. While figures on job multipliers are often uncertain, at least one study estimated that 6,489 people found employment in the private sector because of URS.[37] Others saw Militant's policies as a catastrophe, arguing that it was suffocating the private sector and bringing the city to ruination. One tabloid headlined Liverpool as "A City of Shambles."[38]

Confrontation finally came to a head in the summer of 1985 when the Tories took legal action and inflicted heavy fines on the councilors. By 1987 the House of Lords affirmed those decisions and removed insurgent Labour councilors from power. From that point onward, Liverpool entered another phase. While Labour still held power, the policy emphasis changed. The new strategy encouraged business and stressed the need for public-private partnerships. It also called for a greater concentration of resources on retail, culture, tourism, and commercial development.

These policies were given a boost in the early and mid-1990s through a City Challenge grant. City Challenge modified the tone of urban development by emphasizing business investment. At full speed the grants injected over 250 million pounds ($363 million) into the city.[39] By the late 1990s, City Challenge was succeeded by central government's Single Regeneration Budget. Grants from the Single Regeneration Budget also stressed public-private initiatives and physical revitalization (industrial parks, airport modernization). The flood of money had some impact. Retail outlets and commerce have begun to reappear in the city center, particularly in the vicinity of Clayton Square. Other small projects were directed toward retraining workers and improving local transportation. So quick and frenetic was the spending that jokes abounded about Liverpool as "a city of roundabouts," where everyone moved in circles.

Ostensibly, Liverpool would now compete in regional, national, and international markets. Economic growth absorbed the city's attention. The new city council identified key sectors to be nurtured. These included high technology, telecommunications, pharmaceuticals, and culture.[40] The city that spawned the Beatles would now become Great Britain's "Tin Pan Alley." Liverpool adopted a culture strategy and a newly formed city agency touted rock groups with names like "Frankie Goes to Hollywood," "Teardrop Explodes," and "Echo and the Bunneymen."[41] The logic of this strategy also meant that downtown would receive greater attention.

The biggest story in Liverpool is the redevelopment of its obsolete ports. The now defunct Merseyside Development Corporation, or MDC, began this initiative twenty years ago. Its genesis goes back to the onset of rioting in the city's Gramby ward, where white and black youth paralyzed the city for nearly a week. Known as the Toxteth riots, the massive violence tore the city apart, accelerated middle-class flight, and scared away private investors. Armed with land acquisition, financial assets, and planning power, MDC took charge of 865 fragmented acres of docks that were spread across three different localities. It was also charged with creating housing, building social facilities, developing commerce, producing an attractive environment, and most of all, generating jobs.

MDC was initially given over 200 million pounds ($290 million) to accomplish these daunting objectives.[42] While it was only able to leverage a disappointing 25 million pounds ($36 million) in private capital, the corporation has enjoyed some successes. Liverpool's once great Albert Dock has been restored and made into a tourist attraction. It now features a Maritime Museum, the Tate Gallery, upscale shops, and luxury housing. In spite of shortcomings, "water tourism" has worked to restore a fraction of the city's economy and rebuild fragments of its infrastructure.

While the approach is familiar, MDC did not tow an orthodox line toward the market. It distinguished itself from the staunchly capitalist philosophy of its cousin, the London Docklands Development Corporation, by nurturing a blue-collar constituency and stressing social equity. Along with upscale apartments for "yuppies," MDC built moderately priced housing, retrained workers, and opened up the waterfront to ordinary residents. Land use was tightly planned and MDC showed no inhibition about interfering in the marketplace. It readily consulted with housing associations and local authorities. Indeed, there is some truth to the claim of one MDC official that portside development could be seen as "a socialist initiative" and a step toward a "nationalized waterfront."[43]

Finally, Liverpool's infusion of cash has been complemented by the European Union. Along with parts of Sicily and former communist cities in Germany, the city ranked as having just 75 percent of average European income. This enabled it to receive from the EU the dubious status of an Objective 1 city. The new designation is supposed to funnel some 650 million pounds ($943 million) directly into the city. With matching funding from central government and private investors, an estimated 1.68 billion pounds ($2.43 billion) will pour into the city. The strategy is based on identifying five "economic drivers" within the city — big companies, small companies, technology transfer, leisure industries, and human resources.

Objective 1 has opened the city to the possibilities of further collaboration with private enterprise and stimulated regional cooperation (see chapter 9). Large enterprises will be given strategic development assistance such as site preparation and infrastructure investment. Small and medium enterprise will be eligible for venture capital funding. "Pump priming" resources are also offered to all types of business for marketing, management, and technical assistance.[44] A substantial amount of funding is also allocated for training and job retention. Criteria for Objective 1 stipulate that companies should be encouraged to invest in people and to assist them in the "protection" and creation of jobs."[45] All told, Objective 1 shares funding between market-centered initiatives at 56 percent and social-centered purposes at 44 percent.[46] Social initiatives remain an important component, among which is an effort to combat "social exclusion." Last, we should not confuse EU or national policies with diffuse, uncoordinated development. To the contrary, these policies are purposeful, targeted, and place oriented. Business is channeled into the center city and cannot do as it pleases. Asked what happens should a company refuse to settle in the inner city, an official responded, "Well we've turned them down and will do so in the future, and if business thinks it can go to the suburbs it is mistaken. Why, we just show these fellows the door."

City Challenge, Single Regeneration, and Objective 1 policies have had a visual and pocketed effect on the city. Nevertheless, the underlying conditions have yet to be transformed, and the city is still in the trough of depression. None of Liverpool's key indicators of distress has changed and much of the city is utterly poor. According to one study, gross domestic product within the city "fell further behind national and European Union norms."[47] Unemployment has been virtually unaffected within recipient areas and there has been no effect on the reduction of crime. There is some lag between the implementation of policy and its results. The critical questions are whether Liverpool can be saved; whether a center city strategy can work; and, whether putting money into Merseyside can compensate for the "region's inherent weakness?"[48]

Moderately Social- and Market-Centered Cities: Glasgow and Milan

GLASGOW: THE REGIONAL GAMBLE

Glasgow's priorities have shifted substantially over thirty years. Casting their lot with powerful agencies of the Scottish Office, city officials became enmeshed in a regional gamble for revitalization. At different times this regional approach has steered moderately in both social- and market-oriented directions.

During the 1970s officials sponsored large integrated inner-city programs that favored low-income groups in the poorest neighborhoods. This came after a dramatic shift in national urban policy, which reversed the postwar policy of dispersing people and housing by building new towns. In 1974 the Scottish Office launched a regional approach that gave priority to inner-city renewal. Local government was reorganized, providing Glasgow with an elected regional council (Strathclyde) that took over master planning and some services, such as roads and transportation, leaving the city's district council as a major housing authority and provider of common services. The lion's share of power and resources over urban development was given to a Scottish Development Agency (SDA), an arm of the Scottish Office.

The major SDA-sponsored program in the city was the Glasgow Eastern Area Renewal program (GEAR). Started in 1976, it eventually became the largest urban renewal program in all of Western Europe. Unlike conventional downtown renewal programs, GEAR sought to target most assistance to some of Glasgow's most impoverished inner-city areas. It had the explicit objective of regenerating the area economically through spending on job training, industrial location, and transportation. Social programs also provided housing and family assistance. The Scottish Office spent over 375 million pounds ($544 million) in a city with fewer than a million people.[49] Although led by SDA, local officials were closely involved in the planning and implementation of this initiative. This effort was also supported by regional council action to provide some resources to help support Glasgow's declining tax base and restrict industrial and residential relocation to new suburban centers.

During the 1980s there was a big swing away from equity-based development. When the GEAR project ended in 1986, the Scottish Office did not replace it. Instead, SDA priorities shifted to stimulating growth in areas that had the greatest market potential and would most easily attract private-sector investors—generally in the new towns, suburban areas, and the Central Business Districts (CBDs) of major Scottish cities. In 1991 the SDA was reorganized and renamed Scottish Enterprise (SE) to promote this pro-growth strategy. At the same time, it launched a new strategy that focused on upgrading social services in the inner city.

Even before this policy shift, Glasgow officials placed priority on revitalizing the city's commercial downtown. They employed land clearance, attracting new businesses, and used advertising to redefine the city's image as a place of culture, art, and tourism. The "Glasgow's Miles Better" campaign won international recognition as a successful example of how an old industrial city could become an exciting center of culture. Throughout the 1980s, city and SDA officials worked furiously to implement one major downtown renewal project after another. This included revitalizing the Merchant City historic district and building downtown shopping centers and high-end retail malls (encouraged by subsidies from SE), conference centers, and office developments. Glasgow promoted investments in cultural institutions, such as art galleries, museums, and theaters.

Although Glasgow's "culture strategy" remains ascendant, city officials have maintained commitment to some deprived neighborhoods through a variety of small-area programs. Yet these are far less ambitious and they receive limited funding. The local office of SE, the Glasgow Development Authority (GDA), leads an alliance of government agencies that is dedicated to promoting greater attention to eight deprivation areas outside of the city center. The GDA became an advocate for improving brown field industrial sites in the city—a priority of the local council. Overall, local, and regional authorities have sustained several modest public investment programs in housing, job creation, small business development, training, and social services. These are usually targeted at the city's peripheral housing estates, which are among the most deprived areas. Yet these programs do little more than cope with the social fallout generated by more robust market-centered initiatives of the city and regional agencies.

MILAN: URBAN POLICY ITALIAN-STYLE

Unlike Glasgow or Liverpool, Milan has made fewer efforts to target social assistance.[vi] Nevertheless, the local council has steered a moderately ambitious course by drawing upon extensive powers to give attention to social as well as market objectives in Milan's transformation into Italy's northern economic capital. Yet planning Milanese style is also permeated by political disagreement. Conflicts among politicians at the city and higher governmental levels together with bureaucratic rivalries among different agencies limit the reach of the city's efforts.

Like other Italian cities, Milan has very substantial powers over land use. National governmental agencies also play a powerful role in guiding the local economy through their investment activities in transportation, land development, and business, especially banking. These forms of state intervention give local officials potentially powerful tools for influencing the city's social and economic modernization. The elected Lombardy regional council also is an important actor in the economy of metropolitan Milan, yet it pursues a limited agenda. By law it must defer to the Milan council on city development issues. The regional government, which is primarily concerned with health-care issues, has few powers to influence city development, except in the area of transportation. Its main contribution to the city's development has been the expansion of the *Malpensa* airport into a major European hub over the past decade.

With the election of left-leaning administrations in 1975, Milanese officials used new laws from Rome to impose greater restrictions over housing and commercial development. Disregarding pressure to further concentrate business in the historic center, the Communist-Socialist coalition in power favored forcing business development into a polycentric pattern around the central business area. They hoped to relieve overcrowding, recycle derelict industrial areas, and create green space and cheaper housing in the city's periphery. Officials wished to achieve important social objectives while supporting market-led development.

During this period a major transportation project, the Passante, was initiated. The Passante would provide an underground high-speed train that arcs across the central city and links several train stations. This so-called through-line would help transform Milan into a multicentered metropolis by facilitating intracity travel and intercity train connections. Started in 1982, the Passante became the counterpoint for various redevelopment schemes along the route of the subway. At the same time, public agencies and private investors sought to modernize portions of Milan's central area (moving the stock exchange, expanding an exhibition center, creating a center for the fashion industry and related activities). Planners also launched schemes to redevelop derelict industrial districts. Such districts constituted 27 percent of the total land area of the city as late as 1987, providing enormous opportunities to decentralize the city's business centers.[50] By the 1980s Milan engendered a whirlwind of plans, projects, and proposals to remake the most important business areas of the city. At the same time, project planners were expected to do this while safeguarding Milan's historic integrity, protecting residents, and providing greater public amenities.

In most cases, social objectives (green space, public amenities, peripheral neighborhood improvements) became important ingredients of Milanese development. Nearly all of the major physical renewal schemes were initiated by public agencies under tight political control. They were overseen by bureaucrats employing infrastructure investments and public corporations to guide the projects. Since the schemes for enlarging and dispersing commercial activities were carried out only in abandoned industrial areas, there was virtually no displacement of residents and no encroachment on valued historic districts. At the same time, most of the renewal sites were planned to increase city green space and sometimes provide new housing opportunities.

Once the Passante became the centerpiece of Milan's renewal, an elaborate plan was approved in 1984 that essentially laid out eight scattered urban renewal areas, some of which were linked to the train route. These plans specified the responsibilities of public- and private-sector developers; they detailed public amenities and regulated the projects' impacts on residents. In general, the municipality carefully defined the proportions of land and cubic space devoted to particular functions, such as culture, retailing, finance, hotels, and business services. Further planning reviews specified even more details, accomodating some of the demands of the concerned neighborhood councils.

Planners were able to promote social objectives that are often ignored in cities with less regulated urban renewal. The area projects usually required that private investors also contribute to public projects. Widespread use of developer exactions enabled the city government to limit risk and sometimes to project a profit through development partnerships. In a many cases public corporations have played a key investment role by controlling land and investing in the new developments. One area redevelopment scheme (Bovisa) is dominated by publicly owned

Milan Polytechnic, which moved 43,000 students into the project. Similarly, the city's main exhibition center was expanded into the nearby disused industrial zone. The latter area was owned by the municipality and two public corporations. One, the Ente Fiera Milano, owns and operates the city's vast exhibition halls; the other, Sistemi Urbani, is part of a giant public holding company.[vii] Another derelict district (Bicocca) was recycled as a university site and for a new theater to host La Scala performances during the historic opera house's restoration. As part of the public-private deal, the landowner (Pirelli) provided buildings and infrastructure and in exchange obtained planning permission to construct a large office and residential complex.

Throughout the 1980s and 90s various area projects were modified to take account of resident objections and criticisms. This frequently led to the scaling down of commercial segments, expansion of green space and housing components, and alteration of designs to accommodate the physical impact on adjacent residential areas. In the case of the expansion of the exhibition center, for example, the project was halted after construction had begun on part of its facilities; plans now call for relocation to an adjacent municipality. In the case of a mixed-use residential-commercial complex, the office component of that development was eliminated.[51] At the same time, extensive public ownership of land and strict regulations limited eviction, stabilized rents, and contained property speculation by real estate interests and developers.

What most deflates Milan's planning is that so few of its programs have been realized. Thirty years after it was initiated, the ideal of a polycentric city remains a distant vision. Also, the modernization of Milan's central area has moved at a slow pace. The stock exchange has remained in the city's historical center, the fashion center is still at the planning stage, traffic and pollution have worsened over time. The Passante project was proposed in 1967, but by 2000 only a few stations were open and only one allowed for transfer to other transit systems. Although a third subway line did open during the 1980s, the city managed to implement few of the area projects. It was most successful in cases where a public authority owned the land (Bovisa), where the project was mostly in the hands of a single developer (Pirelli-Bicocca), or where money from Rome and the prod of a national timetable forced completion (expanding San Siro stadium for the 1990 World Cup).

The state-centered planning process often produced stalemate. Unstable political majorities in the local and regional governments, and widespread corruption, stalled projects for decades. Party factions often served as veto groups, slowing or stopping projects that were underway in order to wring concessions over jobs or on unrelated policy matters. Ironically, public inefficiency helped salvage the city's historic fabric.

Policy disagreement and governmental instability moderated the city's market-centered policies and bent them toward social priorities that otherwise might have been overlooked. Treasured historic areas in the downtown were preserved, residential areas remained untouched by urban renewal, and the city avoided overdevelopment. Milan never experienced the kind property bust that rattled cities like New York and London after developers defaulted, yet still managed to slough off most of its industrial past and acquire a vast service sector. Policy Italian-style is never as it appears. Grand plans are created on a strong head of public steam. Over time much energy dissipates and Milan is left with a fraction of its original hopes. But the city prospers.

Moderately Social-centered, Highly Market-centered: New York City

NEW YORK'S "MANHATTAN STRATEGY"

New York policymakers are absorbed in finding ways to promote growth. They struggle to manage a powerful, yet very volatile, economy. Still, public policy rarely reflects unqualified boosterism; local political realities force consideration of compelling social pressures. The result: a market-led strategy that usually incorporates important compromises with a social edge.

Even though New York is one of the world's financial capitals, policy elites do not take this for granted. Globalism has produced a roller coaster economy, which affords an unstable base for making public policy. The mid-1970s fiscal crisis occurred when recession years coincided with rising governmental expenditures and debt burdens. This led to years of austerity, cuts in services, and the hand of outside fiscal monitors who preempted elected officials. After 1981 New York entered boom years that led to the restoration of many services and a return of politics as usual. All this ended in October, 1987 when the stock market crashed. This period was followed by years of job loss as companies moved out of town or contracted their operations, office vacancy rates climbed, and city budgets were slashed. The city lost 350,000 private sector jobs from 1988 to 1992. During the late 1990s, however, New York's economy reignited. Fueled by a booming stock market, the economy generated budget surpluses that had not been seen in decades. The downward cycle of the roller coaster economy commenced again after the shock of September 11. Given such ups and downs, there is little wonder that the state of the local economy absorbs the attention of those who govern the city.

Ironically, the city's status as a global command post lends itself to economic uncertainty. New York is increasingly dependent for wages and revenues on a highly cyclical job sector. By the mid-1990s finance, insurance, and real estate (FIRE) accounted for 15 percent of the city's jobs, but 27 percent of the wages; the securities component accounted for only 4 percent of jobs, but 14 percent of wages. Overall, Wall Street provides about a third of New York City's tax revenues.[52]

Intergovernmental arrangements do not favor the city, leaving it to fend for itself in important economic matters. This also focuses policy attention on promoting the city's standing in the marketplace. Since the late 1970s federal aid to the city fell from nearly 21 percent of total revenue to little more than 9 percent. Federal programs, such as the Urban Development Action Grant program (UDAG) and the Community Development Block Grant, were cut back or eliminated during the 1980s. The only significant federal economic development program to come to New York in recent years is the Empowerment Zone program. In 1993 the city was designated as one of six federally designated Empowerment Zones, enabling it to qualify for many millions of dollars to assist an area that stretches from Harlem to part of the Bronx. This program has yet to actually receive and spend most of the promised monies and it has attracted little business interest.

In the wake of federal retrenchments, state aid plays a larger part in financing the city, although it has not made up for the net shortfalls. The state is strongly tied to the city's economy. Half of the state's tax revenues and about 40 percent of all jobs in the state are found in the city.[53] Despite this, New York's influence in state politics declined throughout the period of our study. Suburban voters steadily diluted the weight of New York voters in gubernatorial elections and in state legislative representation.

State regional agencies undertake some economic activities that benefit the city, but they are inadequate and undependable, and they often move in directions opposed by city officials. For example, the Port Authority of New York and New Jersey attempted to expand its regional economic development role during the 1980s. Under the leadership of Peter Goldmark, it launched a series of initiatives that moved the Authority beyond its traditional role as toll collector and builder of profit-making projects. Yet this did not always help the city. The Authority spent millions during the 1980s in expanding and modernizing New Jersey's airport instead of those located in New York. The Authority also refused to sell its valuable World Trade Center, depriving the city of millions in tax revenues yearly. The Authority's regional development programs shrank during the 1990s as revenues fell flat. Finally, the Authority's attempts to impose regional economic cooperation failed. In 1991 it succeeded in brokering a "nonaggression pact" among the governors in the tri-state region surrounding New York City, which required them to avoid business incentive programs designed to "pirate" companies from each other. The pact lasted four days. Unable to enforce this agreement, the Port Authority's leadership stood by as the pact was repeatedly violated.[54] Ultimately, New York City leaders must chart their own course.

The hand of the private sector looms all over New York. So conscious of growth promotion are city political leaders that nearly all important public programs—including zoning, tax, business incentive, infrastructure, housing, and transportation—are designed in ways that facilitate the leveraging of private sector investment.[55] New York is a high-tax city, but taxes are routinely reduced through abatement programs, land-write downs, and other exemption techniques. The most important programs for economic development are run by appointed Public Benefit Corporations (PBCs) that have considerable fiscal and political autonomy and are sensitive to investors. Unelected, these "money-generating governments" plan, build, own, and operate a host of development projects.[56] Responsible mainly to the bond holders who finance their projects, New York's network of PBCs makes sure that whatever happens, things will be built.

The dominant strategy has been to use city money and regulation to support the transformation of the economy into a world capital of corporate finance. This orientation has found officials concentrating their energies on attracting and retaining jobs in Manhattan with some overflow funneled into downtown Brooklyn. In pursuit of this "Manhattan strategy," they launched new business incentive programs during the 1970s to provide tax breaks to developers and commercial property owners.[57] During recent years, city leaders expanded the use of discretionary business incentives, almost always in order to attract large corporate employers. Few large business expansions or major developments take place in New York City without substantial tax breaks, loans, and other benefits.[58]

The city's "supply-side" packages of benefits to lure business are often negotiated in high-profile deals that are coordinated by the Public Development Corporation, a mayoral agency. They frequently amount to many millions of dollars and are taken up even by businesses that one might think are already well anchored in New York. In 1987 Mayor Edward Koch struck a deal with the National Broadcasting Company (NBC), which threatened to move its 4,000 jobs to a site in New Jersey after thirty-five years in prestigious Rockefeller Center. The network said that its existing headquarters were antiquated and claimed that there were cheaper sites outside of the city. From the city's perspective, if NBC left, other broadcasters might follow. Eventually, NBC decided to renew its Rockefeller Center lease and modernize its facilities there. In return, the city provided NBC with a package of assistance that included a tax break worth $72 million in real estate taxes over a thirty-year period and $800 million in bonds that were exempt from taxes. In addition, the deal also provided NBC with a freeze on future property taxes, while forgiving part of its commercial rent tax and freeing it from paying city sales taxes on at least $1.1 billion on the purchase of new equipment. All told, keeping NBC cost city taxpayers nearly $100 million in lost potential revenues.[59] Similar and even larger packages of benefits have been dealt out to financial companies, entertainment enterprises, office-building developers, credit card firms, banks, and sundry other businesses.

In pursuit of the Manhattan strategy, zoning regulations were revised in order to promote Central Business District (CBD) growth in parts of Manhattan.[60] During the 1980s "bonus zoning" became a popular technique for increasing commercial densities and building heights. Under this scheme, developers who left open space at ground level were given an upper space "bonus" that enabled them to exceed building heights. The mammoth skyscrapers made possible by bonus zoning blocked out the sun during early afternoon and created massive wind tunnels throughout the day. Although bonuses were supposed to be contingent upon the provision of public amenities, such as park-like plazas, these public benefits were often quite minimal in content.[61] Nevertheless, the use of bonus zoning mushroomed because city zoning law often granted these "as-of-right" without much public scrutiny. Similarly, ordinances were enacted that allowed air rights to be freely traded in high-density districts, enabling developers seeking to add floors to do so by purchasing the space from low-rise building owners. City zoning laws became so filled with complex loopholes, rights, and exceptions that builders and planners found them unpredictable and driven by capricious case-by-case judgments. Overall, however, they strongly favored private sector pressures.[62]

Other land-use modifications created new space for development in mid-Manhattan. The once open air and free space of Times Square were filled with buildings and electronic billboards. Its bawdy street life and peep shows were replaced with Disney-like facades and colorful glitter. Within a decade Times Square was transformed into a middle- and upper-class tourist attraction with new hotels, upscale shops, refurbished theaters, and family entertainment. All to be encircled by more skyscrapers, whose office rentals commanded premium prices.

With the recycling of strategically located commercial areas, luxury housing for corporate workers has become a high priority. Together with huge residential projects built adjacent to Wall Street (Battery Park City), upscale housing dominates the marketplace. Also, zoning regulations have been rewritten to permit legal conversions to luxury residential use. This includes the transformation of loft spaces into luxury apartments. These conversions fed by "J 51" and other programs granted tax abatements for renovating old manufacturing spaces. Further, conversion of single-room-occupancy (SRO) properties occurred through administrative neglect of code enforcement,[63] resulting in the displacement of thousands of low-income tenants. Most old SRO buildings became converted into luxury rentals in high-demand neighborhoods.

To some extent, the Manhattan strategy is a creature of market forces, not explicit city policy. Intense competition for jobs, the decentralization of many service operations to the suburbs, and the high demand for living spaces contribute to this phenomenon. To counter it, public officials have attempted to moderate market-led development by granting concessions — often very significant ones — to neighborhoods, tenant associations, and other citizen groups.

For most of the twentieth century, liberal traditions maintained interventionist policies that softened the sting of poverty. A large municipal hospital system provided free health services. Free university education at the city's public colleges was available to city residents. Access to a sprawling subsidized mass transit system of subways, elevated trains, and buses facilitated inexpensive commutation. Some of these commitments were reduced during the years following the city's fiscal crisis, but most remain intact. Despite a brush with municipal bankruptcy, the city's high taxes supported these services and continue to provide generous assistance.[64]

Although some city hospitals closed during the 1970s, the system largely remained. The City University of New York began to charge (low) tuition, but a policy of open admissions fueled its dramatic growth. Beginning in the late 1970s the city government took into public ownership thousands of units of low-income housing that were abandoned by landlords. Many of these so-called "in-rem" properties were often rehabilitated by the city and returned to the private sector, many under tenant management. In an effort to shield low-income tenants from growing housing abandonment, city hall became New York's largest slum landlord. In accordance with state law, the city government is obliged to provide shelter to anyone who is homeless — a responsibility that led city officials to build a vast shelter system during the past two decades. The city's rent control law still protects long-standing tenants, and redevelopment is subject to extensive public scrutiny. In the latter case, virtually all private development must run a gauntlet of review by neighborhood community boards in an elaborate process that enables citizen groups to easily challenge new building. This has kept policy choices from falling entirely into the hands of business.

Citizen activism frequently forces compromises that temper market-led initiatives. During the 1980s activists stopped a massive highway (Westway) project that would run along the West Side to facilitate access into the lower Manhattan business district. Westway was not just a means for transporting cars and trucks, but was supposed to accommodate apartment and office towers along its peripheries. Most important, Westway was expected to become a strategic artery for fulfilling the city's Manhattan strategy, enabling expansion of prime commercial and residential areas. Construction unions and developers stood to reap a bonanza from the project, but were defeated by a tireless citizen lobby and by law suits. More recently, developer Donald Trump proposed huge high-rise development on Manhattan's upper West Side. The Trump Plaza development, located on old New York Central Railway yards, recycles one of the last large plots of prime real estate in the center city. After negotiations with the city and the neighborhoods, Trump granted concessions to the public. These included smaller building size, expanded green space, contribution to modernizing a nearby subway station, and low-income housing units.[65]

In sum, while the Manhattan strategy is sometimes punctuated by social objectives, it is enormously aggressive. Development may be scaled back and additional benefits may be skimmed for activist neighborhoods, but they are rarely abandoned.

Least Social-centered, Most Market-centered Cities: Detroit and Houston

DETROIT: FACTORIES FOR JOBS AND MEGA PROJECTS FOR DOWNTOWN

Detroit went through its postwar history making the same mistakes and suffering the same consequences as other faltering American cities — only more so. The city was always scant on mass transit and had no commuter rail system. Detroit was, however, among the first American cities to introduce expressways into its central business district. With the encouragement of the motor industry, Detroit financed highway construction well before national legislation supported it. Local boosters believed highways, ramps, and parking lots would decongest downtown, make the city more accessible, and enliven business.[66] Exactly the opposite occurred as retail outlets left for suburban malls and offices moved to edge cities.

Detroit's experience with urban renewal was little better. Land clearance eliminated more low-income housing than it replaced, bringing about displacement of small business and more racial segregation. Between 1960 and '67, nearly 26,000 dwellings were demolished because of highway construction and urban renewal, while just 15,000 housing units were built.[67] As so often happens, new parcels of land were occupied by large, powerful institutions like Wayne State University and the Detroit Medical Center.

Popular dissatisfaction with the radical surgery was exacerbated by too little or too late citizen consultation. Segregation, poverty, and white flight created early foundations for a polarized social order. Toward the end of the 1960s, it became conspicuously evident that blacks had absorbed an overwhelming proportion of the displacement and had little to show for it, except pent-up social pressure. The lid blew off in the wee hours of July 22, 1967, and racial rioting engulfed the city for ten days.

For the next thirty years federal programs poured into Detroit. Among these were Model Cities funding, Community Development Bloc Grants (CDBGs), Urban Development Action Grants (UDAGs), and most recently, the city's designation as an Empowerment Zone (EZ). State and city resources often complemented the development package with supply-side sweeteners. Today some 1300 acres have been set aside as a "renaissance zone." The idea is to create a little Hong Kong in America's Midwest by lifting taxes, reducing land-use restrictions, and relaxing environmental regulations. Those businesses choosing to locate in the zone can receive waivers for every state and local tax, and are unhindered by zoning or architectural standards.

These initiatives do reveal a pattern of how elites go about decision making, how they apply past practices to current problems, or what Jones and Bachelor call "solution sets."[68] Typically, the formula consists of using public money to subsidize private capital around a few mega projects. All of Detroit's modern-day mayors adopted this solution set, and used it to form pro-growth coalitions. This included Albert Cobo (1950–57), Louis Miriani (1957–61), Jerome Cavanagh (1962–70), Roman Gribbs (1970–73), Coleman Young (1974–93), and Dennis Archer (1994–2001).

From this assembly Coleman Young emerges as Detroit's consummate builder, having cut a deeper path than his predecessors. He was, however, a builder who responded to actions taken in corporate board rooms. And in many ways he conformed to corporate beliefs that private capital and jobs were a singular solution to the city's problems. "There is noting wrong with Detroit," he exclaimed, "that three or four factories can't solve."[69]

The best-known and perhaps the starkest case of Young's proficiency was his success in attracting General Motors to a site called Poletown. When General Motors announced it was looking for a new Cadillac plant, Young jumped at the opportunity. Selected from among a number of competing sites, the Poletown neighborhood had the advantage of holding vacant parcels, an abandoned automobile plant, and proximity to railroad sidings and interstate highways. Eventually, General Motors and the city selected a 465-acre land mass and designated it as the Central Industrial Park, or CIP.

There were obstacles to making CIP a reality. Land acquisition and financing could be difficult, but these were overcome. With the help of the state, Young succeeded in invoking Michigan's "quick take" law. This law allowed municipalities to acquire property before actually reaching agreement with individual owners. By using the "quick take law," Young could avoid being preempted by competitors and strike an immediate deal with General Motors. Public finances could also guarantee performance on the deal. Detroit committed itself to at least $200 million in direct expenditures and a dozen years of tax abatements.[70] CDBG and UDAG benefits furnished some of the direct public funding, while the city bore responsibility for tax increment financing and other reductions.

Another difficulty with the CIP was that people still lived in the neighborhood and its institutions were still vital. The Poletown episode generated a good deal of local protest, but eminent domain prevailed, and the neighborhood was eliminated. Having made the social sacrifice, the city has found the economic benefits to be dubious. Cost overruns, balloon payments, and increased payments for land acquisition continue to be borne by the city. A reluctant city council has continued to grant tax abatements for new plant equipment, and new bonds have been issued for the tax increment financing district. So committed was Detroit to this market endeavor that the city followed through on its plans despite revenue shortfalls. While the subsidies poured into CIP, Detroit did curb allocational spending by laying off police. By most accounts CIP has fallen far short of expectations, but it is now touted as a symbolic achievement — a "loss leader" that is supposed to yield other benefits.[71]

Young continued along the same strategic path. Within just a few years, he had embarked upon another version of Poletown. Soon afterward, Chrysler announced its intention to close a landmark plant on Jefferson Avenue. Much of the Jefferson Avenue neighborhood was vacant, and the city owned more than a quarter of the parcels, so there was no protest. The new facility covered 637 acres, with an investment of over $1 billion and state-of-the-art robotics.

The "solution set" that Young used for Poletown was now applied to Jefferson Avenue. The support given to Chrysler's Jefferson Avenue plant consisted of tax abatement, loans, revenues from bond sales, job training, and land write downs. The city acquired 400 acres of land, relocated about 2,000 residents, cleared over 800 houses, and supplied the infrastructure. The property was then sold to Chrysler for $5 million, estimated at half its market value. At the time public assistance amounted to $200 million, though cost overruns now put the figure at $264 million.[72] An analyst for the city council put the cost per job at $124,57176.[73]

The mayor was elated at the prospect of having two brand new automobile plants in his city. He pointed out that new housing could be put up in the area and declared, "There can be no dispute that the parlaying of General Motors-Poletown and Chrysler-Jefferson has grandly preserved Detroit's tradition as the Motor City."[74] In 1992 the new Chrysler plant opened with less than a quarter of that work force, and the anticipated spinoffs of new industry have yet to materialize.

One Clinton-era project to be leveraged was Detroit's Empowerment Zone or EZ. In 1996 Detroit successfully bid for "empowerment" status by offering tax incentives, easy finance, wage credits, and technical assistance to potential investors. While Washington put up $100 million, the city obtained $2 billion in commitments or pledges from private sources (mostly from the auto industry and banks). Detroit targeted this initiative within a large swath of eighteen square miles, comprising 13 percent of the city's land area. Most of the investments have been geared toward the revitalization of manufacture, and again automobiles take the lead. Eleven EZ investments are concentrated in either the Big Three auto producers or second-tier manufacturers (metal stamping, electronics, drive lines). A remaining six investments are in general industry.[75]

In recent history leading businessmen have been automobile moguls, like Henry Ford and Max Fisher, or prominent developers like Albert Taubman. Their strategy was to build along the downtown riverfront and anchor investments within mega projects. Additional pieces of the strategy could be taken up by other developers, the city, or public authorities.[viii] At the outset, Ford took the lead in building Renaissance Center, while Fisher and Taubman developed Riverfront West.

Renaissance Center was conceived in 1970 by twenty-three business executives. Led by the Ford Motor Company and high-ranking executives, the strategy envisioned a massive, self-contained commercial complex built along the waterfront and connected to the suburbs by a series of autoroutes. Within a few years Ford put together a "RenCen" partnership worth nearly $300 million. The investors included America's insurance industry, some of the nation's largest banks, and Detroit's motor car giants. The city played a peripheral role and was limited to drawing up technical plans for land clearance and preparation.

Since then, RenCen had a checkered history. At one time the project's backers defaulted on the mortgage, and it was sold for a mere $72 million to General Motors. Today RenCen seems to have recovered from financial trauma. It occupies thirty-three acres that hold a seventy-three-story hotel, a number of office towers, retail stores, and restaurants. Looking at the skyline, RenCen is an impressive site. A closer view shows that it is surrounded by miles of still dilapidated, boarded-up buildings. More tellingly, RenCen is blocked off from the rest of Detroit by an eight-lane freeway. Its suburban work force can drive into it and just as quickly dash out without stepping foot in the rest of the city. Today, it struggles to find its place downtown and plans are underway to reattach the complex to the downtown mainstream.

Meanwhile, Fisher and Taubman planted their anchors at another end of the Detroit River. They opted to build upscale apartments in twenty-nine-story twin towers. Now called Riverfront Towers, this complex features tennis courts atop a parking garage, a health club, swimming pool, and boat marina. Moreover, the project is guarded by twenty-four-hour security. These luxuries were made possible by private bank loans, city-issued development bonds, tax abatements, and federal mortgage guarantees.[76] Detroit's boosters have also been joined by Michael Ilitch, chief executive of Little Caesars pizza company and owner of two sports teams. Ilitch endeared himself to the locals by moving his corporate headquarters into the city, keeping his teams there, and supporting a local theater.[77]

Development strategy is heavily geared toward building mega projects downtown and along the waterfront. On paper the pieces are in place. Renaissance Center and Riverfront Towers are accompanied by Cobo Hall (convention center) and nearby Millander Center (retail outlets and other uses). Added to the mix is Joe Louis Arena (home of the Red Wings hockey team). To build Joe Louis Arena, Young convinced the federal government to lend the city $38 million — to be repaid by advances on federal aid and parking bonds. While property and ticket revenues were supposed to cover the debt, these have not met projections. Pulling this together, a light rail system, or "people mover," circulates along nearly three miles of elevated track, covering major tourist attractions. The stops include restaurants and shops in nearby Greektown, the exhibition and sports complexes of Cobo Hall and Joe Louis Arena, and the hotel/office towers of Renaissance Center.

The downtown strategy has continued well past the Coleman Young era. His successor, Dennis Archer, began his term in 1994. Archer has a softer manner and knows how to reach out to business, not just within the city, but he had also put the touch on suburban money. Archer had continued plans to build a large retail-office complex, dubbed Campus Martius, located minutes from the waterfront. With his deft manner, well-honed on the golf course, the new mayor convinced a major high-tech company to move into Campus Martius. The company, called Compuware, will bring several thousand employees into the complex and become its anchor tenant. During his eight years in office, this was Archer's great coup—he had managed to persuade the company's owner, who had grown up in Detroit, to leave the suburbs and return to the city. While Campus Martius still searches for other tenants, Compuware's return has been billed as a larger movement back to the city. At least one other company has cooperated in Archer's corporate gentrification. General Motors has already moved its offices into other parts of the downtown.

Detroit's market strategy has other powerful, more radical, components—gambling and still more sports. With permission of Michigan voters, the city decided to adopt casino gambling. Three casinos have gone up and have been "temporarily" located in the downtown or waterfront area. One of these casinos is supposed to be moved to nearby Greektown. The city has an 8 percent tap on gambling revenue, while another 7 percent goes to the state. Eventually, the casinos are supposed to generate over 10,000 jobs. Sports prompted a different set of responses, designed more to keep existing business from leaving than attracting new ones. When both of Detroit's professional teams threatened to leave for more lucrative locations, local and state authorities responded. They generously offered to pay nearly half the $500 million it will cost to build separate, side-by-side baseball and football stadiums. City, county, and state officials reasoned that over 3,000 construction jobs and $354 million in hoped-for revenues were worth the immediate price tag of $240 million.

Despite its elite qualities, development in Detroit is hardly cut and dried. Assembling land on the waterfront is difficult and subject to legal contest or bureaucratic obstacles. While Detroit's mayors promise the world, the bureaucracy puts a drag on almost every initiative. The city is faced with a huge surplus of vacant office space and too few renters. Indeed, during his last term in office, Archer was put in the embarrassing position of not being able to spend federal EZ money. Citizens complain about lack of involvement, and corruption is endemic. The police are enmeshed in scandal, and the state has taken over Detroit's failing schools. While it appears that Detroit is a phoenix about to spring form the ashes, recent initiatives are hardly enough to compensate for thirty years of decline. When asked about all the publicity over Campus Martius, an insider put matters in perspective: "One major project in the last ten years? For a city of this size, that's pathetic."

It is still too early to know whether Detroit's strategy of selling itself out of poverty will work. Statistics for the late 1990s show a mixed picture, but there are some indications of improvement.[78] One matter is certain. Detroit's neighborhoods are still devastated and they have paid a price for downtown investment. Traveling through the city, one is struck by the contrast between a few glittering mega projects and vast stretches of empty ruin. On the summer day that Coleman Young announced he would not run for reelection, city residents were asked what had been the mayor's "greatest accomplishment" and his "greatest failures." They listed his great accomplishment as "downtown development," while his biggest failure lay in "ignoring the neighborhoods."[79]

HOUSTON'S COWBOY CAPITALISM

With an impressive skyline, a roster of international employers, and mazes of highway interchanges, Houston looks like an economic powerhouse. Indeed, it is now the nation's fourth largest city. Still, as described in chapter 3, it lacks the economic diversity and international character of "command post" cities. This reality was underscored during the 1980s when a serious recession hit Houston. The city lost 150,000 jobs — 10 percent of its economic base — in 1982–83 and more jobs later in the decade. Most of these job losses occurred as a result of falling oil prices in a city where energy remains the largest industry.[80] The city's mixed economic character leaves local officials and boosters decidedly aware of economic limits and reinforces pro-growth traditions. It is no exaggeration to say that Houston celebrates capitalism and leans to the market as its problem-solver.

This attitude toward the private sector has kept city officials at a greater distance from entangling federal assistance compared to other cities. City boosters have always drawn on federal assistance for infrastructure but not much else. As other forms of federal aid to cities expanded during the 1970s, Houston remained at the bottom. When federal social assistance diminished during the 1980s, the city generally did not attempt to make up the difference.[81]

Houston's relations with the state are important, but state government rarely plays a compensatory economic role. Texas has a strong home-rule tradition along with a restrained view of state power. Except for local school districts, local governments like Houston get almost no revenues from the state. Instead, the city is authorized to employ a wide range of taxes and user fees that usually do not compete with state revenue sources. The state provides legal authority to the city that facilitates its wide discretion in economic matters.[82] Most important, state officials have traditionally granted the city wide powers to annex unincorporated areas, enabling Houston to grow rapidly to capture tax rateables as they spread beyond the city borders, eliminating the possibility of becoming strangled by a ring of suburbs.

Now a mature metropolis, Houston must actively manage its problems. Despite decades of high growth, public intervention continues to be guided by traditions of small government and free enterprise. During the postwar years, Houston firmly established a free-market strategy. This had three components: free market development, aggressive annexation of unincorporated areas, and a policy of low taxes and services. Although city boosters have made liberal use of public funds for highways and defense, other forms of public intervention have been avoided.[ix] Most important, lack of public land-use regulation has led to continuous dispersal of populations and business. Today Houston has a population density of less than 2,000 people per square mile, only one-third of that of Los Angeles. Most of this growth was developer-initiated and supported by self-financing Municipal Utility Districts (MUDs), relieving the city from paying for much of the infrastructure in new growth areas. Although deed restrictions imposed some order, wildcat development became an article of faith.

Market-led growth was coupled with vigorous annexation of peripheral areas in order to preclude suburban incorporation. Houston acquired expansive authority under its home rule charter to wield liberal annexation power. The city council could annex outlying areas on a majority vote of the city without the consent of the subject community. Further, the city could extend its borders by imposing Extra Territorial Jurisdiction (ETJ). While this precluded annexation by another municipality, it did not obligate Houston to provide public services to the affected areas. Until 1980 the population of metropolitan Houston and Harris County doubled every twenty years. Together with Houston's dominant representation on such county and regional bodies as the Port of Houston Authority, these powers extended the city's control over the region.

Throughout its evolution Houston doggedly pursued a policy of low taxes and low public services. At the same time, the growing economy allowed the city to generate more tax monies without altering its low-tax commitment. Despite growing city wealth, Houston's spending on social services, education, and amenities remained very low. Instead, city leaders turned elsewhere and looked to state government to provide improvements.

More recently, these minimalist policies have been challenged. The combination of low-density living and an absence of mass transportation has brought traffic congestion to the point of suffocation. Adding to these burdens, the city has been forced to borrow millions to obtain water. And decades of aggressive annexation have now brought a price. These escalating service demands coincided with the dramatic slump in Houston's economy during the 1980s. A real estate bust wiped out thousands of businesses, including huge numbers of local savings banks and developers. Local politicians had no choice but to increase real estate, sales, and property taxes. Houston's combined tax burden on local residents is now close to the average for metropolitan areas. Its local debt burdens now exceed national averages.

City boosters sought ways of diversifying the economy. Officials began to make more use of subsidies to attract corporate jobs, rather than rely on a low tax, minimal governmental environment. Even as the city was experiencing a revenue shortfall, the city put together a $225 million package of business incentives to keep Compaq Computers in Houston.[83] Annexation is no longer a solution to ensuring growth.

Despite their compromises, officials have not dramatically veered from their highly market-centered posture. Planning remains minimal and largely a private-sector matter. The city planning commission and small department staff do not undertake comprehensive planning, but react to private initiatives from developers. Their major function is to review and approve land subdivision plats and plans. Project engineers, who are invariably employed by developers, do most of the certification for construction projects. As it turns out, the chamber of commerce has become Houston's de facto planning agency.

Houston continues to defer to the private sector. Proposals for a zoning ordinance have been repeatedly rejected. When last debated and rejected in 1993, Houston was the only major American city without this land-use tool. Although the city has struggled to improve mass transit, neither the financial nor political support has arisen for major investments. The city's bus system is inadequate. Proposals for a rail system that would serve downtown areas were defeated in the 1980s by officials of the MTA board. This has made Houston an essentially automobile city. City, county, and state officials scramble to keep up with the city's growing traffic congestion by upgrading roads, building toll roads around and through the city, and debating how to regulate off-street parking problems. City legal staff continue to fight off federal environmental officials who demand that something be done about Houston's notoriously low air quality.

Attention to social policy usually takes a back seat to growth. Attempts to direct greater resources to needy neighborhoods improved after the election of mayor Robert Lanier in 1991. He started a "Neighborhood-to-Standards" drive aimed at upgrading inner-city areas and improving their streets. But Houston still remains a low-service city, where most public projects are expected to pay their own way. The largest recent investments have been in toll roads and airport expansions—all financed by user fees or noncity taxes.

Social services, which are mostly state financed, remain minimal and public amenities tend to be spotty. Although Houston is the fourth largest American city, it has ranked twenty-third in libraries and eighteenth in museums among the top twenty-five metropolitan areas. In 1993 Houston purchased the fewest number of new volumes per capita in its libraries of any of the top twenty-five metropolitan areas. In contrast, Houston rated sixth in professional ballet and eighth in professional sports, both of which are heavily supported by private contributions.[84]

Laissez-faire government continues to this day, even as public policy has been changing in recent years to accommodate Houston's economic maturity. As we describe later, recent decades have witnessed greater recognition of the need to do something about the inevitable problems of an older big-city economy, such as environmental decay, traffic congestion, infrastructure deterioration, crime, and the lagging quality of public services. As city officials have cast about for solutions, taxes have gone up and the size of government has grown. Nevertheless, Houston's romance with limited government and the virtues of capitalism still dominate the city's approach to development.

Least Social-centered and Least Market-centered City: Naples

NAPLES: CLIENTELISM AS URBAN POLICY

"See Naples Before It Dies," quipped a newspaper headline in a play on Goethe's famous words about the city.[x] Until recently, Naples paid little attention to upgrading the social lives of its citizens or to promoting business prosperity. Yet this performance is not for want of public funds. Naples and its region have been the recipient of massive public assistance from the national government to modernize its economy. These national aid programs were sustained by the fact that Naples and much of the South formed a massive voter base of the powerful Christian Democratic party. While these aid programs have diminished, Naples has been receiving greater aid from the European Union.

The city has a long history of projects left on the drawing boards, and funds dissipated by inefficient bureaucracies or siphoned off by pervasive corruption. During 1974–84 the region received large amounts of aid from the European Union, but it could spend only 33 percent of these funds. In the following decade funds devoted to the region were greatly increased, but its ability to spend allocated funds did not improve.[85] Lack of planning, poor administration, political instability, and organized crime were among the forces at work.[86] The planning, audit, and evaluation procedures required by the European Union have been so difficult for Neapolitan bureaucrats to meet that funds remain unspent.

Despite these obstacles, local politicians cast about for programs to sustain industrial activity and look for ways of coping with the region's deindustrialization. After national policies turned away from reliance on state-sponsored industrialization during the 1970s, Neapolitan officials put priority on stimulating service job growth in the city. First, they allowed more flexibility in the planning rules. For example, by relaxing environmental regulations they made room for several public works projects, in particular a new university campus, which was built in the city despite its originally planned location outside the city boundaries.

Second, they made use of state urban development programs. In the 1980s and early 1990s Rome financed new public investments in Naples. The focus was on large-scale projects that were carried out with little regard for established master plans. They included a new university campus, renewal of the city's soccer stadium and related infrastructures, a new ring road around the city, and a new business center, the Centro Direzionale, described later. These various projects were expressions of a de facto urban policy that saw large-scale capital improvements as keys to city revitalization, an idea that dominated Italy's postwar programs to aid the Mezzogiorno.

The building of large-scale projects was also favored for political reasons, namely to feed the clientelistic relationship between politicians and their constituencies. Particularly in the 1980s, political leaders and heads of the private and state-owned companies benefited from big construction projects. Included in the dominant policy coalitions were the Neapolitan ministers in Rome, local politicians in Naples, as well as national and local entrepreneurs in construction and related businesses. The beneficiaries also included organized crime. During the 1980s and 1990s organized crime became heavily involved in the local economy and infiltrated the political system. According to a CEO of a local construction company testifying before a judicial court, 3 percent of the nominal value of each contract was paid to politicians. In the area controlled by the Camorra, an additional 3 percent was due and paid to this organization. Neapolitan urban policy was essentially a by-product of the public funds made available under various national "emergency" programs, chiefly within the framework of the post-earthquake reconstruction program. National leaders with electoral constituencies in the region channeled these financial resources to the area and distributed them to companies (mainly builders) involved in the redevelopment process and to local bureaucracies and dominant political parties.

During the dozen years following the 1980 earthquake, Naples received a $10 billion share of the national government's massive $33.3 billion reconstruction program.[87] The planning and spending of this emergency aid virtually displaced all other economic development activities. City and regional governments focused on demolishing damaged housing, resettling families, and building nearly 21,000 units of new housing. Authorities used emergency legislation and funding to undertake a wide range of land clearance and infrastructure projects.

Despite the efforts, these projects were heavily burdened by lack of planning, huge cost overruns, and shoddy construction. By the end of the 1980s Naples was studded with useless roadways, incomplete viaducts, waterless swimming pools, and a derelict infrastructure. Even when completed, cost overruns and corruption took their toll. Renewal of the city's stadium for the 1990 World Cup cost three times as much as originally estimated. In subsequent investigations, the courts found that systematic corruption led to grossly inflated costs. Fifteen members of parliament from the region, including some from Naples, were brought to trial in 1994 and some were convicted.[88]

Even in the face of appalling corruption and waste, local and national politicians continued to advocate expansion of reconstruction projects. They proposed turning the redevelopment machine to target the city's historic center in an ambitious project named "Neonapoli." The first initiative was intended as a comprehensive program for the regeneration of the historical center of the city. Large parts of the center were to be torn down in order to make room for new high-cost apartment complexes. The second aimed to convert the abandoned Italsider steel plant in Bagnoli into a site for tourism and a technology park. These plans, however, were undermined by anticorruption investigations that swept through Naples and its region during 1992–93. By 2000 only the Bagnoli project came back on the drawing boards.

Throughout the past three decades, a major renewal project, the Centro Direzionale, came underway. It was planned to turn a derelict industrial area near the railway station into a modern commercial hub. This bold project had everything going for it. Public agencies dominated its development and financing. Most of the property was in public hands and the area divided into two giant parcels. A western part was owned by a state-managed company called Italstat, while a larger eastern part was almost entirely owned by the municipality. Without any private land ownership problems, the proposal to build a business center took shape in the early 1960s.

The actual planning of the project began only twenty years later, however. In this long incubation period powerful vehicles for public intervention were trundled in to steer the project. A mixed, but essentially public, corporation called Mededil was formed that gradually acquired land in the area. As Mededil came under the control of the state, it was endowed with the necessary development capital. Second, efforts to advance the project were given a boost with a decision to build new

Law Courts for the city in the Centro. The location of the Law Courts was supposed to attract other public bodies and private offices and to provide an additional rationale for the extension of public transportation to the area. After the project was included in the city's master plan, funds for it were made available through a special national program in 1981.

More than thirty years after it was first proposed, however, the Centro Direzionale is only half finished—mostly consisting of the portion not owned by the state. By 2000 the built portion has failed to spark much economic development, leaving the city with a White Elephant of sorts. Job creation in the Centro has been disappointing, considering the huge investment of public monies. Most of the jobs are not new, but the result of companies' relocation from other parts of the city. Few shopping facilities appear in the area, visibly indicating that the Centro Direzionale has not yet attracted the critical mass of people moving through it to lure shopkeepers. Nor has the clustering of companies from the city's other districts into the Centro generated new real estate development and commercial enterprises. The relocation of public offices is far from complete, delaying the generation of related services. Only in 1999 did a single new employer decide to locate in the Centro—significantly it is a newly formed state agency, rather than a private company. Current estimates of vacancy rates confirm the difficulties ahead in making the Centro Direzionale a prominent location for business.

Elections in 1993 brought Communist Antonio Bassolino to the mayoralty. Until 2000, when Bassolino left Naples for the presidency of the region (Campania), he vigorously pursued institutional reform, establishing orderly public policy and building public confidence in the city. While he proved unable to move the glacier-like pace of government, Bassolino sought to mix social and market strategies. Local development shifted from large-scale public works to low-cost micro projects. The mayor blocked construction in the fragile historic center of the city, where speculators were poised to begin slash-and-burn-style redevelopment. The council approved plans to transform the city's abandoned steelworks. Once cleared and cleaned from industrial pollution, the huge site is scheduled to be turned into a park surrounded by hotels, shops, and a conference center. The mayor also pledged to complete construction of the Centro Direzionale. City hall now intends to complete undeveloped sections at a lower density under guidelines defined by a new master plan.

Since Bassolino's election it is evident that professional planning has enjoyed a renaissance. The master planning process has begun to form the basis for policy-making, helping local players identify new strategic alternatives. The current plan envisons the regeneration of the city periphery and renewal of abandoned industrial areas. Most projects are to be managed by newly dedicated agencies controlled by the municipality.[89] The agencies are also expected to be prime actors in using new policy instruments to obtain financial resources from the central government and to form public-private partnerships whenever possible. During recent years under reformer Bassolino, the municipal government displayed a strong hand in redefining the main strategies and policies for the city. What remains to be seen is whether his successor, Mayor Rosa Russa Iervolino can continue to steer the city in the new direction. Naples is far from dead, but the struggle to revive it faces formidable obstacles.

IS THERE A DUAL URBAN POLICY STRUGGLE?

Our review of thirty years of policy highlights important differences and similarities in local responses. What stands out most is the variation in policy. Some cities asserted an ambitious social agenda while others favored economic growth. Still others followed a middle path, incorporating social and economic agendas. This variation suggests the importance of local politics in playing the global development game. Despite its force, global economic restructuring has not homogenized local politics.

Figures 4.1 and 4.2 show how our cities compare in development policies. The figures respectively display degrees of social-centered and market-centered strategies along with policy highlights for each city. In social-centered policy, Paris and Toronto lead the pack. These cities are followed by Marseilles and Liverpool. Glasgow, Milan, and New York occupy intermediate positions. Naples, Detroit, and Houston are clustered near the bottom. In market-centered policy, the American cities — Houston, Detroit, and New York — are at the top. Glasgow and Milan occupy intermediate positions. Toward the bottom we find Liverpool, Paris, Toronto, and, last of all, Naples.

A glance at these figures helps us answer the question of whether there is a dual struggle over urban policy. Scholars frequently depict urban development as a struggle between different classes of citizens over specific objectives. So-called "pro-growth" programs are presented as competing alternatives to "progressive," or "community," strategies.[90] The reasons for this vary. Some theorists believe that choices over economic development catalyze inherent conflicts over core values. Left-wing theorists contend that pro-growth programs reflect the capitalist market preference for "exchange" rather than "use" value.[91] If one strategy is to prevail, the other must necessarily yield.[xi]

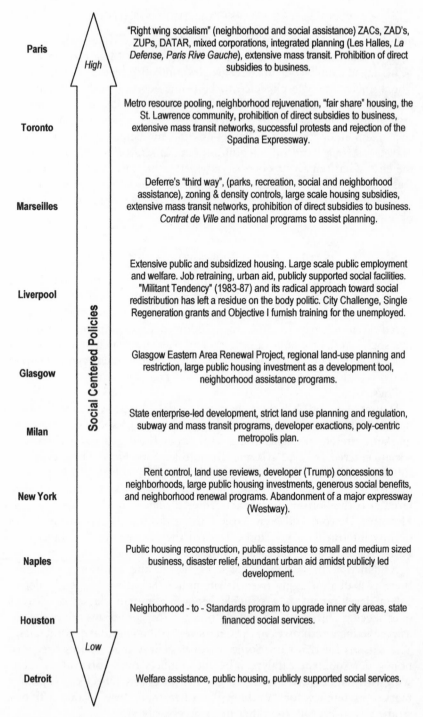

Figure 4.1. Social-centered Policies in Ten Cities.

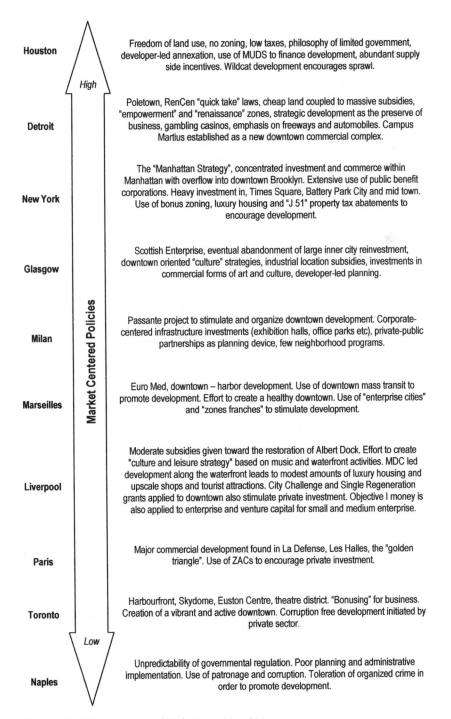

Houston	*High*	Freedom of land use, no zoning, low taxes, philosophy of limited government, developer-led annexation, use of MUDS to finance development, abundant supply side incentives. Wildcat development encourages sprawl.
Detroit		Poletown, RenCen "quick take" laws, cheap land coupled to massive subsidies, "empowerment" and "renaissance" zones, strategic development as the preserve of business, gambling casinos, emphasis on freeways and automobiles. Campus Martius established as a new downtown commercial complex.
New York		The "Manhattan Strategy", concentrated investment and commerce within Manhattan with overflow into downtown Brooklyn. Extensive use of public benefit corporations. Heavy investment in, Times Square, Battery Park City and mid town. Use of bonus zoning, luxury housing and "J 51" property tax abatements to encourage development.
Glasgow	Market Centered Policies	Scottish Enterprise, eventual abandonment of large inner city reinvestment, downtown oriented "culture" strategies, industrial location subsidies, investments in commercial forms of art and culture, developer-led planning.
Milan		Passante project to stimulate and organize downtown development. Corporate-centered infrastructure investments (exhibition halls, office parks etc), private-public partnerships as planning device, few neighborhood programs.
Marseilles		Euro Med, downtown – harbor development. Use of downtown mass transit to promote development. Effort to create a healthy downtown. Use of "enterprise cities" and "zones franches" to stimulate development.
Liverpool		Moderate subsidies given toward the restoration of Albert Dock. Effort to create "culture and leisure strategy" based on music and waterfront activities. MDC led development along the waterfront leads to modest amounts of luxury housing and upscale shops and tourist attractions. City Challenge and Single Regeneration grants applied to downtown also stimulate private investment. Objective I money is also applied to enterprise and venture capital for small and medium enterprise.
Paris		Major commercial development found in La Defense, Les Halles, the "golden triangle". Use of ZACs to encourage private investment.
Toronto	*Low*	Harbourfront, Skydome, Euston Centre, theatre district. "Bonusing" for business. Creation of a vibrant and active downtown. Corruption free development initiated by private sector.
Naples		Unpredictability of governmental regulation. Poor planning and administrative implementation. Use of patronage and corruption. Toleration of organized crime in order to promote development.

Figure 4.2. Market-centered Policies in Ten Cities.

Mainstream theorists believe that there is a social tradeoff between equality and efficiency in economic policy.[92] Peterson views redistributive programs as essentially counterproductive in promoting a community's market position.[93] He contrasts them to developmental policies that can enhance the wealth of the locality. For these scholars, cities must choose between development or redistributive strategies, and it is apparent that development will win. Regime and coalition theorists also see a struggle between social priorities (anti-growth) and market priorities (pro-growth). They believe that pro-growth coalitions systematically exclude nonbusiness interests and that asymmetrical power relationships always favor business.[xii]

Our comparative analysis does not lend support to the idea of a dual struggle, at least on a cross-national level. In most cases local government responses are not bimodal. Market-centered cities do not always neglect social objectives and social-centered cities do not always reject market considerations. A tendency to operate in a mutually exclusive strategic direction did occur in four out of ten cities (Detroit, Houston, Toronto, and Paris), while six cities showed no such inclination.

Table 4.2 and Figure 4.3 show our ten cities arrayed along social- and market-centered categories. The table displays this variation in ordinal rankings by column, while the figure shows cities located along a continuum.

Detroit and Houston promote strongly market-oriented options while giving little attention to social priorities. Toronto and Paris exhibit opposite tendencies. Elsewhere city politicians mix and match, so to speak, and in one city — Naples — there is little emphasis given to either strate-

TABLE 4.2
Policy Orientation in Ten Cities: Social and Market

City	Social-centered Policy	Market-centered Policy
Paris	High	Low
Toronto	High	Low
Marseilles	Moderate	Low
Liverpool	Moderate	Low
Glasgow	Moderate	Moderate
Milan	Moderate	Moderate
New York	Moderate	High
Naples	Low	Low
Detroit	Low	High
Houston	Low	High

Social Centered

Low					High
Houston Detroit	Naples	New York City	Glasgow Milan	Liverpool Marseilles	Paris Toronto

Market Centered

Low			High
Paris Toronto Naples	Marseilles Liverpool	Glasgow Milan	New York Detroit Houston

Figure 4.3. Social- and Market-centered Cities, 1970–2000.

gic direction. Glasgow, Milan and Marseilles promoted both development strategies in reasonably equal proportions. As of late, Liverpool shows this tendency. New York leaned more toward the market strategy, yet it remained moderate in social-centered development.

When local officials in our "mix and match" cities were asked about different policy orientations, few expressed an awareness that they might be running in different directions. By and large, officials did not see business growth and social benefits as competitive choices. One Scottish official explained, "Scottish Enterprise has a clear outlook. We look for opportunities presented by the marketplace and act accordingly. We think that everybody gains by that practice."

Even Toronto does not see itself in a single strategic corner. Referring to a period when the city actually encouraged downtown development, one official described the action as "a real balancing act" in which "enough money needed to be generated in order to support social programs."

Overall, European officials were less inclined than North Americans to view business and social enhancement as mutually exclusive or in the least bit competitive. This was particularly true for Italian cities, where mixed public-private corporations led or even dominated many of the largest development projects. While these officials frequently understood community development in terms of social class competition, the actual formulation and implementation of programs were rarely understood as a matter of making tradeoffs between capital and community. It was widely assumed that most projects could not succeed unless local, regional. and even national officials played a powerful supervisory or supportive role. As one Milanese councilor put it,

Nothing here happens [in development] without the big public agencies —
like the state railroad, the fair authority, the ATM [subway], and the planners — starting things up. Then come the regular bureaucrats, party people,
and the special interests. The problem with the Milanese business community is that the old leadership is no longer there as it once was. They want
to be led.

For the French, the dichotomy between development and redistribution hardly exists. This is true in both Paris and Marseilles, where officials believe that social strategies assist economic growth. Their strategy
rests on the assumption that growth can take place only under conditions of social equality and general well-being. The Cartesian logic is to
beautify the neighborhoods, build more metro lines, create better housing for all, and invest in an economic plan that is inclusive. As one
planner commented, "One cannot have economic prosperity in a social
order that operates at two different speeds." In fact, new business districts are built with this philosophy in mind. Les Halles and La Défense
are quintessential examples of vast social expenditures built into the
fabric of commercial sites. The most recent example of this is in Seine-
Sud-Est, which combines a massive national library with sports, recreation, and commercial development.

American cities show a distinctly different view. In New York officials
regularly expressed the idea that the city's social-benefit traditions severely burdened opportunities for promoting business growth. As one
planner put it,

This is a great city, but it simply can't do everything. Without business,
we're dead. Doing social good sometimes has to take a back seat until we
capture the jobs.

In more purist market-oriented Houston and Detroit, the single-strat-
egy rationale was more apparent. Here, officials often expressed belief
that community development projects, neighborhood renewal, state-led
investment schemes, and other forms of social-centered policy had a
marginal role in stimulating economic growth. A number of officials in
Houston thought that it could even discourage business interest in the
city. As Robert Lanier, a former Houston mayor, put it,

This is a business town and always has been. If you want jobs, you have to
let them figure out how to bring them in. It just makes sense not to get in
their way with unnecessary government.

The Detroit view was similar but more cynical, and born of hardened
experience. Recalling how his city has been hurt by interlocal place
wars, former mayor Young talked about his limited choice:

This suicidal competition (among cities) has to stop, but until it does I mean to compete. It's too bad we have a system of dog-eat-dog and the devil take the hindmost. But I'm tired of taking the hindmost.

CONCLUSIONS

While four cities did adopt relatively "pure" strategies, a dual struggle over urban policy is less frequent, and does not capture most policy responses. Rather than a matter of either-or policy choice, the majority pattern is more complex and contains a hybrid of choices.

This, of course, does not preclude cities from accenting certain policies and restraining others. Some adopted highly social-centered policies, while others put greater faith in the marketplace. Pro-growth cities do not necessarily neglect social agendas, nor do cities with ambitious social development programs pay little attention to growth. American cities do constitute an exception to this observation, and they strongly tilt toward growth. European and Canadian cities did not show evidence of a singular concern with growth. Instead, they pursued both policy directions, viewing them as complementary and "muddled through" their policy choices in order to achieve some balance. We now turn to this task of understanding why cities differ in their policy choices.

NOTES

i. The technical translations sometimes may be different from the descriptive translations used above. Technically, ZAC stands for Zone d'Aménagement Concertée, or zone of concerted development; ZAD stands for Zone d'Aménagement Différée, or zone of differential development; ZUP stands for Zone Urbaine de Priorité, or zone of priority development, and POS stands for Plan d'Occupation de Sol, or plan of occupation. Recently passed legislation strengthens many of these tools. Thus, the POS has been replaced by the Plans Locaux d'Urbanismes or PLU. The PLU permit municipalities to better integrate an ensemble of projects and simplifies planning for citizens.

ii. DATAR stands for Délégation à l'Aménagement du Territoire et à l'Action Régionale.

iii. HLM stands for Habitat de Loyer Modéré or moderate rental housing.

iv. For details, see chapter 6.

v. The legislation includes the "Loi Voynet" and "Solidarité, Renouvellement Urbaine" (Solidarity and Urban Renewal). For details see Délégation à l'Aménagement du Terrioire et à l'Action Régionale, "Premiers Rencontres Nationales Agglomeration (Loi Voynet) Paris," 30 March 2000 and "Présentation de la Loi Rélative à la Solidarité et au Renouvellement Urbain, *Le Moniteur*, 26 January 2001.

vi. This segment on Milan is coauthored with Serena Vicari Haddock.

vii. IRI stands for *Istituto Ricostruzione Industriale* (Institute for Industrial Reconstruction). Together with ENI (energy and chemicals) and EFIM (manufacturing industry), IRI makes up the group of holding corporations that were once the responsibility of the ministry for state holdings.

viii. The city supported this strategy and did its best to invest in the area. Mayor Coleman Young was especially enthusiastic and was purported to have said, "Revitalize the riverfront, and I guarantee you'll revitalize the whole city" (Wheelan and Young, *Detroit and New Orleans*, 11).

ix. For years city leaders refused federal support for urban renewal programs. But they eagerly sought interstate highway monies, research and development spending for the NASA space center, as well as various other Cold War–era programs.

x. *The Sunday Times* [London], January 11, 1970, p. 17. This segment on Naples is coauthored with Serena Vicari Haddock.

xi. Some scholars see social-centered concessions as efforts to deflect working-class demands rather than genuinely accommodate a different strategy. In the end, argues Fainstein (*Restructuring the City*), competition over "the use of real estate for human activity and its market role" dominates the contest over urban space.

xii. Mollenkopf, *Contested City*; Elkin, *City and Regime*; Stone, *Regime Politics*, "Urban Regimes." These scholars generally reject the idea that there are inherent economic trade-offs between pro-growth and egalitarian economic policies (Elkin, *City and Regime*, 98–99; C. Stone, *Regime Politics*, 214–15). Regime theorists argue that there are systemic biases that spring from governing dynamics that make social-centered development incompatible with pro-growth coalition politics. They believe that unless regimes are changed to include non-business interests and provide wider participation in making development policy, community-oriented values will be shortchanged. Otherwise, public officials will gravitate toward building alliances with business interests, especially land interests, and both will work to keep participation and policy agendas closed to alternative strategies (Stone, *Regime Politics*, 206; Ferman, *Challenging the Growth Machine*; Elkin, *City and Regime*, 42). Indeed, once regimes are established, suggest Jones and Bachelor (*Sustaining Hand*, 249–51), pro-growth policies tend to crowd out consideration of competing alternatives because "solution-sets" are adopted that narrowly frame the city's policy options.

1. Houston: Freeway approach, circa 1990s. Photo/Paul Kantor

2. Paris: City Hall Today. Photo/H. V. Savitch

3. Milan: The Garibaldi Repubblica. Photo/Ambrogio Gualdoni

4. Paris: Metro Station at Paris Rive Gauche. Photo/H. V. Savitch

5. Paris: Bibliothèque nationale at Paris Rive Gauche. Photo/H. V. Savitch

6. Milan: Polytechnic buildings in Bovisa. Photo/Paul Kantor

7. Liverpool: City Hall. Photo/H. V. Savitch

8. Liverpool: Skyline at Prince Albert Dock. Photo/H. V. Savitch

9. New York: South Street Seaport. Photo/Paul Kantor

10. Liverpool:
Clayton Square
and Radio Tower.
Photo/H. V.
Savitch

11. Marseilles: The port. Photo/H. V. Savitch

12. Marseilles: Inner-city neighborhood about to be renewed. Photo/H. V. Savitch

13. Naples: Centro Dirizionale with Mount Vesuvius in background.
Photo/Paolo DiStefano

14. Naples: Old Spanish Quarter. Photo/Paul Kantor

15. Glasgow: Backcourts, Drumchapel Housing Estates. Photo/Glasgow City Council

Chapter Five

DRIVING AND STEERING URBAN STRATEGY

I claim not to have controlled events, but confess
plainly that events have controlled me.
—Abraham Lincoln

CIRCUMSTANCE AND CHOICE

Why do our cities pursue different urban strategies? Our theoretical perspective suggests that we should examine both circumstance and choice. Cities differ in their policy agendas. Some communities may place a value on free-market approaches to problems of employment, growth, and the environment, while others see these as matters of strict governmental regulation. Yet choices in policy are also a function of circumstances. In a world of global economic change and regional restructuring, cities are necessarily junior partners in a development game that is strongly shaped by forces over which they have limited control. By virtue of their economic prowess and political muscle, some cities enjoy many bargaining advantages. Other cities lack assets and are subject to what Wirt has called the "compulsion of necessity."[1] They struggle to realize very limited policy choices within environments that leave them in a weak bargaining position.

In this chapter we examine how circumstance influences choice in light of our bargaining theory. We are especially interested in whether cities with particular kinds of resources will move in expected policy directions. These resources are explained by our *driving* and *steering* variables. Both constitute critical resources that enable cities to pursue specific development strategies.[i]

Recall that driving forces arise from a city's market condition and its intergovernmental arrangements, while steering variables encompass popular control and local culture. Driving resources empower cities by conferring advantages in the capital marketplace; they derive from the city's economic attraction and its capacity to leverage those assets with aid from other governments. Steering resources enable cities to tap local activism and public opinion in order to sustain their particular strategies. Focusing on these variables should help us uncover why some cities adopt an ambitious social agenda, while others give greater weight to market appeal. Our bargaining model posits three major propositions.

First, cities with significant driving resources should also have greater choices over policy. Local governments that hold powerful economic positions or draw upon substantial intergovernmental support will be in a better position to deal with private investment markets. Accordingly, they ought to be able to use a greater proportion of their resources to achieve ambitious social agendas. As a corollary, poorer cities with weak market positions and limited intergovernmental assistance are less able to resist business demands in favor of public-sector priorities. With fewer resources and limited political support from higher level governments, they should be more inclined to let markets drive their development strategies.

Second, cities with greater steering resources should have a greater disposition and ability to pursue social-centered policy directions. From a theoretical perspective, high participation and postmaterialist cultures should encourage as well as empower city governments to promote social-centered policies. High-resource cities with an activist citizenry and widespread acceptance of "public regarding" values should be more inclined to incorporate social-centered objectives into their strategies. These same conditions also provide the support required for a social centered agenda. Activist citizens who have the means to keep local officialdom accountable, ought to make officials bargain harder for public benefits, especially in a culture where postmaterialist values dominate. In contrast, where steering resources are weak, public leaders can be expected to concede greater prerogatives to business. Low-resource cities, with limited popular control and materialist cultures, ought to lean toward market-centered policies.

Third, these driving and steering forces should have a cumulative effect. Such an effect provides a city with a context through which it can exploit greater bargaining advantages, thereby expanding its policy choice. Cities with abundant bargaining advantages, operating in favorable contexts, can be expected to entertain policy options that less endowed urban places can only envy. Precisely how these driving and steering variables empower or limit city governmental strategies should become apparent as we study how they interact.

Do Driving Resources Structure Choice?

Exogenous forces are extrinsic to a given system. We consider market condition and intergovernmental support as exogenous driving influences because they are a product of economic and political circumstances beyond the reach of a given city. Although circumstances change over time, this generally happens slowly. Even though cities may experience short-term economic cycles, their market positions require the passing of generations before real shifts occur in the regional or global pecking order. Similarly, national urban policies occur in response to the election of new administrations, but large-scale alterations in intergovernmental relations usually take much longer. The "Roosevelt Revolution," which began in the 1930s and greatly expanded federal aid to United States cities, took more than thirty years to produce results. Many urban programs proposed during the days of the New Deal were not enacted until the 1950s and 1960s. These driving forces imposed important structural conditions that still frame how city governments play the development game.

How do these driving forces expand or limit city policy choices? We claim that economic and intergovernmental circumstances will constrain city policy-making by influencing the distribution of bargaining advantages between public and private actors. Over time, local players will take into account the kinds of policy directions that can be pursued in light of their bargaining resources. We first look at how economic and intergovernmental circumstances affect city policy separately and then examine them together. This allows us to see how economic and governmental forces contribute independently as well as collectively to our bargaining model.

Do richer cities, ones that enjoy strong economies, promote different policies than poorer ones? One hypothesis states that cities with favorable market positions should support more ambitious social agendas compared to cities that lack this advantage. Further, economically favored cities should give less attention to market-centered policies because they have already established themselves as attractive locations for jobs and money.

Despite this seemingly obvious connection, this simple proposition is questionable. Rich cities with booming economies do not necessarily favor ambitious social agendas compared to less favored cities. Houston enjoys a relatively powerful market position, but is among the least social-centered of our cities. Milan and New York also own favored positions, but they are only moderately social centered. In contrast, Marseilles, Liverpool, and Glasgow are all disfavored, declining economies, but they are moderately social centered. Evidence of a direct link between market conditions and urban policy is tenuous, though there may be an indirect, more complex tie (to be discussed later).

Intergovernmental support plays a more important independent role than local economic conditions. Cities having integrated intergovernmental support are more inclined to pursue social-centered policies and to be less attentive to market strategies than cities with diffuse intergovernmental arrangements. There is, in fact, a relationship between the availability of intergovernmental resources and urban policy.

To begin, we focus on the relationship between intergovernmental

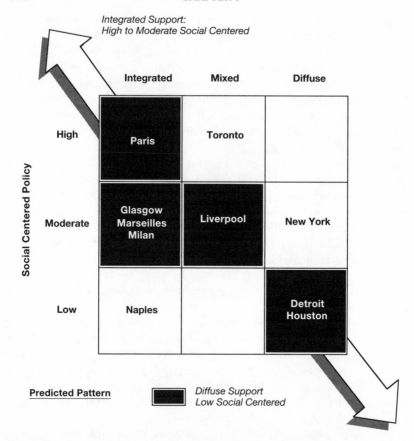

Figure 5.1. Intergovernmental Support and Social-centered Policy.

support and social-centered policy. Figure 5.1 displays this relationship by comparing cities with varying degrees of intergovernmental support against those with high, moderate, and low social-centered policies.

All told, seven of our ten cities move in the predicted direction. Paris, Glasgow, Marseilles, Milan, and Liverpool all enjoy integrated or mixed intergovernmental support and pursue high or moderate social-centered policies. At the other end of the spectrum, Detroit and Houston have diffuse intergovernmental support and show little or no disposition toward a social-centered strategy. The remaining two cases (New York and Naples) stand as exceptions.

Next, we focus on market-centered policies. When we match varying degrees of intergovernmental support with market-oriented or pro-growth strategies, the relationship is somewhat stronger. Figure 5.2 shows that eight of our ten cities promote market-centered strategies

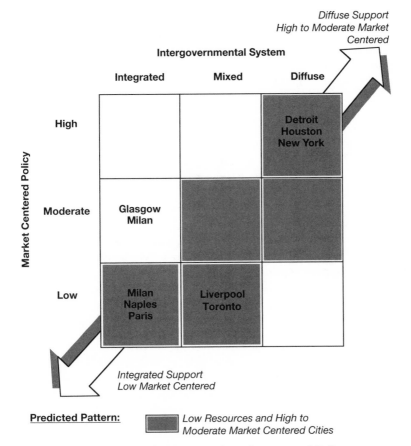

Figure 5.2. Intergovernmental Support and Market-centered Policy.

more or less in proportion to their intergovernmental advantages. Here six of the eight cases are clustered at either the extreme upper right (diffuse support and high market-centered) or the extreme lower left (integrated support and low market-centered).

There is a fairly clear division between North American and European cities. With their diffuse governmental systems, American cities run on their own economic steam and are inclined toward growth and away from policies that incur social liabilities. By comparison European cities with integrated governmental support are less susceptible to this kind of economic pressure. Marseilles, Naples, and Paris are low in market-centered policies. Liverpool and Toronto with their mixed systems are also low market-centered. Glasgow and Milan stand as exceptional cases. All told, not a single European city fits a high market-centered pattern.

The particularly accented link between intergovernmental systems and market-centered policy suggests the importance of political institutions in structuring city-business power relations. National and regional programs help cushion all of the European cities from some of the fiscal effects of capital flight and enable them to resist business demands for concessions in return for their investments. In diffuse systems, businesses are more easily able to play one city against another in order to extract privileges. Whether rich (New York and Houston) or poor (Detroit), American cities are heavily market centered, and this is clearly a product of their diffuse intergovernmental arrangements.

As noted in chapter 4, our interviews revealed that officials in American cities expressed widespread recognition of the idea that city governments were obligated to cultivate a "positive business climate." Much of this stemmed from apprehension over revenue raising compounded by fear that other localities would raid local capital. This feeling was much less common in the European cities. While European officials wanted to improve employment opportunities, they frequently saw this as a public function that was only remotely linked to meeting business preferences in making local development policies. As one Scottish official put it,

> Business leaders really are quite unaware that we want them to be part of our regeneration work here in Glasgow. They see their own bottom line, so to speak, and that's all. For our part, we look to the big public agencies to set expectations. All the talk now is about regionalism, pulling together and being partners with business. But this is government talk. I don't think that business people want to be bothered with telling us what to do.

Similarly, in Milan there was little sense that local planners ought to respond to business preferences in setting policy agendas. One council member commented,

> Who knows what business wants? They're all different anyway. We're elected to serve everybody. The idea of trying to anticipate what will bring more jobs is something we've been doing more of since the 1980s, but mostly we do it on our own. It's not something that business does. You need a broader perspective for this. Planning is important in Milan and people respect it. But it really is a government function.

There are good reasons why integrated political environments help create such expectations about the role of the marketplace. In all of our European cities largesse from higher governments permits local politicians to distribute benefits to local constituencies without seeking donations from the private sector. Mayors, council members, and bureaucrats use the taxing capacity of other governments to cement partisan loyalties. This is true for both right- and left-wing partisans, especially in the French and Italian cities. Paris's Chirac (right, Gaullist) and Marseilles's Deferre (left, Socialist) are mayors who used national resources to feather the nests of their loyalists. Even in Italy, where national urban programs are often in flux due to shifting coalitions Milan's Carlo Tognoli (center, Socialist) and Naples's Antonio Bassolino (former Communist) found that funding from central sources can go a long way toward winning elections. During the 1980s Tognoli used public works contracts throughout the city to cut deals with developers and suppliers who supported his electoral coalition.[2] Naples's Bassolino won voters by capitalizing on special national funding to clean up the city in anticipation of a meeting of the G-7 ministers. He also spent money on things that were highly visible to citizens, such as paving streets, creating pedestrian malls, fixing street lights, and opening up public swimming pools.

British cities are more constrained in their use of national programs for partisan purposes. Yet it is not unknown. Liverpool Labourites, for example, did not hesitate to use the city's payroll and public housing accounts during the 1980s to help compensate for the city's chronic unemployment. In contrast, American mayors were frequently worried about attracting private-sector jobs and concerned about holding back expenses. Once we understand who pays the bill, it is hardly surprising that American cities are so enthusiastic about growth.

A brief comparison of Naples and Detroit shows how intergovernmental systems structure political responses to business and shape the quest for urban aid. Naples and Detroit are among the poorest cities in the West. Both struggle with severe unemployment that extends into double digits. But their orientations toward securing help are fundamentally different. In Naples, the search for governmental money dominates all political activity. The focus on exchanging local votes for national resources encourages Neapolitan parties to broker the distribution of public money. In fact, one Italian writer describes local politicians as *mediatori* — brokers or mediators who help citizens negotiate the public realm.[3] Intraparty factions and governing coalitions nearly always rise or fall over the division of public spoils, and they have little to do with either seeking business support or supporting business.

In contrast, Detroit's relations with the state and federal governments are more distant. The city's politicians are inclined to seek direct help from business. After the 1968 riots, the city turned to the private sector to alleviate racial tensions. A coalition of business and black leaders formed "New Detroit" in order to stanch the downward spiral. Detroit's immediate reflex was to find contracts for minority firms, encourage business investment, and bolster property values. The city's most recent effort at revival through its designation as a federal "Empowerment Zone" also exemplifies this approach. Millions of dollars have been solicited from automobile companies. Business has been asked to set up plants and headquarters within the urban core, and a "One Stop Capital Shop" has been established to assist interested investors.[4] In motor city politics, business leaders have used their powerful presence to demand a prominent role in local governing coalitions. Under Coleman Young, a network of economic development agencies and committees was established to closely enmesh city governmental and corporate decision makers. City plans to revive the sagging fortunes of the downtown complemented the efforts of business players, especially the auto executives. True, initiatives to attract private investment are required by national legislation. But this, too, is a political act that conditions the local response or nonresponse to business and shapes expectations.

BARGAINING CONTEXTS

In the real world, cities do not bargain over development by mobilizing discrete resources. Rather, they navigate within bargaining contexts that distribute advantages between public and private actors and create expectations about power relationships. The impact of intergovernmental support may have an effect on city social policies when this resource is combined with other bargaining resources, such as favorable market conditions. Some bargaining contexts supply abundant advantages to city governments, while others confer few. All told, driving forces line up in different configurations to shape bargaining.

Table 5.1 outlines four bargaining contexts: dirigiste, dependent public, entrepreneurial, and dependent private.

Each is based on a conjunction of our two driving forces — the ability of a city to raise capital through its market condition and public capacity to influence that economy through intergovernmental support. Located in the upper left quadrant, the dirigiste context presents the most advantaged bargaining context. The term connotes public intervention to a point where development is orchestrated by political elites. Cities functioning in this context hold both favorable market positions and enjoy a high degree of intergovernmental support. These crucial advantages permit cities to exact demands upon business. Going down to the next category, we find the dependent public context, which deals cities a mixed hand. These cities have weak economies, but they are able to draw upon access to governmental networks for fiscal assistance and regulatory muscle. This governmental resource partially offsets their economic weakness. As noted earlier, cities operating within an integrated governmental context show little interest in offering supply-side incentives to business, either because they can draw fiscal sustenance from public coffers or because they stand to reap few direct benefits by chasing after business.

TABLE 5.1
City Bargaining Contexts

	Intergovernmental Support	
	Integrated/Mixed	*Diffuse*
Market Condition		
Favorable	DIRIGISTE (Paris, Toronto, Milan)	ENTREPRENEURIAL (New York, Houston)
Unfavorable	DEPENDENT PUBLIC (Marseilles, Glasgow, Liverpool, Naples)	DEPENDENT PRIVATE (Detroit)

In the upper right quadrant, an entrepreneurial context furnishes liabilities and assets to cities. City governments face severe constraints on their use of public intervention because they must contend with a competitive marketplace without much intergovernmental support. In order to keep up the bidding, these cities can be expected to aggressively pursue private capital—often with the lure of supply-side incentives. This disadvantage is partially offset by favorable market conditions, which may boost their bargaining leverage. However, the vulnerability of cities to shifts in private investments limits this bargaining resource.

Finally, a dependent private context is one of near desperation. This context affords neither a strong market position nor does it provide cities with sustained or comprehensive support from higher-level governments. Cities sharing these circumstances suffer an acute shortage of both private and public capital, and they are least able to assert bargaining demands with business.

The advantages and liabilities that spring from each bargaining context hold tangible policy consequences. Figure 5.3 outlines how bargaining is linked to strategic choice. It indicates the relative position of cities in each context. As advantages shrink, so too do choices. A dirigiste context offers the widest latitude, allowing cities to shape the built environment through a combination of public control (tight planning, open spaces, building moratoria) and bountiful private investment. Dependent public and entrepreneurial contexts offer different kinds of freedom. A dependent public context offers durable control for cities, but hamstrings them by a paucity of private investment. An entrepreneurial context frequently offers abundant private investment for cities, but denies them durable control. A dependent private context provides neither sufficient private investment nor control. As such, it holds fewer choices for cities.

Our ten cities are scattered over all four of these environments. Paris, Toronto, and Milan are most advantaged, operating in a dirigiste world.

Figure 5.3. Context, Bargaining, and Strategy.

The least favored city is Detroit, lacking market and intergovernmental advantages in a dependent private situation. Marseilles, Glasgow, Liverpool, Naples are all poor cities that struggle for position in dependent public environments. Finally, New York and Houston compete in entrepreneurial contexts.

The effects of different bargaining contexts on policy choice can be seen in the next figures. Figure 5.4 shows the relationship between bargaining context and social-centered policy. Figure 5.5 shows this relationship for market-centered policy. Observe the "pull" of driving forces on the social- and market-centered directions of our ten cities.

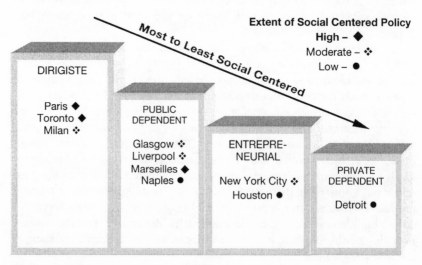

Figure 5.4. Bargaining Contexts and Social-centered Policy in Ten Cities.

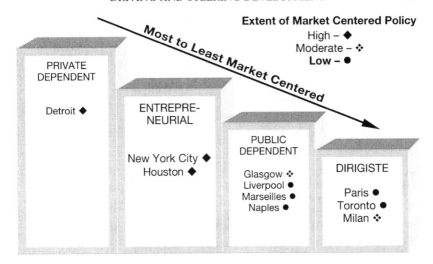

Figure 5.5. Bargaining Contexts and Market-centered Policy in Ten Cities.

Our theory posits that as bargaining advantages increase, cities are more likely to follow social-centered policies. This is illustrated in figure 5.4, where the dirigiste context holds the most social-centered cities. This pattern progressively descends in dependent public and entrepreneurial contexts. Note, too, that the least advantaged context, dependent private, holds no social-centered city. Put another way, almost all high and moderate social-centered cities are found in the two most favorable bargaining contexts. Paris, Toronto, Milan, Marseilles, Glasgow, and Liverpool and are located in either a dirigiste or public dependent contexts. New York is the sole exception.

Turning to figure 5.5, we find an obverse pattern for cities with market-centered policies. That is, as bargaining advantages decrease, cities are more likely to be market centered. Moving from left to right, we see a consistency in this pattern for market-centered strategies. All the high market-centered cities are located in either a dependent private context (Detroit) or an entrepreneurial context (New York and Houston). Only moderate market-centered Glasgow and Milan can be found in advantaged contexts.

There are some lessons here. First, the most exuberant social-centered policies are held by cities with enviable market positions. This is especially valid for Paris and Toronto, but the observation also pertains to strategically moderate cities like Milan and New York. We can say the most fervent social-centered policies require urban wealth to support them. A strong local economy seems to be a necessary but not a sufficient condition for an aggressive social agenda. We should emphasize, however, that the converse to this proposition does *not* hold. Social agendas are not only supported by rich cities but also by some poor ones. This answers the puzzle posed at the outset of this chapter, where we also found poorer cities like Marseilles, Glasgow, and Liverpool adopting social-centered policies, while wealthier cities like Houston refrained from a social agenda. Wealth counts, but it does not ensure or preclude a social strategy. Moreover, less well-off cities with a high degree of intergovernmental support can and do pursue a modicum of redistributive policies.

In the language of classic comparative research, economic requisites play a necessary role in advancing more ambitious social agendas. Without wealth, cities will find it difficult over the long term to sustain those agendas.[5] Liverpool is a dire example of this proposition. Given its limited wealth, Liverpool could only maintain its radical social agenda by bankrupting itself. As described in the previous chapter, that strategy backfired. Herein lies the tension between pro-growth advocates wishing to limit social expenditures and social agenda promoters seeking to augment them (see chapter 9).

The second lesson is that intergovernmental support, or the lack of it, has a particularly lopsided effect on development policies. It enables city governments to avoid engaging in highly market-centered activities, although it is not always sufficient to enable them to pursue ambitious social-centered strategies. Cities that are cushioned by fiscal and regulatory support need only say no when business comes knocking at their doors. This is but a passive political act, and public indifference can wear away private initiative. In contrast, when it comes to collective social benefits, cities must be proactive. This requires an act that involves changing the status quo by balancing private benefits with public goods and engaging in the complexities of interest group mediation. It is here where integrated intergovernmental relationships can support public actors in bargaining with business. No doubt, higher levels of governments can play a critical role in supporting social agenda. But as we later show for Glasgow and Toronto, the intergovernmental blade can cut both ways. There are no guarantees, and higher levels of government can sometime push localities in directions that city leaders do not necessarily want (see chapters 6 and 7).

Third, this exploration of bargaining contexts suggests that development strategies are a product of a particular political economy. It is the interaction of economic conditions and intergovernmental arrangements that generates bargaining advantages for local governments. Most cities pursue policy strategies that are roughly consistent with bargaining advantages that arise from their market position and their external political support. In the short run, local officials may be able to enjoy latitude and "muddle through" on particular issues. They may cut deals that veer off in different policy directions, but over time cities will tend to adapt to the limits of their bargaining resources. One way or another, choice is constrained. That constraint may come from higher-level governments, from the market place, or from a combination of these pressures.

CONTEXT, CHOICE, AND ACCOUNTABILITY

While bargaining context widens or narrows urban choice, all cities are accountable to some type of institution. Cities may find their choice expanded by dealing with other levels of governments rather than private business. But in the final analysis no city is free of restraint, and the real issue rides on the extent and subject of accountability.

Dirigiste choices are conditioned by the direction that governments at other levels wish to follow. In Paris nothing of importance is built without the guidance of a master plan and approval by appropriate ministries. Public officials have enormous latitude in whether, where, and how to build, and this discretion has shifted from time to time. During the "golden age" of the 1960s and 1970s, government moved heavy industry out of the city, invoked building moratoria, and used differential taxes to shape development. All of this radically changed the city's landscape. By the 1990s, the public sector decided to reverse direction. Government relaxed building restrictions, initiated massive construction of "smart office buildings," and supplied infrastructure to support the new initiatives.[6]

Toronto's dirigiste context is looser, but here, too, master plans, transit systems, and the watchful eyes of the province and (former) metropolitan government guide development. During the 1960s and early 1970s, the city aggressively pursued development. The downtown business district and the harbor were radically changed, and there seemed no end to growth. But by 1976 the "growth machine" was stopped dead in its tracks. The city invoked a moratorium on office construction, limited building heights, and required underground parking. Led by a left-wing council and by "Red Tory Mayor" David Crombie, Toronto adopted measures to promote amenities and enhance the quality of urban life. A study of Toronto's downtown development demonstrates the expectations imposed on the process by the Ontario Municipal Board, local planners, the city council, and alert citizen groups.[7] Milan's choices also are broad, although the city government has not used its extensive powers and the city's economic prowess to launch aggressive social agendas on the scale of those of Paris or Toronto. Still, this dirigiste context has not allowed for anything like the vigorous market-centered programs found in the American cities.

Entrepreneurial bargaining leaves cities very much alone in an erratic marketplace. Both New York and Houston have ridden up and down on roller coaster economies. Their respective low points were due to fiscal crises (New York), falling prices and real estate busts (Houston), and other regional economic dislocations. During the mid-1970s New York was rocked by overextended borrowing, and the threat of municipal bankruptcy forced city hall to constrict its social agenda. By the mid-1990s, a surging stock market brought the city to a new economic plateau. Real estate skyrocketed, and a diversified economy enabled the city to revive its moderate social agenda. Houston boomed during the 1960s and 1970s, then slumped during the 1980s when local banks took on risky mortgages and falling oil prices undermined the local economy. During this "depression" the city had to adjust by raising taxes and cutting programs severely. Houston recovered during the 1990s with the return of full employment and a more diversified high-tech economy.

A public dependent context allows economically weak cities to rely on the largesse of central or regional government. Like its counterparts in the rest of France, Marseilles is tied to a process set by national ministries and infrastructure provided by a regional council. Unlike its more prosperous counterparts, Marseilles lacks powerful development corporations, and this poses difficulties for renewal of the city. Marseilles's efforts to develop the waterfront have been stymied by the reluctance of private corporations to commit themselves.

Liverpool fits much the same pattern of control without the diverse liveliness of private capital. Since the fall of Militant Tendency, both Whitehall and the Merseyside Development Corporation have been the leading actors attempting to make up for the city's abandonment by the private sector. The harbor still has limited activity. Liverpool's prime real estate can only be described as spotted development, interspersed by expanses of vacant, neglected land. A major American corporation, Loews Hotel, was refused central government subsidy and eventually abandoned its project for a five-star hotel. Nevertheless, Liverpool does not support many American-style programs that subsidize private business.

Naples also has had to cope with a hollowed out economy. It has tried to substitute public investment for private capital by relying on regional aid programs for Italy's poor Mezzogiorno and national political connections. Glasgow's dependence on regional and national governments has spared the city from the worst effects of economic decay. Its mix of social- and market-centered policies is linked to national aid and regional economic intervention. Despite hard times, the city has been able to sustain a steady flow of social services. In recent years regional decision makers have grown keen about the marketplace and have begun to work with business—so too has Glasgow.

Last, cities in a dependent private context are squeezed on both sides of the development game. They must accept whatever is offered by private investors or rely on relatively meager public help. Detroit exemplifies this dilemma. The city's use of "quick take" laws permits large investors to build where they choose. Its history of weak, segregated public housing also demonstrates the ad hoc character of development.[8] Gaming casinos and sports stadiums are ways of churning revenues. Meanwhile, government aid is supplied in fits and starts, and even during the best of times it has minimal effect. After the 1968 riots, antipoverty legislation suffused the city with "soft money" jobs. By the 1980s that money dried up. With the onset of federally supported "Empowerment Zones" the 1990s has given Detroit another bite at the government apple, but the city continues to shuttle between one big benefactor and another.[ii]

How Cities Steer: The Cumulative Effects of Bargaining Resources

Our view of development suggests that steering and driving variables are interactive and cumulative. For the moment, however, we focus on steering resources. We view these as endogenous sources of bargaining leverage. Popular control and local culture are rooted within the social, demographic, and political confines of a locality. Some of our cities are characterized by extensive citizen participation, while others lack these assets. Some cities have political cultures that support postmaterial tastes, while others are more materialistic.

As explained earlier, these differences in political capacity affect how city governments make use of bargaining opportunities. So long as private or public investment can be obtained at the bargaining table, popular control and local culture will guide choices over what, where, and whether things are built. And by this logic, cities with high steering resources will be better able to influence the application of collective goods and social amenities.

Figure 5.6 shows how cities match up to our steering variables.[iii] The figure displays how cities compare by ordinal rankings. Areas are shaded to distinguish cities with high, moderate, and low resources.

Milan, Paris, Toronto, New York, and Marseilles are the most resource-laden cities. Each of these is characterized by activist popular control and supports postmaterialist values. Given our propositions, we would expect these cities to be the most social centered. In contrast, Liverpool, Naples, Detroit, and Houston are the least. Given their lower popular control and materialist culture, we would expect them to pursue a market-centered strategy. In the middle is Glasgow, whose consis-

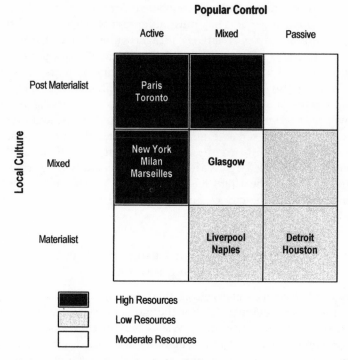

Figure 5.6. Steering Resources in Ten Cities.

tently mixed participatory and cultural characteristics differentiate it from both city groups.

In fact, there is a strong association between steering resources and social-centered policies. Eight of our ten cities pursue social-centered policies that are directly proportional to their steering resources. Five of the cities with substantial steering resources follow a high to moderate social-centered direction, while cities with scant resources follow a low social agenda. Even Glasgow pursues a moderate agenda with its modest resources.[iv]

This brings us to the cumulative impact of all our variables on social-centered policy. We expect that cities with ample steering resources are most able to pursue social-centered policies in a bargaining context that affords advantages. As these advantages mount, cities should be better able to pursue social-centered policies. By the same logic, market-centered policies should be linked to a lack of cumulative resources. As these advantages decline, cities should be more inclined to pursue market policies.

The cumulative effects are examined by separating our cities into two groups — those that have higher steering resources and those with lower

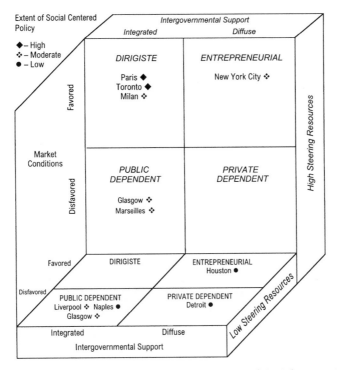

Figure 5.7. Steering Resources, Bargaining Contexts, and Social-centered Policy.

resources. Since Glasgow consistently stands out as a mixed case, it is folded into both higher and lower steering groups, permitting us to consider this city in both ways.

Figure 5.7 displays these relationships along two plains, which show contrasts between cities with high and low steering resources. High-resource cities are located on the upright plain and low steering resource cities are at the bottom. Note the symbols designating the high ($\blacklozenge$), moderate ($\clubsuit$), and low ($\bullet$) direction of urban policies.

In both groups, social-centered strategies are linked to bargaining contexts and to steering resources. Among the higher steering-resource cities, all but one of the cities that are highly or moderately social centered are found in the most advantageous bargaining contexts (dirigiste and public dependent). And the most exuberantly social-centered cities, Paris and Toronto, are located in this most advantageous context. Significantly, there are no social-centered cities in the weak private dependent context. New York is able to steer toward moderate social policies with entrepreneurial advantages. The cities with low steering resources

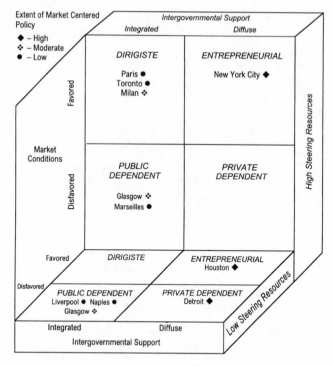

Figure 5.8. Steering Resources, Bargaining Contexts, and Market-centered Policy.

also display a resource-bound pattern. Three out of five lower steering-resource cities are also low in social-centered policies. The only cities that are moderately social centered also share the advantages of a public dependent bargaining context. Note that Glasgow follows a resource-bound pattern whether we place it among the high- or low-resource cities.

When we turn to market-centered policies there is a similar pattern. Steering resources have their greatest impact when cities also possess advantageous bargaining contexts. Figure 5.8 shows that cities generally are less market centered when they enjoy greater steering capacity *and* operate in more favorable bargaining contexts.

Examining cities with higher steering resources, we can discern the pattern. The only highly market-centered city — New York — is lodged in the least advantaged bargaining context. Two of the three low market-centered cities, Paris and Toronto, are in favorable dirigiste contexts. All of the low and moderate market-oriented governments are in the two most advantageous bargaining circumstances (dirigiste or public dependent).

Turning to cities with lower steering resources, we find that only cities that are in relatively favorable public dependent contexts manage to steer away from market-oriented policies (despite their disfavored economies). By contrast, those in less favorable entrepreneurial and private dependent contexts steer toward robust market policies.

Overall, cities tend to pursue urban strategies in ways that are linked to the interaction of steering and driving forces. The availability of ample steering resources helps local governments to steer in social-centered directions, but cities that have an advantaged bargaining context are more able to follow this pathway. In comparison, market-centered strategies are linked to the scarcity of steering resources, but cities that lack economic muscle and have little help from higher-level governments are most inclined to allow business and investment to shape policy.

The Agency / Structure Debate

Are city governments really able to choose their pathway of development? Or are they so constrained by structure that choice does not matter? We find that the question of agency versus structure actually poses a false dichotomy. Both matter. Cities are neither creatures of their bargaining circumstances nor are they masters of their policy choices.

We point out that political agency is resource bounded. Over the long run, city governments do not treat development policies in a piecemeal fashion or as a simple product of immediate political interests. While cities are sometimes likened to "growth machines" driven by powerful political interests, this metaphor does not capture some essential complexities.[9] In reality, cities take into account their structural context and pursue policy strategies that are roughly consistent with their resource capabilities. Cities behave strategically. While political leaders may shape agency resources and convince citizens to support particular strategies, popular support is rarely sufficient to sustain long-term policy directions. Cities require tangible assets with which to build or provide social amenities. These are the preserve of well-endowed cities, often sustained by regional, provincial, or national government.

While structure is important and cities are resource bounded, this does not eliminate political agency. In practice, agency and structure are difficult to separate. What stands out is the cumulative nature of the resources that bear on urban policy. Economic prowess accounts for only a small part of policy variation. Rather, policy is influenced by political elites who collaborate across different levels of government. The latter plays an especially powerful role in limiting or expanding policy choices over extended periods of time.

Further, the skills of local leaders also count. Local politics enables

cities to exploit whatever structural opportunities they find. Steering resources play a crucial role by empowering communities to negotiate
with capital investors. Urban strategies are dependent upon leaders who
take advantage of popular opinion to advance political agendas. Steering resources are tools for politicians who know how to capitalize upon
cultural values. Urban policy is best explained by the reinforcing impact
of multiple variables. Paris and Toronto are scarce examples of cities
that have been able to tap citizen participation and a popular appetite
for social intervention. In contrast, Houston's materialism, its passive
politics, and its need to struggle in a "go it alone" governmental scenario help explain the city's reliance on markets. In between are cities
encountering complex combinations of assets and liabilities that present
their own challenges.

Conclusion: Why Cities Are Neither Prisoners Nor Masters

Our analysis tells us that driving variables bear heavily on city choices.
This is particularly true for intergovernmental support and its role in
cushioning cities from the pressures of interlocal competition. Social
agendas are more easily pursued where localities find help from higher
governments. We also find that market-centered policies are not fully
explained by a city's economic condition, but also depend on whether
cities are located within integrated intergovernmental networks. While
aggressive social-centered policies require economic resources, the converse does not hold. Not all cities that hold economic resources pursue
aggressive social agendas. This explains some of the distinctions between European and American cities. The influence of our four variables is cumulative, and strategic direction cannot be explained by a
single resource.

Development strategy can be also understood in terms of cities bringing local steering resources to specific bargaining contexts. Dirigiste, dependent public, entrepreneurial, and dependent private environments
reflect a descending order of advantage and choice. Governments that
enjoy ample steering resources *and* an advantageous bargaining environment have greatest choice, and are found in cities with the most
ambitious social agendas. As advantages decrease, city governments
tend to become more market centered. In between are cities with mixed
bargaining hands, some in public dependent and others in entrepreneurial contexts.

These findings tell us that structure and agency do not fit easily into
opposing dichotomies. Both factors interact in multiple ways due to the
cumulative effects of driving (exogenous) and steering (endogenous) forces.
While these variables constrain local leaders, they also afford them a degree

of discretion. Most cities are neither prisoners of their environment nor masters of their fate, but are subject to varying degrees of choice.

How the forces of agency and structure interact is crucial to further understanding urban development. Thus far we have seen that city governments struggle to devise strategies that take account of their bargaining position. But *how* do they accomplish this? Do some cities exploit their bargaining opportunities better than others? If so, what makes the difference? Do cities with different assets and liabilities also have different systems of decision making and power? Or do cities tend to resemble each other in their internal politics? Most important, is it possible for cities to change strategic direction? Or do city officials simply accommodate their place in a larger hierarchy? These questions beckon us to examine the nexus between agency and structure by probing the politics of coalitions and regimes.

NOTES

i. Ordinal rankings for driving and steering variables are taken from chapter 3. Ordinal rankings and the categorization of social- and market-centered policy are drawn from chapter 4.

ii. While these patterns suggest how different bargaining contexts constrain urban policy-making, they leave unanswered questions, especially those concerning the degree to which some cities lean toward a social or market direction. For example, New York and Houston share similar entrepreneurial contexts. Yet New York, despite its market economy and limited intergovernmental support, maintains moderate social-centered policies, while Houston does not. By the same token, Milan is no more social-centered than New York, even though it enjoys a powerful dirigiste bargaining context similar to more socially centered Paris and Toronto. Naples is an outlying case in both policy tendencies. It exhibits low commitment to both social- and market-centered strategies. We recognize the complexities of these issues, and suggest that while bargaining contexts furnish partial explanations they do not explain degrees of outcome.

iii. In discerning patterns among our cities, we treat policy strategies and resources consistently. To do this, the category of "moderate" is included with both social and market approaches. Thus, social-centered approaches are composed by using "high" and "moderate" cities, while market-centered strategies are composed by using "low" and "moderate" cities. Resources are composed by selecting only "high" and "low" resource localities respectively for social- and market-centered cities.

iv. Using these rules we present the following figure comparing steering resources and social-centered policy. Note that Paris, Toronto, New York, Milan, and Marseilles support social-centered strategies commensurate with their steering resources. Three cases fall in the opposite direction. This is also consistent with our expectations. With low steering resources, Detroit, Houston, and Naples are the least social centered.

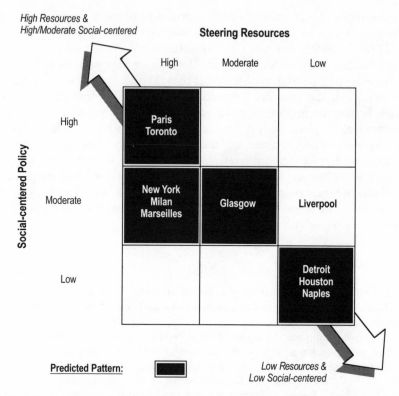

Figure 5.iv. Steering Resources and Social-centered Policy in Ten Cities.

Chapter Six

DIRIGISTE AND ENTREPRENEURIAL BARGAINING

> I've been rich and I've been poor.
> Believe me, rich is better.
> — Sophie Tucker

How city governments exploit their strategic policy opportunities is somewhat like a card game. In poker, each player is dealt a hand of cards that may be strong, weak or somewhere in between. Yet the game is far from over once hands are in place. Particular players deploy their cards differently, some skillfully, others not. Under the right combination of players, strategies, and circumstances, likely losers can become winners. Similarly, in urban development a city is also dealt a hand of structural constraints. These consist of economic and political variables and are encapsulated in our bargaining contexts. Although these structural conditions provide particular advantages and liabilities, it is up to a city's leadership to make the most of them. Urban politics may begin with structural constraints, but it hardly ends with them.

Within this schema regimes fulfill the role of agency. As mentioned in chapter 2, we use the concept of regime in its most limited and original sense — as a regularized pattern of political cooperation for mobilizing city resources in support of a common, agenda.[1] This enables us to focus on how regimes use steering and driving resources in navigating the international marketplace. Put somewhat differently, we see regimes as mobilizing city assets and pursuing opportunities in support of chosen bargaining objectives.[i] In varying ways, regimes frame a city's development agenda and fulfill it. They compose the dominant governing coalitions that bring together the city's economic power, governmental advantages, and local politicocultural resources to fulfill the public agenda. Regimes also function to work out terms of cooperation between segments of the social order, including those that are public, semipublic, nonprofit, and private.

By examining regime behavior we are able to reveal their political dynamics and biases regarding urban development. Of course, the types of regimes in our cities might function differently when they function elsewhere. We recognize that political agency matters, and that governing coalitions might change how they exploit their bargaining environments in response to the challenges at hand.

Nevertheless, we also suggest that regime dynamics are likely to follow limited pathways. Structural constraints limit but do not dictate choices. Decision makers take into account the distribution of bargaining advantages that shape their encounters with the international marketplace. Over time, market conditions, intergovernmental support, popular control, and local culture set expectations about bargaining relationships. As players navigate these structural constraints and mobilize resources, they discover that certain political configurations are more efficacious than others. These configurations become institutionalized as the values, traditions, norms, and practices of a regime.[ii] Partnerships emerge, ways of dealing with the marketplace evolve, and various approaches to development take root. Structural conditions help shape regimes and limit their choices.

Thus, regime politics is a matter of seeking agency discretion and accommodating structural constraints. Change is possible. Opportunities are always on the horizon. Local political leaders may forge coalitions around strategies to obtain assistance from higher-level governments or they may draw upon the city's economic assets in order to influence capital investment. Changes in local partisanship, citizen participation, and other forms of civic activism may present new possibilities for mobilizing public support. Further, slowly changing cultural norms may alter the character of critical publics, leading to pressure for new political agendas. As steering capability grows, regime leaders have opportunities for charting out new directions.

In this chapter and the next, we examine how agency and structure shape the behavior of dominant regimes. This enables us to highlight how local governments exploit their strategic alternatives. It also allows us to show how regimes influence their structural context and may be capable of bringing about changes in community development.

We begin by examining cities that are best able to exploit favorable positions in the international marketplace, namely those found in dirigiste and entrepreneurial bargaining contexts. While all regimes operating in these two contexts enjoy favorable market positions, they organize their politics differently. We see a variety of types. Some assert active, hands-on management of the marketplace. Leaders, bureaucrats, and professional planners employ state power to strongly shape development. Other regimes try to assert this kind of control over the marketplace because they also are endowed with abundant resources. But these regimes lack the political capacity to realize many of their objectives. Still other regime types avoid active planning. They play either a mediating role in managing economic and political cross-pressures or they simply defer to the marketplace to direct development policy.

In dirigiste contexts we point up the presence of "planner type 1 and type 2" regimes. Cities that successfully assert strong control over market forces are treated as type 1 regimes. These cities act prospectively on their development futures, often converting market forces to their own ends. We classify cities that attempt, but frequently fail to realize their objectives as type 2 regimes. These type 2 regimes are often caught in the snare of internal political disagreements that limit regime cooperation due to such things as fractious party politics, interest group rivalry, or even political corruption. One might say that planner type 2 regimes are flawed and frustrated versions of their type 1 cousins.

In an entrepreneurial context we find mercantile and free enterprise regimes. Mercantile regimes take a broad and activist view of public power and aggressively promote business in order to maximize local wealth.[iii] At the same time their encompassing view of public power also prompts mercantile regimes to respond to citizen or neighborhood interests. Caught between the cross pressures of business and popular interests, these regimes often turn out to be fairly volatile. Finally, city governments that follow the marketplace and rely on its signals to manage policy are portrayed as free enterprise regimes. These regimes may well sympathize with business, but resist intervention in the marketplace. Rather than asserting a big public role, this kind of regime concentrates on providing freedom for business to exploit its own interests.

The Dirigiste Context

Planner-type 1 and 2 Regimes

Cities in dirigiste contexts are at the top of the urban hierarchy. Their powerful market positions and intergovernmental advantages provide them with potentially wide policy choices. They can also muster strength from supportive constituencies that embrace postmaterialist values. Still, how and if these resources are exploited depends very much on the kind of regime that plays the development game.

Planner-type 1 regimes are particularly adept at mobilizing an array of capacities in order to advance broad social agendas because they hold substantial steering resources. Toronto and Paris constitute such regimes. Although they differ in many respects and reflect markedly different national cultures, they share commonalities as regimes in their governing coalitions, in the attention they give to their built environments, in their penchant for planning, and in how they approach the marketplace. Their next of kin, a planner-type 2 regime, can be seen in Milan, which always seems to be trying, but is less able to realize its many bargaining opportunities.

The imprints of activism. Toronto was always considered a trail blazer in urban development. Going back to the nineteenth century the city showed a remarkable pride in taking the lead among Canadian cities. It was the first city to put up street lighting (1843), build public libraries (1866), hire a public works staff (1876), build public mass transit (1919), and establish property codes (1936) and take responsibility for public housing (1945). A strong commitment to local government, a self-image of innovation, and a disposition toward activism are deeply embedded in its body politic.[2]

Development politics is carried out through multiple governments, coordinated through overlapping jurisdictions, operating in tandem to realize specific objectives. Nothing better illustrates this proposition than Metro government, established on January 1, 1954. The initiative began with the province and the Ontario Municipal Board, or OMB. Straight away Metro's makers rejected amalgamation because it might suffocate democratic vitality within the area's six cities. Instead, it opted for a federation of jurisdictions, whose council was indirectly elected and chosen from its member units.

As it functioned, the political system contained elements of centralization, which facilitated control, as well as elements of decentralization, which promoted citizen accountability. Ontario generally took on the chore of redistribution and commanded long-range planning. The province did this by issuing mandates and bringing its considerable finances to bear on objectives like building and dispersing public housing. Metro took charge of what could best be described as coordination and control of area-wide functions. This included strategic planning and the all-important provision of infrastructure (development usually follows water, sewer, and utility lines). Metro also managed public transit, major roadways, housing, and economic development. For their part, the municipalities stayed close to their constituencies by handling issues related to local zoning, subdivisions, minor variances, local parks, and recreation and community centers. In some cases, such as planning and zoning, both metro and the individual municipalities shared authority.[3]

Despite the seemingly crazy quilt of authority and geography, the system cohered in remarkable ways. A combination of factors made it all work and determined how an area of 252 square miles would be shaped. Making up the mix was a finely attuned division of labor in which responsibilities were synchronized with area and constituent interests. Toronto's general prosperity and local culture injected an extraordinary comity among its leaders and a concern for general rather than particular benefits.

Innovation created leaders who established pathways of conduct and precedents for policy. Metro's first chair was Frederick Gardiner. Known locally as "Big Daddy," Gardiner has been compared to New York's Robert Moses, as Toronto's publicly designated "master builder." Indeed, Gardiner had met and conversed with Moses. Like Moses, he was an appointee, but this did not stop him from being brash and demonstrating an aggressive willpower. Gardiner also displayed a passion for expressways—proclaiming at one time that he would "cut five or six feet off many sidewalks, shove the poles back, and create two new lanes for traffic."[4]

Apart from these characteristics the comparison ends. For one, both the scale and substance of Gardiner's policies were different. While Gardiner was not above building roads, his initial projects minimized neighborhood disruption. He believed road building could be achieved within a context of "balanced transportation," and he cut a path for rapid transit. The Metro chairman fulfilled his hopes by working tirelessly for transit subsidies and succeeded in gaining support from Ontario. With this accomplished, he began a planning process for a rapid transit (subway) system that yielded results twenty years later. Thus, while growth was important and roads could serve as a stimulant, there were limits to how far this could be pressed. As Gardiner himself put it,

> It is the experience of every large city in America that a succession of new expressways is not the answer to efficient and economical movement of traffic. Each successive one is filled the day it is opened. The irresistible fact is that you cannot provide sufficient highways and parking space to accommodate every person who desires to drive his motor vehicle downtown and back each day. . . . Additional rapid transit is the only answer. It is a snare and a delusion to keep on spending tens of millions of dollars on highways because the province will subsidize them 50 percent. . . . We know that beyond a certain stage $1 spent on rapid transit is worth $5 spent on more arterial highways and parking facilities.[5]

Gardiner prided himself in having a sense of proportion and in seeing the city as a vital center. Neighborhoods were important and bulldozers not always the answer. The Metro chairman was careful to keep a distance from slash and burn practices that destroyed so many neighborhoods south of the border. In this sense he was ahead of his time in pressing for neighborhood retention and rehabilitation. At Gardiner's urging, public housing was put in the suburbs. He combined this strategy with a policy of exactions on developers. By 1955 Gardiner had fees imposed on subdivisions in order to pay for infrastructure and services.[6]

Gardiner then set a pace for other Metro chairs. At least two of his successors used the chairmanship aggressively and could channel development by skillfully applying the tools of planning, infrastructure, rapid transit, and housing policies. There were other occurrences that enhanced Metro's status. Through the 1970s thirteen municipalities had consolidated into just six, and this made it easier to unify the public sector. By 1988 the Metro council was directly elected and its thirty-four members served virtually full time. Previously, Metro councilors were drawn from the individual municipalities and tended to defend their own city's vested interest. Direct elections later became especially important for metro power because members could run in separate districts with a pledge to support a metropolitan wide agenda. Now the Metro council could more forcefully cater to its own constituent base, represent its own conceptions of common interest, and interpret its power in new ways. Tangibly and psychologically, Toronto Metro had matured and acquired a collective identity. Over the longer run this would prove to be a mixed blessing (see the next sections), but for the time being it was heady stuff. With help from the province and cooperation from the municipalities, Metro could unite a powerful public bloc around a common set of policies.

The triple alliance at work.   It was this cooperative confluence of power among province, Metro, and city that directed development up through the late 1990s. The provincial role began with the Ontario Planning Act. Modified over the past thirty years, the act mandated that localities carry out planning and spelled out certain "matters of provincial interest" that would justify intervention. These included environmental protection, energy conservation, financial stability, and the equitable provision and distribution of social services.[7] Also put within the broad grasp of planning are matters related to "community improvement" (urban renewal), land-use controls, and local subdivisions. Ontario's procedures required free and open consideration of local issues. Localities were required to inform the public fully about planning matters, to hold public hearings, and to disseminate information. When challenged, Ontario could bare its teeth and bite very sharply, bringing localities into compliance with mandated planning. The Ontario Municipal Board (OMB) served as watchdog and court of appeals for these procedures, hearing complaints from citizens and agencies and allowing local planning decisions to be contested.

In one of its most notable decisions, the province responded to years of popular opposition against the Spadina Expressway by finally canceling it in 1971. The Spadina was supposed to link downtown Toronto to suburban North York. While Metro and OMB had approved the highway plan, spontaneous demonstrations erupted throughout the city against more road building. Most of the opposition to Spadina was concentrated in the municipalities of Toronto and York. A broad coalition of neighborhoods, tenant associations, ratepayer groups, and environmentalists festooned the city with demonstrations. The collective popular weight came crashing down on decision makers. It is a testimony to the resilience of the system that protestors were not just listened to, but that Metro went ahead with Ontario's decision and subsequently applied the highway funding toward mass transit.[iv]

Despite the embarrassment of Spadina, the Metropolitan council continued to make up the middle link of the triple alliance. Over the years Metro's successes brought it considerable support and legitimacy. This was true across the spectrum of the polyglot metropolis, from traditional groups of European stock to newer immigrants from South and East Asia. While the Metro did not adopt a strategic plan until 1980, it did work with a series of drafts that set out its mission and objectives. Through its considerable powers and a strong chairman the council was able to

- reinforce the downtown as the region's commercial and cultural hub, while promoting subcenters and emphasizing mixed-use development in outer municipalities like North York and Scarborough
- allow for and encourage high-density living outside the city center, particularly in the suburbs
- put limits on neighborhood clearance in favor of preservation
- control sprawl and conserve land throughout the metro area

The adoption of an official plan in 1980 reinforced Metro's operations. Through the decade rapid transit continued to link outer municipalities to the center. In 1955 Toronto's mass transit operated along just 46.5 million square miles. By 1980 its operating square miles reached 101.4 million, and by 1987 it climbed to 120.3 miles.[8] Moreover, the system has not been the exclusive purview of downtown interests, but extended throughout the outer municipalities. Today roughly 62 percent of subway riders are from the outer municipalities.[v] Toronto's rail system is supplemented by light rail and other mass transit. Trams and buses reach into neighborhoods throughout the area.

Housing was also used as a tool to disperse population and diminish lower-income concentrations. Both the province and Metro had their own housing authorities, and they could launch fairly aggressive schemes. Their decisions were not without controversy, and municipalities often resisted. Over time the conflicts subsided, and some consensus emerged over the benefits of fair-share housing. Agreement over these objectives was strengthened by the conversion of questionable public housing projects into less obtrusive assistance. Cooperatives, nonprofit housing, and rent supplements became more acceptable ways for mitigating social segregation.[9]

The demographic and commercial push toward Metro's peripheries was combated by scarcity of land as well as by political actions taken on infrastructure. The installation of septic tanks was subject to strict environmental controls and zoning. Large swatches of green space were made into local or regional parks. This not only dampened the urge to sprawl, but allowed development to keep pace with the outward extension of lake-oriented sewer and water services.[10]

Canadians also learned from the American experience with urban renewal and disliked its abuses. The "slash-and-burn" style of renewal that devastated neighborhoods in many cities south of the border was never part of Toronto's agenda. The city's diversity of ethnic groups had enriched neighborhood life and those communities enjoyed unusual solidarity. Italians, East Europeans, and East and South Asians settled not only near downtown but also throughout the metropolitan area. These newcomers enjoyed a strong sense of ownership in their communities and they formed a natural alliance with metropolitan government, which they saw as a protector of urban diversity. Whether they resided in York, East York, Etobicoke, North York, or Scarborough, they identified as Torontonians, and the best way to do that, in their view, was through Metro.[11]

The last link in the triple alliance were the six municipalities, and at its core is the powerful City of Toronto. During the Metropolitan experience Toronto grew rich and healthy. Its downtown boomed and its cultural life flourished. Canada's financial institutions had begun to concentrate in the downtown as foreign banks, trust companies, and trade association moved into the center. Provincial and Metro politics had worked all too well, and some felt Toronto was becoming "too hot." The proliferation of high rises, mounting congestion, and an invasion of gentrifiers into working-class neighborhoods all seemed to threaten stability.

By the 1970s reformers had won a number of seats on the city council. Antidevelopment sentiment was in the air. Led by the "Red Tory" Mayor David Crombie (1972–78) and later by populist Mayor John Sewell (1978–80), the reformers were determined to slow down or at least better control growth. Within a short time, the city council imposed limits on building height and size, placed a freeze on office construction, and abolished the city's office of economic development.

By 1976 the city's actions were encapsulated in what had become known as the "Central Area Plan." As passed by the council and OMB, the plan called for downtown density limitations, the deconcentration of office towers, and the construction of affordable housing, and low-rise neighborhoods.[12] Other parts of the plan shifted development to underused portions of the city and called for the revitalization of lost manufacture. As the plan wended its way through the legislative process and as it was later implemented, its stringency would soften.

Some neighborhood groups and staunch reformers were opposed to any compromise and the reform movement split into "radical" and "moderate" wings. After public hearings and full discussion, the moderates won out and the Central Area Plan modified. Both Crombie and Sewell were willing to compromise with developers and trade on various advantages (taller buildings for affordable housing). A series of "loopholes" allowed developers to treat hotels as both residential and commercial buildings. The city permitted developers to build "as of right" and surpass density controls in certain areas. Also, planners introduced the idea of "density transfers," giving developers the possibility of exchanging bigger buildings in one area for smaller buildings in another.

All told, the plan was a reasonable one that limited development without harshly penalizing business. The most prominent member of the reformers, Mayor John Sewell, pronounced his contentment with the plan. More importantly, the process revealed a great deal about Toronto politics. As Frisken tells it: All potential influences on city government decision making played a role:

> Neighbourhood and professional groups who participated in the reform movement defined the issues. . . . Even spokespersons for working-class neighbourhoods had influence on the city strategy. . . . Development interests, on the other hand, relentlessly reminded local office holders of the costs to the city treasury and ultimately to the taxpayers. . . . City staff members played a crucial role in translating the concerns of neighbourhood and professional groups into planning principles and then finding ways to reconcile those principles with the aspirations of developers and their allies on the council. They brought to their efforts a professional concern for promoting good design and landscaped open space in the core and for preserving low-rise neighbourhoods outside of it.[13]

While often disagreeing, members of the triple alliance worked well together. Skeptics might point out that Metro was closer to the outer municipalities than central city interests, and would add that Toronto bore too many burdens for the rest of the area. Warts and all, the benefits of intergovernmental cooperation were immense. Provincial, Metro and municipal governments molded common positions on land use, mass transit, housing and infrastructure. This mutually reinforcing, symbiotic coalition allowed Metro Toronto to be counted among the few older North American cities to withstand the suburbs. Metro's six municipalities were often protected by provincial mandates and supported by metropolitan dollars. For their part the municipalities reciprocated by standing up for Metro when it counted and demonstrating loyalty to its planning principles. All this however, was about to come to an abrupt end.

Down with Metro. While Metro Toronto had thrived from the 1950s to the 1980s, so too had the rest of the region known as the Greater Toronto Area or GTA. Forty years ago Metro's share of the GTA population was 77 percent. Today it amounts to just 54 percent, and during the next twenty years it is expected to drop to a third.[14] Besides this, the GTA was badly hit by a recession during the 1990s, and complaints mounted over property tax inequities. People began to wonder whether the Toronto area could do better, be better organized, and compete globally.

Provincial authorities, under the reform-minded New Democratic Party (NDP), decided to take another look at economics and government in the Toronto region. By 1995 the NDP premier appointed a task force to examine the problem and allowed it eighteen months to complete its work. In the interim a new provincial government was elected, led by neoconservative Tory, Mike Harris. While the Tories looked askance at the task force, they did not terminate it. Instead, they shortened its tenure to just four months.[15] When finally presented, the report recommended abolition of Metro government in favor of an extended upper-tier unit that would encompass the entire GTA. This new upper-tier government would cast its nets across a wider region, but it would also be a relatively loose federation of indirectly elected representatives chosen from fifteen municipalities.[16]

Given the limited time in which to draw conclusions, the Task Force unmasked a good deal of information about the region, and came up with a plausible set of recommendations addressing property tax inequities, municipal responsibilities, regional coordination, and a host of other issues. But the Harris government would countenance few, if any, of its suggestions. And there were good political reasons behind the Tory rejection. Harris's neoconservatives were different than their Progressive-Conservative predecessors. These new Tories came to office on a small-town suburban vote, bolstered by an intellectual cadre that wanted to undo the welfare state. Anything that smacked of Toronto's social agenda was looked upon with suspicion. Besides this, the more distant suburbs and small towns opposed an upper tier linking them to Toronto. Adding to the neoconservative rejection was a concern that a GTA-wide authority containing almost half of Ontario's population would be too powerful a competitor.[17] "We were concerned," said one Tory official, "about creating what would be like a small country, along a small province."[18] Logically too, the neoconservatives wanted to put their own stamp on government. Harris admired the Thatcher revolution, calling for simplicity, low taxes, free enterprise, and less government. The Tories had issued a manifesto called the "Common Sense Revolution," which outlined their program, and they were determined to make a distinct mark.

The Harris cabinet deliberated over a variety of ideas and by December 1997 gave their answer. The result was something of a shock. The Tories decided to take a radical step by abolishing Metro, eliminating its six municipalities, and amalgamating everything into a single, unified "mega city." The City of Toronto Act or Bill 103 was introduced into the provincial legislature. If passed, over 2 million people would find themselves under one municipal roof. The newly amalgamated city would have an elected mayor, a forty-four member city council, and a combined bureaucracy of thousands of civil servants. Riding herd over the transition was a board of trustees that would monitor existing municipal councils, approve expenditures, and arbitrate the change.

The seemingly arbitrary process and the content of Bill 103 rubbed against the local grain. Torontonians were not accustomed to be ordered from on high to discard their local democracy. Amalgamation evoked an unprecedented wave of protest. At least ten citizen groups were mobilized into opposing Bill 103. Hundreds of meetings, and marches were held, with most consistently drawing between 1,000 and 2,000 participants.[19] By far the most significant organization was Citizens for Local Democracy, designated by the acronym C4LD.

Leading the charge was John Sewell. The former mayor was a brilliant tactician, and he framed the issue as a blatant attack upon local democracy. C4LD organized benefits and marches, and published a regular newsletter. Many of the participants were middle class and middle aged, and lived close to the downtown. They were generally well educated, reasonably well off, and deeply aggrieved by the threat to their government. While this stratum of the population was most active, it was not alone. Popular support or at least acceptance of the anti-amalgamation movement mushroomed throughout the six municipalities. One municipality, Scarborough, challenged the legality of appointing a board of trustees to oversee them and took the province to court.[vi]

At Sewell's urging, all the municipalities held nonbinding referenda on amalgamation. Surprisingly, turnout was reasonably high across all localities. The City of Toronto's turnout was 36 percent while suburban North York brought out 40 percent of its voters. York and East York attracted 40 and 42 percent respectively, while turnout fell off to roughly 20 percent in Scarborough and Etobicoke. Most significantly, every municipality overwhelmingly rejected the province's move to amalgamate them and abolish Metro. Despite Harris pouring over $4 million dollars into publicizing his cause, anti-amalgamation garnered an astounding 76 percent of the vote.[20]

Up with amalgamation and mega city. All this proved to be of little avail. In April of 1997 the City of Toronto Act was passed and by January 1, 1998 the new mega city was operating. Some amendments were added to quell the opposition. The city council was composed of forty-four members from each of the existing Metro wards plus a mayor elected at-large. The powers of the transition team and board of trustees were watered down. Sneaking into the legislation on a third reading was a provision for six "community councils," drawn from each of the former municipalities. These councils were designed to maintain what was left of local identity; they could make decisions about local zoning variances and grant minor adjustments.[21]

The most startling aspect of the legislation was its lack of study, the paucity of preparation, and its swiftness of passage. From introduction to enactment, Bill 103 took only four months and was adopted with barest deliberation. Despite Tory proclamations about greater efficiency and the elimination of duplication, study after study showed amalgamation would not achieve any savings and could even cost more.[22] Why the haste to abolish the Metro government that had served the area so well for forty-four years and what was behind it all?

Some attribute amalgamation to sheer political animosity of the Harris government toward Toronto. Toronto's city council was fiercely anti-Harris, to the point of giving its employees a day off to mount protests against the province. Harris was then getting even with his opposition, by overwhelming the City of Toronto with more suburban and more conventional constituencies in the outer municipalities.[23]

There were other compelling political and policy reasons. A major rationale behind amalgamation was the so-called "disentanglement and downloading." Over the years, the province had come to support a wide variety of social programs through a series of categorical grants and other assistance. Eliminating Metro through amalgamation could also introduce policy changes. The idea put forth by Harris was to "disentangle" the province from these programs and "download" them to the newly amalgamated government. In return Ontario would pick up costs for education. Presumably, once the new government was responsible for its own social services, it would act more frugally. The addition of more conservative, suburban legislators into a common council would also blunt Toronto's social policies.

Finally, the most alluring motive was the drive to become more economically competitive — both locally and globally. Amalgamation was supported by business and the chamber of commerce, as well as by

Toronto's big newspaper. Developers were peeved at the restrictions put on them by left-leaning city councils who also were behind it. Amalgamation would make it easier to deal with one big government that was likely to be more friendly toward business. Numerous reports, including the earlier GTA task force study, demonstrated a concern for making Toronto competitive in the international market place, and amalgamation was appealing. This touched the provincial government. As one study commented,

> Harris was convinced that Toronto had to reduce its costs to be competitive in the global market, and to the Tories it was obvious that one level of local government had to cost less than seven (Ministry of Muncipal Affairs and Housing, 1996). The provincial government even hired a private consultant to produce a document that supported this assumption.[24]

Whether or not these suppositions will work out is another matter. It is still too early to determine whether institutional change will usher in a deeper regime change. The newly amalgamated city shows some sympathy for business and for the need to compete. It has elected a strong mayor, Mel Lastman, and a new city council that may push for those objectives. Lastman has gone on to political stardom, winning concessions from the province, and his public perception is quite favorable. Notwithstanding this new status, Toronto's attachment to popular control and postmaterialist values are intact. Its community councils have begun to emerge as protectors of these principles. According to one account, the general pattern is that "recommendations from the community councils are never rejected — or even discussed — by the full council.[25] The Tory strategy for bringing about a more entrepreneurial city may or may not work. But again, we can only wait and see.

PARIS: A PLANNER-TYPE I REGIME

Le système Chirac. Even the brashest American boss would have envied Jacques Chirac for the political apparatus at his disposal. Chirac ruled Paris for eighteen years, and did so efficiently, authoritatively, and with political cunning. By any standard, *le système Chirac* was forward looking, dynamic, and extraordinarily popular. Yet it was also monopolistic, single-minded, and managed with an iron fist. Chirac's regime was a strange bundle of contradictions — an old-fashioned city boss who cut across class lines and enjoyed unquestioned popular support, a bureaucracy that thrived on democratic approval, and a conservative coalition that championed municipal socialism.

At the regime's base was the Parisian city council, most of whose 163 representatives were members of Chirac's Gaullist party. Chirac's party held 57 percent of the votes, and it would often be joined by centrists who lifted the Gaullists tally still higher.[vii] As mayor, Chirac controlled a budget of approximately $6.5 billion and commanded 37,000 functionaries.[26] He held power over housing, jobs, and urban development.[viii] By European local standards those were immense prerogatives, and Chirac parlayed them into other arenas.

The mayor's powers were based on an organization of reinforcing political pillars. The first of these pillars carried Chirac's influence into each of the city's twenty arrondissements (neighborhoods). Each arrondissement had its own mayor and local city hall, which drew resources from the central administration. Local mayors held discretion over the distribution of half the social housing in their neighborhood. They also drew on a host of municipal benefits like community development funds, assistance to the needy, and programs to modernize apartments. Chirac knew how to apportion those favors. Over the course of his tenure, Chirac's weight could be felt in almost every neighborhood. What he could not command his centrist allies held for him.

The second pillar strengthened Chirac's hand within the city council. Each neighborhood mayor had a dual role on the city council and served as both a voting representative and as a deputy mayor. Other council members could also be appointed as deputy mayors; in a typical year a total of forty-eight legislators served in that capacity. Deputy mayors were an integral part of Chirac's coalition and extended his legislative influence. Added to the incentive for cooperation were the sheer emoluments of office. Deputy mayors received additional salary, held court in lavish private offices, employed a secretarial and professional staff, and enjoyed the use of a chauffeur-driven automobile.

Not all the deputy mayors were equal. Foremost among them was Jean Tiberi, who served as first deputy mayor. Tiberi was especially influential, and as a young man he helped Chirac climb onto the national political ladder. Initially Tiberi was in charge of general administration. He would go on to manage relations with each of the neighborhood mayors, grant general favors, and serve as the mayor's confident and alter ego.[27]

Another set of political pillars reached into the very heart of government and the ministries. This was made possible through accumulated offices or the *cumul des mandats*. At one time Chirac himself held offices simultaneously as mayor, prime minister, member of the national assembly, and head of his party. His allies on the city council also exercised the *cumul des mandats*. At one time, four municipal councilors served as ministers in the national government, six served as senators, nineteen held office in the national assembly, and twenty-one sat on the regional council.[28] The extent of overlapping offices was astounding and amounted to an interlocking directorate of Chiraquians. *Le système Chirac* pointed the way to intergovernmental influence and showed how this could be used to ply resources and authority from the rest of the nation.

The last, but no less important, pillar was located inside the Gaullist party. Over the years Chirac managed to infiltrate the party and command its heights with operatives from city hall. By the mid-1980s, ten of the twenty-nine of its leading officials also held a Parisian office. The party's secretary general came from the Parisian city council. When, as prime minister, Chirac formed his government, he brought in five ministers from the Paris city council.[29] Indeed, Chirac was accused of using Paris to run the rest of the nation and controlling a "state within a state."[30]

Le système Chirac was not just confined to city hall—it extended into every realm of government. Beyond this, Chirac enjoyed intangible powers and prestige. The national acclaim of being mayor of France's single great city was inestimable. In that role Chirac was not just a national host. He greeted foreign dignitaries and became a European celebrity. Moreover, the press and media were located in Paris and reported on his actions. Everything Chirac did was on display, and since most of his eighteen years were perceived as a period of glorious achievement, the mayor was close to unassailable.

Chirac, of course, had his limitations. He would have to deal with other parties like the centrists when they won the presidency in the 1970s; or he would need to negotiate with the socialists when they took control of national government in the 1980s. But from his perch atop city hall, the mayor could coordinate efforts among municipal, regional, and national governments. As an arch bureaucrat Chirac knew how to get along with the opposition and work across governmental lines.[ix] This was made easier because both the Left and Right viewed public power and market intervention in much the same way.

Searching for a new equilibrium.   Like most conventional politicians of the time, Chirac was haunted by the popularity of the Communist Party. The Communists had a foothold in working-class suburbs and in poor neighborhoods in the north and east of the city. Both the central government and the heavily middle-class citizenry feared a left-wing victory.[x] Much like in other French cities, Parisian Communists succeeded in shaping political discourse and ultimately influenced urban policy. Chirac campaigned for mayor against what he saw as a threat from "collectivism" and "sociocommunism."[31] Clearly, if centrists and rightist politicians were to succeed, they would have to offer a viable populist alternative. The irony was that the more Chirac opposed the left, the more he began to imitate their policies. The sociocommunists favored social housing, and so, too, did Chirac; sociocommunists supported free day-care and so did Chirac; sociocommunists fought for publicly supported cultural events, and so too did Chirac. Finally, sociocommunists argued for a more humane, smaller-scaled environment, and Chirac was already ahead of them.

Whatever else Chirac might do for the city, he was determined to show that he could build a livable Paris. During his first mayoral campaign he laid out this conception.

> Paris needs a mayor who can study and treat its problems. It also needs national intervention if Parisians are to stop the incursion of cement onto the streets of Les Halles, halt the destruction of the quays on the Left Bank, and stop the developers from putting up towers.[32]

Coming from the Right, this may have sounded strange. Critics might counter that Chirac's statements were campaign rhetoric, but they were consonant with the Gaullist regard for a strong state. Intervention and direction of the economy were accepted techniques for realizing public objectives. Besides this, Paris had a powerful impact on the publlic and Chirac's own psyche. Years later, Chirac would reflect on his earliest observations:

> At last I had discovered Paris — a city that I had previously ignored. I realized that Paris was composed of a multitude of villages, where people could cultivate personal relations. Then during the course of my campaign I was surprised and seduced by the enthusiasm about the city, and I said to myself this is tremendous. Another idea struck me about these villages. At bottom Paris was a great city that was trying to fight against the inhumanity that is engendered by being a great city. We had to help Paris do that by favoring communities that would enable people to meet each other and talk to each other.[33]

This attitude was enforced by action. The new mayor relied on a key agency to research and lay out planning strategy for the city. The agency, APUR, was headed by a professional named Pierre Ligen.[xi] Both Ligen and his successor, Nathan Starkman, published highly regarded studies concerning architecture, planning, and urban design, and they had begun to influence local elites.

Chirac and the people around him used APUR's findings to address problems in the oldest, built-up areas of the city. The general idea was to revive the center and then move toward the eastern neighborhoods around it. Over the years, new development had markedly shifted toward the western edge of the city and its newer arrondissements. Many of the city's mega structures, including a grand convention hall, new office buildings, and luxury apartment houses were built in the west and both the pace and scale of development seemed to be accelerating. Chirac and planners at APUR were anxious to reverse this. The idea of finding a new equilibrium in the center and pushing it toward the east seemed feasible.

Through the 1970s and 1980s Chirac and the national government began their efforts at the very epicenter of the city. Public elites had decided to build huge cultural, recreational and commercial centers at Les Halles and at nearby Centre Pompidou. Mixed Corporations, ZACs, and ZADs were used to acquire the land, clear it, and conduct its basic design.[xii] Both the city and the state established the parameters of development and coordinated its massive infrastructure (including rail and metro lines). After these components were in place, private investors, developers, and prospective purchasers were invited to make their bids.[34]

Within a short time, Les Halles and Centre Pompidou had become the most celebrated attractions of the city. Tourists and citizens flocked to the shops and open spaces at Les Halles. They visited the library, media laboratories, and artworks at the Centre Pompidou. Restaurants, hotels, and neighborhoods around Les Halles-Centre Pompidou blossomed. While these projects had their detractors, most were human-scaled and designed for the population at large.[35] Just as important, these projects revitalized the city center and brought new life into adjoining arrondissements. As time went on and the threat from the Left receded, the Gaullists turned to larger projects, especially as the need to balance development toward the east became more important.

The case for rebalancing or readjusting development was compelling. The east was poorer and filled with obsolete factories, marginal workshops, and worn commercial outlets. Large stretches of land on both the right and left banks of the Seine were vacant. Much of this land had been used by the national railway system and was located in the twelfth and thirteen arrondissements. Consolidation and modernization left a good deal of acreage in reserve and relatively few residences were located in those sections. These eastern areas along the river were perfect for creating new neighborhoods and attracting commerce.

During the 1970s APUR began conducting studies for the area along the eastern banks of the Seine. Within a short time the Parisian Prefect bought huge tracts in that area and APUR formulated plans for its development. By the 1980s Chirac's city hall had negotiated with the national government to develop a segment of that terrain along the right bank (twelfth arrondissement). The area, called Secteur Seine Sud Est, was rebuilt through a number of ZACs. Eventually housing, light industry, and office facilities filled the area. Capping off the scheme was a large sports complex designed to accommodate twenty-four different activities. The national government also moved its sizeable Ministry of Finance into the Secteur, followed by a bevy suppliers, banks, and restaurants.[36] Within a short time the predicted synergies had occurred, and part of the formerly deserted eastern frontier, flourished.

Through the beginning of 1990s the city continued to prosper, buoyed by development and what Parisians called the "golden age." Secteur Seine Sud Est created a happy and successful precedent. By now Chirac and his team at APUR set their sights on the east's left bank and laid out grand plans for the area, later baptized Paris Rive Gauche. The prescription called for offices, housing, parks, and sports and cultural facilities linked by rapid transit.[37] The national library, named after President François Mitterand, stood above all else.[xiii]

Times were good and Paris Rive Gauche was supposed to give every major party something. Socialists in the national government supported it, especially since the name of their leader would adorn its major edifice. Gaullists in city hall and the region saw it as an economic locomotive and a way to attract a middle class into the east. Centrists viewed the project as good planning and as containing the right mix of commerce and residence. At the time only the communists and green party shared misgivings about Paris Rive Gauche, finding it wasteful and too large.

Politically, Paris Rive Gauche was in the hands of Chirac and his Gaullists. The usual formula for conducting development was put into operation — collaboration between different levels of government, interlocking directorates of public officials, special zoning and public finance. The project's location in the thirteenth arrondissement placed it within the bailiwick of Jacques Toubon, a Chirac loyalist who held posts as minister of justice, deputy mayor, neighborhood mayor, and municipal councilor. ZACs sprang up in the project area, and their implementation was carried out by a mixed corporation under the acronym SEMAPA.[xiv] Here, too, Toubon would play the pivotal role by serving as SEMAPA's president, thus insuring Gaullist control. Toubon was the city's operative and SEMAPA was a partnership among multiple governments or agencies — 57 percent of its shares belonged to the city, 20 percent was owned by the national railway, and 5 percent was held by the state and the region. The rest was kept by miscellaneous owners.[38]

Everything appeared to be on track until recession struck in 1993. More corporations headed toward the exurbs, unemployment began to climb, and city revenues were on the decline. Worse yet, city hall realized that it had a surfeit of office space on hand and property values began to fall. The average real estate loss amounted to 11.6 percent. Some of the steepest declines were in the "golden triangle" (eighth arrondissementt), where property fell by 23 percent, and in the most western neighborhood (seventeenth arrondissement), where the drop amounted to 17 percent.[39]

Chirac was forced to take the rare step of raising municipal taxes. The mayor adjusted local regulations and lowered density, so that more building space would be used. He also took measures to convert commercial space into residential quarters. While some journalists and partisans exaggerated the extent of decline, the recession did weigh on the city. The "golden age" seemed to have ended or at least abated, and the city would have to modify its development strategy. The time was ripe for some change. By 1995 Chirac was off to the Palace Elysée as president of the republic. While Chirac would have preferred a more graceful exit, the city was ready for a successor. In that same year Jean Tiberi — Chirac's former first deputy mayor — was elected as Paris's next mayor.

Gaullist loss and socialist victory.   Despite Chirac's success, he had not left Tiberi with much political capital. Parisians were discontent with the local economy, with their city's fiscal condition, with rising crime, and with the direction of urban development. Tiberi entered office with a plurality of just 35 percent of council votes.[xv] With help from the center he could muster a majority, but like everyone, he knew the Socialists were posing a real challenge. A left coalition, led by Socialist Bertrand Delanoe, had won six arrondissements, all within the northern and eastern sections of the city. Four more arrondissements in the center and left bank had drifted toward the Socialists and were considered ripe for a future upset.[40] Already the Socialists had begun to attack Tiberi, claiming that he would be a "transitional mayor" and not strong or popular enough to resist a reinvigorated Left.[41]

Clearly, Tiberi would have to shift direction. Much like Chirac did eighteen years earlier, Tiberi sought to preempt the Left by resorting to populist themes. He emphasized the use of bicycles as a means of transport and advocated the construction of special bicycle paths throughout the city. On Sundays he closed highways and streets for pedestrians, cyclists, and joggers. He talked about priorities for better social housing, stable neighborhoods, open participation, and "urbanism with a human face,"[42] and characterized his goals as follows:

> I want to be a quality of life mayor. This theme will be debated in the city council. Problems related to neighborhood proximity, the struggle against pollution, how to better utilize the Seine . . . above all we have to create a dialogue with Parisians.[43]

At the same time, Tiberi sought to carve out his own path and distinguish himself from his mentor. Chirac was a man who would "dive" into problems, Tiberi confessed, but I "pedal" through them. He then insisted, "I am not a transitional mayor."[44] Tiberi's aspirations for the city would be more modest, but at the same time consistent, and he intended to use the bountiful instruments at hand.

Whether Tiberi would be a transitional mayor depended on how he could resolve difficulties confronting his coalition, and his problems came from all sides. On the left, the Socialists had launched a vigorous campaign against Paris Rive Gauche. The critics were led by Socialist Bertand Delanoe, and his allies declaimed the project for being too expensive, too large, and holding too much office space.[45] The Left was now a significant minority: it had elected socialist councilors from the neighborhood, and it could muster constituent support.

Indeed, the system of decentralized popular control and centralized political accountability seems to have worked — this time against the Gaullists. Citizens made their voice heard at neighborhood city halls and acted through their mayors and local councils. They exerted pressure at general meetings of the city council.[46] Elsewhere, citizen held demonstrations against large projects, and the regime was forced to retreat.[xvi]

Tiberi found himself not only pedaling, but also back-pedaling on Paris Rive Gauche. The project was scaled down, so that two subterranean lanes intended for automobiles were eliminated, its extensions into an historic rail station were cancelled, and its office space was reduced. Despite the cutbacks, SEMAPA faced budgetary deficits, city hall found itself criticized for fiscal mismanagement and for having created a "fiasco."[47]

Tiberi's problems were also exacerbated by his own behavior. A series of scandals gripped his administration. The mayor was legally charged with profiting from contracts given to construction companies. He was accused of helping members of his family obtain subsidized apartments. The most talked about scandal involved Tiberi's wife who was found guilty of accepting $36,000 for a badly written report to a government agency on a subject that she knew nothing about. Tiberi had hoped for an easy renomination as mayor. But his petitions were found to contain nonexistent supporters, so called "phantom signatures."[48]

Clearly, Tiberi had lost his moral stature and his populist image was badly tarnished. In the midst of the scandals he was confronted by challenges within his own party. Jacques Toubon had always been Tiberi's rival and had his own mayoral ambitions. For a time Toubon succeeded in forming a breakaway faction of thirty-three city councilors. Among them were thirteen deputy mayors and five neighborhood mayors. Toubon hoped that he could topple Tiberi or at least prevent him from running for reelection. The effort, dubbed a "putsch" by the press, ultimately failed, but it revealed Tiberi's political fragility. The mayor was able to ward off Toubon's challenge by calling for President Chirac's intercession. When Chirac did come to the rescue, Tiberi boasted "I am untouchable."[49]

But was he "untouchable"? Once Tiberi foundered, Chirac kept a distance from him. The president refused to aid him when the Gaullists finally balked at his renomination. The public was against him. Polls showed that 54 percent of Parisians thought Tiberi should resign, and a substantial proportion felt his personal conduct had compromised the city.[50] The possibility of reelection was slim, and 70 percent of voters said that they would vote against the mayor.[51] Even among his own rightist constituency Tiberi could garner only 7 percent of the vote.

Important politicians at both the center and the right began to defect in preparation for the 2001 elections. In those elections mainstream Gaullists decided to put up a well-known candidate named Phillipe Seguin. A crestfallen Tiberi was about to face an ominous split in his own ranks. Besides this, Seguin was hailed as the lead candidate, and many observers believed he would "gobble up" the Socialists.

But Paris was in for a surprise. Not only had the Socialists won many seats in the last election, but they had been gaining steadily over the years. As they saw it, the city was now in the throes of scandal (whose revelations stretched back to Chirac) the opposition was divided, and momentum was on their side. Betrand Delanoe would just need to topple a crumbling machine. As it turned out, the Socialist prognosis was correct. In March of 2001 they carried twelve of twenty arrondissements. The leftist coalition won ninety-two seats in the city council against seventy-one seats for the Right. Ironically, the Left lost the popular vote, but that hardly mattered.[xvii] The Socialists had finally conquered Paris and Delanoe was triumphant.

For all the fanfare and celebration, this was a victory over a man and his errors and not over a system. True, *le système Chirac* was defeated, but was it really gone? The Socialist inherited the same powers, discretion, and political arrangements that Gaullists had enjoyed. While Delanoe had pledged to clean up corruption and to run an honest government, many of the same practices would hold. The Socialists' platform was either a variation of their Gaullist predecessors or quite technical. Delanoe had promised transparency, modernization, security, a better environment and still more gardens. What Parisian could possibly argue with that?[52]

MILAN: A PLANNER-TYPE 2 REGIME

Frustrated politics.   On a summer day in 1980 Mayor Carlo Tognoli took a group of journalists on a helicopter tour over Milan. For the popular cigar-smoking Socialist mayor with a flair for publicity, the event was part of a series of media campaigns to show off the government's new vision of the city. During the tour he described the left giunta's plans for special projects that would radically transform Milan. His plans were a major break from previous years when city hall was more devoted to preserving Milan's industrial past. Indeed, for the past five years the left-leaning administrations struggled to find policies that would cushion their voters from the fearful social effects — especially unemployment and displacement — of the city's relentless transition into one of Europe's major centers of finance, services, and high technology. No longer able to oppose these changes, Tognoli helped forge a new consensus in favor of promoting and controlling them.

More than twenty years later relatively few of the mayor's key projects came to fruition and the goal of a more modern polycentered metropolis remains a distant vision. Like Paris and Toronto, political leaders in Milan have tried to exploit their city's huge economic advantages and political prowess to organize a planner-type 1 regime since the 1980s. Yet despite Milan's position as Italy's northern economic powerhouse and its access to governmental assistance, they have not succeeded. During the 1980s Tognoli did all he could to exploit his formidable political connections with Rome. His close ally, Prime Minister Bettino Craxi, whose power base was also in Milan, even made the mayor Italy's first Minister of Urban Areas. When Tognoli left city hall for Rome, his Socialist successor, Paolo Pillitteri (who is Craxi's son-in-law), pursued similar political strategies.

What often defeats Tognoli, Pillitteri, and other Milanese power brokers is that they are unable to make their government work. Milan has most of the assets of a planner-type 1 regime, but it cannot mobilize crucial steering resources. Almost by default, this planner-type 2 city becomes absorbed in promoting special clientele interests, not governing them. Players find it easy to veto policy change but difficult to bring it about. Although Milan has a reputation for pragmatic government, this image applies more to the way it delivers routine services. Its particular brew of partisanship, bureaucracy, and clientelism concentrates power in a network of state actors but then pulls the regime apart as it makes decisions.

Milanese pluralism and the noncoalition.   Milan's political landscape presents a disjointed profile. It is difficult to speak of a dominant governing coalition because the regime has weak centralizing influences. Even though power gravitates to state-centered institutions and players, they function as a noncoalition who close ranks only on occasion.

As in most of Italy, politicians in Milan are highly organized. They divide into ideological blocs. Party affiliation and perspective essentially anchor participation in the regime, structuring position, place, and decisional networks. The role of partisanship is extended by means of pervasive clientelism for which Italy is famous. The "Clean Hands" investigations of the 1990s was launched by Milan magistrates uncovering widespread favoritism and corruption in the city, eventually resulting in the indictment of scores of public officials, including former mayors Tognoli and Pillitteri. Patronage is organized almost completely by partisan division of spoils. Public agencies and enterprises, such as the city's subway as well as the board of governors for the state university, are always party appointments. Local politicians even appoint the head of the chamber of commerce. Few areas of public life are untouched by party patronage. For instance, the neighborhood councils that were established in the 1970s to extend citizen participation are thoroughly partisan. Their elected membership reflects in the neighborhood the partisan composition of the city council. They are places where local activists often seek to begin party careers, not just forums to promote neighborhood agendas.

Milanese partisanship contributes to the regime's fragmentation and instability. Party politics is competitive, but it is characterized by incessant *trasformismo*, the shuffling of alliances to form administrations. After 1975 center-right coalitions led by Christian Democrats were replaced by left-wing coalitions whose composition changed frequently. Party competition and instability increased steadily after the mid-1980s. Center-left coalitions that excluded the Communists were formed, but they functioned poorly. Even after the return of left giuntas in 1988, party factionalism grew as administrations depended on greens and other small parties for support. The years following 1990 witnessed a quantum leap in party instability. In 1992 Milan became the epicenter of sweeping anti-corruption investigations that eventually spread all over Italy in what journalists termed the *Tangentopoli* (meaning "bribe city") scandal. So pervasive and deeply rooted was evidence of outright bribery and other forms of political corruption found by magistrates that it precipitated deep revulsion among Italy's already cynical voters against the dominant political parties. A crisis of legitimacy occurred, leading to collapse of public support for virtually all of the major parties that governed the country since World War II. A flurry of reforms designed to clean up government and the electoral process and to encourage more orderly governance soon followed. In Milan these years saw the overturning of the old party system, along with the rise of the Northern League, the reform of the Communist Party (which split into other parties), and the birth of new minor parties and factions. But the post-Tangentopoli party system proved no more stable. Voters initially punished the old party regime by electing a Northern League government — an explicitly regional party that seeks a federal state. Yet this new party was unable to build stable center-right alliances due to party defections and an unsettled electorate who turned to another new party, Forza Italia (Go Italy), and to a new mayor in the next election.

Ironically, the reach of party politicians to control government is limited by the strongly clientelist character of politics. Milanese partisans freely mix ideology and patronage politics, but clientelist deal-making assumes such proportions that it takes on a life of its own. Parties, factions, and individual players must maintain elaborate divisions of the spoils and rely on cross-party cooperation in order to do favors and maintain their political base. The upshot is that party leaders are able to control jobs, but they have more difficulty asserting control over policy and bureaucracies. They cannot easily discipline recalcitrant officials without upsetting the existing system of patronage and favors. They lack a stable base for promoting sustained policy agendas.

The local, regional, and central governments play key roles in the noncoalition. In a city where the state looms large in financing and regulating economic activities, public agencies and their professional bureaucracies rival party politicians in matters of governance. Since Milan has few independent revenue sources, it is dependent on finding money for almost any significant capital project from public agencies, especially agencies of the central government. Similarly, local bureaucracies have their own sources of autonomy and power. The city often owns the major public corporations that control its infrastructure. Like all government organizations, however, these agencies advance their own interests.[53] Their power is magnified in a political order like that of Milan, where rampant clientelism, institutional fragmentation, and unstable governing coalitions increase the value of bureaucratic cooperation.

One might expect that national government is a centralizing force in the regime. It is not. Milanese politicians have access to very substantial sources of money and power at higher levels. Despite tight partisan links, central government officials are not very reliable allies with local party machines. Italy not only lacks an urban policy, but the bulk of public expenditures and development assistance is distributed by the field agencies of the national ministries in Rome, state holding companies, public enterprises, and special agencies. The Italian civil service has no uniform training, hierarchy of remuneration, or career mobility. Bureau responsibilities are fragmented due to the tradition of individual agencies having direct links in regions and cities. This permits tight linkages between particular agencies and their client groups at the local level.[54] There is no legal requirement for coordination among state projects, and local officials receive intervention from on high in a process that is at the discretion of particular agencies.

National politicians in Rome have a limited interest in coordinating this system. They display greater attention to redistributing resources to weaker economic regions and doing favors for clients.[55] Partisan rivalry adds to the possibilities for obstruction, especially when different parties govern in Milan and Rome.[56] The effect on Milan is highly negative. Fragmentation of functional competencies and Roman indifference to bureaucratic obstruction leaves Milanese officials scrambling to make deals with strategically placed agencies in order to make the city work. Although the regional government has sometimes been able to assume a role in mediating among these interests, its limited resources and perceived bias in favor of governments on the periphery diminish its ability to overcome governmental fragmentation.[57]

Outside of this dominant core of partisans and bureaucrats, there are other organized interests, especially business groups, good government-style associations, and citizen associations. Unfortunately, these organizations remain marginal because none of them can build alliances, as American "pro-growth" coalitions are able to do. Rather, these groups pursue limited ends and hope to veto occasional decisions that they do not like. This is not for want of organization. Civil society in Milan is highly organized.[58] Rather, these interests stay at the margins because it is such an uphill task for private interests to build policy alliances in a system that is socially at odds and dominated by partisanship.

Business is dwarfed by public actors that can unilaterally change the parameters of decisions.[59] Particular business interests are unable to muster much cohesion in this system. The big industrial groups — such as the state holding companies like IRI with its many subsidiaries, such as ITALSTAT or STET, or corporate giants like Pirelli, Montedison, and Falk — are not homogeneous in their interests and do not express a corporate view. When they have real estate projects to promote, their participation is a minor part of much larger corporate financial portfolios. They look to party chieftains to define the issues.[60] Few took a very active role in managing renewal plans even when they had a direct interest.

Since developers and real estate interests have a large stake in obtaining speculative advantages, they have close ties to party politicians, which were a source of many corruption scandals during the 1980s. Even they do not act as part of a "growth machine." The system of planning regulation prevents private speculation and there is extensive public ownership of land. Public, quasi-public, and mixed corporations are often the main investors in renewal projects all over Milan, crowding out many private developers who are more active in projects outside of the city.[61]

Business finds difficulty acting to promote its own collective interests in local politics. Business leaders realize that if party politicians are unable to succeed, then they can do little better. Like the parties, business has its own internal disagreements. For instance, top business leaders proposed to move the Milan stock exchange in the mid-1960s. The exchange lacked space and modern equipment, including air conditioning, at a time when Milan was rapidly becoming a key center of finance in Europe. Ninety percent of the security trading in Italy takes place in Milan. Yet the matter took more than twenty years to settle.[62] After years of stalemate, regional government mediators nudged business leaders to expand the stock exchange on its existing site. If key business interests are unable to achieve much unity on an issue of such immediate economic importance, they can scarcely pursue more distant collective political agendas.

Lack of cohesion spurred creation of some new organizations to bring together private and public players during the 1980s. One of these partnerships, L'Associazione degli Interessi Metropolitani (AIM) organized banks, corporations, and other business interests into a public-private roundtable with the region and commune. Similar groups of varying persuasions also blossomed.[63] Yet none of these provided venues for coalition building to support specific policies. Most have party linkages and they defer to professional politicians in matters of governance.[64]

Finally, citizen groups are significant players. Since the late 1960s, as social turmoil and demands for direct political participation have escalated, citizen and neighborhood groups have proliferated. Milan's "soft deindustrialization" experience (little unemployment or displacement of the poor) helped undercut vigorous citizen opposition to city development plans. But NIMBYism is pervasive. By the 1980s neighborhood groups were no longer as inclined to depend on party politicians to represent them. Groups without partisan or ideological affinities mobilized over specific issues and were able to win concessions and sometimes even defeat proposals that were perceived to harm valued neighborhood interests.[65] For example, one group was able to eliminate a proposal for a light rail line that was to link with the refurbished San Siro stadium for the 1990 World Cup.[66]

Mobilizing pluralism and Passante. In planner-type 2 politics it is relatively easy for players to protect special interests, but difficult for them to mobilize coalitions in order to realize public agendas. As explained earlier, this arrangement has enabled the regime to cushion vulnerable groups from some of the negative social consequences of economic re-structuring. As the city turned to find ways of stimulating economic growth, the extensive opportunities for public oversight, regulation, and control of projects ensured wide consideration of interests that might be marginalized in less pluralistic regimes. Significant policy change is possible, but it requires a broad consensus among key party and bureaucratic players. It is also critical to generate many side payments, such as jobs and contracts, in order to sustain cooperation among political entrepreneurs. This means cutting almost endless deals that transcend local, regional, and national politics. Only after this is under way does the private sector become much of a player—and usually at the margins of the game.

Since these conditions are difficult to achieve, the regime has limited reach in policy development. The city's experience with building the Passante, the underground train to subway and train stations, into a single network offers a glimpse of the regime in action.[xviii] As noted in chapter 4, this project became the backbone of Milan's economic modernization drive and polycentric expansion. It was expected to facilitate the movement of people and commerce as well as stimulate the redevelopment of underused or derelict areas just outside the Central Business District (CBD). By 2000 the project was well along, but the entire line and its stations of interchange were incomplete after decades of activity. It represents an instance of how planner-type 2 politics can partially succeed.

The project was first proposed in 1967 after disagreements among mayors of communes in the region had led Milan's leaders to focus on transportation as a way out of their stalemate. In succeeding years this program was fought over by public agencies that had a direct stake in the transportation plan. But coalition politics virtually excluded prominent private interests. Even at the height of media attention to the project during the early 1980s, there was little newspaper reporting of details and conflicts among specific interests nor was there any attempt to consult with the business community. Indeed, even though this multi-billion-dollar project was expected to influence property values and alter land uses all along its path, a survey showed that Milan's business leaders expressed little interest in it.[67]

Until the mid-1970s major interests could not agree on what to do with the proposal. Dominant parties opposed the Passante in favor of a vast expansion of the subways and surface transportation. Some parties, like the Christian Democrats and Socialists, were bent on trying to save industrial jobs and were also hesitant to allow the state railroad to assume a leading role in the scheme. Others, like the Communists, wished to contain fare increases and favored other mass transit ideas. This position was also taken by the Metropolitana Milanese, which constructs, but does not operate, the subways. This agency believed that Passante would threaten plans for subway expansion. Similar reasoning led the public corporation that operates the subway system to disregard the plan. The State Railroad, a national agency with ample resources for actually building the line, had other priorities in its national transportation plan. Finally, the private North Milan Railway, which operates north of the city, was also ambivalent. Although the Passante had the support of some partisans and many professional planners, its prospects looked bleak.

Several fortuitous changes eventually brought about a convergence of interests. Most important, left giuntas, elected during the mid-1970s, saw the Passante as a means of accommodating inevitable postindustrial change while opening up opportunities to experiment with the remaking of industrial and residential areas scattered around the city center. The new regional government wished to establish a transportation presence and it took majority control of the North Milan Railway. It saw the Passante as a means of extending the importance of the railroad. When a decision was made by the city to build a third subway line in addition to the Passante, there was little reason for continued opposition by either of the subway agencies. One envisioned a big increase in construction activities since they would build most of the system. The operating authority, which was in fiscal deficit and forced to impose unpopular fare increases, feared excessive passenger traffic after a third subway line opened. The Passante could relieve passenger congestion.

The critical interest to come on board the Passante bandwagon was the State Railroad. Although this agency cared little about the economic value of the project for Milan, it received a huge allocation of money from Rome to deal with rail congestion in urban areas. This largesse changed its priorities. Looking for ways of spending money to assert its new role, the railroad devised a plan to stimulate integration of the regional economy. The Passante was now integral to their plan. They eagerly came up with most of the money for the project.

In effect, the coalition came together after decisions were made to transform the issue of the Passante into a positive sum game where virtually everybody wins. Once the key officials saw benefits and hardly any costs, the project came to life. By being able to exclude or ignore other interests, such as business, neighborhood interests, and other groups who might have had a different stake in the project, bureaucratic elites could pursue their organizational interests without much need to compromise. Similarly, party elites could fulfill their ideological agendas and anticipate huge contracts and patronage opportunities as billions of lira would change hands over many years ahead. Significantly, an agreement was struck in 1983 to set up a committee of coordination representing all the major players to implement the project and oversee the division of spoils.

Not surprisingly, after ground was broken for the Passante in 1984, the project became mired in delay, often due to repeated raids by politicians looking for patronage and payoffs. Most often bureaucrats and party officials whose cooperation was necessary to implement the program used their power to veto or delay critical decisions or approvals. This enabled them to enhance their individual political importance and raise the "price" of their cooperation. This pattern became most salient during the late 1980s. Party factionalism escalated, demands for *tangenti* mushroomed, and deal making had less and less to do with policy-making.

Politics as usual. When Milan's constellation of interests are unable to find a broad consensus on issues, the lure of patronage politics alone is seldom able to carry policy initiatives. Decisions easily get bogged down in conflict and stalemate. Eventually, the need to cope with division and instability in governing coalitions displaces policy considerations.

The city's poor record in implementing most of the area projects that are considered critical to the dream of a multipolar city is suggestive of this reality. Although a detailed master plan to govern the redevelopment of strategic parts of Milan won broad support during the 1980s, only a few of these were realized. Most often the coalition of interests that initially supported area redevelopment plans was unable to hang together as issues of implementation emerged. For instance, a plan to build a modern financial and cultural center around one of the main Passante stations has not yet come to fruition despite the site's strategic location in the CBD. The project had every conceivable advantage. Public agencies owned most of the land. There was broad party support for a project that could begin capturing benefits from the costly Passante project. Since redevelopment of the site would expand the city's financial district, the business community was highly supportive and organized a partnership to promote and invest in the scheme. However, neither the public or private sponsors could maintain agreement. Business interests became divided over the division of property and investor profits, and financial interests reneged on a deal to move the stock exchange there. Public sector players went through continual changes of mind in response to factional rivalries, protests by resident and environmental groups, as well as a corruption scandal involving a major developer. Government agencies that were expected to invest in the project failed to commit at critical times, casting doubt on the viability of the venture.[68] Similar experiences colored other area planning.[69]

Only when exceptional circumstances limit the scope of conflict and when projects can generate huge benefits for nearly everyone has area planning succeeded. For example, the redevelopment of a large site (Bovisa) that is situated at the end of the Passante proved successful. The project was under control of a single investor that happened to be a public educational institution (whose board was appointed by the parties, of course). It planned to transform a grimy and derelict industrial enclave on the edge of a middle-class neighborhood into an upbeat center of schools, culture, and shops while also providing direct subway access to downtown for residents. The only significant opposition came from resident groups seeking to reduce the project's scale and requesting contributions for neighborhood amenities. After pressure from local councilors granted these concessions, urban renewal rolled on.[70]

In the aftermath of *Tangentopoli* and the fall of the old party system, Milan became even more conflict-ridden.[71] This, in turn, has forced politicos to focus on rebuilding the regime's political capacity, not on entertaining bold new economic strategies. New electoral laws enacted in 1993 help centralize power. The mayor became directly elected and parties supporting the winning candidate earned extra representation. Votes of no confidence would result in a new election for the council, but not for the mayor. Further, the mayor's power of appointment was expanded. Nevertheless, recent years continue to witness spreading factionalism within the parties, especially in the new parties struggling to build stable power bases. Although Milan remains an economic powerhouse, its regime severely limits how its citizens can shape the city's future.

The Entrepreneurial Context

Mercantile and Free Enterprise Regimes

The entrepreneurial bargaining context affords regime-builders with mixed opportunities. On one hand, this environment provides cities with relatively favorable economic conditions, encouraging with market power and prospective revenues the possibilities for large public endeavors. Yet, on the other hand, any economic advantages they might enjoy must be constantly weighed against the scant regulatory intervention and fiscal support from higher-level governments that these cities can count on in the development game. The result is an unstable atmosphere for participating in the international marketplace. Governing regimes can easily tack in different directions in finding formulas for political survival. New York's mercantile government sometimes leans Left and supports a big public presence, while Houston's free enterprise politicians favor right-of-center solutions.

Modern mercantilism. During the Middle Ages the cities of the Hanseatic League in Northern Germany were a model of how local governments could mobilize state power to promote commerce and trade. Like these ancient mercantile cities, New York also puts its power behind business, and it endeavors to promote trade in order to maximize its wealth. The leading figure behind this strategy was Robert Moses, who showed how a mix of governmental authority and business acumen could change a whole city. This tradition became all the more acute because of the city's uncertain economic circumstances. As described earlier, the city manages a powerful, but highly volatile, advanced service economy. Though it has global reach, the economy's role in the international marketplace causes it to lurch between boom and bust cycles. Equally important, the city lacks reliable support from national, state, or regional government. The result: private-sector considerations always loom large in public intervention. What happens on Wall Street and the downtown real estate markets plays a central role in public policy.

Although business looms large, politicians are also subject to vigorous cross-pressures from the citizenry. As described in chapter 3, the city's active popular-control system fuels a highly pluralistic politics. Its polyglot political culture adds to these pressures to encourage public-sector solutions.[72] As critics put it, "the overwhelming majority of New York voters sympathize with service-demanders; representatives of money-providing groups stand little chance of gaining a majority of votes."[73] This reality is recognized by business elites. High taxes, large governmental budgets, and a costly system of social services supported by one of the most highly regulated local business environments in the United States are realities that often go unchallenged even by business candidates for public office. The need to constantly juggle these imperatives powerfully shapes New York's regime.

Reconciling cross-pressures. Mercantile politics gives high priority to market-management activities while making important concessions to powerful political interests whose cooperation is important. Business leads. This is most evident on the boards and in the executive offices of Public Benefit Corporations (PBCs) like the bistate Port Authority. These corporations are supposed to be managed like aggressive commercial enterprise, and governors generally have appointed members of the business and legal communities to head them.[74] Business influence goes well beyond mere membership on a PBC. The views and objectives of business leaders are well known in a city where the state of the economy dwarfs all other news. The most salient leaders come from the city's FIRE sector, particularly those who run the investment houses, own much of the city's commercial real estate, and float the billions of dollars in city debt that is issued every year.[75]

A primary institution for bringing together these interests is the New York City Partnership, an organization founded by David Rockefeller during New York's brush with bankruptcy during the 1970s. During the fiscal crisis, business dominated the two state boards that were appointed to monitor and refinance the city's government, the Emergency Financial Control Board (since renamed the Financial Control Board [FCB]) and the Municipal Assistance Corporation (MAC). They virtually ran the city government and imposed austerity programs that led to balanced budgets during the early 1980s.[76] Both institutions have become distant watchdogs as the Partnership has taken the more prominent leadership role.[77] The Downtown Lower Manhattan Association (DLMA) is dominated by Wall Street and strongly influences development decisions in Manhattan.[78]

Business leaders share power with public officials, and together they form the backbone of the mercantile regime. While business provides much of the economic muscle, politicians manage conflict and enlist the support of multiple interest groups (neighborhood associations, "good government" organizations, professional associations, and the media). In this highly pluralistic, variegated system, most important economic policy initiatives must win widespread political acceptance. Elected officials who can put together stable electoral coalitions play an important role in economic policy-making.[79] Public-private cooperation is particularly successful when leaders get behind a pro-growth agenda. But these coalitions ebb during periods of electoral instability.[80]

Electoral politics during recent decades shows how this works. The tumultuous years of Mayor John Lindsay during the 1960s and early 1970s were times of regime conflict. The Lindsay coalition was anchored in liberal voter groups, particularly Jewish professionals and reform Democrats. They joined with lower-income minorities to elect and reelect Lindsay. Although some corporate business players initially backed the mayor, they later abandoned him after the fiscal difficulties began to threaten economic stability. Under Lindsay huge increases in public spending helped precipitate the fiscal crisis.[81] Mayor Abe Beame, who succeeded Lindsay, was unable to build a stable electoral coalition capable of avoiding Lindsay's fiscal dilemmas.

Since the fiscal crisis years, New York mayors have organized voter coalitions that enable them to maintain an alliance with leading business interests while containing the demands of service-demanding groups.[82] However, this is a delicate balance. Popular sentiment often opposes development policies that favor business. The prototype business-government coalition was perfected by Mayor Edward Koch (1977–89). Koch restored the close relationships with corporate business interests that deteriorated during the Lindsay and Beame years. He did so by adopting neoliberal programs. This included fiscal austerity in social services and higher priority for programs to subsidize business priorities. At the same time, Koch forged a voter coalition of middle- and working-class whites, homeowners in the outer boroughs, ethnics, and Catholics. As he cut services to meet fiscal constraints, Koch appealed to concerns about racial turmoil and crime. The coalition proved so successful that it helped him win the Republican and Democrat party nominations in his 1981 reelection bid and again in 1985.

This right-leaning coalition was replaced during David Dinkins's single term. Elected as the city's first black mayor in 1989, Dinkins tried to rebuild something like the old Lindsay coalition. Dinkins did, however, take pains to maintain a tight alliance with the city's business leaders who supported him in order to defuse the racial tensions. While Dinkins pursued pro-business policies, his presence provided powerful symbolic assurances to black voters. Despite his efforts, Dinkins's coalition proved unstable, and conflicts over race plagued his administration. In 1993 he narrowly lost to Rudolph Giuliani.

Koch's old coalition was substantially rebuilt by Mayor Giuliani. The Republican mayor espoused neoconservative ideals, he appealed to many Hispanic voters, and, for the most part, avoided the inflammatory racial rhetoric of the Koch years. The lessons are revealing. Despite some obeisance to a social agenda, most mayors have forged pro-growth voter coalitions, and they have maintained close relations with the city's business leadership.[83] The city's latest mayor, Michael Bloomberg, is a billionaire businessman with liberal credentials.

Nonbusiness groups gain some access to the regime by virtue of the city's pluralist and participatory character.[84] The city's Uniform Land Use Review Procedures (ULURP) allows even weakly organized neighborhood interests to penetrate the governing coalition.[85] Adopted as part of a plan for neighborhood governance, ULURP is an elaborate system of review for all significant land-use changes. The procedure requires that virtually all changes begin with hearings and reviews at the neighborhood planning board level. Although boards can only make recommendations, they carry considerable weight, causing developers to frequently tailor their plans to popular opinion. ULURP also provides for public hearings at other stages of the planning process, including the borough, planning-commission, city-council, and mayoral levels. While some investors feel that ULURP is a developer's nightmare, populists see it as a pluralist's dream.

Officials realize that they can achieve their market management objectives only if they can also satisfy popular opinion. The mercantile regime relies on political institutions that buffer economic policy from voter pressures. PBCs are at the center of decision making. These corporations help insulate major economic programs from voters and the general local government. Financially independent and accountable to capital markets, these corporations plan and operate the city's most important economic development projects. Among these is the Empire State Development Corporation. As a public corporation, it can use its vast borrowing capacity and can override local land-use regulations, including ULURP, to promote economic development.

Since 1970 additional PBCs were created because they serve the governing coalition's market management priorities and they guarantee minimal interference from voters. In 1960 there were only six such authorities in the city. By the 1990s the number of PBCs had soared to thirty-six. Even New York's liberal black mayor David Dinkins sought to create more PBCs, including one such corporation to maintain the city's bridges and another to provide venture capital for private business.[86]

The city government's own participation in development also is structured to buffer it from mass political pressures. It too uses a special agency to package loans, grant tax concessions, and lure jobs into the city. Called the Public Development Corporation, this mayoral agency is not subject to review by the city council. All this is done so that the city can nimbly circumvent public scrutiny and fashion programs tailored to changing business demands.

While the city centralizes some planning, officials have decentralized other parts of the development machine to enhance business control of strategic services. The city has chartered more than a score of Business Improvement Districts (BIDs). These districts function in major commercial areas to permit property owners to assess themselves and fund additional public services (security patrols, capital projects, street repairs, and park renovations). Run on a dollar-a-vote system that excludes nearly all residents, the larger BIDs are located in downtown. They allow businesses to obtain enhanced services and environmental improvements without having to compete for funds in the general budget. One of the most visible BIDs is located downtown and has become a key planner in the Wall Street area. Other BIDs like the Grand Central Partnership and 42nd Street Development Corporation have issued their own bonds to fund capital projects in midtown. Some BIDs can have quite a bit of financial clout. The top executive of one BID received a higher salary than the mayor during the 1990s, and to add to the insult, the BID earned a higher bond rating than the city.[87]

Remaking Times Square.   Officials adopt decision-making strategies that enable them to promote business growth while dealing with the cross-pressures of a participatory pluralist political system. They typically give high priority to market-centered programs. When these issues spill over into the larger political arena, elected leaders or interest groups sometimes are able to challenge business prerogatives.[88] This allows nonbusiness interests to win important concessions. It also helps explain why New York City leans toward highly market-centered policies while also following a moderately social-centered posture. As we described in chapter 4, the story of the 1980s and 1990s was one of remarkable continuity, marked not only by steady dedication to downtown development through a proliferation of supply-side business incentive programs, but also by acceptance of significant social benefit programs.

Regime decision making is vividly illustrated by the Times Square redevelopment.[xix] This project was an important part of the city's strategy of shifting future development from the crowded East Side of midtown to the underutilized West Side of Manhattan. Planners considered Times Square a visual eyesore that stood in the way of attracting more developers and businesses to the West Side. Located in the heart of the city's legitimate theater district, it had become a honky tonk area of street walkers, peep shows, male hustlers, and cheap movie theaters. It also provided some housing to poor residents.

The 1984 Board of Estimate's plan for these thirteen acres of prime real estate called for the construction of four office towers, a wholesale merchandise mart, and a hotel, each of enormous scale. The cost of the project was estimated at more than $2.5 billion. Public assistance in the form of tax breaks and complex packages of incentives to developers were potentially worth billions of dollars.[89] Backing the project were powerhouse authorities, including the State Development Corporation, the city development and planning agencies, and a nonprofit 42nd Street Development Corporation.

The policy struggle shows how business leads but does not dominate. Although the Times Square renewal began as and remains a huge office-tower and commercial construction scheme, it also incorporates some significant public, artistic, and historic preservationist objectives. It preserves nine historic theaters, provides for a renovated subway station, and pursues a cultural theme that is favored by public officials and arts leaders. These were folded into the project as a result of widening public input in planning the project.

The original plan arose from the 42nd Street Development Corporation, a PBC that wanted to revive Times Square as an entertainment district. The corporation began acquiring dilapidated buildings in parts of the area and transforming them into off-off Broadway theaters, restaurants, and arts spaces. Gradually, it lined up corporate sponsorship in favor of a conventional urban renewal plan that would transform the block into an elaborate urban theme park with shows, rides, and high-tech exhibits about the life of the city. Funding for the arts side of the project was to come from the sale of development rights to private developers, who were to build three large office towers.

Despite reservations, the city's culture community saw the new commercial development as the only means of restoring the area's artistic assets. They supported the plan. Developers saw the huge profits that would be generated from recycling one of the city's prime plots of real estate. Only scattered groups of small shopkeepers and residents resisted the project for fear of displacement.

Mayor Ed Koch ultimately refused to support the plan. He contended that its Disneyland cultural vision was for Florida and that New York should have "seltzer instead of orange juice."[90] Koch called for a theme that was more consistent with the city's cultural identity. The mayor also objected that the plan was privately directed with preselected developers and insisted on publicly sponsored planning and competitive bidding.

Following his opposition, project sponsors rolled out a new plan that was similar to the old one except for two critical differences. The new project involved changing the nature of the theme park. Instead of demolishing historic theaters or converting them to high-tech entertainment, they were to be restored, mostly for use as Broadway stages. In effect, the urban theme park was redefined to re-create the Great White Way of old New York, rather than the Disneyland preferred by the developers. The second change anticipated significantly greater new commercial development, including another massive office tower. Further, these office towers were to be supported by new public subsidies — actually far greater than those asked for in the earlier proposal.

The new plan, with its emphasis on preservation and restoration, broadened political support beyond the old pro-growth coalition of developers and public officials. It won the endorsement of civic and professional organizations concerned with historic preservation, the arts, and urban design. Although these groups were unable to get officials to re-create the entire historic district, they obtained their other preservationist goals, especially restoration of the historic theaters.

The significance of these victories became apparent during the 1990s. The 1987 stock market crash and subsequent recession years burst the Manhattan office building bubble. Investors refused to build in an already glutted market. A string of forty-seven lawsuits from opponents held up various parts of the project. Yet the main investor, Prudential

Insurance, had poured $433 million into land acquisition, theater reno-
vation, and retail space before it decided that it no longer wanted to
build. In effect, the cultural interests got what they wanted, but left the
investors holding the bag, so to speak. In 1993, city officials redefined
the project, this time as a retail and entertainment project focusing on
bright, dazzling stores, tourist attractions, and neon signs that re-
created something of Times Square's glory days. Eventually the strategy
paid off. A number of entertainment companies, including Disney, became the lead investors in theaters and tourist enterprises on 42nd
Street. This, in turn, led developers to purchase the office sites from
Prudential and build the new towers that would anchor the modern
Great White Way.[91]

It is easy to be cynical about how much was gained by the so-called
culture community and city officials. Their "arts strategy" helped legitimize an overwhelmingly commercial urban renewal project that grew in
size during its roller coaster history. Public officials also gave away
subsidies that were probably excessive considering the market circumstances.[92] Yet the city could hardly have found a better use for such a
strategic land parcel. Most important, officials, artists and preservationists were able to incorporate some important public values into a project that initially neglected them. In New York's mercantile regime the
market leads, but it does not always rule.

HOUSTON: A FREE ENTERPRISE REGIME

It's the money, stupid.   Like New York, Houston possesses enormous
economic power, but limited intergovernmental support. As described in
chapter 4, Houston's economic muscle is diminished by its relative dependence on energy-related industries and the roller coaster behavior of
the region in the marketplace. The period of bust during the 1980s
seriously challenged the town's habit of expecting unending growth.
Growth consciousness is reinforced by the city's go-it-alone system of
intergovernmental politics.

Unlike New York, however, pressures to pursue growth meet few political barriers. Over fifty years ago, V. O. Key noted that Texans seem
mainly "concerned about money and how to make it, about oil and
sulfur and gas, about cattle and dust storms and irrigation, about cot-
ton and banking and Mexicans."[93] Houston epitomizes this tradition.
Its electorate is historically very deferential to business leadership and
overwhelmingly concerned with making money. Changing social demography has gradually altered the city's traditional character, although
not enough to fundamentally transform it. With its nonpartisan govern-

ment, weak party politics, scant tradition of civic activism, and low voter turnout, mass politics tends to be disorganized, conservative, and more about winning offices than about governing.

A business-centered regime. Free enterprise politics strongly favors private sector leadership and limits mass political cross-pressures that challenge this direction. The days when leading businessmen met in suite 8-F of the Lamar Hotel to informally decide how to govern Houston are gone. The "Suite 8-F crowd" included bankers, oil company investors, contractors, newspapermen, financiers, and was top heavy with real estate investors and developers who saw local politics as an extension of their business activities. In the 1970s more than 150 companies moved corporate subsidiaries, divisions, and headquarters to Houston, making it inevitable that the city's traditional political elite of home-grown businessmen would be eclipsed.

Business domination of the regime continues. Realtors, contractors, and developers overshadow other business players as candidates for political offices. Corporate representatives from the region's vast energy industry, officers of high-technology firms, transportation, the medical sector, and other more recent businesses that relocated to Houston during the postwar decades round out the elite. Unlike of the Suite 8-F crowd, the business elite has become formally organized. Initially they gravitated around the chamber of commerce. The chamber assumed such political importance that ex-mayor Louie Welch said that he "stepped up" to head the chamber after he left the mayor's office.[94]

During the so-called depression of the 1980s, business leaders began to actively recruit companies to the city and coordinate their increasingly diverse membership.[95] In 1984 the chamber of commerce established the Houston Economic Development Council (HEDC), headed by a local developer. Representing the business elite and including a sprinkling of public officials, this organization acted to boost the city and address governance issues. In 1987 the HEDC and chamber of commerce formed the Greater Houston Partnership, an inclusive business organization that covers the seven-county region.

The partnership represents the dominant business players in governing the city, although it is tilted toward the representation of downtown businesses. It has an elaborate system of committees and task forces that together constitute a shadow government. There are specialized divisions that plan, undertake research, and develop policy initiatives in virtually every area related to economic development. One focuses on Houston's intergovernmental relations. There are committees or task forces on tax and fiscal policy, transportation, environmental policy, infrastructure, work training and education, real estate, regional trade, and other issues. Most recently, the partnership has advocated greater attention to regional governmental cooperation and has sought to become inclusive of regional business.[96]

Public officials are also members of the dominant governing coalition, but they do not have a power base that is sufficient to challenge business domination of local economic policy. The power of the mayor and council springs from their ability to organize electoral coalitions around different priorities other than those supported by business players. But their efforts are undercut by the reluctance of many voters to participate in either elections or civic groups or to oppose business leadership. Governmental power is further weakened by the close alliances and relationships between business and elected officials. All but two of Houston's mayors have been local developers. During the 1980s around one third of city council members were associated with real estate and related interests.[97]

As Houston's electorate has diversified and included more migrants from the North, business candidates have been forced to share power with outsiders or broaden their appeal in order to win office. To some extent this has changed the character of winning electoral coalitions. Yet these changes generally have not been sufficient to lead to the election of mayors who depart significantly from the dominant pro-growth development agenda favored by business.

The election of Fred Hofheinz to terms that spanned from 1971 to 1977 marked an important transition for the regime. Unlike his predecessors, Hofheinz was rooted in the moderate wing of the city's business community and fought with the more conservative members of the establishment on social issues, particularly in respect to abandoning the long-standing policy of rejecting federal aid. He won the support of minorities and a coalition of reform-minded whites and blacks. Nevertheless, Hofheinz conformed to pro-growth business policies when he was in office.[98] He was succeeded by a more conservative developer-mayor, Jim McConn.

The election of Kathy Whitmire in 1983 divided the business elite. She promised reform and some liberal social policies that appealed to the city's gays, women, and minorities. This electoral coalition enabled her to beat off a reelection challenge from a more traditional business candidate who headed the chamber of commerce. Whitmire focused on making Houston's government more efficient while avoiding encroaching on business prerogatives. She instituted competitive bidding for city contracts, breaking up the old boy's network, and reduced waste; she also undertook civil service reform and did such things as appoint a black chief of police. At the same time, however, she remained strongly pro-business in her economic agenda. Whitmire maintained low tax, anti-regulatory governmental traditions and did not seek to expand political participation in local governance or promote minority and women's rights in employment. During the city's fiscal crisis of the 1980s the mayor cut services, avoided new taxes, and increased user fees while calling for a local government "run like a business."[99] Eventually Whitmire was grudgingly accepted by the whole business community. Although many liberals, feminists, gays, and environmentalists felt that she was too cautious on their issues, they found the other candidates even less acceptable.[100]

During the 1980s Houston witnessed a large increase in black political representation and increasing citizen dissatisfaction with years of inattention to the neighborhoods. Whitmire's electoral coalition melted in 1991 when black voters went for an African-American candidate while conservative whites turned to a developer, Robert Lanier, who defeated Whitmire. Although Lanier won with almost no black support, he successfully created a governing coalition that was diverse without alienating his conservative base. Lanier doggedly maintained the support of the business community by continuing the city's traditions of limited government. He sometimes broke from downtown interests on transit issues where business interests were themselves divided.

Lanier broadened his appeal to other groups and solidified his support among conservative Anglo voters through a number of initiatives. As a "law and order" candidate, he built up the police department and paid for this by shifting transit funds for this purpose. When crime rates dropped dramatically, his popularity soared everywhere in the city. The mayor reached out to minority voters through his appointments and his defense of affirmative action programs. In his reelection campaigns the mayor captured the support of many minority leaders and voters who previously opposed him. This was enormously helped by his "Neighborhood to Standards" program of reinvesting in inner-city infrastructure that had suffered years of neglect. The program focused on such things as resurfacing streets, adding sidewalks, stop signs, and street lights, and cleaning up vacant lots. This visibly assured minorities that their neighborhoods mattered. He retired with high favorability ratings across all voter groups.[101]

In effect, Lanier's coalition-building skills enabled him to stay within Houston's policy mainstream of limited services, taxes, and regulation while offering other things to strategic voter groups. The 1997 election of Lee Brown, an African-American and former police commissioner, heralded a continuation of biracial politics. Although Brown offers inclusion, he has yet to offend business's economic prerogatives. His reelection in 2001 signaled his success in establishing a broad political base.

Keeping others out. In free enterprise politics, business easily pene-
trates the public sector to drive economic policy while various political
devices impede the influence of other interests. Houston's governmental
structure makes it easy for money interests to wield influence. The city's
system of nonpartisan elections and two-year terms for virtually all offices require officials to constantly raise cash for their campaigns and
depend on endorsements of prominent business groups and newspapers
in order to continue in office. The mayor must raise more than two
million dollars every twenty-four months to get reelected. Most of this
money comes from wealthy individuals and businesses—a result of the
weak city campaign finance laws. Houston has had a mixed at-large/
district system since 1979 when the federal government forced the city
to expand the council to fourteen members, with nine members elected
from districts. Yet the council is a weak player and does not represent
citizens well. The city charter concentrates so many powers in the hands
of the mayor that the bureaucracies have become isolated from political
control and oversight of the council.

Clientelist relations, particularly between developers and city agencies
having anything to do with economic development, are the rule. Until
recent years monies for mayoral campaigns were actually raised by the
director of public works, who then distributed the cash to mayoral candidates favored by developers and contractors—usually to the incum-
bents. Business networks that were centered upon the public works department pressured the agency to resist political control in favor of
rubber stamping developer initiatives.[102]

The city's sacrosanct tradition of privatism virtually ordains business-
centered government. By limiting the scope of the governmental sector,
many matters of public consequence do not become public issues. This
allows private business interests to assert extraordinary influence on
things that interest them. For instance, during the 1980s, the engineering firm of Turner, Collie, and Braden, did so much work for the city
that it became known as "the other public works department." This
company was the chief sewer and water engineer for the city. It headed
planning for the city's airport and led an overhaul of Houston's tax
structure.[103] Since such planning of large projects is done by business
organizations related to the chamber of commerce, it is difficult for
other groups to have much input (since chamber decision making is
considered a private matter).[xx]

When policies touch more directly on nonbusiness interests, programs
generally are structured to make public participation limited and business influence strong. The city's policy of providing infrastructure in
newly annexed areas was kept under the firm control of developers
through the use of Municipal Utility Districts or MUDs, which essen-

tially functioned as mini private governments. The use of deed restrictions, rather than zoning laws, to regulate development makes it difficult for resident groups to mobilize around common causes. Civic clubs (they more or less function like homeowner associations) have arisen to enforce deed restrictions by opposing nonconforming uses. Yet they are a passive form of participation: they serve to enforce policies laid down by developers, not to challenge the status quo that developers have ordained.

Social policies are also structured to keep conflicts over them from spreading. The city's limited responsibility for social programs reduces the need to have to deny demands for their growth. Consequently, there is no large organized political constituency for them. For instance, Houston only had 4,268 public housing units in the late 1980s, including some that were boarded up for demolition. By comparison, Philadelphia had 23,000 units while Atlanta had 15,000. Federal programs for social services (job training, community development) are kept in separate offices and have separate budgets. In contrast, economic development programs are integrated into the traditional city departments where business interests dominate.

This division has made it easy for city officials to let social programs quietly fade away when federal money for them disappeared during the 1980s.[104] Most recently, pressure for school reform led business leaders to find ways of making improvements without encouraging citizen participation. They developed school-business partnerships rather than comprehensive fiscal and governance changes at the system level. The partnerships are individualized to particular schools and are elite-driven by business benefactors. This makes if difficult for community interests to play much of a role in policy-making.[105]

Regime decision-making strategies also keep government in the hands of business leaders. Voters and nonbusiness groups assume some influence mainly when business elites are divided or when voter referenda are required for programs to move forward. In particular, the right to petition — to place issues directly on the ballot for a binding public vote — offers some check on elite influence. But in a city with relatively weak steering resources, challenging business is an uphill climb. This makes Houston's highly market-centered policies difficult to arrest.

Bargaining Texas style: Transportation politics. The chamber of commerce's leadership in developing a comprehensive mobility plan illustrates how market-centered politics works.[xxi] During the 1970s traffic problems grew to alarming proportions after years of unbridled growth, little planning, and lack of investment in mass transit. Traffic congestion was choking commuters, violating federal clean air standards, and even discouraging company relocations to the city. A planning effort was orchestrated by the business community. The chamber of commerce began in 1979 with a special transportation committee to work on a regional plan. They drew together officials from the city, Harris county, the Metropolitan Transportation Authority (MTA), the state highway department, and the turnpike authority.

After more than two years, the chamber unveiled its regional mobility plan. It called for over two hundred projects to be built within fifteen years, including miles of new freeways, 1,400 miles of new streets, a fixed railway to serve downtown, and the addition of two thousand new buses. The cost was estimated at nearly $16.2 billion. To help fund the project, the chamber advocated new taxes, higher bus fares, user fees, and revenue bonds. By 1990 the plan was well on the way to being implemented, in large part because of vigorous political work by the chamber. It helped secure increases from the state legislature in state motor fuel and registration taxes, additional highway funds, and a new county tollroad authority. The chamber also proposed a MTA general transit plan, which was approved by the voters in 1988.

The major snag occurred over the plan's proposed rail project. Though a version of it had won voter approval in 1988, it never promised to provide anything that could service many neighborhoods. As the specifics were hammered out, it became clear that the cost per rider would be very high in low-density Houston and that the system would mainly serve downtown. The plan's fate was sealed when business support faded. Despite support by Mayor Whitmire and some downtown businesses, other business interests led by MTA boss and developer Robert Lanier opposed the project as wasteful. When Lanier became mayor he killed any chance of Houston beginning a rail system.

The mobility plan was essentially a matter of private-sector planning and political coordination. In a city where traffic jams and lack of mass transit are everyday matters of concern, voters still were relegated to the periphery of this political process. Though required referenda and divisions among business power brokers gave the public some influence, citizens were confined to saying yes or no to a minimalist mass transit scheme that only served the downtown agenda.

There are signs, however, that Houston's free enterprise regime is changing. As business diversifies and the citizenry becomes more attentive, the city also becomes more pluralistic. Moreover, economic maturity has engendered demographic diversity. Latino and African Americans now constitute more than half of the voters. The tradition of limited government is fading. The city is adopting more interventionist policies in order to deal with the social costs of unbridled growth. Public tastes for modern infrastructure, better common services, environmental quality, and more social amenities are increasing.

After years of neglect, the need to modernize the infrastructure in central city neighborhoods is almost unavoidable. But doing so invariably precipitates greater political participation by interests that challenge business. In the past, infrastructure was provided by creating MUDs. These special districts allowed developers to steer the entire process and capture the benefits of growth. Today MUDs are inappropriate in older areas, and so the city relies on tax increment financing (TIFs) to renew infrastructure. But TIFs require greater political oversight and neighborhood political participation than do MUDs. State law requires social equity considerations in their administration. This makes developer dominance difficult.[106]

Similarly, the need to diversify Houston's economy has forced business elites to abandon low taxes and limited government. They have accepted greater use of supply-side incentives and special public subsidy deals in order to capture major firms, such as Grumman and Compaq Computer.[107] "Corporate welfare" is now an issue.

As time goes by, changes in Houston's economy, demography, and political culture also mean that government will expand. The city is rapidly acquiring greater steering resources — citizens are becoming more vocal and values may be shifting. Should this continue, the days of free enterprise politics in Houston could be numbered.

COMPARING REGIMES

Regime politics varies among cities at the upper end of the urban hierarchy. Although all of these cities are economically prosperous, they exploit their resources differently. Table 6.1 summarizes how these regimes differ in terms of resources employed, dominant partners, mode of public-private engagement, and development approach. By *resources employed*, we mean the driving and steering variables that a given regime might use to leverage its bargaining. Here we direct our attention toward the resources most heavily relied upon by a given regime (market conditions, intergovernmental support, popular control, and local culture). The next characteristic, *dominant partners*, encompasses the major interests and power brokers that make up governing coalitions. The *mode of public-private engagement*, focuses on how government and business interact over development decisions. We are interested in whether decisions are "open" or "closed" (readily visible to the public) as well as who leads, and whether those decisions are negotiated, brokered, or controlled by a single actor. Also, there may be times when a lead decision maker (government or business) acts independently in constructing the built environment and we include this as a possibility. Our last category deals with *development approach* and harks back to how regimes deal with the marketplace and ultimately with business.

TABLE 6.1
Regimes/Coalitions and Bargaining

Bargaining Context	Regime or Coalition Type	Resources Employed	Dominant Partners	Mode of Public–Private Engagement	Development Approach
Dirigiste	Planner-Type 1 (Toronto and Paris)	Favorable economy, intergovernmental support, popular control, local culture	National or provincial governments, bureaucrats, public corporations	Open/sometimes negotiated. Led by state and public institutions.	Act prospectively to influence or control market forces.
Dirigiste	Planner-Type 2 (Milan)	Favorable economy, intergovernmental support. Ambivalent popular control.	National governments, political parties, bureaucrats, public corporations	Open, state-centered. Led by state and party leaders.	Stalemated, mired in disagreement. Reactive public management of the marketplace.
Entrepreneurial	Mercantile (New York)	Favorable economy, popular control. Ambivalent local culture	Business, government, occasional neighborhood and "good government" groups	Open-to-closed (institutional buffers to popular control). Led by public/private partnerships.	Market intervention is subject to cross-pressures. Overall, support for business by shaping marketplace.
Entrepreneurial	Free Enterprise (Houston)	Favorable economy	Business elites	Closed. Led by business.	Market-led, laissez-faire government.

Here we ask whether regimes act prospectively to control market forces, whether they attempt control but fall into stalemate, whether they act directly to sustain business, or whether they rely on market signals.

Toronto and Paris have planner-type 1 regimes that undertake active roles in managing economic and social change. Elected officials, bureaucrats, professionals, and citizen groups form coalitions that act with considerable independence. In Toronto, development was often conducted by top politicians and more often led by a planning process. This could be seen in the work of the "triple alliance" throughout the 1970s and 1980s. During that time public housing, moratoria on downtown office construction, and preservation of open space were the mainstays of development policy. The "triple alliance" also acted aggressively to build mass transit throughout Metro Toronto and coordinate it with development. In Paris, a powerful intergovernmental alliance of public officials and technocrats used mixed corporations and planning tools to rebuild neighborhoods and shift development toward eastern sections of the city. There, too, publicly built mass transit shaped the location and pattern of development.

Planner-type 2 regimes show somewhat different characteristics. While trying to plan development, Milanese officials had a more sluggish, even reactive, approach and often became mired in stalemate. Party elites led a coalition that supported an extensive governmental role in the city's economy. But this coalition could pull together only sporadically in order to realize public objectives. Officials and bureaucrats attempted to juggle powerful clientelist demands with ambitious plans to modernize Milan. They ended up creating a special interest politics, mediated by the political parties. The ambitous Passante project and the recycling of some old industrial areas were only partially implemented due to political squabbling among bureaucrats and partisan rivalries. Yet the ubiquitous hand of state regulators and party power brokers forced the private sector to accommodate nonbusiness interests in the city's modernization process.

Mercantile politics also constituted a divided regime in New York, where power sharing is the norm. The city's highly pluralist political system competed for attention with powerful private-sector business elites whose influence was institutionalized into partnership arrangements. Corporatist-style institutional buffers were employed to shield market management activities from mainstream electoral politics. But regime players found themselves constantly renegotiating development agendas whenever business-led initiatives became contentious. Promoting the city's global economic engine in Manhattan through land use, urban renewal, business incentives, and other measures often generated concessions to other groups. The city's high-tax/liberal social policy traditions also funneled some of the fruits of downtown growth in directions that business opposes. Finally, Houston's free enterprise politics enabled business-style government to flourish. A relatively closed political process limited the reach of government on matters that business deemed inappropriate. Regulatory, tax, annexation, transportation, and other programs that business deemed important were rarely reversed by opposition groups.

Different Resources/Different Uses

Although all of these cities have formidable economic advantages, some have been able to exercise greater choices than others. Not only have resources differed among cities, but regimes have used them differently. These differences shaped the style of regime politics. Planner-types 1 and 2, found only in dirigiste contexts, were closely managed by public officials and technocrats. The political process in Toronto, Paris, and Milan was relatively open, and the combination of public power and neighborhood pressure acted as a counterweight to business. At times governmental and neighborhood interests could even dominate the process. This was exemplified in Toronto when reformers acted to preserve downtown, mounted successful campaigns against highways, and built assisted housing. It was evident in Paris when popular action reduced or reversed mega projects and successfully protected old neighborhoods.

For the most part, planner-type 1 cities drove their own agendas. There was little preoccupation with the possibility that making public demands would choke off city prosperity. Growth was expected and it was to be controlled. In addition to citizen action, bargaining leverage could be found in intergovernmental fiscal support and in cooperation between different levels of government. Fiscal support and cooperation enabled Toronto and Paris to shape the marketplace through mass transit, publicly conducted development, and an assortment of planning tools. Economic growth gave both cities the luxury of selecting the location and scope of development.

Even planner-type 2, Milan, contained business power, but this did exact a price. Lack of business interest in the city's drive to modernize its transportation system and to decentralize commercial life hampered its ability to realize some important goals. Without a powerful business coalition, politicians were left to their own devices and some projects never materialized. Yet even here Milanese politicians were able to by-pass business by resorting to intergovernmental aid. The Passante was financed and planned entirely by public sector agencies and property speculation was limited. Area redevelopment projects succeeded at least in several places where public investment either substituted for or helped leverage private investment. Despite the regime's limitations, business continues to invest in a very prosperous Milan.

Planner-type 1 and 2 regimes partially differ from one another in their ability to organize steering resources. Officials in Paris and Toronto could draw upon organized popular participation to support programmatic parties or draw upon their support in public hearings and demonstrations. Political elites also used party systems to control patronage and policy within the cities and at higher governmental levels. Supported by postmaterialist cultures that valued public-regarding policies, public elites could dominate city development. In contrast, Milan's fragmented politics made patronage and policy difficult to coordinate.

Regimes that tried to balance business with social interests were limited by a paucity of resources or a poor use of available resources. Mercantile New York and free enterprise Houston struggled to capture private-sector investment, but had little room for maneuvering. Without access to big intergovernmental fiscal cushions, these cities paid the price when economic times turned sour. New York's fiscal crisis during the 1970s and Houston's mini-depression during the 1980s were reminders of the primacy of private-sector investors and the weight those interests carried in policy making. New York leaders struggled for years with unpopular austerity budgets in order to reenter the bond market and disarm state overseers. Houston's governing coalition raised taxes and scrambled to diversify its economy to avoid the consequences of future skids in energy prices. New York and Houston had little choice but to organize regimes that were highly sensitive to the capital marketplace. New York's "partnerships" and Houston's business-style government both functioned to give business interests a leading role in economic management.

Differences in steering resources also played a huge role in shaping these regimes. With a weak civic life, disorganized nonpartisan politics, and extensive voter apathy, there were few impediments to the assertion of business power in Houston. In contrast, New York's mercantile regime had to respond to intense political cross-pressures. Political leaders devised ways of insulating their most important development policies from mainstream politics. But popular pressure also introduced checks on business influence. This made for a shifting policy agenda and opportunities to limit the regime's inclination to lean toward the marketplace.

Structure/Agency and Change

Our regime comparisons point to ways in which agency can be exercised and cities can change. These shifts can be for the "good" or "bad."[xii] Paris during the late 1990s showed a propensity for scandal and corruption. Despite Tiberi's hopes, the regime lost some of its ability to plan and execute. It grew sluggish and the effects of scandal were apparent. By the end of 1999 one could discern a Parisian slide toward a planner-type 2 regime. It is difficult, however, to tell whether corruption is endemic, much less know whether it would riddle subsequent governments.

Toronto presents a different set of facts. In that city a higher level of government became less friendly and exerted pressure on the city to change its policies. To a minor extent this worked. Toronto has recently experienced some movement toward more aggressive, pro-business policies. If provincial pressure is sustained, and the city curtails market controls, Toronto could shift toward a New York-style mercantile regime. For the time being the city still holds its course. Its own mechanisms of popular control and postmaterialist values have kept the city on the same policy trajectory. While it is still too early to know how regime changes will evolve, these cases do underscore the possibility and conceivable direction of transition.

Change does appear to be a function of the availability of resources and how different regimes exercise discretion over those resources. Should Milan's mayor succeed in employing resources more efficiently the city could move toward a planner-type 1 regime. Unstable governments, excessive clientelism, and political fragmentation are being challenged by attempts to centralize power around the mayor, prosecute corruption, and to achieve electoral reforms.

Cities in entrepreneurial contexts are strongly driven by the marketplace, but they also have choices. New York's pluralism and active political participation led policymakers to compromise market-centered policies, even when the city was under enormous fiscal pressure. Regime changes are already taking place in Houston as a result of migration, demographic shifts, rising political participation, especially among Latinos, and rising incomes. Popular control has become more energized and local culture may moderate its materialist character. In many respects, Houston has begun to look like other major urban centers in the United States.[108] Growth in minority political participation and representation as well as the election of white and black reform mayors are visible signs that government may be opening up and diversifying.

Last, we observe that while agency can prompt change, the likely pathways are influenced by the structural context within which city governments bargain. Without major modifications in American federalism, a transition to a planner regime is not likely for that nation's cities. By the same token, change is possible. Houston's evolution toward a mercantile regime through greater public participation seems probable.

By their very nature, planner-type 1 regimes are ambitious undertakings. This kind of politics is difficult to sustain because it requires enormous economic and political capability. Without that capability these regimes can lapse into planner-type 2 or move toward a type of politics that is more directly geared toward economic growth. It stands to reason that active city governments require a sustaining, cooperative, and assertive citizenry. Among the large universe of cities, places like Paris and Toronto do exist but they are relatively rare and subject to considerable pressures, including the urge to compete in the international marketplace. Indeed, Toronto is under such pressure, and given the quest for efficiency, a drift toward a planner-type 2 is not likely for this city. Rather, Tory politics in the province and the international pressures of the marketplace are likely to move that city in the direction of mercantilist politics.

In sum, cities at the top of the urban hierarchy face constraints as well as opportunities. Their likely trajectories of regime change will surely be a byproduct of both. Cities in "dependent" contexts lack such advantages and face different prospects, however. We now turn to them.

NOTES

i. As it has evolved from Krasner's original formulation (see his *International Regimes*), the regime concept has become unwieldy and is almost borderless. See, for example, a critique of the idea's applications by Karen Mossberger and Gerry Stoker in "Evolution of Urban Regime Theory." Our notion of regime differs in important respects from that used by other regime theorists (Sanders and Stone, *Politics of Urban Development*; DeLeon, *Left Coast City*; DiGaetano and Klemanski, "Urban Regimes"; Harding, "Urban Regimes"; Lauria, *Reconstructing Urban Regime Theory*). Along with these theorists, we agree that regimes are the city's lynchpin for bringing about political cooperation and realizing tangible goals—or engage in *social production* (Stone, *Regime Politics*). Yet most regime theorists use this concept to focus on the internal process of business-government relations, while we can also envision regimes as working within a highly variegated public or semipublic sphere. This is not for want of having sustained power, but because the private sector in parts of Europe is often subordinate to the public arm, and in some parts almost nonexistent. Certainly communist or former communist cities like Havana or Moscow experienced their versions of a "regime," and it is difficult to see how anybody could not see these places as valid sites for regime analysis.

ii. From the standpoint of institutional theory, institutions constitute dominant values that give meaning and understanding to political behavior. Over time these patterns of behavior become regularized and tend to reflect a particular organizational logic, although they are not identical with particular organizations. For the institutional view, see North, *Institutions, Institutional Change*; March and Olson, "New Institutionalism," *Rediscovering Institutions*, and

Democratic Governance; Peters, "Political Institutions"; and Pierre, "Models of Governance."

iii. The term "Mercantile" is adapted from its historical use. See the explanation given later in respect to New York.

iv. Obviously the triple alliance did not always cohere. Resentment over suburban dominance of the Metro Council was so strong within the City of Toronto that a majority of voters once passed a nonbinding ballot initiative to withdraw. Others saw Metro as never having recovered from the Spadina controversy. The reversal of the Spadina decision made Metro less sure of its public support and less bold (Anderson, *Summary*). Over the long run, and so far as development was concerned, Metro was invaluable. This is why the municipalities so fiercely and overwhelmingly defended it against abolition.

v. Frisken, "Contributions of Metropolitan Government." In the Toronto context the term "suburbanite" is tricky because the municipalities are socially and economically quite similar (due to Metro policies). Nevertheless, it is used in local parlance, and one writer distinguishes the term by drawing a difference between the older and newer municipalities. Thus North York, Etobicoke, and Scarborough might be considered "suburbs" while Toronto, East York, and York are seen as central cities (Horak, "Power of Local Identity"). For the most part we try to avoid the term suburb and choose instead to distinguish between the central city of Toronto and the remaining five "outer municipalities."

vi. The court did rule in favor of Scarborough, but this turned out to be a Pyrrhic victory when the province changed the title and function of the board of trustees.

vii. During Chirac's last term the apportionment of council seats was: 93 Rally for the Republic (Gaullist); 45 Free Paris (centrist); 17 Socialist; 2 Citizens Movement; 2 Communist; 1 Ecologist; and 3 unaffiliated.

viii. In 1994 the Parisian budget was 32.9 billion francs. At seven francs to the dollar, this amounts to $4.7 billion.

ix. Like other elites, Jacques Chirac was a graduate of the prestigious Ecole National d'Administration or Enarque. These alumni are highly regarded for their technical and political proficiency. One case where that skill came to no avail was in Chirac's desire to build a highway along the Left Bank. Much to Chirac's dismay President Valéry Giscard d'Estaing vetoed the highway.

x. For this reason Paris had been the only French municipality to be denied a mayor since the Revolution. Except for brief interludes in 1789 and 1871, Paris had no mayor; instead, it was overseen by the national prefect. Not until 1975 was a statute passed granting Paris the right to elect its own mayor. Even then, the Prefect of the national police continued to guard the city against any left-wing insurgence.

xi. APUR stands for Atelier Parisen d'Urbanisme.

xii. For a discussion of mixed corporations, ZACs, and other planning tools, see the section on Paris in chapter 4.

xiii. For details, see the section on Paris in chapter 4.

xiv. SEMAPA stands for Société d'Economie Mixed d'Aménagement Parisien. or Mixed Development Corporation of Paris.

xv. *La Croix*, April 7, 1999. For Tiberi, the apportionment of seats was 57

Rally for the Republic (Gaullist); 25 Liberal Democrats (centrist); 9 Union For Democracy (centrist); 43 Socialist; 6 Citizens Movement; 9 Communist; and 14 unaffiliated.

xvi. Tiberi also cancelled a ZAC and the redevelopment of a large complex in the west known as Port Maillot.

xvii. *Le Figaro*, March 19, 2001, p. 11, *Le Monde*, March 20, 2001, p. 38. The popular vote broke down as 50.4 percent for parties on the Right and 49.6 percent for parties on the Left. Both Paris and Marseilles elect mayors indirectly by city councilors representing each arrondissement. It is then possible for mayors to carry a majority of arrondissements while losing the popular vote.

xviii. Factual sources for the following discussion are mainly based on Vicari, "Friction in the Growth Machine"; Vicari and Molotch, "Building Milan"; Fareri, "La Progettzione del Governo a Milano"; Fareri, "Milano"; Fareri, "Milano: Progettualità Diffusa e Difficoltà Realizzativa." In addition, interviews with these authors, Alessandro Balducci and various members of the Milan city government and business community were utilized.

xix. This discussion draws extensively on Reichl's "Historic Preservation" and *Reconstructing Times Square*.

xx. When the Houston Economic Development Council asked for public funding in the mid-1980s, some members objected because this would mean closer public scrutiny of their operations, many of which were kept secret. The HEDC president insisted that companies considering locating to Houston usually like to keep the process secret and he expressed the hope that city officials would respect "the sacred character of our business transactions" (Feagin, *Free Enterprise City*, 168).

xxi. This discussion draws extensively on Murray, Hinnawi, and Donnelly, *Houston Metropolitan Study*; Thomas and Murray, *Progrowth Politics*, 361, as well as interviews with the latter two authors.

xxii. While most would agree that a Parisian shift toward a planner-type 2 regime would be "bad," we draw no necessary equivalent conclusion for a Toronto shift toward business. We see the latter as a personal value judgment.

Chapter Seven

DEPENDENT BARGAINING: PUBLIC AND PRIVATE

For ye have the poor with you always.
— Mark 14:7

Many Western industrial cities are at the periphery of the global marketplace. They not only lack the economic advantages of giants like Paris, Milan, and New York, but they must cope with shrinking economies and attendant social miseries. Their limited assets and weak economic base make them vulnerable to the vagaries of the market place. Cities in dependent bargaining contexts have been jolted by globalization, and often scramble for capital that is siphoned off to more prosperous areas.

Despite these disadvantages, cities do have choices about how to approach development, and regimes will exploit those choices differently. Cities in dependent public contexts can borrow leverage from other governments, enhance their bargaining power, and, in one fashion or another, substitute public aid for private investment. Cities in this particular context may choose to *offset* market disadvantages by enlisting intergovernmental aid and to use available resources to bend negotiations with private capital. Another alternative for these cities is to *accommodate* their market disadvantages by using intergovernmental aid to *ease the pain* of market disadvantages. Used in this sense, accommodation means that cities give up any earnest effort to regenerate themselves. More rarely, cities will choose to *bypass* or *combat* the marketplace in order to resuscitate themselves. They do so by selecting regimes that use resources, like intergovernmental aid or popular control, to challenge capital markets.

Cities operating in dependent private contexts are left with different choices, and their regimes act accordingly. They are less able to tap intergovernmental support on a sustained basis and must attract private sector investors in order to pursue development. Although resistance is sometimes possible, these cities are apt to *submit* to the marketplace and do whatever is necessary to facilitate business. They then use relations with business to sustain themselves and legitimate their achievements.

All of these differences in bargaining opportunities shape a city's approach to the marketplace and to its relations with business. In this chapter we look at how regimes utilize specific bargaining contexts and mobilize resources. Briefly put, city governments that seek to offset market disadvantages and nurture development through public intervention are treated as *grantsman regimes*. City governments that accommodate market disadvantages and rely on public intervention to ease their pains are treated as *clientelist regimes*. City governments that take on the system and attempt to bypass or combat market constraints are treated as *challenger regimes*. Finally, city governments that comply with market demands and make few, if any, demands upon business are seen as *vendor regimes*. As we shall see, regimes are not necessarily static. They can change over time and move in different strategic directions, often despite great odds.

The Dependent Public Context

Grantsman Regimes

Grantsman regimes are strongly oriented toward a single driving resource, intergovernmental support. Public dependence is seen as an opportunity in which governmental leverage can sometimes offset private-sector weakness. Used strategically, this aid might even catapult a city into a competitive international status. These regimes are attentive to building local constituencies, and they also use steering resources to bolster the city's position in the marketplace. One steering resource, popular control, can be employed to garner votes for regional or national candidates. Local regimes ultimately use that clout to obtain national or regional aid. This, in turn, can leverage programs to sustain economic regeneration. Close alliances between unions and party leaders or between neighborhoods and city hall can be built. This sometimes allows grantsman regimes to create powerful political machines that increase their ability to obtain political cooperation, particularly from higher-level governments. Governing elites who can deliver votes will bolster their chances for reelection and acquire more power. They may even initiate new urban strategies and shift development in altogether different directions. Those who cannot produce for their constituents may find themselves replaced or outdistanced by competitors.

MARSEILLES: GRANTSMANSHIP À LA FRANÇAISE

Deferre: The godfather. As the Socialists tell it, Gaston Deferre brought enormous benefits to the city. Upon winning office in 1953, he inherited a city where the green space was limited, the sewer system was incomplete, the housing was substandard, and the treasury was at the brink of bankruptcy. Deferre, himself, governed for thirty-three years and his socialist successors for another nine. During that time he was revered for having built parks, rebuilding the city's infrastructure, sheltering residents in modern housing, and refilling the city's coffers.[1] It was also Deferre who opened up southern portions of the city, along the coastline, to the citizens of Marseilles. He extended highways and public transit to Marseilles's peripheries, enabling cloistered residents to reach southerly beaches. In the process Deferre also created one of the most resilient and political machines in France.

Known as the *système D*, the regime was built on carefully balancing and rewarding the city's major constituencies. For much of the time, Deferre excluded the Communist Party. Instead, he turned to parties of the center and moderate right, giving them control over infrastructure and expenditures affecting the local economy. By doing this, he effectively granted the city's middle class latitude to run business in the center city and its neighborhoods in the posh south. At the time, the Socialists had little to fear from a rightist takeover, and were more concerned about competition on the Left. Having secured the center-right flank, Deferre kept the oversight of all other services for the Socialists — especially housing — and proceeded to cultivate the city's working-class neighborhoods.

His following was built upon a triad of support. The first source of that triad was economic and supplied by tax-supported budgets. These budgets sustained vast subsidies for housing, they fed mixed corporations to carry out development, and they funded public employment. The second was essentially civic — built from the city's dense network of neighborhood organizations and its bountiful social clubs (sports, senior citizens, small business). The third source was political and included the neighborhood mayors, the Socialist Party, and Deferre's own newspaper, *Le Provençal*. Neighborhood mayors were granted their own budgets and discretion in awarding subsidized apartments to constituents. For its part the Socialist Party and its coalition partners could influence the distribution of public jobs. *Le Provençal* put Deferre at the forefront and was a partisan conduit to the voters.

By these strokes, Deferre reserved for himself a cornucopia of patronage and favors. During the height of their power, Marseilles's socialists controlled over 50,000 public jobs, and every public servant could parlay a single partisan preference into multiple ballots. Public housing, or the HLM, was also used to bolster a clientelist regime and ensure local votes.[i] Municipal socialism was more than just an economic platform, but a source of political power. As one writer put it,

This reality gave the socialists an important hold over Marseilles. Forty years of having built so much public housing gave them important paths of communication. It was clear that the more one built HLMs the greater the chances of having a left-wing electorate, which for a long time was Communist.[2]

With these resources Deferre was able to wean communist voters toward the socialist left, while at the same time breaking the back of his communist rivals. Deferre also neutralized Marseilles's bourgeoisie by appointing an adjunct mayor to maintain relations with the banks and the chamber of commerce. Little wonder that Marseilles came to be called the "French Chicago," while the less admiring press referred to the mayor as "*Le Parrain*," or "The Godfather."

The regime was built on blue-collar party loyalists lodged in the neighborhoods and on various members of the bourgeoisie, whose livelihoods were based on the city center and its port. While the *système D* was stable, it was also static. Little or nothing could be invested within the city center without making comparable donations to the city's peripheries. Political courtesy dictated that every government franc put into the center be matched several times over by government francs put into the rest of the city.[3] Grand projects were always hampered by this unwritten formula and by accusations that money for economic development would lead to social segregation.

The *système D* was fueled by state funds. Even when the Gaullists held national power, localities received hefty funds and services — amounting to more than half their budgets. When in 1980 the socialists won the national elections, Deferre stood at the pinnacle. The mayor could now afford to dispense with his center-right coalition and bring the Communist Party into city hall. Under a new socialist-communist coalition, the city pumped up its social agenda for housing, amenities, and public works.

By now the *cumul des mandats* permitted Deferre to become minister of the interior, and, as a member of the government, he sat on the interministerial council. Through these pivotal positions he was able to nurture the city budget with still more national funds. While the initiative for this spending could be traced back to 1953 when Deferre became mayor, the momentum swelled for more than three decades. During Deferre's first decade (1953–65) the budget for development and infrastructure rose by 28 percent, and by his second decade (1966–77) the increase reached 43 percent. City expenditures accelerated by roughly 50 percent though Deferre's third decade (1978–86) and part of the succeeding socialist period (1986–95).[4]

This success in gaining intergovernmental funds made up for the lack of private capital. Streams of public funding would irrigate some development and keep supporters content. Apart from occasional rhetoric,

Deferre's socialism was pragmatic rather than ideological. As mentioned in chapter 4, his policies followed a "third way" and were designed neither for untrammeled capitalism nor doctrinaire socialism. They were rarely, if ever, used to jawbone private capital or force the bourgeosie to relinquish its assets. At times these policies were used to leverage private capital for development. Thus, Deferre sought to build a World Trade Center in the heart of the business district. Deferre's lieutenants envisioned a thirty-story tower built next to Marseilles's stock exchange. The project failed for lack of private interest, but it was to become the harbinger for another development called EuroMéditerranéen. To respond to critics on the Left, Deferre made sure that neighborhoods in the poor north side of the city received money for renovation and public housing. More than anything else, the *système D* maintained social equilibrium by dispersing the fruits of public spending.

Vigourox: The transitional pope.   By the time an accident in 1986 took Deferre's life, the *système D* was waning. Years of decline had taken its toll and party squabbles sapped socialist strength. Deferre's departure left the party tattered and split into numerous factions. One party leader, Michel Pezet, used the situation to attack Deferre and launch a party revolt, while another, Robert Vigourox, carried Deferre's mantle.

The battle between Pezet and Vigourox continued to tear at the seams of the party and each headed separate lists of candidates in the general elections. Vigourox emerged triumphant, but for the Socialists it was a Pyrrhic victory. The new mayor was personally admired for his integrity and honesty (dubbed "Mr. Clean"), but he was also seen as a temporary figure (and called the "transitional pope"). When asked by a journalist whether he would replace Deferre, the new mayor corrected his questioner stating, "No, not replace Deferre I can only succeed him."[5]

Vigourox did have some ideas of his own, but could not bring them to fruition. He saw Marseilles as reaching beyond its municipal boundaries and he began efforts to cooperate with surrounding municipalities. "Our future is not *intra muros*," he proclaimed, "but as a great Mediterranean metropolis."[6] The surrounding municipalities, however, continued to fend for themselves, and this limited Vigourox's political reach. Vigourox also began to open up his regime to the private sector and sought nonpartisan support. He was instrumental in initiating the center for technology at Château Gombert and combating deindustrialization with tertiary services. Always trying to remain above politics, Vigourox could neither remold the system nor stem the tide. In 1995 he gladly retired.

All told, the Socialist regime sustained itself with massive public expenditures, and the benefits were tantalizing. Along with subsidized housing, clean water, and sewerage, public funding also brought jobs, patronage, and contracts. While money poured in from the government, the city matched those contributions and borrowed to meet its obligations. But the price also had to be paid. By 1995 Marseilles's arrears reached 12,777 francs ($2,129) per inhabitant and it was among the most indebted cities in the country.[7]

The paradox of the *système D* was that while the city improved, it also decayed. Better housing and a modern infrastructure helped residents, but the city also lost population and private-sector jobs. For years Deferre had ignored surrounding smaller cities, like Vitrolles and Martigues. Now they were absorbing Marseilles's economic assets. Through the last decade, approximately 10,000 residents left each year and business settled in nearby localities. The unemployment rate in some of the northern arrondissments peaked at 42 percent.[8] The docks continued to experience hard times, handling a fifth as much of the cargo as did comparable ports like Rotterdam.

Moreover, social strains added to economic ones. During the height of the Socialist regime, the city was gripped by a crime wave. Two thirds of Marseilles's residents listed public safety as their greatest concern. Their next greatest concern was immigration into the city, followed by rising welfare.[9] Not surprisingly, the radical right began its electoral ascent. In 1986, the National Front's candidate for the National Assembly won more than 22 percent of the vote. Just two years later the Front's candidate for president, Jean-Marie Le Pen, captured 28 percent of Marseilles's vote.[10]

Gaudin: Coalition or regime? For all of Vigourox's shortcomings, his shift toward new constituencies was portentous. By 1995 Marseilles was in store for a change. This time the challenge came from the center-right's Liberal Democrats, and Jean-Claude Gaudin took charge of city hall. Gaudin exemplified how politicians could use the *cumul des mandats* to catapult themselves into more powerful office. Prior to running for mayor he was president of Marseilles's Regional Council, held national office as Minister of Urban Development, and held a national seat as senator. It was Gaudin, in his capacity as minister, who launched the *zones franches* or enterprise zones, and he was about to inject the city with a similar dose of development.

Upon entering office Gaudin spoke about the need to forge new coalitions, including business. For Gaudin, "clanism" was part of a "bygone era" and he declared his desire to begin a new dialogue within the city.[11] City hall was ready to take on new partners and work equally with neighborhood associations as well as with business. Nevertheless, the mayor knew change would take time and cautioned, "Upon taking office in 1995 we had to deal with forty-three years of municipal socialism or crypto-socialism. And we had to deal with principles that were not our own, particularly on matters of urban development and economic policy."[12]

Gaudin was able to take some early initiatives. He put a halt to building new HLMs and weighed against their political implications saying,

> Marseilles has 56 percent of the department's subsidized housing for 43 percent of the population. That's too much! It's time the socialists understood that we were not elected to uphold their politics. Nor should we concentrate HLMs in Marseilles because neighboring localities do not want them.[13]

Instead Gaudin sought to stimulate the real estate market and bring about what he called the "recentralization" of the city. There were safeguards against overzealous, market-oriented development. The new mayor could not furnish tax abatements or grant free land or increase densities without amending zoning laws. But he could work with the existing framework to set new priorities and recast his resources. These included freeing underused land for development, improving infrastructure, extending mass transit, and doing this while protecting the environment and enhancing the seaport.

At the head of Gaudin's wish list was EuroMéditerranéen. As described in chapter 4, EuroMéd is a massive renewal project that ties the city center to its port. While EuroMéd was begun by his predecessor, Gaudin gave it new meaning by invigorating its politics. Gaudin used previous connections with national ministries to supply infrastructure, lure capital investors, and put pressure on surrounding localities to join the enterprise. He then went about soliciting support from the chamber of commerce, surrounding cities, the regional council, and private investors. Gaudin also opened a dialogue with the neighborhood association and sought their advice.

There is little doubt who runs EuroMéd. It is essentially a public-led venture that enjoins state, city, and regional resources. The EuroMéd initiative is directed by an *Etablissement d'Aménagement Publique* (EPAD) or public development corporation. Unlike American development corporations, French EPADs have substantial public funding and considerable liberty of action. EuroMéd's EPAD is directly tied to the state, which shares its leading role with the localities. As mayor, Gaudin is a key player along with the city's business sector and its port executives. This position close to the political and physical center of Euro-Méd allows Gaudin and his allies to wield a great deal of power and money.[ii] A newly invigorated EuroMéd coupled to a broader vision has brought Marseilles directly into the development game. City hall now uses public funds to leverage private resources to promote development.

This more aggressive approach has brought a different set of actors onto Marseilles's political stage — away from the blue-collar HLMs of the north and toward a new class of citizenry in the south. While not a narrow elite, Gaudin's constituents are middle class, young, and aspiring. Most of them are part of Marseilles's rising house-owning citizens, who already talk about the imminent gentrification of the port area. Within just five years in office, Gaudin has begun to shift Marseilles's governing coalition. But there is a certain continuity of method between Gaudin and his left-wing predecessors. For all his talk of reform, Gaudin has kept a close link with the municipal unions, and he appointed its leader as one of his deputies. Gaudin has also kept a bloated public work force intact, which today reaches 12,700 employees. This valuable source of patronage flies in the face of his renunciation of "clanism."

Indeed, Gaudin is a combination of a modern technocratic and old-fashioned ward healer. And this combination seems to be working well for him. In 2001 he was elected by a handsome margin, and he showed that he could work the crowds as well as any Deferrist. In his bid for reelection Gaudin captured 48 percent of the vote against 35 percent for the Socialists, while the extreme right held just 12 percent of the voters. After the electoral dust had cleared, Gaudin's center-right coalition held a commanding majority, occupying 61 out of 101 seats on the municipal council.[14]

Clearly, Gaudin had established himself as Marseilles's preeminent politician. Even with this clear-cut victory Gaudin follows his recipe of caution by keeping the traditional levers of power intact. Indeed, two photos adorn the mayor's office — one, quite expectedly, of Chirac and the other, quite surprisingly, of Deferre. Speaking of Deferre's portrait, the new mayor admits, "One either loves or hates him, sometimes at the very same time. Perhaps that is my own case."[15]

GLASGOW'S SCOTTISH ENTERPRISE

Grantsman politics. State-centered grantsmanship is what Glasgow's regime politics is all about. Years of deindustrialization have left local officials with a rump economy that is shrinking and out of balance. Regenerating it is beyond the reach of the local government. It lacks the political authority as well as the financial resources for taking on a catalytic role. The result: regime politics converge on a political coalition made up of a hierarchy of public institutions led by the powerful agency Scottish Enterprise or SE.[iii] Since 1974 virtually all major efforts of the

elected district and regional councils have been dependent upon the resources of the SE and its predecessor, the Scottish Development Agency
(SDA). Both agencies had authority to override planning decisions of
local and regional councils in order to realize objectives, although they
were expected to consult with local authorities and build a network of
cooperative planning in the region. This authority was reinforced by
extensive public ownership. Until recent years, most of the large industries in Scotland, such as mining, steel, railways, and transportation,
were in public ownership. Housing was dominated by public provision
in larger cities. SE planning has been supported by the Scottish Office,
which oversees regional development grants and is charged with promoting investment through advertising, subsidies, loans, and other business incentives.

Grantsmanship usually relegates business players to the sidelines of
the regime. Although persons from the private sector serve on various
governmental boards, they have traditionally been subordinate to the
public sector.[16] When the SDA was reorganized in 1991 and renamed
Scottish Enterprise, its relations with business leaders changed. Within a
short time SE set up local enterprise companies throughout Scotland's
urban areas, and the Glasgow affiliate was established as the Glasgow
Development Agency or GDA.

Although the GDA is a private company dominated by business appointments, it functions as a quasi-public authority. It essentially pursues a grants politics in concert with the public players. GDA's director
and board work closely with local officials and is the city's advocate in
relations with SE. Business has little tradition of civic involvement
in Glasgow, where the power of the Labour party is overwhelming.[17] In
fact, GDA now works with local industry to boost an apathetic business
community and encourage it to play some role in Glasgow's planning.
Still, dominant authority has remained with the public sector. The reorganization of the SDA simply redistributed power within the agency; it
did not shift power to private players.[18]

Most recently, SE's role in regional development assumed even greater
importance. The reorganization of Scottish local government in 1996
abolished the regional councils, including the Strathclyde Council,
which encompassed Glasgow's region, and turned over most of their
powers to district councils in a single-tier system. Glasgow assumed
these powers as one of the new single-tier authorities. In 1999 a Scottish
parliament with minor taxing powers was created to serve as a regional
legislature, firmly recognizing the Scottish drive for greater autonomy.

Local officials try to achieve their objectives by seeking to deploy the
political and financial leverage of other government players in the region. They have little choice but to work within the loop of intergovern-

mental arrangements in hopes of getting others to lend their support
and money for city goals. This encourages a pragmatic approach that
reinforces the mainstream tendencies in the local regime. Labour's
agenda emphasizes cooperating with business, polishing the city's cultural image, and seeking the helping hand of government for specific
projects.

This pragmatism is reflected within the Labour Party. During the
1990s, competition over policy centered on two long-time party figures,
Jeanne McFadden and Pat Lally. Both leaders competed for prominence
by offering common-sense arguments about making the city work better. Their pragmatic solutions were intended to get the most out of
whatever programs Scottish Office planners were willing to provide. Although Glasgow development officials may complain, few see intergovernmental politics as "them versus us." For decades nearly all big
program initiatives have been cast in the language of partnership and
problem solving. These terms also dominate the language of most local
regime players.[19]

It is difficult for dissident groups to mount effective challenges to this
get-along style of government. Labour's commanding position, the absence of well-organized party factions, and the city's working-class electorate support the prevailing leadership. The major recent objection to
this regime occurred shortly after Glasgow was designated as the European City of Culture for 1990. The Labour-controlled District and Regional Councils put together a year-long series of special cultural events
celebrating the city's artistic achievements to attract tourists and businesses. Socialist critics, including playwright John McGrath, charged
that this betrayed Glasgow's worker past and ignored how capitalism
was hurting city residents. A "Workers City" group of some forty left-
wing activists emerged as a voice of opposition. This sparked extensive
media coverage and some protests.[20] Within months, however, this
group faded as Labour leadership expressed sympathy with some of
"Workers City" ideas, but continued their booster activities.

A dual strategy.   Glasgow's political entrepreneurs must play by rules
set by more powerful regional politicians, whose policy priorities have
shifted over time. This means that regime leaders have accommodated
increasingly market-centered policy directions. As discussed earlier,
when SDA was launched it favored intervention that focused on bringing jobs to people in Scotland's most devastated and poorest areas. It
mounted a major reinvestment effort, the Glasgow Eastern Area Renewal (GEAR) program. When, after ten years, the program failed to
produce many new jobs, the SDA abandoned this approach.

The agency turned to programs to stimulate growth wherever it

might occur. Regional policies have mostly followed the shift of people
and jobs to the new towns and suburbs. As the SE's support for inner-
city regeneration ebbed, its interest in using small-area programs also
waned. By the late 1980s it wished to end the monopoly of public housing and favored greater personal responsibility, including private home
ownership. Regional officials saw their role as getting residents to
change their attitudes and location, rather than trying to improve job
opportunities at home.[21]

SE policies forced Glasgow's local grants advocates—the GDA and
the city government—to adopt its dual strategy (see chapter 4). This
meant catering to both market- and social-centered constituencies. Private and public investment now promote downtown growth, while casting about for programs to cope with social fallout. Most of the GDA's
activities gravitate toward services and corporate investment schemes
that will expand employment in Glasgow's city center. In recent years
the agency has become an advocate for local politicians demanding
brown field clearance, the regeneration of manufacture, and upgraded
social services.[22] Also, the city's social problems temper any inclination
toward reducing social services. Existing obligations for public housing,
income maintenance, and health care require that the city pay attention
to marginal, blue-collar families.

SE's dual strategy has left the district government with few alternatives. The city government has limited legal authority and a tiny budget
for economic development activities, authority, and is forbidden by law
from using business incentive programs to attract inward investment.
Local politicians have resorted to adopting policies that essentially repli-
cate both faces of SE's dual approach. Officials work to boost the
downtown as a cultural capital, while attending to the social miseries of
decline through small-scale neighborhood social programs. There are
almost continuous promotional campaigns and investments in cultural
institutions, fashion malls, and office developments, supported with
subsidies from SE. Tourism has come to play a large role in Glasgow's
downtown renewal. Tourist trade now accounts for 10 percent of the
city's work force.[23] At the same time, city leaders have become providers
of enhanced community services in the worst-off neighborhoods. In tandem with the far more substantial national safety-net programs a variety of small area programs help to shore up some of the worst enclaves
of poverty. Though earnest in purpose, the poverty-area initiatives have
more symbol than substance.[24] Downtown is where the action and
money are concentrated.

The changing politics of regionalism. Why has grantsmansip become
increasingly market centered—even as the city has continued its virtual

free-fall decline? The regime has done less and less to use public intervention to compensate for Glasgow's weakness in the marketplace. The city's public dependency makes almost everything that happens contingent on the dynamics of the governmental sector. As national and regional practices have changed, local regime players have followed suit.

To some extent, the market-centered policy drift followed the 1979 Conservative electoral victory and the rise of Prime Minister Margaret Thatcher, who was committed to neoliberal directions. Conservative governments pursued years of program changes that aimed to limit government regulation of the economy, reduce the power and autonomy of local government, and favor private-sector solutions to public problems. Tory neoliberalism clearly favored the idea of placing greater emphasis on using commercial efficiency, rather than social equity, in revitalizing urban economies. To a degree, this rhetoric of commercialism found its way into the Scottish Office.

In many respects, however, Scottish development programs were not forced into a neoliberal mold by the national government. Thatcher's radical revision of local government in England never affected Scotland in the same degree.[25] The Scottish system of public-led regional planning was left intact for almost twelve years following Thatcher's election and then merely reorganized with a more private-like veneer. Major SE policies never shifted in a neoliberal direction. Even in the early days of SDA, interventionist rhetoric coexisted with emphasis on commercial viability.[26] Detailed study of agency policies during the years following the Conservative Party victory in 1979 shows continuity in public-sector activity, rather than significant shifts toward neoliberalism.[27] SDA industrial investments were not reduced from their earlier levels of the 1970s. The agency even continued to invest heavily in ailing firms as a means of promoting employment. It is difficult to avoid the conclusion that SDA was guided less by central government than by the agency's own opportunistic principles.[28]

Scottish politics did not conform to changes in national politics for other reasons. Although Tory governments had little partisan political stake in a region that is dominated by Labour, Conservative politicians at Westminster were apprehensive about Scottish demands for greater independence and sought to pacify its advocates. As a result, Scotland has been able to maintain political privileges, including its own ministry, a separate legal system, a distinctive school system, and special housing agencies and programs, among other forms of autonomy. Scottish regional policy has had a bipartisan importance that limits the impact of national politics on Scottish affairs. The huge GEAR program was launched and funded at a time when major inner-city development projects elsewhere in Britain were being rejected or abandoned.[29] In recent years the rise of Scottish nationalist sentiment has made national leaders increasingly reluctant to antagonize Scottish advocates and anxious to find ways of giving Scots greater autonomy.[30] Both parties have embraced concessions for greater regional autonomy. Tony Blair's Labour government supported the creation of the Scottish Parliament in 1999 precisely to deal with the nationalist drift in Scotland.

Glasgow's changes in urban policy are rooted in the dynamics of regionalism itself.[31] Once Glasgow was made dependent upon a regional governmental approach, its fate hinged upon how these officials would view assistance to a poor central city. Over time, however, they saw assistance to Glasgow more as a liability than an asset in their struggle to promote the Scottish economy. This doomed Glasgow's regional gamble.

Political struggle among regime players to define "regional interests" discriminated against Glasgow. Initially, the Scottish Office expected their newly created regional authority to adopt a view that was redistributive, giving priority to black-spot industrial centers like Glasgow.[32] Thus, GEAR assumed a central place in SDA objectives by targeting the city's most needy districts. Yet as these officials began to gain experience, it became clear that revitalizing Glasgow could occur only over the long run, if at all. GEAR's lack of success in creating new jobs or retaining old ones was recognized by SDA officials.[33] Throughout the 1980s the story within SDA is one of gradual redefinition in favor of using public investment almost anywhere in the region in order to maximize job growth.

As a regional agency, SE ultimately measures its performance vis-à-vis other regions and not in terms of its success in aiding Glasgow. Its need to achieve regional growth—regardless of where it takes place—is a powerful constraint. Even if the agency were to succeed in revitalizing inner cities, but without significant improvements in regional economic performance, it would risk the appearance of failure. In the end, the dynamics of grantsmanship must be seen to benefit the region.

In this respect, SE officials were merely conforming to the Scottish Office agencies that managed business incentive programs for luring inward investment. These programs overwhelmingly rewarded private investments in greenfield sites and new towns. As long as private sector investors are believed to prefer sites outside of Glasgow, regional officials find it difficult to work against this market orientation. Thus, the grantsmanship approach has been constrained by the realities of regional development and the marketplace.

This orientation might have been checked by political commitment to older urban areas, like Glasgow, in the hope that better regional economic performance would materialize. While this view was favored by officials in Glasgow, pressures from national, regional, and bureaucratic constituencies made it difficult to sustain.

SE must be responsive to the time horizons imposed on it from above. Although the agency is largely independent of capital markets and does not simply reflect national party politics, it is sensitive to national officials and parliamentary committees. Unless SE can demonstrate achievements, both the agency's financial support and even its political survival are in question. These are hardly remote threats. The agency was reorganized in 1991 because of criticism that its development objectives were lagging. After reorganization, it was prodded to quickly demonstrate new performance capabilities.[34]

Similar political pressures were articulated by the Scottish Office. These officials' interests in the region have not been identical with Glasgow's fate. As a ministry with region-wide responsibilities, the Scottish Office is always under pressure to spread benefits. This discourages concentrating resources in hopes of eventually stimulating long-term diffuse benefits.[iv] Its measuring rod is how well the whole region is doing because regional interests are central to its political enhancement.

Finally, as an agency, Scottish Enterprise does not take a long-term view of regional interests. Since SE does not represent governmental jurisdictions, it does not have to cobble together coalitions from communities in the region. Business professionals and academic economists, who are trained to value market signals, dominate the agency.[35] Their notions of regional interest tend to be shaped by local investors and the corporate business world.

The pressures of these constituencies assumed greatest influence during the mid-1980s when strategic assessment of the first ten years of SDA efforts took place.[36] Disappointed with the results of investment in inner-city regeneration, agency economists took the view that the greater Glasgow region really should be treated as an integrated labor market. They believed that people should move to where jobs are available. The implication was clear: There is little reason to enhance the competitive ability of Glasgow, as long as other parts of the region can attract new jobs.[37]

In sum, the dynamics of grantsmanship worked against Glasgow. Pressures to achieve economic growth in the larger region led to more market-centered policy directions over time. Glasgow continues to decline while the region grows. Local politicians find that they are riding the tail of regional decision makers whose head has changed direction. They continue to try to offset the city's decline, but grantsmanship does less and less to address its social consequences.

Clientelist and Challenger Regimes

Some regimes may give up on reviving themselves through economic development. They may view public dependence as a way of coping with adverse conditions or as managing failure as best as they can. Given this scenario, regimes turn upon themselves. They become so swallowed in corruption or reliant on handouts that clientelism becomes an end in itself. Development then disappears as a viable and serious policy choice. Alternatively, regimes can turn against the system and challenge its legitimacy. Out of sheer frustration these regimes function as counterelites and attempt to overthrow existing relationships. Both clientelist and challenger regimes have one characteristic in common — they have lost confidence in the ability of both government and the marketplace to remedy their condition. Indeed, clientelist and challenger regimes may oppose programs that increase the importance of private capital, especially if it undermines valued political relationships and institutions. At one time or another, Liverpool and Naples have displayed the clientelist approach, and for a brief episode Liverpool took on the role of a challenger. Today, Liverpool struggles toward change. We take a longer-term perspective and, for heuristic or comparative purposes, emphasize the challenger aspects of Liverpool's history (see also chapter 9). In the following pages, we see how different regimes can sometimes blend with one another or replace a given coalition with a rival approach.

LIVERPOOL: CLIENTELIST, CHALLENGER AND STRUGGLING TOWARD GRANTSMAN

Collapse of political stability and the "lost decade." There was a time in the latter nineteenth and early twentieth century when Liverpool had a vibrant middle class. During that era the city was Great Britain's second largest port. Its merchants and industrialists blossomed with the rising prosperity of the city, and they weighed heavily in decisions to build a mighty infrastructure and design grand Victorian buildings. That middle class managed to prolong its influence through the early post–World War II years and work through the Conservative Party. Through the 1950s and 1960s Tories alternated power with Labour. Protestant workers continued to vote for Conservatives while Catholics found a home in Labour's right wing.[38] For a while this rotation of power seemed feasible. Labour was under the grip of the legendary "Braddock machine," which kept members content with patronage, graft, and incremental gains. For their part the Tories accepted mild social intervention. Coexistence was made possible by grants from the central government, supported trade for the bourgeoisie and public housing for the workers.

After their long dominion over the city, the Tories went through a rapid eclipse. Political stability collapsed soon after 1970, in the wake of Liverpool's devastating economic fall. Liverpool had always been regarded as a city with branch plants, but this grew worse. For most of its industrial life an estimated 51 percent of manufacturing firms were absentee owned; by the 1970s that proportion had risen to 71 percent.[39] The shrinkage of locally owned business was aggravated by shutdowns and departures. From the 1970s onward, port traffic dwindled, hundreds of businesses closed, and the city's politics became more brittle. The drop in the number of local proprietors also meant the glue of social cohesion was evaporating. The city's blue-collar majority was divided between Protestants and Catholics, between left and right wings of the Labour Party, and between unions associated with one movement or another. Even Liverpool's small but visible black minority of 30,000 became enmeshed in the social fray.

With the loss of its white-collar constituents, the Tories became nearly extinct, but Labour's reputation for faction and corruption kept it from victory. The Liberal Party stepped into this breach and was extraordinarily successful at the polls. Liberals took up the cause of community politics and began battling for neighborhood revitalization and rent stability. Notwithstanding this appeal, the new Liberal-versus-Labour competition failed to create a healthy rotation of office. Instead, the parties found themselves locked in a standoff. Between 1974 and 1983 no single party held real control, and Liverpool was paralyzed by "hung councils." Even when Labour became the largest single municipal party it refused to take control, leaving the city's business to minority-ruled councils (Liberals or Liberal-Conservative coalitions).

This was a period that one writer called "the lost decade," and for good reason.[40] Municipal services lapsed, public buildings went unrepaired, the schools system continued to deteriorate, and there was little room for planning, much less for economic progress. The only development that appeared to survive was housing construction. As Labour had done for its constituency, the Liberals now used housing to secure votes. During these years, the joke around the city was that the Liberals indeed had a definitive housing strategy — to build houses for sale in Labour wards and houses for rent in Tory wards.[41]

The "lost decade" was but a prologue for more dramatic events. The first of these showed that the "Braddock machine" and the old Catholic right wing were on the way out. Their departure was accelerated by young, energetic, ideological socialists — many of whom belonged to a national group of Trotskyites called Militant Tendency. The new recruits were drawn from the trade unions, they rigorously defended their right to belong to the Labour Party, and their exuberance gradually gave them control. As one early leaflet put it,

> Militant supporters call for Labour to introduce a 35 hour work week to create one million jobs, a 90 pound minimum wage to end poverty, a massive scheme of public works to build homes, hospitals and schools. . . . Join the Labour Party and help ensure it becomes a mass workers party committed to socialist policies. Make sure the right wing of Labour leadership do not succeed in wrecking Labour's chances. . . . Help build a mass campaigning party which fights against the Tories, unemployment and poverty.[42]

The next group of events consisted of strife with the trade unions. In a city where the council employed a third of the work force, centrist parties were bound to clash with the unions. Through much of the decade the city was wracked by strikes. In 1978 social workers went on prolonged strikes over salary issues followed by secretaries and typists who also struck over wages. More radical blue-collar unions also fought with the Liberals over working conditions. Militant Tendency used these clashes to build a power base with both white- and blue-collar unions.

While Militant was building, the streets were coming apart. The condition of the city's black population had gone from bad to worse, and they were now joined by unemployed white youth. In 1981 the Granby ward, known also as Toxteth, exploded. A local policeman had shot a black youth and furious rioting quickly broke out. The incident evoked national attention and the police were forced to use CS gas in order to quell the disturbance. After two weeks the rioting had left one dead, hundreds wounded, and 11 million pounds in damages.

Toxteth was a shock to Liverpool's body politic, and the central government recognized its portent. Shortly after the riots, Michael Heseltine, named himself minister for Merseyside. Liverpool was still operating under a Liberal-Conservative coalition, whose makeup was palatable for Whitehall. Heseltine began funneling money into select projects, most notably to create the Merseyside Development Corporation (MDC) and to begin an enterprise zone at Speke. But this was to little avail. Rebellion was in the air, the mood had grown ugly, and anger was waiting to be fed.

Standing up to the "bitch in London." Thatcher's rightist policies provided the necessary fodder. The Tory platform called for cities to put a ceiling on taxes (rate capping), privatize their work force, and free up local markets. And the Tories showed every indication of sticking to their promises. Before Thatcher's ascension to power in 1979, central government provided nearly 62 percent of Liverpool's income. Just four years later, that share was slashed to 44 percent.[43] With less and less money from Whitehall, Liverpool would face severe revenue shortfalls. To make up for the deficit, tax rates would have to be forced up, rents ratcheted upward, and the municipal labor force shrunk.[v] This was a survive-on-your-own-or-be-dammed approach, and so far as Thatcher was concerned, there was little point in backing losers. Liverpool just might not make it and, like any unsuccessful business, should be allowed to die off.[44]

Liverpudlians were not inclined to agree with Thatcher's assessments, and in May 1983 they turned toward a more ideologically committed Labour party. Having gained 51 out of 92 seats on the council, this time Labour took clear control and readied for the fight. Resistance was made starker by Militant Tendency, whose leadership would have a strong, if not dominant, voice. Two partisan firebrands led the charge — council leader Derek Hatton and the more technocratic chair of the finance committee, Tony Byrne.

Hatton and Byrne were the key figures on the council and led the resistance against any increase in tax rates and any decrease in municipal workers. Their choice was both simple and dangerous — cut or combat — and they chose to fight. The council would not diminish the municipal work force and would limit tax increases to an absolute minimum. From Militant's point of view, central government was responsible for the crisis, and they would rather bankrupt the city than vote for an austerity budget. Indeed, they were backed up by a popular upsurge. Through the early months of 1984 massive demonstrations were held around the city, mostly by trade-union allies. The demonstrations reached a pinnacle in March when more than 50,000 people rallied at town hall to support resistance.

Meanwhile Hatton and Byrne began negotiations with Minister of the Environment Patrick Jenkin. The Militant position was steadfast in arguing that there was nothing left to cut and that withholding aid was tantamount to stealing from the city. Jenkin was equally unwavering and refused to make concessions. Hatton was alleged to have threatened that if Liverpool was not given additional funds, violence would spill onto the streets of Liverpool and attacks would even occur in front of Jenkin's own home. The episode became a national cause célèbre and Thatcher brought the issue to parliament suggesting, "The threats of violence will not help Liverpool, indeed will do Liverpool great damage."[45]

Whatever Thatcher's admonition, Liverpool was not listening. In May 1984 Liverpool Labour triumphed once again at the polls, this time with an increased majority of council seats and a record voter-turnout of 51 percent. Opinion polls showed massive support for fur-

.ther resistance, at least among Labour voters. Surveys of these voters showed that 68 percent favored occupation of council offices by workers who had lost their jobs; 62 percent favored street demonstrations as a means of showing general dissatisfaction; 55 percent supported a general strike; and 48 percent were willing to undertake rent and rate strikes.[46] Even Liberal voters showed significant support for resistance with roughly a quarter of them favoring building occupations and some kind of strike action. Among both groups of voters opposition to Whitehall was high and well over half of all respondents felt Liverpool had been wronged. As one Liberal expressed it, "I can't stand the Militant, but at least somebody is standing up to the bitch in London."[47]

After the rhetoric died down, Byrne sat down with Jenkin to work out a compromise. Liverpool paired down or cancelled plans for spending. It also resorted to creative accounting by using reserve funds to reduce the deficit and recalculating figures for inflation. Byrne also moved some housing expenditure from a revenue to a capital budget, which allowed for further reductions in the deficit. For its part, Whitehall increased aid to Liverpool, provided subsidies for interest payments on demolished housing, and allowed the city to use some aid to continue projects. The agreement allowed Byrne and Jenkin to walk away claiming some sort of victory.

Confrontation and collapse. Unfortunately, the matter was far from settled. First, the psychological rivalry was so great that it spilled onto the public stage. Thatcher made no secret of her displeasure at having to deal with a bunch of left-wing rogues, and Jenkin portrayed the dispute not as a technical difference, but as a Militant plot to upset the system. In his view, Militant "had to eat their words . . . and blackmail had failed." Liverpool claims were also inflammatory. The district leader of Liverpool Labour gloated that the Tories had "backed down in the face of a mobilized city" and said that they should be prepared for "future battles."[48] Derek Hatton boasted,

> There is no way even Thatcher can take on the might of the working class in this city. And this is just a start. Next year we will see not only the defeat of rate capping . . . but we will start to see the kicking out of Thatcher herself.[49]

Second, Liverpool stood as a national symbol and it was now stuck in that position. Left-wing councils from around the country pointed to Liverpool as a way to bring capitalism to a grinding halt. Militants from Liverpool were invited to address Marxist and left-wing councilors in other European cities. The national press also created the image of a daring, pugilistic victory for the Left. *The Daily Mail* wrote,

If a week in politics is a long time, then the past fortnight for Environment
Secretary Patrick Jenkin must have been a pulverizing eternity. He is now
sporting not one but two lovely black eyes. Bang! The Trotskyites and
others of the hard left who run Liverpool had the best of the fight with him
in their threat to defy the law on that city's overspending.[50]

Third, underneath the jingoism there were deep policy differences.
The hard right wanted to radically curtail public spending, believing
that such spending hurt Liverpool, while the hard left saw radical public
spending as Liverpool's only salvation. Thatcher and Jenkin were persuaded that there would be no more soft options and were determined
to root out "municipal Stalinism." Hatton and Byrne vowed to bring
about real socialism and were bent on repeating past tactics with a ven-
geance. Each side had grasped an opposite lesson from the experience.

Those lessons were about to clash. By the end of 1984 Liverpool had
prepared a go-for-bust budget. Led by Militant, the council adopted an
Urban Regeneration Strategy (URS), which pumped the city with public
spending. As mentioned in chapter 4, URS was based on building thousands of publicly supported housing units, but it was also more than a
plan for modern shelter. The idea was to use housing as a wedge to
create nursery facilities, parks, and recreational centers and to refurbish
the city's sanitation services. The city's youth were to be treated to a
brand-new publicly supported educational system. Secondary schools
and adult training were to be overhauled and fitted with free meals,
books, tutoring, and field trips.

There was, of course, a strong political component to URS. The benefits were targeted directly and exclusively on Labour's heartland—
blue-collar neighborhoods where old housing would be demolished and
new flats would be filled with trade unionists. Student leaders were also
brought together with union leaders and given time off to collaborate
on common projects. Finally, URS was a way to bring about full employment and reward the trade unions. Elected union leaders would
select workers for jobs, and this extended to the council's own work
force. Hatton had declared his preference for "socialist managers" and
a portion of the city's administration was nominated by the unions.[51]

To get some immediate cash, the Militant-led council arranged for the
sale of housing mortgages to a French bank. It also front ended expenditures so that capital could be put immediately into public projects. As
the year 1985 rolled on Liverpool continued its defiance. Newspapers
around the country wondered how central government could submit to
"mob criminality."[52] Emboldened by the publicity, Militant refused to
reduce the work force or raise housing rents, and it joined with other
councils to resist Thatcher's rate capping scheme.

With every passing day the deficit loomed, and the council went through most of the year without even setting a tax rate. In British law, refusing to set a tax rate is an act of willful misconduct, subject to removal from office and severe penalties. In the event of such a crime Whitehall had the power to send commissioners into the city, displace the council, and take over municipal affairs.

Clearly, Liverpool was not willing to go just to the brink but beyond it. Popular sentiment seemed to support Militant's actions. Throughout the spring the trade unions came out in massive demonstration along with 25,000 high school students who staged a strike. Liverpool's security forces and caretakers made it known that they would lock out any commissioners sent from London to administer the city. Hatton bragged that commissioners sent from London would never be let off the motorway. Whitehall knew it faced massive resistance and was fearful of creating a national calamity.

Hatton sought to use mass demonstrations and the potential for disorder to force Whitehall's hand. By June, the council met and finally adopted a tax rate. Their answer was nine percent and no more. It was evident that a hike of just nine percent would not put the slightest dent in the city's deficit, and Hatton was trying to compel central government to make up the difference. But Thatcher would have none of that. "These people must be put down," she thundered.

Within weeks the axe had fallen. The district auditor charged forty-seven Labour councilors with "willful misconduct." In the auditor's view the council had not set a rate on time and had failed to set an adequate rate. Because of this, the Crown had lost millions of pounds in delayed collection and interest payments. The penalties for the councilors were severe—barred from serving in public office for five years, an imposed surcharge of 106,000 pounds and an additional imposition of 242,000 in legal costs. The courts upheld the verdict and to tearful watchers the House of Lords concurred and dismissed the councillors.

For the remainder of 1987 Militants tried to mobilize support. The trade unions held a series of votes on whether to wage a general strike. For a while, Hatton managed to secure strike votes and the shop stewards backed him. But the strategy backfired and the unions wound up split between an aggressive blue-collar contingency and reticent white-collar personnel. As the tensions mounted, the unions finally spoke. Workers voted 7,284 for striking and 8,152 against a general job action.[53] Notwithstanding the loss, Hatton still had a desperate card to play. He persuaded the unions to agree to a massive, all-in-one-swoop dismissal of Liverpool's municipal workers. By December some 30,000 workers received redundancy notices. Hatton and his union allies reasoned that fired workers would collect more than their usual salaries in severance benefits, and that once spring rolled around they could be rehired. Liverpool would gain publicity, send the establishment into shock, and create a crisis that would break the logjam. Again the strategy backfired. The press and the public mocked the December redundancies as a vile Christmas gift from Militant.

For a while Labour hung on and even managed to elect another council in 1986. Militant could even claim to have won victories in other cities. But the revolution was spent. Mainstream Labour renounced Militant and expelled the radicals from the party. For five years Liverpool had waged a policy revolution that defied the market. In the end, municipal radicalism was vanquished.

A vacuous aftermath and a glimmer of hope. Through the late 1980s and early 1990s factional fighting eviscerated the locus of power. The Labour Party continued to tear itself apart, and was split between a mainstream group, a smaller cluster of dissidents, an assemblage of Militants, and a suspended bunch of mavericks called "Ward Labour." The Conservatives disappeared and lost their remaining seat. Liberals survived the mayhem through occasional alliances with the Social Democrats.

The Liberal-run council had managed to ease relations with business and forge lines of communication. But the system was in tatters. As one article put it, "In Liverpool the real political contest is between three forces — the Labour Party, Liberal Democrats and apathy."[54] The apathy could readily be seen in voter turnouts. From a high of 51 percent in 1983, just 22 percent of the citizenry went to the polls in 1998. There may have been good reasons for the apathy. Liverpool has the highest property taxes in England and a bloated public payroll. Vestiges of Militant remained through the mid-1990s, and so too did political sniping. The city's middle class continued to shrink and even public officials chose to live outside the city. City services were thought to be awful. Schools continued to deteriorate, housing was poorly managed, and social services were inefficient. Also during the last decade a long dock strike racked the city. The docks dispute resulted in the sacking of 500 workers.[55] Nearly fifteen years after the collapse of Militant policies, the city administration was broken and powerless.

Any effort to fill the vacuum was taken up by church leaders and regional agencies. Protestant and Catholic clergy persuaded government officials and voluntary groups to take a firmer hand in running the city. The Merseyside Development Corporation managed to renew the docks and some residential development has begun to flourish in that area.[56] These and other events have offered some glimmers of hope.

By 1998 Liverpool politics began to shake out loose factions and develop some coherence. The alliance of Liberals and Social Democrats held, and a new party of Liberal Democrats consolidated power within the city council. They now control 70 out of 99 seats on the council and have taken a firm administrative hand. The Liberal Democrats claim to be pragmatic with "no hang-ups" on whether a public or private approach to development is best. By and large their politics is eclectic, and they proudly adopt the accolade of "libertarian socialists." While recognizing that market forces will not catapult the city into prosperity, Liberal Democrats do appreciate the dynamics of free enterprise. Their strategy is to make the most of grants from central government, and leverage them with whatever business investment can be mustered. Objective 1 money is crucial to this approach, and the Liberal Democrats have used it to establish business incubators, "hot lines" for easier licensing and permits, and links with the booming economy, just across the straits, in Ireland. There is, too, another significant component to this strategy, centered on community participation and neighborhood ownership. Liberal Democrats have worked to create local area committees and encourage tenant management, housing cooperatives, and neigborhood-owned companies.

Together with a new cadre of administrative officers, Liberal Democrats take an aggressive attitude toward public service. They enthusiastically advertise that city hall has changed, and so too has its attitude toward municipal services. "Everyone out there is our customer, not our prisoner," says one party leader. Liberal Democrats have also taken pains to hire a hard-nosed, tough-driving chief executive, David Henshaw. Among Henshaw's earlier acts was a reorganization of the local bureaucracy and the sacking of nearly 1,500 municipal employees. To some, Henshaw is an efficient, no-nonsense manager, but for others he is a "ruthless, uncaring bureaucrat" who does "what he wants" and controls the council's agenda.

While Labour has lost seats and is now a minority party, it too has begun to transform itself into a moderate and effective opposition. The local opposition is now led by a popular member of the city council with ties to the national movement of New Labour. Still, attached to much of the socialist ideal, the local Labour Party seeks to make politicians more accountable and argues for political reform. Labour wants city hall to hold a referendum on whether to adopt an elected mayor system, and hopes that a popularly chosen head of the city can make sure investment reaches the neighborhoods. All well and good says one journalist, but what happens "if Derek Hatton, still popular in some parts of the city, were to be elected?"[57]

NAPLES: CLIENTELIST POLITICS

Accommodating decline. Regime politics in Naples mostly seeks to accommodate, not challenge, the city's decay. Facing crushing poverty but having access to great public-sector aid, Neapolitan politicians have little choice but to cast their lot with government. Yet regime leaders usually do not seek to use the hand of the state to improve the city's economy. With limited resources for sustaining collective public action, it is difficult to build the political cooperation necessary for bargaining with capital. Officials usually find it more rewarding to exploit opportunities to reinforce the traditional political status quo. The result is a regime that is absorbed in patronage, favors, and individual political rewards.

The city's weak steering resources incline it toward patronage politics. As noted earlier, Neapolitan citizens are highly partisan, yet they are characterized by alienation and low levels of trust in the state. Voters share a radically materialist view of politics that stresses primary group relations. They devote little activity to voluntary associations and there is widespread acceptance of favoritism as normal.[58] Party politics is seen mainly as a channel of patronage and defense of small-group interests. For their part, political elites are inclined to see their role as the occupation of as many key positions as possible, "not to transform society but to exercise patronage as a symbol of their power."[59] Patronage extends to almost all levels of society and tends to displace competing forms of political relations.

Ambitious politicians generally see local and regional politics as way stations to the power and fortunes of national officialdom. A premium is put on knowing legislators, top elected politicians, influential bureaucrats, and leaders in the big national parties. Close personal links between local party chieftains and national politicians are crucial in playing the aid game. Although there is some dual office-holding (the recent mayor, Antonio Bassolino, was also minister of labor), national influence is more commonly sustained by means of partisan connections and favors. Political parties serve as ladders of mobility, as networks in which negotiations can be conducted, and ultimately as important decision makers.

Ironically, years of public sector dependency have contributed to clientelist expectations. The ad hoc character of Southern aid programs makes long-term planning nearly impossible. Rome's presence in the region lacks predictability. Rome's role usually is of an "emergency" nature. Most funding by the national government addresses specific problems or responds to local crises. Quite suddenly, money lands on the desks of local officials. The largesse is supposed to refurbish a stadium for the soccer World Cup games, build a light rail extension, or provide badly needed sewer infrastructure. But somehow these "exceptional" programs are really quite ordinary and their unpredictability does not help get things done.

Clientelismo and political parties. Neapolitan clientelism is highly organized. Political parties constitute the organizations through which virtually all competing regime interests are mediated. Throughout the postwar years Naples constituted a major stronghold of right-wing strength in Italy. First Monarchist and then Christian Democratic (CD) bosses organized a very effective political machine that ran the city for thirty years. In 1975 the Communists became the city's major party and formed a coalition with the Republicans and Social Democrats, which ran the city until 1983. Various unstable coalitions of parties with the Christian Democrats at the center governed until 1993 when the Democratic Party of the Left (reformed communists) regained power.

Until 1993, when electoral reforms and corruption scandals overturned the postwar party system, local elections were seen fundamentally in terms of local patronage. There was only a weak association between the social and economic characteristics of voters and partisanship, except among the Communists. Voters do not shift from one party to another and this produces very reliable followings.[60] Usually percentage-swings amount to only 2 percent of the balloting (compared with 7 percent in Great Britain). Once the new parties get established, loyalties may well reemerge.

At the top, however, this system of fiefdoms produces governmental instability. Party factions and constant maneuvering among political chieftains for petty advantage are a fundamental part of the system's dynamic. Unstable governing coalitions occur because the parties in power are unable to maintain the alliances necessary to govern. The most common cause is a breakdown within the factions of a given party. When this occurs, a new round of bargaining takes place to produce a new governing coalition.

This system of power does not encourage local politicians to be "boosters" of the economy or promoters of programs. Political success depends more on maintaining and extending one's patronage networks than seeking power through appeals to broader interests. Further, there is only limited and sporadic accountability to voters. Given the nature of coalition politics, voters cannot easily determine who is to be *sindaco* or mayor (until 1993 the mayor was selected by the city council). The *giunta* or executive council that heads the government constantly changes, along with the governing parties, with little relation to election results or the performance of incumbent administrations. The most severe instability occurred in 1984. In that year five different mayors ran Naples — one Communist, one Social Democrat, two Christian Democrats, and one Socialist — in addition to a provisional government appointed by Rome.

The modern Neapolitan boss system emerged during the 1950s under the leadership of Achilles Lauro who relied on demagoguery and personal patronage. The system was extended by the Christian Democrats (CDs) led by the Gava family. By the mid-1970s Silvio and Antonio Gava constructed a system of power that integrated politics, the economy, and administration through a network of clientelist relations. The Gava order survived by using state money intended for modernization of the Southern economy. It tied together not just contractors but also local banks, public finance agencies, and the professional classes, such as engineers, architects, and judges. Furthermore, it was vertically integrated through the party system to elected and appointed officials in Rome who promoted the machine's interests and kept the money rolling into the city.[61] Until the political upheaval of the 1990s, Antonio Gava continued to dominate the boss-ridden CD party.

As Naples became a bailiwick of the CD, its access to national governments grew. By the 1980s several Neapolitan politicians achieved powerful cabinet positions, including those of prime minister and budget chief. This enabled them to assume a powerful role in local politics as well. A Byzantine-like pyramid of national, regional, and local politicians emerged in which networks of *capi-elettori* (electoral agents) and *grandi-elettori* (boss agents) supplied "recommendations" that enabled them to exchange jobs for power while maintaining an elaborate division of the patronage. Local officials often were able to bypass regional officials and go directly to their national governmental contacts.

This system became more entrenched during the 1980s. The Communist administrations led by mayor Maurizio Valenzi during the late 1970s and early 1980s were politically isolated by opposition parties.[62] After the earthquake in 1980, emergency aid programs pumped vast amounts of assistance into Naples and its region for reconstruction. This fueled the system of payoffs, patronage, and partisanship. The return of Christian Democratic-led administrations carried this politics to extremes.

The other interests who participate in the regime do so mostly through party mediation. Since Naples has weak civic group life, many voluntary associations serve as extensions of party leaders who frequently head the local clubs and associations. They are used more to promote the careers of individuals rather than the interests of the group.[63] The more independent civic associations are often marginalized by the regime. The major voluntary association that extends social services to families who live in the decaying old Spanish Quarter is a case in point. The director complains of being ignored and unfunded by the local council, even though it is the main social service organization in one of the poorest neighborhoods in Naples. It depends mainly on European Union and charitable funding for support.

Since the local business sector is not highly developed, Naples is dependent on public-sector activities or on branch plants based in Northern Italy. While the public sector dominates, its size is difficult to determine.[vi] State enterprise alone is huge, and it comprises about 55 percent of Naples's manufacturing. The most active of these are the state enterprises and mixed government-private corporations, such as the Bank of Naples and the development consortium Mededil. But these enterprises are controlled by boards and firms that are appointed as party patronage. The construction industry is the most prominent and powerful player. This industry is highly integrated, incorporating not just builders but also real estate and finance as well. It too depends heavily on political connections to function.

Finally, organized crime is part of the governing regime. As described in chapter 3, the influence of the Camorra is pervasive. This organization infiltrates government and contributes votes to campaigns. In return, mob leaders are able to receive government contracts and to develop protection rackets and other illegal enterprises. Some investigations in recent years portray the Mafia and the Camorra as closely connected and more powerful than local government — at least on matters important to the mob.[64]

Clientelismo *and reconstruction.* When a high local official was asked "Who governs Naples?" the response was swift and certain: *"Nessuno"* (nobody). He explained that there was very little governing capacity in a regime that relies so heavily on patronage politics alone to support governmental action.[vii] Political cooperation is possible for only limited ends, and the scope for neglect, mismanagement, obstructionism, and corruption in public endeavors is vast.

Clientelismo works in two directions. One focuses on using the public sector to maintain and expand the horizontal networks of *clients* that form the base of political cooperation. The other seeks to manage the supply of resources through the maintenance of vertical political networks that bring together national and local-party power brokers.

Clientelismo reached a crescendo when unprecedented amounts of state money poured into the region during the 1980s. Response to the earthquake that struck Naples at this time reveals how the regime works. Prior to this calamity there was uncertainty and intense competition among political leaders in Naples, especially among the city's national players. The weakening of the Gava clan's hold on the city during the 1970s precipitated factional strife among groups of breakaway CD politicians who became powerful national figures. This led to control of the council by a Communist-led coalition headed by Mayor Valenzi. It also shifted power to new factional leaders within the CD who needed to assert their control over local politics in their climb to national power.

The new power brokers included several influential cabinet ministers and even one prime minister. Perhaps the key figure was Paolo Pomicino who led the CD faction that came to support the minority Communist administration in Naples. Pomicino won election as deputy, and he quickly climbed to important national posts, eventually becoming Naples's Rome boss. He and several other politicians from Naples in the CD and in some of the other parties stood in strategic positions to influence the national government's response.[65]

They enabled vast amounts of reconstruction assistance to line the pockets of local politicians and their clientele. Although Naples was not particularly hard hit by the earthquake, it was included along with other severely damaged areas in the lineup for emergency treatment. At the time, Pomicino was the budget minister who approved financing for post-earthquake reconstruction. He also had an interest in companies fronted by local politicians that did work in Naples.[66] Another CD boss was given the job of coordinating policies for local government and for proposing reconstruction measures. As minister of culture and environment, he had a new law passed that entrusted implementation of renewal works to two ministers, one reserved for himself.

Naples's party bosses in Rome worked to authorize the aid programs, so that enormous discretion in carrying them out was allocated to local players while they retained oversight. Even the Socialist governments led by Bettino Craxi preserved the privilege of Neapolitan CD politicans to keep a firm grip on aid programs to the region.[67] Overlapping networks of politicians ensured city access to ill-monitored emergency aid programs. This lasted more than a dozen years. Various laws were written so that there was a wall of separation between national overseers and those implementing projects. This duplicitous legal order enabled high officials to escape accountability for public works, while they essentially "outsourced" management functions to local consortia of public and private contractors connected to the regime.[68]

At the local level, the mayor of Naples and the president of the Campania region were appointed as special commissioners in charge of reconstruction. As huge sums of money poured into the region and restrictions were lifted by Rome, a political free-for-all broke out. Local politicians working with political interests in the national government, courts, and bureaucracies cut deals and parceled out shares of what eventually amounted to more than $42 billion over ten years,[69] not counting aid from ordinary government revenues and from charitable sources. The city's 1972 master plan for renewal was ignored as one project after another was justified as a matter of emergency.

Corruption in subcontracting usually involved local politicians serving as mediators in complicated networks. Larger firms, usually from the North, subcontracted with smaller companies (often owned by the mob) and made payments to obtain the consent of local Camorra bosses in the work zones. Local politicians acted as brokers by distributing and extracting payoffs from all of these players for their "services."[70] Costs quickly inflated. Rules governing labor contracts for large public works were changed to pay a large percentage in anticipation of costs, rather than for work actually done. Consequently, many projects were never completed.

All this led to a power shift among players in the regime — but without fundamentally altering the regime itself. A business-political bloc emerged in which private actors assumed greater importance in determining the rules of the political game.[71] With local politicians firmly enmeshed in complicated deals with corporate businesses, construction interests, and suppliers, the pay-for-politics system gave business players a bigger voice. Party politics also changed. The earthquake aid programs led to an increase in contributions from business that altered party finances and reinforced the hand of the city's Rome bosses.[72]

So much money was dumped into a political system that lacked capacity for collective public action, that it also shifted power to organized crime and shady business. As Camorra families formed construction companies and led building consortiums, legal and illegal business interests freely mixed. Politicians were easy prey for mob bosses who were able to forge links with the dominant party machines.[73] This in turn led to years of exploding conflict within organized criminal factions, including killings and fights among big clans.[74]

Not all decision making displays this degree of corruption. Nonetheless, *clientelismo* of the Neapolitan variety is a constant barrier to sustained governmental action. After more than thirty years the city's major urban renewal project, the *Centro Dirizionale*, remains only half finished. This is a strategic project designed to turn a derelict industrial area near the railway station into a modern commercial center. When completed, the project would relieve congestion in downtown and increase badly needed office employment. Even though the local government owns most of the land, only the private half of the project has been successful. The portion under city hall's control has been mired in neglect or obstruction.[75]

An emerging grantsman? Since 1993 the regime has shown signs of change. After corruption scandals sent scores of Neapolitan politicians to jail, new electoral laws were passed and voters punished incumbent politicians. The old party system collapsed and power shifted to the mayor, who is now directly elected. Something like a mayor-council system has emerged under the leadership of reformer and former Communist Antonio Bassolino. After beating Alessandra Mussolini (the daughter of the dictator) in the mayoral election, Bassolino moved to centralize power.[76] His policies have been intended to appeal to investors and good government. In effect, he seeks to make Naples into a grantsman regime, explicitly vowing to mobilize private sector interests to renew the city. Bassolino has worked on a broad front to challenge favoritism and illegal activities and to create a positive business climate.[77] Dubbed "Saint Anthony," his election mantra called "for a normal and legal city."

A recent crisis exemplifies Bassolino's leadership. After Naples's brush with bankruptcy left it with a $1 billion deficit and austerity, the mayor looked for inexpensive ways of boosting the city. He reinvigorated old, neglected reconstruction projects. In some cases he needed to do little more than open virtually finished roadways, swimming pools, sewers, and other improvements that had been ignored during the go-go days of reconstruction and corruption. This proved very popular with voters whose neighborhoods saw visible improvement after years of inattention.

Under Bassolino's leadership Naples became the first Italian city to issue its own municipal bonds. The city floated a $195 million bond issue to raise funds that tripled the city's aging bus fleet. When Naples was chosen as the site of the G-7 meeting in 1994, new money became available from the national government to clean up the city. The mayor used the funds for new public works intended to make the city shine, such as creating pedestrian zones, paving streets, and attacking signs of physical neglect, including turning on the city's fountains and repairing broken street lights. He also waged a battle against illegal activities and imposed symbols of social order. Mob hirelings who controlled parking in front of the former royal palace were booted out, the piazza was closed to traffic and 200 meter maids were hired to collect fees that previously went to the gangs. Finally, this rule-breaking former Communist mayor even moved to privatize the city's airport.

While many of these changes are more symbolic than substantive,[78] they are having consequences. *Clientelismo* is giving way to an extent that has not been witnessed in Naples for generations. Whether this change is transient or permanent remains a question. After Bassolino left Naples for the regional presidency his successor, Rosa Russo Iervolino, was elected mayor in 2001. Her challenges are formidable.

THE PRIVATE DEPENDENT CONTEXT

Cities in private dependent contexts are marked by plant closings, boarded-up shops, and falling property values. Scarce bargaining resources exacerbate these difficulties, placing these cities at the margins of private investment. Political isolation reinforces economic abandonment. With scant access to a consistent supply of intergovernmental resources, the public sector is incapable of offsetting economic liabilities, leaving these cities with limited strategic choices.

Private dependency accents the necessity to comply with private capital.[viii] These circumstances can give rise to vendor regimes or coalitions. Vendor regimes seek solutions to their problems by marketing public assets for whatever can be obtained. Free land, tax abatements, and the removal of entire communities are some of the chips put on the negotiating table. Vendor regimes see lowering the costs for business as a way to retain old capital and attract new investors. Political leaders see their role as one of facilitating business preferences, and they are often put in the position of reacting to private initiatives.

Detroit as a Vendor City

In riot's wake.   It was a hot and humid July morning in 1967 when rioting broke out in Detroit. A month earlier rumors abounded that police had shot a black prostitute and the neighborhood seethed with anger. When the police raided an after-hours drinking club called the "Blind Pig," the tinder exploded. It did not take long before mayhem enveloped the city. At times over three thousand rioters spilled onto the streets, retail shops were looted, snipers fired freely across blocks, and arsonists set buildings on fire. Before it was over, more than 5,000 national guardsmen occupied the city, and tanks were used to quell the violence. The toll was heavy — forty-three people killed and over $40 million in damage.[79] Worse, Detroit was shattered. The riots set off an exodus of commerce, manufacture and the middle class from which the city has never recovered.

While Detroit's mayor, Michigan's governor, and the nation's president used soldiers to stop the rioting, rebuilding the city was left to the business elite. As parts of the city lay smoldering, a coalition of business leaders, already named New Detroit took charge. For a while New Detroit tried to deal with the situation by giving assistance to the local "war on poverty," but it soon turned its attention toward downtown revitalization.[80] Detroit's last white mayors, Jerome Cavanaugh and Roman Gribbs, dealt with racial and rebuilding issues in different ways. Cavanaugh sought to build biracial coalitions and work closely with New Detroit. Gribbs favored a law and order strategy, and by 1970 had begun working with a newly established business group called Detroit Renaissance. But the trauma of the riots and white flight persisted. The mood was too ugly and too saturated with racial distrust for any clear improvement. City hall would have to recompose itself and reflect a new racial alignment before the trauma could be eased.

Bargaining and nonbargaining with business. When Coleman Young became mayor in 1974, he brought a plan for healing. Young believed he could build an equal coalition with business, put that coalition at the service of the city, and satisfy his constituents. Everything seemed so possible and so complementary — rejuvenate manufacture, develop the riverfront, resuscitate downtown commerce, and deliver jobs for residents. Indeed, Young succeeded in some of these endeavors. He has been described as a "messiah mayor," a great "civic booster," and a "master builder."[81] There is something to be said for Young's role in crystallizing development and creating something out of desolation. Young was particularly effective in bringing money into the city project by project. He enjoyed a close relationship with former heads of government, like Governor William Milliken and President Jimmy Carter. The new mayor was able to use those relationships to build a light rail system ("People Mover") around the downtown and create grand facilities for conventions, exhibitions, and sporting events.

In theory Young should have been able to work wonders with business and, as Atlanta's mayors had done, create coalitions between a black majority and business.[82] As in Atlanta, Detroit's business community is powerful and has a history of tight, effective organization. During its formative period, Detroit business was bound by kinship, social ties, and interlocking directorates on corporate boards.[83] The modern elite is more permeable and less rigid. While the automobile industry still constitutes the core of the establishment (Henry Ford, Max Fisher) and old personalities are still important (developer Al Taubman, and head of Stroh Brewery, Peter Stroh), business has been invigorated by newcomers like sports team owner Michael Ilitch and aggressive Greektown luminaries. As in Atlanta, key business people have a stake in the city; and some of them hold seats on the board of Detroit Renaissance.

But theory does not always conform to reality, and Detroit is not Atlanta. For one, Detroit does not have the strong, indigenous black middle class that typifies Atlanta. This lack of an educated, well-off popular base limits the city's ability to generate home-grown small business and mobilize local opinion. Steering resources are particularly weak in the city. Second, Detroit's automobile companies have a national and international scope. These companies are more inclined to seek opportunities elsewhere. Third, Detroit proportionately has a larger number of absentee owners, professional managers, and faceless stockholders, whose personal ties to the city are tenuous. Last, Detroit is not as diversified as Atlanta, and instead is highly dependent upon automobile manufacture. Power relations between business and city hall are highly asymmetric, and this creates a different dynamic.

Beyond the surface of Young's persona, he had little leverage, and the business establishment knew it. Business had profits to make and its own survival to ensure. Young would soon find out that private interests do not always coincide with public ones; that interlocal competition could be more compelling than loyalty to his city: and that markets could be more powerful than political will. Young would also realize that he would have to scramble to please investors and that Detroit would pay a price.

Behind the facades of Joe Louis Arena and twin sports stadiums lies a story of Detroit struggling to persuade sports teams to remain in the city. Young had hoped that team owners could be attracted to a new waterfront and a promise of new facilities. Years earlier, the Detroit Lions football team had moved nearly forty miles outside the city to Pontiac. Now the Pistons basketball team and the Red Wings hockey team were threatening to move. Team owners were cool to the city or at least plying a tough bargaining stratagem. A Pistons chief executive officer declared, " I want to make it clear we have made no commitment to Detroit, even if a riverfront arena is built." The Red Wings owner candidly announced that his team "should be moved to the suburbs."[84] Before the negotiations were over, Young made the teams an offer they could hardly refuse. The mayor borrowed money, tapped into city surpluses, and used bonding authority to house the city's sports teams. Detroit had set a precedent, and one owner delightfully predicted that "there will never again be a stadium built by private enterprise."[85]

Young would also discover that he might not have the opportunity to bargain, and he came to describe Detroit as a "beggar" in a "three piece suit."[86] The mayor would learn that business could go its own way and ignore him. During the 1980s Detroit Renaissance adopted a $75 million strategic development plan for Detroit without even bothering to consult city hall. Most of the money came from the big three automobile manufacturers.[87] An exasperated Coleman Young refused to implement parts of it. The plan's impact was minimal, but the episode revealed the deep fault lines between business and the city.[88] Despite some diversification, Detroit was still the motor city. A standard political understanding is that once the auto industry decides, city hall is sure to follow.

When business does work with the city, it follows a series of stratagems. At the outset, it announces alternative locations outside of Detroit. Next, business identifies its development objectives, sets a partial price, expects the city to make up the remainder, and stands apart from the ensuing fray. While the dust settles the city gets to work — identifying potential sites, searching for inducements, and trying to arrange its best deal.

For the most part, Young was forced to respond to initiatives taken by the private sector. Referring to the paucity of development during the 1980s, DiGaetano and Klemanski sum up the situation by suggesting, "Those projects that were built were largely reactions to opportunities that presented themselves to the city rather than the implementation of a shared vision between regime partners."[89]

Making way for General Motors. The most telling case of development in the Motor City is Poletown.[90] The genesis of the project goes back to when General Motors Chairman William Murphy invited Mayor Coleman Young and Governor William Milliken to his office. Murphy wanted to brief the two politicians on the deteriorating state of the automobile industry. Years earlier General Motors had relocated its St. Louis facility without alerting local officials, and more recently the company moved a transmission facility to a nearby suburb. People were deeply concerned about the fate of the city and feelings were rubbed raw. Besides, General Motors was considering other sites in Michigan, and state law prohibited other localities from granting concessions to a departing company without the consent of the affected community.

This time Murphy was ready to allow the city to prepare a plan and bid. This strategy allowed General Motors to minimize its own time and costs, compare Detroit's offer with other competitors, and exact maximum concessions from the city. Murphy also insisted that Young act immediately and knew that General Motors could bow out gracefully should the city not be able to meet his requirements. Both Young and Milliken were taken aback, and the mayor's response was blunt:

> You know we can't do that. When you ask us to do something and give us 24 hours, you know up front we can't produce. When will the day be when you come to us and say, here are our plans; let's sit down and plan together.[91]

Partially persuaded by their entreaties, the General Motors chairman agreed to give Detroit greater consideration:

> I'll tell you what I will do. The next plant — the next facility — the next time we do something, we're going to give you guys a shot at it. We're going to let you guys participate, but you will have to move quick.[92]

Later when General Motors announced it was looking for a new plant site, the city responded. Initially, nine sites were considered, and the choice was narrowed down to a site within the Poletown neighborhood. As mentioned in chapter 4, Poletown was strategically located between transportation crossroads. The neighborhood bordered the nearby city of Hamtramck, and its housing stock consisted of modest, single- or two-family dwellings. Churches, small stores, and bars dotted the neighborhood, and small manufacturing firms employed some of the local population. While most of the white population were home owners of Polish origin, the neighborhood also had significant concentrations of Albanian and Arab immigrants. A substantial black population also inhabited a corner of the neighborhood — mostly in public housing. For both white and black residents, churches were the mainstays of social life.

Planning the Central Industrial Park (CIP), as the General Motors site came to be known, might have rolled smoothly had a neighborhood not been in the way. Most of the Polish-American home owners were determined to resist and relied on the Poletown Neighborhood Council to press their case. For its part, the city's Economic Development Corporation (EDC), run by Emmett Moten, took charge.[ix] The fight over Poletown then would be waged, on one side, by Coleman Young and his representative Emmett Moten, and, on the other, by the Poletown Neighborhood Council or PNC.

The contest was highly uneven. Coleman Young was a strong mayor who could have his way with the city council. Everyone knew the council was dependent on executive agencies for advice, constrained by their own lack of information, and pressured by General Motors tight timetable. Because council members were elected at large, there was little incentive for protecting neighborhoods — particularly a small, white ethnic community. If anything, council deliberations on the issue were more theater than reality. It came as little surprise when it passed a resolution declaring that General Motors new plant would "fulfill a public purpose" and authorized the acquisition of property.

True, the PNC could and did use the courts to press their case, taking their complaint to the state's highest tribunal. But Michigan law favored development. Politics is what mattered, and any political struggle would be uphill because of divisions within the neighborhood. Some local business and institutions believed that they could obtain high buy-out prices and favored the project. Besides this, the PNC could not bridge the racial divide. Black residents had been earlier victims of urban renewal, particularly by the city of Hamtramck. They were not about to side with a population they perceived as privileged.

The outspoken mayor was able to capitalize on these splits and Poletown's uncertainty. On several occasions Young made it clear that urban conflict was racial conflict, and he would not be manipulated into supporting the wrong side. A Central Industrial Park would provide jobs for everyone and help balance the racial scales. The mayor even dealt offhandedly with attempts to portray the destruction of Poletown as a populist cause. When consumer advocate Ralph Nader weighed in on the controversy, Young denounced him as a "carpet bagger." As if to underline the racial and economic implications, the mayor went on to say, "Nader doesn't live here. He comes in, he sues, he leaves."[93]

Like the dog that never barked in a Sherlock Holmes mystery, the real revelation is what did not happen. No political body came to the defense of Poletown. No compromises were offered to the residents, not even the most meager face-saving gestures. Young never really bargained with General Motors. The corporation conceived the project, set the costs, determined the financial conditions, and established the deadlines. Efficiently, skillfully, and with gusto the mayor delivered. During the court proceedings, the director of city planning testified that his office was only minimally involved. The reasons offered were the constraints imposed by General Motors' and his own reluctance to jeopardize the company's deadlines. EDC director Moten testified that General Motors criteria had been accepted and, though he tried to be flexible, he could not deviate from the corporation's "footprint." Moten added that "developers state the criteria. It is not peculiar to this project."[94]

In the end the toll was heavy. To create the promised 6,000 jobs, the city moved 3,000 residents, obliterated 143 institutions, and demolished over 1,000 buildings. Detroit's bargaining with General Motors resulted in one lost neighborhood and a gain of an automobile plant—all under what one dissenting judge labeled as the "guiding and sustaining, indeed controlling hand of the General Motors Corporation."[95]

Old solutions and new solution sets. As mentioned in chapter 4, the decision on Chrysler's Jefferson Avenue plant followed a past practice that had been applied to General Motors for the Poletown site. The familiar opener was for Chrysler to point out that there were other choices. Its director of governmental affairs suggested that "it would have been a heck of a lot easier to build this plant in a farm field," but added, "we felt an obligation to the very people who supported us over the years."[96]

Like Poletown, the Jefferson Avenue plant was heavily subsidized with tax abatements, loans, land acquisition, and clearance. Chrysler was well aware of how bargaining was carried out in Detroit, and was quick to request comparable benefits. When the city council balked and rejected tax abatements for the company, Chrysler painted a dire picture. A Chrysler spokesman suggested that should the city not grant the concessions it would "be faced with a big vacant field out there, a barren desert."[97]

There was another ingredient to this bargain, which concerned the money to be made in negotiating its complex finances. Up until the Chrysler episode, Young had maintained a reputation for efficient, relatively honest administration. The Jefferson Avenue project broke that image by exposing a scandal on property appraisals. It turned out that local businesses were padding inventories and overpaying for equipment. In addition to the bloated claims, an auction of appraised equipment bought by the city returned only five cents on the dollar. Everyone who could was drawing from the public trough, and cost overruns ran into millions of dollars. To cover the deficit the city dipped into the general fund and borrowed money from a local bank.

To make matters worse, the scandal oozed out of the press, slowly and painfully. When the media requested documentation and the city refused, the courts intervened and forced compliance. An investigation revealed that the administration had failed to provide the council with full information, and both the council and the mayor were berated by the press for "bad management" and a "lack of proper oversight."[98] Chrysler's Jefferson Avenue project backfired on the mayor, partly because it was difficult to hide the waste, but also because participants had learned how to exploit the process.

There was room for new solution sets on other matters. Gambling casinos had built Las Vegas out of desert sand and created a boomlet in parts of depressed Atlantic City. Young thought Detroit could be the third partner of an urban gambling triumvirate. The benefits of gambling are quite mixed. While it does increase property values, it is also associated with higher crime rates and higher living costs.[99] Clearly the idea was not popular with Detroit residents—especially churchgoers. Despite public reluctance, Young criticized opposition to gambling as a reflection of neighborhood "ignorance." The mayor continued to campaign for gambling, urging people to be "open minded" about the subject, and he vetoed a city council ordinance attempting to ban it.[100]

Detroit's bargaining position may have forced Young to accept business edicts. He might have traded public assets in order to achieve what he considered to be a greater public good, but he was no quisling and realized opportunities when he saw them. Young was willing to deal with any private investor, and gambling interests could be as good as any. Indeed, gambling could provide an activity for the creation of new investor coalitions and break the automobile monopoly. During Young's tenure three local referenda on gambling were defeated, but he did get the public used to the idea.

By the time Dennis Archer became mayor in 1994, Detroit was ready. Archer took up his predecessor's effort to revitalize the city by any means possible. Two years later Archer turned to the state's electorate, and Michigan voters approved a gambling proposition. The city council followed suit, approving a $1.8 billion plan to make Detroit the largest American city to legalize casino gambling. Not surprisingly, some of the gambling franchises have gone to groups that had lobbied for the project.[101]

For all his publicized success, Archer did have his problems. For one, Archer's expansion of the development frontier onto the waterfront encountered unremitting obstacles. Despite business attempts to quietly acquire waterfront parcels, problems of land assembly and bureaucratic inertia continued to block development. These difficulties embarrassed Archer, and he began to wear thin. For another, Archer had always received plaudits from outside reporters, who knew little of the city's problems. But the local press was far more critical, especially in the wake of poor municipal services, police scandals, and failing schools. Last, white elites who were more distant from the city had a higher regard for Archer than local activists who saw him as a "silk stocking black." Other locals criticized him for being weak and indecisive. By the spring of 2001, the mayor's political verve had worn out, and he announced he would not run for reelection. Elected to succeed Archer is a young Detroit-raised politician named Kwame Fitzpatrick. The new mayor is hoping to recruit more business into the city and puts high-technology corporations at the top of his wish list.

COMPARING REGIMES

Different Resources/Different Uses

Regimes tap different resources and use them in different ways. Grantsman regimes like Marseilles and Glasgow rely heavily on intergovernmental support and popular control to leverage finances. In both cases popular control was tied to political parties, while leadership was vested in government. Those governmental elites may have been from different sources (Marseilles at the city level and Glasgow at the city and regional level), but they had a strong public character. In both Marseilles and Glasgow, public-private cooperation was made possible by government-led negotiations, and the public sector (mostly technocrats) played a dominant role in financing, planning, and determining site location. Significantly, both cities struggled mightily to offset market disadvantages. Marseilles did this with substantial investments in neighborhoods, construction of public housing, and massive public investments in Euro-Méditerranéen. Glasgow also used public finances to support public housing and rebuild neighborhoods, coupling that effort to a downtown strategy. In recent years that same intergovernmental support has pushed Glasgow toward a regional solution—quite possibly to the detriment of the city.

Similarly, clientelist Naples used intergovernmental support, but the city vested it with party and local political elites. Naples tied its partners to small business and organized crime; party brokers brought it all together. The city's local culture tolerated sidepayments and corruption, which deepened its clientelist character. These features were consonant with the closed and selective nature of cooperation, and with an accommodating ease-the-pain approach to development. All this was amply demonstrated by Naples's handling of earthquake reconstruction, where party brokers awarded contracts to small business and underworld families. The process meant huge delays in reconstruction and relatively small accomplishments.

Still a sharper distinction in regime can be seen in challenger Liverpool. At least for a time, Liverpool combined intergovernmental support with a strong disposition toward socialism. Here council leaders, who were members of a party faction, worked with labor unions to take control of development. Having lost faith in the marketplace, leaders mostly ignored business and sought other allies. Cooperation was openly solicited with trade unions, neighborhood groups, and the public sector to build housing, create social centers, and redo education. During this period, Militant leaders launched an effort to bypass, indeed combat, market pressures. Liverpool's Urban Regeneration Strategy (URS) consisted of public housing and targeted neighborhood rehabilitation—done with intergovernmental money, loans, and deficit financing, which paved the way toward bankruptcy.

At the other end of the spectrum is vendor Detroit. Scarce intergovernmental resources pushed that city toward business. Essentially, the mayor's partners were business leaders—usually drawn from automobile manufacturers and a group of business executives called Detroit Renaissance. Cooperation was a closed affair and made possible by giving business its best deal. Selling Poletown to General Motors, offering Jefferson Avenue to Chrysler, and opening up gambling to Las Vegas casino interests are stark but no less revealing cases of how Detroit works.

Table 7.1 presents a summary of regime characteristics relative to the kind of bargaining they can carry out. In addition to previously mentioned bargaining contexts and regimes types, the table depicts regimes in terms of resources employed, dominant partners, mode of public-private engagement and development approach.[x]

All cities operating in dependent public contexts used intergovernmental aid to buttress development. As the only major source of capital, intergovernmental aid fostered publicly led development, though with different ends in mind. For Marseilles and Glasgow, this aid was a means to a development end, which could be used to point up regime accomplishments. For Naples, intergovernmental aid was a means to sustain other means (graft sidepayments) and legitimate the regime with the promise of still more favors. For Liverpool, intergovernmental aid could be used to reward party loyalists (jobs and public housing during a clientelist phase) or serve as a means of protest (spending the city into

TABLE 7.1
Regimes/Coalitions and Bargaining

Bargaining Context	Regime or Coalition Type	Resources Employed	Dominant Partners	Mode of Public–Private Engagement	Development Approach
Dependent Public	Grantsman (Marseilles, Glasgow)	Intergovernmental support, popular control	National/regional government, bureaucracy, political parties	Open/negotiated Led by government	Offset market and business disadvantages
Dependent Public	Clientelist (Naples)	Intergovernmental support, local culture	Political parties, small business, organized crime	Closed/brokered Led by political parties (corruption)	Accommodate and ease pain of market and business disadvantages
Dependent Public	Challenger (Liverpool) 1983–87	Intergovernmental support, local culture	Political parties and factions, labor unions	Open/ignored Led by parties and city council	Bypass market and combat business disadvantages
Dependent Private	Vendor (Detroit)	Scarce or nonexistent	Business	Closed/controlled Led by business and mayor's office	Comply with market disadvantages and facilitate business

bankruptcy during its challenger phase) or promoting its development (struggling toward grantsman phase).

Our sole city operating in a dependent private context, Detroit, had sparse intergovernmental funds and, ironically, had little reason to aim its anger toward other governments. Its bargaining impulse was channeled into the marketplace, and it chose to comply with business. If instead Detroit had launched a challenge, it too would have been directed toward the marketplace. Dependency then is a double-edged sword. While regimes may be sustained by a benefactor, that same benefactor can become the target of protest once a city feels deeply aggrieved. Whether it is better to challenge the government or business is another matter. Liverpool did succeed for a while, and might have continued to fend off Thatcher's government by playing a more subtle political game. Instead its city council went to extremes, allowing themselves to be painted as a bunch of irresponsible radicals. Cities that challenge the marketplace are in a far more tenuous position, because markets are both more omnipresent and seemingly "nonpolitical." Attacking an elusive target like the marketplace is a bit like Don Quixote chasing windmills and frequently ends in frustration.

Another bargaining difference between public and private dependency contexts is that governments find it more difficult to conceal their agenda than does business. Public dependent Marseilles and Glasgow could be reasonably sure about what central government was willing or unwilling to do. Even Liverpool and Naples knew when cuts or emergency aid were likely to be forthcoming. These cities exuded a certain confidence in dealing with other governments because everybody was playing by the same rules. But dependent private Detroit never knew where it stood with business, and was never sure where to draw the line on inducements. Automobile manufacturers and sports team owners always let it be known that they could move elsewhere and, true to form, always considered other sites. As a result, the city bargained blindly and out of apprehension. It might very well have overdone already generous offers. This posed a considerable bargaining disadvantage for Detroit, and it paid the price. There were few ways to overcome that liability, but one option was to diversify private investment. Gambling then became a rational choice for a distressed city whose bargaining leverage was very light.

Structure/Agency and Change

Our survey of regimes suggests that structural circumstances powerfully shape politics, but political agency is also important — even in the poorest cities. For one, the viability of political leaders depends upon their ability to satisfy constituents and keep their cities afloat. Given their varying skills and inclinations, leaders in the cases under study were bound to employ available resources with different emphases and in different ways. This accounts for why, despite similar resources at their disposal, cities chose different development approaches.

Second, new political leaders eventually brought about significant regime changes. All of the cities responded to change, often as a result of political challenges by new faces and new interests. After years of political corruption and patron-client politics, Neapolitan voters chose to dispense with the old party bosses and support a reformer who sought to create something like a grantsman politics. Liverpool's radical guard was also forced from power. The city's newest leaders have rejected radicalism in favor of partnerships with central government and with business. In recent years Marseilles and Glasgow have shifted away from statist solutions in favor of building regimes that run closer to the marketplace.

While political leaders are constrained by structure, they can assess opportunities and move their cities to take advantage of them. We can find likely pathways of regime transformation if we consider a city's structure and agency characteristics. The shifts in both Marseilles and Naples tell us that once city governments become more proactive or energize development, they may move toward planner or grantsman regimes. This logic hinges on an assumption that cities will eventually strive for more effective and efficient development. Vigorous development requires commitment, capital, and diversity of interests. If these elements are to be realized, cities need new and invigorated blood. Older, tempered cities, like Deferre's Marseilles, would have to recruit new actors, while retaining continuity with the statist tradition of France. A logical progression for Marseilles is to move toward a planner regime. More sluggish cities, like Naples, would also notch up by showing tangible results, while holding onto the Italian practice of generous intergovernmental aid. If its political reforms take hold, the most likely progress for Naples is to move toward a grantsman-like approach.

Examined from another perspective, these pathways tell us that leaders can act as agents of change, but probable transformations will be constrained by structural circumstances. Thus Detroit is not likely to move toward a Parisian/Toronto planner regime. Despite its flirtation with the market, Glasgow is not likely to become another Houston. Regimes do change, but they are inclined to do so within the gravitational orbit of their bargaining context.

Finally, this is not to say that progress is necessarily linear or that better conditions are inevitable. Some cities might also fall into decline and notch down. Other cities could languish in inertia and remain stuck in the same pattern. Our regime typologies are not meant to lay down laws of change, but to offer guidelines that suggest possible directions. The next chapter addresses issues of direction in greater detail. Where are Western postindustrial cities headed?

NOTES

i. HLM stands for Habitation du Location Modérée, or moderate income housing.

ii. Notwithstanding this influence, Gaudin faces political rivalry from regional and state actors. Among these are national ministers, the regional prefect, and the Socialist Party.

iii. SE and SDA are acronyms used interchangeably throughout this discussion unless it is necessary to be specific for clarity in the history of the agencies.

iv. This compelling institutional interest does not change easily. During the 1960s, Scottish Office policy favored the decentralization of people and jobs to achieve regional balance. It continued to support this policy through regional grant assistance and New Town development even as it embarked on the inner city–oriented programs of the 1970s and 1980s.

v. Tax rates and rents actually were increased in preceding years to meet the shortfalls, and these increases would have to continue during the foreseeable future.

vi. Official figures show that the public sector employs only around 10 percent of the work force. But this excludes vast governmental sectors, such as municipal firms (garbage collection, gas, and water, etc.), state enterprises, quasi-public agencies, and universities (Bianchini, *Urbanization and the Functions of Cities*, 14).

vii. Of course, not all citizens support this system. Throughout Italy, during the 1990s, angry voters used their power to express their opposition to this form of politics. Yet popular opposition is easily marginalized in a political system that is driven by individual payoffs and must cope with the limited opportunities presented by the city's decaying economy.

viii. Challenges to the marketplace are not unknown and have occurred in Mon Valley, Pennslyvania. See Levdansky, *Plant Closings*; Portz, *The Politics of Plant Closings* and Savitch and Kantor, "City Business."

ix. Officially, the neighborhood was represented by a Citizens District Council (CDC), whose composition was determined by the city council.

x. These categories are explained in the previous chapter, but here we furnish an abbreviated and modified explanation: By *resources employed*, we mean the driving and steering variables that a given regime might use to leverage its bargaining (market conditions, intergovernmental support, popular control, and local culture). Dominant partners comprise major interests in governing coalitions. The next characteristic, *mode of public-private engagement*, focuses on how government and business interact over development decisions ("open" or "closed") and whether those decisions are negotiated, brokered, or controlled by a single party. Also, there may be times when a lead decision maker (government or business) chooses to ignore the other party, and we include this as a possibility. Our last category deals with *development approach* and whether regimes try to offset market/business pressures, accommodate them, bypass/combat them, or comply with them and facilitate business demands.

Chapter Eight

ARE CITIES CONVERGING?

The only thing worse than being exploited
by American imperialism is not being
exploited by American imperialism.
— A Socialist member of the Liverpool City Council

LOOK-ALIKE CITIES

The streets of the Merchant City historic district in Glasgow display a harmonious blending of modernity and tradition. Eighteenth-century tobacco warehouses, cobbled mews, and buildings with neatly restored architectural detail sit cheek by jowl with trend-setting boutiques offering London's latest fashion. Tourists from abroad and workers from nearby offices frequent upscale restaurants decorated with hanging plants and staffed by crisp-looking waiters.

Yet for all its charm Merchant City is not very unique. Similar spaces blending history and commerce are found in almost all of our ten cities. New York's South Street Seaport brings together old docks and clipper ships with big-name clothing shops, specialty boutiques, and expensive restaurants. Paris's Les Halles offers recreation, shopping, and culture in a historic setting. Liverpool's Albert Dock now accommodates an art gallery, a maritime museum, and a television news station. The refurbished dock gives this still grimy city a new facade, ironically facing away from Liverpool and toward the ocean. The same fast-food franchises repeat each other in every city, and sometimes the only way of distinguishing an American from a European city is whether the French fries are doused with catsup or mustard. Whereas cities heretofore resisted these trends, they have now succumbed. Naples is feverishly adding pedestrian malls in its historic center, refurbishing public monuments, upgrading visitor facilities, and accommodating fast-food concessions.

Look-alike mixes of history and retail trade sprout up for the obvious reasons of attracting tourists and creating a new image. Led by market-wise convention and visitor bureaus, officials realize that old historical assets have commercial value. Cities are also starting to look alike in myriad other ways. Downtown property markets are developing in similar rhythms. Nearly identical office buildings in U.S., Canadian, and European business districts come off the same fashionable architect's drawing board. As manufacturing activities ebb in the postindustrial West, cities scratch around for a new role. But their game plans often have much in common: downtown shopping malls, gentrification of older neighborhoods, cultural centers, and the ever-present renovated waterfronts, complete with old-fashioned moorings for ships that never seem to arrive.

A key reason for these similarities is the need to replace an exhausted physical environment with one more suited for postindustrial services.[1] Earlier we described how global transformation has changed cities and brought about a service economy. This has created a vast conversion of the built environment to accommodate the hoped-for influx of office workers, tourists, and professional services. Pushing the conversion is an international marketplace that caters to investors, architects, and developers. International conferences and tourism convince local elites that success lies in altering the city's image, so enabling it to conform to the needs of potential investors. Added to the necessary complement of social assets are attractive business districts, electronically sophisticated "smart buildings," and convention centers, luxury hotels, and modern airports.

Copy-cat building practices reflect a heightened competition among cities. At the same time business is presumed to have enhanced its advantages. Corporate directorates scatter different parts of their production to multiple overseas locations. Business mobility reduces the effectiveness of local and even national controls. In competing for a niche in this new world, cities often exploit the same techniques. No wonder big cities seem to look so much alike. The real question is what these look-alike qualities really mean. Do these similarities symbolize something more deeply rooted or are they superficialities that mask real differences?

POLITICAL CONVERGENCE DEFINED AND DEBATED

By political convergence we mean that urban policies, development strategies, and leadership behavior become more uniform across time and space. If cities are converging, variation among them should begin to disappear. Turning to the opposite side of the coin, divergence would mean that cities either remain differentiated or become more dissimilar. Under divergence, we would expect distinctions to increase. Depending upon what factors are being measured, it would be easy to generalize and argue for one side or the other. Thus, one scholar convincingly argues that London is moving "toward a New York model" and world cities are becoming more alike.[2] Another researcher just as cogently points out that major European cities are leaning toward greater divergence.[3] Both writers may well be correct, but then again one of them is referring to the city's built environment, while the other is concerned with local economy. For purposes of clarity and consistency, our reference points are (1) national policies and intergovernmental arrangements that impinge upon a given city, (2) development strategies adopted by cities, and (3) local governance and the changing roles of leaders and regimes within our ten cities.

Extraneous or "greater forces" are often seen as pushing cities toward convergence. Almost by definition globalization standardizes commodities and, ultimately, governments and political behavior. The same products, films, and newscasts are consumed in all parts of the global village. "Best practices" are often adopted across cultures and policy can be transferred across governments. The sheer dynamics of globalization leads us to believe that everything is becoming homogenized. Some scholars suggest that as cities become engaged in an internationalized marketplace, their governments and citizens have little choice but to submit to the hegemony of its competitive pressures — or be left behind.[4] The need to remain competitive encourages — perhaps even compels — governments to act in similar ways.[i] Although there is hardly universal agreement, most convergence theorists share the following rationale:

- In regard to national and intergovernmental roles, convergence fosters a withering away of development controls. This is because greater international competition forces governments to find ways of enhancing their positions in global markets. From the perspective of the national economy, urban policies must become more "efficient."[ii] National urban policies should not restrict business location and ought to avoid tax, regulatory, environmental, and social programs that excessively burden business or cause them to relocate elsewhere. Cuts in fiscal assistance to local governments and the decentralization of governmental responsibilities are employed to stimulate local economic adjustment.[iii]

- Concerning urban development strategies, convergence entails a radical shift away from social- toward market-centered policies. Social policies have inherent disadvantages and are antithetical to strong growth. They lead to higher taxes, they incur lost revenues, and they hamper a city's ability to compete. Alternatively, market-centered strategies enhance growth, revenue, and jobs, and they make cities more competitive. Cities that fail to adopt strong growth policies will lose revenue and jobs.[5] Sooner or later urban policymakers will realize this and market policies will squeeze out social policies.

- As for local governance, major changes should occur in order to facilitate political adaptation to economic convergence. Pressures to champion commercial growth and greater efficiency should lead to greater concentration of power in the hands of a single leader. Entrepreneurial mayors should arise to fill the need for new economic leadership. Less cooperative regimes should be replaced by regimes that facilitate economic adjustment and business power. Local politicians seek to insulate economic decision making from citizen demands in order to allow unencumbered, efficient economic management.[6] Citizen participation ebbs because voters see little point in trying to influence policy agendas that are severely constrained by economic considerations. In the end, regimes are restructured to give business a bigger political voice.

There is, of course, an equally compelling rationale for divergence. Part of the argument rests on historical context. Internationalization of the economy need not ordain the homogenization of local politics.[7] Free trade and exchange are not new. The industrial revolution of the nineteenth and early twentieth centuries also unleashed new international market pressures. Yet the era of the industrial city is often considered a golden age of political innovation and variation.[8] The postindustrial order also affords new opportunities for cities and stimulates new ways of adaptation.[9] The flexible production processes associated with postindustrialism increase the need for governmental intervention, and these interventions are likely to address idiosyncratic needs.

According to its critics, convergence theory is too deterministic. It assumes that the international marketplace drives cities in the same political direction. This determinism neglects the fact that economic change brings about corrective actions and encourages political countermovements.[10] Societies make political choices about their economic welfare because most people refuse to be victimized by an unregulated market economy. Market integration heightens feelings of insecurity among broad segments of society, putting pressure on government to mitigate dislocations and prevent socially unacceptable results. Government regulation often imposes costs on business, but it also provides benefits that are recognized by financial markets and business interests. Prosperity is dependent upon social stability, property rights, human capital, and good government — not just the operation of a marketplace. Garrett found that nation-states largely responded to domestic political pressures during the 1980s as they coped with economic integration.[11] There was no simple "race to the bottom" by governments seeking to become "competitive" at all costs.[iv]

City governments also may be able to capitalize on this political reality. In earlier chapters we saw how urban communities are not equally placed in capital markets. Their ability to exploit different resources enabled them to chart divergent development strategies. These same bargaining resources may empower cities to lean against the winds of homogenization. The argument for divergence can be summarized in the following ways:

- In regard to national and intergovernmental roles, public intervention may grow as a means of regulating the social consequences of the new marketplace. Fears of social and economic dislocation strengthen government's protective role in providing a social net for citizens. Although national governments seek competitive economic advantages, this is likely to be counterbalanced by political demands that excessive competition be controlled or limited.

- Concerning urban development strategies, local choice is a function of a city's bargaining resources, and social policies will remain ascendant in cities that have adopted them. Government is capable of "learning" and strengthening its bargaining capacity by making cities more attractive to investors and promoting intergovernmental cooperation. Those cities with abundant resources should be able to maintain social-centered policy strategies and hold down cutthroat competition. Indeed, development can be "smart" and furnish a city with complementary assets. There is no necessary dichotomy between growth and strong social policies.

- As for local governance, tendencies to centralize governmental power and favor business can be checked by competing political demands. The spread of information should increase citizen awareness, making leaders and regimes more accountable. Postindustrialism also means a growing and well-educated middle class, which is likely to resist giving up their say in running government.[12] This also holds true for governing coalitions. Regimes are as much a product of political demands as economic ones. Given reasonable levels of intergovernmental cooperation, regimes need not slavishly conform to the marketplace.

Our survey does not permit unequivocal resolution of this debate. Still, thirty years of political development in ten major cities should not be ignored for what it offers — a big picture of responses to the international marketplace in a wide variety of localities. The next three sections examine how empirical evidence from our ten cities stacks up to the arguments at hand.

NATIONAL URBAN POLICY AND INTERGOVERNMENTAL ORBITS

While scholars talk about the hollowing out or decline of the national-state, it still remains crucial in the conduct of local affairs. National urban policy can create a powerful governmental presence within cities. National and regional governments often regulate local activities and shape development with money, supervision, and political authority. These governments also set expectations about relations with the private sector and create organizational frameworks through which those relations are carried out. National urban policy is an instrument for extending central influence into intergovernmental relations and it can work in two directions. Vertically it extends national influence directly into local affairs. Horizontally it provides a framework that shapes relationships among localities.

As elaborated in previous chapters, both vertical and horizontal integration contribute to a context through which bargaining is carried out, and they keep localities within national and intergovernmental orbits. Any change in these orbits will influence local bargaining and a city's own position in the international marketplace. The question is whether these orbits have begun to weaken. As a way of getting at this issue we inquire whether national urban policy and its intergovernmental manifestations have begun to fade or change coloration. Are cities breaking away from their national and intergovernmental orbits? How different are national policies and practices from one another? If indeed we are on the road toward convergence, are cities clustering around an "American model"? Is it that the United States has so well positioned itself in the global era that it sets the pace for the postindustrial world?

The American Model

During the 1960s the United States embarked upon a bold venture called the "Great Society." Led by Lyndon Johnson's Democrats the federal government sought to extend itself into every big city with community action agencies, model cities programs, and a host of social policies. A multitude of "paragovernments" arose in America's urban cores that directly linked Washington to neighborhood organizations.[13] The results were disappointing, if not personally painful for Lyndon Johnson, and by the end of his term the president confided that these were "hardly his favorite programs."[14] Endemic rioting, boiling social tensions, and a disastrous war in Vietnam soon spelled the collapse of these efforts. By the mid-1970s the Great Society was well on its way to dismantlement. The United States would reverse policy direction. Under Richard Nixon the Republicans had pulled up stakes in the neighborhoods and were speeding away from social intervention and toward decentralization. Whatever was left of urban policy would be geared toward market-oriented development and left to the discretion of the localities. The new approach would emphasize federal revenue sharing, block grants, housing vouchers, and leveraging private capital. Leading the way were Urban Development Action Grants (UDAGs), Community Development Block Grants (CDBGs), and assistance from the Economic Development Agency (EDA). The block grant approach, UDAGs, CDBGs, and economic assistance emphasized the urban physical environment rather than social needs.[15] These programs usually helped localities reduce business cost and were market driven. Urban policy was bereft of any semblance of national planning and instead driven by congressional pressures to disperse funds.[16] As it turned out, this was a first step in Washington's effort to distance itself from the cities.[v]

During the 1980s the federal withdrawal accelerated. The election of Ronald Reagan led to further diminution of Washington's involvement in the cities. Reagan's conservative electoral coalition largely excluded the big cities, and his policies largely consisted of retrenchment and greater devolution of problem solving to states and localities. Revenue sharing was scuttled and budget reductions shrunk the remaining block grants. Other budget legislation slashed domestic spending and induced a wave of fiscal tightening in cities.[17] Between Reagan's ascension to power in 1980 and his departure eight years later, funding for community development fell by 26 percent.[18] From the late 1970s and to the mid-1980s, federal aid plummeted. Twelve of America's older, industrial cities lost an average of 46 percent in federal funding during this period.[19] Years later a Republican-led congress would retract more than sixty years of federal commitment in aiding the poor. Democratic President Bill Clinton signed the Personal Responsibility and Work Opportunity Reconciliation Act. Welfare entitlement and long-term payments were replaced by what had come to be called "temporary assistance," "time-limited benefits," and "mandatory work requirements." Most welfare recipients were located in urban counties, and between 1994 and 1999 that caseload dropped by 40.6 percent.[vi]

Instead of direct aid the Republicans championed "Enterprise Zones."[vii] Reagan era policy hoped Enterprise Zones would convert vacant industrial sites into unregulated imitations of pre-communist Hong Kong. While Enterprise Zones never saw the light of federal law, thirty-two states created more than 1,400 of them.[20] Washington had clearly set a new tone, and many states followed suit, expecting more aid to flow into their neoliberal experiments. Again, Democrat Clinton adopted aspects of the Republican platform and offered a version of an Enterprise Zone. His biggest initiative was Empowerment Zone legislation. This program also stressed tax reduction, economic development, and job stimulation by targeting federal incentives to a limited number of major cities and scores of smaller Enterprise Communities.[21]

In many respects the American experience provides a textbook example of what globally induced convergence might look like: steady withdrawal of central government from the cities, low taxes, an emphasis on economic development, an unbridled marketplace, low social expenditures, and an expectation that cities should stress their competitive advantage. Apart from marginal programs and more substantive spending for highways and defense, cities would have to go it alone. Decentralization of authority down to states and localities evoked a new paradigm of being "lean and mean" and self-sustaining in a more competitive world.[22]

British Experimentation

At least during the 1980s Great Britain moved furthest in the direction of American-style urban policies. But even here the central government maintained a firm grip on this policy and continued to cushion cities from most of the fiscal consequences. Britain's postwar urban policies targeted national assistance to deprived areas and relied extensively on elected local governments to renew cities. The big break from this pattern occurred during Prime Minister Margaret Thatcher's administration. After 1979 Tory governments did cut domestic programs and aid to cities. During Thatcher's tenure urban aid was cut by nearly 10 billion pounds.[23] The Tories also followed a consistent pattern of reducing local political authority while introducing a greater role for market mechanisms.[viii] Local governments were forced by new national policies to retrench and adopt measures to increase efficiency (competitive bidding, privatization). This limited their powers and opened up decision making to nonelected groups and market pressures.[24]

Urban Development Corporations (UDCs) epitomized this approach. Appointed by the national government with strong business representation, these quasi-governmental organizations assumed the lead role in planning, financing, and implementing urban regeneration schemes. Intended to attract private-sector investment, the UDCs have had extensive powers to acquire land, build, and finance development. UDCs shifted local efforts strongly in favor of stimulating growth.[25]

Also undertaken were initiatives to involve localities in small-area regeneration. These also were made more "market"-oriented. City Challenge Grants and Single Regeneration Grants were overtly competitive and designed to strengthen economic development. These programs were awarded through competitive bidding and based on the ability of cities to come up with a "comprehensive and integrated" development strategy.[26] Under competitive bidding, central government aid was conditioned upon localities entering into partnerships with the private sector.[27] Few of these programs involved new money or long-term governmental commitments. In 1997 Labour took control of the central government. For the most part it continued this approach of prodding localities to become more entrepreneurial. Labour's major departure was to provide new money for programs and to give greater assistance to poorer areas.[28]

Clearly, Britain's newer urban policies represent a shift in favor of more market-oriented development and have the ring of an American-style approach. Even Blair's Third Way resembled Clinton's own centrism. But there are crucial differences. Most important, the British intergovernmental system was never restructured to decentralize political authority or make cities heavily dependent on the marketplace. Rather, local governments continued to receive the bulk of their revenues from the central government, which also remained the sole provider of funds for capital projects. This insulated local governments from dependence on bond markets. National officials closely monitored the activities of the development authorities. Local planning and land-use matters remained subject to official oversight by the Department of the Environment and other national agencies with power to override local decisions. Planning and development arrangements for Scotland continued to reside with special regional agencies having vast power over economic development.

In fact, market-oriented changes in British urban policy were also accompanied by greater, not less, centralization.[29] Central government pushed, prodded, and threatened local authorities, but it did not allow the private sector to dominate them. Even the UDCs remained strongly tethered to national officials through central government finance, appointments, and mandates.[ix] At the same time, the fiscal safety nets that help shield local governments from economic troubles — national financing of most local services and national responsibility for health, public assistance, job training, unemployment relief, and even housing — were essentially preserved. Even during the Thatcher years, spending for social welfare represented a consistently higher proportion of the gross national product in Great Britain than in the United States.[30] Why it is that urban policy never really slipped off the national agenda as it did in the United States is largely attributed to a stronger culture of government intervention and a moral code of "doing the right thing."[31]

All said and done, nothing like a go-it-alone policy was pursued. Unlike the United States, where fiscal retrenchment and diminution of federal authority went hand-in-hand, British urban policy meant expansion of central control and modest experimentation with special market-led urban programs. Even when British politicians talked boldly about monetarism and freeing up private enterprise, they always seemed to pull back — especially during the Blair years. British adaptation to the new era was pronounced, though it was hardly an American copy.

Italy's and France's Own Way

On the surface, it might also seem that Europe was following an American path. Europeans were talking more and more about "policy transfer," and both Italy and France undertook varying degrees of decentralization and fiscal tightening. But it would be a mistake to equate these national changes with those transpiring in the United States. For one, both national actors, along with those in the European Union, remain sensitive to the impacts of globalization. They recognize the tendency of free trade to depress wages and accentuate social polarization. Accordingly, wage deregulation has been opposed on the Continent and income floors have been established. While the United States was clamping down on welfare and would soon abolish it as a long-term entitlement, Europeans were guaranteeing minimum income floors. France established minimum incomes during the 1980s and Italy followed suit.[x] The image of polarized American-style ghettoes evoked a good deal of concern, and "socially excluded" neighborhoods were the target of national and European Union-wide legislation.

Next, political decentralization and fiscal relationships have been adapted to indigenous conditions, and they have distinct national manifestations. While words like "decentralization" and "fiscal deficit" are uttered by Italian or French politicians, they are drawn from a different context and have a different meaning. The intent of national policy is also different and so too is its impact on cities. Rather than a loosening of national involvement, these changes mean that national government would be involved in different ways. In Italy and France "the state" never withdrew from cities, market intervention continued, and business was never put in charge of the development agenda.

In Italy, despite the passage of decentralist measures, relatively little occurred. Civil disturbances inspired parliament during the early 1970s to authorize local governments to create neighborhood councils. Various attempts were made to relax central oversight of local government decisions, but these hardly broke the stringent limits imposed on localities.[32] A network of regional governments was created in 1970. But the regions never assumed a large role in the urban development activities, and they never acquired much legislative or fiscal autonomy.[xi]

Italian policies favoring governmental decentralization also sprang from domestic political pressures having nothing to do with making cities more market oriented. Unlike Britain or the United States, proposals for decentralization reflected attempts to enhance local political participation in the wake of civil strife, student agitation, and pressure from left-wing parties — an effort to open up an encrusted local government system. Policies to cut economic aid in the Mezzogiorno were due to tensions between the North and the South. This was especially true after electoral victories by the Northern League and a surge of provincial nationalism.

Fiscal relations between national and local governments tightened considerably throughout the past three decades, forcing Italian cities to struggle harder to make ends meet. But Italian fiscal retrenchment has never had the effect of limiting the national governmental financial role. Instead of decentralizing fiscal responsibilities, Italy acted to centralize them at the outset of the 1970s. The entire system of intergovernmental finance was reorganized to all but eliminate reliance on local tax revenues.

While Rome continued to hold the fiscal cards, it became less generous. This was followed by changes in national policy to rein city spending. Fiscal tightening on state spending began during the 1980s in the face of growing local government deficits. This tightening increased dramatically after 1992. The national government privatized giant state holding companies. This liberalization resulted in gradual termination of subsidies to state industries in the South and the closing of plants. In the 1990s the special fund for the South was eliminated along with a drive to reform the welfare state. Faced with retrenchment and the elimination of programs, local governments struggled with revenue shortfalls.

Fiscal tightening also occurred because the national government was obliged to fulfill its European agenda. Italy came under pressure to reduce its budget deficit and national debt in order to meet conditions of entry into the European Monetary Union. This pressure accelerated in 1993 after Italy signed the Maastrict treaty and the single European market was established. Italy's scheduled participation in the single currency later in the decade increased fiscal constraints even further. A climate of almost permanent fiscal emergency fostered economic austerity, but it did not bring about a new urban policy.[33] Central finance remained dominant in local politics.[34]

France also adapted in its own unique way. In 1980 François Mitterand's new socialist government adopted measures to decentralize political authority. These changes lasted through the mid-1980s. Decentralist policies diminished the power of nationally appointed prefects and gave greater authority to locally elected officials in the cities, the departments, and the regional councils. Mayors and presidents of local councils were the major beneficiaries of this devolution. The cities enlarged their scope of policy discretion with new funding, while the departments and the region took charge of vital infrastructure, planning, and modernization.

No longer would the prefects exercise *la tutelle*, or guidance, over local officials or have the final word over budgets. Still, the national government has not vanished from city hall. Prefects continued to play a role, but it is one of monitoring local authorities, assuring consistency in the application of national rules, and guiding the stream of planning assistance. Prefects, for example, could guide appeals on land-use ordinances and continue as vital links in communicating with the state.[35]

These actions left prefects in pivotal positions of influence. After decentralization, local government was not the same, and the prefects had changed from "power holders" to "power brokers."[36]

Meanwhile, a new era dawned on French city halls. Decentralization gave mayors power to issue building permits and control zoning densities. It also put more money at local discretion. Taxes on property and auto sales were transferred from the state to local authorities. Henceforth, mayors would be able to collect taxes from business, renters, and landlords. Decentralization thus brought about an enlarged revenue stream for mayors, and they could exercise enormous discretion over its application.[37]

No doubt, the funding windfall was applied to economic development, and new projects sprung up throughout urban France. American writers might be prone to see this as the beginning of American style-economic development and as a "competitive pro-business strategy."[38] But we should also point out that this was not competition at all costs or a lurch toward "place wars."[39] Social expenditures also rose and so too did appropriations for public amenities. By and large, French cities maintained control over the development agenda through traditional vehicles for controlling development. This control has enabled them to enhance collective action and counteract the fragmentary effects of decentralization.

In fact, while the French national government decentralized local government in order to enhance democracy, it also pulled together local governments in order to bolster their control over land use and development. Current legislation goes well beyond the established regional councils by specifying how localities can carry out an array of collective actions. As described elsewhere, these laws facilitate cooperation among localities on such matters as strategic development, tax sharing, and telecommunications modernization. As an inducement, the state provides additional funds to localities that join in collective regional agreements with additional funds.[xii] Other legislation establishes the means whereby cities can take collective action through "communities of cities," urban communities, and regional communities. Fiscal inducements are provided to those localities that choose to organize themselves in some cooperative form. National government has also created a system of "contract cities" (*contrat de ville*) in which cities are encouraged to establish cooperative planning with their respective regions and departments. Still more recent national legislation (Solidarité, Renouvellement Urbaine) requires that localities equalize development and encourage social integration through subsidized housing.

Another difference for French cities concerns their approach to public and private capital. During the early years of decentralization, some cities supported their own industrial enterprise to compensate for abandoned private capital. While localities sought to stimulate economic development, they did not treat public expenditures as a means of leveraging private capital. Public monies were supposed to be used for public purposes, and French mayors continue to stand on that principle. Sophe Gendrot comments on the Franco-American comparison:

> The American principle is that each dollar furnished by the state must bring in eight private dollars. . . . For our part, we are willing to let go of economic benefits, and up through the present city politics has been led by social concerns.[40]

Nothing so illustrates the use of the same words linked to a different context and resulting in a different meaning as does the creation of the *zones franches*. Announced by the government in 1996, the *zones franches* were an effort to inject national assistance into more than twenty distressed localities. Like America's "Empowerment Zones," the plan called for stimulating economic development and creating jobs within these locales. The economic stimulus was to be brought about by tax relief, and to this extent it paralleled the American approach. On close scrutiny, however, job development was a part of a much larger scheme calling for subsidized housing, neighborhood rehabilitation, public infrastructure, aid to education, and increased police protection.[41] Moreover, the establishment of *zones franches* was couched in the language of social rejuvenation. Phrases like the restoration of "social cohesion" and the struggle against "social exclusion" typified the French approach toward development. By this time France had also shown some concern about too great a decentralization of political power. When it came to urban development, newspapers and public officials were already speaking about "the return of the state."[42]

Canada: Still Exceptional?

In Canada the provinces play the "overseer role" in urban development, and they jealously guard that prerogative.[43] Up through the mid-1990s one could fairly say that Ontario shaped Greater Toronto with social-centered policies. No grand plan guided this strategy, and it was carried out through incremental but consistent policies. Ontario managed to limit sprawl, succeeded in clustering growth within bounds, helped Toronto maintain the vitality of its center and the integrity of its neighborhoods, supported mass transit, and built publicly assisted housing in the suburbs. When Metro Toronto failed, Ontario was there with grants, regulations, and political action.[44]

For twenty-five out of the past thirty years, Ontario confidently influenced Toronto's development and assured its continuity. The past five years, however, were pregnant with change. As globalization advanced, the city fell into a slump. Officials expressed alarm about losses in employment, falling house values, and skyrocketing office vacancies. One report expressed alarm at the specter of "a U.S. style decline in our urban core."[45] Ironically, when Mike Harris's Tories captured the province in 1995, they chose American tactics to fight those threats.

The new provincial government might have read from some pages of Ronald Reagan's policy strategy. Harris ran on a platform of reducing the size and cost of government, balancing the budget, and cutting provincial income taxes. Using a rationale of greater efficiency and increased competitiveness, the Tories amalgamated Metro Toronto into a single mega city. Part of this reorganization entailed a decentralization of responsibilities from the province to the newly amalgamated Toronto ("downloading"). As it turned out, "downloading" meant that the province would absorb education expenses while the city took on welfare and other costs. In theory, the changes were supposed to be revenue-neutral. The Harris government promoted amalgamation as a reallocation of responsibilities rather than as a cutback, and Toronto was not supposed to lose funds. Provincial authorities have argued that within time property taxes will be equalized across the larger region, and this will put the higher taxed city in a more competitive position with its lower taxed suburbs. A new funding formula introduced by Ontario will also split the costs of the regional commuter system between Toronto and its suburbs. As the dust has begun to settle, Ontario has embarked on a course of fiscal stringency but nonetheless has retained regulation of local affairs. Despite the fiscal clouds, the intergovernmental system has not dispersed into an American-style withdrawal. To this extent Harris departs from the Reagan script.[46]

Torontonians are still worried that Harris has given them a little bit of sugar to take along with a larger dose of bitter medicine. Opponents disagree with the supposition that amalgamation will be revenue-neutral and claim that the real costs have yet to be felt. "Downloading" has important social implications. Mass transit and housing subsidies have been cut, the costs of social services have been pushed onto the city, environmental regulations have been relaxed, development has been allowed in environmentally sensitive areas, and privatization has been encouraged. For the first time in recent history, homeless people can be seen on the streets of the city. Moreover, the Harris government has begun to undercut provincial planning. It has softened restrictions and allowed localities more discretion on development. Harris also did away with requirements that new residential developments contain a specified component for affordable housing.[47] The upshot of these policies is predictable. Development has begun to slip past smaller suburbs into a formless sprawl, and suburbs like Mississauga and Vaughan are heating up the competition for development dollars.[48]

Ontario has made its intentions clear. It is, however, too early to know how far those intentions will be carried or what form they will take. A host of decisions remain to be settled that will set a future course. On the one hand, the neoliberal momentum is continuing. A bill has just been introduced into the provincial legislature that would give towns and cities the ability to act like private corporations. The bill would eliminate prohibitions against tax incentives to lure business and allow localities to form partnerships with private business for development purposes.[49] On the other hand, Tory supporters are growing edgy about threats to the environment and about rampant sprawl. Harris maintains a fragile coalition and public attitudes still look askance at American-style development. Local culture counts a great deal, and Canadians remain sensitive about melding into an imitation of their powerful southern neighbors.[50]

Is There National Policy Convergence?

Our ten cities most certainly have changed during the past three decades. As convergence theorists would expect, most nations showed some movement toward decentralization. The United States exemplified the strongest decentralist proclivity and policy withdrawal. Elsewhere, decentralization either did not occur or meant very different things. While Great Britain did adopt fiscal austerity measures, it also recentralized urban policy and national ministries exercised more control in local affairs. In Italy and France, decentralization was not a zero-sum game, and both center and periphery appeared to be more fully engaged. National governments continued to show a remarkable presence, and localities sometimes received even more funding as they faced global competition. In France, the state even helped organize localities for collective action. By and large, where national policy and intergovernmental systems were well integrated, they continued to show resilience. During the past five years, Toronto's provincial government showed a distinct inclination to adopt some aspects of the American model by "downloading" costs, but it did not relinquish its role in local fiscal affairs.

Similarly, every national government positioned itself for a more competitive environment. But even in this respect, competition was pursued differently. The United States structured urban and intergovernmental aid so that localities emphasized economic development. Great Britain tilted toward this pattern, and so, too, did Canada's Ontario province (during the past five years), but their effects are still unclear. Elsewhere, national policy did not follow a single market-centered track. In Italy and France, national policy guarded social gains and even emphasized them as a more effective way to compete.

A word should also be said about the supranational role of the European Union or EU. Thus far, predictions that the EU would evolve into a "United States of Europe," promoting laissez-faire policies, have not been borne out.[51] If anything, the EU has pursued interventionist polices by designating some distressed cities with Objective 1 or 2 status. This status entitles cities to receive social and economic funding in order to reduce interlocal disparities and strengthen their participation in the global economy. While the EU's success is yet to be established, there can be little doubt about its intentions — "hands off" policies are still nowhere in sight and interventionist modes of policy are used to strengthen the weakest cities.

The big picture is one of continuing differences in national and intergovernmental politics. National and intergovernmental orbits have held, and higher-level governments still maintain enormous sway over their localities. While we see some shifting in Great Britain and Canada, divergence is alive and quite robust. Both Great Britain's central government and Canada's Ontario government have continued to regulate local affairs, fiscal and otherwise. Traditions and institutions within a given nation are quite durable and often guide future actions. They constitute established pathways for coping with challenges and shape the manner in which cities adapt to change.

LOCAL DEVELOPMENT STRATEGIES

Neoliberalism can be a powerful impetus for development. Under certain conditions low taxes, reduced business regulation, and open competition will attract investors. There is also little doubt about the increasing recognition, if not appeal, of some version of the neoliberal idea.[xiii] In all of our cities journalists, policymakers, and attentive publics reflected on its possibilities. While not without its critics, neoliberalism had its defenders in newspapers, magazines, consultant studies, and retrospective evaluations. At the very ground levels of policy-making, bureaucrats and elected officials expressed a need to make their cities more competitive.

Furthermore, expanding competition was regarded as a sine qua non for a better European Union. Cities have been encouraged to take charge of this new mission by creating agencies to court businesses or encourage tourism. They have established task forces to find ways of improving their image and staged media events to boost their recognition. As one Italian official put it,

> We used to think of ourselves as a political class, and party was always first. But things have changed. The rest of Europe is pushing past us and Italian businesses can't be protected like they were years ago. So our city must find a new economic niche and compete like everyone else. Everybody knows that officials like myself have to become economic innovators for promoting our city. It's not just a matter of party politics anymore.

The general impulse toward competition is clear, but its conceptualization and implementation leaves enormous room for difference. This leads to a number of questions. When people talk about neoliberalism, exactly what do they mean? Given difficult choices, are they willing to sacrifice social benefits for more economic growth or trade greater social equality for more wealth? How do urban policymakers translate those meanings into action? Are the effects of these policies similar across different cities and do they bear a modicum of resemblance to one another? Finally, how can we put this in the context of the convergence debate?

The American Model

There is a tendency to see neoliberalism as an American idea and to equate European policy with its American counterpart.[52] While there are similarities there are also profound differences, and local development in America has its own particular setting. To begin with, the national presence in American cities is minimal. Washington exerts little influence on what transpires in city hall. Additionally, many cities (especially older, industrial urban cores) are estranged from their surrounding localities. The separation is not just legal or economic, but touches on attitudinal discrepancies between cities and suburbs. Opinion polls in New York show that most suburbanites hardly visit the central city and care little about it. In one survey more than half of the respondents said that they visit the city less frequently than they did five years ago. The proportion of suburbanites who read a city newspaper was also down to just 35 percent. A majority of suburbanites never lived in the city and approximately two-thirds of them said that they never visit relatives there.[53] Whether such attitudes toward New York will deepen in the wake of the terrorist events of September 2001 is something that only time will tell. In Detroit the alienation goes well beyond indifference and tends toward hostility. One study shows pronounced differences between central city and suburban attitudes toward government and reports that the area is "separated by formidable social, political, and economic chasms."[54] The psychosocial gulf between these worlds is summed up by one suburban official who made it clear that he "view(ed) the values of people in Detroit as completely foreign."[55]

As a consequence American cities see little choice but to go it alone and count on private wealth to enable them to compete. The first recourse of mayors and their political supporters is to seek mutually beneficial deals with private investors. Going back to the days of urban renewal, cities have grown accustomed to assuming risks and supporting private developers with public cash. Aggressive market-centered development is likely to dominate the agenda and over the years private investors have formed close working relationships with urban renewal agencies. Typically economic development projects were separated from socially oriented programs like public housing projects (often located at the other end of town). These alliances have become institutionalized in what has come to be known as "growth machines" and "pro-growth coalitions."[xiv] In U.S. cities they are manifest in Detroit's Greater Downtown Partnership, New York's, Downtown Lower Manhattan Association, Houston's Greater Partnership.

To make this work, American cities resorted to low-tax, supply-side strategies. Growth machines would be sustained by shedding social programs. The social agenda needed to be held down, if not reduced by discouraging the poor from remaining or settling in highly valued property. Where possible, cities would try to reduce dependent populations (welfare recipients, chronically unemployed). In some instances the poor would be displaced by urban renewal or by gentrifying old central city neighborhoods.[56] What we call social shedding is in keeping with national cuts in intergovernmental aid and welfare assistance throughout the 1980s and 1990s. Houston was always a low-tax haven and continued to keep low social expenditures, but other cities were more generous. Upon coming to office, New York's Mayor Giuliani cut taxes on commercial rents, abolished the unincorporated business tax, and permitted other levies to expire. By the close of the year 2000 New York's Republican mayor had reduced the tax bill by close to $2 billion. Giuliani also eliminated more than 15,000 jobs in social services and cut welfare by more than half.[57] Consistent with Detroit's reputation as a city bereft of decent public services, Mayor Archer kept taxes down and promised further reductions.[58] Between 1994 and 1999 Detroit's welfare load was cut by over 50 percent.[xv]

We emphasize that not all American policymakers support neoliberal development strategies. But in so far as neoliberalism is followed, it should be defined within its indigenous social and political moorings. The American model can be summed up in several ways. The role of "the state" is very much diminished in almost every aspect of local affairs. Cities are viewed as little more than federated units, responsible for their own upkeep and actions. Interlocal competition is often encouraged and the race belongs to the fittest. Private wealth is the vehicle for driving public prosperity. The private sector reigns supreme and is supported by the belief that business is inherently more efficient. Bureaucracy is the enemy and marketplace accountability is seen as superior. Growth and growth machines are to be valued, and a strong social agenda may be antithetical to those values. Furthermore, growth can be invigorated by a certain amount of social shedding and by minimizing dependence on the public sector.

Figure 8.1 portrays a trajectory of major developments in three American cities. The figure ranks these projects according to whether they are predominantly social centered (interventionist) or market centered (neoliberal). Those projects located at or closer to the middle band contain elements of both characteristics. The figure is intended as a time line covering thirty years, and it does not account for the magnitude or context of these developments.[xvi] Accordingly, it should be interpreted narrowly — as an illustration of strategic direction.

Detroit and Houston held steady throughout the period. These cities experienced little divergence from market-centered developments, and most of their projects are located in the lowest (most aggressive) band. Almost every project served to reinforce the "American model," and this trajectory continued right through the 1990s. New York, however, is less typical of that model. Its development moved up and down the scale, and it often carried out social- and market-centered projects simultaneously (mix and match).

The European Way

At least during the Thatcher years (1979–90), there was a certain likeness between American and British neoliberalism. Fiscal cuts to stimulate growth and an emphasis on the private sector ran deep in both nations. Despite the common thread of an "Anglo-American approach," the resemblance cannot be carried too far. Even the most ardent Tories kept a strong and engaged state. Moreover, unlike American cities, British localities resisted the cuts and many of them continued to support social expenditures. One might talk about "compulsory bidding" or "selling off" council housing or "monetarist incentives," but the social net was never lowered all that far. Even during this period of Anglo-American parallel, the role of "British state" remained paramount. Pierre Bourdieu put these differences in characteristic European terms by referring to the complementary tasks of the state's "left and right hands":

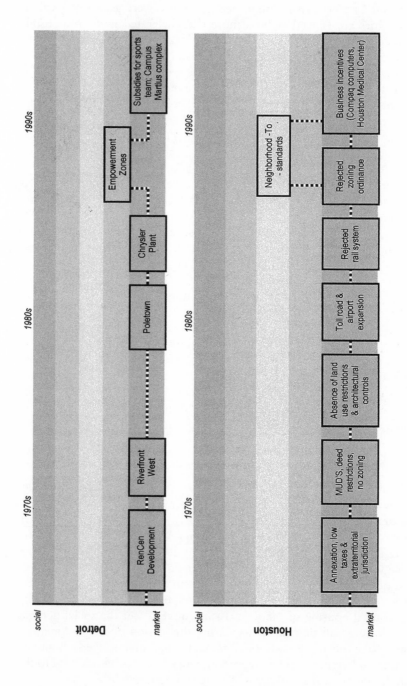

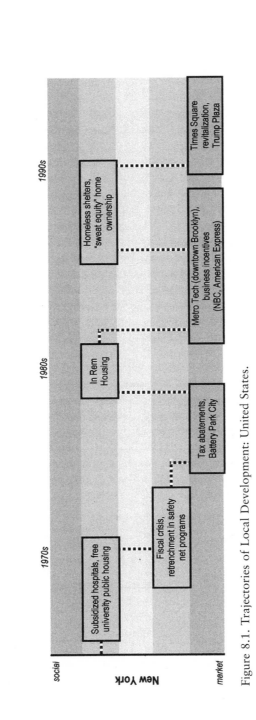

Figure 8.1. Trajectories of Local Development: United States.

On the one hand, we can see the logic of economic development by taking account of international constraints and competition. On the other hand, we can continue to uphold various forms of public intervention in order to deal with poverty and social exclusion.[59]

Clearly, while the American state could deftly apply only its right hand to the problem, British cities followed more ambidextrous solutions and were closer to the European model. The most acute example of this is in land-use policy. Where Americans were prone to sprawled, helter-skelter development, British localities went to considerable extent to contain and concentrate development. Even pro-development British elites pointed to America as a negative example. When Marx and Spencer proposed to build a retail outlet on the outskirts of one city, politicians flatly refused and warned business representatives that the city would block any such proposal. "I think we've learned a lot from what's happened in the states," commented one official, "and it's not going to happen here."

In the rest of Europe, both right and left hands worked with equal vigor. Localities continued to see public goods and national government as the major source of sustenance and rejuvenation. As one Italian analyst observed,

> [Local] decision-making bodies . . . are extremely unfamiliar with the possibility of obtaining more resources from sources other than external grants. . . . [They] are consequently led to consider the real or estimated need of public goods or services as their principal, if not only, point of reference. This is not to say that the problem of resources does not arise for them, but it is presented and seen as an external factor concerning relations between the local authority, which needs funds, and the state or the regions, which do not provide sufficient funds.[60]

Naples differed substantially from American cities like New York. For instance, Neapolitan Mayor Bassolino won national headlines when Naples became the first Italian city to issue its own bonds. But these securities were not used to borrow for traditional development purposes, like business subsidies, airport construction, or infrastructure. Instead, Bassolino used the money to buy a fleet of new buses to upgrade the city's creaky mass transit. Further, the bonds were easily marketable because the taxing power of the national treasury in Rome stood behind them. In contrast, mayors in New York focused their energy on public development corporations rated by Wall Street for their profitability. The New York strategy was to finance pay-as-you-go, income-generating projects like convention centers and airport improvements.

We can see contrasting priorities revealed through different patterns

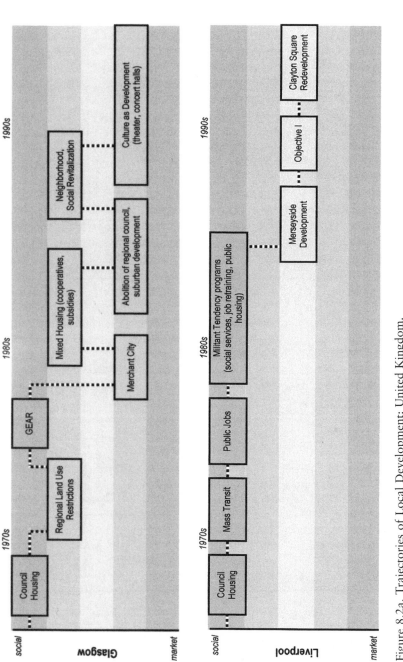

Figure 8.2a. Trajectories of Local Development: United Kingdom.

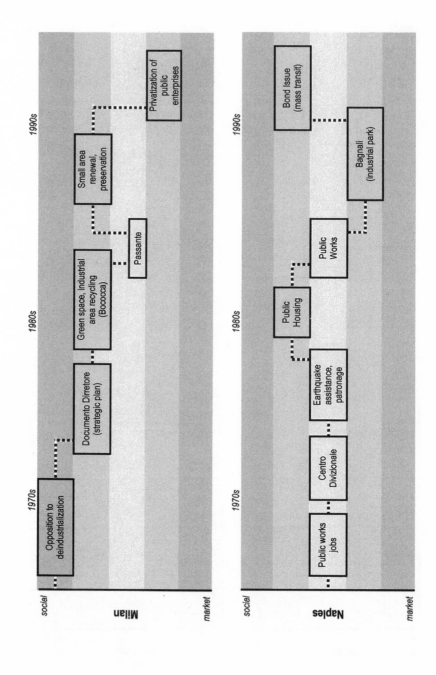

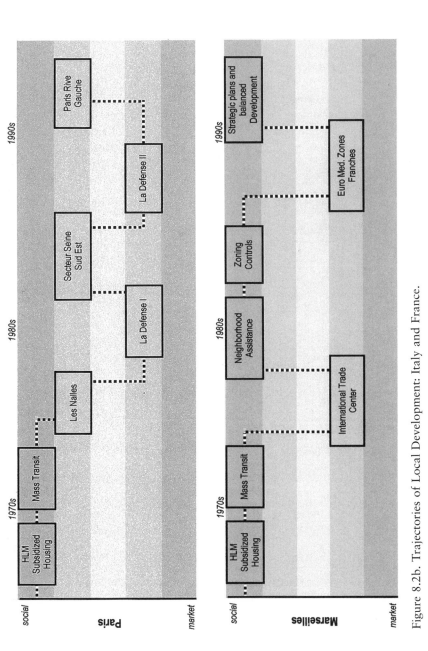

Figure 8.2b. Trajectories of Local Development: Italy and France.

of development. Figure 8.2 presents those patterns for European cities as a trajectory over three decades. Like the previous figure, it shows the frequency of social- and market-centered projects, and it should be viewed as an illustration of strategic direction.

The overall picture is quite different from the American model, exemplified by Detroit and Houston. Social polices are visible across all European cities, and they continued at a relatively aggressive level (uppermost band) though the year 2000. Even when Europeans turn to market-oriented projects they are generally not at the most aggressive level (lowest band). True, during the 1990s there is ratcheting toward market-centered projects. British scholars detected a trend toward place marketing throughout the country, and the experience of Glasgow and Liverpool confirm that.[61] But even this ratcheting reflects flexible mix-and-match policies rather than an abrupt shift. Italian and French cities were steadfast in continuing social-centered policies. Their overall pattern could best be described as sustaining social commitments, but engaging the market in strategic ways. Here, too, we see a continuance of mixing and matching rather than an ideologically driven thrust in another direction.

In any case, we can see that Europeans neither shun market-centered projects nor do they ignore competition. Rather, they view it differently. It can fairly be said that Americans use competition to promote direct short-run returns on investment. Europeans emphasize their competitive edge in terms of long-run investment and ways of reducing social polarization. This can be seen in different ways of managing poverty. While American cities saw radical cutbacks in welfare of 40 percent or more during the 1990s, European cities held steady. In Italy governments at all levels sought ways to increase social assistance. Special emphasis was given to rising unemployment, single-parent families, and excluded immigrants. Attempts to reform abused pension systems were thwarted. Even the prolific "invalid" pensions that prop up poor cities in the South were left intact. State supported minimum income floors are administered by the municipalities, and Naples is a participant. Naples also joined the EU programs to combat social exclusion and promote social solidarity. The city's poorest neighborhoods are targeted for assistance and social integration.

An even stronger social agenda continued in France. In Paris assistance to the poor between 1991 and 1996 actually increased by 68 percent.[62] During this period the greater Parisian region began to bolster its public assistance to the poor with annual increases in the number of beneficiaries of more than 8 percent.[63] Further, despite a surfeit of French academic literature declaiming spatial segregation, allocations to the poor were reasonably distributed throughout the Paris region.[xvii]

With roughly 20 percent of the region's population, Paris collected 29 percent of its social assistance.[xviii] Nearby suburban departments like Haut-de-Seine held 13 percent of the greater region's population and collected 12 percent of its assistance to the poor. The poorest suburban department, Seine-St.-Denis, held 13 percent of the regional population and collected 20 percent of its assistance to the poor.[64] While discrepancies exist, the gaps are not huge and compare favorably to those in the United States.

Much the same story could be told for Marseilles. Between 1990 and 1995 assistance to the poor doubled.[65] By the mid-1990s the proportion of that city's population receiving assistance reached 7.5 percent. Comparable figures for Marseilles's suburbs were 5 percent. To be sure, both Marseilles and Paris have distinctly disadvantaged neighborhoods—usually confined to the northern sections of each city. But compared to those in the United States, their regional discrepancies are mild.

Moreover, the existence of subsidized housing softens social polarization. Investment in assisted housing has always been a mainstay of European social policy and reveals a good deal about local strategies and underlying values. While national governments provide grants to localities for housing, the cities actually implement and bear responsibility for those policies. Housing lies heavily within the purview of localities and is largely initiated at their discretion. A willingness to support socially assisted housing also provides a perspective on how different actors view development.[xix]

Table 8.1 shows the proportion of housing assistance offered in our ten cities as of 1990. The cities are grouped by nation from most to least housing assistance. The sharpest divisions are by nation or region. American cities devote considerably less investment to housing assistance than their European counterparts. New York and Detroit do reach double digits, but Houston falls to just 5.7 percent. By comparison, once we go north of the border into Canada, we see that Toronto rises to 15.5 percent. The contrast is still greater across the Atlantic. British and French cities have the highest proportion of socially invested housing ranging from a high of 51.34 percent (Glasgow) down to 21 percent (Paris). True, Italian cities are lower than their European cousins, but they do compare favorably to their American counterparts.

What accounts for the ability of cities to resist convergence? Our bargaining model suggests that cumulative resources help insulate cities from market pressures and expand choice. All of the cities with the highest cumulative resources—Paris, Toronto, and Milan—along with moderately endowed Marseilles, have been able to maintain social-centered policies. Other cities with moderate resources—Glasgow and New York—were able to sustain some kind of social agenda, while

TABLE 8.1
Assisted Housing in Ten Cities, ca. 1990

City	Percent of population
New York	14.1
Detroit	12.1
Houston	5.7
Toronto	15.5
Glasgow	51.34
Liverpool	37.27
Marseilles	46.30
Paris	21.00
Milan	17.50
Naples	18.20

Liverpool showed some movement toward market policies. In contrast, cities with low cumulative resources either pared down social commitments or kept them at a low level.[xx]

We cannot be sure about the mix and weight of these variables, but it is striking that policy convergence closely follows differences in intergovernmental support. All of the cities in nations with integrated governmental systems pursued a divergent path. We also see that European cities were guided and supported by other levels of government. The conclusion seems inescapable: national, provincial, and regional regulation of local development mitigates social shedding.

Toronto: Resisting or Drifting?

Toronto illustrates the importance of supportive intergovernmental arrangements as a necessary, but hardly sufficient, resource for sustaining social-centered strategies. In Toronto intergovernmental support is a double-edged sword. The Harris government's effort to download social services has not yet caused the city to modify its social agenda, though the signs are ominous. So far Ontario has provided grants and loans to Toronto in order to keep amalgamation revenue-neutral. This has enabled the city to keep its recreation programs free for children and waive user fees for adults in the poorest neighborhoods.[66] The city has also stuck to its neighborhood-oriented, urban-centered strategy by engaging citizens in the planning process and using in-fill housing to populate vacant areas. New market rate housing is used to help defray the costs for assisted housing and homeless shelters.

It appears that bottom-up resistance to Tory policy has worked until now, but pressures from the top have caused some modifications in approach. The city has already begun a campaign to retain business through more aggressive marketing and selective rezoning.[67] It has also streamlined the development process and improved infrastructure for business. Pressures could mount in the near future. The "soft" social services now absorbed by the city are open-ended and popular demand for them could increase, particularly if there is a downturn in the economy.[68] Mayor Lastman has promised no tax increases for three years and that reprieve has expired. Torontonians face a 5 percent tax increase and other fiscal headaches. The city will have to pay back previous loans and gear up for new investment in infrastructure and human capital. Some observers believe that either Toronto will have to raise taxes again or begin to cut back social programs. Given the local culture, the city may well opt for a tax increase, but this cannot be pushed too far and too much into an indefinite future. Resistance could give way into a slow drift away from the city's historic commitments to a social agenda.

Figure 8.3 provides a view of that city's development trajectory. Like the preceding figures, it portrays major developments through the 1990s and situates them by social- and market-centered criteria.

As we can see Toronto pursued an aggressive social agenda through the 1980s. Like some of its European counterparts, it did promote a number of moderate market-centered projects and continues to do so. While the market direction is counterbalanced by a sustained social agenda, there is some drift toward greater market engagement and we cannot be sure how far this will go.

Is Local Development Policy Converging?

The idea of competition has acquired resonance. Globalization has brought on real changes in outlook and in policy. Governments now intervene not only to compensate for market failure but also to sharpen a city's competitive edge. At the same time, the change is not unidirectional nor is it uniform. Our cities are not marching together like toy soldiers into a common frontier. Rather, they face multiple frontiers that are divided by national and continental fault lines. America is on one side of fault line and comes closest to encompassing purist forms of neoliberal principles. Detroit, Houston, and, to a lesser extent, New York followed solitary paths, embraced local growth machines, and, in varying degrees, embarked upon social shedding. Canada's Toronto may occupy another side of a fault line. Though the lines are less clear and still forming, Toronto continues to resist go-it-alone policies and Harris's Tories have not yet pulled back from a regulatory role. Toronto has sped up its growth machine, but without social shedding. Our Euro-

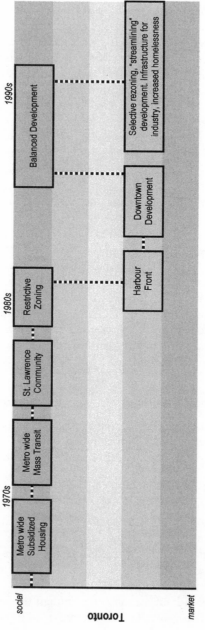

Figure 8.3. Trajectories of Local Development: Canada.

pean cities occupy still other sides of fault lines. British cities like Glasgow and Liverpool were not left to their own devices and, while they both moderated their social agenda, they resisted social shedding. Continental cities have neither gone it alone, nor have they embraced growth machines or shed social policies. To the contrary, French and Italian cities have tried to reduce social disparities and, despite a flirtation with neoliberalism, are quite sensitive about its downsides (social exclusion, threats to social cohesion, etc.).

CHANGING GOVERNANCE VIA LEADERS AND REGIMES: CONVERGENCE?

Globalization and its attendant forces also ushered in changes in how cities govern themselves. New directions for mayors, new styles of operation, and new kinds of regimes are supposed to have taken root.[69] A number of typologies have been used to try to capture these changes. Some writers see the mayor as the central figure and as employing an assortment of skills and assets in order to pilot the city.[70] Other scholars focus on the larger combination of forces that support mayors. They see the action as occurring within regimes or governing coalitions These regimes are pictured in a number of modes—as staying with traditional blue-collar groups, favoring old business elites, or pursuing middle-class social reform.[71] Social scientists are well aware that leadership is not static and that it must constantly resolve competing claims and tensions. We examine this movement in the light of convergence and whether an American-style of urban governance has been adopted elsewhere.

Entrepreneur Mayors American-Style

The alleged rise of "entrepreneurial mayors" provides a useful test for one convergence proposition. Entrepreneurial mayors take on the role of city boosters and image promoters. They sometimes travel far and wide, selling their cities to potential investors. Entrepreneurial mayors often serve as the political focal points, and this means enhanced executive power. Sensing the economic insecurities of citizens, entrepreneurial mayors become messiahs preaching ways to make the city more competitive. Usually this means supporting leaner government and promoting a friendlier attitude toward business.[72] Terry Clark sees a new breed of mayor arising: socially liberal, politically dynamic, but fiscally conservative, and always ready to respond to "new challenges."[73] In the course of that pursuit, these mayors frequently search for ways of "reinventing government," privatizing functions, and pursuing partnerships with business.

Houston's mayors epitomized this style. Recent mayors like Robert

Lanier and Kathy Whitmire expressed dedication to market-led ideas as an article of faith, even as they built multiracial political coalitions demanding the inclusion of other social agendas. Beginning in the early 1970s, every New York mayor pursued a high profile in negotiating packages of tax concessions and business incentives with corporate employers. The mayor became the city's key economic statesman whose reputation depended on boosting New York's business fortunes. This leadership style blurred party differences. The 1989 and 1993 mayoral campaigns saw Democratic black liberal David Dinkins run against Republican white conservative Rudolph Giuliani. Despite differences in their social agendas, neither candidate differed in support for programs to help business.[74] While running for office they tried to outbid each other in promising tax breaks and loans to business and trying to lure more jobs into town. In New York promoting business is good bipartisan politics.

Detroit long had a tradition of entrepreneurial mayors. Coleman Young stood for economic development and pursued a "corporate-centered" strategy, though his image was tarnished by racial animosity and he never rose above the grit of local politics.[75] His successor Dennis Archer was especially exuberant about business and economic development. While Archer lacked Young's fire, he promoted no tax hikes, job development districts, and hailed the city's new sports stadiums and gambling casinos. With over 200 sales trips to his credit, Archer was criticized as an absentee mayor who paid little attention to daily operations. *Newsweek* saw this differently and, because of his development prowess, named Archer one of the nation's top twenty-five mayors.[76] While Archer did have problems making the city run, he had no problem promoting downtown mega projects. In referring to the "rebirth of the city," the mayor boasted about its future:

> Detroit's central business district will soon rival those of other major cities, with three world-class casinos, two state-of-the-art sport stadiums, a new and thriving theatre district, linked river parks, a billion-dollar office and commercial complex, and several renovated office towers.[77]

Great Britain: Rising to the Occasion

Pressures have mounted on British cities to become more aggressive and act more efficiently. The old distinction between policy-making and administration seems to be fading or at least changing. The idea of council leaders patiently conferring with local legislators and then transmitting their policy decisions to a neutral town clerk and local officers is under question. More and more the British talk about better political management carried out by a "strong political executive."[78] An elected mayor presumably would give more energy to local government and be more accountable to the voters. In theory at least, the office of an elected mayor should become a focal point for more contacts with business and other governments, and invigorate local initiatives. The Local Government Act now offers cities a choice of staying with the "council leader" system or adopting various kinds of "strong political executive" models, including the ability to elect a strong mayor.

Thus far Liverpool has been slow to act. The Liberal Democrats, led by Mike Story, are not anxious to press for an elected mayor, mostly because they are content with holding control of the council as it is presently constituted. The Labour Party is in opposition, and some of its leaders view an elected mayor not only as a source of political opportunity but also as a vehicle for strong leadership. Whatever voters choose, it is clear that central government regards the old system as a product of a bygone era. Prime Minister Tony Blair is at the forefront of this effort, encouraging localities to be more innovative and more energetic.

Glasgow shows many of the same tendencies — slow to respond but now on its way. Until the 1980s, a plodding and unimaginative succession of Labour politicians generally held the offices of council leader and lord provost (mayor). But after young and politically ambitious Provost Michael Kelly assumed office in 1983, he launched a bold campaign to reconstruct Glasgow's image. Kelly hired public relations experts and started the "Glasgow's Miles Better" slogan as the new upbeat symbol of the city. The campaign proved enormously successful. He led marketing efforts to proclaim to the world that Glasgow was a leading center of culture, the arts, business services, education, and publishing.

Kelly's success in image remaking never earned him large political rewards, but succeeding council leaders and mayors all paid unwavering heed to his formula. They actively promoted arts and cultural events to attract tourists and investment to the city. A whole new language of entrepreneurial discourse emerged. The city's dusty blue-collar socialist political traditions were traded for newer images associated with place marketing. After Glasgow won designation as 1990 European City of Culture, Council Leader (later provost, or Mayor) Pat Lally boasted,

We are going to use the title for maximum advantage — we are going to milk it for all it's worth. We are using the title to open up employment opportunities in cultural industries and in tourism. We have succeeded in attracting 2 billion pounds worth of investment to Glasgow: we need more and 1990 will help to get it.[79]

Entrepreneur Mayors: Spotty but Visible in Italy and France

Mayoral entrepreneurship has a spottier experience on the Continent, but is gaining recognition. The Italian and French Left have a long history of distrusting markets as problem solvers; even right-leaning parties have little tradition of mixing business with government. Still, entrepreneurial mayors have begun to emerge in most of our cities. On occasion this new leadership style has become an established fixture of local politics.

In Milan mayors paid increasing attention to business relations during the 1980s after Socialist Carlo Tognoli led his party away from old party commitments to reindustrializing the city. Tognoli regularly used public relations to make business aware of the "new" Milan. He helped establish novel partnerships with Milanese business leaders in planning development projects and in examining the city's social and economic challenges.

During the 1990s leaders of the new postreform parties explicitly supported campaigns to increase Milan's competitiveness in preparation for fuller participation in the European Union. Northern League Mayor Marco Formentini warned that Milan's position in Europe would not weather the winds of economic integration. He appealed over the heads of party leaders and factions to establish a "nonpolitical" style of mayoral leadership among voters and business leaders.

In Naples Antonio Bassolino became the first mayor to use business boosterism to expand his political base. In the past, Neapolitan mayors normally had low political profiles. They either had short political lives or they were bosses whose power depended almost exclusively on patronage. This changed in 1993 when reforms made it easier for Italian mayors to govern without party coalitions. The old party system was in disarray. The city was sinking economically. Bassolino drew upon his broad-based support and combined it with entrepreneurial appeals to build a wide voter following. He made trips abroad to court international business, and he explicitly tied his campaign to improving the image of the city as a place of business.[80] He also appointed many people with professional experience outside politics to posts in the executive *giunta*, which governs the city. As one of the mayor's political advisors put it,

> Bassolino sells hope. There is no money because the city is broke. So he tries to symbolize what people in Naples want most—some promise that life will get better, that jobs will come, and that they will have respect again. The city has been down so long, but he shows how it can come up.

Under Jacques Chirac, Paris glowed. For a long time its economy needed little boosting and its image needed little polishing. Chirac was one of France's premier politicians reigning over France's leading city in one of Europe's eminent "capitals." Throughout most of the past thirty years Paris was always an easy "sell" and needed no aggressive salesmanship. On the surface, Mayor Chirac was above commercialism, and he left the promotion of investment to adjuncts or the professionals.[81] Having been mayor of the city for nearly two "golden decades," Chirac was not an easy act to follow. His successor and protégé Jean Tiberi adopted a more modest pose. When first elected, Tiberi campaigned on behalf of an environmentally sane Paris and for the rights of local consumers. Tiberi's socialist successor, Bertrand Delanoe, is not likely to tout entrepreneurship. While it is still to early to know what Mayor Delanoe will do, he is personally more sympathetic to incremental, social reform than to big-splash mega projects. The new mayor has already begun to insist that wealthier arrondissements absorb a fair share of subsidized housing and has promised that he will integrate those areas.

Marseilles's Jean-Claude Gaudin shows a glint of entrepreneurship, but only a glint.[xxi] Gaudin has been careful not to upset the existing system of political rewards and patronage. He has retained Deferre's cautious approach to politics and is considered to be just as shrewd. Nevertheless, as a mayor from the classic Right, Gaudin has broken new ground. He was instrumental in shepherding legislation for the *zones franches*, and he proudly promotes the economic virtues of Marseilles as the Mediterranean's great port city. He roundly takes credit for the mega project EuroMéd and calls it the "key to Marseilles's future."[82] Gaudin is also careful to talk about rebalancing the city, revitalizing its center, and rebuilding poorer neighborhoods in the north. When Gaudin speaks about the future, he means change in both economic and social dimensions:

> In spite of budgetary strictures there are certain necessary expenses for the good of the city. Municipal services must always be kept up along with the maintenance of our infrastructure and our common heritage. . . . Any change will always be in the daily lives of our citizens, in their security, their neighborhoods, their public services, their schools, their nurseries, their retirement homes, and their culture.[83]

Canada: Starting along the Path

Until amalgamation, Toronto could hardly be said to have entrepreneurial leadership. The chair of Metro was a weak office, made powerful on occasion by some of its personalities, and the City of Toronto was largely in the hands of an activist council. Lastman, however, has given panache to the office, and he may very well stand as a model of an entrepreneurial mayor.

The new mayor has the background for the role. Lastman is a product of working-class Toronto. With limited education and meager beginnings he began as an appliance salesman. Eventually he managed to buy his own store, built a chain of retail outlets, and became a multi-millionaire. Lastman always had a flare for publicity and saw it as the key to business success. As an upstart he stood on a street corner in a black-and-white striped prison suit, offering passersby two-dollar bills in exchange for one dollar. At first pedestrians ignored this bizarre spectacle and thought it a trick, but upon discovering the offer was genuine they soon mobbed him shouting, "It's real, it's real!" On that day Lastman gave away 500 dollars in just fifteen minutes, but he gained an even greater value in advertising. On another occasion he flew up to one of Canada's northern reaches in order to prove he could "sell a refrigerator to an Eskimo." Lastman made good on his claim, returning with just a few fish and a polar bear skin but with an abundance of public attention.[84]

As mayor of North York, the flamboyant Lastman continued these tactics. He drove a white Rolls Royce, smoked big cigars, and was a constant source of ideas and exhortation. Inspired by the slogan "I love New York," Mayor Lastman invented a counterpart "North York: The City With Heart."[85] When Metro Toronto was amalgamated, Lastman sensed his opportunity. He ran for the mayoralty of the new mega city and won. Since then Lastman has embarked on a world-wide sales pitch: "Toronto is open for business and I want the world to know that the place to expand is right here in the heart of Ontario."[86] Lastman has gone on to court the film industry, to attract high-tech investors, and to press for a 2008 Olympic bid.[xxii]

At home in Toronto, Lastman has taken up the cudgels for efficiency and promoted privatization. Despite the fact that he ran with Conservative blessing, the new mayor is no dyed-in-the-wool conservative. He readily denounces the Tories for their social cuts, he tries to secure shelter for Toronto's increasing homeless, and he remains socially liberal. The mayor approvingly marched in a Gay Pride parade and rails against sprawl. The question of whether this is posturing may be less important than the question of whether it works. In Toronto's most recent election, Lastman proved that it did by taking 80 percent of the vote.

The American-centric Regime

Does the surge of entrepreneurial-style leadership signify more profound changes in regime politics that favor business, as convergence theory suggests? If this were the case, we would expect to see a drift over time toward types of business oriented regimes. In earlier chapters we found that the regimes most favorable to business demands were vendor, free enterprise and mercantile. Vendor regimes permit business to play a dominant role and determine the development agenda. Free enterprise regimes place business at the center of decision making and subject it to relatively weak checks. In both vendor and free enterprise regimes, business often "captures" the city and can influence policy through side-payments and bribes to politicians. Mercantile regimes are less favorable to business and are cross-pressured by a variety of interests. While not captured by business, city hall is highly sympathetic to it.

Somewhat more insulated from business are grantsman and clientelist regimes. These regimes are able to maximize governmental assistance and exercise more discretion over development. Grantsman regimes are interested in economic growth and are more likely to solicit business cooperation, even though their access to public resources affords some independence. Clientelist regimes are more deeply attached to constituent groups and somewhat less inclined to work with business coalitions in promoting the city's agenda. Whatever cooperation occurs between the regime and business is usually in the form of payoffs rather than policy. In this case it is the regime that squeezes business rather than the other way round.

Most insulated from business pressure are planner and challenger regimes. Planner-type 2 regimes enjoy favorable market conditions and strong intergovernmental support. They are however, beset by political fragmentation, deal making, and sluggish implementation. Planner-type 1 regimes combine a series of advantages including favorable market conditions, strong intergovernmental support, and an active, cohesive citizenry. Challengers go furthest to blunt business. They are at odds with business participation and sometimes openly hostile to it. In both planner and challenger regimes, government sets the development agenda, albeit with varying degrees of success.

Figure 8.4 shows regime types with arrows pointing to regime stability or change between 1970 and 2000. Regime types are shown in two parallel sets of boxes, representing different time periods. The vertical alignment runs from maximum to minimum business influence. Straight unbroken arrows show regime stability. Diagonal dotted arrows show actual or possible regime change.[xxiii] We also note that regimes hardly change over night. It often takes a while for regimes to formulate and gel, and it is not always easy to determine at exactly what point that occurs. Over the past thirty years Liverpool has shifted most often and is still in the process of change.

We see that American regimes are most influenced by business and remain stable over time. Vendor Detroit and mercantile New York re-

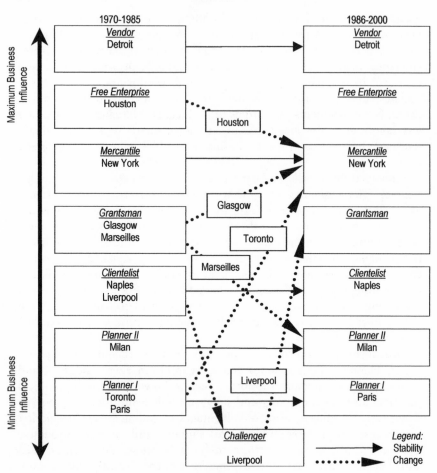

Figure 8.4. Direction of Regime Change.

tain a pro-business stance. While Houston seems to be moving toward some form of moderated pro-business position, it still is firmly within the business camp. In the United States one of the vehicles for that influence is the public-private partnership. American partnerships often leave the public sector in a subordinate position. Referred to in the literature as "unequal partnerships," they often harness public money to support private initiatives.[87] These partnerships are usually a product of local chambers of commerce. Detroit banked its waterfront development on a Greater Downtown Partnership. New York developed similar partnerships to rebuild sections of downtown Brooklyn and lower and mid Manhattan. Houston is immensely influenced by its chamber of commerce, which spawned the Greater Houston Partnership. A staff member at the Houston Partnership explained just how the game of musical chairs between government and business is carried out:

> The partnership board takes a big view of things; they are smart people who know how the city works, after all. And we are appreciated by city and state officials because they see it that way too. You know that when Louis Welch left the mayor's office to become president of the chamber of commerce, he said that he was "moving up" to higher office! Well, maybe he was joking, but you can't deny that the government has to anticipate where business is going. So why not start there?

Regime Change in Europe

As Figure 8.4 suggests, our two British cities, grantsman Glasgow and clientelist Liverpool, show some inclination toward business, though not nearly to the extent of their American cousins. Both cities have made themselves accessible to business, but change is gradual and they are still firmly in the hands of public-sector elites.

In Italy and France we discern no sharp movement toward regimes dominated by business. Milan and Paris remained stable, while Marseilles appears to be moving toward a planner-type 2 regime. For the most part the public sector remained the foremost actor. While regimes appear to be friendlier toward business, we see no headlong rush toward adopting American-style vendor or free enterprise regimes or coalitions. If regimes were changing, they were headed toward a cautiously moderate pro-business orientation (Glasgow, Liverpool) or trying to reinvigorate their own public sector (Marseilles) or simply struggling with a dominant public sector (Naples).

We should also recognize that historic antagonism toward business appears to have dissipated. Ideological regimes have faded and new coalitions have softened their position against business collaboration. By and large localities began to work more collaboratively with business, without being subordinated to it. This may explain the clustering in figure 8.4 toward mercantile regimes. These regimes are capable of opening up toward business, but can also check it with countervailing constituencies.

The comparative uses of public-private partnerships provide a glimpse of how relationships with business may be evolving. Europeans began to build their own version of public private partnerships. British partnerships are still led and supported by government, mostly because chambers of commerce are so weak. British business is highly decentralized and not capable of mounting growth machines comparable to those in the United States. Between 1981 and 1987 British government gave partnerships 1.9 billion pounds in order to keep them alive.[88] Glasgow's Development Agency is nominally private, though it draws mainly on public funds. Liverpool has also turned to the "partnership principle" through its "business link," but it, too, is in the hands of public actors.[89]

The experience of partnerships in Italy and France provide still more distinctions. These partnerships are rooted in different traditions and ways of carrying out development.[90] In Italy, where business has not been active in formal governance, the partnership ideal has begun to ascend, but it is clearly subordinate to the state. In Naples, there were signs of emergence. A business-sponsored partnership, Il Regno del Possibile (The Realm of the Possible), was organized during the early 1990s. Funded by the banks, businesses, and government, Il Regno functioned as a committee to plan the renewal of the city's shabby central historic district. Although this group ultimately fell apart, it constituted a new private-sector initiative. Milan's modernization also generated a proliferation of public-private initiatives. Typically, they brought together elected officials and business leaders to take part in master planning and form consortiums in order to stimulate private investment. Not the least significant, the current mayor, Gabriele Albertini, is a former leader of the local chamber of commerce, and he has appointed a coterie of new business managers to head city government. It remains to be seen, however, whether fraction-ridden Milan will allow business to institutionalize power.

In France, the ideal of a strong, central state remains incontestable. In fact, French chambers of commerce are considered public bodies and receive funding by the state. Typically a powerful state works in collusion with large enterprise at the very peaks of authority. Obligations, risks, and benefits are usually spelled out and outlined in a formal public plan.[91] Government is accustomed to mixed public and private investment and is in the habit of taking the lead. As the French see it, public-private partnerships are not terribly novel. In Paris and Marseilles mixed economic corporations and EPADs led most development initiatives and are integral to the national fabric. This is a particularly French way of engaging private investors. So long as the participants know who possesses the ultimate authority, there is little to be added.

The development of the Rive Gauche in Paris provides some insight into how one French public-private partnership works. A mixed corporation, run by the city, took the lead. A basic plan laid out the scale of the project, set out the locations, and established the proportions of housing, commerce, and industry. The plan also specified particulars like open space, building heights, and infrastructure. Public hearings were conducted and the plan approved by the city council. Only after these elements were in place was the private sector invited to submit competitive bids for development rights. Once contracts were awarded, they were governed by a series of "controls" or compliance standards. Public officials were active at every stage of the project and had to approve construction permits. Housing in the project has been equally divided between low, moderate, and market-rate housing. Commercial development and market-rate housing have been used to subsidize socially assisted housing. While Rive Gauche had its difficulties in getting off the ground, it is now an overwhelming success. Private demand for development rights far exceeds the supply, and over recent years prices have substantially risen.

Continuity and Transition in Canada

As mentioned earlier, provincial pressures toward neoliberalism have caused some ripples. For this reason, figure 8.4 shows some movement toward a mercantile regime, though whether Toronto will actually land in a mercantile box remains to be seen. Some Canadian writers have already sounded the "pro-growth" alarm. They argue that developers are already "beyond the reach of local democracy" and can build with "impunity."[92] The new city council is weak, and Harris's Tories hold a substantial minority of seats on it. Whether the current regime will absorb a tax shock and remain intact is also in question. Despite the alarm bells, to date there is not enough evidence to warrant such a dramatic conclusion. Planning is strong and the social agenda still alive. Certainly, the city has shed its anti-business proclivity, but this is a far cry from being in the hands of business. The notion of public-private partnerships has not fully caught on simply because Canadians have different traditions than their giant neighbor to the south. While some Canadian politicians may speak of public-private partnerships, the public role is very much alive. Quite tellingly, Toronto's economic development strategy contains a resilient and inclusive public component. It explicitly states the city must "Mobilize . . . collective resources through partnerships with public agencies [and] the private and volunteer sectors."[93]

Are Mayors and Regimes Converging?

If there is anything to spot over the past thirty years, it is rise of entrepreneurial mayors. Some form of entrepreneurial leadership arose in many of our cities (save Liverpool, Paris, and perhaps Marseilles). We should see this as a significant occurrence, and an indication of an American "pull" on other cities. How deeply this reaches is another matter. One can point to entrepreneurial mayors as an illustration of how other cities are following the American lead. Furthermore, we might see this as the tip of an iceberg and argue that regimes sooner or later will fall into the American wake. We might also cite evidence of rising partnerships with business. After all, is this not an effect of globalization?

We think, however, that such an interpretation would be misplaced. It is relatively easy for mayors to adopt an entrepreneurial style and sell their city. Closer scrutiny also tells us that mayors may be selling their cities in different ways. Houston's Lanier and Detroit's former Mayor Archer will necessarily have a different "pitch" than Marseilles's Gaudin and Toronto's Lastman. While American entrepreneurs stress low taxes, generous facilities, and business dynamism, their non-American counterparts will point to a very different set of assets. The differences are not simply matters of emphasis but are related to the substance of what these cities are about.

Moreover, the fact that most regimes have been slow to change tells us something about the dent entrepreneurship has made. This resistance should not be attributed to "lag" but to deeply rooted differences in local culture related to the role of business. On the whole, public-private "partnerships" have a different meaning in European cities than in America. In the United States the notion of "partnership" implies that city halls cannot do without the leadership and resources of private business. Cooperation between local development agencies and business is therefore seen as an opportunity for public officials to learn from business and for the private sector to lead the way. In Europe it is the other way around, and leadership resides on the public side. Planning and development are inherently governmental activities. They require political coordination, collaboration, and, above all, attention to the interest of the larger commonweal. Business may facilitate and can advise, but it does not govern. The predicate of public rule is key and so is public confidence. As one Scottish official put it,

> Is there a strategy that guides the market in Glasgow? Yes, of course. The private sector wants to know what is going to happen. They like planning, contrary to the stereotype. So our job is to present goals and then look for opportunities to bring the private sector on board. . . . Without planning the private sector would be rudderless in doing anything for this city, but they would still drive everything. Things would be far worse than they are. Far worse, indeed.

Conclusions

Patterns of convergence and divergence can be likened to an elaborate tapestry. One can find threads of convergence and these would be very real. After all, the past thirty years have brought significant changes to cities and we should see some common threads of experience. Words like "competition," "neoliberalism," "entrepreneur mayors," and "public-private partnerships" are general enough and accurately describe trends in many of our cities. On closer inspection many of those threads turn out to be quite different from one another, and they take divergent turns. They also have a very different content and are better defined by their indigenous contexts. While the "American model" may be easily recognized, its applications are limited. Europeans and Canadians have adapted to the international marketplace in their own ways, and these should be fully appreciated.

These distinctions have profoundly different effects. In Europe, the state has an enduring meaning and it continues to play a central role in establishing local policies. Cities have not traded in social- for market-centered policies, and they view development strategies quite differently than their American counterparts. Governance has not become the handmaiden for business or growth machines. Despite adopting some American practices, Canadians show a similar propensity to follow indigenously carved paths. Notwithstanding pro-growth initiatives, Ontario has not distanced itself from Toronto or its region and continues to be highly interventionist. For both Europeans and Canadians, cities will continue to be strongly guided in the international economy by higher-level governments, and those cities are likely to work collaboratively with neighboring localities and regions. In varying degrees they are bound to retain social-centered policies.

Divergence is very much alive. National policies continue to be heterogeneous. City resources are quite variable and that variation influences strategic alternatives. Even entrepreneur mayors sell their cities in different ways. The drift toward pro-business regimes by some cities is counter balanced by the movement of other cities in a different direction. Our tapestry does have very broad and bold threads of convergence. But the sturdier and more numerous ones are divergent.

What does this tell us about city bargaining? We know that continuing diversity means that bargaining with business will take place on different terms. In dealing through the international marketplace, cities will use different resources and probably reach different outcomes. This means that cities will stress different kinds of comparative advantage, and this is likely to lead to different development strategies. Trade-offs between "fast growth" and "slow growth" will also occur as well as trade-offs between economic vitality and social stability. We now turn to an examination of those strategies and their possibilities.

NOTES

i. See Garrett, *Partisan Politics*, 791–93 for a review of convergence theory in respect to the nation-state. Some urban scholars have been quick to point out that city governments and societies still have choices, but the empirical support for their claims has been mostly anecdotal or based on single-case studies.

ii. Even national governments now encounter new difficulties in managing economic policy. In a world where interest rates are constrained by global capital movements, monetary authorities have fewer options in setting national targets (Frieden, "Invested Interests"; Havrileski, *Pressure on American Monetary Policy*). Fiscal policy has ebbed as a national policy tool, because international trade and competitiveness limit tax and budgetary alternatives (Peterson and Rom, "Macro-economic Policy Making"). Local governments must contend with economic shocks and pressures without as much national assistance because higher-level governments are more absorbed in managing problems of national competitiveness.

iii. Of course, these same theorists recognize that internationalization also produces important forms of divergence. Economic restructuring unleashes inequalities because cities are not equally positioned to exploit the same economic roles. For example, Sassen suggests that a "new geography of centrality and marginality" is emerging (*Globalization and Its Discontents*, xxvi) as a small number of global financial centers, such as New York, London, and Tokyo, take on coordinating functions, leaving most other cities at the margins of the world system and playing more specialized roles. Nevertheless, this only qualifies the convergence hypothesis because even these so-called global cities face severe economic competition as a result of trends toward the consolidation of world financial centers. Indeed, it has been predicted that one day there may be only three major financial centers, one for each world time zone (see *Economist* article "Capitals of Capital," August 22, 1998, p. 2).

iv. Similarly, in the highly integrated U.S. market there is no evidence of state governments converging in tax rates around a minimal mean. Rather, there is dispersion, and low-tax states are generally not the best economic performers. See the discussion in Garrett, "Global Markets and National Politics," 818.

v. The period was interspersed with some federal activism under Carter (Goetz and Clarke, *New Localism*, 44–46). During this interim the federal government tried to combat social distress through an Urban Development Bank and Comprehensive Employment Training Act, but these were relatively short-lived and mired in controversy. The place-based character of most new programs actually stimulated and subsidized local governmental economic competition for jobs, rather than helping to equalize it.

vi. During this period the national welfare caseload dropped by 51.5 percent (Allen and Kirby, "Unfinished Business").

vii. Curiously, Enterprise Zones were a British invention, though they never became very well established in that nation. America, however, embraced the idea and sought to use them to abolish taxes and regulations within designated areas.

viii. Scottish urban policy followed a different track, as noted later and described in chapter 7.

ix. The UDCs are unlike American-style public benefit corporations. The latter are expected to operate as a business in that revenues generated by their projects are dedicated to repaying private sector bond-holders.

x. The French and Italian policies are broadly similar. In 1988 France adopted the Revenu Minimum d' Insertion and in the 1990s Italy adopted the Reddito Minimo di Inserimento.

xi. Hine, "Federalism, Regionalism"; Gario, "Intergovernmental Relations." Italy's tradition of complex and elaborate rules, regulations, and oversight of local governments by national officials ensured that the regional governments could not grow in ways that could challenge national power. Legal restrictions from Rome curbed their administrative discretion. The regions were dependent on specially earmarked funding coming from central government transfers, rather than their own fiscal resources. Most of the latter consist of special supplementary funding exercised through national party networks, rather than through automatic grant formulas (Hine, "Federalism, Regionalism," 115).

xii. "Premiers Rencontres Nationales Délégation à l'Aménagement du Térritoire et à l'Action Régionale, Agglomération." The Loi Voynet was passed in March 2000. Paris is not included because it is governed by its own statutes. The fourteen designated cities are Bordeaux, Brest, Caen, Dunkerque, Grenoble, Lille, Lyon, Marseilles, Montbellard, Nantes, Orléans, Perpignan, Poitiers, and Rennes.

xiii. Policy as an idea involves the diffusion of a consensus among policymakers in favor of common direction for governmental innovation. See the discussion in Derthick and Quirk, *Politics of Deregulation*, and Mayhew, "U.S. Policy."

xiv. Mollenkopf, *Contested City*; Logan and Molotch, *Urban Fortune*. It is not by sheer coincidence that "growth machine" literature originated and grew up in the United States. This is because America has had the most vigorous progrowth politics in the Western world. Since its American invention, the term has translated into non-American contexts, but these remain rather pale imitations. See the original article on the subject by Molotch, "City as Growth Machine," and subsequent responses edited by Jonas and Wilson, *Critical Perspectives*.

xv. Allen and Kirby, "Unfinished Business." Welfare cuts were due to federal and state initiatives. Nevertheless, as mentioned in chapter 3, we view cities as a composite of multiple variables. Intergovernmental actions are an important part of that component, and local policies are often a product of those relationships.

xvi. These projects are selective and limited in scope. They do not include the overall context of policy or the array of policy tools available to cities. While figures 8.1, 8.2, and 8.3 roughly conform to our evaluations of cities adopting social- and market-centered policies, there may be minor discrepancies. For a description of each project or event, see chapter 4 as well as this chapter.

xvii. Brun and Rhein, *La Ségrégation dans la Ville*; Seguad, Bovalet, and Brun, *Logement et habitat*. These allocations were offered and made by national government. As mentioned in note xv. we view this as form of local support and as part of a composite that accounts for city behavior.

xviii. By the "greater Paris region" we mean the eight departments of the Ile-de-France. Public assistance for the poor is the Revenue Minimum d'Insertion or RMI. As mentioned, this assistance was first adopted by the national government in 1988. This is one of many social programs in France, but it is the most notable and closest policy to American welfare assistance.

xix. We should also recognize that subsidized housing in some European cities has not worked well and is stigmatized, especially in Great Britain. Over the past two decades British cities have sold off "council housing" to former tenants. Subsidized housing in France has a much better overall record, though it too has been stigmatized by mega housing projects called *les grands ensembles*.

xx. The distribution of cumulative resources among these cities is explained in chapter 5.

xxi. Entrepreneur mayors have won office in other French cities, like Strasbourg, Lille, and Bordeaux.

xxii. Toronto made a good showing for the Olympic bid, but lost out to Peking.

xxiii. Possible change does not indicate an outcome but rather a process and probable direction.

Chapter Nine

STRATEGIES FOR
THE INTERNATIONAL MARKETPLACE

Progressive societies outgrow institutions
as children outgrow clothes
— Henry George

BARGAINING AND STRATEGIC THINKING

Strategic thinking allows us to attach means to ends, and to do so while taking into account a larger environment. By thinking strategically we can set our sights on the problem at hand, sharpen our focus, and bring a particular approach to bear. Good strategic thinking also begins from a subjective viewpoint and fits into a larger scheme of things. Our own perspective springs from a bargaining model of urban development, and it tells us that cities are heavily dependent upon their ability to negotiate in an international marketplace. The issue is how can localities best deal with this situation.

There is no shortage of suggestions for how cities might cope with the vicissitudes of the marketplace. Indeed, the list proliferates with every passing year. The most familiar are "supply and demand" strategies. These strategies focus on growth, and they respectively seek to stimulate private investment by lowering business costs or by exploiting new markets.[1] Other strategies often complement the supply and demand approach. "Cluster" strategies seek to reach a critical mass and create a mix of related businesses within a given location, enabling cities to build upon their competitive advantages of location and density.[2] "Place marketing" strategies concentrate on selling a city's image in order to attract investors.[3] "Human resource" strategies call for educating a work force in order to draw upon new knowledge economies.[4] "Amenities" strategies recommend that cities enhance themselves with recreation, culture, and open space in order to attract clean industry.[5] "Niche" strategies advise cities to match their strengths with some aspect of market demand and play up unique abilities.[6] "Deregulation" and "efficiency" strategies advise cities to impress business with their superior performance.[7]

These strategies urge cities to sharpen their competitive edge, but they have their uses as well as shortcomings. Instead of a broad-ranged approach that softens, redirects, or rolls back market forces, they come closer to a tactical compliance with it. Our approach is somewhat different. Rather than subordinating cities to market pressures, we underline how cities might strengthen themselves vis-à-vis business and cope with market stings. We focus on how cities can maximize their bargaining resources in the international marketplace and, most crucially, how they might expand choice. Cities may be compelled to bargain with private benefactors, but they need not magnify their weakness. Instead they can leverage their strength.

Taking this perspective is important because, in our judgment, the deliberation over city strategy has been one sided. The public sector is often blamed for its inability to attract business and faulted for its rigidity. Government is admonished to be more efficient and behave like a business. When reformers urge public officials to be more business-like, they mean cities should reduce taxes and work more flexibly to accommodate industry. Seldom do they intend that cities adopt business practices such as having localities merge their resources in order to compete more effectively with business. Even less frequently do they mean that cities should be more aggressive in dealing with business or protect themselves from bidding wars. Rarely do we find strategies designed to improve a city's position in the international marketplace through democratic, participatory institutions.

Is it possible to strengthen a city's bargaining hand? Evidence from our ten cities tells us that some cities have been able to do this and that structural impediments can be modified, if not changed. A sound, long-term strategy is important. The trick is in knowing limitations and making the most of opportunities for cities — both individually and collectively. It is also in knowing what can or cannot be done, in recognizing that not all cities can or should pursue the same course of action, and in setting goals more attuned to the nature of the city than slavishly following fashions of the moment.

CHOICES ABOUT GROWTH, MARKETS, AND DEMOCRACY

The "choice" between growing or dying is not a choice at all but a trap. The ability to choose is crucial to any good strategy. That choice needs to be made in accordance with a city's existing resources and its potential to enhance those resources. Granted, most cities would prefer to grow, and they may even be compelled to seek growth by political pressures. The literature amply demonstrates that growth is aggressively promoted by coalitions of realtors, developers, bankers, utilities, newspapers, and schools.[8] And its allure is potent for good reason. Growth makes politicians happy and officials would much rather cut ribbons than budgets. At least in some systems, it may be difficult to provide

even a meager social agenda without development. Growth may be unequal and lead to enormous social disparities, but most citizens would
rather have something to redistribute than nothing at all. Finally,
growth is propelled by a powerful psychology, feeding on both the fear
of being left behind and the hope of being at the forefront.

Journalists and scholars equate progress, quality, and prestige with
growth.[9] Cities are periodically ranked by their population growth and
carefully watched with each count. Newspapers and electronic media
are quick to announce the "fastest growing cities." We should be careful about these diagnoses and faulty parallels. Growth may be right in
some instance and wrong in others. Growth is neither automatically
good nor bad. It may simply be more appropriate for some cities and
less appropriate for others. Growth can also be misunderstood and mis-
applied. As we point out in chapter 1, some mature cities have lost
population over the past three decades and actually prospered. Paris,
Milan, and preconsolidated Toronto exemplify this pattern. Kenneth
Jackson elucidates this nicely when he points out that Manhattan's population dramatically declined after 1910 because densely occupied space
was filled with landmarks like Rockefeller Center.[10] Statistically, Manhattan was in decline, but in fact it was immensely enriching itself with
soaring property values, public transit, and skyscrapers.

Leo and Brown bring the broader lesson home, showing that Vienna,
Copenhagen, and Rome have been demographically stagnant or have
lost population over the past few decades.[11] By this criterion these cities
would be classified as failing. In reality their magnificence has continued
to this day. Even vastly successful commercial centers like Brussels,
Frankfurt and Hamburg have been demographically stagnant while
continuing to prosper. Since its success with the Olympics, Barcelona is
considered to be one of the most vibrant cities in Europe, yet it incurred
slight population losses between 1981 and 1996.[12] Other cities with
stagnant or decreasing populations are neither booming nor depressed
but reasonably well off. Indianapolis, Winnipeg, Cologne, and Stuttgart
spring to mind.[13] Besides these examples, cities like Detroit, Liverpool,
and Glasgow have actually lost population and endure real decline.
Sharp reductions in population can signal serious deterioration, and
cities need to take strategic action to reverse the trend, but much depends on the circumstances of the city. The point here is that there are
vast differences between different types of cities, and a prescription for
growth carries vastly different consequences. The remedies are different
for different situations, and so should be the choices.

It makes sense that cities should think carefully before rushing headlong into a competitive race for growth. If governments are to exercise
choices over growth, they will have to create strategies that enable them

to act collectively in the international marketplace. There are multiple reasons why this should and can be done. The first is psychological, and part of that psychology requires putting to rest the twin pessimism of determinism and fatalism. With globalization we have reified the marketplace and by now believe its operations are inexorable and its makeup inviolate. Contrary to the stereotype, the international marketplace is not as one-dimensional as some would have us believe. Governments, regional associations, central banks, and international financial institutions (World Bank, International Monetary Fund, World Trade Organization) frequently step into the international marketplace and change it. Also, the movement of international capital is not nearly as untamed as some believe. Most nations have restrictions on where it can flow and encourage where it ought to flow. The U.S. bailout of Mexico during the 1990s, the EU's regulation of monetary policy, and OPEC's curbs on petroleum production are just a few examples of how global markets are regulated. Cities may not yet be major players, but evidence from our study shows that localities can work in tandem with higher-level governments to control larger forces. They can buffer themselves against adverse markets and prevail against raw supply and demand factors. This capacity should be understood and exploited.

Markets are efficient and productive. There is no question that by playing to highly decentralized arenas and to optimally sized populations, markets have outperformed bulky, centralized bureaucracies. And by using the lubricant of rational self-interest and profit, these markets have created record-setting levels of wealth. But markets have also produced huge disparities and unchecked waste. Markets can also fail or ignore whole populations and entire cities. The effects of these imbalances are not only manifest within cities but operate between cities, widening differences and inflating the power of one area to the detriment of another. Markets are plutocracies and respond to those who can turn on or shut off the money spigot. As such, they work for the strong and disregard the weak with consequences that magnify over time. In the 1970s there were differences among our ten cities. Rain-soaked Glasgow and Sunbelt Houston, for example, were never really alike, but both were economically viable and part of a larger world economy. Glasgow survived by brute industrial strength and Houston basked in oil wealth. Toward the end of the century much had changed. Glasgow was industrially broken and marginalized, while Houston glistened with clean industry and had become one of many core cities on the world market.[14]

Markets clear a path for technological progress, but at considerable human cost. Even within the same nation, we see devastating social polarization exacerbated over time. In terms of social affluence the distance between Houston and Detroit was not great during the 1960s. Both cities were populated by blue-collar workers and a stratum of powerful business executives. Over the past three decades the social distances between those cities grew into chasms. Detroit became a sinkhole for wasted industry and Houston thrived as a Sunbelt boomtown. Much the same analogy could be drawn between Milan, which has steadily risen to become a city of high affluence, and Naples, which is mired in poverty and struggling to keep some kind of industrial base. Across nations the distances can be more glaring. Nothing illustrates this better than a comparison of Toronto with Detroit. Both began the 1970s as major cities and both were major centers for automobile manufacture. These cities are not a great distance from one another, located at different sides of the Great Lakes, but today they are worlds apart. Toronto entered the era in sound social condition and by 2000 it had grown into Canada's most upscale sophisticated city. Detroit also entered the era as a reasonably well off union town, led by a powerful industrial elite, but by 2000 had become America's symbol of urban blight. While market conditions accounted for some of the difference, regional and national policies could hardly be discounted in making some areas prosperous and others indigent.

Growth Politics and the Art of Balancing Trade-offs

Only politics allows us to deal with the effects of and compensate for market failures. Good politics can concert local action and bring cities together for mutual cooperation. Collective action can make cities aware of complementary strengths, enable them to assess parameters for growth, and help them set a strategic course. This is no simple matter because development policies are fraught with tradeoffs. Highly competitive market practices can sometimes provide quick injections of capital, invigorate industry, and provide jobs. Yet at the same time they can increase social polarization, tilt imbalances still further, and degrade the environment. It is true that cities require growth in order to redistribute wealth and enjoy the privilege of managing growth. But it is equally valid to be wary of frantic growth or growth at any cost. Cities need to know what they obtain in exchange for the favors they grant investors. Do growth policies yield commensurate payoffs? Do the policies bring "high value" entailing permanent well-paying jobs or "low value" involving intermittent low-paying jobs? Do the benefits serve central city residents or do they leapfrog into more affluent suburbs?

While the scope of our study does not permit us to trace the effects of multiple policies in each of our cities, we can obtain a broad picture. If market policies do anything, they are supposed to create jobs for those

TABLE 9.1
Employment and Unemployment in Dependent Cities, 1991–97

		City	Employment Lost	Percent Change	Unemployment Rate
Market Centered	most	Detroit	− 10,863	− 4.00%	7.90
		Glasgow	− 30,003	− 11.40%	9.87
		Liverpool	− 23,011	− 15.97%	10.37
		Marseilles	− 11,614	− 4.70%	23.30
	least	Naples	− 13,746	− 4.65%	43.00

in need of them. Investment is supposed to "trickle down" to the unemployed and add jobs. For some clues we turn to cities with an unfavorable market position, those that operate in what we call "dependent contexts" (see chapter 7).[i] Using the experience of these cities, we can draw an association between their exuberance for pursuing market policies and their success in garnering employment. Table 9.1 provides a snapshot of how dependent cities and their surrounding suburbs have fared in regard to this criterion over a recent period. The data should give us an idea of how earlier market policies have worked. The table lists cities from most to least market centered.[ii]

As we can see, all of the dependent cities lost jobs. Detroit lost the least number and was down by nearly 11,000 with an unemployment rate of 8 percent. By comparison Glasgow and Liverpool lost 30,000 jobs and 23,000 jobs respectively, and their unemployment rates were slightly higher than Detroit's. During the same period Marseilles and Naples lost 12,000 and 14,000 jobs respectively and their employment rates were well into double digits. As a proportion of total employment, the most market-centered cities lost about as many jobs as the least market-centered ones. We can say that highly market-centered Detroit was able to fend off decline somewhat better than its European counterparts. While Detroit's performance was marginally better, during this period its poverty rate hovered at about 33 percent.[15] All the while substantial development benefits accrued to the suburbs rather than the central city. During this same period, Detroit's suburbs added over 200,000 jobs and experienced half the unemployment.[16] Racial segregation between central city and suburbs remained among the highest in the nation.[iii] Suburbanites were also likely to be the heaviest beneficiaries of subsidized office towers, assembly plants, new waterfronts, and stadiums. They constitute the city's white-collar work force, they hold the highest-paying jobs, and they alone can afford high-priced tickets for sporting events.

While we should not blame market-centered policies for Detroit's problems, they did not appear to be alleviating them. Certainly, when we turn to Europe, the benefits of a market approach are mixed, if not questionable. In Europe the more market-oriented cities fared better on unemployment, but worse on job retention. In fact, social-centered Marseilles and nonmarket-centered Naples do better at holding jobs than more market-centered Liverpool or Glasgow. Moreover, Marseilles shows signs of recovery. Its port has been revived, which has spilled into some downtown rejuvenation. Since the early 1990s cargo increased by close to 50 percent and the port has begun to add jobs.[17]

The paradox of more jobs together with more unemployment may reveal something about social-centered patterns. We see this contrast in two prosperous cities—Paris and New York. During the past decade Paris added 3 percent to its employment base, while New York added less than half that proportion at 1.1 percent.[18] At the same time Parisian unemployment stood at 10 percent while New York's rate was considerably lower at 7 percent.[19] No doubt other governmental policies also influences this outcome. Social benefits tend to be higher on the Continent than in the United States or Great Britain. Generous social benefits in Europe make it more likely that workers will stay home and collect stipends rather than accept lower-paying jobs. Laid-off European workers can often collect 70 or 80 percent of their ordinary wages plus health coverage. Also, the French have reduced the work week to just thirty-five hours without commensurate reductions in pay. This has the effect of maintaining higher-paying jobs, but doing less to offset unemployment. In European eyes it is better not to work than to work at marginal wages.

Other policies may also soften social polarization. Common amenities, free services, and discounted rail fares for the needy can go a long way toward promoting a feeling of equalization. When Europeans talk about social coherence they mean policies that enable diverse classes to partake in similar privileges. James White makes this case for both Europe and Asia, arguing that Paris and Tokyo mitigated social division by focusing on collective benefits and a cultural agenda.[20] Both cities provided high-powered social policies that cut across class lines and absorb masses of people. This strategy stresses social investment, and it can lead to expenses that are difficult to maintain.

These differences in approach provide a clue to our earlier supposition that market-centered policies may be producing an abundance of "low-value" jobs in order to stimulate development, but also producing other liabilities. The market strategy emphasizes short-term, powerful monetary incentives in order to fill urban vacuums with mega projects, but falls short on long-term benefits for the central city. It may hold down unemployment, but it can also exhaust physical and human resources.

To be sure this type of development may draw taxes, revenue, and indirect income. Tangible and immediate renewal can be appealing, and some cities are likely to go it alone in promoting spectacular projects.[21] But is this a smart way to grow? We think not. For one, central-city growth needs to be done in conjunction with suburban growth. Only then can localities exploit complementary strengths and bargain more effectively. Second, if growth policies are to yield substantial returns, interlocal bidding wars must be halted. That is the only way cities can harvest benefits, because whatever else cities may gain by supply-side incentives, they lose in higher taxes, questionable land-use practices, and other costs. Third, localities must learn to share gains so that every participant is rewarded. That is the best way to encourage sound city-building. "Beggar thy neighbor" policies will not do, and are likely to scare away more affluent collaborators. Last, "saving the central cities" requires that central cities also save the suburbs and that each save each other. Much as businesses may form cartels, establish alliances with suppliers, create holding companies or pool information, so too must cities adopt parallel practices. Like business they can do so by showing the divisible and singular benefits to be gained by collaboration.

Before beginning our discussion of strategic alternatives, we underscore that if cities are to bargain effectively, they must have someone at the other end of the negotiating table. Good bargaining requires that cities have viable and confident private investors with whom they can deal. Our approach is neither "pro-business" nor "anti-business," but intended to achieve balance in the bargaining process. Business should neither be so weak as to withdraw from development nor so strong as to dictate development. We seek to avoid the extremes of Liverpool, circa 1980, when private enterprise was forced out of development, as well as the extremes of contemporary Houston, where business exercises unrestrained control over development. Accordingly we believe that there is a role for supply-side incentives. However, those incentives should not be used to pirate industry from one locale to another but to attract fresh capital. Better yet, in an age where localities may be put at a disadvantage, public money can be used to correct bargaining asymmetries.

We now take up some alternate strategies for helping to accomplish these ends. We view bargaining through different territorial, or jurisdictional, scales. We then consider strategies according to their most appropriate territory or jurisdiction. These scales consist of the community territory, the region, and the nation-state. Although international institutions such as the European Union are also of consequence, that scale is beyond the scope of this analysis. These scales often overlap with each other, so that cities can strengthen their bargaining capacity in multiple and complementary ways. They can be viewed as a series of concentric, strategic nets designed to keep cities from falling to the bottom of the bargaining hierarchy.

COMMUNITY DEVELOPMENT APPROACHES

Unlike strategies that stress growth, community development partnerships (CDPs) focus on developing social capital. This usually takes the form of creating small area-programs, community development corporations, and other neighborhood-based activities in "partnership" with public and/or private agencies to upgrade social and economic life in target areas. It has a compelling logic. Poor communities need social organization to obtain economic opportunity. They cannot simply rely on others to revitalize their neighborhoods. Private investors find them unattractive or are unaware of their economic potential. Government agencies find it easy to neglect these disadvantaged areas because they have little political clout. Urban renewal projects often remake poor areas without much attention to their needs and problems. Even when cities succeed in rejuvenating their economies, benefits gained from that renewal are not passed onto neighborhoods. The answer: Get inner-city neighborhoods to invest in themselves and the jobs will follow.

CDP advocates often draw upon the work of Robert Putnam who has highlighted the importance of social capital—associations and norms that enable people to act together effectively to pursue shared objectives.[22] Putnam has shown how social capital played a large role in economic and political development in Italy and in the United States, especially in helping low-income communities get ahead. Accordingly, community development proponents encourage participation in neighborhood organizations and small area-renewal programs to develop the internal social bonds needed for sustaining new economic activities. These organizations are also expected to obtain connections with private foundations, corporations, and government agencies, enabling CDPs to attract resources and investments.[23]

In theory, community development is supposed to engage the poor. Community organizations represent the mobilization of new social capital. To the extent that organizations acquire a grass roots constituency and succeed in many of their objectives, they should increase the capacity of local political problem-solving. As they forge links with important decision makers, they become capable of making claims for a share of power.[24]

It is difficult to generalize about CDPs because there are so many varieties. In Western Europe they are often publicly led; in North America they are often more independent of government and have links with foundations, business corporations, and other private-sector actors. They range greatly in size and resources, from multimillion-dollar operations with large professional staffs to fledgling storefront groups led by volunteers. Some mostly build and manage housing while others are advocacy groups that battle discrimination by lenders and government agencies. The most ambitous ones have comprehensive goals and assume responsibility for job creation and retention, helping small business startups and coordinating social services. Most receive or seek some kind of financial support from government or private-sector "partners" who may also lend technical and political assistance.[iv]

Judged by their recent proliferation, community partnership is an idea whose time has come. In the United States alone more than 2000 community development corporations are up and running.[25] The federal Empowerment Zone program adopted in 1993 officially embodies the community development idea in its strategic rationale.[26] In New York, CDPs dot Harlem, the South Bronx, Bedford Stuyvesant, and other poor neighborhoods. While Houston has been less supportive of these organizations, they have been encouraged in Detroit.[27]

In our European cities, community-based initiatives also proliferated, especially after "social exclusion" became an EU priority. Cuts in expenditures, a self-help philosophy, and devolutionary policies stimulated local partnerships in Liverpool and Glasgow neighborhoods. In Liverpool, the Liberal Democratic majority promoted "bottom-up" policies encouraging communities to formulate "neighborhood plans." One community in the north of the city established a cooperatively owned furniture factory while another established a community-owned housing regeneration company. In Parisian working-class suburbs, some municipalities began community-based factories and cooperatives. Italian cities made less use of CDPs, but some neighborhood councils in Naples and Milan established neighborhood regeneration programs.

Does Community Development Expand Choice?

We lack detailed evidence needed to evaluate all these various community initiatives in our cities, but it is possible to assess their impact on bargaining. From this perspective, we sound a cautionary note. Social capital is not a property of an individual or a group. It is a process that supports a network of relationships that can facilitate access to resources.[28] Thus, increases in social capital matter only when they are enmeshed in a larger system of power.

As a bargaining resource, community development must go beyond mobilizing neighborhood interests and contribute to the formation of what Stone calls "civic capacity."[29] Civic capacity entails building social capital at territorial levels beyond the neighborhood, enabling urban communities to bridge group differences and support broader interaction. As such, cities with ample civic capacity have considerable steering resources. Social capital, partnerships, and popular control allow civic capacity to grow.

Fostering Civic Capacity

Community development operations face major obstacles in contributing to civic capacity. For one, they are by definition quite parochial. Left to themselves, they foster an inward-looking politics, making it difficult to mobilize these constituencies for community-wide cooperation. Failure to take a broader view can only result in community parochialism and what has come to be known as the NIMBY syndrome ("not in my backyard").

Community-style development succeeds only when it becomes part of a broader set of policies and institutions. In his search for the appropriate unit for a democratic political system, Robert Dahl has likened the polity to a set of Chinese boxes. In the smaller boxes of government, political participation is easy, but the issues are often trivial. In the larger scale ones, the matters are more important, but participation must be reduced — perhaps to little more than a single act of voting. As Dahl so aptly puts it, "At one extreme the people vote, but they do not rule; at the other, they rule but there is nothing to rule over."[30]

CDPs also are vulnerable to cooptation. Whether they are dependent upon government or private assistance, community development leaders juggle contradictory political pressures. To mobilize social capital, CDPs must develop a grass roots constituency. At the same time, they need to maintain vertical linkages with resourceful external partners. The dilemma is that the "partnership" aspects of community development — developing networks with resourceful government agencies — discourages leaders from utilizing protests, political campaigns, and advocacy, which may stimulate a mass following but alienate elites.[31] In North American cities, the struggle for grants and private-sector assistance frequently displaces advocacy.[32] Area-based initiatives in our European cities commonly were dependent upon local and national governments. These formal governments usually solicited neighborhoods to overcome anticipated resistance to previously agreed-upon objectives.[33] Not surprisingly, sustaining citizen participation in these programs is a common problem.

Extending the Circle of Community

Given these limitations, community development activities must be linked to organizations capable of aggregating these interests to build civic cooperation around broad issues. In practice *CDP initiatives are contingent on building inclusionary governing regimes that can achieve civic capacity.* CDPs are most successful when supported by friendly regimes that incorporate their goals. For instance, the success of community development organizations in New York's South Bronx was tied to that mercantile regime's support for relatively social-centered housing policies. Although the South Bronx once suffered through devastating abandonment, it has begun to support neighborhood renewal. The most infamous of all streets in the South Bronx, Charlotte Street, was a small revitalization effort run by a neighborhood group taking part in a city-run "sweat equity" project.[v] The success of Charlotte Street prompted other neighborhood organizations to take charge of their streets.

Yet the South Bronx's revitalization was contingent upon the support of a regime that decided to fight housing abandonment. This occurred under the administrations of conservative mayors like Edward Koch and Rudolph Giuliani as well as liberals like David Dinkins. Although these mayors can be criticized for doing too little, it is doubtful that anything could have been achieved without their intervention.[34]

Bargaining, Regimes, and Community Development Politics

Neighborhood success depends on bargaining context and the type of regime sitting at the negotiating table. In entrepreneurial and private dependent contexts, key investment decisions remain largely in private hands. To succeed, CDPs are constrained to make their inner-city areas more competitive and attractive to private capital. Accordingly they focus on finding private benefactors and securing political concessions from benefactors with strong market orientations. By contrast, in dirigiste and public dependent contexts, key investment decisions are lodged in the public sector. In these cases, CDPs function to democratize a highly bureaucratic process. Their success is contingent on securing political incorporation of neighborhood interests in a planning process that is already disposed to public-sector solutions.

A comparison of community development politics in Paris and New York highlights these differences. Paris's planner regime aggregates neighborhood interests through neighborhood city halls and the party system. Neighborhood city halls hold great power in the larger municipal council and in political parties, which is often extended into neighborhood projects. The massive rebuilding of secteur Seine-Sud-Est was led by Jacques Toubon. A member of the municipal council, he served as the mayor of that particular neighborhood and was a leader in the Gaullist Party. Incorporation of neighborhood interests was a natural consequence of Toubon's own power and the city's institutional structure. As these neighborhood interests bargained with national politicians and bureaucrats, they stood a reasonable chance of making their voice heard.

New York's community organizations struggle to balance competing constituencies—sustaining a grass roots presence, obtaining financial support from private and public benefactors, and acquiring political "recognition." To realize these objectives community organizations need resourceful allies, especially in the private sector. Consequently, the largest CDPs include on their boards of directors distinguished political figures, bankers, clergy, foundation representatives, and corporate executives. To take one example, sitting on the board of the renowned Bedford Stuyvesant Restoration Corporation are the chairmen of IBM and Citibank, a former treasury secretary, the head of CBS, and a half dozen other blue-chip corporate and foundation leaders.[35] Though most CDPs do not share such a high profile board, few are without important private sector links, especially to the world of commerce, foundations, and churches. In New York the community struggle is dominated by the need to increase the community's "political value" among the city's luminaries.[36] Here, the most productive strategy may be to obtain legal mandates to require neighborhood consultation in the planning process and raise expectations about the legitimacy of neighborhood claims.

Viable community development also requires adapting civic enhancement to political realities. CDPs must take into account the dynamics of coalition building and interests of politicians. Without securing a place in dominant regimes, minority and neighborhood interests are unlikely to win concessions on their own.[37] For instance, checking bureaucratic power to make room for neighborhood interests is important in planner regimes because professional experts play a central role in decisions. In contrast, CDPs in Houston must seek an expansion of the role of public bureaucracies in economic development—as a means of countering corporate-centered coalition politics.

Although it is difficult to make broad prescriptions, CDPs almost invariably gain by strengthening the role of one institution that we found to be at the core of popular control in our cities—the political party. In every one of our cities party politics influenced civic capacity. Where party politics was more competitive, organized, and capable of bridging diverse groups, it was also a vehicle for expanding citizen participation. No other institution seemed capable of performing this role as well—a finding that has been echoed before.[38]

In this respect, American cities have something to learn from their European counterparts. In virtually every European city, party politics facilitated public power and assisted neighborhood organizations. In Milan the partisan hand in city governance was sufficient to contain business power and facilitate regular neighborhood access. By comparison loose parties or nonpartisan systems in America actually hampered neighborhoods. Only in New York, where elements of competitive party politics remained, did neighborhoods enjoy reasonable access. In nonpartisan Houston, citizen groups and neighborhood advocates had few places to go for help and were powerless in the face of business-led coalitions. Detroit's nonpartisan system also dampened neighborhood activism and relegated those groups to the sidelines.

METROPOLITAN OR REGIONAL INITIATIVES

Three Vehicles for Regionalism

By regionalism we mean the ability of multiple localities within an identifiable geographical setting to work collectively toward common ends. Localities may combine their efforts through loosely organized regional pacts or in more firmly entrenched regional associations. The ends that any regional pact or authority adopts may be broad or narrow. Essentially we are talking about a range of institutional forms that can engage in interlocal cooperation on a metropolitan or regional scale. The means for achieving cooperation can be quite varied. They include 1) multitiered government, 2) linked functions, and 3) complex networks.[39]

Beginning with the *multitiered* vehicle, localities can band together to establish an umbrella institution with metropolitan-wide functions. Under this arrangement localities retain a number of existing functions, but another level of government takes on a discrete set of responsibilities. The "umbrella tier" can be independently elected or separately appointed, and it runs its own bureaucracy that either supplants or supplements responsibilities of "lower-tier" governments. One way to view multitiered government is not as a division between "lower levels" or "higher levels" of authority, but as the formation of different kind of authority designed to deal with "narrow" and "wide" kinds of issues.[vi] One could very well imagine such an authority taking on responsibility for land use, development, and environmental policies. These responsibilities are largely regulatory and developmental in nature, and they accomplish the larger ends of reducing bidding wars and evening out investment. The Greater London Council (1964–86) Metro Toronto (1954–98), and the current Minneapolis/St. Paul Metro are examples of multitiered government.

Next, the *linked functions* vehicle hinges on an agreement between a higher-level government and a single city. Usually the link is developed over a limited set of objectives or responsibilities. The French government uses this extensively to assist cities in realizing particular objectives through a system of contracts with individual cities (*contrat de ville*). These contracts may cover ways in which a city can advance a particular industry (*technopole*), rejuvenate neighborhoods, or adopt strategies for combating social exclusion. Localities voluntarily enter into a *contrat de ville*, and in return for committing themselves to the resolution of a problem receive funding from the national government. This type of linked function has the advantage of flexibility and the ability to address unique needs. The same flexibility and targeted approach has been used in the United States at a metropolitan level. There linked functions have allowed single cities to enter into agreements with their counties in order to share taxes (Louisville), provide services (Charlotte), or support cultural activities (Pittsburgh). In many ways the establishment of a public authority by a state in cooperation with a locality is a type of linked function (see discussion of New York later in this chapter).

A third vehicle for cooperation lies in the *complex networks* approach. Here no tier of government of any substantial nature is added. Rather, officials of existing independent localities make decisions through multiple, overlapping webs of interlocal agreements. Sometimes those agreements can be converted into a single confederation, where officials from existing localities assemble to act in concert. Complex networks are based on voluntary action carried out through horizontal connections. The idea emphasizes efficiency through competitive advantage and synergy by allowing localities to trade on each other's strengths. Complex networks are particularly popular in the United States where local independence is highly valued. Its advocates claim localities can retain independence while also reaping the benefits of cooperation through a rich and intricate net of interlocal agreements or confederations.[40]

None of these institutions is without liability. Multitiered government may appear to reconcile divergent objectives between localism and regionalism, but it has its problems. Efforts to impose regional solutions on "locals" have met resistance. Small cities dislike being told that they must accept an unwanted incinerator or low-income housing for the good of the metropolis. National, state, and provincial authorities have overridden metropolitan governments, presumably for overstepping their bounds. Also, aggressive regulation or redistribution can engender resentment or fears of political competition. Politicians at higher levels of government may look askance at regional or "middle-level" politicians who can command sizeable constituencies. Not surprisingly, metropolitan tiers often find themselves crushed between the grindstones of local and higher levels of government. While metro governments look good on paper, the record is mixed. They appear to do best during their initial years of operation and act with great gusto, but as time goes by the glitter fades. Metropolitan tiers in London and Toronto have been abolished, while the Minneapolis/St. Paul Metro has found itself under fire.[41]

Likewise, linked functions and complex networks are also handicapped. Their partial, flexible, and selective approach can create an impression of being temporary, "band aid" measures. Another difficulty with these approaches is their reliance on self-direction and voluntarism. The perception is that self-direction is also no direction. An absence of comprehensive, agreed-upon objectives can lead to helterskelter policies. Critics would argue that without any central authority, there would be no assurance that regional problems would be addressed. Without strong enforcement, localities could simply disregard any order with which they disagreed.[42] Moreover, weak compliance can only rationalize the status quo. Anything localities do can be explained, ex post facto, as an effort to address regional issues. Last, the *complex networks* approach ignores the stubborn problem of collective accountability: the question of which localities or networks determine overall performance is left open.

Even while taking account of these liabilities, these institutions also have substantial assets. Metropolitan tiers accomplished a great deal when they were given adequate support. London's authority ran the underground, built housing, carried out strategic planning, and defined Greater London by a Green Belt that preserved open space. All this was done with remarkable skill and success. Despite missteps, the Greater London Council was quite popular and its abolition was vigorously opposed.[43] Little more than ten years after abolition, London has turned again to a metropolitan strategic authority led by an elected mayor. Toronto's Metro government also could point to a similar list of accomplishments like fair-share housing, land preservation, and equalized social services. It too enjoyed popular support, and, in the face of abolition, Torontonians came to Metro's defense. Now that it is gone and Toronto's metropolis has expanded, politicians struggle with the need for a regional tier of government. Indeed, it was not so much policies that undid London's and Toronto's multitiered governments, but political punishment from opposition leaders who cultivated a different constituency. While regional governments encounter political problems they are often seen as quite desirable — at least for reasons of good policy and service delivery.

For all the criticism against linked functions and complex networks, both forms of cooperation have steadily gained ground. And while the detractors have a point, they do underestimate the possibilities of these vehicles. Thus, by focusing solely on the ability to compel, critics ignore that localities can find common ground and use that to achieve mutually compatible ends. Voluntarism can be a powerful tool because it is incremental, nonthreatening, and capable of growing by trial and error. Complex adaptation to local conditions may be a good thing, because it is organic and it has the potential to improve the accretion of mutual benefits. There is also a more dynamic issue to be addressed. As metropolitan areas grow outward and into more complex suburbs, new towns, or edge cities, realistic alternatives will be needed for eliciting their cooperation. Complex adaptation permits localities to address what has come to be called the "new regionalism" — an agenda focusing on urban sprawl, the environment, land-use controls, and social equity.[44] The "new regionalism" also explores ways in which governmental institutions can more creatively bring localities together.

Government, Governance, and Regionalism

Both the linked-function and complex-network approaches point up the need to think of regional institutions as more flexible, resilient, and adaptable to rapid change. The urgency is fed by a sharpening dichotomy between notions of government and those of governance. The classic idea of *government* entails formal institutions, elections, established processes of decision making, and administrative structures. Government is an elaborate machine that operates through hierarchical layers of political authority and accountability. Heretofore, most efforts to introduce metropolitan or regional government meant an addition of brand new layers of authority — staffed by a chief executive, a legislative body, and a bureaucracy.[vii] Government is a fairly encompassing form of organization — a legitimate monopoly that takes responsibility for both providing and producing public services. By contrast, *governance* conveys the notion that existing institutions can be harnessed in new ways, that cooperation can be carried out on a fluid and voluntary basis among localities, and that people can best regulate themselves in horizontally linked organizations. Governance also recognizes that localities can provide public services without necessarily producing them. This is accomplished by using other governments or private corporations to undertake interlocal governmental partnerships or public-private partnerships. At least in theory, regional and market power can be joined and enlisted in the service of cities.[viii]

In sum, whereas *government* is vertical and firmly institutionalized, *governance* is flat and flexible. Whereas *government* is formal and directed from above, *governance* is informal and self-regulating. Whereas *government* connects to localities through demarcated procedures, *governance* is looser and less confined by boundaries. *Government* emphasizes the centralizing features of regionalism while *governance* stresses the decentralizing virtues of local cooperation. By and large the multitiered approach is a form of *government*, while complex networks, linked functions, and public-private partnerships are types of *governance*.

We see governance not as a replacement for government, but as an additional mechanism for promoting interlocal cooperation. In many ways governance can bolster strategic nets for cities and enable them to harness or coordinate their bargaining strength. We also note that some types of governance have drawn a good deal of attention because of their adaptability to the global economy. Globalization calls for a simultaneous ability to unify local governments and combine resources, but also plays to their diversity and responsiveness. Smaller governments that can combine resources as the need arises yet innovate under pressure are best suited to the global era.[45] With some degree of success, localities in Europe and North America have used regional institutions to forge partnerships and meet global challenges.[46]

Whether localities are organized through multitiered arrangements or by linked functions or complex networks, our survey suggests that regionalism can enhance citizen choice if it also lends itself to sustaining the bargaining capacity of cities in the capital marketplace. At least in theory, regional intergovernmental cooperation ought to promote the bargaining leverage of localities in several ways.

First, it can broaden the local fiscal base. This enables local governments to more easily substitute public-sector investments for private-sector investments, and it allows cities the opportunity to shift the cost of providing services to governments with a larger and more elastic revenue base. Fiscal regionalism ultimately could encourage local governments to undertake longer-term perspectives in fashioning urban development strategies — in turn, giving greater attention to social priorities rather than just going after every last tax dollar to cover tight local budgets.

Second, regional institutions can expand the territorial reach of regulatory programs aimed at checking the mobility of private capital for public purposes. In Paris, regional institutions worked in consort with the national government to control the movement of industry during the 1970s (through differential taxation, specialized zoning, and the placement of infrastructure).

Third, greater regional cooperation may also limit self-destructive intrametropolitan economic competition that simply moves jobs around without adding any new wealth to the region. For example, throughout the past three decades, New York was unable to stop other localities from luring jobs. Business freely played local governments off against each other and sports teams moved to New Jersey. If a regional prohibition on this form of "sheep stealing" were enforced, there is little doubt that it would have strengthened the bargaining hand of local governments.

Regional institutions have the potential of talking truth to power by conducting policy research. They can enable localities to share information on tax abatements and supply-side inducements to business. They can conduct cost benefit analyses and enable officials to make intelligent decisions about the value of granting tax abatements and the payoff in offering supply-side incentives. They can search for ways to enable localities to merge resources, establish technical training, and maximize public investment. At the very least such cooperation would give localities information needed to make intelligent decisions or launch new initiatives.

Is there evidence that regionalism can actually work in the way theory predicts? Regional governmental intervention was significant in most European cities. In our North American cities it was most significant in Toronto, it played a minor role in New York, a weak role in Houston (functioning through the municipality's vast size), and it was virtually absent in Detroit. Because regionalism is bound up with so many other institutions, it is not easily distinguished from other forms of public intervention, and the effects of regional efforts are all the more difficult to ascertain. Nevertheless, we can trace its strands and offer some generalizations. Most of our cities provide some kind of track record. We begin with the strongest regional efforts.

Putting Regional Theory to Practice

France illustrates complex forms and variations of regionalism. As mentioned in chapter 3 and elsewhere, intergovernmental relations defy neat dichotomies between centralization and decentralization. Indeed, these two traditions can complement each other. In different ways cities are products of each tradition, and regional institutions find themselves at the juncture of local and national action. In Paris, an umbrella tier of regional institutions receives funding from the state and works in collusion with the city and other departments within an enormous area of nearly 5,000 square miles (known as the Ile-de France). Two distinct institutions — a regional council and a social-economic council operate across local boundaries. These institutions assist in infrastructure and transportation, they help build new towns, and they even recruit industry. Almost every major project around and in Paris has been undertaken with regional cooperation. La Défense and, most recently, Paris Rive Gauche are two notable examples.

In Marseilles, regional institutions have grown by increments since the early 1990s. As membership expands, these institutions more closely resemble a complex network. Beginning in 1992, Marseilles began working with three surrounding localities through a public corporation. In this early stage interlocal cooperation focused on minor projects like roads and traffic. Gradually, and with incentives from the state, that cooperation grew and by 2000 it encompassed eighteen localities. What has come to be known as a Communauté Urbaine, is now overseen by a common regional body drawn from the local mayors and councilors of the region's constituent municipalities. Marseilles's Communauté Urbaine now collects a common tax on business, substantially eliminating the incentive for localities to bid against one another for private investment. Interlocal funds are now used to build infrastructure, provide amenities, construct social housing, and stimulate development. The grand project opening the city to the sea, EuroMéditerranéen, is also supported and represented by this newly emerging form of regional governance.

French regional institutions also show some capacity for intelligence gathering. Both Paris and Marseilles have research agencies that gather data, conduct examinations of policy alternatives, and serve as important conduits of information on planning and development. These organizations also search for ways in which interlocal cooperation can reach beyond national boundaries. While, they are not equipped to conduct extensive cost benefit analyses, they have the potential to do so.

Toronto also presents a case for regionalism based on a multitiered approach. For decades the Toronto region was served by a triple alliance between province, Metro, and city. It was formed when the City of Toronto was one-half of the region's population and held about three-quarters of its tax base. As an umbrella tier of government, Metro Toronto guided the area's growth. It assumed responsibility for overall land-use planning, transportation, and infrastructure systems within a 240-square-mile jurisdiction. Acting in cooperation with the province, Metro Toronto displayed all the capability one could expect of a regional government. It provided regional revenue sharing, dispersed social housing, and funneled capital investment into strategic areas — all done without subjecting its constituent governments to severe "place wars."[47] In recent years Metro's position was undermined when the provincial government refused to allow its jurisdiction to expand beyond its original 240 square miles. The province also turned down proposals for a regional complex network of local governments and is now debating whether to put one in place.[48]

The Greater Toronto Area now has a population of 4.5 million and is scattered over 2,700 square miles of city, suburb, and rural areas. Without a regional institution, the bargaining capacity of consolidated Toronto has begun to diminish. Not surprisingly, the city has begun to shift toward market-centered approaches. If past experience is any guide, Toronto's success in managing growth, equalizing revenues, and resisting rapacious intrajurisdictional competition could be weakened. Whether based on a multitiered institution, a complex network, or a linked function, only a regional institution can fully rekindle those policies.

In other European cities regional approaches show a spotty record of helping poor central cities. While Italian regional institutions played only a marginal role in development, they have been able to exert some influence. An umbrella tier, called the Lombardy Regional Council, was able to assert an important mediating role in planning transportation within Milan. Another umbrella tier, the Campania Regional Council, coordinated earthquake assistance in Naples. These instances of partial achievement suggest that regionalism can work with some moderate effect. Milan and Naples might profit from expansion of regional governance — but this has not yet occurred.

The difficulty with Italian regional institutions lies in their inability to effectively implement broader mandates, and do so honestly. In the Neapolitan region, the history of development policies is strewn with haphazard planning, internal bickering, and corruption. In an effort to rescue regionalism, the European Union helped set up the Naples Integrated Operation. This consisted of an attempt to rationalize the administration of extant public services and public investments. Despite this effort, vast sums of money were misdirected or left unspent. Unfortunately the EU's efforts were terminated during the 1990s without leaving much of a mark.

At least in theory, one of the more potent regional strategies occurred in Glasgow. An umbrella tier of government, called the Scottish Development Agency (SDA), aggressively shaped the city's development. It dwarfed the role played by the smaller Strathclyde Regional Council. Unfortunately, Glasgow's regional gamble did not pay off, as theory would predict. True, the SDA initially sought to check the city's decline by undertaking various compensatory measures, and it targeted investments into the worst black spots. Over time, however, SDA policies promoted indiscriminate growth throughout the region. It seemed that the SDA umbrella was much too wide, and this only fueled suburban development, leaving Glasgow behind. The SDA also catered to the private sector, forcing city officials to place their bets on downtown job strategies that bypassed the neighborhoods.

To Glasgow's south lies Liverpool. As with other local governments in England, a type of linked function exists between Liverpool and the central government over land-use controls. All planning applications in excess of 100,000 square feet must be submitted to and approved by a central ministry. The process is an elaborate one involving a planning inspector, a public inquiry, an official report, a planning decision, and possible judicial review. Cities have an opportunity to comment on those applications and often do voice their criticisms and objections. In Liverpool suburban retail malls have been turned down, and it is by now common knowledge that very few have a chance of being approved. This helps curtail sprawl and prevents investments from being drained away from the city. Also, a complex network called the Northwest Regional Assembly has begun to support efforts to modernize the rail system and rebuild infrastructure. The assembly also facilitates discussions with nearby Manchester over concentrating urban development within designated areas and sharing resources.

Obviously America's relationship to regionalism is different. In New York very attenuated forms of regional cooperation are at work — mostly as a linked function between localities and the states of New York and New Jersey. The major effort at developing these links centers on the bistate Port Authority of New York and New Jersey and a single state agency called the Metropolitan Transportation Authority. Both of these agencies deal with a narrow set of functional responsibilities. The Port Authority manages regional bridges, airports, and some mass transit lines. It is largely concerned with facilitating and stimulating economic development. The Metropolitan Transportation Authority confines its responsibilities to rail transportation, mostly between the city and a vast array of surrounding suburbs. While these agencies manage development at the margins, both are creatures of their respective states. With limited discretion and power confined to functional tasks, neither of these agencies has been able to exercise a bold regional strategy.

Even by American standards Houston's efforts at regionalism are weaker and characterized by entirely different dynamics with an altogether different result. It is largely confined to absorbing taxable territory and embracing new development. Although technically not a regional government, Houston's political control over more than 625 square miles functionally gives it enormous range. As Houston's territorial boundaries have grown, however, economic and political pressures have militated against the city acting like a regional government — at least as reformers conceive it. The city has continued to pursue its traditional pro-growth strategies of expanding into the region, even at the cost of depriving older inner areas of attention. Measures to resist further annexation come from the state government, pressured by suburban voters wanting to remain apart. The idea of balanced development, equity, and the restoration of central city neighborhoods seems alien to Houston's regionalism. Taken alone and without the reinforcing policies of the larger region, the state, or the nation, Houston's "single-city regionalism" is narrowly gauged to enhance market-centered policies.

The experience of our cities with regional institutions shows some positive outcomes. Regionalism works well in some integrated intergovernmental systems. This is particularly true of France, where there is a great deal of overlap among programs. French localities are covered with a net of sustaining programs, and regionalism is an important part of this net. Also, regionalism has grown in importance, and it is looked upon with increasing favor by both elites and a larger public. A certain degree of redundancy may help create a healthy political environment for regionalism. It may be that a tiered (umbrella) organization, linked functions, and complex networks can work to reinforce each other, plugging holes or picking up tasks where that becomes necessary. In both France and Italy regional cooperation is a way of democratizing development or providing a measure of equity among localities. By our own reckoning, reforms encourage political participation, add to the steering capacity of local government, and enhance its bargaining power.

Toronto also shows that a certain degree of redundancy may have favorable results. After all, Toronto's success was based on a triple alliance among the province, the city, and Metro government. In effect, multitiered government and linked functions operated simultaneously to sustain development and support social-centered strategies. While we would be cautious about predicting a similar outcome for a looser form of governance between consolidated Toronto and other localities, we would suggest that provincial support is critical.

Used appropriately, regionalism can also assist in retaining scarce capital. Liverpool's embryonic efforts toward recovery are helped by central government keeping the suburbs from sprawling around it. This encourages development and concentrates infrastructure where it is most needed. Moreover, regional efforts show promise that advances can be sustained with each success. The EU, the central government, Liverpool's Liberal Democrats, and its chamber of commerce all press for regional cooperation, and it has become the focus of elite attention in that city. Here outside interests and linked functions have provided a thin edge of a wedge that has been used to stimulate other forms of regional cooperation, such as the initiatives taken by the Northwest Regional Assembly.

Applied inappropriately, regionalism has a downside. Glasgow found that SDA officials became increasingly absorbed in helping fast-growth suburbs in its "Silicon Glen" corridor rather than in trying to revive inner-city neighborhoods. In a more general way Glasgow's experience tells us that when a regional institution is very extensive and less accountable to localities, it can fail to help cities. There are instances where regional institutions bolster their own particular identities and compete as regions with other largely scaled regions. Regional organization then takes on a life of its own as a supragovernment. This "big box" view of regional interests is unlikely to give high priority to cities that do not contribute to regional economic performance. The wider the regional boundaries, the more likely it will respond to big suburban voting blocs. Politics being what it is, powerful interests will discourage "big-box governments" from becoming reliable urban allies.

The case for regional strategy seems to make most sense for fairly compact metropolitan areas where it can be demonstrated that there are salient common socioeconomic interests served by greater regional governance. Here, it may be possible that highly visible social interdependencies, which actually generate common issues and sharing of interests, help bring about political support for policies to enhance fiscal equity and regional development. Common problems and reasonably homogeneous populations then seem to be best served by regional efforts. Similarly, limited forms of cooperation, such as the *contrat de ville* in France, may also create a firm foundation for strengthening cities.

What is clear is that while regionalism can help it is no magic bullet. It is simply a tool that can be used or misused. Also, regionalism is a product of local attitudes and culture (those of France versus those of Italy), it can be overdone and work against cities (as in Glasgow), and it can change over time (as in Toronto). Last, regional reform requires choosing appropriate forms of regional cooperation for each specific political context. In some cases it can help promote other regional efforts (as in Liverpool), but it must be shaped to accommodate particular political and economic realities.

NATIONAL INITIATIVES

Why National Urban Policy

The nation-state is by no means becoming helpless. Despite fears about the weakening or "hollowing out" of the national state,[49] our survey shows national governments to be enormously resilient. Central governments in France, Italy, and the United Kingdom have a commanding presence in their cities, and Canada continues to share national presence with its provinces. Nations lacking a strong national hand, like the United States, have chosen to withdraw from central-city problems. That the United States is a powerful economic actor suggests that there is a difference between weak government and limited government. Some governments choose to limit their scope of policy action and devolve power to localities and regions. Yet, as the European cases show, that is a far cry from sloughing off national responsibilities. Devolution can also mean redefinition of national power with the nation-state coordinating and supporting specific local roles.

Cities and regions are sometimes portrayed as replacing the nation-state as the essential actors on the global stage.[50] This mirror-image thinking rests on the assumption that if one party is gaining another must be losing. As a matter of course, both city regions and nation-states have become more active on the global stage, and their mutual presence is complementary. Nothing reveals this as much as the activities of the European Union, which has forged multisided partnerships among nations, localities, regional associations, and private enterprise. In North America, provinces and states are helping localities function in the international marketplace. Trade delegations, financial alliances, cultural exchanges, and globing warming treaties are the embryonic manifestations of a cooperative public presence in the international arena. The truth is, globalization has brought a proliferation of multisided partnerships and policy adaptations responding to its pressures. In many ways we are experiencing what could be called "pooled sovereignty," enabling individual states to undertake collective action at a supranational level. Seen from this perspective, the importance of the nation-state in taming the international marketplace has been enhanced rather than diminished.

One should be cautious about assuming the benevolence of national governments. While national intervention may limit city dependence on the capital marketplace, it also increases dependence on the public sector and it can subject local citizens to the vicissitudes of a national constituency. Furthermore, national decisions that shape the future of particular cities are made at a distance and their regulations can suffocate local initiative and effectiveness. Too often, national policies become centralized policies and treat all cities as if they confronted the same problems. This policy straight jacket forces local officials into a numbing mindset of conforming to regulations and squirreling away outside money, instead of addressing problems at hand.

There are other difficulties with national urban policy. While national policy can help cities to expand choices, it also can be turned against them. This occurred in Great Britain, when Thatcher governments turned against the demands of poorer cities. It happened in the United States, especially after the election of Ronald Reagan, when big cities became marginalized in national elections and subordinated to a suburban dominated Sunbelt. Similarly, in Italy the past ten years or so have witnessed pressure for national flight from the problems of cities in the country's poor South.

Having expressed these caveats, we also point out that only national government can provide stable, long-term and encompassing protections for cities. There are many reasons for this.

First, only national governments can provide critical regulations, such as minimum wages and social safety nets that have uniform impact throughout the nation. This not only softens disparities among classes, but it also dissuades employers from seeking low-wage and low-benefit locations. While national protections of this kind do not prevent companies from moving abroad, they do dampen the urge to play city labor markets off against each other. National grants in aid play a similar function, limiting bidding wars over private capital. In the United Kingdom most local taxes are passed along to the central government and then "rebated" back to localities in the form of needs-based grants. This ensures a minimum level of public resources for all cities, dampening the need to chase so-called tax ratables. Recently, this has been enormously important to Liverpool, allowing it to hold onto its scarce capital instead of having it slip off to the suburbs. While France allows mayors to retain local business taxes, its system of subventions to local government and restrictions on bidding for business dampens any capital flight.

Second, national policies are necessary for many regional and community-based efforts to succeed. Whatever the advantages of regional strategies, they run the risk of diminishing over time as they are adopted by many jurisdictions. If this happens, tax and job competition on a regional scale simply replace intercity rivalry. Given this scenario, business interests would be likely to play one region against another, much as they do with cities today. There is also a more localized reason for national intervention. Working at the national scale also helps cities at the neighborhood level because tax sharing and equalization enables revenue-starved municipalities to respond to narrower neighborhood claims.

Third, national urban policies can spark new initiatives that increase the city's choices. As local economies have become more competitive over the past thirty years, many national governments have provided policy support to enable cities to revitalize themselves without paring down social commitments. In Paris and Marseilles national governments supplied the backbone of a social agenda while supplying funds to rebuild decrepit rail yards and sagging waterfronts. In Glasgow a Labour government launched inner-city initiatives, resulting in the birth of a special development agency to regenerate the city's most impoverished neighborhoods. In Liverpool, City Challenge grants were essential for beginning the revitalization of its downtown, the effect of which has now begun to spill into adjoining neighborhoods. Even in the

United States, Urban Development Action Grants helped spark the revitalization of downtown areas in Detroit and New York. National policies to save ailing savings and loan institutions helped prevent losses in Houston's property markets, enabling the city to undertake new strategies for economic diversification during the 1990s. These successes have now begun to flow into other parts of the city.

Fourth, national governments can supply equal access to the fiscal and political resources that enable cities to pursue a wider choice of development strategies. This enabled even poor cities, like Marseilles, to combine smart growth, concentrated development, neighborhood preservation, and port revitalization in renewing its economic base. Marseilles's options contrast dramatically with those of Detroit. Left largely to its own devices over the course of thirty years, Detroit found itself devoting its resources to build sports stadiums, gambling casinos, and luxury office towers at the expense of education and city services. Long-term human capital approaches to urban development require "patient" commitments of resources that are difficult to sustain without the help of national governments with their large and elastic tax bases.

Fifth, only national government investments can make cities truly indispensable. National governments control vast resources that transcend local, provincial, and regional boundaries. In Europe national presence is felt in every major city through mega development projects, public housing, government institutions, roads, ports, and, not least of all, a rail system. Simply put, other governments cannot duplicate the enormity and scope of national activities in infrastructure investment and social safety nets. In most of Europe nationally sponsored rail lines nurtured urban rejuvenation. Almost every major development in Paris and Marseilles is captioned by extended rail lines, renovated rail stations, and high-speed trains — all of which are connected to local metro systems.[ix] France's great pride, the TGV, can transport people from downtown Paris to downtown Marseilles in little more than three hours.[x] The TGV is luxurious, its fares are surprisingly inexpensive, and the ride is splendid. Most importantly, this kind of transportation makes cities more vital. What economists call a "positive externality" gives the city unmatched strategic importance and makes it an invaluable site for business.

National Policy Transfer

It would be naive to believe that European-style policy could be or even should be duplicated in the United States or Canada. Still, from the standpoint of urban development, vertically integrated governments have many advantages. As we saw in previous chapters, European-style policies have enabled cities to bargain and entertain policy alternatives that few cities in federal governmental systems could match. Unitary systems can force tax sharing, regulate local and regional economic competition, and award urban aid with enormous latitude.[xi] These systems also have disadvantages. Central control may stifle local policy initiative, excessively concentrate power, and breed local conformity. Nevertheless, the American and Canadian federal systems could borrow from European successes in managing competition by adapting a more indigenous approach.

Even federal systems could do more to curtail harmful intralocal bidding wars, especially when these wars result in merely moving jobs around without adding productivity. While national governments lack the policy and administrative finesse to directly make such distinctions, they could act indirectly through tax policy. Thus, national government could legitimately tax the value of supply-side benefits given to corporations by localities that have lured them away from other places. Again, this would only apply to relocating businesses, but it could include bites into tax abatements, free land, and specially provided infrastructure. From the standpoint of tax theory, this makes good sense because supply-side benefits constitute assets given to a corporations and entail a reduction of ordinary expenses. Normally these inducements would be subject to tax. While these measures might not eliminate all giveaways, the accelerated costs for such gifts would dampen the propensity to offer them.

In the event business is provided with incentives to move to another locality, government might also initiate social/economic impact reviews or SIRs.[51] Like environmental impact reviews, SIRs would assess both positive and negative results of a corporate move. This would include the provision of additional jobs, possible revenues that would accrue to a locality, the need for additional housing, social dislocation, and the like. At the very least, SIRs would constitute a formal step in informing the public about the consequences of bidding wars. Maximally, it would encourage the citizenry to become more directly involved in decision making, enabling them to lobby for beneficial outcomes. Measures of this kind also would have offshoot public benefits. They would stimulate government agencies to disseminate information, inform localities about making cost benefit analyses, and offer a comparative picture of how cities are affected.

When corporations do move they often leave behind unemployment lines, falling property values, disused roads, rail spurs, and other undepreciated infrastructure—the cost of which is born by localities. National policies should be careful about obstructing the free movement of capital, but more could be done to reimburse localities for the social costs of business relocation. European governments have been able to socialize these costs by spreading them across society and by including a tap on corporate profits. In America tax charges could work in tandem with capital investment to ensure that corporations help pay off undepreciated infrastructure and that money could be put in a special fund and used to generate new development.

The tax code could also be made as neutral as possible with respect to subsidizing capital relocation. Accordingly, companies that relocate to other localities should be limited in the amount of tax credits and deductions they can apply for the cost of new plants and equipment. As part of a tax policy approach, the French have used differential taxes to provide place-based incentives or penalties. This was applied in France to decentralize industry from Paris, and taxes were lifted in the central city while commensurately reduced in peripheral areas. Place-based tax policy could be applied in the United States in an opposite manner, so that higher taxes are levied on the development of valuable green space and commensurately reduced in central cities.[xii]

Perhaps the most valuable ways of deploying national assistance to enhance city bargaining is through national fiscal programs that lessen reliance on local revenue sources. National programs that distribute revenues to local authorities on the basis of need-based formulas ensure a minimum standard of public services for all communities. By limiting local property and sales taxes in preference for national tax sharing schemes, localities would be less inclined to sacrifice public amenities and environmental protections. Tax equalization via national revenue sharing would give local regimes new bargaining opportunities. Our own findings overwhelmingly suggest that a certain degree of revenue independence changes the bargaining atmosphere and enables localities to negotiate quid pro quos like green space, height limitations on buildings, and responsible architectural standards.

Equally desirable is the idea of introducing a public presence into capital investment for public development agencies. National, state, or provincial governments should invest in these projects, and where appropriate guarantee bonding, as they do in Britain and in the Continental nations. This would free local development officials from the narrow investor perspective for which they are famous, yet provide accountability for their activities.[52]

Finally, national transportation policy can be altered to make the most of the economic and social value of cities. Americans have loved highways but at enormous social cost. With the adoption of the National Interstate and Defense Highway Act of 1956, highway expenditures have dominated national transportation budgets. This had a profound impact on cities because the character of highways means that development patterns will be extremely fluid. Automobiles expand the uses for land, making settlement patterns more explosive — almost randomly apportioned by points along fluid highway corridors. To appreciate that argument, think of the multiple exits one can take along interstate corridors and the local roads onto which people can fan. Compare this to rail terminals, which are relatively fixed and where settlement is clustered around set points, such as traditional cities, small villages, and new towns. In Europe a national railway system makes compact development possible, and this is one reason why France, Italy, and Great Britain have been able to concentrate development in cities and new towns instead of sprawling suburbs.

Obviously, not all of America or even Canada are proper candidates for mass rail transportation. Feasible mass transportation requires reasonable masses of people who can use a system efficiently. But urban corridors are proper candidates for a state-of-the-art rail system coupled to local mass transit. A national policy of capital investment in heavy and light rail would give cities an immense boost. Once accomplished, cities would recapture their competitive advantage and add to national well-being.

While we have placed our attention on policy transfer from Europe, there are also things Europeans can learn from North American free markets and federalism. One talent Americans display is the ability to create social slack for innovation and creativity. Heavily centralized government can suffocate healthy change, and cities need to breathe in order to attract a vital amalgam of ideas and capital. Europeans might allow for unused factories and warehouses to be more easily converted into nonmanufacturing or residential uses. Outright prohibitions of land-use conversions are bad enough, but European taxes on the transfer of property can be onerous. Also, freezing land prices and surcharges on land speculation does stifle entrepreneurship and cultural creativity. While often done for good reason, Europeans could be more alert to the tradeoffs between protecting existing uses and opportunities for inventing new, productive uses.

Used strategically, supply-side incentives can also be an excellent tool for bargaining and development. Basically, these incentives should not be used to move industry from one locale to another but to form new capital. America's Urban Development Action Grants (UDAGs), Community Development Bloc Grants (CDBGs), and, to a lesser extent, Empowerment Zones (EZs) sometimes succeeded in attracting new development by providing flexible formulas for joining public and private capital. In many ways they have provided a stimulus for well-placed projects in the central city.[53] New York's South Street Seaport and the area around Grand Central Station are examples of how public and private money can be combined to regenerate derelict structures and extend renewal into adjacent areas.

Finally, Europe recently has rediscovered regionalism, and national governments have encouraged greater political devolution.[54] The reasons for this vary, but we do see a renewed appreciation for smaller-scale and more flexible regional governance. North American federalism has long experience with territorial decentralization and has developed highly innovative forms of public entrepreneurship.[55] More flexible forms of local cooperation like complex networks have been able to borrow on the differing strengths of localities and sometimes use private firms or nonprofit organizations to provide public services. Federally sponsored Metropolitan Planning Organizations have been able to work across jurisdictions in bringing about compliance for clean air standards. These possibilities are worthy of consideration.

CONCLUSIONS

Although market-centered growth attracted a good deal of attention, these policies had substantial downsides and achievements were spotty. In many ways market-centered policies engendered deeper social inequalities and reinforced the distance between city and suburb. At least in the poorer or dependent cities, we find that localities choosing to retain their social agendas did about as well as their market-centered counterparts. Our initial observation that good growth is "smart growth" appears to bear up to thirty years of experience. Above all, balanced strategy is critical for achieving equilibrium between growth and preservation.

Growth is certainly important for the redistribution of wealth and may be valuable for some cities, but it should not be pursued for its own sake or uncritically accepted. We find that cities are best off adopting a strategic approach to growth, and we have outlined three scales or strategic policy nets through which development can be approached. Taken alone, these strategies are not likely to change urban fortunes. Cumulatively they could make a substantial difference. Community-based, regional, and national urban policies work best when they are done in conjunction with one another. Community-based strategies furnish critical social capital, citizen involvement, and flexibility. They can also be used to enhance local representation at the bargaining table. Regional strategies can provide important coordination among localities and can control local bidding wars. A national strategy can furnish an encompassing and embracing foundation from which cities can build bargaining strength. Again, there are no guarantees that strategies will always work as they are theoretically portrayed. The world is filled with unintended consequences and much depends on specific political, social, and economic contexts.

NOTES

i. We use these cities because they have experienced similar distress. Also, de-industrialization has led them to pursue different strategic routes toward recovery. This provides a useful, albeit incomplete, test for how well market policies have fared.

ii. Employment is shown by place of work while unemployment is by place of residence. As a general rule, employment is confounded by national and regional trends, so the results should be interpreted with caution.

iii. For metropolitan Detroit the racial index of dissimilarity in 1990 was .83, which means that 83 percent of the black population would have to move into white areas in order to achieve complete integration.

iv. In the United States foundations, corporations, and individuals contributed more than $2 billion to support community development efforts between 1970 and 1990 (Pierce and Steinbach 1990).

v. Mittiga, "Revitalization in the South Bronx"; Rooney, *Organizing the South Bronx*. "Sweat equity" projects were sponsored in New York by city hall. This program sold abandoned houses for one dollar. These organizations then rebuilt derelict buildings and passed ownership to those who had worked on the project.

vi. A division of labor among tiers is key to this type of government. Some services may be better provided at a higher or lower level depending upon whether the goal is to maximize efficiency, effectiveness, equity, or accountability. Further, this often depends on the type of service, whether capital or labor intensive, and the local context.

vii. For purposes of this chapter we use the terms "metropolitan" and "regional" synonymously.

viii. Some accounts of governance view this arrangement more narrowly, as a method of launching mostly public-private partnerships, and are worried about its implications. In particular European scholars see it as robbing public power and diluting state sovereignty. American scholars view it more benignly, as a way of making local governments more efficient as well as encouraging local cooperation to manage new problems. We do not take up a more critical analysis in this section because our objective is to search for viable strategies rather than engage in a critique. For a critique of regionalism and governance see *Journal of Urban Affairs*, 23, no. 5 (2001), issue titled "Regionalism Reconsidered," edited by Frances Frisken and Donald Norris." See especially Frances Frisken and Donald Norris, "Regionalism Reconsidered," and Donald Norris "Prospects for Regional Governance under the New Regionalism: Economic Imperative Versus Political Impediments," and Todd Swanstrom, "What We Argue About When We Argue About Regionalism."

ix. In Milan the city's ambitious plan to decentralize business activity was predicated on taking advantage of investments in national rail links (see chapter

4). Great Britain has lagged behind the rest of Europe in modernizing its rail system, and some would say it is in shambles. Nevertheless, it is a functioning system that covers the nation. Liverpool's own effort at downtown regeneration is centered near a new rail station. Because Britain's rail service has been privatized in recent years, however, rail closures have had devastating effects on many cities.

x. TGV stands for "*le train de grande vitesse*" or, fast train.

xi. In Europe this is also accomplished by the European Union. In Canada, bans of this kind were established at the provincial level, and in America, states like Michigan do have legislation that makes it difficult for localities within the state to raid one another with supply-side incentives.

xii. In a federal system this kind of tax policy would be more appropriate for individual states than national government.

Chapter Ten

CONCLUSIONS: CITIES NEED NOT BE
LEAVES IN THE WIND

It may be that without the pressure of social forces,
political ideas are stillborn: what is certain is that
these forces, unless they clothe themselves in
ideas, remain blind and undirected.
— Sir Isaiah Berlin

Putting Globalization in Perspective

During the Summit of the Americas in April 2001, thousands of protesters took over the old city of Quebec. As they voiced their objections
to a proposed Free Trade Agreement, the crowds struggled against riot
police whose use of tear gas and truncheons dominated media images.
Journalists and officials saw this as an extension of the civil disturbances and demonstrations launched a year earlier in Seattle at the meeting of the World Trade Organization (WTO).[1] The Seattle confrontation
was even worse: police in full riot gear moved into the crowd with
armored personnel carriers while firing tear gas and rubber bullets.
While some of the protests involved peaceful teach-ins, masked youths
also rampaged through the streets, smashing shop windows. The city
was placed under curfew. Seattle's mayor declared a civil emergency and
the governor called in the National Guard. In response, human rights
activists set up a people's tribunal that indicted Union Carbide, the Gap,
and other firms for "crimes against humanity."

Normally opposition to international capitalism in the West is sporadic and less violent. But heightened fear and violent opposition to
global capitalism has marked the turn of our new century. Campaigns
against its institutions have become commonplace, and distrust of free
trade has mounted. International organizations, such as the WTO and
the World Bank, are under intense scrutiny. Political operatives from all
sides of the spectrum — conservative as well as liberal — often share suspicion of the new international economy no matter what their senti-
ments on domestic economic issues. Apprehension is everywhere. Price
wars, massive rates of immigration, expanding multinational corporations, the power of supranational organizations, threats of global recession, and rising social imbalance raise severe doubts about the wisdom
of a global strategy. Antiglobal movements are growing and the events

in Seattle and Quebec have been followed by volatile protests in Prague, Goteborg, Genoa and, Brussels.

Are these protests justified? Does globalization menace our cities? Do radical swings of boom and bust compromise the economic stability of our cities? Can urban democracy survive when footloose capital and expanding international competition limit the importance of place? What does an age of interdependence portend for the future of local democracy? These questions beg for answers.

We cannot predict the future, much less be sure about all of our answers. From what we have been able to gather, however, these fears appear misplaced. Our study suggests that globalization is not an inexorable, limiting force, and we should be careful not to reify it. The future will depend at least as much on the decisions governments make as on the dynamics of the international marketplace. Critics of the new global economy frequently discount the importance of politics in shaping this phenomenon. Yet governments at all levels continually engage global markets, and in doing so will define and shape them.

In previous chapters we described thirty years of sustained participation in the international marketplace by cities, their citizens, intergovernmental allies, and supranational organizations. Our major conclusions are simple, though they conjure up a raft of meanings and inferences. Cities have choices, those choices vary with differential resources, and they are not without constraint. But they are nonetheless choices that can be applied. And most importantly, urban choices are not immutable, but capable of expansion, constriction, and modification. Or to put the emphasis somewhat differently, cities are not mere leaves in the wind of internationalization, but political entities that in many different ways shape economic outcomes.

These observations are consistent with Karl Polanyi's trenchant insight about the industrial revolution and its aftermath.[2] Writing about the relationship between markets and society, Polanyi observed that societies do and must play an active role in determining how markets will work. Polanyi went on to describe how the modern social order evolved and achieved two distinct objectives: one to organize a self-regulating market, and second, to modify it through political intervention, shaping it for social ends. In debunking market utopianism, Polyani saw that economic revolutions are as much about politics as they are about economics. Current globalization is no exception. Examined in historical context, discussions about globalization should not be about conforming to a new order thrust upon us by impersonal forces, but about how to manage its turbulence, shape it dynamics, change its impact, and ultimately use its power for human betterment.

Our ten cities show how government, people, and policy adapt to globalization. We have described how the great transformation of the last thirty years unleashed new forces. It precipitated a vast restructuring of urban centers, widespread deindustrialization, a thorough decentralization of city populations, and the creation of national and cross-national interdependencies. Governments were not passive nor were they relegated to simply mediating larger economic forces. On the contrary, government exercised control over the use of land, the infusion of public capital, and the allocation of critical assets. Furthermore, politicians at all levels mobilized populations, entered into complex arrangements with business, and managed capital investment. In doing so, they shaped the built environment, the social order, and the local economy. Bargaining between cities and capital was not an exception, but an integral and crucial part of city building.

Although we found evidence of policy convergence among our cities, their continuing diversity also stood out. We began this volume by purposely choosing cities that were quite different from one another and proceeded to travel along their paths of development. Now at the end of that voyage we find that diversity has continued. Rather than responding uniformly to global change, our ten cities have shown an ability to forge altogether novel responses. Some localities adopted strong market-centered strategies; they played to private enterprise and the unrestrained swells of the economy. Other cities resorted to equally powerful social-centered strategies; they placed their bets on public direction and the controls of a mixed economy. Some provided enormous social and collective benefits for their citizenry, while others paid attention to revenue streams. All of these responses touched on the deepest matters of public policy involving taxation, economic development, housing, open space, historic preservation, and the very prosperity of cities.

Indeed, we discovered that globalization could be used in more than one way — either to apply newfound prosperity toward social policy and collective benefits or to rationalize market driven solutions and inducements for business. Again, we were able to confirm that urban policy is not ordained by a raw interpretation of globalization, but by particular institutions, attitudes, conditions, and power groupings within a city. In the broadest sense, politics defines how global pressures are treated.

The physical differences among our cities abound. Paris, Toronto, and Milan resisted dramatic skylines and corporate dominance of their urban cores, instead choosing to retain much of their historic character. Other cities like Houston and New York were far more accommodating to anything business would throw their way. Naples tended more to internal political exigencies than to industry, while Glasgow focused on a culture strategy to refurbish its downtown. Socioeconomic values also differed. For some cities economic growth was a sine qua non, while others stressed a strong cultural agenda. More commonly, cities did not perceive this as an either-or choice but combined and complemented strategic policies. Thus, "mix and match" approaches were liberally blended to optimize city bargaining.

We found that differences in strategy are linked to a city's bargaining resources, treated in our conceptual schema as *driving* and *steering* variables. The driving variables of market conditions and intergovernmental support gave cities the wherewithal to finance collective benefits and great projects. The steering variables of popular control and local culture allowed them to decide exactly what to pursue and what was to be most valued. These were not mechanistic decisions, but the product of human action and coalition building. Local regimes sailed the winds and tides of our variables in different ways—some regimes took substantial advantage of intergovernmental aid, while others made substantially less use of it; some regimes maximized popular preferences while others generally ignored them.

How Cities Vary in the International Marketplace

Our survey of ten cities revealed that some localities have greater choices than others. The international marketplace is not of one piece, and cities engage it on different terms. Variations in bargaining permit some local governments to muster considerable leverage over capital investment, while others must struggle against the odds. Specific bargaining contexts may empower or disable cities. Paris and Toronto enjoyed a felicitous confluence of economic, political, and social advantages, and this enabled officials to set the terms of negotiation. More than a few times urban planners had the luxury of turning aside proposals for office buildings, shopping centers, and other job-producing investments. By contrast less fortunate places held far fewer resources and faced hard decisions. Forced to accept less, the most desperate cities engage in bidding wars for tax revenues and jobs. These factors have consequences for how cities remake themselves, what they are able or unable to do for their population, and whether they can respect the physical environment.

Overall we observed that while faced with underlying constraints (structure), cities do have discretion (agency) and political elites maneuver between these poles. Cities can have an abundance of resources but not put them to full or good use. It is possible to have the levers of powers in sight, but not be able pull them. Milan's position as one of Europe's economic powerhouses did not ensure it could employ its bargaining resources efficiently, much less optimally. Much of this could be attributed to the inaction of its politicians and to the inertia of clientelism.

By the same token resources can be scarce but optimally employed.[3] Some cities with moderate or few bargaining resources have used them with considerable skill, allowing us to show how much agency can count. Marseilles and Liverpool mobilized resources to manage the prevailing market conditions. Marseilles appears to be succeeding because it is tactically prepared to shift economic forces and can rely on intergovernmental support. Liverpool at first dismally failed because it launched a frontal, naive attack on the market, and its intergovernmental allies had gone sour. Most recently, Liverpool has set out a path of recovery, deftly trying to manipulate the market with public power and the help of intergovernmental allies. How far it can take this is still an open question, but the efforts have borne some fruit.

Evidence from our ten cities tells us there is some slack in how structure works. Politics does have muscle, but it can only move so much so far. The extent of slack in any system is also affected by the vagaries of chance, moods of the electorate, and swings in economic cycles. Even so, slack can be stretched by pooling resources and working with other levels of government.

Despite all the declarations about declining national sovereignty, we find that in varying ways nation states are alive and well. The claim that supranational organizations erode national sovereignty may well be overstated or may work in more complex ways than is realized. On the face of it, national sovereignty may be constrained or "perforated" by supranational organization, but it may also be enhanced by the capacity to pool sovereignty and strengthen the collective capacity of nation-states to tame market forces. High levels of governmental integration can muster the political wherewithal to manipulate global forces and carve out "third-way" politics. Collectively the European Union offers testimony that international markets can be managed. Individually, the policies of France, Italy, and, to some extent, Great Britain also show how larger forces can be moderated.

On another plain, we have seen that national sovereignty continues to provide a framework for local development and furnishes cities with a great many cues and controls (finances, restriction, mandates, accepted practices). Localities may have more policy discretion, and national sovereignty may be more selectively applied, but it is no less determinative. Nation-states still define the nature of intergovernmental relations and influence elite behavior. The policy implications for this kind of coordination are considerable, and differences between the United States and Canada, for example, reveal some vivid contrasts (Detroit versus

Toronto). One can spot these distinctions by simply traveling from one nation to another.

Why Cities Bargain in the International Marketplace

We can glean more abstract conclusions from this study. Cities have collective interests. They are more than arenas of power in which different interests battle for rewards, but indeed they have a defining identity and a perceptible behavior. We can best appreciate this by stepping back and understanding how our cities evolved over a period of thirty years. All of our cities showed remarkable patterns of continuity and acted within definable historical, political, and social settings. Elites and citizens responded to common threads of experience. Even while adapting to global pressures, development trajectories in each of our cities rarely took a radical change of direction. Those cities that bargained in a dirigiste context continued to provide collective benefits and placed great value on the use of space. Paris, Toronto, and, to some extent, Milan exemplified this experience. Those cities that bargained in entrepreneurial or dependent private contexts provided meager collective benefits and were more apt to squander space. Houston and Detroit best exemplified that pattern. Cities in public dependent contexts — Glasgow, Marseilles, and Naples — adopted public-led strategies that enabled them to veer in quite different directions as they coped with their poverty of investment assets. Yet none of them followed the kind of market-driven impulses found in other cities. The telling point is that so long as bargaining context was unchanged, cities pursued relatively consistent patterns of development. In a sense, all of these localities were products of their bargaining position.

The relationship between policy choice and bargaining capacity reveals a good deal about the process of change. When development patterns did change, we usually discerned a change in a city's bargaining context. That is, the tools, methods, and resources at the disposal of a city were plainly altered. The most poignant examples are Toronto and Paris. In Toronto an abrupt shift in intergovernmental support between the province and the city had begun to manifest itself in a shift toward market-centered policies. Paris moved in the opposite direction, tightening its relationship with the central government, working more closely at a regional level, and integrating its policies with quasi-public bodies.

Cities have a stake in promoting their bargaining position to realize their own objectives. This interest is systemic. It derives from the reality that cities must obtain bargaining capacity in order to realize their policy choices and to avoid being whipsawed by market forces. Just as nation-states seek to obtain bargaining advantages to realize objectives in international politics, local governments must also possess resources to bargain in capital markets.[i] In both cases bargaining resources are not ends in themselves, but means needed to pursue local democracy.

This finding differs fundamentally from the economic logic of development, expounded in chapter 2. Recall that this logic asserts a normative proposition that city policies *ought to* give priority to promoting economic growth. According to this proposition, cities should maximize economic opportunities because such an approach is best for everyone. The economic logic also has an empirical side. It posits that cities *do*, in fact operate by the rule of growth on the supposition that any other policies will bring dire consequences, such as unemployment or lost revenues.[ii]

We differ with these propositions on both normative and empirical grounds. In our view economic growth *ought* to serve good politics, not the other way around. Only an advantaged bargaining position can permit local governments to pursue a range of policies that can be guided by popular preferences. Without choices, cities are slaves to a single-track growth strategy with little opportunity to realize alternatives. Policy alternatives are important for cities that wish to shape how they will grow; they are important for cities whose growth is excessive; they are important for cities where growth is unwanted; and, they are important for cities that want aggressive growth. The cities that encounter such challenges are not just a few and scattered exceptions, and their decision making takes place within a significant universe of policy choice, both in North America and Europe.

The empirical aspects of economic logic are also doubtful. Our findings demonstrate that it is possible for local governments to influence the impact of the marketplace upon their communities by mobilizing critical bargaining resources and deploying them in strategic ways. For this reason we are unable to accept the notion that cities must adhere to an economic logic that gives priority to unqualified growth for fear of being left behind. To the contrary, we believe that cities *promote their bargaining position so that they do not become captive to any single strategy*. In effect, this conclusion reverses the economic logic of urban development — cities compete to have choices, not to reflexively and unthinkingly grow.

Previous chapters show that cities often *do* successfully resist unregulated growth and often give priority to collective benefits. This was not only true of prosperous Paris but also of hard-ridden Marseilles. For the most part it was true of prosperous Toronto and down-and-out Naples. To a partial extent New York could be added to these examples. Throughout the past thirty years that city repeatedly acted to blunt the edges of its ambitious growth policies. New York's preservationist housing policies, its comparatively vast public health investments, and its effort to build collective benefits into some development projects are noteworthy, especially considering its limited intergovernmental resources. These exceptional social policies are best explained as a product of New York's pluralism, its tradition of political participation, and its left-of-center heritage.

In all of these cases, the resources available to these cities were critical in understanding how each city bargained with business. Steering resources played a major role in enabling cities to "break the rules" of economic logic. High rates of citizen participation and postindustrial social values were crucial in supporting the development paths taken by Paris, Marseilles, Milan, and Toronto. So long as cities possessed the willingness to pursue another direction and muster aid from other sources, they moved against prevailing economic currents.

The interest of cities in promoting their bargaining capacity is where the politics of development begins, not where it ends. Bargaining simply reflects the reality of a governmental interface with a larger political economy. In and of itself, this says little about how cities employ resources, chart new possibilities, or realize their core interests. From our perspective, urban theory should take this into account.

GLOBALIZATION, INTERNATIONAL CITIES, AND THE SHOCK OF SEPTEMBER 11, 2001

As shown in chapter 1, every age has its currents and countercurrents — its good and bad effects. Globalization is no different. Its myriad forces have yielded complex and unpredictable responses. Many of these can be seen in the contradictions of wealth and poverty, opportunity and inequality, collective security and individual vulnerability.

We find certain ironies in these contradictions. In many ways globalization has changed the rules of urban political economy. Cities have begun to act as mini sovereignties, moving about to compete for the Olympic Games, court multinational corporations, or sell their products abroad. Our ten cities have begun to operate in a free-floating "borderless" world, searching for capital markets, political influence, or wider recognition. Within this world other actors seek opportunity, and they too are working under different rules, sometimes with unfortunate consequences. The ease of travel across international borders, the capacity of electronic communications to mobilize disaffected individuals, the open nature and fragile interdependence of postindustrial society, and the facility to turn technology against its progenitors have made international terror possible. Urban densities, the role of cities as nerve synapses of the international economy, and the place they hold as media centers make cities highly prized targets.[4]

The bigger the city and the more significant its role in the world market, the more attractive it is as a target of terror. International cities magnify the message of terror, they broaden its meaning, and they engulf more participants. An attack on Wall Street, a massacre in Piccadilly Circus, or the bombing of the Eiffel Tower arouses international alarm. And if terrorists thrive on anything, it is widespread recognition.

There are other parallels between the rise of international cities and the ascension of international terror. Just as cities have attained a strategic niche in a fluid and impersonal global economy, so, too, has terror found a place to launch an inchoate, formless war. International terror may represent the underside of globalization, but it is no less a part of this changing and mixed world. In a macabre twist, the events of September 11, 2001 joined some of the best and the worst aspects of globalization. On that day, four passenger airplanes were commandeered by terrorists. Each aircraft was turned into a guided missile. Two of them were flown directly into the twin towers of New York's World Trade Center; another was targeted into the Pentagon, located in the Greater Washington Area; while the last aircraft never reached its intended target and crashed onto a rural field in Pennsylvania.

Within the short span of an hour on that fateful morning, a part of New York's downtown business district was devastated, and Washington, D.C. was considered too dangerous for the President of the United States to inhabit. By far New York suffered the worse loss. The twin towers were turned into a blazing inferno that unleashed a blizzard of cement, steel, and glass. The immense buildings that had towered more than a thousand feet into the city's skyline soon collapsed. A chasm was left in downtown Manhattan, and its once fabled silhouette suddenly shrunk.

All told, the terrorists killed over 3000 people, they injured many more thousands, and they wrought incalculable damage The widespread panic that the terrorists had intended did not materialize, though they managed to shut down the stock market for the longest period in its history. The nation's air transportation was paralyzed and pushed to the brink of bankruptcy, stock markets around the world accelerated their downward spiral, and economies sputtered. The president of the United States declared the attack "an act of war" and mobilized military forces for action abroad.

Meanwhile, New York was left to cope with its own wreckage. Aside from the incalculable human costs, the aftermath was grim. The city's economy sustained an estimated loss of $83 billion and 125,000 jobs.

Over 25 million square feet of office space was either destroyed or damaged (including 15 million from the World Trade Center). The positive synergies that ignited the city's economy were set into reverse. Like a row of dominos, financial services fell (losing $4.2 billion), followed by tourism (losing 25,000 jobs) and retail trade (losing $7.6 billion), causing collapses in small business and the nonprofit sector.[5] Vacancy rates in the downtown area are estimated to climb from the current 6.4 percent to over 13 percent over the next few years.[iii]

In the immediate run, the attack on New York accomplished terrorist objectives. Urban terror was made possible through a kind of armed jujitsu — apply intense pressure precisely to a limited area and watch the larger body politic twist into convulsions. The attack on just sixteen acres of one of the world's greatest cities made this possible, and its shock waves changed the course of international events.

Nineteen hijackers had flown unhampered along America's busiest urban corridor, known as the Bos-Wash complex, and launched a suicide attack. It seems apparent that these men relied on extensive global networks to carry out their work. The networks may cover an arc stretching from the southern Philippines up through Pakistan, Afghanistan, the Arab Middle East, and into Turkey. Terrorist cells connected to the attack are also thought to be operating in key European cities like Hamburg, Milan, and Paris. Just before the attack on New York, terrorist assaults had occurred in Istanbul and Srinagar (Kashmir, India). Since the attack on New York, terrorists have wreaked havoc in New Delhi's parliament building and massacred civilians in Tel Aviv and Jerusalem (whose human toll was proportionately far worse than anywhere else). Evidence obtained by international intelligence services suggests more attacks might have been planned for London, Paris, and Berlin.

Ironically, the new international terrorism does not diminish the importance of place. Rather, it signals how globalization is enlarging the significance of cities and local politics. New York was undoubtedly targeted for terror because it is an international symbol of capitalism and could be used to make a statement of global scope. Since the attack, local governments everywhere are rethinking the city-building process in order to forestall future terrorist threats. Political leaders are embarking on more active management of urban space to realize new security objectives. Local choices will matter now more than ever.

In some quarters an antiurban bias has crept into the dialogue over the reaction to terror, and some planners are talking about a development strategy of "defensive dispersal."[6] Reminiscent of the 1950s rationale for building freeways to quickly flee from a nuclear attack, this strategy suggests that low densities and spread development would remove attractive targets for terrorists. Still other critics advocate an "end to tower buildings."[7] They suggest that skyscrapers are not only dangerous, but also undesirable. Investors have already begun to withdraw plans for the largest skyscrapers and a good many people feel the twin towers should be replaced by something more modest. Politicians argue that Wall Street and its adjacent financial offices should be dispersed to other parts of the city. While some of these propositions are worthy of consideration and others are not necessarily bad, they do suggest reduced expectations and dampened ambition.

Similarly, some cities face critical choices in rebuilding in the wake of terrorist attacks. In New York new intergovernmental linkages are being forged and new private resources are being mobilized in support of yet-to-be-determined rebuilding plans. It will take a decade before the site of the World Trade Center is rebuilt and years before the downtown recovers. Through the calamity Mayor Rudolph Giuliani became a national hero and the first mayor in history to address the United Nations. Faced with a steep budget deficit, the mayor froze future increases in city expenditures. The governor joined him in asking Congress for $53 billion in emergency aid. As matters stood, the federal government would give the city a fraction of that amount.[iv] Like the fiscal crisis of the 1970s, business would be called in to provide counsel and offer solutions. As of this writing, proposals for a public reconstruction authority have been rejected in favor of market-oriented incentives. Giuliani's successor, Mayor Michael Bloomberg, summed up his development strategy:

> The money that's going to rebuild is all private money. So what's this (public) agency going to do: tell private enterprise what they can do with their money? What you have to do is look for other industries — biotech, media, fashion. And that's what a private developer will do.[8]

How to Prepare for Change

Earlier chapters showed how cities adapted to global change. In most cases institutional and policy change occurred by increments rather than by radical jumps in one direction or another. Once cities head down a particular path, they generally hold to that course. Urban collective behavior appears to be embedded in familiar and routine ways of doing things. When change does occur, it is often pretested by trial and error. Cities take guarded steps, as if they were sticking their toes in cold, rushing waters, readying themselves for the shock. While change took place through existing practices, those practices could also be reformed to meet international challenges.

How might cities prepare for change? A major finding is that while bargaining circumstances are stable, they are not permanently fixed. Ultimately, building better cities depends on investments in political capital. By investing in political capital we mean making a concerted effort to modify institutions, structures, and practices that will enable cities to bargain more effectively and expand choice. Actions of this kind can be carried forward to influence the distribution of advantage within international markets.

Chapter 9 outlined some strategies for achieving this. As we see it, globalization has continued apace and international, national, and local political institutions should be advanced to keep up with it. Basically we focused on how different jurisdictions or territories might be rescaled in order to assist cities. Rescaling the city would also enable governments to work at multiple levels. Our approach hinges on concerting collective action. This has already begun at a supranational level and, despite misgivings, is likely to continue. The European Union has already adopted urban policies and, in time, NAFTA-style treaties could also follow suit.

At the national and middle levels government, a stronger integration of intergovernmental networks and interlocal cooperation made a big difference for cities. Coordinated national and regional policies would complement these actions. Overlapping policy nets linking national, regional, and local authorities have been effective in rebuilding European cities, and this technique could be perfected as well as applied cross-nationally.

Rescaling should not just be carried upward but also moved downward into the grass roots. Ordinarily local regimes carry out two basic functions. One is to navigate the city's external bargaining environment and take advantage of strategic opportunities. A second is to win citizen support. Regimes would be best off linking these functions and engaging citizens directly in the bargaining processes. This would not only enhance democratic legitimacy, but would also enable elites to enlist citizen support and expand ideas for the application of investments.

There are other ways through which investments in political capital (institution building) could be translated into enhancing social capital (changing values to enhance human cooperation). This would entail a modification in social behavior so that citizens work more closely to realize collective benefits. Just as globalization has brought about a closer integration of economic functions, new institutions might also encourage behavioral cooperation. A key to this approach is to enhance steering variables like popular participation and local culture. We are embarking upon an age that will bring a radical shift in social demography (older population, increased longevity, greater diversity, more gender equality). This will undoubtedly change the political composition of cities. Better education, stronger socialization, and civic engagement must keep up with those changes and can make a difference for governing coalitions.

Whatever else occurs in the international marketplace, it is likely to expand, to become more pluralistic. New actors constantly enter the bargaining arena. International organizations have played a burgeoning role. The Organization for Economic Cooperation and Development (OECD), the World Bank, the International Monetary Fund (IMF), the World Trade Organization (WTO), and the G-8 have already begun to fill the international governance vacuum. This organization elite is now joined by nongovernmental organizations, nonprofit groups, regional associations, and cross-national confederations of cities.

These organizations can take up a more specific urban agenda and direct their attention to conditions affecting migrant or guest labor, the need for work force training, and the growth of transnational cooperation among cities. In the wake of international terrorism, these organizations have begun to cooperate in combating the negative side of globalization. Governments at all levels could join in partnerships with new international actors to realize more positive objectives.

Ultimately, freedom and economic well-being will not depend on escaping the international marketplace or obstructing the tide of globalization, as some protesters seem to believe. Our conclusion is that it depends on intelligent political management of global interdependencies by citizens, especially in the cities where their governments bargain over critical choices.

NOTES

i. The classic modern description of state interests in the international order is Morganthu, *Politics Among Nations* and Kenneth Waltz, *Theory of International Politics*. More recent examinations of this idea include Peter J. Katzenstein, Robert O. Keohane and Stephen D. Krasner, "International Organization and the Study of World Politics." *International Organizations*, and John J. Mearsheimer, "The False Promise of International Institutions." *International Security*. Of course, the analogy between cities and nationa states should not be carried too far. Unlike nation states struggling for power on the international stage, city governments need not always compete at the expense of other cities. Urban communities do not seek to forge coalitions with other cities in order to deprive others of power over them. The international marketplace is so vast and the impact that any one city can have on the global system is so remote and indirect that it makes little sense to speak of a zero-sum competition even though some resources, especially capital, are finite.

ii. Tiebout, *Pure Theory of Local Expenditure*, Bish, *Public Economy of Metropolitan Areas*; Peterson, *City Limits*. While economic logic oversimplifies reality and there are substantial exceptions to its generalization, it does contain a strong element of validity for many American and even some European cities. Once put in a comparative, cross-national context, however, it falls substantially short because it does not take account of the full panoply of resources available to cities. These shortcomings have far-reaching consequences for a theory of urban development because they tell us that the economic logic argument rests on a narrow set of circumstances. Our own framework suggests ways in which cities might change those circumstances.

iii. At the time the offices space was a sellers' market and the downtown area was in an unprecedented boom. See *The Wall Street Journal*, December 19, 2001, p. 1.

iv. The implications of federal aid to cities in the wake of terror is discussed more fully in John Harrington and Ronald Vogel's *Political Change in the Metropoli* (New York, Longman, 2000).

APPENDIX

TABLES AND FIGURES SOURCES AND NOTES

CHAPTER 1

Table 1.1. Air Passengers and Cargo

Note:

Passengers = total passengers emplaned and deplaned, passengers in transit counted once.

Cargo = loaded and unloaded freight and mail (in metric tonnes).

NA = not available.

Source: Airports Council International, Annual Worldwide Airport Traffic Report (Geneva, Switzerland, 1991 and 2001).

Table 1.3. Population and Condition

Note:

1. The figures for Berlin include both East and West Berlin. Data for Dublin ca. 2000: 1996 census data from Dublin Corporation: Profile http://www. dublincorp.ie/profile.htm. Data for UK cities ca. 2000: 1994 estimates from United Nations (1998) Demographic Yearbook.

2. London data are for Greater London. Data for U.S. cities ca. 2000: 1998 estimates, U.S. Census Bureau, Population Division. Data for Brussels Capital Region ca. 2000: http://www.brussels.com/. Data for Toronto ca. 2000: City of Toronto, Key Facts — http://www.city.toronto.on.ca/ourcity/keyfacts.htm.

3. Toronto data are for Metro Toronto.

Sources: Cheshire, Paul, Carbonaro, Gianni., and Hay, Dennis (1986), "Problems of Urban Decline and Growth in EEC Countries: Or Measuring Degrees of Elephantness," *Urban Studies* 2 (1986): 131–49. Commission of the European Communities (1992), *Urbanization and the Functions of Cities in the European Community*, European Institute of Urban Affairs (Liverpool: John Moores University). Nathan, Richard P., and Adams, Jr., Charles F. (1989), "Four Perspectives on Urban Hardship" *Political Science Quarterly* 104 (3): 483. U.S. Census Bureau (various years), *Statistical Abstract of the United States* Washington, D.C.: U.S. Government Printing Office. Data for European cities ca. 2000: 1997 — 1999, Thomas Brinkhoff: City Population, http://www.citypopulation.de.

Table 1.4. Major Banks and Bank Holdings

Note:

NA = not available.

Sources: "Top 100 World Banking Companies," American Banker 1999, www.americanbanker.com. "The Top 500 Banks in the World," American Banker, July 29, 1993.

Figure 1.1. Secondary and Tertiary Employment
Sources: Commission of the European Communities (1992), *Urbanization and the Functions of Cities in the European Community*, European Institute of Urban Affairs (Liverpool: John Moores University). U.S. Census Bureau (various years), *City County Data Book*. Washington, D.C.: Government Printing Office.

Figure 1.2. Urbanization and Gross Domestic Product
Sources: World Bank (1994), *World Tables 1994* (Baltimore: John Hopkins University Press). World Bank (1991), *World Tables 1991* (Baltimore: John Hopkins University Press). World Bank (1980), *World Tables 1980*, 2nd ed. (Baltimore: John Hopkins University Press). United Nations (1995), *World Urbanization Prospects: The 1994 Revision*, Department for Economic and Social Information and Policy Analysis, Population Division, New York.

CHAPTER 3

Table 3.1. Office Markets
Notes:
Occupancy rate is calculated as follows: Occupancy Rate = 100%-Vacancy Rate.

Index is calculated as follows: Value of 100 assigned to the highest figure in the column and value of 0 assigned to the lowest figure in the column. The indices in between these two are assigned values from 0 to 100 using the following formula: $X = (Y\text{-}Ymin)^*100/(Ymax\text{-}Ymin)$ where X = standardized index, Y = figures for each city, $Ymax$ = maximum value of Y, $Ymin$ = minimum value of Y. The indices for each city are summed and the total divided by 2.

New York figures are for Midtown 1996; Houston figures are for 1996; Detroit occupancy rate figure is for 1996 (cost/sq. foot figure is for 1995); Paris figures are for "golden triangle" 1996; Marseilles figures are for 1994; Milan figures are for 1996.

Sources: For New York, Detroit, Houston, Toronto, Paris, Milan, and Marseilles: ULI Market Profiles 1995 and 1997, Urban Land Institute, Washington, D.C.

For Glasgow: Glasgow Economic Monitor and The Glasgow City City Council Spring 1998:30–31; Richard Ellis Research Consultancy — Glasgow Market Bulletin. Jones Lang Wooten, New York, N.Y., 1998.

For Liverpool: Jones, Lang, and Wooten, London, March 1998. Richard Ellis Inc., Liverpool, December 1998.

Table 3.2. Civilian Labor Force

Sources: For Detroit, Houston, New York: U.S. Bureau of the Census, *City County Data Book* (Washington, D.C.: U.S. Government Printing Office, 1970–94).

For Toronto: Institut d'Estudis Metropolitais de Barcelona, Cities of The World, 1988.

For Liverpool: Glasgow, Census 1971: England and Wales: Report for the County of Merseyside" (London: Her Majesty's Stationery Office, 1975); General Register Office, Edinburgh, *Census 1971: Scotland: County Report Glasgow City* (Edinburgh: HMSO, 1975); British Office of Population Censuses and Surveys, *Census 1981: County report: Merseyside: Parts 1 and 2* (London: HMSO, 1983); *Census 1991: County report: Merseyside: Parts 1 and 2* (London: HMSO, 1993); General Register Office for Scotland, *1991 Census: Strathclyde region: Part 1 (Volume 2 of 2) and Part 2* (Edinburgh: HMSO, 1993); Institut d'Estudis Metropolitais de Barcelona, *Cities of the World*, 1988.

For Paris, Marseilles: Direction de l'Urbanisme et des Actions de L'Etat, Sous-Directions des Affaires Economiques, Bureau de l'Action Economique, Préfecture de Paris, *Paris: Chiffres*, edition 1993, donnés au 31 decembre 1991; Ville de Marseilles et Agence d'Urbanisme de l'Agglomeration Marseillaise, *Marseille en Chiffres*, edition 1995; Institut d'Estudis Metropolitais de Barcelona, *Cities of the World*, 1988.

For Milan, Naples: Istat, Censimento generale della popolazione (1991), *Popolazione in condizione professionale per ramo di attivita economica*; Istat, Censimento generale della popolazione (1971), *Popolazione in condizione professionale per ramo di attivita economica*; Istat, Censimento generale della popolazione (1981), *Popolazione in condizione professionale per ramo di attivita economica*; Istat, Censimento generale della popolazione, 1971, 1981, 1991.

Labor force data for Toronto, Liverpool, Glasgow, Milan, Naples: 1971, 1981, 1991; Marseilles: 1968, 1982, 1990; data for Liverpool 1990 is based on 10% sample.

Table 3.3. Intergovernmental Aid

Note:

For Naples and Milan, data is an estimate for the decade of 1980. For Paris and Marseilles, data is an average of intergovernmental aid for 1986–95. For Detroit, New York, and Houston, data is an average of intergovernmental aid for 1985–94. For Glasgow and Liverpool, data is an average of intergovernmental for 1974–89. For Tonronto, data is an average for 1979–88 and 1991–92.

Sources: Milan and Naples: Enzo Sanantonio, *Italy: Central and Local Government Relations*, edited by Edward Page and Michael Goldsmith (London: Sage, 1987). New York, Detroit, Houston: U.S. Bureau of Census, "City Government Finances," 1994.

Paris, Marseilles: Vincent Hoffman Martirot and Jean Yves Nevers, "French — Local Policy Change in a Period of Austerity," in *Urban Innovation and Autonomy*, edited by Susan Clarke (Newberry Park, Calif.: Sage, 1989); Remy

Prud'homme, "La France, Pays' Le Plus Décentralisé?" *Le Monde*, May 17, 1994.

Glasgow, Liverpool: Paul Carmichael, *Central—Local Government Relations in the 1980s: Glasgow and Liverpool* (Brookfield, Vt.: Ashgate, 1995).

Toronto Municipality of Metropolitan Toronto, *Briefing Notes for Members of the Council*, 1988, p. 26, and *Key Facts: 1995*, City of Toronto Urban Development Services, "Municipal Financing" VII.

Table 3.4. Electoral Participation and Party Competition

Note:

Index is calculated as follows: Value of 100 assigned to the highest figure in the column, and value of 0 assigned to the lowest figure in the column. The indices in between these two are assigned values from 0 to 100, according to the following formula: $X = (Y\text{-}Ymin)*100/(Ymax\text{-}Ymin)$ where X = standardized index, Y = figures for each city, $Ymax$ = maximum value of Y, $Ymin$ = minimum value of Y. The indices for each city are summed and the total divided by 2.

Sources: For Houston, Detroit and New York: *The New York Times*, November 9, 1989, November 3, 1993, and November 5, 1997; Houston Board of Elections; and *Newsday*, November 1997; Detroit Board of Elections. For Naples, and Milan: Carol Mershon and Gianfranco Paquino, *Italian Politics* (Boulder, Colo.: Westview Press, 1995); Il *Corriere della Sera; l'Unità; Quaderni dell'osservatorio elettorale* (a cura della Giunta Regionale Toscana, dell'IRPET e del Gruppo di Studio sul Elettorale in Toscana), n. 25, 1991 and n. 34, 1995; Ministero dell'interno, Direzione centrale per i servizi elettorali. For Toronto: Ontario Municipal Elections, http://www.canoe.com/cnewsontario/ontmayors.htm.; Greg Essenssa, Toronto Board of Elections, Toronto Canada, November 5, 1998. For Paris: Ville de Paris Elections Municipales, 1989, 1995. For Marseilles: Les Elections Municipales Marseilles June 1995; Agence d'Urbanisme de l'Agglomeration Marseillaise; Les Elections Municipales Marseilles March 1989, Agence d'Urbanisme de l'Agglomération Marseillaise. For Glasgow: Strathclyde Regional Council 1982 and 1985, and Glasgow District Council, 1980 and 1984. For Liverpool: the City of Liverpool, Electoral Registration Officer, 1998.

Table 3.5. Persons in Poverty

Notes:

Data for Liverpool, Paris, Milan, and Naples are estimated or derived from nonnational souces (see below) . Liverpool figure is for 1991; Paris is for 1989 and 1994 respectively. Marseilles is for 1993. Milan is for 1994, and Naples is for 1995. Toronto data is for 1976 and 1986. For Paris, data are for 1989 and 1994. NA = not available.

Sources: For Detroit, Houston, and New York: U.S. Census of Population and Housing 1970 and 1990, U.S. Census of Housing 1970 and 1990.

For Liverpool: Poverty estimate derived from Liverpool City Council, *The Liverpool Quality of Life Survey* (Liverpool, 1991). Also cited in Richard

Meegan's "Liverpool—Sliding Down the Urban Hierarchy," International Sociological Association, Research Committee 21, University of California, Los Angeles, April 23–25, 1992.

For Toronto: Families below poverty line data from "COPCOP, A Special Report for Metro" (Toronto, 1992); Clarence Lochhead and Richard Shillington, "A Statistical Profile of Urban Poverty," Centre for International Statistics, Canadian Council on Social Development, Ottawa, Ontario K2P 2H3.

For Milan, Naples: Istat, Statistiche dell'attività edilizia (1990–1994), "Fabbricati non residenziali di nuova costruzione secondo la destinazione d'uso (volume in metri cubi vuoto per pieno)"; Istat, Censimento genearl della popolazione (1991), "Poplazione in condizione professionale per ramo di attività economica"; Istat, Censimento generale della popolazione (1971), "Popolazione in condizione professionale per ramo di attività economica"; Istat, Censimento generale della popolazione (1981), "Popolazione in condizione professionale per ramo di attività economica"; Istat, Censimento generale della popolazione, 1971, 1981, 1991.

For Paris: Institut National de la Statistique et des Etudes Economiques (INSEE), "Revenue et Patrimoine des Ménages," p. 42, edition 1997.

For Marseilles: Institut National de la Statistique et des Etudes Economiques (INSEE), *Le Bas Revenus à Marseille*, December 1995 (Paris: INSEE, 1996).

Table 3.6. Average Number of Persons per Household

Note:
Marseilles figures are for 1968 and 1990. Other ca. 2000 figures are: New York, Detroit, Houston—2000, Glasgow—1997, Liverpool—1998, Marseille and Paris—1999, Naples, Milan, Toronto—1996.

Sources: For Detroit, Houston and New York: U.S. Census of Housing 1970 and 2000, Bureau of the Census, Washington, D.C., 2000. For Toronto: City of Toronto Planning Board, "Research Bulletin No. 3: Occupied Dwellings (Households)" (Toronto, November 12, 1973); Statistics Canadian, 2000.

For Liverpool and Glasgow: British Office of Population Census and Statistics, "Census 1971: England and Wales: Economic Activity County Leaflet: Lancashire," "Census 1971: England and Wales: Economic Activity: Sub-regional Tables," "Census 1971: England and Wales: Report for the County of Merseyside" (London: HMSO, 1975); General Register Office, Edinburgh, "Census 1971: Scotland: County Report Glasgow City" (Edinburgh: HMSO, 1975); British Office of Population Censuses and Surveys, "Census 1981: County Report: Merseyside: Parts 1 and 2" (London: HMSO, 1983); The Urban Audit, www.inforegio.cec.eu.int/urban/audit/.

For Milan, Naples: Istat, Statistiche dell'attività edilizia, 1990–94. "Fabbricati non residenziali di nuova costruzione secondo la destinazione d'uso (volume in metri cubi vuoto per pieno)"; Istat, Censimento generale della popolazione, 1991, "Popolazione in condizione professionale per ramo di attivita economica"; Istat, Censimento generale della popolazione, 1971, "Popolazione in condizione professionale per ramo di attivita economica"; Istat, Censimento generale della popolazione, 1981, "Popolazione in condizione professionale per ramo di attivita economica"; Istat, Censimento generale della popolazione, 1971, 1981, 1991. The Urban Audit, www.inforegio.cec.eu.int/urban/audit/.

For Paris: Atelier Parisien d'Urbanisme (APUR) le Recensement de 1990 à Paris Premiers Resultats, p. 47 (Paris, France, September 1991), Atelier Parisien d'Urbanisme (APUR), *Paris: 1954–1990* (Paris France); INSEE, www.insee.fr, and Atelier Parisien d'Urbansime (APUR) Le Recensement de 1999: Population et Logements (Janvier 2000) p. 12.

For Marseilles: *Marseille en Chiffres*. p. 9; Ville de Marseilles et Agence d' Urbanisme de l'Agglomération Marseillaise, *Recensement de 1968 Population Legale*, tome I (Paris: INSEE, 1969); INSEE, www.insee.fr.

Figure 3.1. Population Growth and Loss

Sources: Detroit, Houston, New York: U.S. Bureau of the Census, "*City County Data Book, U.S. Counties*, and *Population Estimates, "A Comparative Analysis of America's Great Cities"*. (Washington, D.C.: U.S. Government Printing Office, 1970, 1990, 2000); *United Nations Demographic Yearbook* for years 1970, 1971, 1999.

Toronto: Metropolitan Toronto Planning Department, "Space and Employment Characteristics: Greater Toronto Area" (April 1992); Metro Toronto Planning Department (Research and Special Studies Division), *Key Facts, 1995* (May 1995); City of Toronto Urban Development Services, "Profile Toronto" (May 1997); www.population.com (c. 1999); "Access Toronto" public information service; U.S. Census Bureau; Population Estimates; *United Nations Demographic Yearbook* for years 1970, 1971, 1999.

Glasgow, Liverpool: British Office of Population Census and Statistics, "Census 1971: England and Wales: Economic Activity County Leaflet: Lancashire," "Census 1971: England and Wales: Economic Activity: Subregional tables," "Census 1971: England and Wales: Report for the County of Merseyside" (London: HMSO, 1975); General Register Office, Edinburgh, "Census 1971: Scotland: County Report Glasgow City" (Edinburgh: HMSO, 1975); British Office of Population Censuses and Surveys, "Census 1981: County Report: Merseyside: Parts 1 and 2" (London: HMSO, 1983); "Census 1991: County Report: Merseyside: Parts 1 and 2" (London: HMSO, 1993); General Register Office for Scotland, "1991 Census: Strathclyde Region: Part 1 (Volume 2 of 2) and Part 2" (Edinburgh: HMSO, 1993); Physical and Economic Regeneration Services of Glasgow City Council; Population Department of Office of National Statistics, "Population.com," available online: www.population.com (c. 1999); *United Nations Demographic Yearbook* for years 1970, 1971, 1999.

Paris, Marseilles: Institut National de la Statistique et des Etudes Economiques (INSEE), *Recensement de 1968: Population Légale: Statistiques Communales Complémentaires: Evolutions Demographiqes 1962–1968 et 1954–1962*, tome 1: Ain à Charente, (Paris: Imprimérie Nationale); Atelier Parisien d'Urbanisme (APUR), *Vingt Ans d'Evolution de Paris: Donnees Statistiques 1954–1975: Paris et Arrondissements: Population, Logement, Ménages* (Paris, 1975); INSEE, *Recensement Général de la Population de 1975: Resultats du Sondage: Population, Ménages, Logement, Immeubles*, tome II: Aveyron et Creuse (12 et 23);

APUR, *Premiers Resultats du Recensement de 1982 à Paris: Population et Logements* (Paris, 1983); INSEE-Provence-Alpes-Côte d'Azur Service Etudes et Diffusion, *L'Agglomération Marseille-Aix-en-Provence au Recensement de 1990*; INSEE, *Recensement Général de la Population de 1990: Commune de Maresilles: Population-Activité-Ménages: Le Department et ses Principles Communes, Bouches-du-Rhône*; APUR, *Le Recensement de 1990 à Paris: L'évolution de la population, Les caracteristiques démogrpahiques et sociales, Le parc de logements: Premiers Resultats* (Septembre 1991); Direction de l'Urbanisme et des Actions de l'Etat, Sous-Direction des Affaires Economiques, Bureau de l'Action Economique, Préfecture de Paris, *Paris: Chiffres* (edition 1993), donnés au 31 décembre 1991; Fédération Nationale, Institut d'Aménagement et d'Urbanisme de la Région d'Ile-de-France, et APUR, *Tableau de Bord des Agglomérations Françaises: Region Ile-de-France* (Paris, 1994) INSEE-et des Etudes Economiques Provence-Alpes-Côte d'Azur, Chambre Régionale de Commerce et d'Industrie de Provence-Alpes-Côte d'Azur-Corse, Sécretariat Général pour les Affaires Régionales de Provence-Alpes-Côte d'Azur, et Conseil Régional de Provence-Alpes-Côte d'Azur, *Données Economiques et Sociales: Resultats 1994, Bouches-du-Rhône.* "Population.com," available online: www.population.com (c. 1999). *United Nations Demographic Yearbook* for years 1970, 1971, 1999.

Milan, Naples — Istat, Statistiche dell'attivita edilizia (1990–1994), "Fabbricati non residenziali di nuova costruzione secondo la destinazione d'uso (volume in metri cubi vuoto per pieno)"; Istat, Censimento generale della popolazione (1991), "Poplazione in condizione professionale per ramo di attività economica"; Istat, Censimento generale della popolazione (1971), "Popolazione in condizione professionale per ramo di attività economica"; Istat, Censimento generale della popolazione (1981), "Popolazione in condizione professionale per ramo di attività economica"; Istat, Censimento generale della popolazione, 1971, 1981, 1991; "Population.com", available online: www. population.com (c. 1999). *United Nations Demographic Yearbook* for years 1970, 1971, 1999.

Figure 3.2. Second Sector Change

Note:
Data not available for Toronto agglomeration.

Sources: Detroit, Houston, New York: U.S. Bureau of the Census, *City County Data Book, U.S. Counties, A Comparative Analysis of America's Great Cities* (Washington, D.C.: U.S. Government Printing Office, 1970, 1990).

Toronto: Metropolitan Toronto Planning Department, "Space and Employment Characteristics: Greater Toronto Area" (April 1992); Metro Toronto Planning Department (Research and Special Studies Division), *Key Facts 1995* (May 1995); City of Toronto Urban Development Services, "Profile Toronto" (May 1997).

Glasgow, Liverpool: British Office of Population Census and Statistics, "Census 1971: England and Wales: Economic Activity County Leaflet: Lancashire," "Census 1971: England and Wales: Economic Activity: Subregional Tables," "Census 1971: England and Wales: Report for the County of Merseyside" (London: HMSO, 1975); General Register Office, Edinburgh, "Census 1971: Scotland: County Report Glasgow City" (Edinburgh: HMSO, 1975); British Office of Population Censuses and Surveys, "Census 1981: County Report: Merseyside: Parts 1 and 2" (London: HMSO, 1983); "Census 1991: County Report: Merseyside: Parts 1 and 2" (London: HMSO, 1993); General Register Office for Scotland, "1991 Census: Strathclyde Region: Part 1 (Volume 2 of 2) and Part 2" (Edinburgh: HMSO, 1993).

Paris, Marseilles: Institut National de la Statistique et des Etudes Economiques (INSEE), *Recensement de 1968: Population Légale: Statistiques Communales Complémentaires: Evolutions Démographiqes 1962–1968 et 1954–1962*, tome 1: Ain à Charente (Paris: Imprimérie Nationale); Atelier Parisien d'Urbanisme (APUR), *Vingt Ans d'Evolution de Paris: Données Statistiques 1954–1975: Paris et Arrondissements: Population, Logement, Ménages* (Paris, 1975); INSEE, *Recensement Général de la Population de 1975: Résultats du Sondage: Population, Ménages, Logement, Immeubles*, tome II: Aveyron et Creuse (12 et 23); APUR, *Premiers Résultats du Recensement de 1982 à Paris: Population et Logements* (Paris, 1983); INSEE-Provence-Alpes-Côte d'Azur Service Etudes et Diffusion, *L'Agglomération Marseilles-Aix-en-Provence au Recensement de 1990*; INSEE, *Recensement Général de la Population de 1990: Commune de Maresilles: Population-Activité-Ménages: Le Department et ses Principles Communes, Bouches-du-Rhône*; APUR, *Le Recensement de 1990 à Paris: L'évolution de la population, Les caracteristiques démogrpahiques et sociales, Le parc de legoements: Premiers Resultats* (Septembre 1991); Direction de l'Urbanisme et des Actions de l'Etat, Sous-Direction des Affaires Economiques, Bureau de l'Action Economique, Préfecture de Paris, *Paris: Chiffres* (edition 1993), donnés au 31 décembre 1991; Fédération Nationale, Institut d'Aménagement et d'Urbanisme de la Région d'Ile-de-France, et APUR, *Tableau de Bord des Agglomérations Françaises: Région Ile-de-France* (Paris, 1994); INSEE-et des Etudes Economiques Provence-Alpes-Côte d'Azur, Chambre Régionale de Commerce et d'Industrie de Provence-Alpes-Côte d'Azur-Corse, Sécrétariat Général pour les Affaires Régionales de Provence-Alpes-Côte d'Azur, et Conseil Régional de Provence-Alpes-Côte d'Azur, *Données Economiques et Sociales: Résultats 1994, Bouches-du-Rhône.*

Milan, Naples: Istat, Statistiche dell'attività edilizia (1990–1994), "Fabbricati non residenziali di nuova costruzione secondo la destinazione d'uso (volume in metri cubi vuoto per pieno)"; Istat, Censimento generale della popolazione (1991). "Popolazione in condizione professionale per ramo di attivita economica"; Istat, Censimento generale della popolazione (1971), "Popolazione in condizione professionale per ramo di attività economica"; Istat, Censimento generale della popolazione (1981), "Popolazione in condizione professionale per ramo di attività economica"; Istat, Censimento generale della popolazione, 1971, 1981, 1991.

Figure 3.3. Tertiary Sector Change

Note:

Data not available for Toronto agglomeration.

Sources: Detroit, Houston, New York: U.S. Bureau of the Census, *City County Data Book*, *U.S. Counties, "A Comparative Analysis of America's Great Cities"* (Washington, D.C.: U.S. Government Printing Office, 1970, 1990).

Toronto: Metropolitan Toronto Planning Department, "Space and Employment Characteristics: Greater Toronto Area" (April 1992); Metro Toronto Planning Department (Research and Special Studies Division), *Key Facts 1995* (May 1995); City of Toronto Urban Development Services, "Profile Toronto" (May 1997).

Glasgow, Liverpool: British Office of Population Census and Statistics, "Census 1971: England and Wales: Economic Activity County Leaflet: Lancashire," "Census 1971: England and Wales: Economic Activity: Subregional Tables," "Census 1971: England and Wales: Report for the County of Merseyside" (London: HMSO, 1975); General Register Office, Edinburgh, "Census 1971: Scotland: County Report Glasgow City" (Edinburgh: HMSO, 1975); British Office of Population Censuses and Surveys, "Census 1981: County Report: Merseyside: Parts 1 and 2" (London: HMSO, 1983); "Census 1991: County Report: Merseyside: Parts 1 and 2" (London: HMSO, 1993); General Register Office for Scotland, "1991 Census: Strathclyde Region: Part 1 (Volume 2 of 2) and Part 2" (Edinburgh: HMSO, 1993).

Paris, Marseilles: Institut National de la Statistique et des Etudes Economiques (INSEE), *Recensement de 1968: Population Légale: Statistiques Communales Complémentaires: Evolutions Démographiqes 1962–1968 et 1954–1962*, Tome 1: Ain à Charente (Paris: Imprimérie Nationale); Atelier Parisien d'Urbanisme (APUR), *Vingt Ans d'Evolution de Paris: Données Statistiques 1954–1975: Paris et Arrondissements: Population, Logement, Ménages* (Paris, 1975); INSEE, *Recensement Général de la Population de 1975: Résultats du Sondage: Population, Ménages, Logement, Immeubles*, tome II: Aveyron et Creuse (12 et 23); APUR, *Premiers Résultats du Recensement de 1982 à Paris: Population et Logements* (Paris, 1983); INSEE-Provence-Alpes-Côte d'Azur Service Etudes et Diffusion, *L'Agglomération Marseilles-Aix-en-Provence au Recensement de 1990*; INSEE, *Recensement Général de la Population de 1990: Commune de Maresilles: Population-Activité-Ménages: Le Department et ses Principles Communes, Bouches-du-Rhône*; APUR, *Le Recensement de 1990 à Paris: L'évolution de la population, Les caracteristiques démogrpahiques et sociales, Le parc de logements: Premiers Resultats* (Septembre 1991); Direction de l'Urbanisme et des Actions de l'Etat, Sous-Direction des Affaires Economiques, Bureau de l'Action Economique, Préfecture de Paris, *Paris: Chiffres* (edition 1993), donnés au 31 décembre 1991; Fédération Nationale, Institut d'Aménagement et d'Urbanisme de la Région d'Ile-de-France, et APUR, *Tableau de Bord des Agglomérations Françaises: Région Ile-de-France* (Paris 1994); INSEE-et des Etudes Economiques Provence-Alpes-Côte d'Azur, Chambre Régionale de Commerce et d'Industrie de Provence-Alpes-Côte d'Azur-Corse, Sécrétariat Général pour les Affaires Régionales de Provence-Alpes-Côte d'Azur, et Conseil Régional de Provence-Alpes-Côte d'Azur, *Données Economiques et Sociales: Résultats 1994, Bouches du Rhône.*

Milan, Naples: Istat, Statistiche dell'attività edilizia (1990–1994), "Fabbricati non residenziali di nuova costruzione secondo la destinazione d'uso (volume in metri cubi vuoto per pieno)"; Istat, Censimento generale della popolazione (1991), "Popolazione in condizione professionale per ramo di attività economica"; Istat, Censimento generale della popolazione (1971), "Popolazione in condizione professionale per ramo di attività economica"; Istat, Censimento generale della popolazione (1981), "Popolazione in condizione professionale per ramo di attività economica"; Istat, Censimento generale della popolazione, 1971, 1981, 1991.

Figure 3.4. Educational Attainment

Note:
Actual years: Detroit, Houston, New York: 1990; Marseilles, Milan, Naples: 1991 Toronto, Glasgow, Liverpool: 1996; Paris: 1998.

Sources: Detroit, Houston, New York: U.S. Census Bureau, www.census.gov.

Glasgow, Liverpool, Marseilles, Milan, Naples: Urban Audit: Assessing Quality of Life of Europe's Cities, http://www.inforegio.cec.eu.int/urban/audit/.

Paris: "Ile-de-France—Effectifs de l'enseignement supérieur," INSEE, www. insee.fr.

Toronto: "Statistical Profile of Canadian Communities," Statistics Canada, http://www.statcan.ca/.

Figure 3.8. Professionals and Managers

Sources: Detroit, Houston, New York: U.S. Bureau of the Census, *City County Data Book, U.S. Counties, "A Comparative Analysis of America's Great Cities"* (Washington, D.C.: U.S. Government Printing Office, 1970, 1990).

Toronto: Metropolitan Toronto Planning Department, "Space and Employment Characteristics: Greater Toronto Area" (April 1992); Metro Toronto Planning Department (Research and Special Studies Division), Key Facts 1995 (May 1995); City of Toronto Urban Development Services, "Profile Toronto" (May 1997).

Glasgow, Liverpool: British Office of Population Census and Statistics, "Census 1971: England and Wales: Economic Activity County Leaflet: Lancashire," "Census 1971: England and Wales: Economic Activity: Subregional Tables," "Census 1971: England and Wales: Report for the County of Merseyside" (London: HMSO, 1975); General Register Office, Edinburgh, "Census 1971: Scotland: County Report Glasgow City" (Edinburgh: HMSO, 1975); British Office of Population Censuses and Surveys, "Census 1981: County Report: Merseyside: Parts 1 and 2" (London: HMSO, 1983); "Census 1991: County Report: Merseyside: Parts 1 and 2" (London: HMSO, 1993); General Register Office for Scotland, "1991 Census: Strathclyde Region: Part 1 (Volume 2 of 2) and Part 2" (Edinburgh: HMSO, 1993).

Paris, Marseilles: Institut National de la Statistique et des Etudes Economiques (INSEE), *Recensement de 1968: Population Légale: Statistiques Communales Complémentaires: Evolutions Démographiqes 1962–1968 et 1954–1962,* Tome 1: Ain à Charente (Paris: Imprimérie Nationale); Atelier Parisien d'Urbanisme (APUR), *Vingt Ans d'Evolution de Paris: Données Statistiques 1954–1975:*

Paris et Arrondissements: Population, Logement, Ménages (Paris, 1975); INSEE, *Recensement Général de la Population de 1975: Resultats du Sondages: Population, Ménages, Logement, Immeubles*, Tome II: Aveyron et Creuse (12 et 23); APUR, *Premiers Résultats du Recensement de 1982 à Paris: Population et Logements* (Paris, 1983); INSEE-Provence-Alpes-Côte d'Azur Service Etudes et Diffusion, *L'Agglomération Marseille-Aix-en-Provence au Recensement de 1990*; INSEE, *Recensement Général de la Population de 1990: Commune de Maresilles: Population-Activité-Ménages: Le Department et ses Principles Communes, Bouches-du-Rhône*; APUR, *Le Recensement de 1990 à Paris: L'évolution de la population, Les caracteristiques démogrpahiques et sociales, Le parc de logements: Premiers Resultats* (Septembre 1991); Direction de l'Urbanisme et des Actions de l'Etat, Sous-Direction des Affaires Economiques, Bureau de l'Action Economique, Préfecture de Paris, *Paris: Chiffres* (edition 1993), donnés au 31 décembre 1991; Federation Nationale, Institut d'Aménagement et d'Urbanisme de la Region d'Ile-de-France, et APUR, *Tableau de Bord des Agglomérations Françaises: Region Ile-de-France* (Paris 1994); INSEE-et des Etudes Economiques Provence-Alpes-Côte d'Azur, Chambre Régionale de Commerce et d'Industrie de Provence-Alpes-Côte d'Azur-Corse, Sécrétariat Général pour les Affaires Régionales de Provence-Alpes-Côte d'Azur, et Conseil Régional de Provence-Alpes-Côte d'Azur, *Données Economiques et Sociales: Resultats 1994, Bouche-du-Rhône*.

Milan, Naples: Istat, Statistiche dell'attività edilizia (1990–1994). "Fabbricati non residenziali di nuova costruzione secondo la destinazione d'uso (volume in metri cubi vuoto per pieno)"; Istat, Censimento generale della popolazione (1991). "Popolazione in condizione professionale per ramo di attività economica"; Istat, Censimento generale della popolazione (1971). "Popolazione in condizione professionale per ramo di attività economica"; Istat, Censimento generale della popolazione (1981), "Popolazione in condizione professionale per ramo di attività economica"; Istat, Censimento generale della popolazione, 1971, 1981, 1991.

CHAPTER 8

Table 8.1. Assisted Housing

Notes:
Toronto, Milan, and Naples data for housing units is actually assisted households. Actual years: Detroit (74/89), Houston (76/91), New York (76/91), Toronto (1996), Naples (80/90).

Sources: U.S. Annual Housing Survey (1974, 76, 89, and 91): Housing Characteristics for Selected Metropolitan Areas, Toronto *Key Facts* (1995).

For Liverpool and Glasgow: British Office of Population Census and Statistics, "Census 1971: England and Wales: Economic Activity County Leaflet: Lancashire," "Census 1971: England and Wales: Economic Activity: Subregional Tables," "Census 1971: England and Wales: Report for the County of Merseyside" (London: HMSO, 1975); General Register Office, Edinburgh, "Census

1971: Scotland: County Report Glasgow City" (Edinburgh: HMSO, 1975); British Office of Population Censuses and Surveys, "Census 1981: County Report: Merseyside: Parts 1 and 2" (London: HMSO, 1983); "Census 1991: County Report: Merseyside: Parts 1 and 2" (London: HMSO, 1993); General Register Office for Scotland, "1991 Census: Strathclyde Region: Part 1 (Volume 2 of 2) and Part 2" (Edinburgh: HMSO, 1993).

For Milan, Naples: Istat, Statistiche dell'attività edilizia (1990–1994), "Fabbricati non residenziali di nuova costruzione secondo la destinazione d'uso (volume in metri cubi vuoto per pieno)"; Istat, Censimento generale della popolazione (1991), "Popolazione in condizione professionale per ramo di attività economica"; Istat, Censimento generale della popolazione (1971), "Popolazione in condizione professionale per ramo di attività economica"; Istat, Censimento generale della popolazione (1981) "Popolazione in condizione professionale per ramo di attività economica"; Istat, Censimento generale della popolazione, 1971, 1981, 1991; also estimates of Assisted Housing (interview, February 2001).

For Paris: Atelier Parisien d'Urbanisme (APUR), Le Recensement de 1990 à Paris Premiers Résultats. p. 47 (Paris, Septembre 1991) and Atelier Parisien d'Urbanisme (APUR), Paris: 1954 – 1990 (Paris).

For Marseilles: Marseilles en Chiffres. p. 9; Ville de Marseilles et Agence de Urbanisme de l'Agglomération Marseillaise; Recensement de 1968 Population Légale, tome I (Paris: INSEE, 1969).

CHAPTER 9

Table 9.1. Employment and Unemployment

Notes:

Actual years are as follows: Marseilles: 1990–1999; Glasgow and Liverpool 1991–1996; Detroit: 1991–1997; Naples: 1981–1991.

Sources: Detroit: State of the Cities Data Systems: Current Labor Force data, SOCDS Special Extract from County Business Patterns; http://socds.huduser.org/index.html.

Marseilles: Recensement de la population 1999, Exploitation principale, Copyright INSEE:http://www.recensement.insee.fr/.

Naples, Glasgow, and Liverpool: Urban Audit: Assessing the Quality of Life of Europe's Cities; Directorate General for Regional Policy and Cohesion of the European Commission by ECOTEC Research and Consulting Ltd. http://www.inforegio.cec.eu.int/urban/audit/.

AUTHOR-SOURCE NOTES

CHAPTER 1
THE GREAT TRANSFORMATION AND LOCAL CHOICES

1. Knight and Gappert, *Cities in a Global Society*; Judd and Parkinson, *Leadership and Urban Regeneration*.
2. Population Action International, *Global Migration*.
3. Stoltz, "Europe's Back Doors."
4. A.T. Kearney, Inc., "Globalization Index."
5. Sassen, *Cities in World Economy*.
6. Savitch, *Post-industrial Cities*; Sassen, *Global City*.
7. Swanstrom, "Semisovereign Cities"; Hill, "Cleveland Economy."
8. Gappert, *Future of Winter Cities*.
9. Dangschat and Obenbrugge, "Hamburg."
10. Bernard and Rice, *Sunbelt Cities*; Ruble, Tulchin, and Garland, "Globalism and Local Realities."
11. Gotttman, *Megalopolis*.
12. U.S. Bureau of the Census, "Population of the 100 Largest Cities"; State of the Cities Census Data Systems.
13. Sternlieb and Hughes, *Post-industrial America*; Kantor with David, *Dependent City*; Kantor, *Dependent City Revisited*, chap. 6.
14. Mumford, *City in History*; Jacobs, *Death and Life of Great American Cities*; Gans, *Urban Villagers*.
15. Savitch, "Global Challenge."
16. Sassen, *Global City*, *Cities in a World Economy*; A.T. Kearney, Inc., "Globalization Index."
17. Held, "Democracy."
18. Knight and Gappert, *Cities in Global Society*; United Nations Centre for Human Settlements, *Indicators Newsletter*.
19. Smith, *Transnational Urbanism*.
20. Savitch and Ardashev, "Does Terror Have an Urban Future?"
21. Webber, "Order in Diversity."
22. Kresl, "North American Cities International"; Sassen, *Cities in World Economy*; Glickman, "Cities and International Division of Labor."
23. Prud'homme, "Les sept plus grandes villes du monde"; Savitch, "Cities in a Global Era."
24. European Foundation for the Improvement of Living and Working Conditions, *Living Conditions* (1986); Baugher and Lamison-White, *Poverty*.
25. O'Connor, *Fiscal Crisis of State*; Saunders, "Central Local Relations."
26. Judd and Fainstein, *Tourist City*.
27. Schumpeter, *Capitalism, Socialism and Democracy*.
28. Swyngedouw, "Mammon Quest"; Ascher, *Metapolis ou l'Avenir des Villes*.

29. Polanyi, *Great Transformation.*
30. Logan and Molotch, *Urban Fortunes.*
31. Rubin and Rubin, "Economic Development Incentives."
32. Mollenkopf, *Contested City.*
33. Williams and Adrian, *Four Cities*; Swanstrom, "Semisovereign Cities."
34. Muzzio and Bailey, "Economic Development"; Clavel, *Progressive City.*
35. Clark and Inglehart, "New Political Culture"; Clark, "Structural Realignments."
36. Miranda, Rosdil, and Yeh, "Growth Machines."
37. Peterson, *City Limits.*
38. Stone and Sanders, *Politics of Urban Development*; Stone, *Regime Politics*; Swanstrom, "Semisovereign Cities"; Logan and Molotch, *Urban Fortunes.*
39. Leo, "City Politics"; Clarke and Gaile, *Work of Cities.*
40. Gurr and King, *State and City.*

Chapter 2
Toward a Theory of Urban Development

1. Savitch, *Post-industrial Cities*; Judd and Parkinson, "Leadership and Urban Regeneration"; Keating, M., *Comparative Urban Politics.*
2. Tiebout, "Pure Theory of Local Expenditures"; Bish, *Public Economy of Metropolitan Areas*; Peterson, *City Limits*; Schneider, *Competitive City.*
3. Peterson, *City Limits.*
4. Ibid., p. 15.
5. Sanders and Stone, *Politics of Urban Development*; Swanstrom, *Crisis of Growth Politics*; Logan and Swanstrom, *Beyond the City Limits.*
6. Swanstrom, "Semisovereign Cities."
7. Imbroscio, *Industrial Growth*; Taylor, "Structure, Culture and Action."
8. Peterson, *City Limits.*
9. Sanders and Stone, *Politics of Urban Development.*
10. Lindblom, "Still Muddling."
11. Kantor, *Dependent City*; Elkin, *City and Regime.*
12. Ostrom, Tiebout and Warren, "Organization of Government"; Peterson, *City Limits*; Stiglitz, *Economics of the Public Sector.*
13. Lindblom, "Market as a Prison."
14. Crenson, *Un-Politics of Air Pollution*; Vogel and Swanson; "Growth Machine"; Stone, *Regime Politics*; Ferman, *Challenging the Growth Machine.*
15. Mollenkopf, *Contested City*; Fasenfest, "Community Politics."
16. Logan and Molotch, *Urban Fortunes*; Sanders and Stone, *Politics of Urban Development.*
17. Cummings, *Business Elites.*
18. Dunford and Kafkalas, "Global-Local Interplay"; Parkinson, Foley, and Judd, *Regenerating the Cities.*
19. Cox, "Globalisation, Competition and the Politics."
20. Piore and Sabel, *Second Industrial Divide*; Storper, *Capitalist Imperative.*
21. Sassen, *Mobility of Capital and Labor*; *Global City*; Noyelle and Stanback, "Economic Transformation."

22. Pyrke and Lee, "Place Your Bets."

23. Thrift, *Spatial Formations*.

24. Muzzio and Bailey, "Economic Development."

25. Drier and Keating, "The Limits of Localism."

26. Savitch, "Global Challenge."

27. Warner and Low, "Factory in the Community"; Schulze, "Role of Economic Dominants."

28. Fogelsong, *Married to the Mouse*.

29. Pickvance and Preteceille, *State Restructuring*.

30. Kantor, *Dependent City Revisited*; *Dependent City*.

31. Savitch, *Post-industrial Cities*.

32. Savitch, *Post-industrial Cities*; Elkin, *City and Regime*.

33. Healy and Williams, "European Urban Planning Systems"; Barlow, *Public Participation*.

34. Keating, *Comparative Urban Politics*, 15–16.

35. Wong and Peterson, "Urban Response."

36. Danileson, *The Politics of Exclusion*; Kantor, *Dependent City Revisited*.

37. Goldsmith, "Central and Local Government Relations"; Healy and Williams, "European Urban Planning Systems."

38. Levine and Van Weesop, "Dutch Urban Planning."

39. Caro, *Power Broker*; Walsh, *Public's Business*.

40. Sharpe, *Local Fiscal Crisis*; Page and Goldsmith, "Center and Locality"; Pickvance and Preteceille, *State Restructuring*.

41. Rhodes "Power Dependence Theories," *Control and Power*.

42. Thoenig, "Pouvoir d'Etat et Pouvoirs Locaux."

43. Riesman, *Lonely Crowd*.

44. Walsh, *Public's Business*.

45. Simmie, *Power, Property and Corporatism*; Berger, *Organizing Interests*; Cawson, *Organized Interests*.

46. Putnam, *Making Democracy Work*; Fukuyama, *Trust*.

47. Clark, "Structural Realignments."

48. Savitch, *Post-industrial Cities*.

49. Wolman and Goldsmith, *Urban Politics and Policy*.

50. Vicari and Molotch, "Building Milan."

51. Banfield and Wilson, "Political Ethos Revisited"; Putnam, *Making Democracy Work*.

52. Webber, "Order in Diversity."

53. Mollenkopf, *Contested City*; Logan and Molotch, *Urban Fortunes*; Vogel and Swanson, "Growth Machine"; Ferman, *Challenging the Growth Machine*.

54. Krasner, *International Regimes*.

Chapter 3
Ten Cities, Thirty Years

1. Hall, "Creative Cities."

2. Hall, "Global City Regions."

3. Bish, *Public Economy*, Stiglitz, *Economics of the Public Sector*.

4. Trachte and Ross, "Crisis of Detroit."

5. Newman, "Lessons from Liverpool"; and City of Liverpool, *Annual Report*.

6. Parkinson and Russell, "Economic Attractiveness and Social Exclusion," 12.

7. City of Liverpool, *Annual Report*.

8. Donzel, "Regeneration in Marseilles," 289.

9. *Fortune* Magazine, November 14, 1994; November 13, 1995; November 11, 1996; and November 24, 1997.

10. GTA Task Force, *Toronto*.

11. Gilbert and Stevenson, "Governance and Economic Performance."

12. Jones and Bachelor, *Sustaining Hand*; Darden et al., *Detroit*.

13. Jacobs, *Cities and the Wealth of Nations*, 32.

14. Savitch and Vogel, *Regional Politics*; Barnes and Ledebur, *Local Economies*.

15. Keating, *City that Refused to Die*; *Economist*, August 22, 1998.

16. Confort, "Economy of Merseyside."

17. Reich, *Work of Nations*.

18. Feagin, *Free Enterprise City*.

19. U.S. Bureau of the Census, 1995–96.

20. U.S. Bureau of the Census, Census of Governments, 1992.

21. U.S. Bureau of the Census, 1995–96; Savitch and Thomas, *Big City Politics*.

22. Darden et al., *Detroit*.

23. U.S. Bureau of the Census, Census of Governments, 1992.

24. Darden et al., *Detroit*, 245.

25. Thomas, *Redevelopment and Race*, 214.

26. Wood, *1400 Governments*; Danielson and Doig, *New York*.

27. Berg and Kantor, "New York."

28. Goldberg and Mercer, *Myth of the North American City*, 124.

29. Duffy, *Competitive Cities*, 158.

30. Kaplan, *Urban Political Systems*; Rothblatt and Sancton, *Metropolitan Governance*; Frisken, "Contributions of Metropolitan Government."

31. Ashford, *British Dogmatism*; Page and Goldsmith, *Central and Local Government Relations*.

32. Gurr and King, *State and the City*.

33. Carmichael, *Central-Local Government Relations*.

34. Ashford, *British Dogmatism*.

35. Donzel, "Regeneration in Marseilles"; Judd and Parkinson, "Leadership and Urban Regeneration."

36. Keating, *Nations Against the State*.

37. Harvie, *Scotland and Nationalism*; Jeffrey, "Decentralization Debate."

38. Savitch, "Encourage then Cope."

39. U.S. Bureau of the Census, 1991–92.

40. Orr and Stoker, *Urban Leadership and Regimes*, 15.

41. Ewen, *Corporate Power and Urban Crisis*: Jones and Bachelor, *Sustaining Hand*.

42. Thomas and Murray, *Progrowth Politics*, 94.

43. Welch and Bledsoe, *Urban Reform*.

44. Thomas and Murray, *Progrowth Politics*, 88.

45. Allum, *Politics and Society*, 255.
46. Pecorella, *Community Power.*
47. Fowler, "Community Board Wrap Up."
48. *Le Monde*, March 8, 1988.
49. *Le Monde Diplomatique*, June 1993.
50. *Le Point*, June 18, 1994.
51. Patsias and Quesnel, "Associations de Citoyens et Construction d'une Citoyennette Quotidienne."
52. Musterd and Ostendorf, "Dutch Welfare State"; Magnussen, "Radical Municipalities."
53. Dogan and Pelassy, *How to Compare Nations.*
54. Crenson, *Un-Politics of Air Pollution*; Kunstler, *Geography of Nowhere.*
55. Muzzio and Bailey, "Economic Development"; DeLeon, *Left Coast City.*
56. National Advisory Commission on Civil Disorders, *Report.*
57. Thomas, *Redevelopment and Race*, 141.
58. Ibid., 184.
59. Fasenfest, "Community Politics."
60. Bledsoe and Welch, *Urban Reform and Its Consequences*, 23.
61. DiGaetano and Lawless, "Urban Governance."
62. Fleming, "Who'll Take on Liverpool Now?"
63. Carmichael, *Central-Local Government Relations*, 167.
64. Allum, *Politics and Society*, 19–87.
65. Dal Piaz, *Napoli.*
66. Allum, *Politics and Society.*
67. Feagin, *Free Enterprise City.*
68. Roncayolo, *Les Grammaires d'une Ville.*
69. INSEE, *Information Economiques*, no. 109.
70. Roncayolo, "Les Grandes Villes Françaises"; Donzel, "Regeneration in Marseilles," 114.
71. Brand, "Politics in Glasgow."
72. Keating, *City that Refused to Die.*
73. *Economist*, August 22, 1998; Varady, "Neighbourhood Regenration."
74. Gendrot, "Grass Roots Mobilization."
75. *L'Evenement du Jeudi*, August 20–26, 1998.
76. *Le Parisien*, September 16, 1998.
77. The *Economist*, May 19, 1990; Frisken, "Contributions of Metropolitan Government."
78. Frisken, "Politics of Urban Policy-Making."
79. Vicari, "Friction in the Growth Machine," 17.
80. Miranda, Rosdil, and Yeh, "Growth Machines"; Clark and Inglehart, "New Political Culture"; Clark, "Structural Realignments."
81. Clark and Hoffman-Martinot, *New Political Culture.*

CHAPTER 4
SOCIAL- AND MARKET-CENTERED STRATEGIES

1. Easton, *Systems Analysis of Political Life.*
2. Goetz, "Type II Policy and Mandated Benefits"; Stone; *Regime Politics*;

Capek and Gilderbloom, *Community versus Commodity*; Clavel, Pitt, and Yin, "Community Option"; Miranda, Rosdil, and Yeh, "Growth Machines."

3. Logan and Molotch, *Urban Fortunes*.

4. Haegel, *Un Maire à Paris*.

5. Savitch, *Post-industrial Cities*; Noin and White, *Paris*.

6. *Les Echos*, September 28, 1994.

7. Noin and White, *Paris*.

8. *Libération*, December 12, 1994, sec. M2.

9. *Le Monde*, December 22, 1992.

10. *Le Monde*, April 4, 1994.

11. *Le Figaro*, January 26, 1996.

12. Renaud, *Paris, Un Etat dans l'Etat?*

13. Lindblom, "Science of 'Muddling Through,'" "Still Muddling Not Yet Through."

14. Goldberg and Mercer, *Myth of the North American City*.

15. Quoted in Holden, "Why Toronto Works."

16. Frisken, "Contributions of Metropolitan Government."

17. Ibid., 277.

18. Metropolitan Toronto Planning Department, *Metropolitan Toronto: Key Facts*.

19. University of British Columbia, *St. Lawrence: 1974–79*.

20. Frisken, *City Policy-Making*, 84.

21. Frisken, "Politics of Urban Policy-Making."

22. Gilbert and Stevenson, "Governance and Economic Performance."

23. Morel, "Marseilles aux Tournants du Siècle."

24. Tulasne, "Trois Decennies de Planification."

25. Ibid., 58.

26. Ville de Marseilles, *Marseilles en Chiffres*.

27. INSEE, 1997.

28. Donzel, *Marseilles: L'Expérience de la Cité*, 120.

29. *Le Figaro*, 26 Janvier, 1996, 29.

30. Donzel, "Regeneration in Marseilles."

31. Donzel, *Marseilles: L-Expérience de la Cité*.

32. *Les Echos*, January 21, 1998, p. 11.

33. Guillermin, *EuroMéditerranée, Au Coeur de la Métropole*.

34. Parkinson and Russell, "Economic Attractiveness."

35. Parkinson and Bianchini, *Cultural Policy*; Parkinson and Evans, "Urban Regeneration."

36. Parkinson and Evans, "Urban Regeneration."

37. Taaffe and Mulhearn, *Liverpool*.

38. *Daily Express*, September 16, 1985.

39. Russell, *Liverpool City Challenge*.

40. Parkinson and Russell, "Economic Attractiveness."

41. Parkinson and Bianchini, *Cultural Policy*.

42. Harding, "Urban Regimes."

43. Parkinson and Evans, "Urban Regeneration."

44. Merseyside 2000, *Merseyside Development*.

45. European Social Fund, *Merseyside Objective 1.*

46. Boland, Mannin, and Wallace, "Merseyside."

47. Evans, "Governance."

48. Ibid.

49. Brindley, Rydin, and Stoker, *Remaking Planning*, 127–32.

50. Fareri "Milano," 62.

51. Ibid.

52. O'Cleireacain, "Private Budget," 27–31.

53. Ibid., 28.

54. Berg and Kantor, "New York."

55. Rogowski, Berkman, Strom, and Maniscalco, "New York City's Outer Borough Development Strategy."

56. Kantor, "Dual City as a Policy Choice."

57. Savitch, *Post-industrial Cities.*

58. Fainstein, *City Builders.*

59. Kantor, *Dependent City Revisited*, 1–3.

60. Savitch, *Post-industrial Cities.*

61. Toti, "Politics of Zoning."

62. Ibid.

63. Mollenkopf, *Contested City.*

64. O'Cleireacain, "Private Budget."

65. Berg, *Politics of Economic Development.*

66. Thomas, *Redevelopment and Race*, 169.

67. Ibid.

68. Jones and Bachelor, *Sustaining Hand.*

69. Ibid., 249.

70. Fasenfest, "Community Politics."

71. Jones and Bachelor, *Sustaining Hand.*

72. DiGaetaeno and Klemanski, *Urban Governance.*

73. Jones and Bachelor, *Sustaining Hand*, 226.

74. Young and Wheeler, *Hard Stuff*, 252–53

75. U.S. Department of Housing and Urban Development, *Empowerment Zone.*

76. Darden et al., *Detroit.*

77. DiGaetano and Klemanski, *Urban Governance.*

78. U.S. Department of Housing and Urban Development, 1999.

79. Thomas, *Redevelopment and Race*, 169.

80. Murray et al. *Houston Metropolitan Study*, 70.

81. Thomas and Murray, *Progrowth Politics*, 248–49.

82. Ibid., 248.

83. Turner and Garber, "Responding to Boom," 15.

84. Stein, *Houston Metropolitan Study*, 21.

85. Cavola and Vicari, "Business Center Project."

86. Dal Piaz, *Napoli, 1945–1985*; Barbagallo, *Napoli Fine Novecento.*

87. Kantor, Savitch, and Vicari, "Political Economy of Regime Politics."

88. Cavola and Vicari, "Business Center Project," 21.

89. Cavola and Vicari Haddock, "Naples: City on the Edge."

90. DeLeon, *Left Coast City*; Clavel, *Progressive City*; Clavel, Pitt, and Yin, "Community Option."

91. Logan and Molotch, *Urban Fortunes*; Harvey, *Urban Experience*; Fainstein, *City Builders*.

92. Okun, *Equality vs. Efficiency*.

93. Peterson, *City Limits*.

CHAPTER 5
DRIVING AND STEERING URBAN STRATEGY

1. Wirt, *Power in the City*.

2. Bocca, *Metropolis*.

3. Gribaudi, *Mediatori*.

4. McCarthy, "Revitalization of the Core City."

5. Lipset, *Political Man*.

6. Renaud, *Paris, Un Etat dans l-Etat*; Noin and White, *Paris*.

7. Frisken, *City Policy-Making*.

8. Sugrue, *Origins of Urban Crisis*.

9. Logan and Molotch, *Urban Fortunes*.

CHAPTER 6
DIRIGISTE AND ENTREPRENEURIAL BARGAINING

1. Krasner, *International Regimes*.

2. Kaplan, *Urban Political Systems*; *Reform, Planning and City Politics*.

3. Feldman, "Metro Toronto."

4. Colton, *Big Daddy*, 164.

5. Ibid., 160

6. Ibid.

7. Frisken, "Planning and Servicing the Greater Toronto Area."

8. Frisken, "Contributions of Metropolitan Government."

9. Frisken, "Planning and Servicing the Greater Toronto Area."

10. Ibid.

11. Siemiatycki and Isin, "Immigration, Diversity and Urban Citizenship."

12. Frisken, "Toronto at a Crossroads."

13. Ibid., 98.

14. Isin and Wolfson, "Making of the Toronto Megacity."

15. Ibid.

16. GTA Task Force, *Toronto*.

17. Horak, "Power of Local Identity."

18. Sancton, *Merger Mania*, 120.

19. Horak, "Power of Local Identity."

20. Ibid.

21. Isin and Wolfson, "Making of the Toronto Megacity."

22. Sancton, *Merger Mania*.

23. Horak, "Power of Local Identity."

24. Isin and Wolfson, "Making of the Toronto Megacity," 71.

25. Sancton, *Merger Mania*

26. *Libération*, April 12, 1994.

27. LaGroye, *Le Système Chirac*.

28. Guiral, "Le conseil de Paris."

29. LaGroye, *Le Système Chirac*.

30. Renaud, *Paris, Un Etat dans l'Etat?*

31. Haegel, *Un Maire à Paris*, 72.

32. Ibid., 75.

33. Ibid., 192.

34. Savitch, *Post-industrial Cities*.

35. Cornu, *Le conquête de Paris*; Madelin, *Le Clan des Chiraquiens*.

36. Savitch, *Post-industrial Cities*.

37. Atelier Parisien d'Urbanisme, *Paris Projet*.

38. Madelin, *Le Clan des Chiraquiens*.

39. *Le Journal des Finances*, June 5, 1993, p. 769.

40. *Le Monde*, April 13, 1999.

41. *Libération*, August 10, 1999.

42. Guiral, "L'attente des législatives conforte Tiberi en sa mairie."

43. *Le Figaro*, January 31, 1996.

44. Ibid.

45. *Conseil Municipal*, January 22, 1996, p. 133.

46. *Conseil Municipal*, October 23, 1996, 757–58.

47. *Le Parisien*, January 17, 1996, p. 6.

48. *Le Parisien*, September 16, 1999, p. 3.

49. Guiral, "Tiberi, le boulet de la Chiraquie."

50. *Le Parisien*, October 26, 1999, p. 2

51. *Paris Match*, July 8, 1999.

52. *Le Parisien*, March 20, 2001, p. 4.

53. Wilson, *Bureaucracy*. Perulli, *Atlante Metropolitano*, 211.

54. Tarrow, *Between Center and Periphery*, 89.

55. Dente, *Istituzioni*, 110.

56. Pompili, "Milan," 309.

57. Dente, *Istituzion*: 107.

58. Martinotti, Micheli, Vicari, Muti, and Natale, *Milano Ore Sette*.

59. Bellaviti, "Pubblico e Privato"; Dente, *Istituzioni*, 112–13.

60. Fareri, "La Progettzione del Governo a Milano," 207.

61. Bianchini, *Urbanization and the Functions of Cities*, 36; Fareri, "Milano: Progettualità Diffusa e Difficoltà Realizzativa," 214.

62. Dente, *Istituzioni*, 61–64.

63. Fareri, "Milano: Progettualità Diffusa e Difficoltà Realizzativa," 163–220.

64. Goldstein, *Urbanistica come Regolazione Sociale*, 86–87.

65. Bellaviti, "Pubblico e Privato," 125; Fareri, "Milano: Progettualità Diffusa e Difficoltà Realizzativa," 79.

66. Fareri, "Milano: Progettualità Diffusa e Difficoltà Realizzativa."

67. Vicari, "Friction in the Growth Machine"; Vicari and Molotch, "Building Milan."

68. Bellaviti, "Pubblico e Privato," chap. 1; Fareri, "La Progettzione del Governo a Milano," 167.

69. Fareri, "La Progettzione del Governo a Milano."

70. Bellaviti, "*Pubblico e Privato,*"chap. 1.

71. Magatti, *Corruzione Politica*, chap. 2.

72. Kasnetz, *Carribean New York*; Jones-Correa, *Between Two Nations*.

73. Brecher and Horton, *Setting Municipal Priorities*, 108.

74. Danielson and Doig, *New York*.

75. Fitch, *The Assassination of New York*.

76. Bellush and Netzer, "New York Confronts Urban Theory."

77. Shefter, *Political Crisis*.

78. Berg, "Politics of Economic Development."

79. Mollenkopf, *Phoenix in the Ashes*; Berg and Kantor, "New York."

80. Fainstein, "Changing Character of Community Politics"; Shefter, *Political Crisis*.

81. Siegel, *Future Once Happened Here*; Morris, *Cost of Good Intentions*.

82. Green and Wilson, *Struggle for Black Empowerment*; Mollenkopf, "New York."

83. Sites, "Limits of Regime Theory."

84. Sayre and Kaufman, *Governing New York City*; Bellush and Netzer, "New York Confronts Urban Theory."

85. Pecorella, "*Community Power.*"

86. Kantor, *Dependent City Revisited*, chap. 6.

87. Zukin, *Cultures of Cities*, chap. 1; Rogowski et al., 1998

88. Brecher and Horton, *Setting Municipal Priorities*, 124–26.

89. Reichl, "Historic Preservation," 520.

90. Ibid., 523.

91. *New York Times*, April 5, 1998, sec. A1, B3.

92. Ibid., B-3; *New York Times*, March 31, 1998, sec. A1, B2.

93. Key, *Southern Politics*, 254.

94. Shelton et al., *Houston*, 38.

95. Greater Houston Partnership, staff interviews, April 22, 1998.

96. Greater Houston Partnership, *At Work*.

97. Feagin, *Free Enterprise City*, 154.

98. Thomas and Murray, *Progrowth Politics*, 191–92.

99. Feagin, *Free Enterprise City*, 155.

100. Murray et al., *Houston Metropolitan Study*, 188.

101. Murray, "Power in the City," 35; Longoria, *School Politics in Houston*.

102. Thomas and Murray, *Progrowth Politics*, 197.

103. Burka, "Why is Houston Falling Apart?"

104. Thomas and Murray, *Progrowth Politics*, 299–300.

105. Longoria, *School Politics in Houston*.

106. Thomas and Hawes, "Changing Coalition Politics."

107. Greater Houston Partnership, *At Work*, 6.

108. Kantor, *Dependent City Revisited*.

CHAPTER 7
DEPENDENT BARGAINING: PUBLIC AND PRIVATE

1. Roncayolo, *Les Grammaires d'une Ville.*
2. Viard, *Marseilles, une Ville Impossible*, 240.
3. Ibid., 249.
4. Donzel, *Marseilles: L'Expérience de la Cité.*
5. *Le Monde*, July 15, 1986.
6. *Le Quotidien de Paris*, June 27, 1990, p. 10.
7. *Le Figaro*, January 26, 1996, p. 29.
8. *Le Monde*, June 5, 1998.
9. *Le Figaro Magazine*, December 5, 1987.
10. Donzel, *Marseilles: L'Expérience de la Cité.*
11. *Le Figaro*, July 23, 1997.
12. *Le Monde*, June 5, 1998.
13. *Le Monde*, August 21, 1999.
14. *Le Monde*, March 20, 2001, pp. 12, 49.
15. *Le Monde*, May 9, 1996.
16. Keating and Boyle, *Remaking Urban Scotland*, 19–21.
17. Keating, *City that Refused to Die*, "Disintegration of Urban Policy."
18. Kantor, "Can Regionalism Save Poor Cities?"
19. Lever, *Glasgow*, "Local Authority Responses"; Boyle, "Regeneration in Glasgow"; "Changing partners."
20. McClay, *Worker's City*; Boyle, "Relentless Boosterism."
21. Turok, "Continuity, Change and Contradiction"; Robertson, "Pulling in Opposite Directions"; Great Britain, Scotish Office, *New Life for Urban Scotland.*
22. Glasgow Regeneration Alliance, *Shaping the Future*; Glasgow Development Agency, *Annual Report*, 1996.
23. *Financial Times*, October 1, 1996; Webster, *Housing, Transport and Employment.*
24. Kearns and Turok, "Power, Responsibility, and Governance"; Kintrea, "Whose Partnership?"; Hastings, "Unravelling the Process of 'Partnership.'"
25. Lawless, "Urban policy."
26. Keating, "Disintegration of Urban Policy," 523.
27. Halkier, "Development Agencies and Regional Policy," 16–23; Great Britain, Her Majesty's Treasury, *Government's Expenditure Plans 1990–1991 to 1992–93*, p. 10; Great Britain, Depts. of the Secretary of State for Scotland and the Forestry Commission, *The Government's Expenditure Plans, 1996–1997 to 1998–99*, Apendix 7.
28. Kantor, "Can Regionalism Save Poor Cities?"
29. Lawless, "Urban policy"; Brindley, Ryden, and Stoker, *Remaking Planning*, 7.
30. McCrone, "Regionalism and Constitutional Change."
31. Kantor, "Can Regionalism Save Poor Cities?"
32. Lever, "Reurbanization."
33. Boyle, "Changing Partners," 312–13; Scottish Development Agency, *GEAR Project Evaluation.*

34. Great Britain, House of Commons, Scottish Affairs Committee, *Operation of the Enterprise Agencies*: xxxv–xxxvi.

35. Hayton and Mearns, "Progressing Scottish Enterprise," 311; Wilson, *Bureaucracy*, 50–71.

36. Lever, "Local Authority Responses"; Boyle, "Changing Partners."

37. Scottish Development Agency, *GEAR Project Evaluation*, 45; Webster, *Home and Workplace*, 3–5.

38. Dye, *150 Years in Struggle*.

39. Parkinson, *Liverpool on the Brink*.

40. Ibid.

41. Ibid.

42. Taaffe and Mulhearn, *Liverpool*, 59–60.

43. Parkinson, *Liverpool on the Brink*.

44. Newman, "Lessons from Liverpool," 36.

45. Parkinson, *Liverpool on the Brink*, 48.

46. Ibid.

47. Taaffe and Mulhearn, *Liverpool*, 135.

48. Ibid., 156.

49. Parkinson, *Liverpool on the Brink*, 108.

50. Taaffe and Mulhearn, *Liverpool*, 152.

51. Ibid., 168.

52. *Daily Mail*, September 16, 1985

53. Taaffe and Mulhearn, *Liverpool*.

54. *Economist*, April 18, 1998, p. 54.

55. Dye, *150 Years in Struggle*.

56. Fleming, "Who'll Take on Liverpool Now?"

57. *Economist*, November 6, 1999, p. 59.

58. Putnam, *Making Democracy Work*; Allum, *Politics and Society*.

59. Allum, *Politics and Society*, 327.

60. Ibid., 147; Barbagallo, *Napoli Fine Novecento*.

61. Barbagallo, *Napoli Fine Novecento*, 15.

62. De Lucia, *Napoli: Cronache Urbanistiche*.

63. Allum, *Politics and Society*, 255.

64. Della Porta, "Politics, the Mafia, and the Market," 180.

65. Barbagallo, *Napoli Fine Novecento*; Becchi, "Difficult Reconstruction," 117;

66. Barbagallo, *Napoli Fine Novecento*, 71–72

67. Becchi, "Difficult Reconstruction," 119–20; "L'Economia della Catastrofe."

68. Barbagallo, *Napoli Fine Novecento*, 73–78.

69. Becchi, "Difficult Reconstruction," 123.

70. Giorgino, "Opere Pubbliche Prima e Dopo Tangentopoli," 421.

71. Gasparrini, "Napoli," 364–65.

72. Barbagallo, *Napoli Fine Novecento*, 95

73. Sales, *La Camorra, Le Camorre*, 214–22.

74. Barbagallo, *Napoli Fine Novecento*, 57–59.

75. Cavola and Vicari, "Business Center Project."

76. Stancanelli, "Chiamatelo Diego Armando Bassolino"; Marrone, *Il Sindaco*.

77. Goldstein, *Urbanistica come Regolazione Sociale*, 47.

78. Allum, Cilento, and Mattina, "Local Electoral Reform."

79. United States Kerner Commission, *Report*.

80. Darden et al., *Detroit*.

81. Rich, *Coleman Young*, 280; Thomas, *Redevelopment and Race*, 149; Whelan and Young, *Detroit and New Orleans*, 10.

82. Stone, *Regime Politics*.

83. Ewen, *Corporate Power*.

84. Rich, *Coleman Young*, 176.

85. Ibid., 172.

86. Ibid., 142.

87. Orr and Stoker, *Urban Leadership*.

88. DiGaetano and Klemanski, *Urban Governance*.

89. Ibid.

90. Fasenfest, "Community Politics."

91. Jones and Bachelor *Sustaining Hand*, 73.

92. Ibid.

93. Rich, *Coleman Young*, 191.

94. Jones and Bachelor, *Sustaining Hand*, 119.

95. Fasenfest, "Community Politics"; Jones and Bachelor, *Sustaining Hand*, 124.

96. Jones and Bachelor, *Sustaining Hand* (2nd ed.), 222.

97. Ibid.

98. Ibid., 222.

99. Sternlieb and Hughes, *Atlantic City Gamble*.

100. Rich, "Politics of Casino Gambling," 284.

101. Whelan and Young, *Detroit and New Orleans*.

CHAPTER 8
ARE CITIES CONVERGING?

1. Dickens, *Global Shift*; Knight and Gappert, *Cities in a Global Society*.

2. Fainstein, *City Builders*, xi.

3. Lever, "Delinking Urban Economies," 236.

4. Chase-Dunn, *Global Formation*; Kresl and Gappert, *North American Cities*; Pickvance and Pretceille, *State Restructuring*; Pyrke and Lee, "Place Your Bets"; Grieder, *One World*.

5. Castells, "Commentary," *Information City*; Fainstein, *City Builders*; Harvey, *Urbanization of Capital*; Harloe, Pickvance, and Urry, *Place, Policy and Politics*.

6. Smith, *City, State and Market*; Harvey, *Urbanization of Capital*.

7. Cox, "Politics of Globalisation," "Globalisation, Competition and Politics"; Hirst and Thompson, *Globalization in Question*.

8. Teaford, *Unheralded Triumphs*; Suttcliffe, *Toward the Planned City*; Kantor, *Dependent City Revisited*.

9. Savitch, *Post-industrial Cities*, "Cities in a Global Era"; Goetz and Clarke, *New Localism*, 3.

10. Polanyi, *Great Transformation*; Goldberg and Mercer, *Myth of the North American City*.

11. Garrett, *Partisan Politics*.

12. Savitch, "Global Challenge and Institutional Capacity."

13. Kleinberg, *Urban America in Transformation*; Moynihan, *Maximum Feasible Misunderstanding*.

14. Moynihan, *Maximum Feasible Misunderstanding*,142.

15. Wong and Peterson, "Urban Response"; Peterson, *Price of Federalism*.

16. Kantor, *Dependent City Revisited*, 77–111.

17. Kleinberg, *Urban America in Transformation*.

18. U.S. Department of Housing and Urban Development, *State of the Cities 2000*; *Nation's Cities Weekly*, April 2, 1990, p. 6.

19. Teaford, *Rough Road to Renaissance;* U.S. Bureau of the Census, 1977–78 and 1984–85.

20. Barnekov, Boyle, and Rich, *Privatism and Urban Policy*, 121.

21. U.S. Department of Housing and Urban Development, *State of the Cities 2000*.

22. Savitch, "Cities in a Global Era."

23. Lawless, "Urban Policy in the Thatcher Decade," 104.

24. Chandler, "Local Authorities"; Barnekov, Boyle, and Rich, *Privatism and Urban Policy*.

25. Newman and Thornley, *Urban Planning*, 122–123.

26. Kearns and Turok, "Power, Responsibility, and Governance," 176.

27. Le Galès and Mawson, "Contracts versus Competitive Bidding."

28. Kearns and Turok, "Power, Responsibility, and Governance."

29. King, "Government Beyond Whitehall."

30. Wolman and Goldsmith, *Urban Politics and Policy*.

31. Mossberger and Stoker, "Inner-City Policy," 398.

32. Dente, "Sub-national Governments."

33. Ferrera, "Uncertain Future," 231.

34. Della Sala, "Hollowing Out the State."

35. Meny, *Center-Periphery Relations*.

36. Schmidt, "Unblocking Society," 22.

37. Bernier, *Political and Financial Consequences*.

38. Levine, "Transformation of Urban Politics."

39. Haider, "Place Wars."

40. Sophie Gendrot, "La crise dans nos banlieues est loin de celle que connaissent les ghettos aux Etats-Unis."

41. *Le Parisien*, March 29, 1996.

42. *Le Monde*, May 12, 1994.

43. Goldberg and Mercer, *Myth of the North American City*.

44. Frisken et al., *Governance and Social Well-being*.

45. GTA Task Force, *Toronto*.

46. Wolfson and Frisken, "Local Response."

47. Frisken, "Greater Toronto Area in Transiton."

48. Wolfson and Frisken, "Local Response."

49. *Globe and Mail*, November 14, 2000.

50. Garber and Imbroscio, "Myth of the North American City Reconsidered."

51. Goldsmith and Klausen, *European Integration*; Jensen-Butler, Shachar, and Van Weesop, *European Cities*.

52. Levine, "Transformation of Urban Politics"; Kresl and Gappert, *North American Cities*; Fainstein, *City Builders*.

53. *New York Times*, January 2, 1992, secs. A1, B4.

54. Bledsoe, *From One World*, I.

55. Siegel, *Future Once Happened Here*, 78.

56. Anderson, *Federal Bulldozer*; Laska and Spain, *Back to the City*.

57. Seligman, "Giuliani and After."

58. King, "With Rebirth, Detroit Jewels Get a New Sheen."

59. Quoted in Le Galès and Mawson, "Contracts versus Competitive Bidding."

60. Rey and Pola, "Integovernmental Relations in Italy," 382.

61. Bassett, "Growth Coalitions"; Wood, "Analysing the Politics."

62. INSEE, *Ile-de-France dossiers*.

63. Ibid.

64. Ibid.

65. *INSEE*, February, 1999.

66. Thomlinson, "When Right is Wrong."

67. Wolfson and Frisken, "Local Response."

68. Thomlinson, "When Right is Wrong."

69. Cohen et al., *Preparing for the Urban Future*; Hambleton, Savitch, and Stewart, *Globalization and Democracy*.

70. Clarke, "Urban Innovation and Autonomy"; Clark, T. N., *Urban Innovation*.

71. DiGaetano and Klemanski, *Power and City Government*.

72. Teaford, *Rough Road to Renaissance*, 295–307.

73. Clark, "Globalisation and Transformations."

74. Kantor, *Dependent City Revisited*, 12.

75. Rich, *Coleman Young*.

76. McConnell, "Snow Woes Put Archer's Mettle."

77. Archer, "Economic Development Message."

78. Hambleton, "Modernising Political Management."

79. Lally, "Why Glasgow," 6.

80. Marrone, *Il Sindaco*. Pasotti, "Clients to Citizens."

81. Madelin, *Le Clan des Chiraquiens*.

82. Gaudin, *Déclaration sur les orientations de la politique municipale*.

83. Ibid.

84. Welsh, "The Salesman."

85. Ibid.

86. *Toronto Economic Development Strategy*, November 17, 2000, p. 1.

87. Cummings, *Business Elites*; Squires, *Unequal Partnerships*.

88. Lawless, "Urban Policy in the Thatcher Decade."

89. European Commission Directorate General for Regional Policies, *Merseyside 2000*.

90. Heinz, *Partenariats Publics-Privés dans l'Aménagement Urbain*; Pierre, *Partnerships in Urban Governance*.

91. Ascher, *Metapolis ou l'Avenir des Villes*.

92. Thomlinson, "When Right is Wrong," 248.

93. *Toronto Economic Development Strategy*, November 17, 2000.

CHAPTER 9
STRATEGIES FOR THE INTERNATIONAL MARKETPLACE

1. Eisinger, *Rise of the Entrepreneurial State*.

2. Porter, "Competitive Advantage."

3. Pagano and Bowman, *Cityscapes and Capital*.

4. Reich, *Work of Nations*; Clarke and Gaile, *Work of the Cities*.

5. Florida, "Competing in the Age of Talent."

6. Boyle, M. Ross, "Economic Development Targeting."

7. Parks and Oakerson, "Regionalism, Localism"; Savas, *Privatization*.

8. Molotch, "City as a Growth Machine"; Logan and Molotch, *Urban Fortunes*; Jonas and Wilson, *Critical Perspectives*.

9. *Newsweek*, February 6, 1989; *U.S. News and World Report*, November 13, 1989; *Wall Street Journal*, March 27, 1989; Hall and Hay, *Growth Centers*; Summers, Cheshire, and Senn, *Urban Change*.

10. Kenneth Jackson, discussion list e-mail, 1999.

11. Leo and Brown, "Slow Growth."

12. *Urban Audit*, 2001.

13. Ibid.

14. Friedman, "World City Hypothesis."

15. State of the Cities Data Systems, March 2001.

16. Ibid.

17. *Le Monde*, December 5, 2000.

18. State of the Cities Data System, March 2001.

19. INSEE, 1998.

20. White, "Old Wine, Cracked Bottle?"

21. Olds, "Globalization"; Loftman and Nevin, "Going for Growth."

22. Robert Putnam *Making Democracy Work*; "Bowling Alone."

23. Gittel and Vidal, *Community Organizing*.

24. Putnam, "Bowling Alone."

25. Gittel and Wilder, "Community Development Corporations."

26. Lemann, "Myth of Community Development."

27. Hula, Jackson, and Orr, "Urban Politics."

28. Lopez and Stack, 1999: 39; Warren, Thompson, and Saegert, "Social Capital and Poor Communities."

29. Stone, "Civic Capacity," 596.

30. Dahl, "City in the Future of Democracy."

31. Stoecker, "CDC Model of Urban Development."

32. Rusk, *Inside Game, Outside Game*.

33. Di Ciommo, "Economic Actors and City Governability"; Atkinson and Lejeune, "Area-Based Urban Policy Initiatives."

34. Bockmeyer, "Devolution and the Transformation."

35. Rusk, *Inside Game, Outside Game*, 25.

36. Kantor, "Governable City."

37. Browning, Marshall, and Tabb, *Racial Politics in American Cities.*

38. Lowi, "American Business"; Key, *Southern Politics.*

39. Savitch and Vogel, "Paths to New Regionalism."

40. Stephens and Wilkerson, *Metropolitan Government*; Parks and Oakerson, "Regionalism, Localism."

41. Vogel and Harrington, *Political Change in the Metropolis.*

42. Norris, "Whither Metropolitan Government?"

43. Savitch, *Post-industrial Cities.*

44. Savitch and Vogel, "Paths to New Regionalism"; Katz, *Reflections on Regionalism.*

45. Porter, "Competitive Advantage of the Inner City"; Savitch, "Global Challenge."

46. Clarke and Gaile, *Work of the Cities;* Pierre, "Models of Governance."

47. Haider, "Place Wars."

48. Greater Toronto Area Task Force, *Greater Toronto*; Vogel, "Metropolitan Governance."

49. Scott, "Regional Motors"; Harris, "Cities in a Global Economy"; Beauregard and Pierre, "Disputing the Global."

50. Pierce, Johnson, and Hall, *Citistates*; Abu-Lughod, *New York, Chicago, Los Angeles.*

51. Pastore et al., *Regions That Work.*

52. Kantor and Savitch, "Can Politicians Bargain with Business"; Sbragia, Debt Wish.

53. Kantor with David, *Dependent City*; Zukin, *Cultures of Cities*; Boris and Steuerle, *Nonprofits and Government.*

54. Keating, *New Regionalism.*

55. Eisinger, *Rise of the Entrepreneurial State*; Osborne and Gaebler, *Reinventing Government*; Osborne. *Laboratories of Democracy.*

CHAPTER 10
CONCLUSIONS: CITIES NEED NOT BE LEAVES IN THE WIND

1. *Economist*, "New Trade War."

2. Polanyi, *Great Transformation.*

3. Dahl, *Who Governs.*

4. Savitch and Ardashev, *Does Urban Terror Have An Urban Future?*

5. New York City Partnership and Chamber of Commerce, *Working Together to Accelerate New York's Recovery*, 11–15.

6. Quinn, *Growth No Growth.*

7. Kunstler and Salingaros, *End of the Tower Buildings.*

8. Traub, *No Fun City*, 70.

Glossary

Agency — Political action that substantially conveys human volition, personal discretion, and freedom of decision.

Challenger regimes — Local governing coalitions that mobilize to oppose the legitimacy of the political and economic systems in order to advocate revolutionary alternatives. These regimes are radically oriented and their ideologies and their urban development strategy are viewed as vehicles for bringing about systemic change.

Clientelist regimes — Local governing coalitions that view public dependence as a way of accommodating, rather than changing, adverse economic conditions. They are oriented toward exploiting public largesse as a means of building political power around patron-client relationships. They often play down development as a viable and serious policy choice.

Currency exchange rates — Values of European currencies are at the following approximate exchange rates as of January, 2002: one United States dollar equals 7 French francs, 2200 Italian lira, 1.50 British pound sterling and 1.12 Euro dollar.

Dependent private bargaining context — A weak bargaining environment shared by cities lacking access to substantial intergovernmental assistance and lacking a competitive economic position in capital markets. Advantages accrue to business.

Dependent public bargaining context — A moderately weak bargaining environment shared by cities having access to relatively integrated intergovernmental support, but lacking a competitive position in the private capital marketplace. Advantages accrue to higher-level governments.

Diffuse intergovernmental systems — National political systems that substantially decentralize decision-making authority, fiscal relations, and economic regulation to cities, regions, provinces, or other subnational governments, such as in the United States federal system.

Dirigiste bargaining context — A favorable city bargaining environment in which cities enjoy the advantages of positive market conditions as well as access to an integrated and supportive intergovernmental environment. Advantages accrue to local, regional, or national officials.

Driving variables — Contextual forces that furnish investment power to localities. They include economic conditions and intergovernmental systems. Driving variables determine if things can be built and are often derived from the external environment.

Entrepreneurial bargaining context — A mixed city bargaining environment that enables local governments to draw upon positive economic conditions, but without substantial intergovernmental assistance. Advantages are often shared among private and public officials.

Etablissement Publique d'Aménagment (EPAD) — French public development corporations that can be quite aggressive in pursuing development goals. These organizations are usually funded and controlled through public sources.

Free enterprise regimes — Governing coalitions that follow the marketplace and rely heavily on its signals to manage policy. These regimes may well sympathize with business. They resist intervention in the marketplace and focus on providing opportunities for business to exploit its own interests.

Grantsman regimes — Local governing coalitions strongly oriented toward a single driving resource, intergovernmental support. Public dependence is seen as an opportunity where governmental leverage can sometimes offset private sector weakness. At the same time, these regimes are attentive to building local constituencies, using steering resources to bolster the city's position in the marketplace.

Integrated intergovernmental systems — National political systems that provide substantial vertical integration of decision-making authority, fiscal relations, and economic regulation among cities, regions, provinces, or other subnational governments, and the central government.

Intergovernmental support — Practices used by localities in conjunction with regional, provincial, state, or national authorities to intervene in the marketplace. Specific support mechanisms, such as planning, land-use controls, fiscal support, taxation, and other policies are brought to bear in order to influence public control over development.

Local culture — The values and norms found in urban populations that underlie local development priorities and agendas.

Market-centered development policy — Public policies that weigh gains primarily by the criterion of economic growth, placing the highest priority on attracting jobs, increasing population, and adding buildings and revenue. These policies target benefits to business in the belief that they will trickle into the larger population. Supply-side inducement such as tax abatements, free land, and available infrastructure typify this development strategy.

Market conditions — Circumstances or forces that make cities more or less appealing to private capital, influencing a city's competitive position vis-à-vis other cities and regions. This may be due to various reasons, including a city's geographic characteristics, political status, business circumstances, or other vital role in the international marketplace.

Materialist culture — Values and norms shared by a population that favor jobs, income, and other tangible benefits that are easily divisible in development agendas.

Mercantile regimes — Local governing coalitions that take a broad and activist view of public power, aggressively promoting business in order to maximize growth while also using public intervention for coping with political cross-pressures from citizen and neighborhood interests. Governing coalition behavior tends to be fairly volatile.

Mixed corporation — French organizations that combine a majority shares of public capital with private contributions in order to carry out development. Among other things they are often used to build socially subsidized housing.

Planner-type 1 regimes — Governing coalitions that successfully assert strong control over market forces and are capable of acting prospectively on their development futures, often converting market forces to their own ends.

Planner-type 2 regimes — Governing coalitions that share characteristics with type 1 regimes but frequently fail to realize their objectives. These regimes are laden with inertia due to internal political disagreements or clientelism that limit cooperation.

Popular control — Democratic political institutions and practices, such as levels of political participation, organized partisanship, and political competition, which provide a means of making public officials accountable to voters and motivating them to legitimate their actions.

Postmaterialist culture — Values and norms shared by a population that favor preservation of the built or natural environment, and promoting other indivisible community benefits in development agendas.

Regime — The dominant governing coalition in cities. As such, regimes constitute a regularized pattern of political cooperation for mobilizing city resources in support of a common, identifiable agenda.

Social-centered development policy — Public policies that put a priority on public amenities or collective benefits. This is done by seeking to distribute the benefits directly and widely to urban populations. They consist of green belts, low- and moderate-income housing, historic preservation districts, and mass transit. These policies are often supported by material exactions from the private sector.

Steering variables — Steering forces that shape development choices. These include institutions for popular control as well as local cultural values. Steering variables give expression to how, where, and whether things are built.

Structure — Long-term, underlying, and relatively fixed forces that configure decision making and constrain political actions, such as the economic benefits that spring from the geographic location of a city or a city's intergovernmental fiscal support.

Vendor regimes — Local governing coalitions seeking solutions to their development problems by marketing public assets for whatever can be obtained and facilitating business preferences. Political leaders view lowering the costs for business as the major means for retaining old capital or attracting new investors and are strongly inclined toward reacting to private initiatives.

ZACs, ZADs, ZUPs — French zoning tools that are used to carry out development. These are respectively coordinated development zones, special development zones, and priority development zones. These tools enable a cadre of policy-makers and technocrats to pour public money and infrastructure into the city's most strategic sites.

BIBLIOGRAPHY

A. T. Kearney, Inc. 2001. "The Globalization Index." *Global Outlook: International Urban Research Monitor*, April.

Abu-Lughod, Janet L. 1999. *New York, Chicago, Los Angeles: America's Global Cities*. Minneapolis: University of Minnesota Press.

———. 1996. "Administration for the Next Century." *Administration and Society* 30 (3): 248–73

———. 1994. "Agenda." *Urban Affairs Quarterly* 29 (3): 356–82.

———, ed. 1994. *From Urban Village to East Village*. Oxford: Blackwell.

Allen, Katherine, and Maria Kirby. 2000. "Unfinished Business: Why Cities Matter to Welfare Reform." *The Brookings Institution* (July).

Allum, Felia, Marco Cilento, and Cesare Mattina. 1998. "Local Electoral Reform and Local Politics: The Case of Naples." Paper prepared for the European Consortium for Political Research Workshop, University of Warwick, U.K., March 23–28.

Allum, Percy. 1973. *Politics and Society in Postwar Naples*. Cambridge: Cambridge University Press.

———. 1981. "Thirty Years of Southern Policy in Italy." *Political Quarterly* 52 (July/September): 314–23.

Altschuler, Alan A., and Josè A. Gomez, 1993. *Regulation for Revenue: The Political Economy of Land Use Exaction*. Washington: Brookings.

Amin, Ash. 1992. "Big Firms vs. the Regions in the Single European Market." In *Cities and Regions in the New Europe*, edited by Mick Dunford and Grigoris Kafkalas. London: Belhaven.

Amin, Ash, and Nigel Thrift. 1992. "Neo-Marshellian Nodes in Global Networks." *Journal of Urban and Regional Research* 16:571–87.

Anderson, Bill. 1995. "Summary of Municipal Economic Development Activities in the Greater Toronto Area." Introductory Material to GTA Task Force Report.

Anderson, Jeffrey O. 1990. "When Market and Territory Collide: Thatcherism and the Politics of Regional Decline." *West European Politics* 13 (April): 234–57.

Anderson, Martin. 1964. *The Federal Bulldozer: A Critical Analysis of Urban Renewal*. Cambridge: MIT Press.

Archer, Dennis. 2000. "Economic Development Message."

Ascher, François. 1995. *Metapolis ou l'Avenir des Villes*. Paris: Odile Jacob.

Ashford, D. 1982. *British Dogmatism and French Pragmatism*. London: Allen & Unwin.

Atelier Parisien d'Urbanisme. 1990 *Paris Projet: L'Aménagement du secteur Seine Rive Gauche*. Paris Projet Numero 29. Paris: Atelier Parisien d'Urbanisme.

Atkinson, Rob, and Stephanie Lejeune. 2001. "Area-Based Urban Policy Initiatives—the Role of Resident Participation in England and France." Paper presented at the European Urban Research Association Conference—Area-Based Initiatives in Contemporary Urban Policy—Innovations in City Governance—Copenhagen.

Bailey, Robert W. 1999. *Gay Politics, Urban Politics: Identity and Economics in the Urban Setting.* New York: Columbia University Press.

Banfield, Edward, and Wilson James. 1971. "Political Ethos Revisited." *American Political Science Review* 66(4): 1048–62.

Barbagallo, Francesco. 1989. "Un Sistema di Potere Contro lo Sviluppo del Sud." In *L'Affare Terremoto: Libro Bianco sulla Ricostruzione*, edited by Francesco Barbagallo, Ada Becchi, and Isaia Sales. Salerno: Angri.

———. 1997. *Napoli Fine Novecento.* Turin: Einaudi.

Barber, Benjamin R. 1984. *Strong Democracy.* Berkley: University of California Press.

Barlow, James. 1995. *Public Participation in Urban Development.* London: Policy Studies Institution.

Barnekov, Timothy, Robin Boyle, and Daniel Rich. 1989. *Privatism and Urban Policy in Britain and the United States.* Oxford: Oxford University Press.

Barnes, William R., and Larry C. Ledebur. 1994. *Local Economies: The U.S. Common Market of Local Economic Regions.* Washington, D.C.: National League of Cities.

Bartik, T. J. 1991. *Who Benefits from State and Local Development Policies?* Kalamazoo, Mich.: Upjohn Institute.

Basset, Keith. 1999. "Growth Coalitions in Britain's Waning Sunbelt: Some Reflections." In *The Urban Growth Machine: Critical Perspectives, Two Decades Later*, edited by Andrew E. G. Jonas and David Wilson. Albany: State University of New York Press.

Baugher, Eleanor, and Leatha Lamison-White. 1996. *Poverty in the United States: 1995.* U.S. Bureau of the Census, Current Population Reports, series P60–194. Washington, D.C.: U.S. Government Printing Office.

Beauregard, Robert A. 1984. "Structure, Agency and Urban Redevelopment." In *Cities in Transformation*, edited by M. Peter Smith. Beverly Hills: Sage.

Beauregard, Robert A., and Jon Pierre. 2000. "Disputing the Global: A Sceptical View of Locality-Based International Initiatives." *Policy & Politics* 28 (4): 456–78.

Becchi, Ada. 1987. "Napoli contro Napoli: Citta come Economia e Citta come Potere." *Meridiana* 5:143–67.

———. 1989. "L'Economia della Catastrofe, Il Partito della Catastrofe." In *L'Affare Terremoto: Libro Bianco Sulla Ricostruzione*, edited by Francesco Barbagallo, Ada Becchi, and Isaia Sales, 38–67. Salerno: Angri.

———. 1992. "The Difficult Reconstruction of Irpinia." In *Italian Politics*, edited by Stephen Hellman and Gianfranco Pasquino, 110–28. New York: St. Martin's.

———, ed. 1984. *Napoli Miliardia.* Milan: Angeli.

Bell, Daniel. 1973. *The Coming of Post-Industrial Society: A Venture in Social Forecasting.* New York: Basic Books.

Bellaviti, Paola. 1994. "Pubblico e Privato, Centrale e Locale nella Pianificazione per Progetti: Problemi e Opportunità per l'Innovazione delle Politiche Urbanistiche." Doctoral dissertation. Turin: Polytechnic of Turin.

Bellush, Jewel, and Dick Netzer. 1990. "New York Confronts Urban Theory." In *Urban Politics New York Style*. Armonk, N.Y.: M. E. Sharpe.

Bennington, John, and Mike Geddes. 1992. "Local Economic Development in the 1980s and 1990s: Retrospect and Prospect." *Economic Development Quarterly* 6 (4): 454–64.

Berg, Bruce. 1999. *The Politics of Economic Development in New York City*. Draft manuscript, Department of Political Science, Fordham Unversity.

Berg, Bruce, and Paul Kantor. 1996. "New York: The Politics of Conflict and Avoidance." In *Regional Politics: America in a Post City Age*, edited by H. V. Savitch and Ronald K. Vogel. Thousand Oaks, Calif.: Sage

Berger, Suzanne, ed. 1981. *Organizing Interests in Western Europe*. New York: Cambridge University Press.

Bernard, R. M., and B. R. Rice. 1983. *Sunbelt Cities: Politics and Growth since World War II*. Austin: University of Texas Press.

Bernier, Lynne Louise. 1992. *Political and Financial Consequences of Decentralization in France: A Survey of the 1980s*. Prepared for delivery at the Annual Meetings of the Urban Affairs Association in Cleveland, Ohio. Beverly Hills: Sage.

Bianchini, Franco. 1991. *Urbanization and the Functions of Cities in the European Community: Naples*. Liverpool: University of Liverpool Center for Urban Studies.

———. 1994. "Milan." In eds. *European Cities Towards 2000*, edited by Alan Harding et al. Manchester: Manchester University Press.

Bish, R. L. 1971. *The Public Economy of Metropolitan Areas*. Chicago: Markham.

Bledsoe, Timothy. 1990. *From One World Three: Political Change in Metropolitan Detroit*. Detroit: Center for Urban Studies, Wayne State University.

Bledsoe, Timothy, and Susan Welch. 1988. *Urban Reform and Its Consequences: A Study in Representation*. Chicago: University of Chicago Press.

Bocca, Giorgio. 1994. *Metropolis*. Milan: Arnoldo Mondadori.

Bockmeyer, Janice L. 2001. "Devolution and the Transformation of Community Housing Activism." Draft manuscript.

Boland, Philip, Michael Mannin, and John Wallace. 1995. "Merseyside: Implications of Economic Development." Unpublished Report. Liverpool.

Boris, Elizabeth T., and C. Eugene Steuerle, eds. 1999. *Nonprofits and Government*. Washington, D.C.: Urban Institute Press.

Boyle, M. 1995. "Relentless Boosterism—Glasgow's Addiction to Culture-Led Regeneration." Draft manuscript, Strathclyde University.

Boyle, M. 1994. "Economic Development Targeting in the Nineties." *Economic Development Review* 12 (2): 13–22.

Boyle, R. 1990. "Regeneration in Glasgow: Stability, Collaboration and Inequality." In *Leadership and Urban Regeneration*, edited by D. Judd and Michael Parkinson, 109–32. Newbury Park, Calif.: Sage.

———. 1993. "Changing Partners: The Experience of Urban Economic Policy in West Central Scotland." *Urban Studies*, 30 (2): 309–24.

Brand, J. 1968. "Politics in Glasgow." Unpublished manuscript, University of Strathclyde.

Brecher, Charles, and Raymond D. Horton, eds. 1989. *Setting Municipal Priorities*. New York: New York University Press.

Brindley, Tim, Yvonne Rydin, and Gerry Stoker. 1989. *Remaking Planning*. London: Unwin.

Browning, Rufus, Dale R. Marshall, and David H. Tabb, eds. 1997. *Racial Politics in American Cities*. New York, Longman.

Brun, Jacques, and Catherine Rhein, eds. 1994. *La Ségrégation dans la Ville: Concepts et mesures*. Paris: L'Harmattan.

Burka, Paul. 1980. "Why is Houston Falling Apart?" *Texas Monthly* (November): 309.

Burke, Mike, Colin Mooers, and John Shields, eds. 2000. *Restructuring and Resistance: Canadian Public Policy in an Age of Global Capitalism*. Halifax: Fernwood.

Butcher, Hugh, and Ian G. Law. 1990. *Local Government and Thatcherism*. London: Routledge.

Capek, S., and J. Gilderbloom. 1992. *Community versus Commodity*. Albany: State University of New York Press.

Carmichael, Paul. 1995. *Central-Local Government Relations in the 1980s: Glasgow and Liverpool Compared*. Brookfield, Vt.: Ashgate.

Caro, Robert. 1974. *The Power Broker*. New York: Random House.

Castells, Manuel. 1985. "Commentary on C. G. Pickvance's 'The Rise and Fall of Urban Movements' Environment and Planning.'" *Space and Society* 3:13–29.

———. 1989. *The Information City*. Oxford: Basil Blackwell.

Cavola, Lucia, and Serena Vicari Haddock. 1998. "The Business Center Project in Naples." Unpublished paper. University of Pavia.

Cawson, A., ed. 1985. *Organized Interests and the State. Studies in Meso-Corporatism*. Beverly Hills, Calif.: Sage.

Ceci, Francesco, and Daniela Lepore. 1997. *Arcipelago Vesuviano*. Lecce: Argo.

Cerase, F. P., E. Morlicchio, and A. Spamo. 1991. *Disocccupati e Disoccupate a Napoli*. Milan: CUEN.

Chandler, James A. 1993. "Local Authorities and Economic Development in Britain." In *The New Localism*, edited by Susan E. Clark and Edward G. Goetz, 46–64. Newbury Park, Calif.: Sage.

Chase-Dunn, Christopher. 1989. *Global Formation: Structures of the World Economy*. Oxford: Basil Blackwell.

Cheshire, P. et al., 1987. *Urban Problems and Regional Policy in the European Community*. Brussels: Commission of the European Communities.

Cheshire, P., G. Carbonaro, and D. Hay. 1986. "Problems of Urban Decline and Growth in EEC Countries: Or Measuring Degrees of Elephantness." *Urban Studies* (2):131–49.

City of Liverpool 1998. *Annual Report: 1996–97*.

City of Liverpool. 1998. Personal interview with city information officer, December 1.

City of Toronto Housing Department. 1979. *St. Lawrence 1974–1979*. Toronto: City Toronto Planning Board.

Clark, T. N. 1996. "Structural Realignments in American City Politics: Less Class, More Race, and a New Political Culture." *Urban Affairs Review* 31 (3): 367–403.

Clark, Terry Nichols. 2000. "Old and New Paradigms for Urban Research: Globalization and the Fiscal Innovation Project." *Urban Affairs Review* 36 (1): 26.

———. 2001. "Globalisation and Transformations in Political Cultures: How Globalisation Makes Small Governments Beautiful." In *Globalization and Democracy*, edited by Robin Hambleton, H.V. Savitch, and Murray Stewart. London: Palgrave.

———, ed. 1994. *Urban Innovation: Creative Strategies for Turbulant Times*. Thousand Oaks, Calif.: Sage.

Clark, Terry, and Vincent Hoffman-Martinot, eds. 1998. *The New Political Culture*. Boulder, Colo.: Westview.

Clark, Terry Nichols, and Ronald Inglehart. 1990. "The New Political Culture: Changing Dynamics of Support for the Welfare State and Other Policies in Post-Industrial Societies." Draft paper. University of Chicago.

Clarke, Susan E., ed. 1989. "Urban Innovation and Autonomy: Political Innovation and Autonomy." In *Urban Inovation*, vol. 1. Newbury Park: Sage.

Clarke, Susan E., and Gary L. Gaile. 1998. *The Work of the Cities*. Minneapolis: University of Minnesota Press.

Clavel, P. 1986. *The Progressive City*. New Brunswick, N.J.: Rutgers University Press.

Clavel, Pierre, and Nancy Kleniewski. 1990. "Space for Progressive Local Policy: Examples from the U.S. and U.K." In *Beyond the City Limits*, edited by John Logan, and Todd Swanstrom. Philadelphia: Temple University Press.

Clavel, Pierre, Jessica Pitt, and Jordan Yin. 1997. "The Community Option in Urban Policy." *Urban Affairs Review* 32 (4): 435–58.

Cohen, M. D., J. G. March, and J. P. Olsen. 1997. "A Garbage Can Model of Organizational Choice." *Administrative Science Quarterly* 17:1–25.

Cohen, Michael A., Blair A. Ruble, Joseph S. Tulchin, and Allison M. Garland, eds. 1996. *Preparing for the Urban Future: Global Pressures and Local Forces*. Washington D.C.: The Woodrow Wilson Center Press.

Colton, Timothy J. 1980. *Big Daddy: Frederic G. Gardiner and the Building of Metropolitan Toronto*. Toronto, Buffalo, London: University of Toronto Press.

Confort, Trevor. 1982. "The Economy of Merseyside, 1945–1982: Quickening Decline or Post Industrial Change?" In *The Resources of Merseyside*, edited by W.T.S. Gould and A. G. Hodgkiss. Liverpool: Liverpool University Press.

Conseil Municipal. 1996. *Bulletin* January 22: 133.

Conseil Municipal. 1996. *Bulletin* October 23: 757–58.

Cornu, Marcel. 1972. *Le conquête de Paris*. Paris: Mercure de France.

Cox, Kevin. 1992. "The Politics of Globalisation: A Skeptic's View." *Political Geography* 11:427–29.

Cox, Kevin R. 1995. "Globalisation, Competition and the Politics of Local Economic Development." *Urban Studies* 32 (2): 213–24.

Crenson, M. 1971. *The Un-Politics of Air Pollution.* Baltimore: Johns Hopkins University Press.

Cummings, Scott, ed. 1988. *Business Elites and Urban Development.* Albany: State University of New York Press.

Dahl, Robert. 1961. *Who Governs.* New Haven: Yale University Press.

———. 1967. "The City in the Future of Democracy." *American Political Science Review* 61 (4): 953–70.

Daily Express, The. 1985. September 16.

Daily Mail, The. 1985. September 16.

Dal Piaz, Alessandro. 1985. *Napoli, 1945–1985.* Milan: Angeli.

Dangschat, J. S., and J. Obenbrugge. 1990. "Hamburg: Crisis Management, Urban Regeneration, and Social Democrats." In *Leadership and Urban Regeneration*, edited by Judd and M. Parkinson, 88–108. Newbury Park, Calif.: Sage.

Danielson, M. 1976. *The Politics of Exclusion.* New York: Columbia University Press.

Danielson, Michael, and Jameson W. Doig. 1982. *New York: The Politics of Urban Regional Development.* Berkeley: University of California Press.

Darden, Joe T., Richard Child Hill, June Thomas, and Richard Thomas. 1987. *Detroit: Race and Uneven Development.* Philadelphia: Temple University Press.

Dawson, Jon, and Michael Parkinson. n.d. *Urban Development Corporations: The Merseyside Experience 1981–1990, Physical Regeneration, Political Accountability and Economic Challenge.* Working Paper No. 13. Liverpool: European Institute for Urban Affairs, John Moores University.

Délégation à l'Aménagement du Terrtioire et à l'Action Régionale. 2000. "Premiers Rencontres Nationales: Agglomérations (Loi Voynet)." Paris: DATAR, March 30.

DeLeon, Richard. 1992. *Left Coast City.* Lawrence: University Press of Kansas.

Della Porta, Donatella, and Alberto Vannucci. 1995. "Politics, the Mafia, and the Market for Corrupt Exchange." In *Italian Politics*, vol. 9, edited by Carol Mershon and Gianfranco Pasquino, 164–83. Boulder, Colo.: Westview.

Della Sala, Vincent. 1997. "Hollowing Out the State: European Integration and the Italian Economy." *West European Politics* 20 (1): 15–33.

De Lucia, Vezio. 1998. *Napoli: Cronache Urbanistiche, 1994–1997.* Milan: Baldini e Catoldi.

———. 1992. *Se Questa è una Città.* Rome: Riuniti.

Dente, Bruno. 1991. *Istituzioni e Nuovi Modelli di Governo Urbano.* Milan: Angeli.

———. 1997. "Sub-national Governments in the Long Italian Transition." *West European Politics* 20 (1): 176–93.

Derthick, Martha, and Paul Quirk. 1985. *The Politics of Deregulation.* Washington, D.C.: Brookings Institution.

Di Ciommo, Francesca. 2001. "The Economic Actors and City Governability: The Examples of Urban Regeneration in Milan, Naples and Paris." Paper presented at the European Urban Research Association Conference, "Area-Based Initiatives in Contemporary Urban Policy—Innovations in City Governance," in Copenhagen.

Dicken, P. 1992. *Global Shift: The Internationaization of Economic Activity*. London: Chapman and Hall.

DiGaetano, A., and J. Klemanski. 1993. "Urban Regimes in Comparative Perspective." *Urban Affairs Quarterly* 29 (September): 54–83.

———. 1999. *Urban Governance in Comparative Perspective: The Politics of Urban Development in the U.K. and U.S.* Minneapolis: University of Minnesota Press.

DiGaetano, Alan, and Paul Lawless. 1999. "Urban Governance and Industrial Decline." *Urban Affairs Review* 34 (4): 546–77.

Dogan, M., and J. Kasarda, eds. 1988. *The Metropolis Era*. Newbury Park, Calif.: Sage.

Dogan, Mattei, and Dominique Pelassy. 1984. *How to Compare Nations*. Chatham, N.J.: Chatham House Publishers.

Donnison, D., and A. Middleton. 1987. *Regenerating the Inner City: Glasgow's Experience*. London: Routledge.

Donzel, A. 1990. "Regeneration in Marseilles: The Search for Political Stability." In *Leadership and Urban Regeneration: Cities in North America and Europe*, edited by Dennis Judd and Michael Parkinson. Urban Affairs Annual Review, 37. Newbury Park, Calif.: Sage.

Donzel, André. 1992."Urbanisation et Fonctions des Villes: Le Cas de Marseilles." Aix-en-Provence: Centre National de Research Scientifique.

———. 1998. *Marseilles: L'Expérience de la Cité*. Paris: Anthropos.

Downs, Anthony. 1995. *New Visions for Metropolitan America*. Washington, D.C.: The Brookings Institute.

Drier, Peter, and Dennis W. Keating. 1990. "The Limits of Localism: Progressive Housing Policies in Boston, 1984–1989." *Urban Affairs Quarterly* 26 (December): 191–216.

Duffy, Hazel. 1995. *Competitive Cities*. London: E & FN Spon.

Dunford, Mick, and Grigoris Kafkalas, eds. 1992. *Cities and Regions in the New Europe*. London: Belhaven.

Dunford, Mick, and Grigoris Kafkalas. 1992. "The Global-Local Interplay, Corporate Geographics and Spatial Development Strategies in Europe." In *Cities and Regions in the New Europe*, edited by Mick Dunford, and Grigoris Kafkalas. London: Belhaven Press.

Dye, Jim, ed. 1998. *150 Years in Struggle: The Liverpool Labour Movement 1848–1998*. Liverpool: Liverpool Trades Union Council.

Easton, David. 1965. *A Systems Analysis of Political Life*. New York: John Wiley.

Echoes, Les. 1994. September 28.

———. 1998. January 21.

Economist, The. 2001. "The Price of Civic Price." March 10, p. 56.

Economist, The. 1999. "The New Trade War." December 4, pp. 25–26.

———. 1999. "Scouse Honour." November 6, pp. 58–59.

———. 1999. "America's World." October 23, p. 15.

———. 1998. August 22, pp. 47–48.

———. 1998. "Capitals of Capital." Survey of Financial Centers. May 9, pp. 1–35.

———. 1998. "The Name Game." April 18, p. 54.

———. 1990. May 19, pp. 17–20.

Eisinger, Peter K. 1988. *The Rise of the Entrepreneurial State: State and Local Economic Development Policy in the United States.* Madison: University of Wisconsin Press.

Elkin, Stephen L. 1987. *City and Regime in the American Republic.* Chicago: University of Chicago Press.

European Commission Directorate General for Regional Policies. 2000. *Merseyside 2000: Programming Document for Objective 1: 1994–1999.* Merseyside, UK.

European Foundation for the Improvement of Living and Working Conditions. 1985. *Living Conditions in Urban Europe.* Information Booklet Series.

European Foundation for the Improvement of Living and Working Conditions. 1986. *Living Conditions in Urban Europe.* Dublin: Foundation for the Improvement of Living and Working Conditions.

European Research and Development Fund. 1996. *Merseyside 2000: Objective 1, Guidance Notes for Applicants.*

European Social Fund. 1998. *Merseyside Objective 1: Action for Industry Measures 1.2–4.4, Guidance for 1999 Applications.* European Social Fund, Great Britain.

Evans, Richard. 2000. "Governance, Competitiveness and Social Exclusion: Merseyside Objective 1 Programme." Working paper. European Institue for Urban Affairs, Liverpool John Moores University.

Ewen, Lynda Ann. 1978. *Corporate Power and Urban Crisis in Detroit.* Princeton: Princeton University Press.

Fainstein, Susan. 1991. "The Changing Character of Community Politics in New York City: 1968–88." In *Dual City,* edited by John Mollenkopf and Manuel Castells, 315–32. New York: Russell Sage.

Fainstein, Susan S. 1994. *The City Builders: Property, Politics, and Planning in London and New York.* Cambridge, Mass.: Blackwell.

Fainstein, Susan, et al. 1986. *Restructuring the City.* New York: Longman.

Fainstein, Susan S., and Norman Fainstein. 1989. "The Ambivalent State: Economic Development Policy in the U.S. Federal System under the Reagan Administration." *Urban Affairs Quarterly* 25 (1): 41–62.

Fareri, Paolo. 1990. "La Progettzione del Governo a Milano: Nuovi Attori per la Metropoli Matura." In *Metropoli Per Progetti,* edited by Bruno Dente, Luigi Bobbio, Paolo Fareri, and Massimo Morisi. Milan: Il Mulino.

———. 1991. "Milano: Progettualità Diffusa e Difficoltà Realizzativa." In *La Costruzione della Città Europea negli Anni '80,* edited by Credito Fondiario. Rome: Credito Fondiario.

————. 1994. "Milano." In *Le Decisioni di Opera Pubblica e di Urbanistica nelle Città*, ISAP. Milan: Archivo.

Fasenfest, David. 1986. "Community Politics and Urban Redevelopment." *Urban Affairs Quarterly* 22 (1): 101–23.

Feagin, Joe R. 1988. *Free Enterprise City*. New Brunswick, N.J.: Rutgers University Press.

Feagin, Joe R., John Gilderbloom, and Nestor Rodrequez. 1989. "Private-Public Partnerships: The Houston Experience." In *Unequal Partnerships*, edited by Gregory Squires. Albany: State University of New York Press.

Feldman, Lionel D. 1995. "Metro Toronto: Old Battles—New Challenges." In *The Government of World Cities: The Future of the Metro Model*, edited by L. J. Sharpe. Chichester, UK: John Wiley.

Ferman, Barbara. 1996. *Challenging the Growth Machine*. Lawrence: University of Kansas Press.

Ferrera, Maurizio. 1997. "The Uncertain Future of the Italian Welfare State." In *Crisis and Transition in Italian Politics*, edited by Martin Bull and Martin Rhodes, 231–49. London: Frank Cass.

Figaro, Le. 1996. January 26, p. 29.

————. 1996. January 31.

————. 2001. March 19, p. 11.

Fitch, Robert. 1993. *The Assassination of New York*. New York: Verso.

Fleming, Stewart. 1997. "Who'll Take on Liverpool Now?" *New Statesman*. 10 (455): 24–25.

Florida, 2000. "Competing in the Age of Talent: Quality of Place and the New Economy." A Report prepared for the R. K. Mellon Foundation and Sustainable Pittsburgh. Pittsburgh Penn.

Fogelsong, Richard E. 2001. *Married to the Mouse*. New Haven: Yale University Press.

Fortune Magazine. 1994. November 14.

Fowler, Glenn. 1980. "Community Board Wrap Up." *New York Affairs* 6 (1).

Frieden, Jeffrey A. 1991. "Invested Interests: The Politics of National Economic Policy in a World of Global Finance." *International Organizations* 45 (4): 425–51.

Friedman, John. 1986. "The World City Hypothesis (Editor's Introduction)." *Development and Change* 17 (1): 74.

Frisken, Frances. 1988. *City Policy-Making in Theory and Practice: The Case of Toronto's Downtown Plan*. London, Canada: University of Western Ontario.

————. 1990. "Planning and Servicing the Greater Toronto Area: The Interplay of Provincial and Municipal Interests." Urban Studies Programme Working Paper No. 12. Toronto: York University.

————. 1991. "The Contributions of Metropolitan Government to the Success of Toronto's Public Transit System: An Empirical Dissent from the Public-Choice Paradigm." *Urban Affairs Quaterly* 27 (2): 268–92.

————. 1993. "Planning and Servicing the Greater Toronto Area: The Interplay of Provincial and Municipal Interests." In *Metropolitan Governance: American/Canadian Intergovernmental Perspectives*, edited by Donald N. Rothblatt, Andrew Sancton. Berkeley: Institute of Governmental Studies Press, University of California.

———. 1993. "Politics of Urban Policy-Making: Provincial and Municipal." Paper prepared for a symposium on "Toronto Region in the World Economy," York University Urban Studies Program, North York, Ontario, June 24–26, 1993.

———. 1997. "Integrating Economic and Social Development in Metropolitan Areas: Lessons from Toronto." OECD-Toronto Workshop, "Better Governance for More Competitive and Livable Cities."

———. 1998. "The Greater Toronto Area in Transiton: The Search for New Planning and Servicing Strategies." In *Metropolitan Intergovernmental Governance Perspectives Revisited*, edited by Rothblatt Donald and Andrew Sancton Berkely: University of California Press.

———. 1999. "Toronto at a Crossroads, and How It Got There." Unpublished manuscript. University of Toronto, Canada.

Frisken, Frances, L.S., Bourne, Gunter Gad, and Robert A. Murdie. 1997. *Governance and Social Well-being in the Toronto Area: Part Achievements and Future Challenges*. Research Paper 193. Toronto: Centre for Urban and Community Studies, University of Toronto.

Fukuyama, Francis. 1995. *Trust: The Social Virtues and the Creation of Prosperity*. New York: Free Press.

Gans, H. J. 1962. *The Urban Villagers: Group and Class in the Life of Italian-Americans*. New York: Free Press.

Gappert, G. 1987. *The Future of Winter Cities*. Newbury Park, Calif.: Sage Publications.

Garber, Judith A., and David L. Imbroscio. 1996. "The Myth of the North American City Reconsidered." *Urban Affairs Review* 31 (5): 595–624.

Gario, Giuseppe. 1995. "Intergovernmental Relations in Lombardy: Provinces, Regions and Cities." *Political Geography* 4 (4): 419–28.

Garrett, Geoffrey. 1998. "Global Markets and National Politics: Collision Course or Virtuous Circle?" *International Organization* 52 (4): 787–824.

———. 1998. *Partisan Politics and the Global Economy*. Cambridge: Cambridge University Press.

Gasparrini, Carlo. 1991. "Napoli." In *La Costruzione della Città Europea negli Anni '80*. Vol. II. *Rome, Italy*, 337–407. Rome: Credito Fondario.

Gaudin, Jean-Claude. 1995. *Déeclaration sur les orientations de la politique municipale*. Maire de Marseilles.

Gendrot, Sophie. 1987. "Grass Roots Mobilization in the Thirteenth Arrondissment of Paris: A Cross National View." In *The Politics of Urban Development*, edited by Clarence Stone and Hayood Sanders. Lawrence: University Press of Kansas.

———. 1996. "La crise dans nos banlieues est loin de celle que connaissent les ghettos aux Etats-Unis." *Le Monde*. May 22, 1996.

Gilbert, Richard and Don, Stevenson. 1997. "Governance and Economic Performance: The Montreal, Toronto, and Vancouver Regions." OECD-Toronto Workshop, "Better Governance for More Competitive and Livable Cities." The Municipality of Toronto and the Territorial Development Service of the Organization for Economic Cooperation and Development.

Giorgino, Luigi. 1994. "Opere Pubbliche Prima e Dopo Tangentopoli." *Stato e Mercato* 42:413–38.

Gittell, Ross, and A. Vidal. 1998. *Community Organizing: Building Social Capital as a Development Strategy.* Thousand Oaks, Calif.: Sage.

Gittell, Ross, and Margaret Wilder. 1999. "Community Development Corporations: Critical Factors that Influence Success." *Journal of Urban Affairs* 21 (2): 341–62.

Glasgow Development Agency. 1994, 1995, and 1996. *Annual Report and Accounts.* Glasgow: Glasgow Development Agency.

Glasgow Development Agency. n.d. *Strategic Plan, 1995–98.* Glasgow: Glasgow Development Agency.

Glasgow Regeneration Alliance. n.d. *Shaping the Future.* Glasgow: Glasgow Regeneration Alliance.

Glickman, N. J. 1985. "Cities and the International Division of Labor." Working Paper Number 31 Austin: Lyndon B. Johnson School of Public Affairs, University of Texas.

Globe and Mail, The. 2000. "Tories usher in era of privatized cities." November 14.

Goetz, Edward. 1990. "Type II Policy and Mandated Benefits in Economic Development." *Urban Affairs Quarterly* 26:170–91.

———. 1993. "The New Localism from a Cross-National Perspective." In *The New Localism: Comparative Urban Politics in a Global Era,* edited by Edward Goetz and Susan E. Clarke. Thousand Oaks, Calif.: Sage.

Goetz, Edward, and Susan E. Clarke, eds. 1993. *The New Localism: Comparative Urban Politics in a Global Era.* Thousand Oaks, Calif.: Sage.

Goldberg, Michael A., and John Mercer. 1986. *The Myth of the North American City: Continentalism Challenged.* Vancouver: University of British Columbia Press.

Goldsmith, Michael, and K. K. Klausen, eds. 1997. *European Integration and Local Government.* Brookfield, Vt: Edward Elgar.

Goldsmith, Mike. 1993. "The Europeanization of Local Government." *Urban Studies* 30 (4–5): 683–99.

Goldstein, Mattco Bolocan. 1997. *Urbanistica come Regolazione Sociale.* Milan: Masson.

Gottman, J. 1961. *Megalopolis: The Urbanized Northeastern Seaboard of the United States.* Cambridge: MIT Press.

Grant, Gerald A. 1997. "Economic Development and Urban Region Competitiveness — Recent Toronto Initiatives." OECD-Toronto Workshop, "Better Governance for More Competitive and Livable Cities." The Municipality of Toronto and the Territorial Development Service of the Organization for Economic Cooperation and Development.

Great Britain, Departments of the Secretary of State for Scotland and the Forestry Commission. 1996. *The Government's Expenditure Plans, 1996–1997 to 1998–99.* Cmnd. 3214. Edinburgh: HMSO.

Great Britain, Her Majesty's Treasury. 1990. *The Government's Expenditure Plans, 1990–1991 to 1992–93,* chapter 15, "Scotland." Cmnd. 1015. Edinburgh: HMSO.

Great Britain, House of Commons, Scottish Affairs Committee. 1995. *The Operation of the Enterprise Agencies and the LECs*. First Report, vol. 1. London: HMSO.

Great Britain, Scottish Office. 1988. *New Life for Urban Scotland*. Edinburgh: HMSO.

Greater Houston Partnership 1997. *At Work*. Vol. 52, no. 2 (February). Houston: Greater Houston Partnership.

Greater Toronto Area Task Force. 1996. *Greater Toronto*. Ontario: Queen's Printer for Ontario.

Green, Charles, and Basil Wilson. 1989. *The Struggle for Black Empowerment in New York City*. New York: Praeger.

Gribaudi, Gabriella. 1991. *Mediatori*. Turin: Rosenberg and Sellier.

Grieder, William. 1997. *One World, Ready or Not*. New York: Touchstone Books.

GTA (Greater Toronto Area Task Force). 1996. *Toronto: Report of the GTA Task Force, January 1996*. Toronto: Greater Toronto Area Task Force.

Guillermin, B. 1996. *EuroMéditerranée, Au Coeur de la Métropole*. Marseilles: Etablissement Public d'Aménagement.

Guiral, Antoine. 1994. "Le conseil de Paris fait sa rentrée sous le signe des elections." *Libération*, October 26.

———. 1996. "L'attente des législatives conforte Tiberi en sa mairie." *Libération*. February 2.

———. 1999. "Tiberi, le boulet de la Chiraquie," *Libération*, March 5.

———. "Le putsch avorte des pieds nickelés. *Libération*, August 11.

Gurr, T. R., and Desmond S. King. 1987. *The State and the City*. Chicago: University of Chicago Press.

Haegel, Florence. 1994. *Un Maire à Paris: Mise en scène d'un nouveau rôle politique*. Paris: Presses de la Fondation Nationale des Sciences Politiques.

Haider, Donald. 1992. "Place Wars: New realities of the 1990s." *Economic Development Quarterly* 6 (2): 127–34.

Halkier, H. 1992. "Development Agencies and Regional Policy: The Case of the Scottish Development Agency." *Regional Politics and Policy* 2 (3): 1–26.

Hall, Peter. 2000. "Global City Regions in the Twenty-First Century." In *Global City Regions*, edited by Allen Scott. Oxford: Oxford University Press.

Hall, P., and D. Hay. 1980. *Growth Centers in the European Urban System*. Berkeley: University of California Press.

Hall, Peter. 1989. *Urban and Regional Planning*. London: Unwin Hyman.

———. 2000. "Creative Cities and Economic Development." *Urban Studies* 37 (4): 639–49.

Hambleton, Robin. 2000. "Modernising Political Management in Local Government." *Urban Studies* 37 (5–6): 931–50.

Hambleton, Robin, H. V. Savitch, and Murray Stewart, eds. 2002. *Globalization and Democracy*. London: Palgrave.

Harding, Alan. 1994. "Urban Regimes and Growth Machines." *Urban Affairs Quarterly* 29 (3): 356–83.

Harding, Alan. n.d. *Public-Private Partnerships in Urban Regeneration*. Working Paper No. 4. Liverpool: European Institute for Urban Affairs, John Moores University.

Harloe, Michael, Chris Pickvance, and John Urry, eds. 1990. *Place, Policy and Politics: Do Localities Matter?* London: Unwin Hyman.

Harris, Nigel. 1997. "Cities in a Global Economy: Structural Change and Policy Reactions." *Urban Studies* 34 (10): 1693–703.

Harvey, David. 1985. *The Urbanization of Capital.* Oxford: Blackwell.

———. 1989. *The Urban Experience.* Baltimore: Johns Hopkins University Press.

Harvie, C. 1995. *Scotland and Nationalism: Scottish Society and Politics, 1707–1994.* 2nd ed. London: Routledge.

Hastings, Annette. 1996. "Unravelling the Process of 'Partnership' in Urban Regeneration Policy." *Urban Studies* 33 (2): 253–68.

Havrileski, Thomas. 1995. *The Pressure on American Monetary Policy.* 2nd ed. Boston: Kluwer.

Hayton, K., and E. Mearns. 1991. "Progressing Scottish Enterprise." *Local Economy* 5 (4): 305–16.

Healy, Patsy, and Richard Williams. 1993. "European Urban Planning Systems: Diversity and Convergence." *Urban Studies* 30:701–20.

Heinz, Werner, ed. 1994. *Partenariats Publics-Privés dans l'Aménagement Urbain.* Paris: L'Harmattan.

Held, David. 1991. "Democracy, the Nation-state and the Global System." *Economy and Society* 20:138–72.

Hill, Edward W. 1995. "The Cleveland Economy: A Case Study of Economic Restructuring." In *Cleveland: A Metropolitan Reader*, edited by W. D. Keating, N. Krumholz, and D. C. Perry, 53–84. Kent, Ohio: Kent State University Press.

Hirst, Paul. 1994. "Why the National Still Matters." *Renewal* 2 (4): 12–20.

Hirst, Paul, and Grahame Thompson. 1996. *Globalization in Question: The International Economy and the Possibilities of Governance.* Cambridge: Polity Press.

Holden, Alfred. 1995. "Why Toronto Works." *Planning* 61 (3): 4–11.

Horak, Martin. 1998. "The Power of Local Identity: C4LD and the Anti-amalgamation Mobilization in Toronto." Paper presented at the Centre for Urban and Community Studies, University of Toronto, Toronto.

Hula, Richard, Cynthia Jackson, and Marion Orr. 1997. "Urban Politics, Governing Non-Profits and Community Revitalization." *Urban Affairs Review* 32 (4): 459–89.

Hulchanski, J. David. 1990. *Planning New Urban Neighborhoods: Lessons from Toronto's St. Lawrence Neighborhood.* Vancouver: University of British Columbia Press.

Imbroscio, David. 1999. *Industrial Growth.* Oxford: Basil Blackwell.

———. 1999. "Structure, Agency and Democratic Theory." *Polity* 32 (1): 45–66.

Indergaard, Michael. 1997. "Community-Based Restructuring? Institution Building in the Industrial Midwest." *Urban Affairs Review* 32 (5): 662–82.

Institut National de la Statistique et des Etudes Economiques (INSEE). 1997. *Information Economiques.* No. 109. Paris: INSEE.

————. 1998. *Paris en Chiffres: Ile-de-France dossiers.* No. 32, December. Paris: INSEE.

————. 1998. "Hauts-de-Seine en chiffres," "Val-de-Marne en chiffres," "Seine-Saint-Denis en chiffres." In *Ile-de-France dossiers*, No. 33, December.

————. 1999. http://www.insee.fr/fr/insee—regions/idf/rfc/chiffres—cle.htm.

Institut National de la Statistique et des Etudes Economiques (INSEE). 1999. *Le bas revenues dan les Bouche-du-Rhône.* February. Paris: INSEE.

Isin, Engin, and Joanne Wolfson, 1999. "The Making of the Toronto Megacity: An Introduction." Paper presented at York University as the Urban Studies Programme. Working Paper No. 21, Toronto.

Istituto per la Scienza dell'Amministrazione Pubblica. 1984. *Le Relazioni Centro-Periferia.* Milan: Giuffre.

Jackson, Kenneth. 1999. Discussion list e-mail.

Jacobs, Jane. 1961. *The Death and Life of Great American Cities.* New York: Vintage.

Jacobs, Jane. 1984. *Cities and the Wealth of Nations.* New York: Random House.

Jeffrey, C. 1997. "The Decentralization Debate in the UK: Role-Model Deutchland?" *Scottish Affairs* 19:42–54.

Jensen-Butler, Chris, Arie Shachar, and Jan Van Weesop, eds. *European Cities in Competition.* Brookfield, Vt.: Ashgate.

Jonas, Andrew E. G., and David Wilson, eds. 1999. *Critical Perspectives Two Decades Later.* Albany: State University of New York Press.

Jones, Bryan D., and Lynn W. Bachelor. 1986, 1993. *The Sustaining Hand: Community Leadership and Corporate Power.* 1st and 2nd eds. Lawrence: University Press of Kansas.

Jones-Correa, Michael. 1998. *Between Two Nations.* Ithaca: Cornell University Press.

Journal des Finances, Le, 1993. June 5, p. 769.

Judd, Dennis, and Susan Fainstein, eds. 1999. *The Tourist City.* New Haven: Yale University Press.

Judd, Dennis, and Michael Parkinson, eds. 1990. *Leadership and Urban Regeneration: Cities in North America and Europe.* Urban Affairs Annual Review, 37. Newbury Park, Calif.: Sage

Kafkalas, Grigoris, ed. 1992. *Cities and Regions in the New Europe.* London: Belhaven Press.

Kanter, Rosabeth Moss. 1995. *World Class: Thriving Locally in the Global Economy.* New York: Simon & Schuster.

Kantor, P. 1993. "The Dual City as a Policy Choice." *Journal of Urban Affairs* 15 (3): 231–44

Kantor, Paul. 1974. "The Governable City: Islands of Power and Political Parties in London." *Polity* 7:4–31.

————. 1995. *The Dependent City Revisited: The Political Economy of Urban Development and Social Policy.* Boulder, Colo.: Westview.

———. 2000. "Can Regionalism Save Poor Cities? Politics, Institutions and Interests in Glasgow." *Urban Affairs Review* 35 (4): 794–820.

———. 2002. "The Local Polity as a Pathway of Public Power: Taming the Business Tiger During New York City's Industrial Age." *International Journal of Urban and Regional Research.*

Kantor, Paul, with S. David. 1988. *The Dependent City: The Changing Political Economy of Urban America.* Glenview, Ill.: Scott, Foresman.

Kantor, Paul, and H. V. Savitch. 1993. "Can Politicians Bargain with Business: A Theoretical and Comparative Perspective on Urban Government." *Urban Affairs Quarterly* 29 (2): 230–55.

Kantor, Paul, H. V. Savitch, and Serena Vicari. 1997. "The Political Economy of Regime Politics: A Comparative Perspective." *Urban Affairs Review,* January 1997.

Kaplan, Harold. 1967. *Urban Political Systems: A Functional Analysis of Metro Toronto.* New York: Columbia University Press.

———. 1982. *Reform, Planning and City Politics: Montreal, Winnipeg, Toronto.* Toronto: University of Toronto Press.

Kasnetz, Philip. 1992. *Caribbean New York.* Ithaca: Cornell University Press.

Katz, Bruce, ed. 2000. *Reflections on Regionalism.* Washington, D.C.: Brookings Institution.

Katzenstein, Peter J., Robert O. Keohane, and Stephen D. Krasner. 1998. "International Organization and the Study of World Politics." *International Organizations* 52, no. 4 (Autumn): 645–85.

Kearns, Ade, and Ivan Turok. 2000. "Power, Responsibility and Governance in Britain's New Urban Politcy." *Journal of Urban Affairs* 22 (2): 175–92.

Keating, Dennis. 1997. "The CDC Model of Urban Development: A Reply to Randy Stoecker." *Journal of Urban Affairs* 19 (1): 29–35.

Keating, Michael. 1988. *The City that Refused to Die: Glasgow.* Aberdeen: Aberdeen University Press.

———. 1989. "The Disintegration of Urban Policy: Glasgow and the New Britain." *Urban Affairs Quarterly* 24 (4): 513–36.

———. 1991. *Comparative Urban Politics.* London: Edward Elgar.

———. 1996. *Nations Against the State: The New Politics of Nationalism in Quebec, Catalonia and Scotland.* London: Macmillan.

———. 1998. *The New Regionalism in Western Europe.* Northampton, Mass.: Edward Elgar.

Keating, Michael, and Robin Boyle. 1986. *Remaking Urban Scotland.* Edinburgh: Edinburgh University Press.

Keating, W. D., N. Krumholz, and D. C. Perry. eds. 1995. *Cleveland: A Metropolitan Reader.* Kent, Ohio: Kent State University Press.

Key, W. Dennis. 1949. *Southern Politics in State and Nation.* New York: Vintage.

King, Desmond. 1990. "Economic Activity and the Challenge to Local Government." In *Challenges to Local Government,* edited by Desmond King and Jon Pierre, 265–89. Newbury Park, Calif.: Sage.

King, Desmond. 1993. "Government Beyond Whitehall: Local Government and

Politics." In *Developments in British Politics*, vol. 4, edited by Patrick Dunleavy, A. Gamble, I. Holiday, and G. Peele. London: Macmillan.

King, Desmond S., and Jon Pierre. 1990. *Challenges to Local Government.* Newbury Park, Calif.: Sage.

King, R. J. "With Rebirth, Detroit Jewels Get a New Sheen." *The Detroit News*, June 16, 1999.

Kintrea, Keith. 1996. "Whose Partnership? Community Interests in the Regeneration of a Scottish Housing Scheme." *Housing Studies* 11 (2).

Kleinberg, Benjamin. 1995. *Urban America in Transformation: Perspectives on Urban Policy and Development.* Thousand Oaks, Calif.: Sage.

Knight, R., and G. Gappert, eds. 1989. *Cities in a Global Society.* Urban Affairs Annual Review, 35. Newbury Park, Calif.: Sage.

Krasner, Stephen. 1983. *International Regimes.* Ithaca: Cornell University Press.

Kresl, P. K. 1994. "North American Cities International." *A Proposal for Funding on Behalf of the NACI Steering Committee.* Bucknell University.

Kresl, Peter Karl, and Gary Gappert, eds. 1995. *North American Cities and the Global Economy.* Urban Affairs Annual Review, vol. 44. Thousand Oaks, Calif.: Sage.

Kunstler, James H. 1993. *The Geography of Nowhere.* New York: Simon & Schuster.

Kunstler, James, and Nikos Salingaros. 2001. "End of the Tower Buildings." *Planitizen*, September 17.

Lagroye, Jacques. 1986. *Le Système Chirac.* Manuscript.

Lally, Pat. 1990. "Why Glasgow Should Ignore the Hysteria in the Culture Debate." *Glasgow Herald*, June 30, sec. 6.

Laska, Shirley Bradway, and Daphne Spain, eds. 1980. *Back to the City: Issues in Neighborhood Renovation.* New York: Pergamon.

Lauria, Mickey, ed. 1997. *Reconstructing Urban Regime Theory.* Thousand Oaks, Calif.: Sage.

Lawless, P. 1991. "Urban Policy in the Thatcher Decade: English Inner-city Policy, 1979–1990." *Environment and Planning* 9:15–30.

Le Galès, Patrick, and John Mawson. 1994. "Lutte contre l'exlusion et logique de compétition entre villes." *La Société contre l'Exclusion Pouvoirs Locaux* 2 (2): 64–67.

———. 1995. "Contracts versus Competitive Bidding." *Journal of European Public Policy* 2 (2): 205–41.

Lemann, Nicholas. 2002. "The Myth of Community Development." *New York Times Magazine*, January 9, 1974. Reprinted in *The Politics of Urban America*, 3rd ed., edited by Dennis R. Judd and Paul Kantor. New York: Longman, 2002.

Leo, Christopher. 1997. "City Politics in an Era of Globalization." In *Reconstructing Urban Regime Theory*, edited by Mickey Lauria. Thousand Oaks, Calif.: Sage.

Leo, Christopher, and Wilson Brown. (2000) "Slow Growth and Urban Development Policy" *Journal of Urban Affairs.* Volume 22, No. 2: 193–213

Levdansky, D. 1984. *Plant Closings in Southwest Pennsylvania.* Pittsburgh: University of Pittsburgh Center for Social and Urban Research.

Lever, William F. 1992. "Local Authority Responses to Economic Change in West Central Scotland." *Urban Studies* 29 (6): 935–48.

———. 1993. "Reurbanization—The Policy Implications." *Urban Studies* 30 (2): 267–84.

———. 1997. "Delinking Urban Economies: The European Experience." *Journal of Urban Affairs* 19 (2): 227–38

———. n.d. *Glasgow*. Draft manuscript.

Levine, M., and J. Van Weesop. 1988. "The Changing Nature of Dutch Urban Planning." *Journal of the American Planning Association* 54 (3): 315–23.

Levine, Myron A. 1994. "The Transformation of Urban Politics in France." *Urban Affairs Review* 29 (3): 383–410.

Liberation. 1994. December 12.

———. 1996. February 7.

———. 1999. August 10.

Lindblom, Charles E. 1959. "The Science of 'Muddling Through.'" *Public Administration Review* 19:79–88.

———. 1979. "Still Muddling Not Yet Through." *Public Administration Review* 39:517–26.

———. 1982. "The Market as a Prison." *Journal of Politics* 44:324–36.

Lipset, Seymour M. 1981. *Political Man*. Baltimore: Johns Hopkins University Press.

Loftman, Patrick, and Brendan Nevin. 1996. "Going for Growth: Prestige Projects in Three British Cities." *Urban Studies* 33 (6): 991–1019.

Logan, John, and Harvey L. Molotch. 1987. *Urban Fortunes: The Political Economy of Place*. Berkeley: University of California Press.

Logan, John, and Todd Swanstrom, eds. 1990. *Beyond the City Limits*. Philadelphia: Temple University Press.

Long, Norton E. 1958. "The Local Community as An Ecology of Games." *American Journal of Sociology* 64 (November): 251–61.

Longoria, Thomas. 1997. *School Politics in Houston: Conflict, Cooperation and the Development of a Reform Agenda*. Draft manuscript.

Lowi, T. J. 1964. "American Business, Public Policy, Case Studies, and Political Theory." *World Politics* 16:677– 715.

Madelin, Philippe. 1997. *Le Clan des Chiraquiens*. Paris: Seuil.

Magatti, Mauro. 1997. *Corruzione Politica e Società Italiana*. Draft manuscript. Catholic University, Milan.

Magnussen, W. 1989. "Radical Municipalities in North America." Paper presented at the 1989 Annual Meeting of the American Political Science Association, August 31 to September 3. Atlanta, Georgia.

March, James G., and James P. Olson. 1984. "The New Institutionalism: Organizational Factors in Political Life." *American Political Science Review* 78:734–49.

———. 1989. *Rediscovering Institutions*. New York: Free Press.

———. 1995. *Democratic Governance*. New York: Free Press.

Marrone, Titti. 1996. *Il Sindaco*. Milan: Rizzoli.

Marshall, A. 1927. *Industry and Trade*. 3rd ed. London: Macmillan.

Martinotti, Guido, Giuseppe Micheli, Serena Vicari, Emanuela Muti, and Paolo

Natale. 1988. *Milano Ore Sette: Come Vivono i Milanesi.* Milan: Comune di Milano.

Mayhew, David. 1994. "U.S. Policy Waves in Comparative Context." In *New Perspectives on American Politics,* edited by Lawrence C. Dodd and Calvin Jillson. Washington, D.C.: CQ Press.

McCarthy, John. 1997. "Revitalization of the Core City; the Case of Detroit." *Cities* 14 (1): 1–11.

McClay, F. 1988. *Worker's City: The Real Glasgow Stands Up.* Glasgow: Clydeside.

McConnell, Darcy. 1999. "Snow Woes Put Archer's Mettle, Skills to the Test." *Detroit Free Press,* Jan. 21.

McCrone, D. 1993. "Regionalism and Constitutional Change in Scotland." *Regional Studies* 27 (6): 507–72.

Mearsheimer, John J. 1994/95. "The False Promise of International Institutions." *International Security* 19 (3): 5–47.

Meegan, Richard. 1990. "Merseyside in Crisis and in Conflict." In *State Restructuring and Local Power: A Comparative Perspective,* edited by Chris Pickvance and Edmond Pretceille. London: Pinter.

———. 1992. "Liverpool-Sliding—Down the Urban Hierarchy." Paper presented at International Sociological Association, Research Group 21, University of California, Los Angeles, April 23–25.

Meny, Yves, and V. Wright, eds. 1985. *Center-Periphery Relations in Western Europe.* London: Allen and Unwin.

Merseyside 2000. 1996. *Merseyside Development.* Liverpool: Merseyside Development Corporation.

Mershon, Carol, and Gianfranco Pasquino, eds. 1995. *Italian Politics,* vol. 9. Boulder, Colo.: Westview.

Metro Toronto Planning Department. 1995. *The Municipality of Metropolitan Toronto: Key Facts—1995.* Toronto: Municipality of Metropolitan Toronto.

Miranda, R., D. Rosdil, and S. Yeh. 1992. "Growth Machines, Progressive Cities and Regime Restructuring: Explaining Economic Development Strategies." Paper prepared for the 88th Annual Meeting of the American Political Science Association, Chicago, IL: September 3–6.

Mittiga, Sien. 2001. "Revitalization in the South Bronx and Community Development Corporations." Senior honors thesis, Fordham University, New York.

Mollenkopf, John. 1983. *The Contested City.* Princeton: Princeton University Press.

———. 1990. City Planning. In Charles Brecher and Raymond D. Horton, (eds). *Setting Municpal Priorities,* edited by Charles Brecher and Raymond D. Horton. New York: New York University Press.

———. 1992. *Phoenix in the Ashes.* Princeton: Princeton University Press.

———. 1997. "New York: The Great Anomaly." In *Racial Politics in American cities,* edited by Rufis Browning, Dale R. Marshall, and David Tabb. New York: Longman.

Molotch, Harvey. 1976. "The City as a Growth Machine." *American Journal of Sociaology* 82 (2): 309–30.

———. 1990. "Urban Deals in Comparative Perspective." In *Beyond the City*

Limits, edited by John Logan and Todd Swanstrom. Philadelphia: Temple University Press.

Monde, Le. 1986.July 15.

———. 1994. April 14.

———. 1994. "Le retour de l'Etat." May 12.

———. 1994. December 20–22.

———. 1999. April 13.

———. 2001. March 20, p. 38.

Morel, Bernard. 1995. "Marseilles aux Tournants du Siècle." *Libération*, February 15, p. 7.

Morganthau, Hans J. 1973. *Politics Among Nations: The Struggle for Power and Peace.* 5th Edition. New York: Knopf.

Morris, Charles. 1980. *The Cost of Good Intentions.* New York: Norton.

Mossberger, Karen and Gerry Stoker. 1997. "Inner-City Policy in Britain: Why It Will Not Go Away." *Urban Affairs Review* 32 (3): 378–403.

———. 2000. "The Evolution of Regime Theory: The Challenge of Conceptualization." Paper presented at the 30th Annual Meeting of the Urban Affairs Association, Los Angeles, May 3–6.

Moynihan, Daniel P. 1970. *Maximum Feasible Misunderstanding: Community Action in the War on Poverty.* New York: Free Press.

Mumford, L. 1961. *The City in History: Its Origins, its Transformation, and Its Prospects.* New York: Harcourt Brace Jovanovich.

Murray, Richard. 1997. "Power in the City: Patterns of Political Influence in Houston, Texas." In *Perspectives on American and Texas Politics*, edited by Kent L. Tedin, Donald S. Lutz, and Edward P. Fuchs. Dubuque, Iowa: Kendall/Hunt.

Murray, Richard A., Mark Hinnawi, and David Donnelly. 1998. *The Houston Metropolitan Study: Infrastructure Investment and Regional Growth.* Houston: Rice University Baker Institute of Public Policy.

Musterd, S., and W. Ostendorf, 1993. *Ethnicity and the Dutch Welfare State: The case of Amsterdam.* Amsterdam: Amsterdam Studies Center for the Metropolitan Environment.

Muzzio, D., and R. Bailey. 1986. "Economic Development, Housing and Zoning." *Journal of Urban Affairs* 8:1–18.

Nathan, Richard, and Charles Adams. 1976. "Understanding Central City Hardship." *Political Science Quarterly* 91:47–62.

———. 1989. "Four Perspectives on Urban Hardship." *Political Science Quarterly* 104 (3): 483–508.

National Advisory Commission on Civil Disorders. 1968. *Report of the National Advisory Commission on Civil Disorders.* New York: Bantam Books.

Nation's Cities Weekly, 1990. April 2.

Nethercutt, M. 1987. *Detroit Twenty Years After.* Detroit: Center for Urban Studies, Wayne State University Press.

Newman, Peter. 1986. "Lessons from Liverpool." *Planning and Administration* 1:31–41.

Newman, Peter, and Andy Thornley. 1996. *Urban Planning in Europe.* London: Routledge.

Newsweek. 1989. "America's Hot Cities." February 6, pp. 42–49.

New York City Partnership and Chamber of Commerce. 2001. *Working Together to Accelerate New York's Recovery, Economic Analysis of the September 11 Attack on New York City.* November: 11–15. New York: Office of the New York City Partnership.

New York Times, The. 1992. "For many in the New York Region, The City is Ignored and Irrelevant." January 2, secs. A1, B4.

Noin, Daniel, and Paul White. 1997. *Paris.* Chichester, England: John Wiley.

Norris, Donald. 2001. "Prospects for Regional Governance Under the New Regionalism: Economic Imperative Verses Political Impediments." In "Regionalism Reconsidered." *Journal of Urban Affairs* 23 (5): 557–72.

———. 2001. "Whither Metropolitan Government?" *Urban Affairs Review* 36 (4): 532–50

North, Douglas C. 1990. *Institutions, Institutional Change and Economic Performance.* Cambridge: Cambridge University Press.

Noyelle, Thierry, and Thomas Stanback. 1984. *The Economic Transformation of American Cities.*New York: Conservation for Human Resources, Columbia University.

O'Cleireacain, Carol. 1997. "The Private Budget and the Public Budget of New York City." In *The City and the World: New York's Global Future*, edited by Margaret Crahan and Alberto Vourvoulias-Bush. New York: Council on Foreign Relations.

O'Connor, James. 1973. *The Fiscal Crisis of the State.* New York: St. Martins.

Okun, A. 1975. *Equality vs. Efficiency: The Big Tradeoff.* Washington, D.C.: Brookings Institution.

Olds, K. 1995. "Globalization and the Production of New Urban Spaces: Pacific Rim Megaprojects in the Late 20th Century." *Environment and Planning* 27: 1713–1743.

Orr, Marion, and Gerry Stoker. 1992. *Urban Leadership and Regimes in Detroit.* Detroit: Center for Urban Studies Special Research Series, Wayne Sate University.

———. 1994. "Urban Regimes and Leadership in Detroit." *Urban Affairs Quarterly* 30 (September): 48–73.

Osborne, David. 1988. *Laboratories of Democracy.* Boston: Harvard Business School Press.

Osborne, David, and Neil Gaebler. 1992. *Reinventing Government.* Reading, Mass.: Addison Wesley.

Ostrom, Vincent, Charles Tiebout, and Robert Warren. 1961. "The Organization of Government in Metropolitan Areas: A Theoretical Inquiry." *American Political Science Review* 55:831–42.

Pagano, Michael, and Ann Bowman. 1997. *Cityscapes and Capital.* Baltimore: Johns Hopkins University Press.

Page, Edward C., and Michael J. Goldsmith. 1987. "Center and Locality: Functions, Access and Discretion." In *Central and Local Government Relations*, edited by Edward C. Page and Michael J. Goldsmith. London: Sage.

Painter, Joe. 1997. "Regulation, Regime, and Practice in Urban Politics." In

Reconstructing Urban Regime Theory, edited by Mickey Lauria. Thousand Oaks, Calif.: Sage.

Paris Match. 1999. July 8.

Paris Projet Numero 29. 1990. *Paris Projet: l'Amenagement du secteur Seine Rive Gauche.* Paris: Atelier Parisien d'Urbanisme.

Parisein, Le. 1996. March 29.

————. 1999. October 26, p. 2.

Parkinson, Michael. 1985. *Liverpool on the Brink: One City's Struggle Against Government Cuts.* Hermitage, U.K.: Policy Journals.

————. 1990. "Political Responses to Urban Restructuring: The British Experience Under Thatcherism." In *Beyond the City Limits*, edited by John Logan and Todd Swanstrom. Philadelphia: Temple University Press.

————. 1991. *Port Cities in Europe: The Restructuring of the Port of Liverpool.* Liverpool: European Institute for Urban Affairs, John Moores University.

————. n.d. "Urban Leadership and Regeneration in Liverpool: Confusion, Confrontation or Coalition?" Working Paper No. 14. Liverpool: John Moores University.

Parkinson, Michael, and Franco Bianchini. 1990. *Cultural Policy and Urban Regeneration in Liverpool: A Tale of Missed Opportunities.* Liverpool: European Institute for Urban Affairs, John Moores University.

Parkinson, Michael, and Richard Evans. 1988. "Urban Regeneration and Development Corporations: Liverpool Style." Working Paper No. 2. Liverpool: European Institute for Urban Affairs, John Moores University.

Parkinson, Michael, Bernard Foley, and Dennis R. Judd, eds. 1989. *Regenerating the Cities: The UK Crisis and the US Experience.* Glenview, Ill.: Scott, Foresman.

Parkinson, Michael, and Hilary Russell. 1994. "Economic Attractiveness and Social Exclusion: The Case of Liverpool." Paper prepared for the report EUROPE 2000+ for the European Commission. Liverpool: John Moores University.

Parks, Roger, and Ronald Oakerson. 2000. "Regionalism, Localism, and Metropolitan Governance: Suggestions from the Research Program on Local Public Economics." In *State and Local Government Review* edited by H. V. Savitch and Ronald K Vogel. Vol. 32, no. 3.

Passotti, Eleanora. 2001. "Clients to Citizens: Public Opinion Mobilization in Naples." Paper delivered to the Annual Meeting of the American Political Association, San Francisco, September.

Pastore, Manuel, Jr., Peter Dreier, J. Eugene Grigsby III, and Marta Lopez-Garza. 2000. *Regions that Work.* Minneapolis: University of Minnesota Press.

Patsias, Caroline, and Louise Quesnel. 1999. "Associations de Citoyens et Construction d'une Citoyennette Quotidienne." Paper presented at the Annual Meeting of the European Research Association, Paris, France.

Pecorella, Robert F. 1994. *Community Power in a Postreform City.* Armonk, N.Y.: M. E. Sharpe.

Pendall, Rolf. 1999. "Opposition to Housing: NIMBY and Beyond." *Urban Affairs Review* 35 (1): 112–36.

Perry, David C., ed. 1995. *Building the Public City.* Thousand Oaks, Calif.: Sage.

Perulli, Paolo. 1992. *Atlante Metropolitano.* Bologna: Il Mulino.

Peters, B. G. 1996. "Political Institutions, Old and New." In *A New Handbook of Political Science*, edited by R. E. Goodin and H. D. Klingemann. Oxford: Oxford Univeristy Press.

Peterson, Paul E. 1981. *City Limits.* Chicago: University of Chicago Press.

———. 1995. *The Price of Federalism.* Washington, D.C.: Brookings Institution.

Peterson, Paul E., and Mark Rom. 1989. "Macro-economic Policy Making: Who is in Control?" In *Can the Government Govern?* edited by John Cubb and Paul E. Peterson. Washington, D.C.: Brookings Institution.

Pickvance, Chris. 1990. "Institutional Context of Local Economic Development: Central Controls, Spatial Policies." In *Place, Policy and Politics: Do Localities Matter?* edited by Michael Harloe, Chris Pickvance, and John Urry. London: Unwin Hyman.

Pickvance, Chris, and Edmond Preteceille, eds. 1991. *State Restructuring and Local Power: A Comparative Perspective.* London: Pinter.

Pierce, N. R., and C. F. Steinbach. 1990. *Enterprising Communities: Community Based Development in America, 1990.* Washington, D.C.: Council for Community Based Development.

Pierce, Neal R., with Curtis W. Johnson, and John Stuart Hall. 1994. *Citistates: How Urban America Can Prosper in a Competitive World.* Washington, D.C.: Seven Locks.

Pierre, Jon, ed. 1998. *Partnerships in Urban Governance: European and American Experience.* New York: St. Martin's.

Pierre, Jon. 1999. "Models of Governance: The Institutional Dimension of Politics." *Urban Affairs Review* 34 (3): 372–96.

Pinnaro, Gabriella, and Enrico Pugliese. 1990. "Informalization and Social Resistance: The Case of Naples." In *L'Economia Informale in Una Prospettiva Comparativa: Aspetti Macro e Microeconomici.* Rome: Istituto di Studi per lo Sviluppo Economico.

Piore, M., and C. F. Sabel. 1984. *The Second Industrial Divide.* New York: Basic Books.

Point, Le. 1994. June 18.

Polanyi, Karl. 1944, 1957. *The Great Transformation.* Boston: Beacon.

Pompili, Tomaso. 1998. "Milan: The Failure of Agency in the Metropolis." In *European Cities in Competition*, edited by Chris Jensen-Butler, Ave Shechar, and Jan Van Weesop. Brookfield, Vt.: Ashgate.

Population Action International. 1994. *Global Migration: People on the Move.* Washington, D.C.: Population Action International.

Porter, M. 1995. "The Competitive Advantage of the Inner City." *Harvard Business Review* (May–June): 55–71.

Portz, John. 1990. *The Politics of Plant Closings.* Lawrence: University Press of Kansas.

Prud'homme, R. 1994. "Les sept plus grandes villes du monde." Paper no. 94–08. Direction Régionale de L'Equipement Ile de France.

Prud'homme, Rémy. 1994. "La France, Pays le Plus Décentralisé d'Europe?" *Le Monde*, May 17.

Przeworski, Adam. 1982. "The Structure of Class Conflict in Democratic Capitalist Societies." *American Political Science Review* 76:215–38.

Putnam, Robert. 1993. *Making Democracy Work: Civic Traditions in Modern Italy*. Princeton: Princeton University Press.

———. 1995. "Bowling Alone: America's Declining Social Capital." *Journal of Democracy* (January).

Pyrke, Michael, and Roger Lee. 1995. "Place Your Bets: Towards an Understanding of Globalization, Socio-Financial Engineering and Competition Within a Financial Center." *Urban Studies* 32 (2): 329–44.

Quinn, Michael. 2001. "Growth No Growth." *Journal of Planning Education and Research* 4 (10): 52–63.

Quotidien de Paris, Le. 1990. June 27.

Rebeggiani, Enrico, and Susy Veneziano. 1993. "La Disoccupazione in Campania." *Inchiesta* 99:49–60.

Reich, Robert B. 1992. *The Work of Nations: Preparing Ourselves for 21st–Century Capitalism*. New York: Vintage.

Reichl, Alexander J. 1997. "Historic Preservation and Pro-growth Politics in U.S. Cities." *Urban Affairs Review* 32:513–535.

———. 1999. *Reconstructing Times Square*. Lawrence: Univesity Press of Kansas.

Renaud, Jean-Pierre. 1993. *Paris, Un Etat dans l'Etat?* Paris: L'Harmattan.

Rey, Mario, and Giancarlo Pola. 1990. "Intergovernmental Relations in Italy: Recent Institutional and Financial Developments." In *Decentralization, Local Governments, and Markets*, edited by Robert Bennett. Oxford: Clarendon.

Rhodes, R.A.W. 1986. "Power Dependence Theories of Central Local Relations: A Critical Assessment." In *New Research in Central Local Relations*, edited by Michael Goldsmith. London: Gower.

———. 1999. *Control and Power in Central Local Relations*. London: Gower.

Rich, Wilbur C. 1989. *Coleman Young and Detroit Politics: From Social Activist to Power Broker*. Detroit: Wayne State University Press.

———. 1990. "The Politics of Casino Gambling." *Urban Affairs Quarterly* 26 (2): 274–98.

Riesman, David, with Nathan Glazer, and Denney Reuel. 1961. *The Lonely Crowd*. New Haven and London: Yale University Press.

Robertson, D. S. 1998. "Pulling in Opposite Directions: The Failure of Postwar Planning to Regenerate Glasgow." *Planning Perspectives* 13:53–67.

Rogowski, Edward T., and Ronald Berkman with Elizabeth Stom and Anthony Manicalco. 1995. "New York City's Outer Borough Development Strategy: Case Studies in Urban Revitalization." In *Urban Revitalization*, edited by Fritz W. Wagner, Timothy E. Joder, and Anthony J. Mumphrey, Jr. Oaks, Calif.: Sage.

Roncayolo, Marcel. 1996. *Les Grammaires d'une Ville*. Paris: Ecole des Hautes Etudes en Sciences Sociales.

Rooney, Jim. 1995. *Organizing the South Bronx*. Albany: State University of New York Press.

Rothblatt, Donald N. and Andrew Sancton, eds. 1993. *Metropolitan Governance: American/Canadian Intergovernmental Perspectives*. Berkeley: Institute of Governmental Studies Press, University of California.

Rubin, I., and H. Rubin, 1987. "Economic Development Incentives: The Poor (Cities) Pay More." *Urban Affairs Quarterly* 23 (1): 37–62.

Ruble, Blair, Joseph Tulchin, and Allison Garland. 1996. "Globalism and Local Realities: Five Paths to the Urban Future. In *Preparing For The Urban Future*, edited by Michael A. Cohen, Blair A. Ruble, Joseph S. Tulchin, and Allison M. Garland. Washington, D.C.: Woodrow Wilson Center.

Rusk, David. 1999. *Inside Game, Outside Game*. Washington, D.C.: Brookings Institution Press.

Russell, Hillary. 1997. "Liverpool City Challenge: Final Evaluation Report." European Institute for Urban Affairs. September. Liverpool: John Moores University.

Sabel, C. F. 1989. "Flexible Specialization and the Re-emergence of Regional Economies." In *Reversing Industrial Decline*, edited by P. Hirst and J. Zeitlin, Oxford: Berg.

Sales, Isaia. 1993. *La Camorra, Le Camorre*. Rome: Riuniti.

Sancton, Andrew. 2000. *Merger Mania: The Assault on Local Government*. Westmount, Quebec, Canada: Price-Patterson.

Sanders, H., and C. N. Stone. 1987. *The Politics of Urban Development*. Lawrence: University of Kansas Press.

Sassen, 1988. *The Mobility of Capital and Labor*. Cambridge: Cambridge University Press.

———. 1991. *The Global City: New York, London, Tokoyo*. Princeton: Princeton University Press.

———. 1994. *Cities in a World Economy*. Thousand Oaks, Calif.: Pine Forge.

———. 1998. *Globalization and Its Discontents*. New York: New Press.

Saunders, Peter. 1982. "Why Study Central Local Relations?" *Local Government Studies*, 8 (2): 55–56.

Savas, E. S. 1987. *Privatization: The Key to Better Government*. Chatham, N.J.: Chatham House.

Savitch, H. V. 1979. *Urban Policy and the Exterior City*. New York: Pergamon.

———. 1989. *Post-industrial Cities: Politics and Planning in New York, Paris, and London*. Princeton: Princeton University Press.

———. 1996. "Cities in a Global Era: A New Paradigm For the Next Millennium." In *Preparing for the Urban Future: Global Pressures and Local Forces*, edited by M. Cohen et al. Washington, D.C.: Woodrow Wilson Center Press.

———. 1998. "Global Challenge and Institutional Capacity, Or, How We Can Refit Local Administration for the Next Century." *Administration & Society*, 30 (3): 248–73.

———. 2002. "Encourage then Cope: Washington and the Sprawl Machine." In *Urban Sprawl and the Uneven Development of Metropolitan America*, edited by Gregory D. Squires. Washington, D.C.: Urban Institute.

Savitch, H. V., and Grigoriy Ardashev. 2001. "Does Terror Have an Urban Future?" Unpublished manuscript.

Savitch, H. V., and Paul Kantor. 1993. "Urban Mobilization of Private Capital: A Cross-National Comparison." Comparative Urban Studies Occasional Paper, No. 3. Washington, D.C.: Woodrow Wilson International Center.

———. 1995. "City Business: An International Perspective on Marketplace Politics." International Journal of Urban and Regional Research 19 (4): 495–512.

Savitch, H. V., and J. C. Thomas. 1992. Big City Politics in Transition. Eds. Newbury Park, CA: Sage.

Savitch, H. V., and Ronald K. Vogel, eds. 1996. Regional Politics: America in a Post-City Age. Thousand Oaks, Calif.: Sage.

Savitch. H. V., and Ronald K. Vogel, 2000. "Paths to New Regionalism." State and Local Government Review 32 (3): 158–66.

Sayre, W., and H. Kaufman. 1960. Governing New York City. New York: W. W. Norton.

Sbragia, Alberta. 1999. Debt Wish. Pittsburgh: University of Pittsburgh Press.

Schattschneider, E. E. 1960. The Semi-Sovereign People. New York: Holt, Rinehart and Winston.

Schmidt, Vivien A. 1989. "Unblocking Society by Decree: The Impact of Governmental Decentralization in France." Comparative Politics 21(1): 53–72.

Schneider, Mark. 1989. The Competitive City. Pittsburgh. University of Pittsburgh Press.

Schulze, Robert. 1958. "The Role of Economic Dominants in Power Structure." American Sociological Review 23 (1): 3–9.

Schumpeter, Joseph. 1950. Capitalism, Socialism and Democracy. New York: Harper and Row.

Scott, Allen J. 1996. "Regional Motors of the Global Economy." Futures 28 (5): 391–411.

Scottish Development Agency. 1988. GEAR Project Evaluation. Final report by PIEDA and Center for Housing Research. Glasgow: University of Glasgow and Scottish Development Agency.

See Naples Before it Dies. 1970. The [London] Sunday Times. January 11.

Segaud, Marion, Catherine Bonvalet, and Jacques Brun, eds. 1998. Logement et habitat: L'etat des savoirs. Paris: La Découverte.

Seligman, Dan. 2000. "Giuliani and After." Commentary 110 (4): 44–46.

Sharpe, L. J. 1981. The Local Fiscal Crisis in Western Europe. Beverly Hills: Sage.

———. ed. 1993. The Rise of Meso Government in Europe. London: Sage.

Shefter, Martin. 1985. Political Crisis, Fiscal Crisis. New York: Basic Books.

Siegel, Fred. 1997. The Future Once Happened Here: New York, D.C., L.A., and the Fate of America's Big Cities. New York: Free Press.

Shelton, Beth Anne, Nestor P. Rodriguez, Joe R. Feagin, Robert Bullard, and Robert D. Thomas. 1989. Houston: Growth and Decline in a Sunbelt Boomtown. Philadelphia: Temple University Press.

Siemiatycki, Myer, and Engin Isin. 1997. "Immigration, Diversity and Urban Citizenship in Toronto." Canadian Journal of Regional Science/Revue canadienne des sciences régionales (Spring-Summer/Printemps-Eté): 73–102.

Simmie, James. 1981. *Power, Property and Corporatism: The Political Sociology of Planning place.* Macmillan.

Sites, William. 1997. "The Limits of Regime Theory: New York under Koch, Dinkins and Giuliani." *Urban Affairs Review* 32 (4): 536–57.

Smith, M. Peter, ed. 1998. *Cities in Transformation.* Beverly Hills, Calif.: Sage.

Smith, Michael Peter. 2001. *Transnational Urbanism.* Oxford: Blackwell.

Smith, Michael Peter. 1988. *City, State and Market.* New York: Basil Blackwell.

Spotts, Fredrick, and Theodore Wieser. 1986. *Italy: A Difficult Democracy.* New York: Cambridge University Press.

Squires, Gregory D., ed. 1989. *Unequal Partnerships.* New Brunswick: Rutgers University Press.

Stancanelli, Bianca. 1995. "Chiamatelo Diego Armando Bassolino." *Panorama* September 25, pp. 85–87.

State of the Cities Census Data Systems (http://socds.huduser.org).

Stein, Robert. 1998. *The Houston Metropolitan Study: A Report and Recommendations on Amenities in the Houston Metropolitan Area.* Houston: Baker Institute for Public Policy, Rice University.

Stephens, G. Ross, and Nelson Wilkerson. 2000. *Metropolitan Government and Governance.* New York: Oxford University Press.

Sternleib, G., and J. Hughes. 1983. *The Atlantic City Gamble.* Cambridge: Harvard University Press.

Sternlieb, G. and J. W. Hughes. 1975. *Post-industrial America: Metropolitan Decline and Inter-regional Job Shifts.* New Brunswick, N.J.: The Center for Urban Policy Research, Rutgers University.

Stiglitz, J. E. 1986. *Economics of the Public Sector.* New York: W. W. Norton.

Stoecker, Randy. 1997. "The CDC Model of Urban Development: A Critique and an Alternative." *Journal of Urban Affairs* 19 (1): 1–22.

Stolz, George. 2000. "Europe's Back Doors" *Atlantic Monthly,* January, pp. 26–28.

Stone, C. N. 1993. "Urban Regimes and the Capacity to Govern: A Political Economy Approach." *Journal of Urban Affairs* 15:1–29.

Stone, C. N. and H. Sanders, 1987. *The Politics of Urban Development.* Lawrence: University of Kansas Press.

Stone, Clarence N. 1989. *Regime Politics: Governing Atlanta, 1946–1988.* Lawrence: University Press of Kansas.

Stone, Clarence N. 2001. "Civic Capacity and Urban Education." *Urban Affairs Review.* 36 (5): 594–619.

Storper, M., and A. J. Scott. 1989. "The Geographical Foundations and Social Regulation of Flexible Production Complexes." In *The Power of Geography,* edited by S. Wolcott and M. Dear. Winchester, Mass.: Unwin Hyman.

Storper, M., and R. Walker, 1989. *The Capitalist Imperative: Territory, Technology, and Industrial Growth.* Oxford: Basil Blackwell.

Sugrue, Thomas J. 1996. *The Origins of Urban Crisis: Race and Inequality in Postwar Detroit.* Princeton: Princeton University Press.

Summers, Anita A., Paul C. Cheshire, and Lanfranco Senn, eds. 1993. *Urban Change in the United States and Western Europe: Comparative Analysis and Policy.* Washington, D.C.: The Urban Institute Press.

Suttcliffe, Anthony. 1982. *Toward the Planned City: Germany, Britain, the United States and France, 1788–1914*. New York: St. Martin's.

Swanstrom, T. 1985. *The Crisis of Growth Politics: Cleveland, Kucinich, and the Challenge of Urban Populism*. Philadelphia: Temple University Press.

———. 1989. "Semisovereign Cities: The Politics of Urban Development." *Polity*, 21 (1): 83–100.

———. 2001. "What We Argue when We Argue about Regionalism." In "Regionalism Reconsidered." *Journal of Urban Affairs* 23 (5): 479–96.

Swyngedouw, Erik A. 1992. "The Mammon Quest: 'Glocalization,' Interspatial Competition and the Monetary Order: The Construction of New Scales." In *Cities and Regions in the New Europe*, edited by Mick Dunford and Grigoris Kafkalas. London: Belhaven.

Taaffe, Peter, and Tony Mulhearn. 1988. *Liverpool—A City That Dared to Fight*. London: Fortress.

Tarrow, Sidney. 1977 *Between Center and Periphery: Grassroots Politics in Italy and France*. New Haven: Yale University Press

Taylor, Michael. 1989. "Structure, Culture and Action in the Explanation of Social Change." *Politics and Society* 17:115–62.

Teaford, Jon. 1984. *Unheralded Triumphs*. Baltimore: Johns Hopkins University Press.

———. 1990. *The Rough Road to Renaissance: Urban Revitalization in America, 1940–1985*. Baltimore: Johns Hopkins University Press.

Thoenig, J-C. 1978. "Pouvoir d'Etat et Pouvoirs Locaux." *Pouvoirs* 4:25–37.

Thomas, June M. 1997. *Redevelopment and Race: Planning a Finer City in Post War Detroit*. Baltimore: Johns Hopkins University Press.

Thomas, Robert D., and David W. Hawes. 1999. "Changing Coalition Politics in Houston: Municipal Utility Districts to Tax Increment Reinvestment Zones." Paper delivered to the Annual Meeting of the Urban Affairs Association, Louisville, Kentucky, April.

Thomas, Robert D., and R. W. Murray. 1991. *Progrowth Politics*. Berkeley: Institute for Governmental Studies, University of California.

Thomlinson, Neil. 1999. "When Right is Wrong." In *Restructuring and Resistance*, edited by Mike Burke, Colin Mooers, and John Shields. Halifax, Nova Scotia: Fernwood.

Thrift, Nigel. 1996. *Spatial Formations*. London: Sage Publications.

Tiebout, C. 1962. "A Pure Theory of Local Expenditures." *Journal of Political Economy* 64:416–24.

Toronto Economic Development Strategy. 2000. November 17. http://.city.toronto.on.ca/business/econdev/strategy—execsum.htm

Toti, Stephanie. 2000. "The Politics of Zoning and Land Use Reform in New York City." Unpublished senior honors thesis, Fordham University.

Trachte, Kent, and Robert Ross. 1985. "The Crisis of Detroit and the Emergence of Global Capitalism." *International Journal of Urban and Regional Research* 9: 186–217.

Traub, James. 2001. "No Fun City." *The New York Times Magazine*. November 4, p. 70.

Tulasne, Etienne. 1994. "Trois Décennies de Planification (1960–1990)." In *Marseilles, 25 Ans de Planification Urbaine*, edited by Dominique Becquart. Paris: L'Aube.

Turner, Robyn A., and Judith A. Garber. 1994. "Responding to Boom and Bust: Urban Political Economy in Houston and Edmonton." Paper delivered to the American Political Science Association, New York City, September 1–4.

Turok, I. 1987. "Continuity, Change and Contradiction in Urban Policy." In *Regenerating the Inner-city: Glasgow's Experience*, edited by D. Donnison and A. Middleton. London: Routledge and Kegan Paul.

U.N. Centre for Human Settlements (Habitat). 1996. *Indicators Newsletter, 5*. United Nations.

United States Kerner Commission. 1968. *Report of the National Advisory Commission on Civil Disorders*. New York: Bantam Books.

University of British Columbia. 1990. *St. Lawrence: 1974–79*. Vancouver: University of British Columbia Press.

Urban Audit: Assessing the Quality of Life of Europe's Cities. 2001. Directorate General for Regional Policy and Cohesion of the European Commission by ECOTEC Research and Consulting Ltd. Website: http://www.inforegio. cec.eu.int/urban/audit/

U.S. Bureau of the Census. 1970. "Population of the 100 Largest Cities and Other Urban Places in the United States: 1790 to 1990." Population Division Working Paper No. 27 (Washington, D.C., June 1998)

U.S. Bureau of the Census, Dp-4. Income and Poverty Status in 1989–1990. Geographic Area: Detroit city, Michigan. U.S. Census Bureau.

U.S. Department of Housing and Urban Development, 1980. *Deregulating Community Development*. Paul R. Dommel, Michael J. Rich, Leonard S. Rubinowitz, and Associates. Washington, D.C.: HUD, Office of Policy Development and Research.

U.S. Department of Housing and Urban Development. 1997. *Empowerment Zone Performance Reports*. Washington, D.C.: HUD.

U.S. Department of Housing and Urban Development, Office of Community Planning and Development. 1999. Community Development Block Grant Program Directory of Allocations.

U.S. Department of Housing and Urban Development. 1999. *The State of the Cities: 2000*. Washington, D.C.: HUD, Office of Policy Development and Research.

U.S. Department of Housing and Urban Development. 2000. *The State of the Cities 2000: Megaforces Shaping the Future of the Nation's Cities*. Washington, D.C.: HUD.

U.S. News and World Report. 1989. "America's Boom Towns." November 13, pp. 54–64.

Van den Berg, Leo, Jan Van der Borg, and Jan Van der Meer. 1995. *Urban Tourism*. Brookfield, Vt.: Avebury.

Varady, David. 1996. "Neighbourhood Regenration of Glasgow's Southside: Implications for American Cities." *Journal of Urban Design* 1 (2): 201–14.

Viard, Jean. 1995. *Marseilles, une Ville Impossible*. Paris: Payot & Rivages.

Vicari, Serena, and Harvey Molotch. 1990. "Building Milan: Alternative Machines of Growth." *Urban Affairs Quarterly* 14 (4): 602–24.

Vicari-Haddock, Serena. 2002. "Business as Usual: The Naples Business District (Centro Direzionale di Napoli)." *In Urbanising Globalisation: Urban Redevelopment and Social Polarisation in the European City*, edited by F. Moulaert, A. Rodriguez, and A. Swyndegouw. Oxford: Oxford University Press, 2002.

Vicari, Serena. 1986. "Friction in the Growth Machine: The Political Economy of Mass Transportation in an Italian Metropolitan Area." Ph.D. diss., University of California, Santa Barbara.

Vidal, Avis C. 1992. *Rebuilding Communities*. New York: Community Development Research Center, New School for Social Research.

Ville de Marseilles. 1995. *Marseilles en Chiffres*. Marseilles: Agence d'Urbanisme de l'Agglomeration Marseillaise.

Vogel, Ronald K. 2001. "Metropolitan Governance in Greater Toronto: Assessing the New Paradigm." Unpublished manuscript.

Vogel, Ronald, and John Harrington. 2002. *Political Change in the Metropolis*, 7th ed. New York: Longman.

Vogel, Ronald, and Bert Swanson. 1989. "The Growth Machine versus the Anti Growth Coalition: The Battle For Our Communities." *Urban Affairs Quarterly* 25 (1): 63–85

Wall Street Journal, The. 1989. "The New Boom Towns." March 27.

Wall Street Journal, The. 2001. December 19, p. 1.

Walsh, Annmarie. 1978. *The Public's Business*. Cambridge: MIT Press.

Waltz, Kenneth N. 1979. *Theory of International Politics*. Reading, Mass.: Addison Wesley.

Wannop, U., and R. LeClerc. 1987. "Urban Renewal and the Origins of GEAR." In *Regenerating the Inner-city: Glasgow's Experience*, edited by D. Donnison and A. Middleton. London: Routledge.

Warner, W. Lloyd, and J. O. Low. 1946. "The Factory in the Community." In *Industry and Society*, edited by William Foote Whyte. New York: Mcgraw Hill.

Warren, Mark, J. Phillip Thompson, and Susan Saegert. 1999. "Social Capital and Poor Communities: A Framework for Analysis." Paper presented at the conference" Social and Poor Communities: Building and Using Social Assets to Combat Poverty, Fordham University, New York City.

Webber, Melvin. 1963. "Order in Diversity: Community Without Propinquity." In *Cities and Space: The Future Use of Urban Land*, edited by Lowden Wingo, 23–54. Baltimore: Johns Hopkins University Press.

Webster, D. 1994. *Home and Workplace in the Glasgow Conurbation*. Glasgow: The Scottish Urban Regeneration Forum Seminar.

———. 1994. *Housing, Transport and Employment in Glasgow*. Glasgow: Glasgow Regeneration Alliance Roads and Transport Working Group.

Welch, Susan, and Timothy Bledsoe. 1988. *Urban Reform and Its Consequences*. Chicago: University of Chicago.

Welsh, Moira. 2000 "The Salesman." *The Star* (Toronto). Nov. 11.

Whelan, Robert K., and Alma H. Young. 1998. "Detroit and New Orleans: Black Mayors and Downtown Development." Paper prepared for American Political Science Association Conference, Boston, September 3–6.

White, James W. 1998. "Old Wine, Cracked Bottle? Tokyo, Paris, and the Global City Hypothesis." *Urban Affairs Review* 33 (4): 451–77.

Williams, Oliver, and Charles Adrian. 1963. *Four Cities: A Study in Comparative Policy Making*. Philadelphia: University of Pennsylvania Press.

Wilson, James Q. 1989. *Bureaucracy*. New York: Basic Books.

Wilson, James Q., and Edward Banfield. 1971. "Political Ethos Revisited." *American Political Science Review* 66 (4): 1048–1063.

Wirt, Frederick M. 1974. *Power in the City: Decision Making in San Francisco*. Berkeley: University of California Press.

Wolfson, Joanne, and Frances Frisken. 2000. "Local Response to the Global Challenge: Comparing Local Economic Development Policies in a Regional Context." *Journal of Urban Affairs* 22 (2): 361–85.

Wolman, Harold, and Michael Goldsmith. 1992. *Urban Politics and Policy: A Comparative Approach*. Cambridge, Mass.: Blackwell.

Wong, K. K., and P. E. Peterson. 1986. "Urban Response to Federal Program Flexibility: Politics of Community Development Block Grant." *Urban Affairs Quarterly* 21 (3): 239–311.

Wood, A. 1996. "Analysing the Politics of Local Economic Development: Making Sense of Cross-national Convergence." *Urban Studies* 33:1281–95.

Wood, Robert C., with Vladimir V. Almendinger. 1961. *1400 Governments: The Political Economy of the New York Metropolitan Region*. Garden City, N.Y.: Anchor.

Young, Coleman, and Lonnie Wheeler. 1994. *Hard Stuff: The Autobiography of Mayor Coleman Young*. New York: Viking.

Zukin, Sharon. 1995. *The Cultures of Cities*. Oxford: Blackwell.

INDEX

active participation, 76, 79–83, 150, 173
advantaged bargaining, 52, 92, 168. *See also* bargaining
African-Americans. *See* blacks
agglomeration, 7, 55–56, 58, 62, 65, 68, 94
Albertini, Gabriele, 306
amalgamation, 71, 174, 181, 182–183, 280, 294–295, 301–302
American model, xviii, 272–274, 283–285, 292, 309
Amsterdam, 3, 42–43
annexation, 134, 135, 136, 143, 211–212, 217, 286, 334–335
anti-growth strategies, 20, 23, 33, 52, 144, 178. *See also* growth
Archer, Dennis, 76–77, 129, 132–133, 259–260, 284, 298, 308
architecture, 88–89, 105, 114, 129, 186, 248, 267–268, 341
arrondissements. *See* neighborhoods
Asia, 43, 178, 319
Atelier Parisen d'Urbanisme (APUR), 186, 187
Atlanta, 212, 254
automobiles, 20–21, 47, 56, 59, 60, 85, 87, 88, 89, 108, 128, 130, 131–132, 136, 156, 190, 254, 255, 259, 261, 263, 278, 302, 317, 341–342

banking: CDPs and, 321, 325; in Canada, 188; capital and, 316–317; choice and, 314–316; in Detroit, 131, 132, 259; economy and 14; globalization and, 15, 56; growth and, 18, 317, 321; in Houston, 136, 208; in Italy, 73, 120–121, 178, 196; in Milan, 120–121, 196; in Naples, 178, 248, 249, 306; neighborhoods and, 106; in New York, 59, 123, 126, 207; PBCs and, 70; in primate cities, 7; public officials and, 32; suburbs and, 17; transportation and, 22. *See also* financial institutions
bargaining: advantages and, 149; business and, 34, 36, 254–256; city, 309, 341;

342; capital and, xvi, 36, 246, 320, 322; choices and, 27, 150, 151, 271; cities and, 25–26, 27, 149, 163, 164–166, 167, 353; contexts and, 156–161; control and, 149; definition of, xvii, 391; in Detroit, 258, 259, 263; development and, 48, 49, 51, 322–326; diversity and, 309; driving variables and, 150–151; entrepreneurial and, 171–222; government and, xvi, 34, 36, 37, 43, 247, 331, 335; investment and, 31, 32–33; linkages and, 272; markets and, 31, 37, 50, 55; regimes and, 52–53, 171–172, 261; regionalism and, 330; resources and, 31–32, 38–39, 163, 164–166, 223–224, 252–253, 264, 270–271, 293–294, 313, 317; steering variables and, 48, 75–76, 150–151, 164, 165, 166. 168–169, 335; strategic thinking and, 313–317, 320, 321; in Toronto, 332–333; urban development and, 37, 43–46, 92, 313, 323, 342, 343; vertical integration and, 339–340; Western Europe and, 40, 42, 43
Bassolino, Antonio, 79, 140–141, 146, 155, 252, 288, 300, 349–350, 351–353, 356–358
Beame, Abraham, 202, 203
Bedford Stuyvesant Restoration Corporation, 325
benefits, 236, 319–320; collective, 40, 84, 88, 114, 317, 351, 352, 357; indivisible, 83–84, 99
Berlin, 43, 355
bidding, 209, 274, 314, 320, 326–327, 332, 338
Bill 103. *See* City of Toronto Act
blacks, 9, 77, 78, 85, 116, 155, 203, 204, 209, 210–211, 213, 219, 238, 239, 253, 254, 257, 260, 298. *See also* ethnic groups, minorities
Blair, Tony (prime minister), 235, 275, 299
Bloomberg, Michael, 203, 356
blue collar, 5–6, 22, 46, 62, 77–78, 84, 86–87, 89–92, 111, 114–115,